The Discipline Book

A Concise Guide to Discipline

in the

New York State Public Service

by

Harvey Randall

and

Eric D. Randall

Copyright © 2009 Public Employment Law Press

Paperback ISBN 978-1-60145-800-1
Ebook ISBN 1-931511-74-8

Library of Congress Control Number: 2009925852

All rights reserved. No part of this publication may be reproduced, stored in a retrieval system, or transmitted in any form or by any means, electronic, mechanical, recording or otherwise, without the prior written permission of the author.

Printed in the United States of America.

BookLocker.com, Inc.
2009

www.publicpersonnellaw.blogspot.com
E-mail: publications@nycap.rr.com

Readers please take note that:

Consistent with the Declaration of Principles jointly adopted by a Committee of the American Bar Association and a Committee of Publishers and Associations, the material in *The Discipline Book* is presented with the understanding that the authors and the publishers are not providing legal advice to the reader and in the event legal or other expert assistance is needed, the reader should seek such advice from a competent professional.

Also, the reader should be always aware of the fact that subsequent court and administrative rulings, or changes to laws, rules and regulations may have modified or clarified or vacated or reversed the material and the decisions summarized here. Accordingly, these materials should be *Shepardized*® or otherwise checked to make certain that the most recent information is being considered by the reader.

Table of Contents

INTRODUCTION 1

CHAPTER 1: DUE PROCESS RIGHTS OF EMPLOYEES 3

Part One: Who is entitled to due process? 3
1.01 Due process rights depend on appointment status and jurisdictional classification
1.02 Who is entitled to due process?
1.03 Who has no due process rights?
1.04 Due process rights under Section 3020-a
1.05 The concept of tenure
1.06 "Permanent" appointments, probation and tenure in the competitive class
1.07 Permanent vs. probationer vs. provisional
1.08 Probationers' due process rights
1.09 Temporary and provisional appointments
1.10 Jurisdictional misclassification
1.11 Budgetary classification irrelevant to due process rights of employees
1.12 Rights of employees of quasi-government entities
1.13 Veterans' due process rights

Part Two: Forms of due process 21
1.14 Impartial tribunals
1.15 Specificity of charges
1.16 Immunity from discipline
1.17 Right to pre-determination hearing
1.18 Ambiguity of language in Taylor Law agreements
1.19 Right of appeal and timeliness
1.20 Absence from hearings
1.21 Notice of hearings
1.22 Name-clearing hearings
1.23 Due process and optional hearings
1.24 Removal by operation of law
1.25 Suspension without pay
1.26 Authority to discipline
1.27 Pending criminal matters
1.28 Double jeopardy
1.29 Civil rights
1.30 First Amendment rights
1.31 Freedom of information
1.32 Public hearings
1.33 Disciplinary action based on pre-employment misconduct

CHAPTER 2: CONDUCTING AN INVESTIGATION 47
3.01 Forms of evidence
3.02 Hearsay evidence
3.03 Standard of proof: criminal vs. disciplinary hearing
3.04 Standard of proof, Section 75
3.05 Standard of proof, Section 3020-a
3.06 Effect of criminal conviction or dismissal on discipline
3.07 Testimony by the accused
3.08 Best evidence rule
3.09 Tainted evidence
3.10 Confessions and coercion
3.11 Competent and incompetent witnesses
3.12 Opinion evidence
3.13 Foundation for testimony
3.14 Credibility of witnesses
3.15 Conflicting evidence
3.16 Employee surveillance
3.17 Judicial notice
3.18 Disclosure of personal records
3.19 Unsealing criminal records
3.20 Standard of conduct
3.21 Admissions
3.22 Source of documentary evidence
3.23 Privileged communications
3.24 Using polygraph tests in disciplinary actions
3.25 Pitfalls for that a hearing officer must avoid

CHAPTER 3: EVIDENCE 64
3.01 Forms of evidence
3.02 Hearsay evidence
3.03 Standard of proof: criminal vs. disciplinary hearing
3.04 Standard of proof, Section 75
3.05 Standard of proof, Section 3020-a
3.06 Effect of criminal conviction or dismissal on discipline
3.07 Testimony by the accused
3.08 Best evidence rule
3.09 Tainted evidence
3.10 Confessions and coercion
3.11 Competent and incompetent witnesses
3.12 Opinion evidence
3.13 Foundation for testimony
3.14 Credibility of witnesses
3.15 Conflicting evidence
3.16 Employee surveillance
3.17 Judicial notice
3.18 Disclosure of personal records

3.19 Unsealing criminal records
3.20 Standard of conduct
3.21 Admissions
3.22 Source of documentary evidence
3.23 Privileged communications
3.24 Using polygraph tests in disciplinary actions
3.25 Pitfalls for that a hearing officer must avoid

CHAPTER 4: PROPOSING A PENALTY 79
4.01 The Pell standard
4.02 Court review
4.03 Lawful penalties
4.04 Recommending penalties
4.05 Using the individual's employment history in disciplinary action
4.06 Indemnification
4.07 Expiration of the penalty
4.08 Whistleblower protection
4.09 Determining the penalty to be imposed
4.10 Due Process and Progressive Discipline
4.11 Substantial Evidence
4.12 The Pell Standard of Fairness
4.13 Reasons Courts Reject Penalties
4.14 Violations of the Pell standard
4.15. Penalty: reprimand
4.16 Loss of leave credits and other alternative penalties
4.17 Penalty: fine
4.18 Penalty: suspension
4.19 Penalty: demotion
4.20 Time and attendance issues
4.21 Examples of penalties imposed

CHAPTER 5: OBLIGATIONS OF EMPLOYERS AND UNIONS UNDER NEGOTIATED DISCIPLINARY PROCEDURES 106
5.01 Notice of discipline
5.02 The "Bill of Rights" in contracts
5.03 Absence from work during disciplinary activities
5.04 Duty of fair representation
5.05 Procedures under contracts
5.06 Reassignments
5.07 Settlement
5.08 Pre-hearing suspensions

CHAPTER 6: FILING CHARGES UNDER SECTION 75 116
6.01 Key procedural elements
6.02 Charges must be specific
6.03 Employee must receive opportunity to respond

6.04 Right to union representation
6.05 Statute of limitations
6.06 Serving charges
6.07 Pitfalls to avoid
6.08 Criticism is not discipline
6.09 Admission of guilt difficult to retract
6.10 Pending criminal charges
6.11 Choice of law

CHAPTER 7: FILING CHARGES UNDER SECTION 3020-A 126
7.01 Statute of limitations
7.02 Need for investigatory report regardless of merit of allegations
7.03 Risk of libel or slander as a result of investigatory report
7.04 Name-clearing hearings
7.05 Pitfalls to avoid
7.06 Criticism is not discipline
7.07 Procedures in filing charges
7.08 Use of school attorney
7.09 Verdict shopping
7.10 The Section 3020-a process
7.11 Informing the Commissioner
7.12 Hearing panel members
7.13 Pre-hearing conferences
7.14 Characteristics of arbitration

CHAPTER 8: SUSPENDING EMPLOYEES PENDING A HEARING 143
8.01 Suspension without pay – general considerations
8.02 Suspensions with pay, Sections 72 and 75
8.03 "Emergency" Suspensions
8.04 Suspension without pay, generally
8.05 Suspension without pay of unlicensed individual
8.06 Suspension without pay in the event of postponement of disciplinary proceeding
8.07 Suspension of a school superintendent
8.08 Unpaid suspension past 30 days: Conflict with local law
8.09 Suspension without pay, medical
8.10 Suspension without pay
8.11 Effect of criminal actions on suspensions
8.12 Mitigation of damages
8.13 Taxation of a settlement
8.14 Recoupment of cash advances
8.15 Bad faith
8.16 Employment contracts
8.17 Suspension with pay, pending criminal action
8.18 Reassignment pending discipline
8.19 Suspension without pay failure to report to work
8.20 Repayment of salary after being continued on the payroll

CHAPTER 9: PENDING CRIMINAL ACTIONS 157
9.01 Simultaneous prosecution
9.02 Acquittal of criminal charges does not bar disciplinary action
9.03 Criminal conviction bars administrative acquittal of the same charge
9.04 Use of disclosures in criminal trials
9.05 Probationers and criminal charges
9.06 Reinstatement after acquittal
9.07 Settlement to avoid prosecution
9.08 Administrator's immunity
9.09 Collateral estoppel
9.10 Disclosure of records

CHAPTER 10: PREPARING FOR A HEARING 163
10.01 The settlement option
10.02 Selecting a hearing officer
10.03 Pre-hearing legwork
10.04 A pre-hearing checklist
10.05 Hearing in absentia
10.06 Leave to attend hearing
10.07 Mitigation of damages in cases of acquittal
10.08 Taxation of a settlement
10.09 Independent review of facts
10.10 Considering material in a post-hearing brief submitted by a party
10.11 Stay of arbitration

CHAPTER 11: APPEALS 172
11.01 Who may appeal?
11.02 What may appeals concern?
11.03 What standards apply in appeals?
11.04 Forums for appeal
11.05 Challenging a Section 75 decision
11.06 Challenging an arbitration award
11.07 Biased hearing officers
11.08 Deadlines for appeal
11.09 Timely and untimely appeals
11.10 Outcomes of appeals
11.11 Vacating or modifying penalties: The Pell Standard
11.12 Back pay and benefits
11.13 Statute of limitations
11.14 Back salary

CHAPTER 12: NON-DISCIPLINARY TERMINATIONS 183
12.01 Termination for disability
12.02 Section 73 pre-termination due process requirements
12.03 Arbitrating Section 71 and Section 73 terminations

12.04 Other provisions of law
12.05 Considering disability claims
12.06 Termination of a probationary employee

CHAPTER 13: TERMINATIONS WITHOUT A HEARING 196
13.01 Necessity of a license
13.02 Removal by operation of law
13.03 Disqualification for employment because of a criminal conviction
13.04 Irrelevance of criminal history
13.05 Removal after convictions
13.06 Contract violation
13.07 Denial of equal protection?
13.08 Employees-at-will
13.09 Withdrawing resignations
13.10 Name-clearing hearings
13.11 Noncompetitive class employees
13.12 Disqualification, Section 50.4 CSL
13.13 Nature of the offense
13.14 Violation of oath of office
13.15 Reversal of felony conviction

CHAPTER 14: REDRESS AND REMEDIES 213
14.01 Delays in reinstatements
14.02 Back pay
14.03 Reinstatement

CHAPTER 15: DRUGS, DRUG TESTING AND DISCIPLINE 217
15.01 Reasonable suspicion
15.02 Pre-employment testing
15.03 Due process guidelines
15.04 Guidelines on employee privacy
15.05 Observer's presence during testing
15.06 Drug testing and collective bargaining
15.07 Penalties
15.08 Refusal to participate in a drug treatment program
15.09 Libel and slander
15.10 The ADA and human rights laws

CHAPTER 16: SOME SPECIAL PROVISIONS OF LAW 227

CHAPTER 17: PROVISIONAL AND PROBATIONARY EMPLOYEES 231
17.01 Tenure of provisionals by operation of law
17.02 Tenure
17.03 Reviewing probationary employee terminations
17.04 "Permanent probationers"

17.05 Standard of review
17.06 Bad faith determinations
17.07 Separation pay for probationary teachers
17.08 Disciplinary probation
17.09 Light duty and probationary requirements
17.10 Drug use and probation
17.11 Probation and alcoholism
17.12 Probation and stress
17.13 Extension of probation: modified duty
17.14 Traineeships
17.15 Extensions of the probationary period
17.16 Attaining permanent status
17.17 Date of permanent appointment and traineeships
17.18 Non-competitive class employees
17.19 Good faith determinations concerning probationary service
17.20 Notice of termination
17.21 Second probationary periods
17.22 Good faith probationary decisions
17.23 Name-clearing hearings
17.24 Tenure by operation of law
17.25 Transition from probationer to tenured
17.26 Suspension of a probationer
17.27 Rights under a Taylor Law agreement
17.28 Distinguishing between temporary and provisional appointment

CHAPTER 18: CASE SUMMARIES 262

GENERAL INDEX 519

ABOUT THE AUTHORS 529

INTRODUCTION

The Introduction to the First Edition of the Discipline Book sets out the philosophy and purposes underlying the development and publication of this handbook. This edition updates the First Edition by incorporating significant court, administrative and arbitral rulings involving discipline, due process and other important issues concerning the discipline process handed down since the publication of the First Edition.[1]

As the determination of the appropriate penalty to be imposed on an individual found guilty of one or more charges is a critical consideration in satisfying administrative due process requirements, the Second Edition incorporates selected portions of the Penalty Book, the companion volume to the 1999 edition of the Discipline Book.

Personnel administration in New York State in general may be viewed as poised on a three-legged stool: one leg is the Civil Service Law and related personnel statutes; the second leg collective bargaining pursuant to the Taylor Law; and the third leg – federal and state civil rights laws. To neglect considering each of these elements when considering or processing a disciplinary action is to "court disaster."

As stated in the introduction to the First Edition, the discipline of employees is one of the most complex and important areas of employer-employee relations in New York State public employment. To quote from the Introduction to the First Edition: *This book explains the rules governing discipline. Emphasis is placed on the importance of proper procedure, as defined by the relevant laws as well as court rulings and arbitration decisions made under those laws, most notably Section 75 of the New York State Civil Service Law [Section 75] and Section 3020-a [Section 3020-a] of the New York State Education Law. Also covered are disciplinary procedures that take place under alternatives to the statutory provisions that are authorized by collective bargaining agreements negotiated under the New York State Taylor Law (Section 200 et sec of the Civil Service Law.)*

"Discipline is a legal process in which front-line decision-makers typically are not lawyers but lay people -- police chiefs, agency administrators, school superintendents, et cetera. Likewise, union officials who represent employees in the disciplinary process may be assisted by counsel but are rarely lawyers themselves. This book is intended to aid such individuals by demystifying the disciplinary process and cataloging some of the more salient legal issues that can arise in discipline. Also, attorneys who specialize in New York public employment law should find this book a useful reference on both fundamental points and some of the finer nuances in the law of discipline.

"The body of judicial precedent that pertains to discipline in New York State is substantial. Thousands of administrative disciplinary decisions and penalties have been challenged in lawsuits filed under Article 78 of the New York State Civil Practice Law and Rules (CPLR) or, where arbitration is involved, pursuant to Article 75 of the CPLR. Fortunately for those who wish to

---

[1] **N.B.** Subsequent court and administrative rulings, or changes to laws, rules and regulations may have modified or clarified or obviated or vacated or reversed the material, the conclusions or the decisions summarized in this handbook. Accordingly, these material and summaries should be *Shepardized*® or otherwise checked to make certain that the most recent information is being considered by the reader.

understand the principles of discipline, the majority of these lawsuits concern similar questions and issues. Each chapter of this book addresses one of those common questions or issues. Chapter one, for instance, addresses the question: "Did the employee receive due process?" After an explanation of what due process is and why it is important, the chapter explains a number of types of due process issues, usually with reference to a specific New York State or federal court decision that dealt with that issue. Succeeding chapters are organized similarly.

"The information provided in this book is intended to be neither pro-management nor pro-labor; it is the authors' belief the public interest is served if all parties have a clear understanding of the law. For the disciplinary process to have integrity, the principles of fairness and sound procedures should be well-understood by all parties involved -- administrators responsible for personnel management, the leaders of collective bargaining units and attorneys practicing public sector labor law in New York State.

"Cases cited involve a variety of pubic employers including police agencies, school districts, state departments and agencies, and municipalities. Readers are cautioned against ignoring material simply because the type of public employer involved is different from the reader's own. In many cases, identical principles apply regarding proper procedure. In the opinion of the authors, courts will consider the decisions summarized in this handbook as precedents in future litigation involving disciplinary actions.

"New York State Courts made most of the rulings cited in this book. As some readers may be unfamiliar with the hierarchy of the state court system, here is a summary: the first court with jurisdiction on many issues involving public employment in New York State is the New York State Supreme Court. Decisions by any Supreme Court justice may be reviewed by the Appellate Division of the New York State Supreme Court, usually referred to simply as the Appellate Division. Decisions by the Appellate Division are reviewed by the Court of Appeals, which is New York's highest court. Furthermore, federal courts may hear cases in which Constitutional issues are raised.

"Of course, disciplinary procedures do not exist in a vacuum. Actions taken against an employee under a disciplinary procedure may be attacked as being discriminatory in violation of federal or State Human Rights Laws, or as being an unfair labor practice under the Taylor Law. The Americans with Disabilities Act of 1990 applies to public and quasi-public employers and is an additional factor to be considered in disciplinary matters as well.

"The reader should keep in mind that the law governing the disciplinary process is under constant revision. No book can provide a definitive guide to what is lawful and what is not in a given situation. This book is intended, rather, to acquaint readers with the general concepts of administrative due process so that they may make informed judgments in their roles. Readers are urged to seek early legal assistance when faced with an actual or potential disciplinary action."

Harvey Randall, J.D.
Eric D. Randall, M.B.A.
April 2008

CHAPTER 1

DUE PROCESS RIGHTS OF EMPLOYEES

Part One: Who is entitled to due process?

When courts review the lawfulness of disciplinary actions taken against public employees, a single question is the most fundamental: In the disciplinary process, did the employee involved receive all the administrative due process to which he or she was entitled?

Courts view the failure to satisfy any one of the elements required for administrative due process as a complete failure of the process and this will result in the complete frustration of the appointing authority's[1] effort to discipline an officer or an employee.

The vesting of the responsibilities of being an appointing authority is derived from local or state legislation, or the charter of a locality. For example, the appointing authority for a Sheriff's Department is typically the sheriff. In political subdivisions of the State the appointing authority may be the school board, the governing body of a public authority, a town board, the town supervisor or the mayor. With respect to the State as an employer, the appointing authority is usually the agency or department head. In this book, the terms "appointing authority" and "employer" will be used interchangeably.

When courts uncover an error in due process, they will void disciplinary penalties and either dismiss the case or remand (return) the case to the employer for reconsideration. Ignoring due process is costly -- and unfair.

Due process is short for "due process of law." This is an old concept with roots in English common law traditions. Under the common law, individuals could not be deprived of their liberty without due process of law -- notice of the charges and a full and fair hearing before any action could be taken. Freedom from arbitrary action was deemed a form of liberty that must be protected. Over time the concept of liberty was extended to cover property rights. Clearly, a farmer evicted from his property without just cause was denied liberty. In the 16th century, the common law recognized that one's job is a form of property and that keeping one's job is a form of liberty. Under the common law, any person "put from his livelihood" had been denied liberty. Hence, no man could be denied his employment or trade without due process of law.

In modern disciplinary actions, it is essential that employees' due process rights be respected. Employees who are entitled to due process (typically, "permanent" and "tenured" employees) cannot be removed or subjected to any disciplinary penalty unless their incompetence or misconduct has been proved by substantial evidence in a hearing. Like the criminal justice system, administrative disciplinary procedures incorporate fundamental due process concepts such as the presumption of innocence of the accused and the placing of the burden of proof on the charging party.

Section 75 of New York's Civil Service Law, for example, requires notice and hearing, the right to representation, the right to confront and present witnesses, and the right of review or appeal. Similar due process requirements are essential in alternative dispute resolution procedures negotiated through collective bargaining in accordance with the New York State Taylor Law.

Contract disciplinary procedures typically cover only those employees who have rights under statutes such as Section 75 of the Civil Service Law or Section 3020-a of the Education Law. However, some collective bargaining agreements grant due process rights to certain groups of employees, such as provisional employees, who are not entitled to such rights by statute.

This book concerns the discipline of public employees in New York State. Who is included in the public service in the state?

In New York State, one may be employed in either the private sector or the public sector. The public sector in New York has two components: the military service and the civil service. The State's military service is outlined in footnote[2] below.

The civil service consists of the classified service and the unclassified service. The "classified service" comprises the bulk of "civil service employment" in New York State. Positions in the classified service are under the jurisdiction of either the state Civil Service Commission or a local Civil Service Commission or Personnel Officer. Civil service positions that are not under such jurisdiction are deemed to be in the "unclassified service," which includes judges, elected officials, commissioners and teachers.

Finally, the classified service is composed of four classes, known as jurisdictional classes: the competitive class, the noncompetitive class, the exempt class and the labor class. As explained below, an individual's statutory right to due process depends the nature of his or her appointment by the State or a political subdivision of the State.

1.01 Due process rights depend on appointment status and jurisdictional classification

The right to due process is not universal. For example, a substitute teacher employed for a two-week stint does not have the same right to due process as a tenured teacher. Likewise, a provisional civilian police dispatcher does not have the same right to due process as a detective holding a permanent appointment. It should be clear from these examples that the due process rights of an individual employee flow from that individual's appointment status and jurisdictional classification.

Appointment status, also known as employment status, refers to whether one holds permanent, contingent permanent, temporary, or provisional appointment. The appointment status of employees in the public service is considered in "The Concept of Tenure" [See 1.05 below].

---

[2] Although this book essentially addresses discipline in the civil service of the State and its political subdivisions, New York also has a military service. New York's military service has four components: the organized militia, the state reserve list, the state retired list and the unorganized militia. The organized militia consists of the New York Army National Guard, the New York Air National Guard, the New York Naval Militia and the New York Guard. The unorganized militia consists of "all able-bodied male residents between the ages of 17 and 45 who are not members of the organized militia or on the state reserve list or the state retired list." The State's Code of Military Justice, Article 7 of the Military Law, sets out the disciplinary procedures to be followed with respect to members of the organized militia, those on the State reserve list and those on the State retired list.

The term jurisdictional classification[3] refers to whether a position is (a) in the classified service, and therefore subject to the jurisdiction of a Civil Service Commission or (b) in the unclassified service [Section 35, Civil Service Law], and therefore not subject to the jurisdiction of a Civil Service Commission. "Jurisdictional classification" also refers to whether a given position in the classified service is assigned to the competitive, non-competitive, exempt or labor class [Section 2.10 of the Civil Service Law]. Unless placed in a different jurisdictional class by action of a civil service commission or by statute, all classified service positions are in the competitive class.

Issues of appointment status and jurisdictional classification are at the heart of a high percentage of lawsuits involving disciplinary cases. Anyone involved in the disciplinary process should look at these issues first, because an employee's due process rights depend on his or her actual, i.e., statutory, appointment status and the actual jurisdictional classification of the position to which he or she has been appointed. We use the word "actual" because the failure of an employer to properly identify an employee's statutory appointment status or the statutory jurisdictional classification of the individual's position does not expand or diminish the employee's legal rights.

Probationers terminated during the probationary period often claim they were denied due process and constitute another significant body of individuals filing lawsuits against public employers in New York State.

For probationers, one other factor influences the right to due process beyond those listed above: how long the probationer has served in his or her position. Employees in competitive class or the non-competitive class who are serving probationary periods have due process rights only if they (a) not yet completed the minimum period of probation, (b) have become "tenured" by successfully completing their probationary period, or (c) have become tenured by serving the maximum period of probation and continuing to work in the position without having been removed by the appointing authority. Being continued in service beyond the maximum period of service without the appointing authority having taken formal action to confirm or deny tenure in the position is referred to as attaining "tenure by estoppel" or sometimes as attaining "tenure by acquiescence". In fact, Section 65.4 of the Civil Service Law actually provides for an appointee attaining tenure by estoppel under certain circumstances.

In contrast, probationers may be dismissed without due process, i.e., notice and hearing, for any lawful reason or for no reason, if they have completed their minimum period of probation but have not yet completed their maximum period of probation. See 1.05 below, "The concept of tenure," and the successive sections.

The categories of jurisdictional classification in the classified service are the competitive class, non-competitive class, exempt class and labor class. One might wonder why these different classes exist. The answer lies in Article V, Section 6 of the New York State Constitution, which requires that, wherever practicable, appointments and promotions in the civil service be made according to merit

---

[3] The term jurisdictional classification is sometimes confused with "position classification." Position classification deals with the duties and responsibilities of a position and, for State positions, its allocation to a salary grade. See 1.11 below, "Budgetary classification is irrelevant to due process rights of employees."

and fitness. Competitive examinations are used to establish eligibility for such employment. Because competitive examinations are not practicable in every instance, the State Legislature provides guidelines for creating positions outside the competitive class. These positions may be placed in one of three categories: the exempt class, the non-competitive class or the labor class.

"Jurisdictional classification" refers to the decision-making process concerning whether a position belongs in the competitive class or one of the other classes listed above.

In February 1998 the Civil Service Commission proposed a rule to clarify the categories outside the competitive class by establishing these definitions:

Exempt class: "The exempt class is to include those positions specifically placed there by the Legislature, together with all subordinate positions for which there is no requirement that the person appointed pass a civil service examination. Instead, appointments rest in the discretion of the person who, by law, has determined the position's qualifications and whether the persons to be appointed possess those qualifications."

Non-competitive class: "The non-competitive class is to be comprised of those positions which are not in the exempt or labor classes and for which the Civil Service Commission has found it impracticable to determine an applicant's merit and fitness through a competitive examination. The qualifications of those candidates selected are to be determined by an examination which is sufficient to insure (sic) selection of proper and competent employees."

The labor class: "The labor class is to be made up of unskilled laborers in the service of the State and its civil divisions, except those which can be examined for competitively." [NYS Register, Feb. 4, 1998, p.6]

1.02 Who is entitled to due process?

Broadly, the employees entitled to due process are those employees who are specifically granted due process rights under a state statute such as Section 75 of the Civil Service Law or Section 3020-a of the Education Law or a contract negotiated in accordance with the Taylor Law.

Most Taylor Law agreements closely track, or incorporate by reference, either Section 75 or Section 3020-a regarding categories of employees entitled to due process. Those employees who enjoy a statutory right to due process under Section 75 or Section 3020-a are:

1. Tenured teachers in the public schools and BOCES. [Section 3020-a of the Education Law]; see 1.04, "Due process rights under Section 3020-a," below.

2. Tenured administrators in the public schools and BOCES. [Section 3020-a of the Education Law]; see 1.04, "Due process rights under Section 3020-a," below.

3. Employees with permanent and "contingent permanent" appointments to positions in the competitive class of the classified service, provided they have either (a) not yet completed the

minimum period of probation, (b) become tenured by successfully completing their probationary period, or (c) become tenured by serving the maximum period of probation and continuing to work in the position without having been removed by the appointing authority ("tenure by estoppel") [Section 75.1(a) of the Civil Service Law.]

A so-called Section 64.4 or "contingent permanent" employee serves in a position that has been "left temporarily vacant by the leave of absence of the permanent incumbent thereof," and who has been permanently appointed or reinstated to the position in accordance with Section 64.4 of the Civil Service Law. For an example of how these appointments are made at the state level, see Section 4.11 of the Rules of the NYS Civil Service Commission.

4. Non-competitive class employees who have served for at least five years and who are not considered policy-makers or "confidential" under the rules of the state or a local civil service commission.[4]

If a probationary period is provided by the civil service commission having jurisdiction, non-competitive class employees have due process rights only if they have either (a) not yet served the minimum period of probation, (b) successfully completed their probationary period, or (c) served the maximum period of probation and are still working in the position without being removed by the appointing authority ("tenure by estoppel") [Section 75.1(c)]

5. Exempt class employees who are honorably discharged veterans who have served in time of war (WWI, WWII), or in a "police action": Korea, Vietnam, Lebanon, Grenada, Panama or the Persian Gulf; [see Section 85] or are exempt volunteer firefighters as defined in the New York General Municipal Law Section 200. [Section 75.1(b) of the Civil Service Law] However, being a veteran or firefighter will not entitle an exempt class employee to due process if he or she is designated a private secretary, cashier or deputy of any official or department [Section 75.1(b)].[5]

6. Labor class employees who are honorably discharged war veterans or exempt volunteer firefighters. [Section 75.1(b)]

7. Employees in New York City who have served for at least three years as Homemakers or Home Aides in the non-competitive class. [Section 75.1(d)]

8. Police officers who have served as detectives for three continuous years, unless they are reduced in rank for solely economic reasons, or consolidation or abolishment of police functions. [Section 75.1(e)]

---

[4] Those designated "confidential" by PERB constitute a different class of employees and such a designation does not affect their due process rights under Section 75, Section 3020-a and other statutes.

[5] The presence (or absence) of the word "deputy" in an employee's job title, such as deputy sheriff or deputy commissioner, is not predictive of whether or not the person is a deputy under Section 75. The meaning of the term "deputy" for the purposes of Section 75.1(b) refers to the possession of sufficient administrative power, by statute or other authority, to perform duties vested in a principal officer. See Sullivan v Superintendent of Insurance of New York State (64 NY2d 1074) To further complicate matters, courts have frequently relied on the duties set out in job descriptions rather than duties actually performed to determine whether individuals are have "deputy" status.

1.03 Who has no due process rights?

Who is entitled to due process depends on whether statute or a collective bargaining agreement controls.

Section 75 grants no due process rights to employees in the classified service who are:

Temporary employees [See 1.09]

Provisional employees [See 1.09]

Non-competitive class employees who are policy-makers and are designated "confidential" in the rules of the responsible civil service commission

Exempt class employees other than exempt volunteer firefighters and certain veterans

Labor class employees other than exempt volunteer firefighters and certain veterans

Such employees may be entitled to due process rights under collective bargaining agreements negotiated in accordance with the Taylor Law, however.

1.04 Due process rights under Section 3020-a

Section 3020-a, most recently amended by the Legislature effective August 25, 1994, is the equivalent of Section 75 in primary and secondary public education. It provides that tenured teachers and administrators can be disciplined only for just cause and in accordance with the due process procedures set out in Section 3020-a or as provided in alternative disciplinary procedures negotiated under the Taylor Law and set out in a collective bargaining agreement.

Different sections of the New York State Education law grant due process rights as described in Section 3020-a to specific categories of tenured educational personnel. These categories of educators are: generally teachers and supervisory staff of a vocational education and extension board (Education Law Section 1102.3); generally assistant and other superintendents and teachers and other employees of a city school system in cities having less than 125,000 inhabitants (Section 2509); generally assistant and other superintendents and teachers and other employees assistant and other superintendents and teachers and other employees of cities of New York, Buffalo, Rochester, Syracuse and Yonkers (Section 2573); specifically assistant and other superintendents and teachers and other employees of the City of New York, (Section 2590-j); generally assistant and other superintendents and teachers and other employees of school districts employing fewer than 8 teachers, other than a city school district (Section 3012); and specifically assistant and other superintendents and teachers and other employees of board of cooperative education services [BOCES] (Section 3014).

Unclassified service employees of the City and State University systems including community colleges are not covered by Section 3020-a; they are covered by the "trustee's policies" of these institutions or by procedures negotiated in accordance with the Taylor Law.

1.05 The concept of tenure

Although "tenure" is associated most closely with educational settings, the legal concept of tenure is not limited to educators. The vesting of due process rights and other rights in a probationer who has completed the maximum period of probation is often referred to as tenure. Attaining tenure simply means that an employee has successfully completed a probationary period or, under certain circumstances, has not been dismissed prior to end of his or her maximum period of probation.

The concept of tenure originated in a time when a person's political or religious views could result in a termination if they were not consistent with the "politically correct" views of the period. The concept of tenure has endured under a public policy that a civil service meritocracy administered with integrity is preferable to a political machine. In New York State, only incompetence or misconduct with respect to job performance or off-duty misconduct adversely reflecting on the public employer may serve as a legal basis for disciplinary action by a public employer.

The keys to attaining tenure in the public service are (1) permanent appointment and (2) successful completion of any probationary period required by law, rule or regulation.

Tenure can arise through inaction as well as through action. Should the appointing authority neglect to timely notify a probationer that he or she is to be terminated for failure to satisfactorily complete the probationary period on or before the end of the individual's probationary period, the employee is deemed to have obtained tenure by operation of law, also known as tenure by estoppel or tenure by acquiescence.

Tenure is not always permanent. For instance, an individual holding "tenure" in his or her position accused of wrongdoing may agree to be put on disciplinary probation to settle the matter. Violating the terms of the probation can lead to dismissal without notice and hearing notwithstanding the employee's prior tenure status. For instance, state corrections officer Tina Ramos agreed to pay a $1,000 fine and be placed on disciplinary probation for one year to settle a disciplinary case involving improper behavior when escorting a prisoner.

After Ramos was observed carrying her weapon in a hospital examination room in violation of departmental rules, she was terminated without a hearing for violating the terms of her disciplinary probation. [Ramos v Coombe, (Appellate Division, 1997), 654 NYS2d 454, 237 AD2d 713, leave to appeal dismissed 89 NY2d 981.]

1.06 "Permanent" appointments, probation and tenure in the competitive class

Section 63.1 of the Civil Service Law provides that "every original appointment to a position in the competitive class is subject to a probationary period." This language means that the effective date of an individual's permanent appointment to a position in the competitive class occurs on the same day that his or her probationary period begins.

In other words, becoming permanent and becoming tenured are two distinct events. An employee attains tenure upon completing a probationary period. If the employee is in the competitive class, he or she holds a permanent appointment from the first day of his or her probationary period and matures into tenured status upon satisfactory completion of the probationary period.

It follows that even probationers hold permanent appointments. This concept is put into practice when layoffs occur; the employer must measure the seniority of employees from the day they began as probationers, not the day they completed their probationary period.

To illustrate this concept, consider this question: The Civil Service Law states that for the purposes of layoff, a person's seniority is measured from his or her "original date of permanent appointment" to a position in the classified service. When is that? The answer is not the date the employee's probationary term (if any) ended. Rather, it is the day he or she was initially permanently appointed to the classified service position as a probationer.

1.07 Permanent vs. probationer vs. provisional[6]

If a person is going to err thinking about the due process rights of an employee, it is likely to involve confusion of three "P" words: permanent, probationer and provisional. Even supposed experts in the civil service law are prone to errors in mixing up these terms. One of the authors was dismayed when he discovered that an editor substituted the word "provisional" for "probationary" in a chapter he wrote for the New York Bar Association's book, Public Sector Labor and Employment. Here is a review of the definitions:

"Permanent" refers to the nature of an appointment of a person, not the status of the position itself. The term is also used to refer to the nature of appointments of employees in the classified service.

A special sub-class of "permanent" has been authorized by Section 64.4 of the Civil Service Law and is generally referred to as a "contingent permanent appointment." A contingent permanent employee serves in a position that has been "left temporarily vacant by the leave of absence of the permanent incumbent thereof" and has been permanently appointed or reinstated to the position in accordance with Section 64.4 of the Civil Service Law. Such individuals enjoy all of the rights of a permanent appointee except the right to continue in the position upon the return of the individual on leave from the position.

---

[6] A special "appointment status" results when an individual is appointed to a position encumbered by an officer or employee absent for ordered military service. In such situations the position held by a public employee absent on military duty typically is filled by appointing a "substitute employee" to the vacancy. The substitute employee is appointed "for a period not exceeding the leave of absence of the former incumbent and ... shall acquire no right to permanent appointment or tenure by virtue of" such service. For additional information concerning "substitute appointments, see Sections 242 and 243 of New York State's Military Law.

In the competitive class, a "permanent" appointment is typically an appointment made from a list of eligible candidates. These lists include "preferred lists" and other types of lists and "rosters" created as a result of a lay-off of employees and "eligible lists" rankings of people who have taken a civil service examination ("open competitive" or promotion lists). Most appointments in the New York State civil service are permanent appointments in the competitive class because (1) all positions in the classified service are automatically in the competitive class unless placed in another jurisdictional classification by the State Civil Service Commission or by statute and (2) the state constitution mandates that Civil Service positions be filled by competitive examination wherever practical.

In rare instances a permanent employee in the competitive class may be nominated for a noncompetitive promotion examination to a competitive class position. This is permitted when there are three or fewer candidates eligible for the promotion examination.

The term "permanent" for the purposes of the Civil Service Law does not have the common-use meaning of established or long-lasting. Rather, it denotes entitlement -- that the individual is entitled to certain benefits and protections not available to temporary or provisional employees.

In the non-competitive class, employers make "permanent" appointments where the only requirement is that the individual pass a non-competitive exam and satisfactorily complete the probationary period. All appointments in the non-competitive class are permanent unless the appointments were made to encumbered positions. An encumbered position is a position authorized to be established by the appropriate civil service commission and included in the budget whose permanent incumbent is absent, typically because of an authorized leave without pay.

Exempt and labor class employees also are recipient of permanent appointments as long as the appointments were not made to encumbered positions.

As described in the previous section, all employees that receive a permanent appointment must serve a probationary period before achieving tenure. But a probationary employee does not "become" permanent when he or she successfully completes the probationary term; as explained earlier, the appointment is permanent from day one of his or her effective date of appointment.

"Provisional" appointments are made to vacant positions in the competitive class. Technically, provisional appointments may not last more than nine months and are made when there is no appropriate eligible list available to fill the vacancy.

What is an "appropriate" eligible list? A list determined by the civil service department (state or local) to contain the names of individuals qualified for the position. One type of list used to fill a vacancy is a "preferred list" of laid-off employees. Another type is a ranking of people who have taken an open-competitive or promotion civil service exam. There are other types of lists, such as a special military list. To make appointments, employers must follow either the "Rule of One" (selecting the top person or only person on a preferred list or special military list) or the "Rule of Three" (selecting from among three candidates receiving the highest scores). Which Rule the employer follows depends on the type of list certified or, in some cases, the provisions of a collective bargaining agreement.

Where there are at least two more people on the list than the number of positions to be filled by a competitive or promotion examination, this is referred to as a "mandatory" list and the appointing authority must make appointments in accordance with the Rule of Three. Thus, if there are at least three people on an eligible list for a single position, the position is to be filled using the Rule of Three. If there is no mandatory list, the vacancy may be filled on a provisional basis in accordance with Section 65 of the Civil Service Law. More rarely, a vacancy may be filled on a "temporary" basis in accordance with Section 64 of the Civil Service Law [see 1.09, "Temporary and Provisional Appointments"].

"Provisional" refers to the nature of the appointment of a person, not the position in which the person serves or the employee as an individual. One is a "provisional" employee only in the respect that one has a provisional appointment to a position. There is no such thing as a "provisional position" -- rather there is a permanent or temporary position that is vacant, and which may be filled by "provisionally appointing" an individual to the vacancy. Provisional appointments are described in Section 65 of the Civil Service Law.

To illustrate the difference between the personnel concept of "permanent status" and the budgetary concept of "permanent position," it is possible to make a permanent appointment to a "temporary position." Indeed, under certain circumstances it is possible to make a permanent appointment to a position that does not exist. In other words, the permanent or temporary status of a position deals with its funding and does not address the personnel status of the incumbent. [See 1.11, "Budgetary classification irrelevant to due process rights of employees]

In contrast, appointment to an encumbered position, permanent or temporary, is a "temporary" appointment or a contingent permanent appointment, depending of the action taken by the appointing authority and the eligibility of the individual for a contingent permanent appointment.

"Probationary" can refer to either a person or an appointment, but not to a position. You can call someone new to a job a probationary employee or say he or she has a probationary appointment until a certain date of maximum probation. But the position in which he or she serves is not probationary. See Appendix 2, "Provisional and Probationary Employees."

1.08 Probationers' due process rights

It is not uncommon for there to be confusion or misunderstanding regarding the due process rights of probationary employees in the classified service. The rules of the state civil service commission and many local civil service commissions usually specify both a minimum period of probation (typically eight weeks) and a maximum period of probation (as short as 12 weeks or as long as three years, depending on the position and the jurisdiction).

Permanent appointees who have served as probationers can be divided into three categories, each with unique due process rights:

1. Employees who have not yet completed their minimum period of probation. These probationers have full due process rights under Section 75. Courts have voiced the view that it is unfair to dismiss

someone except for cause until they have been given a minimal chance to prove themselves. For an employer to dismiss a probationary employee before he or she has completed his or her minimum period of probation, the employee must be brought up on charges of either incompetence or misconduct and found guilty.

2. Probationers who have completed the minimum period of probation, but not yet completed the maximum period of probation. These employees have virtually no due process rights under state law. Employers may summarily dismiss -- without notice and without hearing -- such probationers as long as the action is not being taken for a discriminatory, arbitrary or otherwise unlawful reason. See, for example, Garrison v Koehler, 555 NYS2d 8, in which a female probationer persuaded the Appellate Division, First Department, that the "insubordination" that led to her dismissal from the New York City Dept. of Corrections was really her refusal to submit to sexual harassment.

Probationary terminations are often challenged by the disappointed employee. In its decision in In re Nilda Munoz, a case involving the interplay between the authority to terminate a probationer and the procedures requiring the evaluation of a probationer's performance, decided March 18, 2003, the Appellate Division, First Department rejected a claim that Section 2573.1(b) of the Education Law provided that a New York City probationary school principal's employment could be terminated only by majority vote of their respective community school boards. Munoz had argued that it was unlawful for a New York City community superintendent to terminate her services as a probationary principal.

The Appellate Division pointed out that Section 2573.1(b), which applies to the New York, Buffalo, Rochester, Syracuse and Yonkers city school districts, does not require a majority vote of the community school board but a majority vote of the board of education. Further, noted the court, the Education Law was subsequently amended by Education Law Section 2590-f.1(c), a provision applicable only to the New York City school district, that specifically grants community superintendents authority to appoint and discharge all employees.

The court said that to the extent the two provisions are inconsistent, the earlier enacted must be deemed superseded by the later enacted provision, citing Garzilli v Mills, 250 AD2d 131.

The court also rejected Munoz's claim that her termination was unlawful because the steps set out in the "Principal Performance Review" procedure (PPR) had not been satisfied. Munoz contended that she was not evaluated at least annually and that she was not given notice of her deficiencies. Accordingly, she argued, the superintendent had not complied with certain procedural requirements incorporated in the multi-step evaluation and reporting process and thus her termination should be overturned by the court.

The court declined to do so, explaining that the PPR is not a rule implementing any law binding on the superintendent but merely constituted "a compilation of explanatory forms and instructions that have no legal effect."

It should be mentioned, however, that local civil service commissions may have rules that restrict the circumstances under which a probationary employee may be dismissed, and employer must honor those restrictions. See the Court of Appeals ruling in Scherbyn v Wayne-Finger Lakes BOCES, 77 NY2d 753.

Likewise, some collective bargaining agreements specifically provide due process rights to probationary employees and other employees not having tenure rights.

3. Employees who have completed their maximum period of probation. These employees are no longer probationers but are "tenured" employees. They have full due process rights under Section 75. They cannot be dismissed except for cause, i.e.: being found guilty of charges of incompetence or misconduct.

A case in which the Court of Appeals clearly addressed these basic rules on dismissal of probationary employees is York v McGuire, 63 NY2d 760.

Notably, the maximum period of probation can be extended. Employers are empowered under the rules of state civil service commission and many local civil service commissions to extend periods of probation as a matter of discretion rather than terminate the employee. This must be done before the employee's maximum period of probation has expired, however.

Generally if a probationary employee is absent, for any reason, with or without pay, his or her probationary period is automatically extended by the number of days he or she is absent. [See, for example, 4 NYCRR 4.5(f).] There are some exceptions, however. If the absence is short -- 10 days (or 20 days if the probationary term or maximum term exceeds 26 weeks) -- Civil Service "Rules" may allow the appointing authority to consider the days absent as "time served." [See, for example, 4 NYCRR 4.5(f). This applies to both authorized and unauthorized absences.

If a probationer is absent due to "ordered military service," his or her military service is to be credited "as satisfactory service" for the purpose of completing his or her probationary period if he or she is honorably discharged or released from active duty. [See Sections 242, 243 of the Military Law] This means that an individual may satisfy his or her probationary period requirements while on military duty. If the individual is appointed or promoted to a position while on military duty, his or her military service is also to be counted as "satisfactory service" for the purposes of probation.

The above applies to all probationary employees in the classified service, those in the non-competitive class, the exempt class, the labor class and the competitive class. In the competitive class, probationary employees include permanent employees who are serving a probationary period upon an initial appointment, or upon promotion, as well as contingent permanent employees.

Sometimes a state law or the civil service commission having jurisdiction over a certain position has set the minimum period of probation and the maximum period of probation to be the exact same amount of time. In such cases, the employee has due process rights under Section 75 at all times or, as some may observe: instant tenure!

A danger in understanding the rights of probationers is to get caught up in nomenclature and assume that because someone is "probationary," he or she does not have due process rights. Often the exact opposite is true. Both employers and employee representatives should be vigilant on this issue.

See Appendix 2, "Provisional and Probationary Employees."

1.09 Temporary and provisional appointments

Temporary appointments in the competitive class are appointments made to an encumbered position. It may be made without competitive examinations for short periods -- usually three or six months -- in accordance with Section 64 of the Civil Service Law. However Section 64 provides for temporary appointment under other circumstances and may even require such appointments to be made from an eligible list.

Provisional appointments are appointments made by a civil service commission to fill vacancies when there is no appropriate eligible list. Forms of eligible lists include lists of people who have taken a civil service exam, preferred lists of laid-off employees and special military lists [See 1.07].

Even if an employee has served years or decades as temporary or provisional, his or her status never "ripens" into a permanent appointment with tenure rights to due process. Temporary and provisional appointments are "merely stop-gap" measures with no possibility of ripening into permanent appointments [Halpin v Reile, 1970, 64 Misc.2d 1023, 316 NYS 2d 819]

There are exceptions to the above, however. Provisional employees can become permanent employees with tenure rights to due process under certain special conditions set out in Section 65.4 of the Civil Service Law. Section 65.4 provides that a provisional employee is automatically "afforded permanent appointment" in the position in the event either of two specific circumstances is satisfied:

1. The provisional employee (a) takes and passes an examination for the position and (b) the resulting list is not a "mandatory list" and (c) he or she is continued in the position for a period greater than the required probationary period for the position; or

2. An individual is (a) on a nonmandatory eligible list for the position and is (b) provisionally appointed to the position and (c) is continued in the position beyond the maximum probationary period for the position.

If a provisional employee attains permanent appointment by "operation of law," he or she will have all the rights of a tenured employee, including the right to notice and hearing for the purpose of disciplinary action. See Roulett v Town of Hempstead Civil Service Commission, 1971, 71 Misc.2d 477, 336 NYS2d 286, affirmed 40 AD 611, 335 NYS2d 1008.]

Is there any exception to a temporary employee being ineligible for due process protections? Only if "temporary" does not truly describe the status of the employee, despite the label. See Spindel v New York City Housing Authority, 1964, 41 Misc.2d 363, 245 NYS2d 506.

Of course, temporary or provisional employees might have special due process rights under a Taylor Law agreement. Also, any individual dismissed or penalized for a discriminatory reason or some other unlawful reason may be entitled to redress under the state Human Rights Law or federal laws such as Title VII, Civil Rights Law of 1964.

Furthermore, it should be remembered that individuals holding a temporary or provisional appointment who are terminated (as well as permanent employees who are dismissed before completing their probationary period) might be entitled to a "name-clearing hearing." See 1.22, "Name-Clearing Hearings."

The following summarizes the basic concepts underlying temporary and provisional appointments:

Typically a temporary appointment is made to a position temporarily vacant or to a position that is not expected to be continued for any extended period of time as generally set out in Section 64 of the Civil Service Law.

A long list of decisions support the holding that an individual "temporarily appointed" to a position pursuant to subdivisions 1, 2 and 3 of Section 64 of the Civil Service Law cannot and does not attain permanent status by operation of law regardless of the duration of such status and regardless of the fact that under certain circumstances the temporary appointment has been made from an appropriate eligible list. Indeed, such an appointment from the eligible list may lawfully have been made without regard to rank on the eligible list, thus avoiding the provisions of Civil Service Law Section 61, which sets out the so-called "rule of three."

Accordingly, it seems clear that except as provided by Section 64.4, a temporary appointment cannot mature into permanent status.

An appointment pursuant to the exception set out in Civil Service Law Section 64.4 is typically referred to as a "contingent permanent appointment." This may be viewed as a "special form of temporary appointment" -- one that provides many of the benefits incumbent upon permanent appointment to the individual appointed to an encumbered position in the competitive class of the classified service but (1) requires that the appointing authority affirmative act to provide for such a "contingent permanent" appointment and (2) requires that the appointee otherwise satisfies the mandates of Section 61.

As the Court of Appeals indicated in Snyder v Civil Service Commission, 72 NY2d 981, a temporary appointee, even if otherwise eligible for such appointment pursuant to Section 64.4, must be appointed specifically as a contingent permanent employee by the appointing authority, which status is granted solely at the discretion of the appointing authority.

In contrast, a provisional appointment authorized by Civil Service Law Section 65, [a provisional appointment may be made only to a position that is wholly vacant], may, under certain conditions, mature into a permanent appointment by operation of law. Section 65.4 sets out the terms and conditions pursuant to which a provisional appointment matures into a permanent appointment. The various terms, conditions and circumstances under which such permanent status obtains are explained in such decisions as Matter of Roulette, 40 AD2d 611, Haynes v Chautauqua County, 55 NY2d 814, Becker v New York State Civil Service Commission, 61 NY2d 252 and La Sota v Green, 53 NY2d 491.

1.10 Jurisdictional misclassification

Many discipline cases involve employees who claim their positions belong in a jurisdictional classification that carries due process rights. In Ficken v VEEB, 90 N.Y.2d 809, Ficken was terminated from her position of "secretary" with the Suffolk County Vocational Education and Extension Board [VEEB] for alleged misconduct. She persuaded the Appellate Division that her dismissal was without notice and hearing in violation of Section 75 of the Civil Service Law.

Although VEEB claimed that the Suffolk Civil Service Commission had designated Ficken's position as unclassified pursuant to Section 35, the Appellate Division affirmed a lower court ruling that "there is no enumerated category under Section 35 within which [Ficken] falls." The court said that "as all positions not defined as unclassified must be classified, [Ficken's] position must be a classified service position" in the competitive class. Hence, Ficken was entitled to due process.[7]

If a local civil service commission or the State civil service commission has jurisdiction, then the commission or its designee has control over all issues of appointment, retention and dismissal concerning the application of the Civil Service Law in a particular situation. For instance, a civil service commission must certify payrolls at least once a year to ensure that each person paid has been lawfully appointed in accordance with the Civil Service Law. The certification attests that the individuals on the payroll were lawfully appointed in accordance with the Civil Service Law. It is a misdemeanor to pay an individual on a civil service payroll if that individual has not been duly appointed and so certified by the responsible civil service commission.

If a civil service commission has jurisdiction over a position, the Civil Service Law dictates the due process rights to which the individual is entitled. Which specific due process rights the individual is entitled to under the Civil Service Law depends on the individuals' employment status (permanent, temporary, provisional, et cetera) as well as the jurisdictional classification of the position and, possibility, the terms of a collective agreement.

1.11 Budgetary classification irrelevant to due process rights of employees

Managers sometimes think that designating a position as "permanent" or "temporary" for budgetary purposes can be meaningful in determining an individual's rights under the Civil Service Law or a Taylor Law Agreement. This is not the case.

The budget status of the position is irrelevant to the status held by the incumbent of the position for the purposes of determining an individual's rights and benefits, including the individual's right to due process. Indeed, for budgetary purposes, all "permanent" positions could be viewed as temporary, as there is no assurance that the funds necessary to pay the incumbent of a particular position will be appropriated for, or authorized for disbursement in, a given fiscal year.

---

[7] This ruling may be viewed as "overreaching," however, because there was nothing in the record to suggest that the secretary was permanently appointed to her position from an eligible list. Being in the competitive class does not bestow due process rights unless one holds a permanent or contingent permanent appointment. In other words, the court did not address the possibility that Ficken held a temporary or provisional appointment in the competitive class, as opposed to a permanent appointment or a contingent permanent appointment in the competitive class.

In fact, a person may be appointed to a budget-maker's "temporary position" on a permanent basis or to a "permanent position" on a temporary basis. The only possible relevance to the budget status of a position is that the abolishment of a position encumbered by a permanent appointee may ultimately result in a layoff and the establishment of a preferred list.

However, the fact that the position has been abolished does not necessarily mean that disciplinary issues may be ignored. As the Appellate Division's decision in Rubtchinsky vs Moriah Central School District suggests, disciplinary action an individual against should not be discontinued simply because he or she has been laid off as a result of the abolishment of a position. Rubtchinsky, a teacher, was suspended with pay pending the outcome of a disciplinary hearing on charges of incompetence and misconduct. He was then advised that a position in his department was to be abolished and as the teacher with the least seniority, his services would be discontinued. A Section 3020-a disciplinary hearing was never held.

The Appellate Division held that Rubtchinsky could get back salary upon reinstatement to his former position if he demonstrated that he was improperly excessed -- i.e., he was not the least senior individual for the purposed of being excessed. Significantly, the court commented that it knew of no reason to abort a disciplinary hearing simply because the individual was laid off from his or her position.

If, on the other hand, the disciplinary action against the employee is prosecuted and the penalty imposed is dismissal, he or she may be declared ineligible for reinstatement from a preferred list. For example, Section 80.7 of the Civil Service Law, in pertinent part, provides that "Notwithstanding any other provisions of this chapter, the civil service department or appropriate municipal commission may disqualify for reinstatement and remove from a preferred list the name of any eligible who ... has been guilty of such misconduct as would warrant his dismissal from the public service...."

Should the civil service agency elect to remove an individual from a preferred list under such circumstances, the law further provides that "No person shall be disqualified pursuant to this subdivision unless he is first given a written statement of the reasons therefore and an opportunity for a hearing at which such reasons shall be established by appropriate evidence, and at which such person may be represented by counsel and present evidence."

As both the Civil Service Law and the Education Law vest a employee who has been laid off with the right to reinstatement from a preferred list, it seems clear that the employer must go forward with the discipline action notwithstanding the layoff of the accused employee or risk his or her reinstatement from the preferred list.

It is important to understand that an individual's appointment (permanent, contingent permanent, et cetera) defines the individual's employment status, not the fiscal status of the position he or she is filling.

A person may even receive a permanent appointment to a position that does not exist and be vested with the rights that ordinarily flow from "permanent appointment." [See the Appellate Division, Fourth Dept.'s decision in Buffalo PBA v City of Buffalo, Motion for leave to appeal denied, 84 N.Y.2d 813.]

Why would such an appointment be made in the first place? As the Buffalo decision explains: To provide for the appointment as a permanent of an individual in anticipation of a vacancy, which may not become available until after an eligible list expires. In this case, the appointing authority made an appointment to a non-existent position and placed the individual thus appointed on a leave of absence without pay (from the non-existent position). When the incumbent retired some weeks later, after the eligible list had expired, the individual was placed in the newly vacant position and returned from leave.

Another situation in which an appointment to a non-existent position might be approved is when there is a "promotion vacancy" but there is no vacancy in a lower grade position in the line of promotion. In such a situation an individual could be permanently appointed from an eligible list to a lower grade title in the promotion line, or reinstated to a title in the promotion line that he or she formerly held, and simultaneously appointed to the higher title as a provisional employee. The reason for this is that if the individual were not permanently appointed to an eligible lower grade title, he or she would not be able to compete in the promotion examination for the title he or she held provisionally but, at best, could only compete in an open-competitive examination for the title, if one were held. Here the significance lies in the fact that a promotion list must be exhausted before an open competitive list may be certified for appointment.

1.12 Rights of employees of quasi-government entities

If all this were not complicated enough, the line between public employment and "private employment" may be blurred in quasi-governmental entities. The general rule is that the officers and employees of a public benefit corporation are employed in the "private sector" and are not subject to the provisions of the State Constitution's mandate concerning selection for employment in the public service on the basis of merit and fitness or the provisions of the Civil Service Law.

Accordingly, employees of an Off-track Betting Corporation are in the private sector and may not claim rights set out in the Civil Service Law. However, the Legislature has specifically granted civil service rights to the officers and employees of certain public benefit corporations. For example, the officers and employees of the New York City Off-track Betting Corporation have been covered by the civil service system by statute.

The important thing for the reader to remember is that it is the individual's employment status and jurisdictional classification that controls with respect to any rights or benefits he or she may enjoy or demand. Other considerations, such as an individual's or an individual's spouse's status as a veteran may also have an impact on an employee's rights.

It bears repeating that in order to determine the rights of a particular individual, whether by statute or by contract, it is essential to first determine that individual's status in the personnel system of the State or a political subdivision of the State.

The failure to make a correct determination with respect to an individual's status could result in a court determination that the employee was unlawfully removed from the position and the appointing authority directed to reinstate the individual with back salary and benefits.

1.13 Veterans' due process rights

Veterans have unique due process rights under New York State law. Section 75 of the Civil Service Law specifically covers veterans who have served in the armed forces of the United States in time of war and who have been "honorably discharged" or released under honorable conditions. Section 85 of the Civil Service Law sets out the definition of a veteran for the purposes of Section 75.

This is a significant benefit if the veteran is in the exempt class or the labor class, because such employees typically serve at the pleasure of the appointing authority and are not entitled to notice and hearing in connection with disciplinary actions. A veteran in an exempt class position [other than one serving as a private secretary, cashier or as the deputy of an official or department] or in a labor class position has been given the same rights with respect to removal and discipline as permanent employees in the competitive class.

Another benefit of veteran's status: If the employee is serving in a non-competitive class position but has not yet served for a sufficient period to qualify for Section 75 rights in such status, he or she may assert their veteran's status to qualify for Section 75 rights.

Section 75 also applies to "exempt volunteer firefighters" as defined in the General Municipal Law employed in positions in the exempt, non-competitive or labor class. Such firefighters are entitled to the same removal and other disciplinary proceedings as apply to permanent employees in the competitive class.

Still, a veteran is not entitled to special due process in the form of a notice and hearing if he or she is removed from his or her position as a probationary employee as the Court of Appeals ruled in Vaillancourt v NYS Liquor Authority, 544 NYS2d 609, 153ADd 531, appeal gr 74 NY2d616, aff 75 NY2d 889.

In Vaillancourt, the Court of Appeals said that Section 75.1(b)'s granting of due process rights to certain veterans did not "abrogate the provisions of Civil Service Law Section 63 requiring completion of a probationary term nor well-established judicial authority denying the right to a pre-termination hearing to a veteran on probation."

Similarly, in 1990 the Appellate Division, Third Department, concluded that the right of a veteran to a Section 75 hearing did not apply if the employee-veteran was terminated during his probationary period. [Waters v NYS Department of Correctional Services, 554 NYS2d 80, 160 AD2d 1112]

Of course, a collective bargaining agreement negotiated pursuant to the Taylor Law may provide due process rights in connection with discipline and dismissal actions to employees in the classified service not covered by Section 75.

Section 75.1.e provides an example of such a benefit that is created by law.

Part Two: Forms of due process

Due process essentially means that an employee is treated with fairness, has the right to counsel, is given a reasonable opportunity to mount a defense and is entitled to call witnesses to testify on his or her behalf. Below we will discuss several forms of due process that should be provided in any disciplinary case.

1.14 Impartial tribunals

One of the most common due process claims challenging disciplinary determinations is that the tribunal that heard the charges was not impartial. Indeed, it is a common practice in New York State for governmental officials to render judgments in cases in which they are personally involved! Typically the appointing authority files charges against a subordinate pursuant to Section 75 alleging misconduct is the same authority issuing the final determination after a disciplinary hearing is held and the hearing officer issues his or her findings of fact and a recommendation as to the penalty to be imposed.

The appointing authority is simply the person or body that has the legal authority to hire and fire. Unless there is provision for some independent agent such as a arbitrator to make the final determination, the appointing authority, be it an elected body such as a school board or a town board, a department head or a public administrator such as a superintendent, police chief or town manager will make the final disciplinary decision concerning guilt and penalty to be imposed. This situation was the genesis of negotiating alternatives to the statutory disciplinary procedures, usually referred to as "contract disciplinary grievance procedures," through collective bargaining under the Taylor Law.

Every so often an employee brought up on disciplinary charges challenges the impartiality of the person making the decision as to guilt and the penalty to be imposed. Less frequent is an employee's challenge to the qualifications of the person designated to review the disciplinary action. The impartiality of the disciplinary tribunal was an issue in Edgar v Dowling, 96 AD2d 510, and addresses both such types of challenges to persons serving as the disciplinary officer.
Edgar was found guilty of misconduct and insubordination and he was dismissed from his position with the Town Highway Department. He was able to get the determination and penalty annulled by the court because the person who had investigated and filed the charges against him, Dowling, had also testified against Edgar at the hearing. Dowling then "reviewed the record of the hearing" and found Edgar guilty dismissing him. The court said that Dowling should have disqualified himself as the decision maker under the circumstances.

The court then directed that a "duly qualified individual, not heretofore involved in these proceedings", review the disciplinary record and recommendation. This was done and again Edgar was found guilty and again he was dismissed from the position.

Edgar appealed a second time, claiming that the individual chosen to redetermine the charges against him had not been "duly qualified" because he had not been formally appointed a deputy town superintendent of highways (See Section 32(2) of the Highway Law.) The court rejected the argument, finding no merit in the claim that the reviewer was not "duly qualified." It held that the determination of the reviewer was supported by substantial evidence. The court then said that while the penalty of dismissal was harsh, it was not so disproportionate to the offense as to shock one's sense of fairness, citing Pell v Board of Education, 34 NY2d 222.

Such practices can suggest at least the appearance of a conflict of interest. Courts have judged such situations on a case-by-case basis and have found denial of due process in some cases but not others. The key issue is whether or not the person or body rendering the final determination was impartial enough to be fair.

For instance, in 1994 the Appellate Division, Third Department, found the sheriff of Ulster County acted improperly when he demoted a corporal who was found guilty of sleeping on the job on two occasions [Stapleton v LaPaglia, 616 NYS2d 679, 207 AD2d 945. Even though an independent hearing officer heard charges, the court said the demotion was excessive because the sheriff both initiated disciplinary charges against Stapleton and made the final determination as to the penalty to be imposed. Notably, the sheriff imposed a harsher penalty than one recommended by the hearing officer. The court ordered Stapleton's reinstatement to his former position with back salary and benefits until a new penalty determination by a designee of the sheriff without any personal involvement in the charges was made.

Similarly, in 1996, the Appellate Division annulled the dismissal of Saratoga County's director of data processing, who had been found guilty of sexual harassment and incompetence. [Ernst v Saratoga County, 651 NYS2d 709, 234 AD2d 764.] The court said the chairman of the county Board of Supervisors denied Ernst a fair and impartial tribunal because the chairman (a) met with the county's attorneys "to discuss the pending investigation," (b) met with the employees involved to, as he phrased it, "relieve their fears;" (c) signed the notice of the charges against Ernst, (d) voted to bring charges against Ernst, (e) served as a witness at the disciplinary hearing and (f) voted to accept a hearing officer's findings of guilt and impose the recommended penalty.

Nevertheless, in some cases courts have been more tolerant of employers being involved in some aspect of the disciplinary process. In Stanton v Board of Trustees, 550 NYS2d 16, the Appellate Division, Second Department ruled that an employee was not deprived of administrative due process even though members of the Board who voted to terminate Stanton also participated in the underlying investigation that lead to charges of misconduct being brought against her. "(A)lthough a 'fair trial in a fair tribunal is a basic requirement of due process'," the court said, "... it has also been recognized that 'mere familiarity with the facts of a case gained by an agency in the performance of its statutory role does not disqualify a decision-maker.'"

In Stanton's case, the Appellate Division noted that although the Board was authorized by Section 75.2 of the Civil Service Law to conduct a disciplinary hearing concerning the charges it had filed against her, it elected to have an independent hearing officer preside at the hearing instead. The court viewed this as evidence of the board's desire to minimize the possibility of bias that might result from the overlapping investigator and adjudicative functions of the board.

In addition, it was noted that members of the board who had testified against Stanton at the hearing did not vote on the question of whether to terminate her employment.

In cases in which a board is the appointing authority and is voting to accept a hearing officer's finding of fact, each member of the board must make an independent review of the record. This means a copy of the transcript must be made available to each member of the board who votes.

The Ernst v Saratoga County case [651 NYS2d 709, 234 AD2d 764] described above illustrates this principle. The court was persuaded that board members failed in this duty because "the only complete copy of the hearing transcript was made available to the Board members at the county personnel office."

Appointing authorities, whether they are individuals or boards, should use common sense in handling disciplinary cases to minimize even the appearance of an impropriety. Besides the risk of litigation, there can be costs in terms of morale and public perception. One need not be an attorney to see that problems could arise with an administrator or a board member serving multiple roles such as accuser, investigator, witness, judge, jury and executioner.

1.15 Specificity of charges

Disciplinary charges and specifications must be sufficient to permit the accused employee to understand the nature of the charges and specifications and prepare his or her defense.

The importance of being precise in drafting disciplinary charges is illustrated by the decision of the Appellate Division in the Fella case [Fella v County of Rockland, 297 A.D.2d 813].

According to the Appellate Division, even in situations where discipline may be warranted, the failure to properly word the charges and specifications may be fatal to the employer's attempt to discipline an employee.

Peter Fella, Rockland County's Commissioner of Hospitals, was suspended for 30 days without pay for allegedly violating the County's Equal Employment Opportunity Policy [EEOP].

According to the court's decision, following an investigation, the Rockland County Director of Employee Rights and Equity Compliance [Director] concluded that Fella had created a hostile work environment by promoting a person with whom he was then having a romantic relationship to a vacant assistant director of nursing position.

The Director held that the Commissioner's action violated the County's EEOP based on a finding that some employees said that they felt uncomfortable at work because Fella had this "romantic relationship" with a co-employee. This, according to the Director, created a hostile work environment and, as such, violated the EEOP. The County Executive adopted the Director's findings and suspended Fella for having created a hostile work environment in violation of the EEOP.

In its decision the Appellate Division noted that the County's EEOP defined sexual harassment as "unwelcome sexual advances, requests for sexual favors, sexual demands or conduct of a sexual nature which 'had the purpose or affect [sic] of unreasonably interfering with an [affected] person's work performance or creating an intimidating, hostile or offensive work environment.'" Citing

DeCinto v Westchester County Medical Center, 807 F2d 304, the court explained that there is no sexual discrimination or harassment involved "where the conduct complained of by the employee involves an isolated act of preferential treatment of another employee due to a romantic, consensual relationship."

The Supreme Court judge commented that while Fella's decision to promote an individual with whom he was having a romantic relationship may constitute poor judgment, it did not constitute a violation of the County's EEOP - the alleged basis for bring the disciplinary action. As the County failed to establish any violation of its EEOP, the Supreme Court annulled the determination of the Rockland County Executive. The Appellate Division affirmed the ruling.

Of particular interest is the Supreme Court's noting that Fella's actions may have served as a basis for discipline, albeit based on other theories of alleged misconduct. While the Court concluded there was no violation of the EEOP and thus the County could not sustain the charges it filed against Fella, the decision suggests that Fella's behavior might constitute a legitimate basis for subjecting him to disciplinary action based on other specifications.

In other words, it is possible that had the County charged Fella with misconduct based on specifications other than violating the EEOP, the court might have allowed its disciplinary action against Fella to survive.

What lesson can be learned from Fella? While the charges and specifications filed against an employee should clearly apprise the individual the alleged "misconduct or incompetence" giving rise to the charge, the specifications should constitute acts or omissions that, if proven to have occurred, would support a finding that the employee was guilty of misconduct or incompetence. In any event, the employer should be reasonably certain that it would be able to prove the allegations, whatever they may be, before initiating disciplinary action against an individual.

Under Section 3020-a as amended, hearing officers are empowered at prehearing conferences to hear requests from employees for a "bill of particulars" including witness statements, notes, district records, student records, exculpatory evidence and other material. [Section 3020-a.3(C)(III)(C)] Normally it is sufficient for the employer to provide enough information to allow the employee to make an informed response.

For instance, if an employee were accused of stealing, it would be appropriate to state what was stolen and when it turned up missing. In an 1899 case, state courts ruled that dismissal for alleged misconduct will not be sustained if the employer failed to state with any certainty the time and place that the alleged misconduct took place. [People v Elmendorf, 42 App. Div. 306, 59 NYS 115]

The Civil Service Law states that accused employees must be furnished with a copy of the charges and be given at least eight days to respond. [Section 75.2, Civil Service Law]

The key issue is whether the employee has been given enough information to defend himself or herself from the charges. In Martinez v Franco, 222 A.D.2d 335, a New York City Housing Authority police officer claimed that the Authority prejudiced his right to be informed of the charges against him when it failed to introduce its Patrol Guide Manual into evidence at his disciplinary hearing.

The Appellate Division disagreed, finding that Martinez "showed an understanding of the charges when he consented to the introduction of the [Authority's] letter setting them forth and waived a formal reading thereof."

Another case dealing with the specificity of charges and specifications is Ritz v Board of Fire Commissioners, Selkirk Fire District, 622 NYS2d 830, 212 AD2d 949 (1995). In Ritz, disciplinary charges against a chief and assistant chief of volunteer firefighters alleged they had improperly conducted a "live" burn training exercise but did not specify any rule, regulation, by-law or policy that allegedly had been breached. Accordingly, the Appellate Division found this violated due process. It held that an individual charged with misconduct must be provided with sufficient information to develop a defense, and that there must be effective communication of any unwritten policy if that policy is to be the basis of disciplinary charges.

1.16 Immunity from discipline

An administrator is sometimes confronted by a situation in which an attempt to discipline an employee seems impossible because the employee claims that he or she has been granted immunity in connection with a criminal proceeding. According to the Appellate Division, disciplinary action may proceed in spite of the claimed immunity (Greco v Board of Nursing Home Examiners, 91 AD2d 1108). The Special Prosecutor granted Greco "transactional immunity from prosecution" in connection with a criminal matter in exchange for his cooperation.

The board later revoked his nursing home administrator's license. The Appellate Division, in a split decision, rejected Greco's argument that his immunity barred revocation of his license.

The court said "a prosecutor cannot divest an independent body of its lawful discretion by promising broad immunity." This is consistent with the view that an administrative disciplinary action based on the same events that may have resulted in a criminal prosecution is not "double jeopardy." Had the board been a party to the granting of immunity, however, it would have been bound by the agreement.

Likewise, statements made by an employee to the police during their investigation of criminal charges filed against the employee constitutes "competent evidence" and may be admitted into evidence during the disciplinary hearing (Dacey v County of Dutchess, 121 AD2d 536).

The reverse situation occurs when a disciplinary action precedes criminal action. If an employer threatens to fire or take other adverse action against an employee if he or she does not answer questions, the employee's answers to those questions are typically automatically shielded from use in a subsequent criminal prosecution under a concept called "transactional immunity" or "use immunity."

1.17 Right to pre-determination hearing

Sometimes it is difficult to determine whether an order given to an employee constitutes discipline and whether the employee is entitled to due process before the order goes into effect. When asked to evaluate such cases, the courts examine whether administrative decision constituted involved a deprivation of a "property interest" or a "liberty interest," or whether the decision was arbitrary and capricious.

For instance, in the Appellate Division's March 1998 decision in Taylor v NYS Dept. of Correctional Services, 248 A.D.2d 799, the court ruled that barring a corrections officer from carrying a weapon while off duty was not a disciplinary penalty that required a pre-determination hearing.

A psychologist advised a correctional facility's superintendent that State Corrections Officer Mark Taylor "was dangerous and may lose impulse control at any time." The superintendent prohibited Taylor from carrying a concealed weapon while off-duty.[8]

Taylor "became belligerent and abusive" when the psychologist refused to give him a copy of a report that he had prepared for Family Court. Taylor refused repeated requests to leave the psychologist's office and ultimately police officers were called and escorted him for the office.

1.18 Ambiguity of language in Taylor Law agreements

Sometimes the wording of a collective bargaining agreement is ambiguous as to whether a certain category of employees is entitled to due process rights. It is a basic tenet of contract law that in cases of ambiguity in contract language, the ambiguity should be resolved against the drafter of the language. So, if the employer wrote language in a collective bargaining agreement that is ambiguous, the dispute would be resolve in favor of the union. If the union drafted the language, the dispute would be resolved in favor of the employer.

For instance, in Leon v Lukash, 577 NYS2d 478, a noncompetitive class employee of Nassau County in a position designated "confidential" by the Nassau County Civil Service Commission sought due process rights and cited an ambiguous section in a collective bargaining agreement between the County and CSEA.

The Appellate Division found that the parties did not intend to grant confidential employees such as Leon pre-termination hearing rights. The court said that to the extent that there was any ambiguity in the language of the agreement, any such ambiguity "should be resolved against the drafter ... CSEA." The court concluded that Leon was not improperly discharged from his position insofar as the disciplinary provisions of the controlling Taylor Law agreement were concerned.

Other cases dealing with ambiguity of contract provisions and due process rights are Taylor v NYS Dept. of Correctional Services [arbitrator should decide whether BOCES teachers serving in its "alternative high school" were teachers covered by the agreement] and Willis v NYC Police

---

[8] The rules of the state Correctional Services Department allow it to prohibit an employee from carrying a weapon while off duty if it determines "the employee's mental or emotional condition is such that his or her possession of a weapon represents a threat to the safety of the employee, the facility or the community." Section 265.20 of the State Penal Law gives State correction officers a statutory exemption from prosecution for criminal possession of a weapon.

Department, 214 A.D.2d 428 [Construing the language of an agreement to extend an employee's probationary period to a specific date against the drafter -- the employer -- Willis was granted an extension of her probationary period to cover 40 days of sick leave that Willis took during her original probationary period].

1.19 Right of appeal and timeliness

Part of due process is the right to appeal. But this right a short-lived one for actions challenging an administrative action are brought under Article 78 of the Civil Practice Law and Rules [CPLR]. Article 78 has a four-month statute of limitations.

Some appeal rights have an even shorter life. For instance, appeals under Section 76 to the civil service commission having jurisdiction must be filing within 30 days, while appeals from Education Law Section 3020-a pursuant to Article 75 of the CPLR must be filed within 10 days [Section 3020-a.5]

If an employee wishes to challenge a disciplinary decision, it is critical that the action be commenced before the expiration of the controlling Statute of Limitations.

The general rule is that the statute of limitations begins to run beginning when a final administrative determination has been received by the individual or by his or her legal representative.

There are exceptions, however. For instance, if the employer agrees to grant a re-hearing of a case, that can change the deadline for filing an Article 78 petition.

In DelBello v NYC Transit Authority, 542 NYS2d 271, DelBello did not attend a disciplinary hearing that resulted in his termination in 1985 because the notice of the hearing had been sent to an outdated address. (See "Absence from hearings", below) The Authority then agreed to give DelBello a new, second hearing but did not reinstate him to his position pending its issuing a determination following the completion of this second hearing and in 1986 sustained its earlier ruling terminating DelBello. When DelBello sued under Article 78, which has a four-month statute of limitations, the Authority argued that he was untimely as he had not brought the action within four months of his termination in 1985.

The Appellate Division, Second Department, ruled that the Article 78 action was timely. If a governmental agency agrees to hold a new hearing at which new testimony is taken, new evidence offered and new matters are considered, an individual may challenge the new determination pursuant to Article 78. In such a situation, the time period allowed to file such a challenge begins to run from the date the new determination is received by the individual.

If the Authority had simply denied DelBello's request to reconsider its decision, he would have been untimely as he had not sued within four months of his receiving the July 1985 determination. By agreeing to hold a new hearing, the Authority exposed itself to an Article 78 challenging its "new determination" in 1986 even though it affirmed its 1985 ruling.

There is a significant difference between granting an individual a new hearing and agreeing to reconsider a prior determination as the decision in Pinto v Town of Greenburgh, 567 NYS2d 98 demonstrates.

Pinto, after being guilty of misconduct and dismissed from his position, asked the Town to reinstate him to his former position. When his request was denied, Pinto sued the seeking reinstatement. The court dismissed his petition, holding that his 1988 request for reinstatement was nothing more than an application for reconsideration of the Town's determination dismissing him from his position.

Affirming the lower court's ruling, the Appellate Division said that Pinto's action was "time-barred," having been brought more than four months after the completion of the disciplinary action in 1986. The general rule: a request for "reconsideration" of a disciplinary determination does not stop the statute of limitations from running for the purpose of filing a timely appeal from the underlying decision.

Another exception involves suing school districts and BOCES. Typically the aggrieved party filing a "notice of claim" pursuant to Section 3813 of the Education Law must precede such actions. Section 3813 bars the initiation of any action for 30 days following the filing of the notice of claim. Accordingly, this extends the last day on which one can file an Article 78 action.

In Cordani v Board of Education, 66 AD2d 780, the Appellate Division decided that the four-month Statute of Limitations set out in Section 217 of the Civil Practice Law and Rules "was enlarged by 30 days in light of the fact that, pursuant to Education Law Section 3813, 30 days must pass after service of the notice of claim before an action may be commenced."

However, there is some disagreement concerning the application of the notice requirements of Section 3813 with respect to initiating judicial action against a school district or a BOCES when a challenge to a disciplinary action is involved.

Section 76 of the Civil Service Law gives a person found guilty of charges brought pursuant to Section 75 a statutory right to appeal the penalty imposed to the responsible civil service commission or, in the alternative, to the courts pursuant to Section 78 of the CPLR.

Notwithstanding this, the Appellate Division's ruled that an employee of a school district or a BOCES in the classified service, as a condition precedent to his or her filing an Article 78 appeal challenging the Section 75, Civil Service Law disciplinary action, must have filed a timely notice of claim with the district or BOCES [Stevens v McGraw CSD, 261 AD2d 698, motion for leave to appeal denied, 93 NY2d 816].

In contrast, in Sephton v Board of Education of the City of New York, 99 AD2d 509, the Appellate Division ruled that "the 'tenure rights' of teachers are ... considered a matter in the public interest and therefore Section 3813 is not applicable to cases seeking to enforce such rights."

New York courts have distinguished between proceedings "which on the one hand seek only enforcement of private rights and duties and those on the other in which it is sought to vindicate a public interest; the provisions of subdivision 1 of section 3813 are applicable as to the former but not as to the latter" (Union Free School Dist. No. 6 of Towns of Islip & Smithtown v New York State Div. of Human Rights Appeal Bd., 35 NY2d 371, 380, rearg denied 36 NY2d 807).

Does challenging an adverse disciplinary determination involve efforts to vindicate a private right or a public interest? It would seem that the fact that the Civil Service Law provides an aggrieved employee with a statutory right to appeal an adverse disciplinary action to a civil service commission or to the courts, he or she should have the same standing with respect to his or her "tenure rights" as are enjoyed by educators under Section 3020-a, or vice versa.[9]

1.20 Absence from hearings

Due process is essentially the right to a hearing. What if an individual who has been served with disciplinary charges fails or refuses to attend the disciplinary hearing that has been scheduled? Has the employee been denied due process?

Not necessarily. "[D]ue process does not require that a petitioner be present at an administrative hearing, but rather requires notice of the charges and an opportunity to be heard," the Appellate Division, Third Department ruled in Mujtaba v NYS Dept. of Education, 538 NYS2d 654. The case involved a pharmacist who claimed, unsuccessfully, that she had been denied due process because, despite the fact that she knew a hearing was scheduled, she elected to go on a religious pilgrimage.

Sometimes an employee served with a notice of disciplinary action refuses to participate in the proceeding or does not appear at the hearing. Courts have held that the employer may proceed with the disciplinary action even though the employee is not present. The hearing may proceed and the employee tried in absentia provided the appointing authority made a diligent effort to contact the employee to inform him or her that the disciplinary hearing had been scheduled and would take place even if he or she did not participate.

Indeed, there is even case law stating that an arbitrator may proceed with a disciplinary arbitration hearing in the absence of the appointing authority and make a final, binding determination. In Hall v Environmental Conservation, 235 A.D.2d 757, the employer boycotted the arbitration because it believed that Hall was not entitled to the arbitration. The court upheld the arbitrator's award in favor of the employee.[10]

---

[9] It should be noted that in CSEA v Lakeland Central School District, the Appellate Division rejected the School District's theory that CSEA's action for damages "for breach of a collective bargaining agreement" should be dismissed because CSEA had not complied with the "notice of claim" requirements set out in Section 3813 of the Education Law. The Court said that "the collective bargaining agreement entered into by the parties contained detailed grievance procedures and this constituted a waiving compliance with that requirement" by the School District.

[10] In its appeal Environmental Conservation [DEC] claimed that its termination of Hall was not subject to being challenged pursuant to the "contract disciplinary procedure" because the State Department of Civil Service had disqualified Hall for employment. Thus, claimed the DEC, Hall's appointment was void and therefore he could not claim any rights under Section 75 of the Civil Service Law or the collective bargaining agreement. A Supreme Court judge granted the union's motion to confirm that portion of the award providing for back pay, holding that the disciplinary proceeding was not rendered moot by the Civil Service Department's action but declined to confirm that part of the award that directed DEC reinstate Hall to his former position. The Appellate Division affirmed the lower court's ruling.

The Mari decision [Mari v Safir, 291 AD2d 298] sets out the general standards applied by the courts in resolving litigation resulting from conducting a disciplinary hearing in absentia.

The decision demonstrates that an individual against whom disciplinary charges have been filed cannot avoid the consequences of disciplinary action being taken against him or her by refusing to appear at the disciplinary hearing. The decision also provides an opportunity to explore a number of factors that should be kept in mind when involved in a disciplinary or other administrative action held "in absentia."

New York City police officer Robert A. Mari was served with disciplinary charges alleging that he (1) engaged in unauthorized off-duty employment; (2) knowingly associated with a person believed to be engaged in, likely to engage in, or to have engaged in criminal activities; (3) intentionally disclosed an informant's identity to a target of police activity; and (4) harassed "a former paramour."

When Mari failed to appear at his disciplinary hearing, he was "tried in absentia" and was found guilty of the several disciplinary charges filed against him. The penalty imposed: termination. Mari appealed, contending that he should be given a "new hearing" because he was not actually present during the disciplinary proceeding.

The Appellate Division, First Department, dismissed Mari's appeal. Conceding that Mari not present at the disciplinary hearing, the court said "a new hearing is not warranted since [Mari] avoided service of the notice of the revised hearing date, and thereafter intentionally absented himself from the hearing."

The general rule in such situations is that if the employee fails to appear at the disciplinary hearing, the charging party may elect to proceed but must actually hold a "hearing in absentia" and prove its allegations rather then merely impose a penalty on the individual on the theory that the employee's failure to appear at the hearing as scheduled is, in effect, a concession of guilt.

In such case, however, the appointing authority is required to make a reasonable effort to contact the employee before proceeding to hold a disciplinary hearing in absentia. It may be that the employee has a valid excuse for his or her nonappearance such as a family emergency or personal illness that would justify the hearing officer granting an adjournment.

The following are factors that should be kept in mind in connection with holding a disciplinary hearing in absentia:

1. Was the employee properly served with the disciplinary charges and advised of the date, time and place of the hearing?

2. If the individual fails to appear at the hearing as scheduled, a diligent effort must be made to contact the individual to determine if he or she has a reasonable explanation for his or her absence before the hearing officer proceeds with holding the hearing in the absence of the accused employee.

3. A formal hearing must be conducted and the employer is required to introduce evidence proving its charges to the hearing officer.

4. A formal record of the hearing must be made and a transcript provided to the appointing authority and, if requested, to the employee.

5. The employee must be advised of the appointing authority's determination and his or her right of appeal if he or she has been found guilty of one or more of the charges.

On the other hand, participating in an arbitration proceeding when one need not do so may have consequences equally serious to those flowing from the failure to appear and participate in the arbitration proceeding. In Suffolk County v SCCC Faculty Association, the Appellate Division pointed out that if a party participates in arbitration when "it did not have to," it couldn't later seek to vacate the arbitration award "because it was not required to submit to the arbitration of the issue."

On another point, assume that an individual served with disciplinary charges pursuant to Section 75 of the Civil Service does not file an answer to the charges and specifications. May the appointing authority impose the proposed penalty without holding a disciplinary hearing? Probably not.

Although Section 75 requires the appointing officer to allow the accused employee at least eight days to file his or her answer to disciplinary charges in writing, this simply gives, but does not mandate, the employee at least eight days in which to prepare and submit an answer to the charges. As Section 75 is silent as to when the accused individual must file an answer, this suggests that the individual may remain mute -- i.e., decline to file an answer to the charges -- without jeopardizing any of his or her Section 75 rights to administrative due process.

Second, and perhaps critical to due process considerations in connection with taking disciplinary action against a public employee, Section 75 provides that "the burden of proving incompetency or misconduct ... (is) upon the person alleging the same."

In other words, the failure of an employee to file an answer to the disciplinary charges, appear at the disciplinary hearing or his or her even refusing to defend himself or herself against the charges at the hearing does not excuse the employer of its duty to prove the employee's incompetence or misconduct before making a determination as to guilt and then imposing an appropriate disciplinary sanction.

Turning to the merits of the disciplinary determination in Mari's case, the court said that "that there was substantial evidence ... to support the hearing officer's findings." As to the penalty imposed, the Appellate Division found that it was not so disproportionate to the offenses of which Mari was found guilty "as to shock this Court's sense of fairness," citing Kelly v Safir, 96 NY2d 32.

Mari also alleged that the department acted in "bad faith" when it accelerated the date of his disciplinary hearing. He contended that the hearing date was improperly accelerated and as a result his pension was forfeited since his termination took place before the effective date of his retirement[11]. The Appellate Division dismissed this branch of Mari's appeal. According to the ruling, that Mari "was found guilty of conduct that took place, and the resulting disciplinary charges were filed, long before [he filed his] application for retirement."

---

[11] Section 13-173.1 of the Administrative Code of the City of New York requires an employee to "be in service" on the effective date of his or her retirement or vesting of retirement benefits. If the employee is not "in service" on that date, he or she forfeits his or her retirement benefits.

1.21 Notice of hearings

The employer is required to make a reasonable effort to notify the employee of the charges and of the date and place of the disciplinary hearing. In the DelBello case, mentioned in 1.19 above, [DelBello v NYC Transit Authority, 542 NYS2d 271] DelBello had moved from the address listed in the Transit Authority's records and did not receive notice of his disciplinary hearing.

The Transit Authority was aware of this fact as its notice was returned to it unopened and marked by the U. S. Postal Service as "Moved, left no address." The Authority did not undertake any further attempts to inform him of the pending disciplinary action.

The Appellate Division, citing Mullane v Central Hanover Bank and Trust Co., 339 U.S. 306, said that "mailing the notice to [DelBello's] last known address was not notice reasonably calculated, under all the circumstances, to apprise [him] of the pendency of the [disciplinary proceeding] and afford [him] an opportunity to present [his] objections.'" The court concluded that the Authority acted in an arbitrary and capricious manner when it treated DelBello's failure to receive the notice of the charges and the hearing as "his problem."

Before conducting a hearing in absentia, the employer is required to make a reasonable effort to locate the employee and serve the charges. It is also advisable for the employer to document the efforts it undertakes in its efforts to notify the employee in such a situation.

1.22 Name-clearing hearings

If adverse information concerning an employee's termination has been publicized by the employer and could be construed as injurious to the reputation of the former employee, the former employee may demand a name-clearing hearing. This applies when no other due process is available. Such cases typically involve non-tenured employees.

A name-clearing hearing is NOT the equivalent of a disciplinary hearing. It is merely the opportunity to clear one's name. No further action is required of the employer should the name-clearing hearing result in the employee's vindication. Although an employer may chose to reinstate the employee after a name-clearing hearing, there is no legal obligation to do.

Much less is at stake in a name-clearing hearing than in a disciplinary hearing. If an employee prevails in a disciplinary hearing, he or she will win something tangible -- typically reinstatement and back pay. If an employee prevails in a name-clearing, the employer is compelled to do exactly nothing. Even if the appointing authority or its designee declares at a name-clearing hearing that the employer was completely mistaken and acted despicably, this statement may be the employee's only reward.

Name-clearing hearings are required in only certain circumstances. First, the employer must have publicized the reason that the employee was dismissed or disciplined. Perhaps a statement was made to a newspaper reporter, or a statement was made at a public meeting. In contrast, such statements made to another administrator who has an interest or responsibility involved does not constitute "publication" so as to justify a name-clearing hearing. Second, the reason given for the disciplinary action must reflect negatively on the employee such that it might hold the individual up to ridicule or impugn his or her reputation or good name and conceivably limit his or her opportunity for future employment.

1.23 Due process and optional hearings

Sometimes a public employer files charges and specifications against an employee and holds an administrative disciplinary hearing even if it is not required to provide the employee with such "notice and hearing" by law or a Taylor Law contract provision. The Appellate Division, Third Department, decided a case in which the due process implications of a "non-mandatory" disciplinary hearing were considered [Christopher v Phillips, 554 NYS2d 370].

The State Commission on Correction, following its investigation of a disturbance at the Orange County Jail, concluded that Christopher, a deputy sheriff-captain with the Orange County Sheriff's Department, "utilized poor judgment and did not respond properly in the incident." The Commission recommended that disciplinary charges be filed against Christopher and the undersheriff.[12]

Christopher was terminated. He was then offered an opportunity to challenge the charges filed against him. The hearing officer found Christopher guilty of six of the eight specifications filed against him but made no recommendation as to any penalty. When the sheriff concurred in the hearing officer's determination, Christopher appealed.

The Appellate Division indicated that in its opinion "the protections of Civil Service Law Section 75" did not apply to Christopher and "in the absence of any other proof establishing [Christopher's] right to protection under ... Section 75" concluded that he could not claim that the hearing provided to him was mandated by that provision. Also noted was the fact that Christopher was not "a member of any civil service bargaining unit" and therefore presumably not protected by any contract disciplinary procedure negotiated pursuant to the Taylor Law [see Section 76.4, Civil Service Law]. The Appellate Division also stated that the termination notice "did not specify that any action was being taken pursuant to the Civil Service Law."

According to the opinion "if a hearing is not required by law, the substantial evidence standard of review does not apply...." Instead, said the Appellate Division, the appropriate standard for the purpose of judicial review [in such a situation] is whether the determination is arbitrary or capricious. The fact that a hearing was held even when not required by law does not alter the applicability of this standard.

The Appellate Division decided that the sheriff's determination, including the sanction applied, termination, was rational and thus neither arbitrary nor capricious. The lesson here is that if an appointing authority elects to provide an employee with "notice and hearing" in the nature of a disciplinary proceeding despite the fact that it is not otherwise required to do so, any determination made as a result of such an action is (1) subject to judicial review and (2) must be found to comply with the "arbitrary and capricious" standard if challenged in order to survive.

---

[12] The Undersheriff apparently had come to the jail during the disturbance "to provide additional supervision."

1.24 Removal by operation of law

In some cases, administrative due process hearings may be pre-empted by statute. A public officer may be subject to removal by operation of law, without regard to administrative due process. Typically, the office is deemed vacant upon the occurrence of a specific event, usually a criminal conviction or his or her failure to maintain a legally mandated residence. In other cases a "separation" or "termination" is, in fact, NOT a dismissal as that term is normally understood in employment situations.

As an example of "removal by operation of law," there presently exist statutes such as Section 30 of the Public Officers Law that mandates removal from public office as the automatic penalty in the event a public officer is found guilty of a felony or the violation of his or her oath of office. (A police officer is a "public officer" for the purposes of Section 30 [Sullivan v Whitney, 25 NYS2d 762; Winkler v Sheriff, 256 AD 770]. It should be understood that while all public officers are public employees, not all public employees are public officers.)

Statutes such as Section 30 contrast significantly with the concepts underlying progressive discipline. The removal provisions of these statutes can be said to constitute a punishment flowing from criminal conduct, wrongdoing or a violation of one's oath of office. These transgressions are sometimes referred to in somewhat archaic legal terms: misfeasance, malfeasance or nonfeasance in office. Loosely defined, these terms are used to describe, respectively, acting unlawfully; doing something badly; and not doing anything when something should be done.[13]

1.25 Suspension without pay

Due process may not be required in certain situations regardless of the status of the employee. An individual may be suspended without pay if he or she becomes unable to lawfully perform the duties of the position because of a lack of, or the loss of, a required license or similar permit.

If an individual has lost the required license or permit, the courts have upheld the right of the employer to summarily place the employee on leave without pay without limitation. "Summarily" in this context means without preferring (issuing) formal charges and providing a due process hearing. Frequently, however, the employee is also charged with incompetence or misconduct, and disciplinary sanctions imposed.

Courts have viewed employees who lack licenses as being "unqualified," in contrast to being "incompetent," to perform the duties of the position. Indeed, it could be argued that the employer has no alternative, as it could be considered unlawful to permit an unlicensed individual to perform the duties for which a license is required.

---

[13] Decisions addressing the issue of the automatic termination of an individual from his or her public office include: Bowman v Kerik, App. Div., First Dept., 4/4/00 [Section 30.1(e) is a self-executing statute and no pretermination hearing was required]; Schirmer v Town of Harrison, USDC, SDNY, February 1999 [police officer had moved his domicile to Connecticut and therefore was no longer eligible for employment]; Foley v Bratton (decided with Griffin v Bratton), Court of Appeals, February 18, 1999 [to the extent that the automatic removal provision of Public Officers Law are inconsistent with pre-termination administrative hearing procedure, the Legislature's determination that a felony or "oath of office" conviction is serious enough, without more, to justify automatic removal" is controlling].

Common examples include the revocation of a truck driver's permit to operate a motor vehicle on public roads, loss of an attorney's license to practice law and the expiration of a temporary permit to teach. All that appears to be necessary in such cases is for the appointing authority to make some reasonable inquiry to determine if the employee may lawfully perform the duties of the position.[14]

The appointing authority also has the option of reassigning the individual to a different position, for which the person is otherwise qualified and for which the license is not required.

Whether the individual is suspended or reassigned, care should be taken that the license is, in fact, essential to the duties of the position.[15]

See also Chapter 8, Suspending Employees Pending a Hearing.

1.26 Authority to discipline

From time to time, the key issue in a discipline case is whether a given administrator has the authority to impose discipline. In Rine v City of Sherrill, 574 NYS2d 641, it was claimed that only the City Commission, consisting of five elected officials and the city manager, had the authority to remove an employee and authorize disciplinary actions.

Rine had been suspended and served with Section 75 disciplinary charges alleging certain off-duty misconduct. The city manager designated a hearing officer to conduct the required disciplinary hearing. Rine objected, claiming that the city manager is not empowered to initiate "removal proceedings."

The city, on the other hand, contended that the Manager had the sole removal authority" and therefore had the power to initiate the hearing. The court agreed with the city. It concluded that although the Charter could have expressly provided that the commission had the exclusive power to remove police officers, it was silent as to such removal authority.

As viewed by the court, the city manager is the city's chief administrative officer and has the power to exercise control over all departments of the city's government. Accordingly, the Manager's power of removal was consistent with the controlling provisions of City Charter.

---

[14] See, for example: Fowler v City of Saratoga Springs, _Misc2d_ (City Engineer lawfully dismissed for failure to obtain Professional Engineer's license by a specified date); Meliti v Nyquist, 385 NYS2d 407, 53 AD2d 951, affirmed 41 NY2d 183 (immediate suspension of teachers was lawful because their teaching licenses had expired); O'Keefe v Niagara Mohawk Power Corp, 714 FSupp 622, (traveling company demonstrator was not discriminated against when a private employer terminated him after his driver's license was suspended).
[15] See Matter of Jerry, 35 NY2d 534 [tenured employee may not be suspended without explicit statutory (or Taylor Law contract) authority] and Matter of Martin ex rel Lekkas, 86 AD2d 712 [if the license is not essential to the duties of the position, failure to have a valid license is not fatal to the employee's continuation in service].

1.27 Pending criminal matters

Sometimes an employer wishes to proceed with a disciplinary action at the same time as criminal charges are pending. Does this constitute "double jeopardy"? Courts have ruled this is not double jeopardy. For example, in Matter of the Haverstraw-Stony Point CSD, 24 Ed. Dept. Rep. 466; the Commissioner of Education ruled that a Section 3020-a hearing panel is not required to adjourn an administrative disciplinary hearing when parallel criminal proceedings are underway.

Chaplin v NYC Department of Education, 48 A.D.3d 226, is another example. Here the Appellate Division said that an employee was not entitled to a stay of the disciplinary case as a criminal defendant does not have a right to stay a related disciplinary proceeding pending the outcome of trial, citing Watson v City of Jamestown, 27 AD3d 1183. Denial of such a stay does not adversely affect the employee's constitutional rights.

The appointing authority has no obligation to postpone disciplinary action simply even if the county District Attorney requests administrative action be postponed. This was the point made by the court in Levine v New York City Transit Authority, 70 AD2d 900 (2nd Dept 1979), affirmed 49 NY2d 747 (1980)] [See also 2.14: "Impact of criminal action on disciplinary action".]

However, it is sometimes advantageous for the appointing authority to wait until the criminal matter has been adjudicated, because a criminal conviction compels an automatic finding of guilt in a disciplinary hearing involving the same offense. If an employee is found guilty in a court of law of a crime such as stealing, and disciplinary charges are filed related to that same incident of theft, there is no legal way for a disciplinary hearing officer to find the employee not guilty of stealing. Probably the leading case illustrating this point is Kelly v. Levin, 440 NYS2d 424. In Kelly the court ruled that is a reversable error for an administrative disciplinary body to acquit an employee if the individual has been found guilty of a criminal act involving the same allegations.

The reason this is true is that the standard of proof required in a criminal proceeding is higher than that in a disciplinary proceeding. In a criminal case, the standard is proof beyond a reasonable doubt; in disciplinary the standard is merely "substantial evidence." See Chapter 3, Evidence, especially 3.06, "Affect of criminal conviction or dismissal on disciplinary outcome."

If the appointing authority elects to pursue a disciplinary hearing at the same time criminal charges are pending, the employee's rights under the Fifth Amendment rights may be a concern. The employee may not wish to testify in his own defense in the disciplinary hearing, fearing his statement could be used against him in the criminal proceeding. In Forte v NYC Transit Authority, 2 A.D.3d 489, a New York State Supreme Court Justice ruled it was improper for a hearing officer to find an employee of the Manhattan and Bronx Surface Transportation Authority guilty and recommend dismissal under such circumstances.[16]

---

[16] It is worth noting that employees who have not been charged with any disciplinary offenses may be compelled to answer investigatory questions or face discipline, regardless of any claims to Fifth Amendment rights, provided that he or she is granted immunity from use of his answer in a subsequent criminal proceeding or is not required to waive such immunity. [See "Refusal to answer questions," 2.06].

Forte had been arrested for allegedly stealing four payroll checks and refused to present a defense in the disciplinary hearing on the advice of his lawyer, citing the Fifth Amendment.

The court was sympathetic to Forte. It said "a central guiding principle since our Nation's birth is that the ultimate injustice to be ever guarded against is governmental injustice. Since the prosecuting agency and the hearing authority are one and the same, there is an obligation incumbent upon the court to insure that the governmental authority has not abused its power and stripped petitioner of the civil remedy to which he was entitled."

Manhattan & Bronx Surface Transportation Authority was ordered to conduct a two-part hearing and determine, as a threshold matter, whether Forte would have had to rely on his own testimony to refute the charges. If it was determined that Forte's testimony was necessary, then by invoking his fifth amendment privilege, Forte did not receive the hearing to which he was entitled and MaBSTOA would have to conduct a new hearing.

According to the ruling, employees of MaBSTOA do not have civil service status. The court found that Forte enjoyed the rights and benefits incorporated in the provisions of MaBSTOA's Managerial Disciplinary Policy and Procedure. These provide, in pertinent part, that "prior to discharge an employee will receive written notice of charges, reason for discharge, and a statement that the employee may respond in writing or in person within two weeks, requesting an informal hearing with his/her immediate superior. When any aspect of the authority's operation is jeopardized by the continued presence of a pre-discharged employee, that person may be immediately suspended without pay pending final determination. After having an informal hearing, the charged employee will receive written notification of the hearing disposition."

1.28 Double jeopardy

If an employee is acquitted in a criminal case, that does not prevent the employer from proceeding with a disciplinary action because the standard of proof is different. (See Chapter 3, Evidence). The very same facts and witnesses might prompt a verdict of not guilty from a reasonable jury yet bring a determination of guilty by a hearing officer.

A case that illustrated this was Police Comm., City of New York, _ Misc.2d _. A police officer [DB] was indicted for perjury in connection with her testimony before a grand jury. A few days after this indictment was returned by a grand jury, DB was served with disciplinary charges that alleged that she committed perjury during the same grand jury hearing in violation of police rules and procedures. Although DB was acquitted of the criminal action, the department proceeded with the administrative disciplinary action.

In considering the department's proceeding with the disciplinary action, the court said, "It is true that DB was acquitted after trial on the criminal charge of perjury in the first degree. Of course, she is entitled to the benefits of this adjudication. However, termination of a criminal case in a manner favorable to a defendant presents no bar to the continuation of a collateral civil service disciplinary proceeding."

The court said that its view was based on the fact that "the standard of proof [substantial evidence] that must be met to sustain a charge at a disciplinary hearing, where the ultimate penalty could be the loss of employment, is not as rigorous as the standard of proof applicable to the trial of a criminal case [beyond a reasonable doubt], where the ultimate penalty could be the loss of liberty."

1.29 Civil rights

Public employers in New York State should be vigilant that they do not violate employees' civil rights while pursuing disciplinary action. Civil rights issues are not uncommon in discipline cases.

In one sheriff's department, the employees' manual contained a rule prohibiting employees from engaging in a "relationship with any inmate, former inmate, [or] parolee ... in any manner or form that is not necessary or proper for the discharge of the employee's duties." Any such conduct was to be reported to the department.

Vega, a corrections officer, was brought up on disciplinary charges alleging that she had engaged in "covert and unauthorized conduct in developing and maintaining an apparent close relationship with an inmate and parolee." The charges noted that Vega was married to the parolee.

Found guilty of the charges, Vega was dismissed from her position. She sued the department contending that her dismissal was arbitrary and capricious and in violation of Executive Law Sections 291 and 296 which prohibits discrimination against an employee because of marital status.

The Appellate Division affirmed a lower court's ruling dismissing the case. It said that although the marriage between Vega and the parolee was noted in the disciplinary charges, the basis for her termination was her violation of the rule prohibiting department employees from fraternizing with inmates, former inmates or parolees. Accordingly, Vega's discipline and ultimate termination was not based on her marriage itself [Vega v Dept. of Correctional Services, 588 NYS2d 202].

1.30 First Amendment rights

A number of public employers have policies in place that require an employee to use an internal grievance procedure before the employee can bring a matter to the attention of the public or other, non-department, public officials. Does such a policy violate the employee's First Amendment rights?

In Sanchez v Santa Ana, 915 F2d 424, a U.S. Circuit Court of Appeals decided that such a procedure did not violate an individual's right to free speech "given the employer's interest in protecting itself from false and unfavorable publicity." Sanchez was a police officer; the agency involved was the Santa Ana Police Department. [For First Amendment rights in the context of disciplinary investigations, see 2.06 and 2.07]

1.31 Freedom of information

Another issue is freedom of information in disciplinary actions. The release of information related to a disciplinary proceeding is a concern to both employers and employees.

While an employee who has been served with disciplinary charges may decide to make such action public, the employer is generally reluctant to disclose the fact that it has served disciplinary charges against an employee and to provide the public or the press with the reasons for its undertaking such action.

When a newspaper learned that a city firefighter had been suspended, it asked the city for information concerning any disciplinary action being taken against the individual. The city refused to provide any information concerning any pending disciplinary action and, in addition, it refused to give the newspaper access to any city records concerning the matter.

The city told the newspaper that the records it wished to obtain "constitute personnel records used to evaluate performance" and cited Section 50-a of the Civil Rights Law and Section 87(2-a) of the Public Officer Law as authority for rejecting the newspaper's request.

The newspaper sued the city claiming it had violated the freedom of information Law [Rome Sentinel Company v City of Rome, 546 NYS2d 304]. The city resisted, arguing (1) the Sentinel was not entitled to documents concerning the suspension of a municipal employee; (2) the employee had a right to privacy that the city had an obligation to protect; and (3) the Sentinel failed to show that the records it sought "are clearly of significant interest to the general public."

The court held that the Freedom of Information Law establishes "specific, narrowly construed instances where disclosure will not be ordered." For example, an agency may deny access to records, which are inter-agency, or intra-agency materials and which are not final agency determinations.

The court said that "under this exemption, the Sentinel would not be entitled to accusations or complaints of misconduct against the fireman; however it would be entitled to the final agency determination concerning his suspension, unless that determination is further protected by Section 50-a of the Civil Rights Law as a fireman's personnel records which are used to evaluate his performance."

The court also said that in balancing the privacy rights of the employee against the public's right to know and considering the decisions in Capital Newspapers v Burns, 67 NY2d 562 and Gannett Co., Inc. v James, 86 AD2d 567, it found that the newspaper was "entitled to disclosure of the final determination in this fireman's suspension hearing, without disclosing all the supporting allegations, complaints or witness names."

The confidentiality of disciplinary records was one of the issues in the Sangirardi case [Sangirardi v Nassau County, NYS Sup. Ct., Justice Alpert, 7/1/02, not officially reported]. In deciding the Sangirardi case, Supreme Court, Nassau County, considered the right of a student complainant to see the "Final Results" of a college disciplinary hearing held following her filing her complaint.

A Nassau County Community College women's basketball team member alleged that she had been sexually assaulted by members of the college's men's basketball team. She asked for audiotapes, videotapes and transcripts of the disciplinary proceeding conducted by the college. The college declined to provide her with these materials, claiming that the federal Family Educational Rights and Privacy Act, 20 USC 1232g, frequently referred to as the Buckley Amendment, although allowing students and parents access to "education records," prohibits their dissemination to the public.

Justice Alpert agreed in part, ruling that the student complainant was entitled to a copy of the "final results" of the disciplinary proceedings. Justice Alpert noted that the Buckley Amendment authorizes the disclosure of disciplinary records to teachers and school officials and of the "final results" of any disciplinary proceeding to an alleged victim.

Suppose a disciplinary action is "settled" and the parties agree to keep the terms of a disciplinary settlement confidential. Is such an agreement a defense to a demand to disclose the terms of the disciplinary settlement?

Reading the Sangirardi decision together with the ruling in LaRocca v Jericho UFSD, 220 AD2d 424, it appears that there is neither a federal nor a state shield to honoring such a confidentiality agreement.

In LaRocca, the School District had filed disciplinary charges against the principal of one of its schools. Subsequently the Jericho School Board authorized its superintendent to negotiate a settlement that would dispose of the matter. A settlement was reached and the Board adopted a motion withdrawing its charges against the principal without prejudice.

Anthony LaRocca, vice-president of the Jericho Teachers Association, asked for a copy of the settlement agreement on behalf of the teachers supervised by the principal. LaRocca's request was denied on the grounds that (a) providing the teachers with a copy "would constitute an unwarranted invasion of personal privacy" and (b) the document relates to "intra-agency or inter-agency materials which the School District is not required to disclose."

LaRocca then sued under the Freedom of Information Law [FOIL] (Article 6, Public Officers Law), contending that all records of a public agency are "presumptively accessible" and the settlement agreement did not fall within any of the recognized exceptions set out in FOIL.

Although a Supreme Court justice dismissed LaRocca's petition [LaRocca v Jericho UFSD, 159 Misc2d 90], the Appellate Division reversed, ruling that the settlement agreement did not constitute an "employment history" as defined by FOIL and therefore is presumptively available for public inspection.

Significantly, the Appellate Division said that "as a matter of public policy, the Board of Education cannot bargain away the public's right to access to public records." The court ruled that the settlement agreement or any part of it providing for confidentiality or purporting to deny the public access to the document "is unenforceable as against the pubic interest."

Moreover, the decision indicates that a public employer may not, by private agreement, limit the public's right to access to records which are otherwise subject to disclosure under FOIL, citing

Anonymous v Board of Education of the Mexico Central School District, 62 Misc 2d 300. In Mexico the court said that an agreement to keep secret that to which public has a right of access under FOIL unenforceable as against public policy.

There may be some aspect of a disciplinary settlement confidentiality agreement that is enforceable, however. In LaRocca, the settlement agreement contained references to charges that the principal denied or were not admitted, together with the names of certain teachers. The Appellate Division ruled that disclosure of such parts of the settlement agreement would constitute an unwarranted invasion of privacy within the meaning of FOIL.

The Court said that the settlement agreement must be redacted [censored] to eliminate such references -- i.e., the disputed charges and the names of the teachers -- prior to its release to LaRocca.

However one member of the Appellate Division panel reviewing the appeal rejected the concept of providing for confidentiality in such cases. Judge O'Brien said that in his view, "Although disclosure of the charges might cause some embarrassment, that is an insufficient basis under FOIL to deny disclosure."

With respect to the availability of public documents pursuant to FOIL, it is well settled that FOIL imposes a broad duty of disclosure on government agencies as noted by the Court of Appeals in Fink v Lefkowitz, 47 NY2d 567.

The general rule: All agency records are presumptively available for public inspection and copying, unless they fall within 1 of 10 categories of exemptions, which, as a matter of the exercise of discretion, permit agencies to withhold certain records.

In other words, the fact that certain records may properly be viewed as falling into an "exemption" category does not mean that the record may not be disclosed pursuant to a FOIL inquiry. The statute merely permits the agency to elect to withhold disclosing an "exempt" document or record.

The Court of Appeals has repeatedly stated that FOIL is to be liberally construed and its exemptions narrowly interpreted so that the public is granted maximum access to the records of government.

Expressly exempted from mandatory disclosure are records that "if disclosed would constitute an unwarranted invasion of ... privacy" (Public Officers Law Section 87[2][b]), including but not limited to "disclosure of employment, medical or credit histories or personal references of applicants for employment."

Although it is clear that a record is not considered an "employment history" merely because it records facts concerning employment, the term "employment history" for purposes of FOIL exemptions is not defined in the statute, nor well interpreted by case law.

However, as the court said in Hanig v State of New York Dept. of Motor Vehicles, 168 AD2d 884, aff'd 79 NY2d 106, its companion term "medical history" has been defined as "information that one would reasonably expect to be included as a relevant and material part of a proper medical history."

By this the court presumably meant that term "employment history" means that "information" that one would reasonably expect to be included as a relevant and material part of a proper personnel record system.

Another element to consider: the courts had held that a payment made to an individual as part of a disciplinary settlement is not to be viewed as the payment of "annual salary."

In Horowitz v NYS Teachers' Retirement System, 293 A.D.2d 861, the issue concerned the impact of making a lump-sum payment to an employee as an inducement to his or her submitting a resignation in lieu of being served with disciplinary charges in determining his or her final average salary for retirement purposes.

In July 1988, the Jericho Union Free School District offered Marc W. Horowitz the opportunity to resign from his administrative position in lieu of his being served with disciplinary charges. As part of the settlement negotiations related to Horowitz's separation, Horowitz was to receive a lump-sum payment of $123,789 consistent with a benefit set out in a then expired agreement between the District and the Jericho Administrators Association entitled the "Resignation-Retirement Incentive Benefit Program."

The Teachers' Retirement System [TRS] refused to include the $123,789 lump-sum payment to Horowitz as part of his "final average salary" [FAS] for the purpose of determining his retirement allowance. TRS viewed the payment "as an inducement for [Horowitz's] immediate resignation" rather than "compensation for accumulated sick time" as claimed by Horowitz.

Horowitz sued, but the Appellate Division, Third Department, sustained the Supreme Court dismissal of Horowitz's petition. Citing Section 501.11(a) of the Education Law, the Appellate Division said an individual's FAS is defined as "the average annual compensation earnable as a teacher during any five consecutive years of state service."

Noting the lesson in Moraghan v New York State Teachers' Retirement System, 237 AD2d 703, the court said that the purpose of the statute is to prevent artificial inflation of an individual's final average salary by payments made in anticipation of a member's resignation.

Accordingly, the Appellate Division held that "a lump-sum payment may be excluded from the calculation of a teacher's five-year final average salary where the circumstances support the conclusion that the payment was made in exchange for resignation rather than in satisfaction of accumulated sick leave", citing Hall v New York State Teachers' Retirement System, 266 AD2d 638, [leave to appeal denied, 94 NY2d 759].

Although Section 5003.2 of the Rules of the Commissioner, [21 NYCRR 5003.2 (b)], provide that "termination pay" is includable computation if it constitutes compensation earned as a teacher," the Appellate Division ruled that 21 NYCRR 5003.2 did not apply in Horowitz's case.

Why not? Because, said the court, the timing of Horowitz's resignation rendered him ineligible for the lump-sum payment provided by the then expired collective bargaining agreement between the District and the Association. This apparently resulted in the District and the Association entering "into a separate agreement designed to facilitate [Horowitz's] resignation."

According to the decision, the so-called "Horowitz Incentive Agreement" provided Horowitz with the same financial benefit that the expired collective bargaining agreement provided to eligible retirees for accumulated sick leave. However, the Horowitz Incentive Agreement described its benefit as "a pay differential equal to one year's salary" rather than the payment of accumulated sick leave credit and Horowitz's resignation was specifically conditioned on the receipt of this payment.

Other distinctive elements noted by the Appellate Division: The Horowitz Incentive Agreement was executed on the same day as the stipulation, provided a benefit for which Horowitz was the only recipient and required Horowitz to act within two business days in order to obtain its benefit.

The Appellate Division ruled that the language and circumstances of the agreements involved here rationally support TRS' findings that the Horowitz Incentive Agreement was tailored to Horowitz's particular situation and was created "solely to induce his resignation." Under these circumstances, said the Appellate Division, Supreme Court did not err in upholding TRS' determination and dismissing Horowitz's petition.

However, the fact that the amount paid to the employee in connection with a disciplinary settlement was not deemed wages for the purposes of calculating the employee's FAS for retirement should not be viewed as suggesting that such the payment is not subject to withholdings for income tax and other purposes.

1.32 Public hearings

May the public be barred from an administrative disciplinary proceeding? The access of the public to a professional disciplinary proceedings held pursuant to the Education Law was considered in Johnson Newspaper Corporation v Melino, 547 NYS2d 915. While the Johnson Newspaper case concerned disciplinary proceedings involving a dentist held pursuant to Section 6510(3) of the Education Law, the decision is instructive with respect to the access of the public to disciplinary proceedings.

The Johnson Newspaper case arose as the result of the State Education Department's Office of Professional Discipline's [OPD] refusal to allow a newspaper reporter to attend the disciplinary hearing. OPD advised the newspaper that such hearings were closed to the public. It indicated that it was the Regent's policy to close all such disciplinary hearings to the public unless "all present agree to public access ... which protects the public good and reduces the potential for irreparable harm to a professional reputation by unfounded accusations."

The Johnson Newspaper decision considered the applicability of "the State's strong public policy of public access to judicial and administrative proceedings" to a disciplinary proceeding under Section 6510(3) of the Education Law. The Appellate Division concluded that there exists "a countervailing presumption of confidentiality with respect to disciplinary proceedings" and "the closure of professional disciplinary proceedings does not violate [Johnson Newspaper's] First Amendment access to government."

This ruling provides some authority to support a decision to deny the public access to a disciplinary proceeding when both parties agree to do so. However, this does not imply that the public is to be denied access to disciplinary proceedings automatically. The opinion also notes that in Matter of Capoccia, 59 NY2d 549, a case involving disciplinary action taken against a lawyer, "the confidentiality of lawyer disciplinary proceedings might be waived." The Appellate Division concluded that the Capoccia ruling "inferentially accepts the confidentiality of professional disciplinary proceedings as to attorneys notwithstanding a similar lack of specific reference to closed hearings in ... [Section 90[10] of the Judiciary Law]."

However, this does not appear to be the case when the employer wishes to have the disciplinary proceedings closed to the public while the accused employee favors an open hearing. For example, in Randall v Toll, 74 Misc.2d 315, the court held that a disciplinary action taken against an employee pursuant to Section 75 of the Civil Service Law could not be closed to the public unless the accused employee agrees or requests that the proceedings be held privately.
Here the employer had decided to close the disciplinary proceedings to the public over Randall's objections. The employer attempted to justify its action by claiming that it was trying to protect Randall's privacy. As noted in the Capoccia decision, any such right to "privacy" may be waived by the accused. The hearing officer ultimately acquitted Randall of all charges and specifications.

In contrast, if the employer wants to have the disciplinary hearing opened to the public and the employee objects, insisting that the hearings be conducted in private, it probably would be best for the employer to agree to close the hearing for the reasons given to support the Regent's policy concerning public access to professional disciplinary hearings.

Where, however, the public's access to a disciplinary proceeding has been limited, or provided for, by an agreement negotiated under the Taylor Law, any deviation from the requirements of the contract should be agreed to by the employer and the union.

Rules promulgated by the Commissioner of Education implementing the recently amended disciplinary procedures for educators [See Section 3020-a, Education Law], provide that disciplinary hearings are closed to the public unless the accused employee elects an open hearing. However, there appears to be no authority in Section 3020-a justifying the "automatic closure" of a disciplinary hearing.

1.33 Disciplinary action based on pre-employment misconduct

In deciding Umlauf v Safir, 286 A.D.2d 267, the Appellate Division considered a rather unique question: what action, if any, may the appointing officer take in consideration of an employee's "pre-employment" misconduct.

Clearly an employee may be subjected to disciplinary action for his or her off-duty misconduct that adversely affects his or her employer. If the employee is found guilty, any one of a number of penalties, including termination, may be imposed. May "pre-employment misconduct" service as the basis for bringing disciplinary action against an employee?

Arthur K. Umlauf sued the City of New York following the Police Commissioner's dismissing him from his position without a hearing. Although Umlauf's petition seeking to annul the Commissioner's action was dismissed by State Supreme Court Justice William Davis, the Appellate Division reversed Justice Davis' decision "on the law."

The Appellate Division ordered Commissioner Safir to reinstate Umlauf to his former position. If the Commissioner wished have Umlauf terminated, said the court, Safir would have to submit a request for such action in accordance with the provisions of Civil Service Law Section 50.4.

Section 50.4 provides for the disqualification of applicants or eligibles by the state civil department or responsible municipal civil service commission for a variety of reasons. The court's decision indicates that the relevant provision in this case is Section 50.4(d). Paragraph (d) authorizes the disqualification of an individual who has been guilty of a crime.

Section 50.4 further provides that "[n]o person shall be disqualified pursuant to this subdivision unless he [or she] has been given a written statement of the reasons therefore and afforded an opportunity to make an explanation and to submit facts in opposition to such disqualification."

The court found that Safir had terminated Umlauf because of Umlauf's pre-employment conduct. This, said the Appellate Division, was improper -- an appointing authority does not have the authority to take such unilateral action. The court pointed out that in this instance Section 50.4 of the Civil Service Law vests the authority to disqualify or remove the individual in the head of New York City's Department of Citywide Administrative Services, not the head of a City department or agency.

Further, the individual may neither be disqualified nor terminated, as the case may be, unless he or she is provided with a written explanation of the reasons for the proposed action and given an opportunity to submit an explanation and facts opposing such action prior to his or her disqualification for, or termination of, employment.

Where the appointing authority seeks to have an individual disqualified or employee terminated for one or more reasons set out in Section 50.4, it should so advise the State Department of Civil Service or the responsible municipal civil service commission, as the case may be, setting out its reasons for seeking the disqualification or termination of the individual.

Is the individual who is to be disqualified or terminated pursuant to Section 50.4 entitled to a hearing before the department or municipal commission? In Mingo v Pirnie, 55 NY2d 1019, the Court of Appeals ruled that no "Section 50.4 hearing" is required where the individual is advised of the reasons for the proposed action and given an opportunity to submit a written explanation and exhibits contesting his or her disqualification or termination.

Another element in this case -- Umlauf had also claimed that he was entitled to a name-clearing hearing. The Appellate Division, citing Swinton v Safir, 93 NY2d 758, agreed. The court said that Umlauf "has sufficiently raised the issues of the partial falsity and overall characterization of information included in his personnel file, the dissemination of such information, both past and future, as well as the presence of 'stigma plus' -- in this case governmental defamatory action in conjunction with loss of employment."

CHAPTER 2

CONDUCTING AN INVESTIGATION

When allegations of misconduct arise, both the employer and the union representing the employee are obligated to investigate.

The employer has a responsibility as a steward of public trust to investigate any allegations of malfeasance (wrongdoing), misfeasance (performing a public duty, but in an improper manner) and nonfeasance (failing to perform one's duty).

The union has an obligation to investigate under its duty of fair representation. The union must ascertain facts in order to adequately represent the individual or make judgments of how to devote resources when multiple union members are involved or perhaps are accusing each other of improper conduct.

This chapter considers the procedures that should be followed in processing disciplinary actions. Specific requirements in individual cases may vary depending on the legal authority used -- Section 75 of the Civil Service Law, Section 3020-a of the Education Law, or an alternative disciplinary procedure negotiated under the Taylor Law [Article 14 of the Civil Service Law] and set out in a collective bargaining agreement.

When the appointing authority is a "body" such as a board or commission, it is not unusual for one or more members of the "body" to participate in an investigation of employee conduct that ultimately results in disciplinary charges being filed against the employee. Has the employee been denied due process if those members of the board or commission who conducted the investigation also participate in the post hearing determination as to the employee's guilt with respect to one or more of the charges and imposition of a discipline penalty?

This issues is explored in Stanton v Board of Trustees, 550 NYS2d 16

In Stanton the Appellate Division, Second Department ruled that an employee is not deprived of administrative due process because members of the Board who voted to terminate Stanton also participated in the underlying investigation that lead to charges of misconduct being brought against her.

The decision states that "although a fair trial in a fair tribunal is a basic requirement of due process ... it has also been recognized that mere familiarity with the facts of a case gained by an agency in the performance of its statutory role does not disqualify a decision-maker."

As to Stanton's other claims in support of her contention that she had been denied due process, the Appellate Division commented that although the Board was authorized by Section 75.2 of the Civil Service Law to conduct a disciplinary hearing concerning the charges it had filed against her, it elected to have an independent hearing officer preside at the hearing instead.

The Court viewed this as evidence of the Board's desire to minimize the possibility of bias that might result from the overlapping investigatory and adjudicative functions of the Board. In addition, it was noted that members of the Board who had testified against Stanton at the hearing did not vote on the question of whether to terminate her employment.

Regardless of whether the legal authority for pursuing a disciplinary action is Section 75, Section 3020-a or a collective bargaining agreement, certain elements are standard in any disciplinary process in New York State.

These elements are:

1. A suspicion of wrongdoing or the receipt of allegations of employee misconduct or incompetence.

2. An investigation and determination as to whether disciplinary action is warranted.

3. The filing of disciplinary charges, including the proposed penalty.

4. Holding the disciplinary hearing.

5. Findings of fact and a determination by a hearing officer or tribunal.

6. Appointing authority accepts, modifies or rejects hearing officer's finding[s] and/or recommendation[s].

7. Challenging the hearing determination through an appeal process.

The remainder of this chapter will describe proper procedures in perhaps the most sensitive part of a disciplinary proceeding: the investigation of allegations. Later chapters will concern other steps in the discipline process.

It is worth noting that collective bargaining agreements typically contain detailed guidelines on procedures to be followed in investigations. Employers sometimes choose to follow the steps in a collective bargaining agreement even for personnel who are not covered by the agreement. For instance, suppose an administrator is investigating an employee for possible misconduct. Although the employee is not covered under the employer's collective bargaining agreement, the administrator may choose to follow the same investigatory steps outlined in the collective bargaining agreement.

There are pros and cons to this approach. On the positive side, following the procedure conveys an intent to be fair and equitable. Also, those steps are well defined and familiar to the administrator. There is no risk of establishing a past practice within the meaning of the Taylor Law if the individual is outside the negotiating unit, because past practice only applies to parties to an agreement.

On the other hand, if the individual involved is a member of the negotiating unit but is not entitled to due process due to his or her employment status there is a strong possibility of establishing a "past practice" by providing due process to individuals in a negotiating unit not entitled to due process under a collective bargaining agreement or by statute.

With respect to those not in a negotiating unit, providing such a procedure to some, but not others, may result in claims of unlawful discrimination by those not accorded such a benefit. For instance, a black employee who is not entitled to due process may cite as evidence of discrimination the case of a white employee who was not entitled to due process yet was granted it anyway while he or she was not accorded similar treatment.

If charges are served on the employee as a result of the investigation, the authority for such action would be set out in a statute such as Section 75 of the Civil Service Law or Section 3020-a of the Education Law or the relevant clause in a collective bargaining agreement.

2.01 Overview: Disciplinary investigations

It is well established that an employer, acting through its supervisory staff, has an inherent power to investigate its employees when it has knowledge of, or a reasonable suspicion, of misconduct.

A disciplinary investigation has three basic purposes: (1) to ascertain whether claims of misconduct or incompetence have a firm basis in fact; (2) to exonerate the innocent and (3) to identify the persons or records that will be relied upon at any future disciplinary hearing.

Most collective bargaining agreements set out in some detail the procedures to be followed in connection with the investigation of a matter that may lead to disciplinary action. Such guidelines for investigations may prove helpful in other disciplinary situations as well.

Where there are no contract provisions concerning investigations, the employer usually relies on Section 61.f the Public Officers Law as authority for conducting the investigation.

2.02 Handling complaints

Employers sometimes receive complaints or allegations of misconduct about employees from members of the public or co-workers. Such complaints should be investigated.

If the appointing authority is satisfied that there is no merit to the allegation, there is no need to pursue discipline or alternative remedies. If the employer believes there is merit to the allegation, it has options besides proceeding with disciplinary charges.

These options include:

Assignment of a mentor

Clarifying duties and responsibilities

Closer supervision

Counseling

Retraining

Transfer or reassignment

2.03 Anonymous allegations

Sometimes an individual is the target of allegations that have been submitted anonymously. An anonymous allegation poses a serious problem for the administrator. The allegations may be false, made as a result of malice or may simply be a mistake on the part of the accuser. Nevertheless, it is necessary for the administrator to assume the charges are valid and undertake an investigation of the matter.

Such an investigation probably need not be as intensive as would be the case were the allegations made by a supervisor in the normal course of business or by a known party. However, the administrator should satisfy himself or herself that there is no substance to the allegation. If the investigation reveals that there is some substance to the allegations, and if true would constitute misconduct, further action should be taken by the administrator.

Anonymous communications that allege improper conduct by an employee place the appointing authority on the horns of a dilemma. If the employer ignores the communication, it may later develop that there was some substance to the allegation, and the employer will be exposed to criticism (or liability) for failing to act "on the information." On the other hand, if the appointing authority confronts the employee, relying solely on the information it received anonymously, it may be criticized for taking adverse action against the employee based on such information alone. Such was the situation that faced the appointing authority after it received an anonymous letter alleging that one it its firefighters, Scott Wilson was using illegal drugs.

Wilson v City of White Plains, 95 NY2d 783, sets out the standard applied by the Court of Appeals when it considered the actions taken by White Plains based on its receiving anonymous information alleging Wilson was using illegal drugs.

White Plains ordered Wison to submit to blood and urine. Ultimately disciplinary charges were filed against Wilson. A hearing officer found Wilson guilty of six charges of misconduct. The Commissioner of Public Safety adopted the findings and recommendations of the hearing officer and dismissed Wilson from his position. Wilson appealed his termination and persuaded the court that his removal was arbitrary.

Noting that "there was no objective evidence which would have suggested that the [Wilson] was abusing alcohol or drugs," the Appellate Division said that under these circumstances, ordering Wilson to undergo such testing "was arbitrary and without even a minimal basis of justification." Finding that Wilson's dismissal was improper under the circumstances, the court directed the department to reinstate him to his former position with back pay and benefits.

In annulling Wilson's dismissal the Appellate Division said that "in directing [Wilson] to submit to blood and urine tests, the fire department officials "relied upon an unsubstantiated and anonymous letter" and that there "was no objective evidence which would have suggested that the [firefighter] was abusing alcohol or drugs."

The Court of Appeals disagreed with the lower court's conclusion and reversed the Appellate Division's determination.

According to the high court, in addition to its receiving an "anonymous letter" concerning Wilson's alleged use of drugs, "the City presented evidence of Wilson's physical manifestations of substance abuse the day he was tested, long record of excessive absences, prior substance abuse problems, reputation for showing up at work under the influence, as well as his understanding that he could be tested if he showed any signs of recurring substance abuse."

2.04 Fairness in investigations

It should be remembered that in the investigatory stage of the disciplinary proceeding it is as important for the employer to attempt to clear the employee as to discover evidence of wrongdoing.

Investigation is essentially fact-finding. While the investigation may have been undertaken as a result of allegations of misconduct directed at a particular employee, it should also be used as a means of exoneration. Indeed, the investigation might uncover the fact that while there was wrongdoing, it was the act of another employee rather than the target of the original investigation.

Typically, the investigation should be conducted and completed before the decision to initiate discipline is made. In any event, discipline action shall be taken as a result of the analysis of the findings of the investigator, and not because of any prejudgment or "instinct" concerning the guilt of an individual on the part of the administrator.

There should be no preconceptions as to the guilt of the employee under investigation or any limit placed on the scope of the investigation with respect to merits of the charges being explored.

2.05 Interviewing employees

The co-workers of the employee as well as superiors, subordinates and others may be interviewed in the course of an investigation. Employees who are not suspected of wrongdoing can be required to provide and sign statements concerning the target of the investigation.

The employer usually cannot compel the cooperation of any non-employee witnesses, however.

2.06 Refusal to answer questions

Case law suggests that an employee may be disciplined for refusing to answer questions, provided that he or she is either granted immunity from use of his answer in a subsequent criminal prosecution or is not required to waive such immunity.

In January 1998 the U.S. Supreme Court ruled that federal government agencies may take silence into consideration and draw adverse inference in discipline cases.

In Lefkowitz v Turley, 414 US 70, the U.S. Supreme Court held that when a public employee is compelled to answer questions or face removal if he or she refuses to do so, the responses are cloaked with immunity automatically, and neither the compelled statements nor their fruits may be used against the employee in a subsequent criminal prosecution. Similarly, a New York Supreme Court justice ruled in Seabrook v Johnson, 173 Misc.2d 15, that it would "offend the guarantee against self-incrimination to require a public servant to answer questions, even relating to the performance of official duties, upon the threat of dismissal, and to make use of the incriminating statements in a subsequent criminal prosecution."

If a person believes information obtained under threat of disciplinary action is going to be used against him or her in a pending criminal proceeding, he or she may request a "Kastigar hearing" to determine whether the prosecution made any use of either a compelled, immunized statement or any evidence derived directly or indirectly from such a statement [Kastigar v United States, 406 U.S. 441.]

Another U.S. Supreme Court case frequently cited concerning this issue is Garner v Broderick, 392 U.S. 273. The High Court held that if an public officer or employee refuses to answer questions specifically, directly and narrowly related to the performance of his official duties and is not required to waive his or her immunity with respect to the use of such answers in a criminal prosecution, the constitutional privilege against self-incrimination would not bar termination for such refusal to answer.

New York's highest court, the court of Appeals, addressed the issue in People v Corrigan, 80 NY2d 326. The Court of Appeals said that under both state and federal law any statement made under the threat of dismissal is protected by the privilege against self-incrimination and is "automatically immunized from use in criminal proceedings." The court said that the immunity that attaches to any statement that a public worker gives under compulsion bars the use of the statement itself, as well as any evidence derived directly or indirectly from it, in any criminal prosecution. See 9.04, "Use of Disclosures in Criminal Trials."

The specifics of the Corrigan case may be instructive, because the court permitted incriminating statements to be used in criminal proceedings. The court reasoned that the incriminating statements were in the form of official reports -- Use of Force reports.

Five corrections officers were indicted in relation to use of force on prisoners. Each officer filed an affidavit asserting that he had been ordered by a superior officer, under threat of job forfeiture, to submit a written "Use of Force" reports about the underlying incidents. Each man claimed that at the time the report was submitted he believed that neither the statement nor any information or evidence derived therefrom could be used in a subsequent criminal investigation.

Not all affirmative duties to report violate the privilege against self-incrimination, the court said. As an example, it noted that "hit and run" statutes requiring a driver involved in an accident to stop at the scene and provide a name and address do not violate the constitutional right against self-incrimination.

The court noted that the rules and regulations of the employer required Use of Force reports to be completed by any officer involved either as a participant or a witness in a use of force incident against an inmate. The court said that the "Use of Force Reports" could be equated to incident reports. Officers involved in incidents were required to complete a written report concerning the event, but such filing did not serve, in and of itself, to make them targets of investigation.

The mere possibility of incrimination is insufficient to defeat the strong policies in favor of disclosure in instances where force is used. The court commented that the "Use of Force Report" is "clearly designed, at least in part, to protect the interests of the individual officer as well as the Department and includes space for the officer to list any claimed injuries." The court ruled that the Department's reporting regulation did not violate the officers' constitutional rights.

Other cases concerning an employee's duty to respond to a superior's questions are Albino v City Civil Service Commission, 565 NYS2d 520 [appointing authority does not abuse discretion by suspending an employee for 20 days without pay for refusing to answer as supervisor's questions]; Shales v Leach, 119 AD2d 299 [police officer accused of bribe can be disciplined for refusal to answer questions], and Altieri v Roberts, 92 AD2d 1028 [former county corrections officer is not entitled to unemployment insurance benefits after being fired for refusing to cooperate in a hearing concerning an alleged assault on an inmate].

2.07 Free speech

Sometimes an employee is disciplined for action that the employee claims was Constitutionally protected free speech. Orange County Deputy Sheriff Christopher Warren was suspended without pay for 30 days after the Department decided that he violated Sheriff Department rules by giving statements concerning the relocation of the County's jail to a newspaper reporter before he obtained his superior's authorization. The Appellate Division said Warren's speech was not protected because it involved his personal concerns with the relocation of the jail and not a matter of public concern.

Employers should be cautious about policies regarding media contacts. A federal district court judge ruled that a public employer violates the First Amendment rights of its employees by requiring "pre-clearance" of any communication with the news media. [Harman v City of New York, USDC SDNY 96Civ846, 1997]

Another freedom of speech case involved a corrections officer with Nazi sympathies. When New York State Corrections Commissioner learned that corrections officer Edward Kuhnel flew a Nazi flag at his home, he suspended him from his position. Two days later charges of misconduct were filed against Kuhnel, seeking his termination.

PERB Arbitrator Robert T. Simmelkjaer ruled that the department could not discipline an employee for his off-duty exercise of his or her rights to free speech without demonstrating that such conduct actually harmed the Department or impaired the individual's ability to perform his official duties.

In Fry v McCall, USDC SDNY, 6/99 [Judge Koeltl], a federal district court judge was asked to determine if a public official statements concerning matters alleged to be of "public concern" served as a shield against his or her removal from the position.

Patricia C. Fry sued State Comptroller Carl McCall alleging that she had been dismissed from her position as Director of the Bureau of Budget Analysis with the Office of the State Deputy Comptroller because she spoke out on a matter of public concern and that her discharge deprived her of her First Amendment right to free speech in violation of 42 U.S.C. Section 1983.

Fry alleged that she had been terminated because she had questioned reports concerning a New York City "budget crisis" in 1993 and 1994 and that the Comptroller discharged her because she expressed skepticism about the accuracy or integrity of those reports.

The Comptroller, on the other hand, contended that Fry "had become insubordinate to her supervisor, disruptive at staff meetings, unwilling to cooperate in the preparation of the OSDC reports, and abusive toward a colleague." In addition, the Comptroller argued that even if he had discharged Fry because of her statements, this "did not violate her First Amendment rights because the State's interest in the effective and efficient operations of the [agency] outweighed any free speech rights [Fry] may have had."

The court said that to win her Section 1983 claim for wrongful termination based on a First Amendment violation, Fry was required to prove by a preponderance of the evidence (a) that the speech at issue was constitutionally protected, and (b) that it was a "substantial" or "motivating" factor in the decision to terminate her employment. Judge Koeltl concluded that "Fry has failed to prove by a preponderance of the evidence that her expressions of concern [regarding the reports] were a 'substantial' or 'motivating' factor in the decision to dismiss her."

The decision notes that there are a number of relevant factors to be considered in such cases, including [a] the time, manner, and place of the speech; [b] the extent of the disruption caused by the employee's conduct; [c] the responsibilities of the employee and [d] whether the employee held a policymaking position...." Significantly, the court observed that "[a] high ranking policy-making employee does not have, and never has had, a First Amendment right to refuse [her] employer's directive to promote agency policy."

In Vezzetti v. Pellearini, 22 F.3d 483, 486 (2d Cir. 1994) the Second Circuit Court of Appeals, which has jurisdiction over New York State, set out a number of guidelines for determining "policymaker status." To resolve the issue, the courts should determine whether the individual:

(1) is exempt from civil service protection,

(2) has some technical competence or expertise,

(3) controls others,

(4) is authorized to speak in the name of the policymakers,

(5) is perceived as a policymaker by the public,

(6) influences government programs,

(7) has contact with elected officials, and

(8) is responsive to partisan politics and political leaders.

The court said that Fry satisfied all of these eight criteria with respect to the issue of her "policymaker" status. Under the Pickering balancing test, said the court, the Comptroller "justifiably terminated Ms. Fry, a policymaking employee whose behavior not only threatened to become disruptive, but had already become disruptive, in order to preserve the efficiency and effectiveness of the OSDC."

Having found that Fry "failed to demonstrate that Comptroller McCall, or indeed any state employee, acting under color of state law, deprived her of her right to free speech in violation of the First Amendment", the court dismissed her action on the merits.

2.08 Self-incrimination and immunity

Forcing an employee to answer questions generally precludes criminal prosecution based on those answers. Testimony obtained under threat of the loss of public employment provides the employee with limited immunity and such testimony may not be used as a basis for subsequent criminal prosecution [Lefkowitz v Turley, 414 US 70].

What about witnesses who may have participated in wrongdoing? Are they automatically granted limited immunity by virtue of their testimony in an administrative procedure? The answer is no. An administrative officer cannot bind the district attorney by a promise of immunity from criminal prosecution in exchange for his or her testimony as a witness at an administrative hearing.

By the same token, the district attorney cannot bind an administrative tribunal with respect to its exercising its lawful authority. If immunity is a consideration, the witness must be granted such immunity by the appropriate authority in order for it to be effective and binding.

The several decisions in Mountain v Schenectady focused on the relationships between a refusal to waive immunity from prosecution and the loss of public office. See 474 NYS2d 612; 453 NYS2d 93 and 428 NYS2d 772.

2.09 Lying by employees

Any cloak of immunity that might attach to an employee's statements dissolves if the employee is shown to have lied in his or her testimony. It is well-settled law that one who is granted immunity in return for his testimony receives no license to swear falsely with impunity under the protection of that immunity.

If the employee supplies information deemed to be cloaked with immunity because it had been compelled under threat of termination, "that immunity would dissolve in the face of false allegations being filed." [Seabrook v Johnson, 660 NYS2d 311.] See also United States v Apfelbaum, 445 U.S. 115.

In 1998 the U.S. Supreme Court ruled unanimously that federal government agencies could mete out harsher discipline to employees who lie while being investigated for job-related conduct. Although only federal employees were involved, the ruling is also expected to influence cases involving state and local employees. Chief Justice William H. Rehnquist wrote that if employees remain silent, citing the Fifth Amendment or some other reason, employers are free to take such silence into consideration and draw adverse inferences in discipline.

2.10 Statute of limitations on discipline

If an employer decides to postpone disciplinary action, the employer should be mindful of the running of the statute of limitations, which under Section 75 is 18 months (1 year for managerial and confidential state employees), except for acts or omissions that constitute a crime. [Section 75.4] Thus, if the employee's alleged misconduct would not constitute a crime under New York or federal law, the employer must file disciplinary charges within 18 months of the act of alleged misconduct or incompetence. After 18 months, the employer is barred from filing charges based on those acts or omissions.

2.11 Legal representation during investigations

Sometimes a person asks to have a union representative or an attorney present when being questioned at the investigatory stage of a potential disciplinary action. However, unless provided for under the terms of a collective bargaining agreement, generally the employee has no right to have an attorney present during an investigatory interview. The employer may allow an attorney to be present, but there is risk that this could be viewed as a past practice and become an obligation in future disciplinary cases.

In 1993 the state Legislature amended the Civil Service Law to address the right to representation. The law states employees subject to potential disciplinary action are entitled to union representation during the investigatory state, and to have representation by an attorney or a union representative in a disciplinary hearing. Section 75.2 provides that an employee "who at the time of questioning appears to be a potential subject of disciplinary action shall have a right to representation by his or her certified or recognized employee organization under article fourteen of this chapter and shall be notified in advance, in writing, of such right.... If representation is requested a reasonable period of time shall be afforded to obtain such representation.... [At a disciplinary hearing] (t)he person or persons holding such hearing shall, upon request of the person against whom charges are preferred, permit him to be represented by counsel, or by a representative of a recognized or certified employee organization...."

The law also provides that accused employees must be furnished with a list of charges and be given at least eight days to respond.

Although a given employee may have no statutory right to counsel in a given disciplinary investigation, Taylor Law contracts may provide that an employee may have attorney (or a union representative) present during a pre-disciplinary investigatory interview.

Generally, though, employees who refuse to answer questions unless legal counsel is present are subject to discipline for refusing to answer. Cases that illustrate that the employer has no obligation to allow the employee's attorney to be present during investigatory questioning are Sundram v Kirschbaum et al, and Sundram v Hallerman, _ AD2d _. In those cases the State Commission on Quality Care for the Mentally Disabled argued successfully that "the courts consistently have rejected the right to counsel before an investigatory administrative body."

The cases involved the death of a patient and the sexual abuse of another at Bellview Hospital Center. The Commission had a policy against allowing attorneys to be present during interviews of employees. The Appellate Division said this was a permissible policy because it viewed the Commission's authority as purely investigatory in nature "as it has no adjudicative functions, existing merely to gather facts, generate reports and make recommendations." The court said: "That disciplinary or criminal proceedings may result from the Commission's investigatory function is insufficient reason to impose a right to counsel."

Suppose an employee is threatened with disciplinary action if he or she does not immediately resign. Is the employee entitled to consult with a lawyer before making such a decision?

In Rychlick v Coughlin, 63 NY2d 643, a case involving a corrections officer, the Court of Appeals ruled that the answer is no. The court pointed out that threatening to do what the appointing authority had a right to do -- i.e., file disciplinary charges -- did not constitute coercion so as to make the resignation involuntary.

Even a contractual right to representative is not absolute, though, as the Appellate Division ruled in Reid v NYS Division of State Police. Reid appealed his dismissal, claiming that his due process rights under the Taylor Law agreement then in force had been violated because counsel did not represent him when he was interviewed by "Division investigators" prior to being served with disciplinary charges.

The Appellate Division said that the interview was an ordinary inquiry by a supervisor, however. The court ruled that an ordinary supervisory inquiry was not governed by the procedural requirements of the collective bargaining agreement.

2.12 Suspension with or without pay

One issue that arises early in disciplinary cases is whether the employer should immediately suspend the employee from his or her position pending the results of an investigation. This is a matter of discretion.

Section 75 provides that an individual can be suspended pending a hearing on the charges and the final determination. The suspension may be without pay for a maximum of 30 days. [Section 75.3] The legislature enacted this rule because of laxness on the part of supervisors in fixing hearing dates. To suspend an employee without pay and then fail to provide for a prompt hearing would place the employee under undue hardship [Morris v Reid, 1960, 210 NYS2d 868]

If the disciplinary proceeding or a settlement has not been completed within 30 days of the beginning of the period of suspension without pay, the individual must be restored to the payroll, even if he or she is not permitted to return to work. [Maurer v Cappelli (2 Dept. 1973) 42 AD2d 758, 346 NYS 2d 154] An exception provides for a pre-hearing period of suspension without pay longer than 30 days if the employee or his or her representative delay the hearing. See, for example, DeMarco v City of Albany (3 Dept. 1980) 75 AD2d 674, 426 NYS2d 860. For other exceptions due to collective bargaining agreements or other reasons, see Winkler v Kingston Housing Authority, NYS App. Div, April 10, 1997, Langhorne v Jackson, 614 NYS2d 627, and Robinson v New York City Transit Authority (2 Dept, 1996) 226 AD2d 467, 641 NYS2d 55.

If the employee is later acquitted, "he shall be restored to his position with full pay for the period of suspension less the amount of any unemployment insurance benefits he may have received during such period" [Section 75.3]. It should be noted, however, that although the civil service law as amended bars consideration of income earned by the employee in determining the individual's back salary, sometimes the courts overlook this change in the law.

If the employee is found guilty, Section 75 lists among permissible penalties a suspension without pay not to exceed 60 days. If such a penalty is assigned, the pre-hearing suspension may be considered "time served" but there is no requirement for the employer to do so [Section 75.3]. An employee found guilty has no right to salary for the period of pre-hearing suspension [Paris v City of New York, 1947, 189 Misc. 445, 74 NYS2d 584].

Under Taylor Law agreements and Section 3020-a, penalties of suspension without pay longer periods that otherwise set out in statute are possible. In the case of a teacher found guilty of helping students cheat on a Regents exam, for instance, the Appellate Division ruled "a two-year suspension without pay was not so disproportionate to the offenses committed as to be shocking to one's sense of fairness." [Earles v Pine Bush CSD, 638 NYS2d 163]

The employer's ability to suspend an employee may depend on the terms of a collective bargaining agreement rather than Section 75. But the existence of a "grievance procedure," alone does not constitute a substitute for Section 75. [Mancuso v Crew, NYS Supreme Court, January 1998, not officially reported].

Section 75.3 provides that an employee may be suspended without pay only if "charges have been preferred." In other words, until a notice of disciplinary charges has been actually served on the employee, the individual must be retained on the payroll. Written charges may be served via a delivery service such as certified U.S. mail or by hand, in which case an affidavit by the deliverer would serve as proof of service of charges on the employee.

There are other alternatives for removing the employee from the workplace. The employer may suspend the employee with pay or reassign the individual to another position for which he or she is otherwise qualified. Either of these actions will usually withstand judicial scrutiny.

See also Chapter 8, Suspending Employees Pending a Hearing.

2.13 Affect of criminal actions on suspensions

Suppose that after disciplinary charges are served the individual is arrested and jailed based on the same acts or omissions. The individual's ability to build a defense would be compromised, and he or she might be unable to attend the scheduled disciplinary hearing.

Even if the individual is released on bail, it is likely that prosecutors would pressure the employer not to proceed for fear of compromising the criminal case. Is the employer forced by such circumstances to return the employee to the payroll after 30 days? The answer is: not necessarily. The employer has the option of withdrawing the charges pending resolution of the criminal case. This can also save the employer considerable effort in proving its case, because a guilty verdict in a criminal court automatically serves to establish guilt in a disciplinary forum. See "Impact of criminal action on disciplinary action, generally", below, and Chapter 3, Evidence.

If the disciplinary charges are withdrawn and the individual remains in jail and thus unable to report to work, the employer can require the employee to use up all his or her vacation, personal leave and other leave (other than sick leave, unless he or she is sick) while he or she is in jail if he or she wishes to remain on the payroll, then suspend the employee without pay because the employee is absent and has exhausted available leave credits.

2.14 Impact of criminal action on disciplinary action, generally

In some cases the incident for which the employee is to be disciplined may also constitute or be related to a crime and there may be a criminal proceeding pending or expected. It is common for prosecutors to ask employers to refrain from proceeding out of fear that the criminal case would be compromised.

There is no legal obligation on the part of the employer to honor such a request. Neither a district attorney nor the employee can require that the administrative action be postponed until the criminal action is completed.

However, if the decision is made to proceed before the criminal action is tried, the agency may find itself having to develop its own evidence. Often the district attorney will refuse to cooperate.

Postponing action can save the employer effort because the standard of proof is higher in the criminal forum, and a guilty verdict in a criminal court automatically serves to establish guilt in a disciplinary forum. [Kelly v Levin, 440 NYS2d 424]

By the same token, a "not guilty" verdict in a criminal proceeding does not prevent the individual from being found guilty in a disciplinary hearing, because the standard of proof differs. The criminal standard is proof of guilt beyond a reasonable doubt, while the standard for disciplinary proceedings is substantial evidence of guilt. [See Chapter 3, Evidence.]

Statements made by the employee to police during investigation of criminal charges filed against the employee constitutes "competent evidence" and may be admitted into evidence during the disciplinary hearing [Dacey v County of Dutchess, 121 AD2d 536].

See also Chapter 9, Pending Criminal Actions.

2.15 Voluntary resignations

A common reaction to the receipt of information that could result in disciplinary action being brought against an employee is for a supervisor to confront the employee and state that charges will be preferred (filed) unless the individual "volunteers" to immediately resign from the position.

An employee may claim that such a confrontation constitutes "duress or threat" that will negate the "voluntariness" of the resignation and make it meaningless. However, case law indicates that in the absence of extenuating circumstances such as excessively lengthy or intense questioning, it is difficult to argue successfully that one's resignation was obtained under duress. In a nutshell, the employer has a legal right -- perhaps even a duty -- to file disciplinary charges. It is not coercive to threaten to do what one has a legal right to do.

The Rychlick case illustrates the point [Rychlick v Coughlin, 63 NY2d 643]. Rychlick, a corrections officer, was alleged to have failed to come to the assistance of a fellow corrections officer during a fight between that officer and an inmate. In the presence of his union representative, he was offered the option of resigning or having formal disciplinary charges filed against him. He was permitted to confer with a union official but when he requested time to consult with an attorney, he was advised that unless he resigned at that moment in time, charges would be filed against him. He resigned. Four days later Rychlick sought to withdraw the resignation, which he claimed had been "forced" from him. The request was denied and Rychlick sued to regain his job. Although a lower court had found "duress" and ordered Rychlick reinstated with back pay, the Court of Appeals held that the "threat to file formal charges ... does not constitute duress."

The decision noted that the appointing authority had the legal right, if not the duty, to press charges under the circumstances and it was not duress to threaten to do what one had the legal right to do.[17]

---

[17] The general rule with respect to an employee seeking to withdraw his or her resignation: Allowing the employee to withdraw a resignation that has be delivered to the appointing authority or its representative is at the sole discretion of the appointing authority. However, a resignation must be in writing in order to be effective; typically courts will refuse to recognize an oral resignation.

2.16 Issuing subpoenas, recording evidence

State officers are authorized under Section 61 of the Public Officers Law to make an "inquiry as to the official conduct of any subordinate officer or employee," also local laws may grant parallel powers to local government officials. In connection with such investigations, the officer has the power to issue subpoenas to require the attendance of witnesses and the production of books and papers relating to any matter under inquiry.

If a person refuses to honor a subpoena, it may be necessary to have a court issue the order. While the administrator or arbitrator issuing a subpoena rarely has the power to "enforce" compliance, a court may hold a person in contempt for such a failure to comply with its order. (Subpoena means "under penalty".) The court can place the offender in jail, fine him, or both for noncompliance with what has now become its order.

2.17 Informants

Sometimes disciplinary action results from information supplied by an informant. Does the accused have the right to know the identity of the informant?

Because "the hearings held in disciplinary proceedings are not governed by the rules obtaining [applying] at a criminal trial" the Appellate Division, First Department, has ruled the answer is no [Coleman v Kramer, 603 NYS2d 140, 198 AD2d 12, leave to appeal den 84 NY2d 801].

The case involved a New York City Transit Police officer who tested positive for cocaine in a test that was administered on the tip of an informant.

The opinion indicates that in the course of the hearing, the administrative law judge "diligently evaluated the reliability of the confidential informant, and the informant's fear for personal safety," in an "in camera" review. An in camera review is a private review (literally: "in one's heart").

2.18 Evidence

Unless there is substantial evidence to support the charges, the employee cannot be found guilty. Accordingly, any defects in the investigatory stages of the disciplinary action may have a significant adverse effect later in the proceeding.

This is true from both the employer's and the employee's perspective.

Sometimes the employee fails to develop or preserve evidence that would tend to exonerate him or her. He or she then may be unable to rebut the evidence presented by the employer at the disciplinary hearing.

See Chapter 3 for more on evidence.

2.19 Recording investigation findings

It is important to maintain accurate records regarding persons interviewed, including dates and times of the interviews as well as the documents examined and the other physical evidence reviewed or observed. Where appropriate, photographs or videotape may be used to preserve evidence.

Having a written sworn statement is also important. If the person is unwilling to provide such a sworn statement (it is best to obtain the statement at the time of interview), it makes the information gathered suspect at best. At worst, if called as a witness, the person may deny having made such a statement or claim it was misunderstood.

While recorded evidence can strengthen a case, introducing written or taped testimony can be problematic if the witness does not appear, because the individual in essence is denied the right to cross-examine the witness. However, the employee must lodge any objections to taped testimony when it is introduced at the disciplinary hearing if he or she is to retain the right to challenge the findings of the hearing officer on this basis in court [Baker v NYC Transit Police Department, Appellate Division].

2.20 Record-keeping

After an investigation has been completed there are three major options available to the administrator:

1. Determine that disciplinary action is unwarranted.

2. Decide that there is insufficient evidence for filing charges but that some other action, such as "counseling the individual" is appropriate.

3. Recommend the filing of disciplinary charges against the individual.
Regardless of the decision or recommendation with respect to going forward with disciplinary action, a formal report of the findings and reasons for the recommendation should be prepared. It is important to do this for a number of reasons.

First, the reasons for undertaking the investigation in the first place might be attacked as an abuse of process, unlawful discrimination or on a number of other theories.

A contemporaneous report concerning the investigation undertaken and the findings may be critical to successfully defending the decision to investigate or to proceed, or not to go forward, with disciplinary action upon the completion of the investigation.

The next chapter will provide guidelines for presenting evidence at disciplinary hearings under Section 75 of the Civil Service Law, Section 3020-a of the Education Law and under collective bargaining agreements negotiated pursuant to the Taylor Law.

2.21 Defamation of employees

Even if the employee decides not to proceed with disciplinary action, an employee who has been the subject of an investigation may claim that he or she has been defamed in a libelous or slanderous manner. [If defamatory statements are written, it could constitute libel; if oral, slander.] The employee could accuse the employer or a co-worker of committing libel or slander.

To prove libel or slander, the individual generally must show that defamatory statements or writings were provided to a third party not otherwise entitled to receive such information. The Fedrizzi decision [Fedrizzi v Washingtonville CSD, 611 NYS2d 584, 204 AD2d 267] considers such a case and briefly summarizes the law with respect to libel or slander.

The Washingtonville Central School District fired Fedrizzi, a school bus driver, after a disciplinary proceeding. He sued, contending that the school district had libeled him. The Appellate Division, upholding a lower court's determination, ruled that "the publication of the offending statements to a third party" is a necessary element to proving libel or slander.

The court said that "words are published within the meaning of the law of libel when they are in writing and are read by someone other than the person libeled and the person making the charges."

As to the law of slander, the court said that "the slanderous words must have been spoken in the presence and hearing of some person other than the one slandered, who is not entitled to hear the defamatory matter."

In either situation, libel or slander, there is no damage within the meaning of the law unless there is some communication to a third party having no interest in the matter.

Among the most common situations are those involving the employee alleging that defamatory statements appeared in internal communications between administrators or between an employee and an administrator. In such cases defamatory written or oral communication between and among administrators and employees may be protected by what is called a "qualified privilege." To overcome a qualified privilege, malice must be shown. Murphy v Herfort, 428 NYS2d 117, is an example of litigation resulting from communications between administrators; Missek-Falkoff v Keller, 545 NYS2d 360, is an example of a case where one employee sued another because of the contents of a memorandum from the second employee to a superior concerning a "problem" with the co-worker.

Likewise, the issue of injury to one's reputation may arise in connection with an employee's former employer supplying information to a prospective employer of the individual in response to a request for "references" [see Buxton v Plant City, 57 LW 2649].

Cases alleging defamation may also involve consideration of whether a "public official" is able to recover damages because of allegedly libelous or slanderous statements.

CHAPTER 3

EVIDENCE

Evidence is the critical factor in any administrative proceeding, including disciplinary actions.

In a disciplinary hearing, the burden of proving the charges and specifications filed against an employee is always on the charging party. One "proves" facts relevant to the case by means of "evidence."

The burden of proof never shifts to the employee; the employee is not required to prove that he or she is not guilty.

However, if the employer introduces evidence that, if unrebutted, would prove that the employee is guilty of the charges, the employee must present evidence in his or her defense. The failure to do so will, in effect, be construed by the hearing officer or arbitrator as an admission that the employee is guilty as charged.

If the charging party presents evidence showing that the employee is guilty as charged, the charging party has established a prima facie case. To show that the employee is innocent, he or she must rebut the prima facie case made by the charging party. This is sometimes referred to as the "burden of going forward," which is distinct from the burden of proof. The employee need not prove his or her innocence; the employee need merely rebut the prima facie case.

Evidence is the key to showing facts that, if believed, establish or disprove the allegations on which the disciplinary charges are based.

"Proof" is the belief or conclusions arrived at by the use of evidence. In a court of law, the "technical rules of evidence" are required to be followed. In an administrative proceeding such as a disciplinary action and in arbitrations, the technical rules of evidence are generally not applied. For instance, hearsay testimony, which typically is barred from testimony in a criminal trial, is permissible in an administrative hearing. (See "Hearsay evidence", below.)

Indeed, in some situations the statute providing for the due process hearing specifically excuses compliance with or the application of the technical rules of evidence.

Still, many judicial traditions are followed in administrative proceedings and arbitrations. For example, in a court of law the party having the burden of proof has the right to open and close the case.

This convention is followed in administrative proceedings and arbitrations where the charging party, if it wishes, makes the opening statement first and may make the final or closing statement to the hearing officer after the accused does so.

3.01 Forms of evidence

There are a number of different forms that evidence can take, including:

Testimonial evidence -- oral evidence given by a witness under oath at a hearing

Documentary evidence -- any printed or written material introduced at a hearing for the purpose of showing the truth of its contents

Real evidence -- all evidence presented to the hearing officer. Real evidence can be "direct," that is evidence which standing alone establishes the facts at issue, or "circumstantial."

Circumstantial vs. direct evidence -- Circumstantial evidence consists of facts which do not directly prove the allegation but which the hearing officer may consider in order to infer facts that may then be used to determine the fact at issue.

"I saw X take the book from the table" is an example of direct evidence. Consider, in contrast: "The book was on the table when I left. When I returned X was leaving the room holding a package and I noticed that the book was no longer on the table" is circumstantial evidence leading to an inference that "X" took the book from the table.

Material evidence -- Evidence may also be classified as relevant or material -- something that may logically be considered to prove or disprove a fact.

Competent evidence --If the evidence is "competent", it is "admissible" evidence. Evidence is termed "incompetent" if it is relevant ("material") evidence but may not be used because it must be excluded from consideration for some reason.

For instance, statements made by an employee to the police during investigation of criminal charges filed against the employee constitutes competent evidence and may be admitted into evidence during the disciplinary hearing (Dacey v County of Dutchess, 121 AD2d 536).

Hearsay evidence -- Second-hand information, e.g.: "Bob told me that Sharon said X," or "Everybody in the office knew Alan and Wynona were having an affair." Although inadmissible in criminal trials, hearsay evidence is admissible in civil proceedings including disciplinary actions.

3.02 Hearsay evidence

Anyone who has watched a courtroom drama knows that "hearsay evidence" is inadmissible in a criminal proceeding. Hearsay (defined above) is an example of incompetent evidence under the formal rules of evidence applicable in the courtroom. But hearsay evidence may be considered admissible evidence in civil proceeding such as an administrative proceeding such as an action under Section 75 or Section 3020-a. ["Compliance with technical rules of evidence shall not be required," Section 75.2; "[R]ules and procedures for the conduct of hearings ... shall not require compliance with technical rules of evidence," Section 3020-a(2)(C).]

In other words, hearsay is "competent evidence" in disciplinary actions.

An administrative agency "can prove its case through hearsay as long as it is believable, relevant and probative." [Riley v Schles, 585 NYS2d 627, 185 AD2d 437 (1992)] Likewise, hearsay evidence may be used against teachers absent any suggestion that the evidence was unreliable [Carangelo v Ambach, (1987, 3d Dept) 130 AD2d 898, app den 70 NY2d 609]

Hearsay evidence was a factor in the Brinson case [Brinson v Safir, 255 A.D.2d 247, motion for leave to appeal denied, 93 N.Y.2d 805]. James Brinson, a New York City police officer, was dismissed after being found guilty of "knowingly and wrongfully associat[ing] with persons know to be engaged in criminal activity."

The evidence against Brinson consisted of hearsay statements of two informants. The statements of the informants were corroborated by police surveillance. The Appellate Division said that such testimony, together with its corroboration, constituted substantial evidence of the charges filed against Brinson and dismissed his appeal.[18]

Another aspect of the appeal involved Brinson's being required to submit to a drug test. The Appellate Division said that "corroborated information" supplied by informants provided a "reasonable suspicion" to require Brinson to undergo drug testing.

Despite its admissibility as competent evidence, an employee may not be found guilty of charges solely on the basis of hearsay; some real evidence is required [Brown v Ristich, 36 NY2d 183; Carroll v Knickbocker Ice Co., 218 NY 435].

Unless expressly required to exclude hearsay under the terms of a collective bargaining agreement, arbitrators will usually permit the introduction of hearsay.

3.03 Standard of proof: criminal vs. disciplinary hearing

The standard of proof for disciplinary hearings is lower than the standard of proof required for criminal proceedings. The reason is that amount to which one's liberty is at risk is lower in a disciplinary hearing than a criminal proceeding. "[t]he standard of proof [substantial evidence] that must be met to sustain a charge at a disciplinary hearing, where the ultimate penalty could be the loss of employment, is not as rigorous as the standard of proof applicable to the trial of a criminal case [beyond a reasonable doubt], where the ultimate penalty could be the loss of liberty." [Matter of Police Commissioner of the City of New York, _ Misc 2d _]

---

[18] Another "hearsay evidence in administrative hearings" case is Derbyshire v Safir, App. Div., First Dept., November 1, 2001. In this appeal, the Appellate Division held that Joseph Derbyshire received a fair hearing and that substantial evidence supported the administrative determination to dismiss him from his position. Derbyshire had argued that certain hearsay evidence against him should not have been considered in making the administrative determination. The Appellate Division disagreed, ruling that "[h]ighly probative hearsay evidence was properly admitted" and thus could be considered in making the determination.

3.04 Standard of proof, Section 75

Section 75 does not set any standard concerning the evidence required to prove the case against the employee. However, the courts generally have been satisfied with the employee being found guilty on the basis of "substantial evidence". [Simpson v Wolansky, 38 NY2d 391]

According to the Appellate Division, substantial evidence is "such relevant proof as a reasonable mind may accept as adequate to support a conclusion or ultimate fact" [Torres v County of Westchester, 582 NYS2d 451].

Blacks Law Dictionary, 4th edition, includes among its definition of "substantial" the following: "Belonging to substance, actually existing; real; not seeming or imaginary; not illusive; solid; true; veritable."

As a matter of procedure, if an Article 78 action is brought alleging that the administrative determination is not supported by substantial evidence, Section 7804(g) of the Civil Practice Law and Rules requires that the case be transferred directly to the Appellate Division. [Johnson v Ward, 507 NYS2d 852]

3.05 Standard of proof, Section 3020-a

In education disciplinary cases, the standard of proof is less rigorous than substantial evidence. Section 6510(3)(c) of the Education Law was amended in 1984, changing the standard to be met from "substantial evidence" to "a preponderance of the evidence" (see Chapter 1018 of the Laws of 1984). Two years later, in 1986, the Court of Appeals has ruled that to determine whether charges were properly brought under Section 3020-a, the proper standard is "preponderance of evidence", not substantial evidence. [Martin v Ambach, 67 NY2d 975]. See also Appendices for Commissioner's Regulations, 8 NYCRR 82, Comment 82-1.10(g).

A preponderance of the evidence is the standard used in civil cases. It simply means evidence for one side outweighs evidence for the other side by some degree, however minute.

"If the evidence is equally balanced, or if it leaves the jury in such doubt as to be unable to decide the controversy either way, judgment must be given against the party upon whom the burden of proof rests." [Roberge v Bonner, 185 NY 265, 269.

According to Black's Law Dictionary, 4th Edition, "The word 'preponderance' means something more than 'weight'; it denotes a superiority of weight, or outweighing." The side with a preponderance of the evidence presents information that "produces the stronger impression, and has the greater weight, and is more convincing as to its truth when weighed against the evidence in opposition ..." [S. Yamamoto v Puget Sound Lumber Co., 84 Wash. 411, 146 P. 861, 863]

One does not provide a preponderance of the evidence merely by calling more witnesses than are called by the other party; New York's Supreme Court has ruled that "witnesses are to be weighed, not counted." [Nelson v Easton & Amboy R.R. Co., 7 Misc. 656, 657, 28 NYS 50, 52]

So far we have been talking about the standard of evidence that applies in proving or disproving a disciplinary allegation. There is also a standard that applies when courts judge whether the employer was justified in bringing charges in the first place. According to the Court of Appeals, the standard is a preponderance of the evidence. [Martin v Ambach (1986) 67 NY2d 975].

3.06 Effect of criminal conviction or dismissal on discipline

In a criminal case the standard of proof is more stringent than in a disciplinary hearing; the prosecutor must prove guilt beyond a reasonable doubt.

The fact that there are differing standards of proof means that a guilty plea or verdict in a criminal case means that the employee is automatically and without exception guilty of parallel charges brought in a disciplinary forum stemming from the same underlying events.

If a jury finds a person to be guilty beyond a reasonable doubt of, say, larceny, a disciplinary hearing officer need hear no other evidence to render a verdict of guilty regarding a parallel charge of theft in a disciplinary proceeding. The decision in Kelly v Levin, 440 NYS2d 424, illustrates this proposition. The reason is that "beyond a reasonable doubt" requirement of the criminal action satisfies a higher standard than is required to be met to establish guilt in an administrative disciplinary forum. If a jury has determined that a person can jump four feet off the ground, there is no need for a hearing officer in a civil proceeding to hear testimony to determine if the person can jump one foot off the ground.

On the other hand, a finding of not guilty in a criminal proceeding does not prevent the holding of a disciplinary hearing. A person can be found not guilty beyond a reasonable doubt and still found guilty under the standard of substantial evidence or preponderance of the evidence in an administrative proceeding.

3.07 Testimony by the accused

Another difference between criminal and disciplinary actions is the inferences that are allowed if the accused declines to be a witness on his or her own behalf or refuses to answer a question if called as a witness.

A disciplinary hearing officer may take the fact that accused declined to testify into consideration when determining guilt or innocence while in a criminal proceeding the accused may claim exercise his or her privilege against self-incrimination without running any legal risk of having such action construed as evidence of guilt.

In other words, an administrative preceding the refusal to testify may be considered by the hearing officer as some evidence that the testimony or response would not be favorable to the employee's case. Indeed, silence may be considered an admission in certain circumstances.

This is frequently the result when an individual against whom the charge has been made, or a witness whom he or she could have called to testify, has been given an opportunity to reply and would be expected to reply if the statement were untrue but does not do so.

If a party deliberately destroys evidence, the hearing officer may infer that the evidence would have been unfavorable to that party. However, sometime records that could serve as evidence have been destroyed for a legitimate purpose, such as making room for an employee lounge. In Matter of Klikocki (NY Department of Corrections, Mount McGregor) 628 NYS2d 876, 216 AD2d 808, the Appellate Division decided that evidence Klikocki claimed would be helpful in his defense that the employer had destroyed was not destroyed in an effort to conceal something but rather occurred in the normal course of affairs.

Of course, state and municipal employers must comply with State and local law controlling the retention, storage and destruction of public records. A number of publications concerning these requirements for counties, municipal governments, public benefit corporations, schools and BOCES and community colleges may be obtained from the Education Department's Local Government Records Bureau. The Education Department's Bureau of Records Analysis and Disposition has a schedule for the retention of personnel and financial records by State agencies. Copies are available from these bureaus. Write to them at the State Department of Education, Albany NY, 12230.

3.08 Best evidence rule

While the technical rules of evidence followed by the courts concern themselves with a number of ways in which written material can be shown to be genuine, in administrative proceeding the documents are usually accepted by the hearing officer or arbitrator with much less formality.

Although following the "best evidence rule" -- introduction of the original document -- may be possible, photocopies of such documents are acceptable, especially when the documents involved are "official records" or "records prepared or maintained in the ordinary course of business" by an employer.

3.09 Tainted evidence

It is well settled that the evidence obtained in the course of an unlawful search cannot be used in a criminal proceeding and the courts routinely approve requests to "suppress" such evidence. But there are conflicting decisions by federal and state courts as to whether such "tainted evidence" may be used in administrative proceedings.

The Appellate Division, Fourth Department, annulled the dismissal of a state trooper on drug-related charges. While off-duty, the trooper had been ordered out of a private vehicle by police who found a small bag of marijuana in the car. Because the disciplinary determination was based on evidence obtained in the course of an illegal search and seizure, the Appellate Division held that the exclusionary rule applies in administrative proceedings. The court said that "the fruits of an illegal search may not be used to support the imposition of civil penalties."

The Appellate Division noted that the Court of Appeals had considered the issue and ruled that "to the extent that the State, or its agents, can bypass the deterrent effect of the exclusionary rule by using the fruits of an illegal search in a 'civil' or 'administrative' proceeding, the incentive for enforcement and investigative personnel to exceed constitutional limitations on their activity remains and the effectiveness of the rule as a deterrent is diminished," citing Piccarillo v NYS Board of Parole, 48 NY2d 76.

3.10 Confessions and coercion

New York courts have held that threatening disciplinary action against an employee for alleged misconduct or incompetence if he or she does not resign from the position does not constitute coercion because the employer has the legal right to file charges against the worker. In Rychlick v Coughlin, 63 NY2d 643, the court said that the threat to file formal disciplinary charges if the employee did not resign does not constitute duress as it is not duress to threaten to do what one has the legal right to do -- file disciplinary charges against the worker.

3.11 Competent and incompetent witnesses

The term "competent" may be used to describe a witness as well as evidence. A competent witness is expected to have actually perceived that to which he or she is to testify, to have the ability to recall events witnessed in the past and to have the power to communicate intelligibly and honestly. Such testimony is given under an oath or an affirmation to tell the truth.

While a witness may not give evidence by reading his or her testimony from a prepared statement, documents may be used to refresh the witness' personal knowledge of a relevant fact. The time when the document was prepared is irrelevant.

However the document used by the witness is subject to inspection by the other party and to cross-examination. If a document is used to refresh the recollection of a witness it may be admitted as an "exhibit" -- a convenient statement of the testimony -- but not as evidence itself.

3.12 Opinion evidence

Sometimes a witness is asked to provide an opinion rather than facts.

Generally the role of a witness is to state facts, not conclusions or opinions. However certain "opinions" may be permitted. These include opinions dealing with the emotional state of another person; that an item had a particular taste or smell; or the identification of another person's voice.

3.13 Foundation for testimony

Usually a "foundation" must be provided for such opinion testimony such as evidence that the witness has some basis for the opinion.

If, for example, the witness is called to give an opinion as to whether or not the he or she heard the voice of a particular individual, it will be necessary to first show that the witness had some basis to conclude that the voice heard was that of the individual in question.

3.14 Credibility of witnesses

The statement of a witness at a hearing may be attacked as inconsistent with a statement made earlier by the witness concerning the same event or fact.

Unless the inconsistency is explained away, the demonstration of such inconsistent statements will not help to establish the credibility of the witness. It should be remembered that the credibility of a witness and the weight to be given to the testimony of the witness is determined solely by the hearing officer or arbitrator.

On the issue of the credibility of witnesses, a teacher was charged with conduct unbecoming a teacher based on allegations that he touched the breasts or buttocks of female students on a number of occasions. When the [old] Section 3020-a hearing panel cleared him of all charges and specifications, the district appealed. The Commissioner upheld the hearing panel's determination [Comm. of Ed. Decision #12399].

One of the issues involved the credibility of the witnesses. As to the testimony of the student-witnesses, the panel said "words are hopelessly inadequate to describe the tinny, artificial, and canned nature of ... [the teacher's] accusers." [The record indicates that teacher was alleged to have repeatedly "patted the rear ends of some of the girls in a classroom full of children and none of the boys (except one whose testimony was discounted by the panel) saw any of this happen."]

As to the testimony of another student, the panel said that "an oath has no meaning for this child whatsoever; she will say whatever she wants, whenever she wants."

On the issue of credibility, the Commissioner said that "where the panel determination rests in a major part on determination of witness credibility, [he] will not substitute [his] judgment for that of the panel unless there is clear and convincing evidence that the determination of credibility is inconsistent with the facts."

3.15 Conflicting evidence

It is not unusual for witnesses to have differing versions of events. It is the purview of the hearing officer or arbitrator to make assessments of credibility. Courts are reluctant to substitute their judgment for that of the hearing officer regarding which witness is more credible.

However, courts may intervene when a hearing officer sees evidence where there is none. The Appellate Division overturned a finding of obstructing justice because there was nothing in the record to support a conclusion by the hearing officer "that the third party was actually in a position to accurately overhear conversations between two people who deny that the conversations ever took place." [Riley v Schles, 585 NYS 627, 185 AD2d 437 (Third Dept., 1992)

3.16 Employee surveillance

The availability of video cameras for employee surveillance is becoming an important issue in terms of employee privacy and the expectation of employees to privacy at the work site.

Two state employees were threatened with disciplinary action when they were observed by a surveillance video camera engaged in sexual intercourse while they were supposed to be working at their respective duties.

It is probable that in the course of a disciplinary action the employer may seek to use such types of surveillance records. For issues concerning use of such records, see DiMichel v South Buffalo Railway Company, 80 NY2d 184, rearg den Poole v Consolidated Rail Corp, 595 NYS 2d 397, cert den 114 SCt 68, 510 US 816, rearg dism 610 NYS2d 156.

3.17 Judicial notice

Certain facts need not be proved through the introduction of evidence at a hearing. The hearing officer may take "judicial notice" of certain things. For example, judicial notice may be taken of "notorious facts" -- facts generally known to the community such as the names of principal government officials.

Also subject to judicial notice are manifest facts -- facts not generally know to the public but which may be quickly determined by reference to some authoritative source. An example of a manifest fact is the "official time" of sunrise on a particular day.

Judicial notice may also be taken of laws, rules and regulations as well as facts specifically known to the hearing officer or arbitrator.

A hearing officer may be requested to take judicial notice of a fact or may do so on his or her own motion.

Where written documents are introduced, authentication may be required if the documents are not "official documents or records."

3.18 Disclosure of personal records

Does an individual brought up on disciplinary charges have the right to review the employer's files for exculpatory information? The Appellate Division ruled in the Connolly case that there is no such obligation because "the hearings held in disciplinary proceedings are not governed by the rules obtaining at a criminal trial." [Connolly v Williams, 618 NYS2d 808, 210 AD2d 19].

3.19 Unsealing criminal records

If a criminal prosecution has preceded a disciplinary action, the employer may obtain records from the district attorney even if the criminal case was dismissed. (See Section 160.50, Criminal Procedures Law.)

For example, after a Special Prosecutor was unable to prove a prima facie criminal case against a New York City police officer, the city Police Department asked the court to unseal the records so that they could be used in a departmental disciplinary action. [Matter of the Police Commissioner, Extraordinary Special and Trial Term, Supreme Court, NYC]. Concluding that the records were essential to the Police Department's disciplinary investigation, the court released the court records but not the records of the grand jury.

Because the standard of proof is less rigorous to prove guilt in a disciplinary hearing, the fact that the criminal charges have been dismissed or the individual acquitted is not dispositive of disciplinary issues. See "Standard of Proof", above.

3.20 Standard of conduct

Certain public employees are subject to "strict discipline," i.e., are held to a higher standard of performance and conduct. Law enforcement personnel and individuals in "positions of trust" such as teachers are generally held to this higher standard. See Poitevien v Brown, _ AD2d _.

The higher standard is sometimes referred to as "moral character." Stedronsky v Sobol, 572 NYS2d 445, concerns such considerations.

3.21 Admissions

Another type of evidence that may be introduced is the "admission" made by the employee -- a pretrial statement that is against the employee's own best interest. Some contract disciplinary procedures prohibit the employer from seeking such "admissions" from the employee prior to the serving of charges. Obtaining such an admission, therefore, may constitute a breach of contract.

3.22 Source of documentary evidence

Documentary evidence includes photographs, affidavits, tape recordings and similar items. The source of documentary evidence can be an issue. Finkelstein v State Personnel Board, decided by the California Court of Appeals, Third District, involved the introduction of material found during the involuntary search of Finkelstein's personal briefcase as evidence in a disciplinary action seeking his dismissal.

Finkelstein was an employee of the California Franchise Tax Board. The Board was moving to new quarters and all employees were instructed not to place confidential materials in attaché cases or anything that could be handled by the movers.

Disciplinary action was initiated when a supervisor, without permission, searched Finkelstein's personal briefcase to make certain that these instructions were being followed found documents setting out a "joint venture agreement with the tax compliance manager of a corporation [Finkelstein] was auditing...."

Finkelstein claimed that the damaging documents should not have been admitted as evidence in the disciplinary hearing under the "exclusionary rule." This rule is usually applied to suppress the use of evidence in a criminal proceeding that is claimed to have been obtained by a law enforcement officer illegally.

The purpose of the rule is to discourage police and other law enforcement officers from using illegal methods to obtain incriminating evidence against a suspect.

Citing O'Connor v Ortega, 48 U.S. 709, which held that a government employer does not need a warrant or probable cause to make a reasonable employment related search of an employee's "workplace," the court said that "[w]e need not decide whether the search of the briefcase was reasonable because, even assuming the search was unlawful, the evidence found in the briefcase was properly admitted in the disciplinary proceeding."

The court reasoned that here the search was motivated by the supervisor's desire to prepare the office for relocation and not any wish to uncover evidence damaging to the employee. "Thus, a rule suppressing such evidence at disciplinary proceedings would not have deterred the search. Exclusionary rule or no, the supervisor would still have examined the employee's briefcase for confidential tax forms. On these facts, the lack of deterrent effect counsels against the application of the exclusionary rule."

Sometimes the investigation of charges or activities underlying the investigation involves the search of an employee, the employee's property or the employee's workstation. Boyd v Constantine, 586 NYS2d 439, considers the issue of search.

3.23 Privileged communications

One area of testimony that may cause some difficulty is the claim of "privileged communication." The claim of privileged communication is available with respect to oral or written statements made by an individual to his or her attorney, or in the course of a patient/physician relationship or between a client and a certified social worker, a registered psychologist or a member of the clergy acting in their "official" capacity.

Even so, the privilege attaches only if the communication was made under circumstances showing an intent that it be confidential and in private. This privilege is personal to the individual and only he or she may exercise or claim it.

Other cases concern the use of confidential information, such as grand jury testimony. Grand jury proceedings are secret and confidential. To protect this confidentiality, the nature and substance of testimony or evidence presented to grand jury is usually not disclosed as a matter of public policy. Only certain individuals, such as a district attorney, members of his or her staff and investigating police officers have access to materials presented to a grand jury. However, a witness is free to disclose his or her testimony given to a grand jury. [Nassau County Police Department, _ Misc2d _]

The Nassau County Police Department initiated "an administrative hearing" against on one of its officers, David Mann. Mann had been indicted by a Nassau County grand jury. The Department's special counsel asked the court to authorize the disclosure of certain testimony and documents presented to the grand jury concerning Mann for use in the administrative disciplinary action being taken against Mann.

Included in the testimony sought was the evidence given by a number of witnesses including an individual named Jill. The special counsel said that he wanted to use Jill's testimony in the administrative hearing but that she had died after the return of the indictment.

The special counsel also asked the court to give Mann's attorney "all prior statements made by his witnesses" who are to testify at the administrative hearing, claiming that this was "Rosario material" [People v Rosario, 9 NY2d 286].

In support of his application, the special counsel submitted affidavits from twelve grand jury witnesses agreeing to the release of their own testimony. In addition, Mann sent the court a letter consenting to the release of his own testimony.

The court said that "disclosure is the exception rather than the rule" and one seeking such disclosure must demonstrate a compelling and particular need for access to grand jury records. Although the witnesses who testified consented to the release of their testimony, the court decided that "the reasons for release proposed by the special counsel do not create the necessary weight to overcome the presumption of confidentiality."

Nor, said the court, did the special prosecutor make a strong enough showing "of a compelling and particularized need" for access to the records concerning the deceased witness, Jill.

The decision notes two other significant points.

1. The court said that Jill's testimony, if offered in the disciplinary proceeding, "would be clearly hearsay." Grand jury testimony "given by a witness not available for trial does not come within the relevant statutory exceptions to the hearsay rule regarding the use of prior testimony" under Section 670.10 of the Criminal Procedures Law; and

2. Insofar as "disclosure" is concerned the Rosario rule is not applicable in administrative disciplinary procedures and there is no duty to "disclose" prior statements made by witnesses who will testify for the employer at the hearing. Further, the accused has the right to cross-examine any witnesses called to testify by the employer.

There are additional aspects of evidence that should be considered such as the method of gathering or obtaining evidence. Unlike the situation in matters to be determined by a court of law, "discovery" is not generally available in administrative proceedings. However, this may be changing. The recently amended Education Law Section 3020-a, which controls in the discipline of educators, however, provides for "discovery."

In general, however, all that the employer usually is required to provide the employee charged with misconduct or incompetence is a statement of the charges and specifications in sufficient detail as to reasonably permit the individual to prepare a defense to such charges and specifications.

Although a subpoena may be issued to compel the production of documents at the hearing or require an individual to appear as a witness, neither the "examination before trial" (EBT) nor discovery are required to be provided in connection with administrative proceedings such as disciplinary actions pursuant to Section 75.[19]

As to the use of the EBT or demands for discovery in connection with arbitration, such procedures are available only to the extent that the contract disciplinary procedure may provide for them.

3.24 Using polygraph tests in disciplinary actions

In Motell v Napolitano, 588 NYS2d 452, one of the issues was the use of a polygraph or "lie detector" test in the course of a disciplinary investigation.

Money that was missing from a wallet turned over to Motell, an employee of the Syracuse Department of Aviation at Hancock Field, as "lost property." In the course of an investigation, Motell agreed to submit to a polygraph test.

Motell was later served with disciplinary charges involving the missing money.

The Appellate Division ruled that the disciplinary hearing officer did not err as a result of allowing the results of the polygraph test to be introduced as evidence. The court said that where the record contains substantial evidence of the reliability of the polygraph machine used and the qualifications of the person administering the test, evidence of the results of such an examination may be considered by the hearing officer in a disciplinary proceeding.

The hearing officer found Motell guilty and recommended that he be dismissed. Neither the findings of the hearing officer nor his recommendation referred to the results of the polygraph test. The appointing officer adopted the findings and recommendations of the hearing officer.

---

[19] Insofar as the State is concerned, if the department or agency does not respond to a request for its documents, the party seeking the documents must obtain a judicial subpoena in order to obtain such records.

The court, affirming the disciplinary determination and penalty, held that there was substantial evidence to support the appointing officer's decision dismissing him, "although the proof against [Motell] was entirely circumstantial." It also said that the penalty of dismissal was not disproportionate in view of "the nature of the charges and the employee's disciplinary history."

In response to Motell's claim that the appointing authority "failed to make an independent appraisal of the record prior to rendering his determination," the Appellate Division said that the appointing authority did have the complete record of the proceedings before him and "the extent to which independent study of the evidence in the record is necessary to the required exercise of informed judgment must be left to the wisdom and practical good sense."

Another polygraph test case is Matter of Donnelly, Appellate Division, Second Department.

Sometimes the employee served with disciplinary charges will agree or in some cases, demand, to take a polygraph test. If the results indicate that the employee is "not guilty" of the charges, is that finding controlling? Not always.

Although Donnelly had "passed" a lie detector test, the hearing officer had found him guilty of certain of the charges and recommend dismissal. The hearing officer had rejected the polygraph test findings because "the questions were asked in such a way that Donnelly could answer them 'truthfully' and yet those truthful answers would not necessarily be evidence of innocence."

The issue was one of "credibility" and the weight to be given such evidence was for the hearing officer to determine said the Court. The Appellate Division ruled that the hearing officer's determination, which turned on Donnelly's credibility, was supported by substantial evidence and upheld the finding of guilt and the penalty of dismissal.

3.25 Pitfalls for that a hearing officer must avoid

In the Goohya case, [Goohya v Walsh-Tozer, 292 A.D.2d 384, 33 A.D.3d 798, motion for leave to appeal denied, 8 N.Y.3d 806] the Appellate Division overturned the appointing authority's adoption of a hearing officer's findings and recommendation because, said the court:

1. Under the guise of making findings of fact, the Hearing Officer merely reiterated the parties' testimony and other evidence submitted at the hearing.

2. Other than the Hearing Officer rejecting one or two portions of the testimony of Goohya's expert, there is no indication of the evidence he relied upon in reaching his ultimate conclusions in deciding the matter.

3. After setting forth all of the evidence in the record, the Hearing Officer merely stated, in conclusory fashion, that each charge was supported by substantial evidence.

Annulling the appointing authority's dismissal of Indrakumar Goohya based on the hearing officer's findings and recommendation, the court returned the matter to the Department "for a new hearing before a different Hearing Officer and thereafter for a new determination" by the appointing authority.

The court said that "[d]ue process considerations mandate that findings of fact be made in a manner wherein the parties are assured that the decision is based on evidence in the record, uninfluenced by extralegal considerations, and that both an intelligent challenge by a party aggrieved by the determination and an adequate judicial review are possible," citing Simpson v Wolansky, 38 NY2d 391.

"While it is clear that strict rules of evidence are not applicable to administrative hearings," the Appellate Division pointed out that an administrative determination may be annulled "where prejudice so permeates the underlying hearing as to render it unfair." Here, said the court, the Hearing Officer "committed errors which so prejudiced Goohya that a new hearing is warranted."

Among the faults attributed to the Hearing Officer by the court was the Hearing Officer's rejection of Goohya's request for disclosure of the medical records of the two patients who testified at the hearing, despite the fact that the Department had access to, and used, these same records at the hearing.

According to the decision, the Hearing Officer had determined that the records were confidential.

On this issue -- the confidentiality of patient records -- the Appellate Division said that the need for maintaining the confidentiality of the patients' records must be balanced against the concern for Goohya's rights and any adverse impact on his reputation, livelihood and future employment. Clearly, confidentiality, on these facts, must yield to Goohya's right to conduct an effective defense to the disciplinary action. Thus, the confidentiality accorded the hospital records of mental patients by the Mental Hygiene Law is not absolute. In a proper case, it must yield to the needs of justice.

Presumably the Appellate Division would apply the same principle and criteria to other types of "confidential records" in appropriate situations.

The Appellate Division also noted that the Hearing Officer ruled that while Goohya's witness qualified as an expert in psychiatry, "his testimony would be accorded diminished weight and he would not in fact be given expert status because he had never before testified in an administrative proceeding." In the words of the Appellate Division: "this ruling has absolutely no basis in law". In addition, the court faulted the Hearing Officer because he "failed to indicate in his report what weight, if any, he gave to Goohya's expert's testimony."

The Appellate Division concluded that these errors, together with the failure of the Hearing Officer to make findings of fact, prevented it from properly reviewing the final administrative determination by the Commissioner, that granting Goohya's appeal and annulling the disciplinary determination was warranted.

CHAPTER 4

PROPOSING A PENALTY

Modern disciplinary procedures seek to correct undesirable employee behavior and to rehabilitate the worker. The term "progressive discipline" is often used to describe this effort, especially in connection with contract disciplinary procedures involving arbitration. Simply stated, unless the offense is extremely serious, the penalty of dismissal is unlikely to be imposed for a first, or even a second, offense. Progressive discipline theory emphasizes behavior modification to rehabilitate the worker by imposing increasing severe penalties for repeated employee misbehavior in recognition of the economic cost to the employer of losing and replacing a trained employee.

The philosophy of progressive discipline makes it incumbent on the employer to be reasonable in assigning penalties. Consistently, courts in New York State have recognized the importance of using progressive discipline. Rulings by the New York State Supreme Court, the Appellate Division of the Supreme Court, and the Court of Appeals, New York State's highest court, suggest that it is particularly bad policy for an employer to be inconsistent when assigning penalties for certain offenses. At the same time, courts recognize that every disciplinary situation is different, and are predisposed to accord "much deference" to the employer's determination regarding the penalty to be imposed [Ahsaf v Nyquist, 37 NY2d 182].

In Gradel v Sullivan Co. Public Works, 257 A.D.2d 972, the Appellate Division upheld the employer imposing a greater penalty that the one recommended by the hearing officer as there was ample evidence in the record to support the employer's decision.

In short, courts are reluctant to substitute their judgment for that of the employer on the fairness of penalties, but will do so if the penalty appears grossly unfair. This standard was established in Pell v Board of Education, 34 NY2d 222.

4.01 The Pell standard

What's fair? The seminal case in New York State regarding standards of fairness is the Pell case [Pell v Board of Education, 34 NY2d 222].

Pell stands for the proposition that a penalty imposed must be proportionate to the offense and not be "shocking to one's sense of fairness." This is a high standard. Although it is common for employees to challenge penalties as shocking to one's sense of fairness, courts almost always uphold the disciplinary penalty imposed by the employer.

What kind of penalties qualify as "shocking to one's sense of fairness" in the eyes of state courts? Such penalties as:

Terminating an employee for being absent without proper authority and failing to document his absence, where the employee involved had an exemplary employment record and had suffered a stroke while visiting relatives in Egypt. [Selim v NYC Transit Authority, 632 NYS 2d 223, 220 AD2d 515]

Terminating an employee for failing to turn in his keys when ordered. [Maher v Hayduk, 630 NYS2d 384, 218 AD2d 700]

Dismissal of a tenured elementary school principal with an "unblemished record for over 15 years" for failing to accurately track revenues and expenditures, and concealing deficits, while service as a probationary Assistant Superintendent for Business. The court said his acts were "isolated incidents in his career and did not involve moral turpitude or fraud." [Perotti v Pine Plains CSD, 631 NYS2d 65, 218 AD2d 803, leave to appeal den 88 NY2d 802]

Terminating a school bus driver who used excessive force to deal with unruly students but who had just received a very positive work evaluation. [Ross v Oxford Academy & CSD, 590 NYS 2d 552, 187 AD2d 898, leave to appeal den 81 NY2d 705]

Suspending an employee for 30 days without pay for engaging in conduct that may result in a safety hazard. [Smith v Hager, 586 NYS2d 41]

Demoting an employee for sleeping on duty on two occasions, although a hearing officer found the employee's supervisor had "condoned" such conduct and the hearing officer had recommended a suspension without pay for three weeks. [Stapleton v La Paglia, 616 NYS2d 679, 207 AD2d 945]

Terminating a corrections officer who used excessive force against a prisoner while going to the aid of a fellow officer who has struggling with the inmate. An administrative law judge had recommended a penalty of suspension without pay for 60 days. [Allman v Koehler, 554 NYS2d 842]

Dismissal of a 17-year employee who failed to report her intended absence on two occasions. "The maximum sanction that could be supported by this record is a suspension without pay for a period of two weeks," the court said. [Rathburn v Onondaga County Library, 456 NYS2d 900, 90 AD2d 971]

4.02 Court review

It is routine for employees found guilty as a result of disciplinary action to ask the courts to review whether a penalty imposed by an appointing authority was unfair or excessive in light of the offenses involved. Only certain circumstances can the employer appeal a penalty if it feels the penalty is not harsh enough.[20]

One example is the somewhat extraordinary case of Greenburgh CSD #7 v Sobol, 654 NYS2d 458.

---

[20] Section 75 provides that the appointing authority or its representative ultimately determines guilt and the penalty to be imposed. Accordingly, only the employee would appeal an adverse decision. If, for example, a "Step 2" grievance decision granting the employee's grievance is made by the supervisor but the appointing authority disagrees with the determination, it could not appeal the supervisor's ruling. It is only in situations where a third party, i.e., an arbitrator or an independent hearing panel, makes the final disciplinary determination and imposes the penalty that it would be possible for the appointing authority to challenge the decision.

In Greenburgh, a hearing panel found a teacher guilty of a number of specifications set out in charges alleging "inappropriate remarks and inappropriate physical contact" with female students by the teacher. The penalty imposed by the hearing panel: suspension without pay for one and one-half years.

The Greenburgh Central School District #7 challenged the Section 3020-a hearing panel's decision by appealing to the state Commissioner of Education and later the courts. [This decision was made under the "old" Section 3020-a that was in effect prior to a revision in 1994.]

The Appellate Division said it would apply Pell standard to determine whether the penalty is too lenient. Finding the penalty neither arbitrary nor capricious, the Appellate Division sustained it. The court said that the underlying facts, coupled the absence of charges ever having previously been filed against the teacher during his 21-year career, supported the Commissioner's determination that the penalty imposed was proportionate to the offenses for which the teacher was found guilty.

4.03 Lawful penalties

Lawful penalties under Section 75 are:

Reprimand

Fine not to exceed $100

Suspension without pay not to exceed two months

Demotion in grade or title

Dismissal

Under Section 75 these penalties are mutually exclusive. For instance, if the employee is found guilty of one or more of the charges and specifications, the employer may impose for a single offense a penalty of suspension without pay or a reprimand, but not both. [Sinnott v Finnerty (2nd Dept, 1985) 113 AD2d 836, 493 NYS2d 504] However, multiple penalties are possible for multiple offenses. [See, for example, Wilson v Sartori (3d Dept. 1979) 70 AD2d 959, 417 NYS2d 329]

There are other possible exceptions to the prohibition on "multiple penalties" being imposed on an individual.

In Seabrook v New York, NYS Sup. Ct., Ia Part 5, Justice Stallman [not officially reported], a case involving efforts to curb chronic absenteeism, the court considered the unilateral adoption of an employer policy that provided that any employee who was out sick more than 12 days in a 12-month period (excluding absences for certain specified reasons), would be deemed to be guilty of "chronic absenteeism" and could lose of one or more of the following discretionary benefits and privileges:

1. Assignment to a steady tour;

2. Assignment to a specified post or duties;

3. Access to voluntary overtime;

4. Promotions;

5. Secondary employment;

6. Assignment to preferential/special units or commands; and

7. Transfers.

The Union sued, contending that the policy violated Sections 75 and 76 of the Civil Service Law.

The Union's theory: The policy imposes disciplinary sanctions without providing the individual with the notice and hearing required by Section 75 as a condition precedent to initiating a disciplinary action.

The court dismissed the Union's petition, holding that the mandates set out in Sections 75 and 76 were inapplicable because the penalties set out in the policy do not include any of the sanctions or penalties set out in CSL Section 75(3) with respect to a correction officer deemed to be a "chronic absentee." [21]

Justice Stallman said that CSL Section 75 specifically limits the imposition of disciplinary penalties to those set out in the section. The employer may not impose penalties exceeding those set by statute. As an example of this principle, Justice Stallman cited Cepeda v Koehler, 159 AD2d 290.

In Cepeda the court held that a penalty consisting of forfeiture of 15 vacation days plus the payment of $1,500 fine violated the penalty provisions of Section 75, which only sanctions the imposition of a "single penalty" from among those enumerated.

In another multiple penalty case, Matteson v City of Oswego, 588 NYS2d 472, the Appellate Division overturned the penalties imposed by the appointing authority and remanded the matter for the imposition of a new, appropriate penalty.

Oswego had imposed the following penalties on Matteson: (1) suspension without pay for 30 days; and (2) demotion to a lower grade position; and (3) restitution of $3,699.48.

---

[21] In contrast, it could be argued that the imposition of any penalty given in response to misconduct requires a pre-imposition hearing in accordance with Section 75 and then only the Section 75 penalties may be imposed if the individual is found guilty of the charge[s]. The mischief implicit in the Seabrook rationale is that an appointing authority could by simply imposing a "non-Section 75" sanction on an individual escape having to provide the employee with administrative due process.

The Appellate Division held that the penalty meted out was contrary to law in that "the imposition of multiple penalties was improper" under 75.3 of the Civil Service Law.

In contrast, in cases involving the imposition of a penalty by an arbitrator pursuant to a "contract disciplinary procedure" the courts have held that the only limitations on the penalty to be imposed is the sound judgment of the arbitrator. Rarely are arbitrators limited as to the penalties or combination of penalties they can assign.

4.04 Recommending penalties

In the New York State public service employers have the burden of proposing penalties, setting penalties or both. It is normal procedure after a disciplinary investigation for the employer to write a letter to the employee that specifies disciplinary charges, and typically such a letter will include a proposed penalty.

Under Section 3020-a an arbitrator or a panel of arbitrators will consider the evidence and the penalty proposed and make a binding decision as to the penalty imposed. Under Section 75 the decision to impose a penalty remains with the employer; hearing officers only make findings of fact and a recommendation as to the penalty to be imposed.

What should an employer consider in proposing or setting a penalty?

1. Employment record. The employee's personnel history may be considered in setting a penalty, provided the employee is advised that this will be done and is given an opportunity to comment on the contents of his or her file. [See Bigelow v Trustees of the Village of Gouverneur, 63 NY2d 470; Doyle v Ten Broeck, 52 NY2d 625]. Relevant questions include: Is this the employee's first offense of this nature, or is there a pattern of offenses? Has the employee been disciplined or served with disciplinary notice in the past?

Notably, a series of petty offenses by a single individual may have a cumulative impact in the setting of a penalty. In fact, courts have approved the dismissal of an employee for a series of misdeeds that if considered individually would not have been viewed as justifying termination. For example, a bus driver was terminated after he reported 30 minutes late to a scheduled class on customer service. While that might seem excessively harsh, the Appellate Division upheld the penalty because the driver was simultaneous found guilty of threatening a supervisor. He was also found guilty of operating his bus ahead of schedule in one instance. A state Supreme Court Justice noted that Robinson had been given a warning and a reprimand prior to being served with the four formal disciplinary charges and "a total of five violations in so short a time weighs heavily here" [Robinson v NYC Transit Authority, not officially reported].

2. Taylor Law agreements. Does the controlling collective bargaining agreement set penalties for this type of offense? Does it provide for harsher penalties for repeated offenses?

3. Employer's records and history. Does the employer have any written guidelines on how certain offenses will be handled? Were other employees who committed similar misconduct subject to disciplinary action? What penalties were imposed for similar offenses involving other employees?

4. Employee's awareness of the issue. Was the employee told of the expected standard of behavior or performance? Was there any change or improvement?

5. Mitigating circumstances. If the employer is aware of any mitigating circumstances, these should be considered.

6. Decisions by other jurisdictions. What penalty was imposed for similar offenses by other jurisdictions? If challenged, were they sustained by the courts and for what reasons. Although every disciplinary situation is unique, research into similar cases is appropriate and can inform the decision-maker on setting of penalties.

7. Relevant laws. In certain cases laws compel dismissal if the employee is found guilty of the charges in some form of legal forum. Section 30 of the Public Officers Law, for instance, operates to remove a public officer from the position without any reference to any administrative proceeding by the employer -- if the public officer has been convicted of a felony or a crime involving the violation of the individual's oath of office. In such cases the employee is not entitled to any administrative due process. The legal argument here is that the individual did receive due process in the criminal proceeding, so due process has not been denied.

4.05 Using the individual's employment history in disciplinary action

The Section 75 hearing officer admitted the accused employee's performance evaluations during the proceeding at the request of the appointing authority, indicating that the evaluations would be considered in determining the penalty the hearing officer would recommend if he found the employee guilty of one or more of the disciplinary charges.

The question raises a number of issues, including the following:

1. May such records be introduced into the record at the disciplinary hearing?

2. If the employee is found guilty of charges unrelated to adverse material in his or her personnel record, may the hearing officer use such information to recommend a penalty to be imposed by the appointing authority?

3. If the employee is found guilty of charges related to an adverse comment in his or her personnel records should further consideration be barred on the grounds of "double jeopardy?"

Introducing the personnel record:

In Scott v Wetzler, 195 AD2d 905, the Appellate Division, Third Department rejected Scott's argument that he was denied due process because the Section 75 hearing officer allowed evidence concerning his performance evaluations to be introduced during the disciplinary hearing.

The court said that "such evidence was relevant to the determination of an appropriate penalty," noting that Scott was allowed an opportunity to rebut these records and to submit favorable material contained in his personnel file.

Considering the personnel record:

Having introduced the employee's personnel records, for what purpose(s) may they be used?

In Bigelow v Village of Gouverneur, 63 NY2d 470, the Court of Appeals said that such records could be used to determine the penalty to be imposed if:

1. The individual is advised that his or her prior disciplinary record would be considered in setting the penalty to be imposed, and

2. The employee is given an opportunity to submit a written response to any adverse material contained in the record or offer "mitigating circumstances."

Is criticism discipline?

In Holt v Board of Education, 52 NY2d 625, the Court of Appeals ruled that performance evaluations and letters of criticism placed in the employee's personnel file were not "disciplinary penalties" and thus could be placed there without having to first hold a disciplinary proceeding.

In other words, the appointing authority's placing correspondence critical of the employee's conduct or performance in his or her personnel file did not constitute discipline.

The basic rule set out in Holt is that a statutory disciplinary provision such as Section 75 of the Civil Service Law does not require that an employee be given a hearing or permitted to grieve every comment or statement by his or her employer that he or she may consider a criticism.

In contrast, alleged "constructive criticism" may not be used to frustrate an employee's right to due process as set out in Section 75 of the Civil Service Law, Section 3020-a of the Education Law or a contract disciplinary procedure.

As the Commissioner of Education indicated in Fusco v Jefferson County School District, CEd, 14,396, decided June 27, 2000, and Irving v Troy City School District, CEd 14,373, decided May 25, 2000:

Comments critical of employee performance do not, without more, constitute disciplinary action. On the other hand, counseling letters may not be used as a subterfuge for avoiding initiating formal disciplinary action against a tenured individual.

What distinguishes lawful "constructive criticism" of an individual's performance by a supervisor and supervisory actions addressing an individual's performance that are disciplinary in nature? This could be a difficult question to resolve.

As the Court of Appeals indicated in Holt, a "counseling memorandum" that is given to an employee and placed in his or her personnel file constitutes a lawful means of instructing the employee concerning unacceptable performance and the actions that should be taken by the individual to improve his or her work.

In the Fusco and Irving cases the Commissioner of Education found that "critical comment" exceeded the parameters circumscribing "lawful instruction" concerning unacceptable performance.

In Fusco's case, the Commissioner said that "contents of the memorandum" did not fall within the parameters of a "permissible evaluation" despite the school board's claim that the memorandum was "intended to encourage positive change" in Fusco's performance.

The Commissioner noted that the memorandum "contains no constructive criticism or a single suggestion for improvement." Rather, said the Commissioner, the memorandum focused on "castigating [Fusco] for prior alleged misconduct."

In Irving's case, a school principal was given a letter critical of her performance and the next day reassigned to another school where she was to serve as an assistant principal.

The Commissioner ruled that these two actions, when considered as a single event, constituted disciplinary action within the meaning of Section 3020-a of the Education Law.

Sometimes an individual alleges that he or she has been subjected to "double jeopardy" because a "counseling memorandum" was placed in the individual's personnel file and later disciplinary charges involving the same event(s) are served upon the individual. Does including or incorporating the events set out in the counseling memorandum as charges constitute "double jeopardy?"

No, according to the Court of Appeal's ruling in Patterson v Smith, 53 NY2d 98. In Patterson the court said that including charges concerning performance that were addressed in a counseling memorandum was not "double jeopardy."

The court explained that a "proper counseling memoranda" contains a warning and an admonition to comply with the expectations of the employer. It is not a form of punishment in and of itself.

Accordingly, case law indicates that giving the employee a counseling memorandum does not bar the employer from later filing disciplinary charges based on the same event.

Further, the memorandum may be introduced as evidence in the disciplinary hearing or for the purposes of determining the penalty to be imposed if the individual is found guilty.

The employer, however, may not use the counseling memorandum or a performance evaluation to avoid initiating formal disciplinary action against an individual as the Fusco and Irving decisions by the Commissioner of Education demonstrate.

4.06 Indemnification

Managers in the public service should be aware that they may be held personally liable for the payment of damages won by an employee who has been unlawfully dismissed from his or her position, unless the managers are able to claim indemnification under Section 17 or Section 18 of the Public Officers Law.

Section 17 of the Public Officers Law provides for the defense and indemnification of State officers and employees, and certain others, if they are sued as the result of their performing, or not performing, an official duty. The section states:

The state shall indemnify and save harmless ... in the amount of any judgment obtained ... in any state or federal court ... or the amount of any settlement ... or shall pay such judgment or settlement; provided, that the act or omission from which such judgment or settlement arose occurred while the employee was acting within the scope of his public employment or duties; the duty to indemnify and save harmless or pay prescribed by this subdivision shall not arise where the injury or damage resulted from intentional wrongdoing on the part of the employee.

Section 18 of the Public Officers Law provides for the "defense and indemnification of officers and employees of public entities" other than the State where the jurisdiction has adopted a local law or taken other appropriate action to confer the benefits available under Section 18 upon its officers and employees.

Under both Sections 17 and 18, however, the key to claiming representation and indemnification is that the individual was acting within the scope of his or her employment. The jurisdiction's chief legal officer typically makes that determination.

4.07 Expiration of the penalty

The Commissioner of Education was asked to resolve an interesting, but rare, penalty issue -- what happens if the penalty imposed is a suspension without pay and the individual is in jail during part of the "period of the suspension?" [Manning v Warsaw CSD, CEd 14071, 1/13/99]

The Warsaw Central School District had served disciplinary charges against a tenured teacher, William Manning, Jr., related to his alleged operating a motor vehicle under the influence of alcohol.

Following a disciplinary hearing and an appeal, on November 22, 1994 former Commission of Education Sobol issued a decision and imposed a penalty of suspension without pay for two years. The decision was sustained by a State Supreme Court justice [Manning v Sobol, August 7, 1995, not officially reported].

Manning, however, was incarcerated in the Wyoming County jail on July 19, 1994. Because he was "unavailable" to work, the district changed his pay status from suspension with pay pending resolution of the Section 3020-a action to suspension without pay effective July 19, 1994.

Released from prison and claiming that his two-year suspension without pay commenced on November 22, 1994, Manning advised the district that he intended to return to work on November 22, 1996. The District said that the two-year suspension period commenced on March 21, 1995, when he was released from prison and therefore he could not return to work earlier than March 21, 1997. Manning appealed.

Commissioner of Education Richard P. Mills said that the two-year suspension imposed by former Commissioner Sobol commenced when Manning was released from incarceration since allowing the suspension to run concurrently with his incarceration "nullifies a portion of the suspension, since [Manning] could not work during that period in any event."

The Commissioner rejected Manning's claim that he was entitled to back salary from November 22, 1996, holding that to do so would abrogate the degree of discipline deemed appropriate by former Commissioner Sobol.

4.08 Whistleblower protection

Disciplinary action may not be used to retaliate against a worker because the employee "blew the whistle." Section 75-b of the Civil Service Law prohibits an employer from taking any adverse personal action against an individual because the employee disclosed information regarding "improper action" by an employer or the employer's violation of a law, rule or regulation where the violation involves a danger to the public's health or safety.

In addition to prohibiting termination or other disciplinary action, the employer may not take any adverse personnel action against the individual involving compensation, appointment, promotion, transfer, assignment, reinstatement to a position or in the evaluation of the worker's performance.

The United States Supreme Court has established a two-prong test with respect to claims of dismissal in retaliation for "whistle blowing" [Conrick v Myers, 461 U.S. 1138]. To win, the individual must prove that (1) the speech is protected; i.e., the speech involved a matter of public concern, and (2) that the protected speech was a substantial factor in motivating the termination. Courts have declined to provide whistleblower protection in cases in which they determined that the matter involved a purely personal concern.[22]

The public interest is also a factor. Section 75-b of the Civil Service Law, provides that a public employer "shall not dismiss or take other disciplinary or other adverse personnel action against a public employee regarding the employee's employment because the employee discloses to a governmental body information regarding a violation of law ... which violation creates and presents a substantial and specific danger to the public health or safety...."

---

[22] Under the First Amendment, public officers and employees typically enjoy "protected speech" in connection with their public comments concerning a State or municipal employer's activities that are a matter of public concern. In contrast, speech by a public officer or employee that merely addresses a personal concern such as the individual's personal unhappiness working for the public employer or for a particular supervisor, or related to the individuals' particular position, work assignments or working conditions, or the individual's personal disagreement concerning the internal operations of the department or agency, that do not rise to the level of speech concerning a "public interest," does not involve "protected speech" within the meaning of the First Amendment.

This does not mean that a whistleblower has carte blanche to engage in misconduct and go unpunished. Section 75-b.4 states that nothing in the section "shall be deemed to ... prohibit any personnel action which otherwise would have been taken regardless of any disclosure of information."

Court rulings suggest that when a "whistle blower" defense is offered or anticipated, the charging party will have to present evidence that its reasons for disciplining the employee are not pre-textual.

4.09 Determining the penalty to be imposed

Some of the most difficult personnel decisions made by public employers in New York State involve the setting of disciplinary penalties. Which forms of misconduct justify firing an employee? When are lesser penalties appropriate? When do circumstances justify imposing a harsher penalty than recommended by a hearing panel or arbitrator?

There are no standards for employers and arbitrators to turn to answer such questions. Although a few Taylor Law contracts set out specific penalties for certain infractions, usually involving time and attendance matters, there is no "penal code" that lays out a range of penalties for various offenses. However, there are lessons to be learned from history. Employers have made a countless number of penalty decisions over the years.

A percentage of these have been appealed to New York State courts, federal court or others empowered to review disciplinary actions, including as the State Civil Service Commission, local civil service commissions and arbitrators. The New York State Commissioner of Education had the power to review and set disciplinary penalties until August 1994, when Section 3020-a of the Education Law was amended.

These judicial and quasi-judicial decisions provide a body of precedent that may be useful to employers and union leaders in setting or negotiating penalties. This handbook contains summaries of such decisions.

4.10 Due Process and Progressive Discipline

To understand why the courts overturned certain penalties and let others stand, it is important to understand the key legal concepts that apply to discipline in New York State. The first concept is due process. This idea dates back to English common law, which held that people could not be deprived of their liberty or property rights without due process of law -- certain procedural steps designed to test the merits of claims of wrongdoing. This was to prevent those in power from exercising arbitrary authority. It is critical that the due process rights of employees be respected in the disciplinary process. Failure to do this often means the courts will overturn findings of guilt and vacate the penalties imposed.

The second key concept is the idea that discipline should be progressive. Progressive discipline theory emphasizes behavior modification to rehabilitate the worker is more productive than the employer having to replacing a trained employee. In effect, progressive discipline provides an employee with a second, and sometimes a third, chance to become a productive worker. For repeat offenders, increasing severe penalties are typically imposed.

Certain offenses are so egregious as to warrant dismissal in the first instance. Fighting on the job, destroying equipment or materials and stealing from the employer are examples of egregious misconduct. But for lesser offenses, the employer should impose a penalty that fundamentally serves as a message to employee: This behavior is unacceptable, and now you have another chance.

When courts are asked to review disciplinary actions, they apply certain tests. The first question is whether the employee should have been found guilty of misconduct in the first place. Generally, courts are reluctant to substitute their judgment for that of the hiring authority on the issue of guilt. Assuming that due process rights have been respected and there is no flaw in the disciplinary process, the rule is that an employer's determination of guilt must be sustained as long as it is supported by "substantial evidence."

4.11 Substantial Evidence

What constitutes substantial evidence? According to the Appellate Division of the New York State Supreme Court, "substantial evidence is such relevant proof as a reasonable mind may accept as adequate to support a conclusion or ultimate fact." (DiCairano v Gandolfo, Appellate Division). For instance, it is improper to consider an employee's record in determining issues of guilt or innocence. The employee's history is not substantial evidence. Suppose one witness says the employee was late and another witness says the employee was on time. It would be improper to consider the employee's attendance history to make a judgment of which witness should be believed. The historical information has no relevance in determining whether the employee was late on the date in question. A person with a reasonable mind would not be expected to say, "The employee was late before, and so he must have been late this time, too."

However, if the employee is found guilty, an employee's record may be used in setting a penalty. In the example above, if the employee was found guilty of being late, historical information about previous disciplinary convictions for time and attendance problems could be relevant in deciding the appropriate penalty. An employer who considers an employee's record in setting a penalty must give the employee an opportunity to comment on that record. (See the Bigelow case in Chapter 2. See also Village of Gouverneur, Doyle v Ten Broeck, 52 NY2d 625.)

"Substantial evidence" is a less rigorous standard of proof that the criminal standard of "proof beyond a reasonable doubt." In addition, the "rules of evidence" used in a court proceeding are typically not required to be followed in an administrative proceeding, including administrative and arbitration disciplinary proceedings. For instance, hearsay testimony is permissible in administrative and arbitration disciplinary proceedings, while with few exceptions, only direct testimony is permissible in criminal trials. Hearsay testimony is second- or third-hand information, such as "John's supervisor told me that John said he would not go to see a doctor." Direct testimony would be: "I heard John say he would not go to see a doctor."

While hearsay testimony is permissible and may be part of what constitutes "substantial evidence," hearsay must be trustworthy and "must be based on more than conclusory statements based on surmise." (Drayton v. Nassau County Department of Public Works). Furthermore, hearsay testimony alone might be deemed insufficient to constitute "substantial evidence" and thereby justify a determination that the employee is guilty of misconduct.

It is routine for litigants to ask courts to review the case facts and judge whether or not the decision was supported by substantial evidence.

4.12 The Pell Standard of Fairness

If a court finds the determination of guilty was not arbitrary or illogical and was supported by substantial evidence, it will turn to the issue of whether the disciplinary penalty imposed should be upheld. The judicial test applied here is the so-called "Pell standard": is the sanction imposed so disproportionate to the offense or offenses of which the individual has been found guilty as to be shocking to one's sense of fairness? [Pell v Board of Education, 34 NY2d 222]

What constitutes a penalty judged to be so shocking? An example of the type of punishment that might be seen as violating Pell would be to fire someone for a minor offense such as a single instance of smoking on the job. On the other hand, everything depends on the circumstances. The unique conditions and requirements of a given workplace must be recognized in judging the fairness of a sanction. Suppose the aforementioned employee who was caught smoking happened to be working in a factory manufacturing gunpowder? Clearly, the unique working conditions of the factory compel the factory's managers to be harsher in handling a smoking infraction than other employers in other industries might be when confronted with the same offense.

Another legal dictum that goes hand-in-hand with Pell is the philosophy that "much deference" is to be accorded to the agency's determination regarding the penalty to be imposed [Ahsaf v Nyquist, 37 NY2d 182]. In short, courts will overturn penalties only if they perceive them to be unfair. And, in general, courts are reluctant to substitute their judgment for that of the employer.

Sometimes an employee who is disciplined will point to another employee who committed the same offense yet received a lighter punishment. Case history suggests this particular argument is not likely to sway courts. However, in at least one case the Appellate Division was persuaded by an argument that a certain penalty was unfair because lesser penalties had been imposed for more egregious conduct [Trotman v Ward, 146 AD2d 236].

Challenges to disciplinary penalties have also been made based on allegations of unlawful discrimination. A worker may claim that he or she received a harsher penalty solely because of the individual's race, religion, gender or some other unlawful consideration.

Uniformity in setting of penalties should not necessarily be the goal of public employers, though. The goal should be fairness, and a rigid uniformity in the penalties an employer assigns for various categories of offenses is not necessarily the same as fairness. On the topic of different penalties imposed for the same offense or similar offenses, judges seem philosophically aligned with Ralph

Waldo Emerson, who said, "A foolish consistency is the hobgoblin of little minds." In Alaimo v Ambach, a case involving an employee who had been found guilty of the felony of perjury and lost a license, the Appellate Division did not accept the argument that the penalty was too harsh compared to penalties given to others committing the same type of offense. In Alaimo, the court said, "The mere fact that others guilty of similar transgressions have escaped with lighter penalties does not justify a modification here."

4.13 Reasons Courts Reject Penalties

Relatively few penalties are rejected by the courts as being fundamentally unfair. It is much more common for courts to either reduce a penalty or require an employer to reconsider a penalty because of procedural defect in the disciplinary process that voids one or more of the findings of guilt. The due process rights of employees must be respected throughout the disciplinary process, and it is essential that both personnel officers and union leaders have a firm grasp of case law to ensure that the rights of employees are fully understood.

For instance, one case considered important by many public employers and attorneys is Matt v LaRocca. In Matt the Appellate Division described circumstances in which an employee may legally refuse to answer questions in a disciplinary investigation. The Matt ruling exposed the limits of Section 61 of the Public Officers Law, a statute that has been relied on by public employers as authority for investigating the activities of its employees and compelling them to talk about work-related events under oath. (See Chapter 2)

Both the filing of disciplinary charges and the determination of the penalty to be imposed may be challenged on the grounds that such action or decision constitutes a violation of Title VII, the Americans with Disabilities Act, the Age Discrimination in Employment Act or any of several other federal and state civil rights laws.

New York State Courts made most of the rulings summarized in this handbook. As many readers may be unfamiliar with hierarchy of state court system, here is a quick review: the first court with jurisdiction on disciplinary matters under various state laws is the New York State Supreme Court. The Appellate Division of the Supreme Court, often referred to simply as the Appellate Division, reviews decisions by the Supreme Court. Decisions by the Appellate Division are reviewed by the Court of Appeals, which is New York's highest court.

The reader is cautioned against assuming that any case described in this handbook is directly parallel to a situation the reader confronts. Decisions in individual cases depend on specific case facts and, often, the language of relevant collective bargaining agreements. Case examples presented in this handbook are intended to serve as illustrations of the legal principles that govern discipline in New York State. An understanding of these principles should serve the reader well.

4.14 Violations of the Pell standard

The "Pell standard" is a holding by the New York State Court of Appeals that any disciplinary penalty authorized by law is permissible as long as it is not so disproportionate to the offense that it is "shocking to one's sense of fairness" [Pell v Board of Education, 34 NY2d 222]. This is, of course, a subjective standard and one, which the courts are frequently asked to interpret. Countless public employees who have been found guilty of disciplinary infractions have filed lawsuits to ask state courts to evaluate whether the penalty imposed on them is "shocking to one's sense of fairness." Only rarely do judges find a penalty so disproportionate, however.

Courts generally are reluctant to substitute their judgment for that of an arbitrator or hearing officer. But sometimes the Courts reduce penalties after finding a procedural flaw that requires one or more findings of guilt to be thrown out. Suppose an employee is dismissed after being found guilty of one charge of smoking in a no-smoking building and one charge of embezzling $100,000. If a court later rescinds the finding of embezzlement, the penalty of dismissal would likely be viewed as shocking to one's sense of fairness. A judge would probably say it is disproportionate to fire someone for one smoking offense.

4.15. Penalty: reprimand

A reprimand is the minimum disciplinary penalty set out in law. Section 76 of the Civil Service Law does not permit employees given reprimands to appeal their discipline cases to state courts.[23] However, the courts have considered certain cases in which the penalty was a reprimand because other issues were involved. And the employer is empowered to appeal the decision of a disciplinary panel or an arbitrator if it believes the penalty is not allowed by law.

4.16 Loss of leave credits and other alternative penalties

Sometimes the penalty imposed involves an employee losing vacation time or other leave credits. A penalty frequently imposed by an arbitrator under a disciplinary procedure negotiated pursuant to the Taylor Law, it is sometimes applied in a settlement of a Section 75 or a Section 3020-a case as well.

4.17 Penalty: fine

The theory underlying imposing a fine as a disciplinary penalty is that the employee will receive a message that is clear and specific and has a direct impact on his or her pocket. As a consequence of the employee's unacceptable behavior, he or she feel the sting of a direct -- albeit temporary -- reduction of his or her paycheck. In imposing a fine, the employer sets a specific value on the seriousness of the infraction, and the employee experiences that assessment as a tangible loss.

---

[23] Section 76.1 of the Civil Service Law, however, allows an officer or employee to appeal the penalty of a reprimand if he or she was suspended without pay prior to the disciplinary hearing if the penalty of a reprimand is "unaccompanied by a remittance of such officer's or employee's prehearing suspension without pay."

4.18 Penalty: suspension

Suspension without pay is a common penalty for a disciplinary infraction. A distinction should be made between suspensions that are the result of a disciplinary process and suspensions that are part of a disciplinary procedure. For instance, the imposition of suspension for 30-day without pay pending a hearing is not viewed as a "penalty" per se, at least at the time it is imposed. If the employee is acquitted of all charges he or she is restored to the position with back salary, less any unemployment insurance benefits received during the suspension [Section 75.3, Civil Service Law.]

However, if the employee is found guilty and assigned a penalty of suspension without pay, the 30 days that the employee has already endured without pay can, at the discretion of the employer, be considered "time served" in fulfillment of the assigned penalty.

Section 75.3 also provides that the appointing authority, as a matter of discretion, may consider the time during which an officer or employee was suspended without pay pending the disciplinary hearing as part of the penalty. Where an alternate to Section 75 has been negotiated pursuant to the Taylor Law (see Section 76.4 of the Civil Service Law) the question of an employee's suspension without pay pending the hearing may go to the arbitrator. If the employee was suspended pending the grievance hearing is found guilty, the agreement may provide that the arbitrator shall also consider the question of whether the pre-hearing suspension was appropriate under the circumstances.

Employees who are suspended pending a hearing and are later given the penalty of reprimand have the right to appeal the reprimand unless the employer reimburses them for the pre-hearing suspension less any unemployment insurance benefits they may have received.

4.19 Penalty: demotion

Typically a demotion is a "permanent" action and the disciplined employee has no rights to reemployment in the higher-level title. In some instances, however, an arbitrator may impose the penalty of demotion for a limited period. In such cases the arbitration award will provide for the reinstatement of the disciplined individual to the higher-grade title if he or she meets the conditions imposed by the arbitrator within a specified period.

As to effecting the penalty of demotion, it may not be as simple as it appears. If there is an unencumbered position in the lower grade, the individual to be demoted can be merely appointed to the vacancy. If, however, there is no vacancy available the situation may be somewhat more complex and a number of procedural alternatives may have to be considered by the appointing authority.

For example, the higher-level position may be "temporarily downgraded" or, less frequently, "reclassified downward," to the lower title and grade and the disciplined employee appointed to it. In the alternative, a vacancy in the lower grade may be created by the promotion of the incumbent of a lower grade position with the simultaneous demotion of the individual to the newly created lower grade vacancy. In such cases the individual promoted frequently will have a "hold" on the lower grade position if he or she was promoted permanently unless any required probationary period is waived.

Such a "hold" will also result in cases where the individual is appointed to the higher-grade position provisionally or appointed as a "temporary employee" from an appropriate eligible list.

Another factor that might complicate matters could be the existence of a preferred list for either or both titles. In such cases the preferred list is "ignored" if its use would result in a layoff of a permanent incumbent, including the individual disciplined. In addition, in some cases a provision in a collective bargaining agreement such as "job bidding" could have an impact on personnel transactions and would have to be considered in determining the rights of the individuals involved.

4.20 Time and attendance issues

Time and attendance problems are among the most common experienced by employers.

Although traditional disciplinary procedures have been followed in attempting to correct an employee's habitual tardiness or absences, some public employers and employee organizations have negotiated special procedures just to handle time and attendance matters.

These agreements typically provide for:

1. Procedures to resolve time and attendance problems outside the contract's disciplinary procedure.

2. Defining what constitutes time and attendance abuse.

3. Setting specific penalties, progressive in nature, for violations of the employer's time and attendance rules. The penalties may range from a warning for the first offense considered under the procedure to suspensions or fines in the employee continues to violate the employer's time and attendance rules. Typically the procedure authorizes termination if the employee refuses or is unable to comply with the attendance rules.

4. Appointing a permanent arbitrator or umpire to consider all time and attendance charges.

5. Waiving the right to appeal an arbitrator's award.

6. Granting the arbitrator the authority to terminate the individual if the conditions set out in the agreement are satisfied.

Where the employee contends that his or her time and attendance problems are due to a disability within the meaning of the Americans With Disabilities Act or the Rehabilitation Act of 1973 or another federal or state law, it will be necessary to determine if, indeed, the individual is disabled and his or her attendance problems are caused by or result from the disability. If so, the employer is usually required to make a reasonable accommodation, which could consist of modifying the individual's work schedule.

As example of a "Time and Attendance Disciplinary Procedure, adopted Section 33.5 of the 1995-1999 agreement between the Civil Service Employees Association [Institutional Services Unit] and the State of New York follows:

AN EXAMPLE OF A TIME AND ATTENDANCE GRIEVANCE ARTICLE

1. All notices of discipline based solely on time and attendance, including tardiness, which have not been settled or otherwise resolved, shall be reviewed by a permanent umpire.

2. The determination of the permanent umpire shall be confined to the guilt or innocence of the grievant and the appropriateness of the penalty. The employee's entire record of employment may be considered by the permanent umpire with respect to the appropriateness of the penalty imposed. The umpire shall have the authority to resolve a claimed failure to follow the procedural provisions of this Article.

3. The decision and award of the permanent umpire with respect to guilt or innocence and penalty, if any, shall be final and binding on the parties and not subject to appeal to any other forum except that, in the case of a decision and award which results in a penalty of dismissal from service, the decision and award may be reviewed in accordance with Article 75 of the Civil Practice Law and Rules. The permanent umpire shall, upon a finding of guilt, have full authority to uphold the penalty proposed in the notice of discipline or to impose a lesser penalty within the minimum and maximum penalties set out in the schedule printed below. In appropriate cases, and in addition to the penalty imposed, the permanent umpire may direct the grievant to attend counseling sessions or other appropriate programs jointly agreed upon by the State and CSEA.

4. The State and CSEA shall mutually select a panel of permanent umpires, who shall serve for the term of this agreement. All fees and expenses of the permanent umpire shall be divided equally between the State and CSEA.

5. Unless otherwise mutually agreed, the permanent umpires shall be available to hold reviews at least once each month on a regularly scheduled basis. At such times, the permanent umpires shall review and finally determine all time and attendance disciplinary grievances which have been pending no less than ten (10) days prior to the permanent umpire's scheduled appearance and are unresolved.

6. An employee is entitled to appear at the review before the permanent umpire and is entitled to have a CSEA representative or an attorney provided at his or her own expense present. Matters scheduled to be heard by the permanent umpire may not be adjourned except at the discretion of the permanent umpire for good cause shown. Any matters that are adjourned shall be rescheduled for the next regularly scheduled appearance of the permanent umpire.

7. Where an employee is to be served a notice of discipline related solely to time and attendance and, within three years of such notice, has been found guilty of or settled [or a combination of both] two prior notices of discipline not solely related to time and attendance, the appointing authority may elect either to pursue such time and attendance notice before the permanent umpire in accordance with the

following Schedule or to serve a notice of discipline and proceed before a disciplinary arbitrator. This provision shall not apply to notices of discipline based solely on tardiness.

8. The penalty level for notices of discipline that contain charges of both tardiness and unauthorized absence shall be the appropriate level within the type of unauthorized absence charge.

4.21 Examples of penalties imposed

Listed below are sanctions approved by the courts imposed on individuals found guilty of a variety of disciplinary charges. These are presented as illustrations only. It must be remembered that each disciplinary penalty must be justified on its own merits.

Listed alphabetically by type of "offense," each entry reports the penalty imposed and the court making the ruling. The listing also demonstrates the fact that different penalties may be imposed for the same type of offense depending on circumstances as penalties should be determined on a case-by-case basis.

Absence, excessive, dismissal, Graham vs. Sands as Administrator, McKinnon v. Board of Educ. of North Bellmore Union Free School Dist. 273 A.D.2d 240

Abuse of sick leave, suspension for three months without pay, Decisions of the Commissioner of Education 11682

Abuse of sick leave, suspension without pay for 60 days and probation, Halligan v NYC Police Department, 567 NYS2d 47

Accidental discharging firearm while at home, dismissal, Hansen v Appellate Division, 3rd Dept.

Alcoholism, dismissal, Decisions of the Commissioner of Education, 11142

Allowing vehicle to run out of gas, two months suspension without pay and a $100 fine, Bollin v City of Kingston, 89 AD2d 658

Assaulting a fellow police officer, dismissal, Hammond v City of Amsterdam, Appellate Division

Associating with a felon in violation of department rules, forfeiture of 10 days vacation, Morrisette v Dilworth, 59 NY2d 449

Attacking a police officer, dismissal, Islar v Koehler, 554 NYS2d 219

AWOL, dismissal, Foust v Village of Port Chester, 211 A.D.2d 717

AWOL and falsifying records, forfeiture of 15 days of vacation, Fusco v Brown, Appellate Division

Chronic lateness, settled - disciplinary probation, Matter of Polistena, Supreme Court, Kings County

Cocaine use, dismissal, Kearse v Brown, 585 NYS2d 27

Collecting football bets, dismissal, Ivory v New York Department of Environmental Protection, Appellate Division, 1st Department

Concealing a criminal conviction, dismissal, Arbitration award

Conduct unbecoming a teacher - appearing intoxicated in classroom, three-month suspension without pay, Decisions of the Commissioner of Education, 10924

Confiscating marijuana without making an arrest, dismissal, Brady v Connelie

Consideration of prior disciplinary records, dismissal, Sapp v Gleason, 590 NYS2d 119

Corporal punishment of student, dismissal, Decisions of the Commissioner of Education, 13166

Criminal conviction, dismissal, Sherman v Yonkers City School District, Appellate Division

Cumulative disciplinary actions, dismissal, Robinson v NYC Transit Authority, NYS Sup. Ct.

Dereliction of duty - falling asleep on the job, dismissal, Grossman v Kralik, 217 A.D.2d 625

Disclosing contents of standardized test, 3-month suspension without pay, Decisions of the Commissioner of Education 11776

Displaying a violent temper, dismissal, Pollman v Fahey, 106 AD2d 771

Disrespectful and contemptuous conduct towards supervisor, termination, In re Tracy 256 A.D.2d 800

Driving police vehicle at excessive speed, suspension without pay for five days, Dwyer v City of White Plains, Appellate Division

Embarrassment of department by employee's actions, 40-day suspension without pay, Dean v Del Castillo, 570 NYS2d 678

Excessive absence, dismissal, Baugh v Stern, 559 NYS2d 243

Excessive absenteeism, suspension without pay for 30 days, Hunter v NYC Board of Education, 190 AD2d 851

Excessive lateness, fine of one month of salary, Decisions of the Commissioner of Education 11174

Excessive use of sick leave, no overtime and shift swapping permitted, De Vito v. Kinsella, 234 A.D.2d 640

Exposing the department to criticism, suspension without pay for forty days, Small v. Human Resources Admin., 299 A.D.2d 238

Failing to be alert while on guard duty, one-week without pay and transfer, Council 82, AFSCME v Dept of Correctional Services, Appellate Division

Failing to comply with civil service law, dismissal, Matter of Johnson, Appellate Division, 2nd Dept., 1983

Failing to follow rules, forfeiture of 10 days of vacation, Negron v Ward, 557 NYS2d 48

Failing to follow supervisor's direct order, suspension without pay for 30 days and disciplinary probation for one year, Condon v Brown, Appellate Division

Failing to pay bridge tolls, dismissal, Dillon v Connelie, Appellate Division

Failing to prepare lesson plans [5 charges], $8,000 fine, Meyer v Charlotte Valley CSD, Appellate Division

Failing to protect property, dismissal, Orkopoulos v Sandler, 552 NYS2d 290

Failing to report and absence from location, dismissal, Mellette v Ward, 547 NYS2d 35

Failing to respond to a supervisor's questions, 20-day suspension without pay, Albino v City Civil Service Commission, 565 NYS2d 520

Failure to attend drug-counseling program, dismissal, Hill v Hartnett, 568 NYS2d 234

Failure to exercise reasonable care, causing an accident, $100 fine and a reprimand, Remillard v City of Watervliet, Appellate Division, 3rd Department

Failure to provide correct information, demotion, Ehmann v Whalen, Appellate Division, 3rd Dept.

Failure to report for medical exam, employee elected 5-day suspension without pay rather than a pay a $300 fine, Santiago v Koehler, 546 NYS2d 625

Falsification of time records, dismissal, McClellan v Alexander CSD, 607 NYS2d 812

Falsifying an arrest record, 60-day suspension without pay, Luedeke v Police Commissioners, Town and Village of New Paltz, Appellate Division

Feigning illness, forfeiture of 25 days of vacation, Matter of Cohen, Appellate Division, May 1983

Filing false accident reports, dismissal, Smith v Delaney, Appellate Division

Filing false sick leave claim, five day suspension without pay, Motala v Connelie

Forgetting to report for medical exam, three-week suspension without pay, Driscoll v Syracuse Department of Fire, Appellate. Division

Fraternization prisoner's family, dismissal, Colon v Sielaff, Appellate Division

Fraud in claiming on-the-job injury, dismissal, Klikocki v Department of Corrections, Appellate Division

Giving police shield to unauthorized person, dismissal, Turkoanje v Ward, 554 NYS2d 185

Harboring a fugitive, dismissal, Fludd v Sielaff, Appellate Division

Hatch act violations, dismissal, Blackburne v GOER, Appellate Division

Hazing of student by teacher/coach, suspension from coaching duties, Matter of Covino, Decisions of the Commissioner of Education 11227

History of discipline, dismissal, Gunther v Mayor of the City of Oswego, Appellate Division, 1983

Ill treatment of prisoners, dismissal, Deputy Sheriffs Local 2390 v St. Lawrence Co., Appellate Division

Illegal activities of spouse, dismissal, Colon v Ward, 554 NYS2d 231

Inability to spell compromises ability to teach, dismissal, Decisions of the Commissioner, 10936

Inability to teach and mental incapacity, dismissal, Matter of Fitzpatrick, Appellate Division

Inability to work cooperatively , dismissal, Schuttak v Village of Endicott, Appellate Division

Inappropriate touching of students, dismissal, Meister v Sobel, NYS Supreme Court

Incompetence, dismissal, Reed v Town of Huntington, Appellate Division

Incompetence, six months suspension without pay, Decision of the Commissioner of Education, 12276

Incompetence after a transfer, dismissal, Kloepfer v Ambach, Appellate Division

Incompetence and insubordination of teacher, dismissal, Dunnigan v Ambach, Appellate Division

Incompetence and misconduct, demotion, Roman v Allen, Appellate Division

Incompetence and neglect of duty, dismissal, Fayville v Ambach, Appellate Division, 3rd Department

Incompetence and other charges, dismissal, Swike v Ambach, Appellate Division

Inflicting corporal punishment on student, loss of six-months salary, Decisions of the Commissioner of Education, 11601

Injuring a patient, dismissal, Yerry v Ulster County, 512 NYS2d 592

Insubordination, 3-days suspension without pay, Scott v Wetzler, Appellate Division

Insubordination, 80-days suspension without pay, Procida v Grinker, 546 NYS2d 367

Insubordination, dismissal, Moccio v State, 606 NYS2d 300

Lack of good moral character as a condition of employment, dismissal, Arana v Constantine, Appellate Division

Leaving post without permission, suspended for six months and prohibited from holding any position as a fire company line officer for two years, Bigando v Board of Fire Commissioners, Kingston, Appellate Division, 3rd Department

Lewd behavior, dismissal, Matter of Shocker, NYS Supreme Court

Loss of teaching license, suspension without pay for one and one-half years, subject to dismissal if she failed to obtain permanent certification by a specified date, 1991, Decisions of the Commissioner of Education, 12454

Making derogatory statements, fine of 10-days of pay for each of 3 offenses, Matter of Meyer, Appellate Division, 2nd Dept.

Making sexually suggestive remarks, dismissal, Connolly v Williams, Appellate Division

Misuse of department's computer, 30-day suspension without pay to be followed by a one-year disciplinary probationary period, Tuzzio v Ward, 554 NYS2d 227

Misuse of family sick leave provisions, suspension without pay for nine and one half months, Decisions of the Commissioner of Education 11111

Misuse of weapon while off-duty, dismissal, Rodriguez v Ward, Appellate Division
Neglect of duty while off-duty, dismissal, Barnes v City of Albany, Appellate Division

Off-duty conduct that discredits an employer, dismissal, Robertson v Eccleston, Appellate Division

Off-duty misconduct, dismissal, Respass v Ward, 551 NYS2d 20

Off-duty misconduct, dismissal, Zazycki v City of Albany, Appellate Division, 3rd Dept

Off-duty police officer failed to stop an apparent rape, dismissal, Sadler v Bratton, Appellate Division

Off-duty practical jokes by supervisor, demotion and a six-month probationary period, Sguanci v Commissioner of Public Works, Broome County, Appellate Division

Off-duty threat with weapon, dismissal, Cocozzo v Ward, 556 NYS2d 328

Patient abuse, dismissal, Welch v Weinstein, Appellate Division

Patient abuse, dismissal, Welch v Weinstein, Appellate Division, 2nd Department

Payoff outstanding parking tickets, settled - disciplinary probation, McCallum v NYC Department of Transportation, App. Div.

Permitting competitive bidding irregularities, dismissal, Segrue v City of Schenectady, Court of Appeals

Placing an individual in danger, forfeiture of 25 vacation days, O'Connor v Kelly, Appellate Division

Playing a practical joke, dismissal, Keith v NYS Thruway Authority, Appellate Division

Playing practical joke with fake spider, suspension without pay for one-year, Decisions of the Commissioner of Education, 10842

Pointing firearm at civilians, suspension without pay for 30 days and disciplinary probation for one year, McKernan v Kelly, Appellate Division

Poor attendance, dismissal, Conte v Koehler, Appellate Division

Poor medical procedure, dismissal, State University of New York v Young, Appellate Division

Positive drug test, dismissal, Joyner v Abate, Appellate Division

Providing fake urine for drug tests, dismissal, Blount v Bratton, Appellate Division

Punching a hospital patient, dismissal, Gonzalez v Carter, Appellate Division

Racist remarks, forfeiture of 15 days of vacation, Gantt v Ward, 565 NYS2d 493

Receiving items without paying for them, 10-day suspension without pay, Williamson v Brown, Appellate Division

Refusal to answer questions concerning official business, 30-day suspension without pay, Mahler v Triborough Bridge Authority, Supreme Court, 1982

Refusal to participate in drug counseling program, dismissal, Akers v New York City Transit Authority, 569 NYS2d 137

Refusal to report for medical exam, 60-days suspension without pay, Rivera v Beckman, Appellate Division

Refusal to report to supervisor's office, 20-day suspension without pay, Albino v City Civil Service Commission, 565 NYS2d 520

Refusal to take a drug test, dismissal, Washington v Dolce, Appellate Division

Refusing to comply with new staffing policy, 30-day suspension without pay, Dejnozka v City of Saratoga Springs, Appellate Division, 3rd Department

Refusing to obey a lawful order, suspension without pay for two months, Murano v Goshen, 589 NYS2d 117

Refusing to take a drug test, dismissal, Felder v Kelly, Appellate Division

Refusing to take a mental examination, dismissal, Lucheso v Dillon, Sheriff, Appellate Division

Resignation does not prevent disciplinary action, dismissal, Decisions of the Commissioner of Education, Decision 12807

Sexual harassment, suspension for time taken off payroll, about 4 months, NYC Transit Authority v Transport Workers Union, 606 NYS2d _

Sexual relations with a patient, dismissal, Ford v CSEA, 94 AD2d 262

Shooting an unarmed civilian, dismissal, Vacchio v Ward, 554 NYS2d 523

Showing pornographic films in class, dismissal, Shurgin v Ambach, 56 NY2d 700

Sick leave violations, dismissal, Silva v Sielaff, Appellate Division

Sleeping on the job, dismissal, NY Transit Authority v Local 100, Transport Workers Union, Appellate Division, 1st Dept.

Soliciting criminal conduct, dismissal, Scheiber v NYC Board of Education, 593 NYS2d 563

Stabbing an inmate, dismissal, Charles Johnson v Ward, 507 NYS2d 852

Taking second job while on sick leave, two-year suspension without pay, Decisions of the Commissioner of Education, 11063

Teacher met with student in a darkroom, $1,000 fine, Decisions of the Commissioner of Education 11407

Threatening to shoot a visitor, settled - disciplinary probation, Matter of Blackwell, Supreme Court, New York

Threats to spouse, 30-day suspension without pay, Stiles v Phelan, Appellate Division, 3rd Dept.

Time and attendance problems, settled - disciplinary probation, Matter of Sepulveda, Appellate Division, 2nd Department

Unacceptable behavior, dismissal, Jackson v Sobel, Appellate Division

Unauthorized absence because of incarceration, dismissal, Trainosky v Department of Taxation and Finance, Appellate Division, 3rd Dept.

Unauthorized absences, dismissal, DeStefano v Village of Port Chester, Appellate Division

Undue familiarity with inmates by correction officer, dismissal, McFarland v Abate, Appellate Division

Unlawful possession of marijuana, dismissal, Boyd v Constantine, Court of Appeals

Unsatisfactory attendance, settled - disciplinary probation, Miller v NYS Dept. of Correctional Services, Appellate Division, 3rd Dept.
Untimely notification of teaching plans, $500 fine, Decisions of the Commissioner of Education 11109

Use of drugs by police officer, dismissal, Murphy v NYC Transit Authority, Appellate Division

Use of employer's property for personal business, demotion, Howland v Schuyler-Chemung-Tioga BOCES, Appellate Division

Use of excessive force by police officer, 20-day suspension without pay and disciplinary probation, Nunez v Ward, 567 NYS2d

Use of excessive force/indecent language by police officer, suspension for 30 days without pay, NYC Transit Authority, Appellate Division

Use of illegal drug, dismissal, Longo v Dolce, Appellate Division

Use of illegal drugs, dismissal, Ruggiero v Brown, 585 NYS2d 25

Use of physical force by teacher, one-month suspension without pay, Decisions of the Commissioner of Education, 12421

Use of vulgar language by police officer, 30-days suspension without pay and six-month probation, Gadway v Connelie, Appellate Division, 3rd Dept, 1984

Using a controlled substance, dismissal, Garnes v State Police, Appellate Division

Using corporal punishment, dismissal, Decisions of the Commissioner of Education 11486

Violating a disciplinary settlement, dismissal, Miller v NYS Dept. of Correctional Services, Appellate Division

Violation of disciplinary probation, termination, Chase v Suffolk County Police Commissioner, 121 AD2d 718

Violation of employer's rules, dismissal, Vassar v Sielaff, Appellate Division, Pagan v Brown, 575 NYS2d 488

Violation of employer's work rules, dismissal, Diaz v Rozzi, Appellate Division

Violation of oath of office, dismissal, Broome County v Conte, 120 Misc 2d 1050

Violation of terms of disciplinary probation, dismissal, Soto v Koehler, [Appellate Division]

Working second job while on sick leave, dismissal, Gailband v Christian, Court of Appeals

CHAPTER 5

OBLIGATIONS OF EMPLOYERS AND UNIONS UNDER NEGOTIATED DISCIPLINARY PROCEDURES

Today the most common type of disciplinary procedure used in New York State public employment is one that has been negotiated by an employer and a union as part of a collective bargaining agreement under the Taylor Law. Such "contract disciplinary procedures," are adopted either in lieu of or in conjunction with Section 75 of the Civil Service Law or Section 3020-a of the Education Law.[24]

Such agreements may grant due process rights to employees not entitled to the protections under statutes (state or local laws) such as Section 75 of the Civil Service Law or Section 3020-a of the Education Law.

Some agreements provide employees with a choice as to the forum to hear the charges. For instance, the employee may be able to choose either a statutory procedure such as Section 75 or the procedure provided by the agreement. For an overview of the statutory processes, see Chapter 6: Filing charges under Section 75 or Chapter 7: Filing charges under Section 3020-a.

Collective bargaining agreements usually require the employer to give the employee:[25]

1. A statement of charges and the proposed penalty

---

[24] **N.B.** In Matter of Patrolmen's Benevolent Assn. of City of N.Y., Inc. v New York State Pub. Empl. Relations Bd., 13 AD3d 879, affirmed, 6 NY3d at 570 and Matter of Town of Orangetown v Orangetown Policemen's Benevolent Assn., 18 AD3d 879, modified, 6 NY3d at 570, the Court of Appeals held that **police discipline may not be a subject of collective bargaining under the Taylor Law when the Legislature has expressly committed disciplinary authority over a police department to local officials.** In the words of the court: *The issue is not, as the unions argue, whether these enactments were intended by their authors to create an exception to the Taylor Law; obviously they were not, since they were passed decades before the Taylor Law existed. The issue is whether these enactments express a policy so important that the policy favoring collective bargaining should give way, and we conclude that they do.*

[25] In Matter of Oxford Employee Support Personnel Association v Oxford Academy & Central School District, 40 A.D.3d 1297, the court pointed out that Civil Service Law Section 76.4 authorizes the negotiation of alternatives to the disciplinary procedures set out in Section 75 of the Civil Service Law. Unless the collective bargaining agreement specifically set out the fact that an alternative disciplinary procedure has been agreed upon, Section 75 controls. Critical to the court's resolution of the appeal was the following language set out in the collective bargaining agreement between the parties: *A grievance shall mean a complaint by an employee in the bargaining unit (1) that there has been as to the employee a violation, misinterpretation or inequitable application of any of the provisions of this Agreement or (2) that the employee has been treated unfairly or inequitable (sic) by reason of any act or condition which is contrary to established policy or practice governing or affecting employees, except that the term grievance shall not apply to any matter as to which (1) a method of review is prescribed by law.* This language, in the opinion of the Appellate Division, precluded processing the disciplinary action initiated against Wall under to the contract grievance procedure. The court, citing Matter of South Colonie Cent. School Dist. [South Colonie Teachers Assn.], 46 NY2d 521, said: "Quite clearly, Civil Service Law Section 75 provides a method of review for alleged employee misconduct and, pursuant to the exclusionary language of the bargaining agreement, relegates the parties to such procedure rather than the grievance/arbitration procedures provided by the bargaining agreement."

2. An opportunity to meet with the administration to discuss settlement and,

3. Arbitration by a neutral party, if the matter cannot be settled. Typically, the decision of an arbitrator or panel of arbitrators is binding under collective bargaining agreements.

The method of selecting an arbitrator or the members of a panel of arbitrators is usually set out in the collective bargaining agreement. For instance, the parties may have agreed to seek the assignment of an arbitrator from a panel maintained by a "professionally neutral" organization such as the American Arbitration Association or from a panel of arbitrators created by the parties. Or the parties may have designated a "permanent arbitrator".

Whenever an alternative to the statutory disciplinary procedure has been negotiated and is used by the parties, the contract provisions will control. That is, if a dispute arises, the courts will look to the provisions of the contract rather than state law to resolve the dispute.

Contract disciplinary grievance procedures vary, so this book is able to consider only some of the more common concepts and provisions contained in such agreements. The reader should carefully review the specific provisions of the collective bargaining agreement in force at the reader's workplace to determine the specific procedures and requirements that must be observed in bringing or defending a disciplinary action.

5.01 Notice of discipline

Most contract procedures initiate discipline with what is called a "notice of discipline." However, it is important to remember that counseling employees about their conduct is not viewed as disciplinary action under Section 75 nor under most Taylor Law agreements. This is an important distinction because only a notice of discipline triggers an employee's right to due process, not by counseling.

Counseling may take written form. A notice of discipline is more formal than a letter sent to an employee and placed in his or her work record. For instance, in the Port Jefferson Union Free School District v United Aides and Assistants, PERB rejected a union's claim that every written criticism of an employee was a "reprimand" and that no penalties could be assigned without a disciplinary hearing. (See "Criticism is not Discipline" in the next chapter.)

A notice of discipline usually lists the reasons for taking disciplinary action and the proposed penalty. The employee must file an objection to the discipline in the form of a grievance if he or she wishes to challenge the imposition of the proposed penalty. The agreement will usually specify a time period for a response. Under Section 75 the employee must be given at least eight days to file a response.

If the employee files a timely grievance, the disciplinary action goes forward. Sometimes there are negotiations regarding the imposition of a different penalty in an effort to "settle the case." This is true with respect to Section 75 and Section 3020-a proceedings as well as there is no statutory bar to "settling the matter." Many times the settlement takes the form of a disciplinary probation period or the employee accepts a penalty less severe than the one proposed by the appointing authority.

What if the employee does not respond to the notice of discipline sent in accordance with the provisions in the collective bargaining agreement? May the employer impose the proposed penalty without holding a disciplinary hearing? The answer is generally yes, depending on the wording of the agreement.[26]

Section 75 does not require employees request a hearing in order to receive one. But Section 3020-a.4 of the Education Law does require that the individual request a hearing otherwise the school board is to "determine the case and fix the penalty." Further, "the unexcused failure of the employee to notify the [school] clerk or secretary of his or her desire for a hearing ... shall be deemed a waiver of the right to a hearing...."

The Section 3020-a model is followed in most alternative disciplinary procedures negotiated pursuant to the Taylor Law. If the employee does not file a timely "disciplinary grievance," the appointing authority usually is authorized to impose the penalty proposed in the "notice of discipline" served on the individual without further action on its part and without referring the issue to arbitration.

5.02 The "Bill of Rights" in contracts

It may be helpful to contrast what could be called typical contract disciplinary clauses with the provisions of a statutory due process disciplinary procedure such Section 75 of the Civil Service Law.

A "Bill of Rights" is frequently included in a negotiated disciplinary procedure. This provision generally sets out some basic due process provisions and concepts that are implied or specifically contained in Section 75 of the Civil Service Law. Many such contract clauses recite such basic principles as the placement of the burden of proof on the charging party or the right to representation at each step of the disciplinary process.

However, representation is not usually provided as a matter of right during any investigatory questioning of an employee by an employer, even though such questioning may lead to disciplinary action being taken against the employee being questioned. In some agreements the right to such representation is triggered if the investigator determines that the individual being questioned is likely to be disciplined as a result of the information being obtained by the questioning.

Cases that illustrate that there is no obligation to allow counsel to be present during investigatory questioning include Sundram v Kirschbaum et al, _ AD2d _ and Sundram v Hallerman, _ AD2d _ . In these cases the State Commission on Quality Care for the Mentally Disabled argued successfully that "the courts consistently have rejected the right to counsel before an investigatory administrative body."

With respect to investigations, sometimes a person asks to have a union representative or an attorney present at the questioning. The availability of such assistance will depend on the terms of the controlling agreement. The employer, of course, could elect to permit such representation even if none is specifically provided for by the agreement. Many employers decline to do so, however, for fear of

---

[26] The general rule in arbitration is that the failure to file an "answering statement" to disciplinary charges shall not operate to delay the arbitration process.

establishing a "past practice" that would obligate them to always allow representation during such meetings with employees.

If the employee refuses to respond to legitimate questions or otherwise fails to cooperate in the investigation, he or she may be disciplined for such actions.

If the employee has a right to counsel or to having a union representative present, but no representative is present, there is a risk to the employer that any information or evidence obtained during the meeting will not be considered ("suppressed") in a future disciplinary hearing involving that employee.

For this reason, it would be advisable for employers confronted with this circumstance to obtain a written statement from the employee to the effect that the individual knows that he or she has the right to obtain assistance from the union or legal counsel but declines to request such assistance. This should be viewed as the administrative due process equivalent of the Miranda warnings associated with the criminal process.

The employee should not be asked to waive such a right, however. The employer should avoid even the appearance that pressure was used to prompt an employee to forsake any right to due process. Failure to comply with due process requirements is always fatal to a disciplinary action, if challenged.

The fact that the employee refuses assistance, or is unable to obtain union or attorney representation promptly, should not prevent the investigation from continuing. If the employee does desire representation, a reasonable opportunity to obtain such assistance should be provided but his or her inability to obtain such assistance in a timely manner should not serve to frustrate the investigation.

A number of agreements permit a recording or transcript to be made if the employee is so advised in advance. The language of the agreement should be examined as to whether the employee merely need be informed of the recording or transcription, or whether the employee must agree to the recording or transcription.

The employee's agreement to the recording or transcription does not appear to be required in connection with investigations being conducted pursuant to Section 61 of the Public Officers Law, however.

Contracts generally prohibit the employer from demanding a "confession." Even if such a prohibition is not in effect, the employer should not ask the employee to sign any admission of guilt which is to be used in a disciplinary action without first giving the employee an opportunity to consult with a union representative or an attorney.

Otherwise, any admission obtained might be subject to suppression. If an admission is challenged, it will probably be suppressed unless it can be clearly shown that the employee was:

1. advised of the effect of such an admission;

2. aware of the fact that he or she could seek legal or union assistance before signing;

3. asked if he or she understood these rights and the effect of the admission; and

4. not coerced into waiving any of these rights.

Accordingly, it would be prudent for the investigator to make a clear and concise record of the fact that the individual was provided with what might be considered the administrative equivalent of the "Miranda warning" that police officers must give to suspects as they are placed under arrest in a criminal investigation. For a confession to survive a challenge, the employee probably will be required also to show that after providing the explanation and a reasonable opportunity to seek assistance, the employee indicated that he or she still wished to make such a statement.

At times it has been necessary to show by evidence other than the statement itself that the employee waived these rights with full knowledge of the consequences of the act. Still, it is always possible for the employee to attempt to repudiate the admission on the grounds that he or she was not informed of these rights, or was coerced into signing the statement, or was misled as to the effect of the signing the statement.

For all these reasons it is often best for the employer to insist that the employee seek assistance, notwithstanding the attractiveness of quickly disposing of the matter by obtaining an admission of wrongdoing from the employee.

5.03 Absence from work during disciplinary activities

Usually the agreement allows the union to designate a co-worker to serve as the employee's representative. If the designated individual is also an employee, that person is usually permitted to participate "on union leave," without charge to personal leave accruals. The employee is not so excused.

As is the case in Section 75 proceedings, under most negotiated agreements the employee must charge any absence from work in connection with the hearing - or the preparation for the hearing - to appropriate leave accruals. Charges to sick leave are not permitted. If the employee has exhausted all leave credits, he or she must be placed on leave without pay. Witnesses, other than the accused, are normally permitted to appear without charge to leave accruals.

5.04 Duty of fair representation

Most Taylor Law agreements include a multi-step grievance procedure. If disputes cannot be resolved at the supervisory or the appointing authority level, the matter is usually submitted to an arbitrator.

The duty of fair representation by unions is significant because generally only a union may demand arbitration or challenge an adverse arbitration award. Typically the individual does not have the right to demand arbitration should the union elect not to do so. This is due to the fact that only the union is party to the contract and the arbitration award. [Soto v Lenscraft Optical Corporation, 7 NY2d 397]

So, it is not uncommon for workers to claim that their union breached its duty to represent them by failing to pursue a grievance or failing to appeal an arbitration award despite its being asked to do so.

The Court of Appeals has ruled that "a union breaches its duty of fair representation when its conduct toward a member of the collective bargaining unit is arbitrary, discriminatory, or in bad faith." [Civil Service Bar Association, Local 237 v City of New York, 64 NY2d 188]

In Alston v Transport Workers Union of Greater New York, 225 AD2d 424, the Appellate Division pointed out that an amendment to the Civil Practice Law and Rules [Chapter 467, Laws of 1990], reduced the statute of limitations for bringing an action against a union for breach of its duty of fair representation from six years to four months [Section 217(2)(a), CPLR]. The four-month period commences to run from the date on which the employee knew or should have known that the breach had occurred or the date the employee suffers actual harm, whichever is later.

Unions do not need to process every grievance filed by an employee to fulfill their duty of fair representation, as in the case of a state Department of Motor Vehicles employee who filed 50 grievances [DiBenedetto v Ryan, 208 AD2d 796]. A union's decision not to pursue a grievance to arbitration is binding on the employee and precludes resort to additional remedies [Commack Union Free School District v Ambach, 70 NY2d 501]

A union's "duty of fair representation" runs only to employees; generally there is no such duty with respect to former unit members such as retirees. [Burnham and UFT, 28 PERB 4590; Lanzillo and Greece CSD, 28 PERB 3048] However, In Baker v Irondequoit CSD, 70 NY2d 314, the Court of Appeals held that a union's duty to process a former employee's grievance, under some circumstances, survives the employee's separation.

The duty of fair representation does not preclude a union from reaching an agreement with an employer on terms that are more favorable to some employees than to others. [Matter of Wayne County Sheriff's Employee Association, 29 PERB 4580; Hoerger v Great Neck UFSD, et al, Hoerger v. Board of Educ. of Great Neck Union Free School Dist. 215 A.D.2d 728, 215 A.D.2d 727, 215 A.D.2d 727.

An employee may demand arbitration or sue the employer directly only if the collective bargaining agreement allows an employee to bring such an action or if the union breaches it duty of fair representation. [Ponticello v County of Suffolk, Appellate Division]

Contract procedures can impose a greater burden on a union than might be imagined. This is illustrated by Ferri v Public Employees Federation, 92 AD2d 1054.

Ferri was given a notice of discipline charging him with misconduct. The proposed penalty was dismissal. When a timely grievance was not filed as required by the contract, he was dismissed without a hearing. He later sued the Public Employees Federation (PEF), claiming it had failed to assist him despite repeated requests for help, violating its duty of fair representation. PEF argued that while it was the employee's exclusive representative for certain things, the contract permitted Ferri to be represented by an attorney of his choice or by the union and therefore it did not breach its duty to Ferri.

The court was not persuaded by PEF's position. According to the court, such a position would effectively relieve the union of any responsibility on behalf of its membership in the area of disciplinary grievances.

What if the employee is represented by a union attorney and is ill served? Can the employee claim lack of fair representation? This was the issue in Salerno v Civil Service Technical Guild Local 375, [not officially reported]. An employee of the New York City Department of Housing Preservation and Development, Salerno was served with a notice of discipline alleging that he was absent from his job without permission, charging the absence to his accrued sick leave credits. In a settlement negotiated by an attorney on retainer to the union, Salerno agreed to resign from his position "effective immediately," waived accrued back pay and vacation pay; and agreed never again "to seek or obtain employment with the City of New York." In exchange the department agreed to drop disciplinary action and agreed that it would not oppose any application submitted by Salerno for "pension benefits."

As it turned out, Salerno could not qualify for a pension. He sued the union for allegedly breaching its duty to him. He said that he would have fought the charges but for the fact that his attorney "assured him that his pension was guaranteed." The court found the local did not breach its duty of fair representation because "there must be a showing that the activity, or lack thereof, was arbitrary, discriminatory or in bad faith." The court declined to hold the union responsible for any alleged malpractice on the part of the attorneys it had provided Salerno in order to assist him.

Another element that may become an issue: Are the terms of the settlement agreed upon by the employee and the appointing authority's representative binding on the appointing authority?

Alfred v Safir, 283 A.D.2d 280, teaches that in the context of the settlement of a disciplinary action, the penalty to be imposed agreed upon by the employee and employer's representative, and made part of the record by the disciplinary hearing officer, may not be binding on the appointing authority.

While in the course of settling a disciplinary matter, the employee typically agrees to plea guilty to some or all of the charges in exchange for a negotiated penalty that the employee and the employer's representative agree will be imposed. The hearing officer usually makes this settlement a part of the record and the hearing is then "closed."

According to the Alfred decision, New York City Police Commissioner Howard Safir suspended Gary Alfred for 30 days without pay and placed him on disciplinary probation for one year following the settlement of disciplinary charges filed against Alfred. Alfred objected, contending that he, the department's representative at the disciplinary hearing and the disciplinary hearing officer had all agreed to the imposition of a different disciplinary penalty.

The Appellate Division, First Department, unanimously affirmed Safir's decision, commenting that "[t]he various determinations and penalties agreed to by [Alfred] and [the department's] advocate and/or hearing officer were not binding" on Safir, the appointing authority, citing Silverman v McGuire, 51 NY2d 228.

As to the penalty ultimately imposed on Alfred by Safir in the course of the disciplinary action, the court ruled that it was "not so disproportionate to [Alfred's] failure to perform the most basic aspects of his assignment as to shock our sense of fairness."

This ruling suggests that where the appointing authority makes the final determination, it would be prudent for:

1. The employer's representative to insist that any settlement of a disciplinary action include a statement to the effect that the settlement is subject to the approval of the appointing authority; and

2. The employee or the employee's representative to insist on a provision spelling out what is to happen if the appointing officer does not agree to imposed the penalty set out in the settlement proposal.

5.05 Procedures under contracts

Most agreements set out in some detail the procedures to be followed in connection with the investigation of a matter that may lead to disciplinary action.

Such detailed guidelines on investigatory procedures are often useful to follow in investigations being done under the authority of statutory laws such as Section 75 or Section 3020-a. For instance, suppose a school district superintendent is investigating a principal for possible misconduct. Although the principal is not covered under the school district's collective bargaining agreement, the superintendent may wish to follow the same steps outlined in the collective bargaining agreement simply because those steps well-defined and should be familiar to the superintendent.

Where there are no contract provisions concerning investigations, the employer usually relies on Section 61 of the Public Officers Law as authority for conducting the investigation.

Contract disciplinary clauses often include the following types of provisions:

1. No "self-incrimination." The concepts underlying this provision are equally applicable in a Section 75 or similar action. Self-incriminating statements may be held to have automatically given the employee a qualified immunity from criminal prosecution if coerced.

2. The burden of proof. This is always placed on the charging party. In an administrative proceeding, the charging party is required to prove the charges by either a "preponderance of the evidence" or by "substantial evidence." The more rigorous "beyond a reasonable doubt" standard used in criminal prosecutions is not used in these proceedings.

The burden of proof should be distinguished from the burden of persuasion. The burden of persuasion shifts from the employer to the employee once the employer has made its case against the employee; the burden of persuasion shifts back to the employer if the employee has provided an explanation of his or her conduct sufficient to overcome the employer's case. The burden of proof is never shifted to the employee; it is always the burden of the charging party.

3. "No reprisal." This type of provision is meant to protect the employee, the employee's witnesses, and possibly "hostile" employer witnesses involved in the disciplinary action from any subsequent adverse action by the employer regardless of the outcome of the disciplinary action.

The suspension without pay provision in the disciplinary contract procedure could be significantly different from the suspension provisions in Section 75 or Section 3020-a. Suspensions without pay may be prohibited altogether. Or suspensions without pay could be authorized for reasons other than those set out in state law. The contract may even permit the employee to elect to be reassigned to a different position in lieu of suspension without pay.

Under some contracts the question of the reasonableness of a suspension without pay may be subject to review by the arbitrator.

Suppose an employer wishes to bar an employee from a work site. Courts have usually upheld the immediate suspension of the employee with pay if there is some danger to the individual, the public or the organization. In some instances courts have permitted suspensions without pay when charges were served shortly thereafter (within 24 hours). Most arbitrators would probably apply a similar standard.

Such "emergency" situations are considered in Section 72.5 of the Civil Service Law. This provision addresses situations in which employees are unable to perform the duties of their position because of a disability and the appointing authority believes that their continued presence at work constitutes some type of danger.

Rather than expose itself to the risk of having improperly suspended the employee, the appointing authority often directs the employee to "take a leave" and to charge such absence to appropriate leave accruals. However, even this action may be challenged later by the employee under a contract grievance procedure. It is usually best to reserve "suspensions" for those situations in which it is necessary to protect the agency, its staff or the public.

5.06 Reassignments

Contract disciplinary procedures often authorize -- and may even require -- an employee to be placed in a different position pending a determination.

A contract may also prohibit disciplinary action in the face of pending criminal charges. Although not so stated in law, the courts have ruled that Section 75 proceedings need not be postponed because a criminal action is already pending or may soon be commenced.

Unless the appointing authority agrees to postpone the disciplinary action, the fact that the employee may simultaneously be facing criminal action will not serve to bar the administrative disciplinary action from going forward. (Matter of Mountain v City of Schenectady, 1982.)

Generally the negotiated agreement requires that the union to be notified if the employee is to be disciplined. Some contracts even require that copies of the charges be supplied to the union. In the absence of such a requirement, no such notice is given to an employee organization in cases involving discipline under Section 75.

Normally the penalty proposed is indicated to the employee under the contract disciplinary procedure.[27]

If the matter is settled, the penalty may be anything agreed upon by the parties in both the contract and statutory proceedings.

If the matter goes to arbitration, the arbitrator is not bound to impose the maximum proposed penalty. An arbitrator may impose any penalty he or she thinks appropriate and reasonable -- even one not provided for in the agreement. In contrast, the only penalties that may be imposed under Section 75 or Section 3020-a are those set forth in the law. If a different one is imposed it will survive only to the extent that it is not challenged on appeal.

5.07 Settlement

Another option or alternative in a contract grievance procedure is "settlement." Prior to or at the conclusion of a contract disciplinary hearing, the representatives of the employer and the employee may agree to enter into discussions to "settle" a matter. The arbitrator, in turn, usually agrees to withhold issuing the arbitration award pending the outcome of these "settlement" discussions.

What if the union negotiates a settlement but the employee later refuses to sign? Has the union failed to bargain in good faith? PERB considered the issue in Town of Henrietta and CWA, 23 PERB 3004. The employer filed a complaint with PERB alleging the union violated its duty to negotiate in good faith when it refused to sign the settlement as required by Section 204.3 of the Civil Service Law [the Taylor Law]. PERB found an oral agreement had been reached. However, the only issue for it to decide, said PERB, was "whether a Taylor Law duty exists to execute the disciplinary settlement agreement reached." PERB ruled that "the duty to execute a written agreement created by Section 204.3 is most appropriately construed as applying to collectively negotiated agreements and not to settlement agreements reached pursuant to the grievance procedure contained in such a collective bargaining agreement."

5.08 Pre-hearing suspensions

A Taylor Law contract may authorize the arbitrator to consider any suspension without pay as a factor in setting the penalty. Until recently, the pre-hearing suspension under Section 75 was generally considered by the courts to be independent of -- and permitted in addition to -- the penalty imposed. Typically, the penalty imposed does not provide "credit" for any period of suspension during the pendency of the charges. More recent decisions seem to indicate "credit" is to be given for such suspensions (see Sinnott v Finnerty, 65 NY2d 780).

---

[27] The new Section 3020-a requires that the employer specify the maximum penalty it will impose if the employee declines to request a hearing, as well as the maximum penalty it will seek if the matter is submitted for hearing.

CHAPTER 6

FILING CHARGES UNDER Section 75

Until the development of contract disciplinary procedures, Section 75 was the most widely used mechanism for disciplining most public employees in the competitive class in New York State.

Some administrators claim Section 75 is difficult to use. Employees and their representatives also tend to dislike the law, pointing out that under Section 75 that the prosecutor also serves as judge and jury. However, the U.S. Supreme Court has ruled that procedures whereby an administrative body both investigates and adjudicates a matter does not violate due process [Withrow v Larken, 421 U.S. 35].

If used properly, Section 75 can provide management with an effective tool for employee discipline and provides employees with assurance of due process. In some cases, Section 75 is still the only disciplinary procedure available to a public employee. One example of this would be an employee designated managerial or confidential under the Taylor Law. Also, if there is a contract disciplinary procedure in place, Section 75 may be applicable to those employees who are not in the unit.

Section 75 is not available to employees of a public benefit corporation, even those who are veterans who served in time of war, unless the Legislature specifically provided that the corporation was subject to the Civil Service Law (Burnes v Quinones, 68 NY2d 719).

6.01 Key procedural elements

The key procedural elements in a Section 75 proceeding are:

1. Providing written notice of the reasons for disciplinary action.

2. Determining if the individual should be suspended without pay or reassigned to another workstation.

3. Notifying the individual of the date of the hearing, the fact that he or she may be represented by an attorney or his or her union representative and that he or she may call witnesses to testify.

4. Notifying the individual of the penalties specified in that may be imposed if the individual is found guilty of some or all of the charges.

6.02 Charges must be specific

Consideration also must be given to the adequacy of the charges and specifications given to an employee. Courts have ruled that charges must be sufficient to allow an employee to properly defend himself or herself. [Montrois v City of Watertown Fire Department, 115 AD2d 248.] It is well established that no person may lose substantial rights because of wrongdoing "shown by the evidence, but not charged." [Murray v Murphy, 24 NY2d 150]

On another point, may an employee be charged with misconduct that had not previously been charged in any previous disciplinary action?

In People v Patino, App. Div., 2nd Dept., 3/1/99, the Appellate Division upheld the conviction of Robert Patino, a former Nassau County police officer, who was found guilty of grand larceny and defrauding the government in connection with his claim of disability in order to obtain sick leave benefits.

Patino had argued that he had been subjected to "selective prosecution" because of the police department's alleged animosity towards him as no one had ever been subjected to criminal action because of such misconduct - here the abuse of sick leave. The Appellate Division upheld his conviction.

The court said that Patino failed to establish that he was singled out by the Nassau County District Attorney's Office for criminal prosecution "based upon an impermissible standard such as race, religion or some other arbitrary classification."

Clearly the fact that an individual is the first to be charged with a certain act of misconduct is not a defense for such misconduct. Further, equally unpersuasive is the argument that other individuals had engaged in the same type of misbehavior but were not disciplined for such action.

Again, unless the individual can demonstrate that such disciplinary action resulted because of some prohibited consideration such as his or her race, color, gender or disability, there is nothing to prevent his or her being the "first" to be so charged.

On a related issue, sometimes an individual will sue his or her employer contending that malice motivated filing disciplinary charges against him or her. This was the allegation made by the employee in Howard v City of New York, App. Div., 1st Dept., 1069

The employer filed disciplinary charges against an employee only to later withdraw the charges. Is the employer guilty of malicious prosecution? As the Howard case demonstrates, it depends on the circumstances.

The New York City Department of Corrections filed disciplinary charges against one of its correction officers, Cheryl Howard. The basis for these disciplinary charges: allegations that Howard had appeared in a pornographic video. When it was subsequently discovered that Howard had neither appear in, nor was involved with, the pornographic video, the Department rescinded and withdrew the disciplinary charges it had filed against her. Howard, however, sued the Department, charging it with malicious prosecution because, she alleged, the Department had conducted a "deficient investigation into the grounds for initiating the disciplinary proceeding against her."

The Appellate Division sustained the Supreme Court's dismissal of her charge of malicious prosecution because Howard did not allege any "special injury." According to the ruling, Howard did not allege any "concrete harm ... considerably more cumbersome than the physical, psychological or financial demands of defending" the disciplinary proceeding.

Further, said the court, Howard did not demonstrate that she had suffered "a highly substantial and identifiable interference with person, property or business."

Another case involving alleged malicious prosecution is Covert v County of Westchester, 608 NYS2d 516. Covert, a Westchester County corrections officer, sued the County for malicious prosecution after he was acquitted of criminal charges of assault base on allegations made by a prisoner that Covert and two other correction officers had subjected him to a beating.

The court dismissed Covert's complaint, holding that "[i]n this instance there was ample evidence in the record to find, as a matter of law, that there was probable cause to believe that Covert had committed the assault."

Although the Covert case involved a criminal complaint being filed against the employee, presumably the same standard would be applied by courts in cases alleging malicious prosecution in connection with administrative disciplinary actions.

6.03 Employee must receive opportunity to respond

Section 75 provides that the appointing officer must allow the accused employee at least eight days to file his or her answer to disciplinary charges in writing.

Does this mean that if an individual does not file an answer to the charges and specifications, the appointing authority may impose the proposed penalty without holding a disciplinary hearing?

To the best of the authors' knowledge, this specific question has not yet been litigated. But a close reading of Section 75 suggests such an action by an employer would not survive judicial review because Section 75 simply does not require that the employee submit any answer to the charges. This suggests that the individual may remain mute without jeopardizing his or her due process rights.

Furthermore, Section 75 provides that "the burden of proving incompetency or misconduct ... (is) upon the person alleging the same." In other words, the failure of an employee to offer a defense does not absolve the employer of the duty to prove misconduct before imposing a disciplinary sanction.

Indeed, it is well-settled that in the event the employee fails to appear at the disciplinary hearing, the charging party must proceed and actually hold the hearing in absentia rather then to merely proceed with the imposition of a penalty on the individual on the basis of his or her failure to appear at the hearing as scheduled. In other words, the failure of the accused individual to appear does not excuse the appointing authority from presenting evidence to support the charges and specifications filed against the individual.

Given that the courts require employers to conduct a hearing if an employee fails to appear at the proceeding, it seems unlikely that the courts would approve imposing a penalty on an individual because he or she failed to "answer."

Moreover, under Section 75 the employee need not ask for a hearing; it is to be provided as a matter of right.[28]

Section 75 also requires that a transcript of the hearing be provided free of charge to the employee.

Most alternative disciplinary procedures negotiated pursuant to the Taylor Law follow the 3020-a model. If the employee does not file a timely "disciplinary grievance," the appointing authority usually is authorized to impose the penalty proposed in the "notice of discipline" served on the individual without further action on its part and without referring the issue to arbitration.

6.04 Right to union representation

In 1993 Section 75.2 of the Civil Service Law was amended to provide that an employee who is represented by a certified or recognized employee organization pursuant to the Taylor Law who, "at the time of questioning" appears to be potentially subject to disciplinary action is to be notified, in advance and in writing, of his or her right to be represented by the union.[29]

Failure to allow an employee to exercise his or her right to have union representation is called "direct dealing" and is improper. Directing can be an unfair labor practice in violation of Section 209-a.1(a) of the Civil Service Law [the Taylor Law].

See, for example, Erie County Water Authority, 24 PERB 4539, (failure to notify the employees involved or their union representatives of the nature of the investigation prior to the questioning and failing to allow employees to consult privately with their union representative prior to their interrogation constituted violations of the "past practice" and was therefore a violation of the Section 209-a.1(d) of the Taylor Law).

Likewise the failure to allow representation can be construed as a violation of the union's right to organize under Section 202 of the Taylor Law. See Local 650 and the City of Buffalo, 30 PERB 3020 [termination violated right to organize under Section 202].

---

[28] Educators should note that Section 3020-a of the Education Law, the statutory equivalent of Section 75 for teachers and school administrators, does require that the individual request a disciplinary hearing. [See Chapter 7.]

[29] In 1994 officers and employees designated managerial or confidential within the meaning of Article 14 (the Taylor Law) covered by Section 75 were given a similar "right to notice" [Chapter 226 of the Laws of 1994].

6.05 Statute of limitations

Under Section 75.4 all employees, other than managerial and confidential employees,[30] may not be served with disciplinary charge more than 18 months after the occurrence of the alleged misconduct unless "the incompetency or misconduct complained of and described in the charges, if proved in a court of appropriate jurisdiction, (would) constitute a crime."

It is extremely important to understand the language of the law in Section 75.4. Key points:

1. For the purposes of automatic termination pursuant to Section 30(1)(e) of the Public Officers Law a "crime" is a felony -- not a misdemeanor unless the misdemeanor constitutes a violation of a public officer's oath of office.

2. To ignore the statute of limitations, the law speaks hypothetically about the alleged act constituting a crime; it does not require a criminal conviction.

Suppose evidence arises that an employee embezzled money four years ago. Under Section 75.4, the employer would be able to initiate a disciplinary action. The reason: embezzlement, "if proved" in a court of law, would be "a crime," i.e.: a felony.

In contrast, suppose the employer discovered that four years previous an employee had been propositioning a subordinate and promising he would use his power in the office to do "nice things" for the employee if she cooperated. Under Section 75.4, the employer would be not able to initiate a disciplinary action. The reason: quid-pro-quo sexual harassment, "if proved" in a court of law, would not "constitute a crime." While assault is a felony, sexual harassment absent assault is not a felony. Sexual harassment is civil violation.

To return to the embezzlement example, suppose the employer contacts the District Attorney, and the D.A. declines to prosecute. Such a decision would have absolutely no effect on the employer's ability to file disciplinary charges. Again: the law does not require a criminal conviction.

Suppose several years after the alleged embezzlement the D.A. does pursue a criminal conviction, and the employee is acquitted. May the employer proceed with disciplinary charges nevertheless the fact that the individual was acquitted in the criminal action?

In a word Yes! Why? Because the standard of proof is lower in administrative proceedings than criminal proceedings. (See Chapter 3, Evidence). The fact that embezzlement was not proved in a court of law does not prevent the employer from determining that if the embezzlement were proved in court, the transgression committed would be felony. The seriousness of the allegation permits the employer to ignore the statute of limitations.

---

[30] In 1995 Section 75.4 was amended to provide that the statute of limitations for filing Section 75 charges against managerial or confidential employees was one year, except where such charges, if proved in a court of law, would constitute a crime [Chapter 197, Laws of 1995].

However, there may be an implied statute of limitations with respect to bringing Section 75 disciplinary action after 18 months (or one year for "management confidential" employees). Probably courts would apply the same statute of limitations that would control in bringing the criminal action for the alleged offense.

How far may one look back for the purpose of initiating disciplinary action against an employee? The DeMichele case [DeMichele v Greenburgh CSD #7, 2nd Cir., 2/17/99] involved "looking back" 20 years.

Section 3020-a(1) of the New York State Education Law provides that "no charges ... shall be brought more than three years after the occurrence of the alleged incompetency or misconduct, except when the charge is of misconduct constituting a crime when committed."

In the DeMichele case, a teacher in the Greenburgh Central School District #7 was found guilty of having inappropriate sexual contact with female students in incidents occurring more than 20 years earlier. The Second Circuit U.S. Court of Appeals sustained the school board's decision to dismiss the teacher, even though the teacher had not been convicted of any "criminal act."

Following the same logic as New York State courts applied in addressing similar issues involving statutes of limitation under various disciplinary provisions, the federal court observed that the law does not require the individual to be found guilty of a felony in a criminal court for disciplinary charges to be filed after the three-year statute of limitations has expired.

Rather, the law merely characterizes the nature of the allegation. The law says that if a Section 3020-a hearing officer or disciplinary panel finds an individual guilty of an act that fits the definition of a felony under relevant criminal statutes, then a penalty may be imposed even if the disciplinary charges were brought after the three-year statute of limitations has expired (see Re Board of Education of City School District of the City of New York, Opinions of the Commissioner of Education No. 11353 [1984]).

Section 3020-a(1) of the Education Law also requires that disciplinary charges be filed "during the period between the actual opening and closing of the school year" during which the employee is normally required to serve.

The 20-year-old sexual misconduct charges arose after a newspaper reported that Greenburgh #7 teacher Robert DeMichele had been restored to the payroll in 1996 after serving one and one-half year disciplinary suspension. The article noted that the suspension without pay was imposed as a penalty after DeMichele was found guilty of having inappropriate conduct with female students during the 1991-92 and 1992-93 academic years.

After the article appeared, two women contacted district officials and alleged that DeMichele had sexually abused or molested them when they had been students in the district decades earlier -- during the 1972-73 and 1974-75 school years. There was no dispute that the district was unaware of these allegations prior to its receiving the February 1996 reports. On March 11, 1996 the district initiated a second Section 3020-a disciplinary action against DeMichele. The hearing officer found DeMichele guilty of all but one of seven specifications set out in the charges. As a result DeMichele was dismissed. The disciplinary determination was reported to the press.

The hearing officers ruled that (1) each instance of misconduct alleged in the second disciplinary proceeding constituted a crime when committed and (2) Section 3020-a does not require that the misconduct actually be the subject of a criminal prosecution. Rather than appeal the hearing officer's determination, DeMichele sued in federal district court claiming that the second disciplinary action violated his rights under 42 U.S.C. Section 1983. He contended that his rights were violated because:

1. The district forced him to defend charges concerning events that occurred more than 20 years ago, which left him unable to defend himself in violation of his right to due process under the Fourteenth Amendment; and

2. He was deprived of a liberty interest without due process under the Fourteenth Amendment when the district's prosecutor disclosed the results of the hearing to the media.

In an unpublished decision, a federal district court judge granted the district's motion for summary judgment and thus dismissed DeMichele's petition without a hearing on the merits of the complaint. The Circuit Court of Appeals affirmed the lower court's decision.

The Circuit Court said that to show a violation of due process as a result of delay in a hearing, New York State law requires the subject of an administrative disciplinary proceeding demonstrate that delay in initiating proceedings caused "actual prejudice" to his or her ability to defend against the charges. The court suggested that if the school district had known about the 1970s allegations before 1996 but delayed proceeding with discipline, DeMichele might have been able to show that his ability to defend himself had been compromised.

The court also addressed DeMichele's claim that the dissemination to the media of the results of his second disciplinary hearing stigmatized him and wrongfully deprived him of his liberty interest under the Fourteenth Amendment. The court noted that this argument rested on the assumption that the results of the disciplinary proceeding were not a matter of public record, but instead were part of his "employment history" which could not be released under New York's Freedom of Information Law, [Public Officers Law, Article 6, ("FOIL")].

However, the decision noted that New York courts have found that the disposition of misconduct charges does not constitute part of an employee's "employment history" as that phrase is used in FOIL, citing LaRocca v. Board of Education of Jericho Union Free School District, 632 N.Y.S.2d 576. The Circuit Court ruled that under the circumstances, the dissemination of the background and result of the first disciplinary hearing to the press did not deprived DeMichele of any liberty interest and dismissed the appeal.

6.06 Serving charges

If the charges are not served upon the employee personally, it is advisable to mail them by certified or registered mail, return receipt requested, to the employee's address on record with the agency.

If the charges are served on the employee personally, an "affidavit of service" or written statement to that effect should be obtained from the individual who actually delivered the charges to the accused employee.

Sometimes new or additional charges or specifications are to be filed against the employee after he or she has been served with an original charge. If such is the case, the additional charges may be combined with the original charge -- if additional time to respond is provided -- and if it will not adversely affect the employee's ability to develop a proper defense. Any scheduled hearing should be postponed if there is any question of the employee not having had sufficient time to adequately prepare a defense regarding the additional charges. In the alternative, the appointing officer can elect to proceed independently with the new charges and hold a second hearing to hear the additional charges.

Usually the charges are made by, or in the name of, the appointing authority. The hearing may be conducted by the appointing authority or by a designee.

How specific and accurate must the charges be? In a case involving the Westchester County Correctional Facility, charges against an employee specified that she "had hit and choked her supervisor." The hearing officer determined that the employee had "physically assaulted her supervisor" and that "the nature and degree of the assault and injury is not as important as the fact that it took place at all." The Appellate Division was not troubled by this deviation [Langhorne v Jackson _ AD2d _].

Nevertheless, it should be obvious that the employer should endeavor to be as accurate and specific in charges as possible.

6.07 Pitfalls to avoid

By the time an administrator is prepared to recommend or prefer charges against an employee for incompetence or misconduct, reasonable efforts must have been made earlier to acquaint the employee with the expected standards of performance. If the employer fails to follow what is generally accepted as appropriate personnel and human relations procedures to advise workers of expected standards of performance and behavior, this omission may mitigate the imposition of a disciplinary penalty or under some circumstances, exonerate the individual. For instance, an employer may give an individual a counseling memorandum indicating the nature of the problem and the employer's expectations as to improvement. Criticism is not discipline (see below).

Employee appraisals may be used by either party to bolster its case. If the employee has been rated "satisfactory" for his or her performance or behavior, it may compromise a subsequent effort to claim in a disciplinary hearing that performance during the same or proximate time period was unacceptable or constituted misconduct. Unless a new supervisor has taken over and has been unsuccessful in his or her attempts to modify the employee's behavior, the employer will have a difficult time explaining why the employee's heretofore "satisfactory" behavior is now the subject of a disciplinary action.

Another pitfall to avoid is uniformly relying on counseling for first offenses, even if the offense is egregious. While discipline should be progressive, a significant exception to this general rule involves conduct so egregious that the individual may be presumed to know it was wrong, e.g.: striking a co-worker or stealing from the employer. In such cases, the appointing authority may be viewed as condoning the misbehavior or being irresponsibly lax if it fails to file formal disciplinary charges.

6.08 Criticism is not discipline

Employer's counseling memoranda have been challenged on the grounds that it constituting disciplinary action. The courts have rejected the notion that such an action constitutes discipline. An employee is not entitled to hearing before a letter critical of the worker's performance is placed in his personnel file, where no punishment is involved. [Hoffman v Village of Sidney (3 Dept. 1997) __ AD2d __, 652 NYS2d 346]

Similarly, if the same behavior is later cited as grounds for discipline, courts have said that this is not double jeopardy. [Holt v Board of Education, 52 NY2d 625; Patterson v Smith, 53 NY2d 98]

It may be useful to consider the alternative. If the rule in such cases is that a memorandum critical of an employee did constitute "discipline," it would be necessary for an employer to bring formal disciplinary action against an employee, hold a hearing and if the employee is found guilty, determine that the penalty to be imposed would be placing a critical memorandum in the employee's personnel folder. Courts have said such formality is uncalled for.

6.09 Admission of guilt difficult to retract

It is difficult for an employee who admits guilt to retract that statement. The Stedronsky case is an illustration of this.

A teacher, Stedronsky admitted to a private investigator that while employed as a teacher, "he engaged in inappropriate conduct with a male student, to wit, sexual contact and other behaviors in an attempt to obtain sexual gratification."

However the record indicated that the private investigator falsely told Stedronsky that "there was incriminating evidence of his sexual misconduct with his students and that if he failed to admit that he engaged in such conduct or if he sought counsel, the School District would pursue a criminal conviction rather than merely seek his resignation."

Stedronsky's efforts to suppress these admissions at the administrative hearing that followed were unsuccessful. Ultimately the Commissioner of Education revoked Stedronsky's license to teach based on a Hearing Panel's findings that Stedronsky engaged in inappropriate conduct with students and lacked adequate moral character. The Commissioner also adopted the panel's recommendation that Stedronsky be given the opportunity to reapply for a teaching license in three years following appropriate therapy. The Appellate Division concurred in this reasoning. [Stedronsky v Sobol, 572 NYS2d 445].

6.10 Pending criminal charges

If criminal charges are pending against an employee, does the employee have the right to demand that administrative disciplinary action involving charges based on the same acts be stayed until the criminal action is resolved? And if an employee is acquitted of a criminal charge, does this preclude pursuit of disciplinary action based on the same actions?

The answer to both questions is no.

An employee has no right to have a disciplinary action delayed pending a criminal decision because a "not guilty" verdict in a criminal proceeding has no bearing on the outcome of an administrative disciplinary action.

While criminal proceedings require proof beyond a reasonable doubt for an individual to be found guilty, the standard of proof in disciplinary action is merely substantial evidence or, at times, a preponderance of the evidence. And certain forms of evidence such as hearsay evidence that are not admissible in a criminal proceeding are admissible in an administrative disciplinary action. So it is possible for someone to found not guilty in a criminal court of a given act, say larceny, and yet be found guilty in disciplinary proceeding.

On the other hand, suppose an individual is convicted of a crime by a court of law. Is it possible for the individual to be acquitted of disciplinary charges involving the same facts and allegations?

Absolutely not. Why? Because the standard of proof is greater in a criminal trial, a guilty criminal verdict automatically triggers a guilty verdict in an administrative disciplinary proceeding, as long as the facts and allegations are the same. [Kelly v Levin, 440 NYS2d 424]

6.11 Choice of law

What happens if a penalty chosen by an appointing authority is legal under a local law but illegal under Section 75? The challenge here is for the appointing authority to determine which law controls, or takes precedence. When a "special statute" conflicts with a general act, the provisions of the "special statute" control (take precedence). [Nieves v Haera, _ AD2d _]

It appears that the only means of modifying the disciplinary procedures of a "local or special law" such as those set out in the Rockland County Police Act is to seek its repeal or to negotiate an alternative disciplinary procedure pursuant to the Taylor Law.

CHAPTER 7

FILING CHARGES UNDER Section 3020-a

After an investigation has been completed there are three major options available to the education administrator:

1. Determine that no disciplinary action is warranted.

2. Decide that there is insufficient evidence for filing charges but that some other action, such as "counseling the individual" is appropriate.

3. Recommend the filing of disciplinary charges against the individual.

If charges are filed against an individual the following key steps must be followed:

1. Written charges should be submitted during the school year to the school board via the clerk or secretary of the school district.

2. The school board is to be immediately notified. Within five days after receipt of charges, the employing board, in executive session, shall determine, by a vote of a majority of all the members of such board, whether probable cause exists to bring a disciplinary proceeding against an employee.

3. If the board votes to proceed with disciplinary action, a written statement specifying the charges in detail must be sent to the employee.

4. The employee must be advised as to the maximum penalty that would be imposed if he or she does not request a hearing.

In addition, the individual is to be told the penalty that the board will seek to have imposed if he or she found guilty of the charges after a hearing. The letter must also describe or outline the employee's rights under Section 3020-a.

5. Such information is to be sent to the accused employee by certified or registered mail, return receipt requested or served by personal delivery to the employee.

7.01 Statute of limitations

Charges must be brought within three years of the occurrence of the alleged incompetency or misconduct, except when the misconduct, if proven, would constitute a crime. [Section 3020-a(1); see also Re Board of Education of City School District of the City of New York, 1984 Op Comr Ed No. 11353]]

The law also requires that charges be filed "during the period between the actual opening and closing of the school year for which the employed is normally required to serve." [Section 3020-a(1)]

7.02 Need for investigatory report regardless of merit of allegations

Regardless of the decision or recommendation regarding going forward with disciplinary action, a formal report of the findings and reasons for the recommendation should be prepared. It is important to do this for a number of reasons.

First, the reasons for undertaking the investigation in the first place might be attacked as an abuse of process, unlawful discrimination or on a number of other theories.

A contemporaneous report concerning the investigation undertaken and the findings may be critical to successfully defending the decision to investigate or to proceed, or not to go forward, with disciplinary action upon the completion of the investigation.

7.03 Risk of libel or slander as a result of investigatory report

Is there any risk of being sued for libel because such a report is created and shared among administrators? In libel and slander cases, there is no damage within the meaning of the law unless there is some communication to a third party not otherwise privileged to such information. In a work situation, written or oral communication between and among administrators and employees alleged to be defamatory is typically protected by what is called a "qualified privilege."

However, such qualified immunity will be lost if the information is distributed beyond those who need to know it for bona fide business reasons. Any claim to a "qualified privilege" that might otherwise be available to an individual will be lost if there is a discussion or the distribution of a letter or other communication to unprivileged persons or to both privileged and unprivileged persons. [Fedrizzi v Washingtonville CSD, _ AD2d _]

Another example of litigation resulting from communications among administrators is Murphy v Herfort, 428 NYS2d 117. Also, Missek-Falkoff v Keller, 545 NYS2d 360, is an example of a case where one employee sued a co-worker because of the contents of a memorandum from the co-worker to a superior concerning a "problem" with the employee.

The issue of libel may also arise in connection with an employee's former employer supplying information to a prospective employer of the individual in response to a request for references.

Even providing a positive job reference can be dangerous for an employer. This was shown in a somewhat extraordinary case of Randi W., decided by the California Supreme Court on January 27, 1997. A school vice principal named Robert Gadams allegedly molested a 13-year-old named Randi W. The parents of Randi W. won a lawsuit in which they contended that Gadams' former employer, the Muroc Joint Unified School District, committed a fraud by providing a placement office with a positive evaluation of Gadams despite the fact that Gadams had been accused of making sexual remarks to female students and touching them inappropriately.

The California Supreme Court ruled that the writers of letter of recommendation have a duty to be accurate, and that this duty is owed anyone who would be hurt by misrepresentations, including both prospective employers and third parties such as Randi W.

7.04 Name-clearing hearings

Dismissal of an individual who is not entitled to a Section 3020-a hearing because he or she does not have tenure frequently results in litigation.

While the individual may not be able to demonstrate that his or her dismissal was in violation of law or arbitrary or capricious, he or she may be able to obtain a right to a "name-clearing hearing."

In Matter of Stanziale, 55 NY2d 735, the Court of Appeals ruled that while Stanziale was not entitled to a disciplinary hearing under either Section 75 of the Civil Service Law [a statutory equivalent of Section 3020-a] or the controlling union contract, he was entitled to some due process so that he could "clear his name" because the basis for dismissal was of a stigmatizing nature.

However, that was the extent of the relief to which an employee is entitled under such circumstances. An individual cannot demand reinstatement even if he or she were to prevail at the name-clearing hearing.

Thus, where the reason for the dismissal is made public by the employer, there is a tendency for the courts to provide a hearing to persons not protected by a Section 3020-a or Section 75 type of law or a Taylor Law agreement if the court views the reasons for the termination as stigmatizing the individual. However, the "name-clearing" type of hearing has not to date resulted in an employee winning a reinstatement.

7.05 Pitfalls to avoid

As was suggested in an earlier chapter, the following concerns should be kept in mind during the investigation process:

By the time an administrator is prepared to recommend or prefer charges against an employee for incompetence or misconduct, reasonable efforts must have been made to acquaint the employee with the expected standards of performance or behavior (both at work and while off-duty) and the area or areas in which the employee has failed to meet or comply with the minimum standards required.

Unless the employer follows what is generally accepted as appropriate personnel and human relations procedures to advise workers of expected standards of performance and behavior, this omission may mitigate the imposition of a disciplinary penalty or under some circumstances, exonerate the individual.

Accordingly, there must be effective supervision. If the employee can rightfully claim that "no one ever told me my work was unacceptable" or "no one ever told me what I was expected to do," it will be extremely difficult, if not impossible, to discipline the employee -- unless the charge involves misbehavior or incompetence so egregious and obvious that any claim that "I didn't know it was wrong to do (or not do) that" by the employee would be ludicrous.

Another problem may arise when an employee has been rated "satisfactory" for his or her performance or behavior and later the subject of disciplinary charges on the grounds that such performance or behavior is unacceptable or constitutes misconduct. Unless a new supervisor, who is unhappy with such conduct, has taken over and has been unsuccessful in his or her attempts to modify the employee's behavior, the employer will have a difficult time explaining why the employee's heretofore "satisfactory" behavior is now the subject of a disciplinary action.

How can this be done?

Frequently an individual will be given a counseling memorandum indicating the nature of the problem and the employer's expectations as to improvement. Criticism is not discipline.

7.06 Criticism is not discipline

Employer's counseling memoranda have been challenged on the grounds that it constituting disciplinary action. The courts have rejected the notion that such an action constitutes discipline. Similarly, if the same behavior is later cited as grounds for discipline, courts have said that this is not double jeopardy. [Holt v Board of Education, 52 NY2d 625; Patterson v Smith, 53 NY2d 98]

In Port Jefferson Union Free School District v United Aides and Assistants, PERB rejected a union's claim that every written criticism of an employee is a "reprimand" and therefore can only result after the imposition of a penalty following disciplinary action.

Sometimes it may be difficult to determine the location of that thin line that separates lawful "constructive criticism" of an individual's performance by a supervisor and supervisory actions addressing an individual's performance that are disciplinary in nature.

The Commissioner of Education decided that the administrator's actions constituted discipline rather than constructive criticism in two cases, Matter of Fusco, Comm. of Ed. Decision 14,396, June 27, 2000 and Matter of Irving, Comm. of Ed. Decision 14,373, May 25, 2000.

As noted earlier, the Court of Appeals has ruled that a "counseling memorandum" that is given to an employee and placed in his or her personnel file constitutes a lawful means of instructing the employee concerning unacceptable performance and the actions that should be taken by the individual to improve his or her work [Holt v Webutick Central School District, 52 NY2d 625].

In other words, comments critical of employee performance do not, without more, constitute disciplinary action. On the other hand, counseling letters may not be used as a subterfuge for avoiding initiating formal disciplinary action against a tenured individual.

In the opinion of the Commissioner of Education, the employers "crossed the line" in both the Fusco and Irving situations.

According to the ruling in Fusco, Jefferson's superintendent, Dr. Wayne Jones, prior to his leaving the district in October 1997, had evaluated school administrators. Fusco was not evaluated by any of the district's acting superintendents who served following Jones' departure.

On July 29, 1998 the school board gave Fusco a memorandum entitled Board Evaluation of Principal Work Performance in which the board characterized Fusco's performance during both academic 1996-1997 and 1997-1998 as "unsatisfactory." The board's examples of Fusco's unsatisfactory performance set out in the evaluation included allegations that Fusco:

1. Demonstrated "unsuitable judgment;"

2. Exhibited unsuitable behavior;

3. Engaged in insubordinate and disrespectful behavior; and

4. Exhibited poor leadership.

The board placed a copy of its evaluation in Fusco's personnel file and Fusco appealed to the Commissioner. Fusco argued that:

1. Only the superintendent of schools is authorized to evaluate her performance and thus the board's action constituted a violation 8 NYCRR 100.2(o); and

2. Assuming that board could conduct such evaluations, the evaluation, when placed in her personnel file, constituted "an impermissible disciplinary reprimand, issued without complying with the procedural protections of Education Law Section 3020-a."

The board defended its action, contending that (1) it did, in fact, have authority to evaluate Fusco's performance and (2) its action was "constructive criticism" of Fusco's performance permitted by law and thus did not constitute disciplinary action within the meaning of Section 3020-a.

The Commissioner agreed with the board in part. First he pointed out that while 8 NYCRR 100.2(o) requires that the superintendent "develop formal procedures for the review of the performance of all personnel of the district", there is nothing in the regulation that requires the superintendent to conduct the evaluation.

Accordingly, the Commissioner ruled that in the absence of a provision that would "prohibit a board of education from doing so," a school board can itself conduct such an evaluation.

What of Fusco's second claim -- that the evaluation constituted unlawful disciplinary action and thus must be removed from her personnel file?

The Commissioner said that while the general rule is that personnel given critical administrative evaluations by a supervisor is not entitled to Section 3020-a protections, a disciplinary reprimand couldn't be issued without a finding of misconduct pursuant to Section 3020-a.

Did Fusco's evaluation constitute disciplinary action without the benefit of the protections of Section 3020-a? Yes, ruled the Commissioner, it did.

The Commissioner said that "contents of the memorandum" did not fall within the parameters of a "permissible evaluation" and despite the board's representation that it was "intended to encourage positive change" in Fusco's performance, it "contains no constructive criticism or a single suggestion for improvement." Rather, said the Commissioner, the memorandum focused on "castigating [Fusco] for prior alleged misconduct."

Instead of "constructive criticism," the Commissioner concluded that the evaluation "chastised [Fusco] for serious misconduct," including "improper release of confidential information, harassment of staff members, damaging district/union relationships...and poor leadership."

The district was directed to remove the evaluation from Fusco's personnel file as it "does not constitute a performance evaluation" but rather "an impermissible reprimand."

The Irving appeal followed action by Troy City School District Superintendent Armand Reo. After discussing letters of complaint received from parents and other concerns with the school board and Elementary School Principal Mozella Irving, Reo gave Irving a "letter of counseling" in which he, among other things, said:

You are hereby counseled that in future dealings with the parents of our students you must avoid a confrontational attitude ... avoid making rude or inappropriate comments to parents and you should generally make every attempt to accommodate reasonable requests [received from] parents. A copy of this letter was placed in Irving's personnel file.

The next day, October 8, 1999, Reo gave Irving a second letter in which he told her that she was transferred to a different school, where she would serve as assistant principal effective October 14, 1999 and that such action was being taken "in the best interest of the school district."

Protesting that her involuntary reassignment and demotion "was disciplinary in nature" and illegally deprived her of her rights to due process as set out in Section 3020-a of the Education Law, Irving appealed Reo's action to the Commissioner of Education.

The Commissioner sustained Irving's appeal, holding that the record convinces me that disciplinary action was taken and that Irving was deprived of her rights under Education Law Section 3020-a.

Conceding that Sections 1711 and 2508 of the Education Law authorize a superintendent to transfer personnel, the problem here, said the Commissioner, was that Irving's alleged "staff mistreatment" and "parental mistreatment" were the only reasons for reassigning and demoting Irving set out in the record.

The Commissioner pointed out that the several meetings between Reo and Irving, and Reo and the board, and the two letters given to Irving by Reo, "are all part of a single process, and it is inescapable that the sole reason for [Irving's] transfer was her alleged misconduct as a principal."

Considering all of these circumstances as a whole, the Commissioner concluded that Irving was entitled to the protections of Section 3020-a, including the right to contest formal charges, "and those rights have been violated here."

Another consideration that the Commissioner found persuasive: all of the materials submitted by the board in responding to Irving's appeal were "directed toward demonstrating misconduct on the part of [Irving]. This, the Commissioner pointed out, was exactly the type of proof that the district would have been expected to introduce in a Section 3020-a disciplinary hearing.

Rejecting the district's argument that Irving's "transfer was for the good of the district" and thus not disciplinary in nature, the Commissioner said this theory "misses the mark." He observed that "one would hope that every school district disciplinary action or proceeding, taken in good faith, is for the good of the district."

The Commissioner annulled Irving's reassignment from her position as principal of School 2 to assistant principal of School 14 "without prejudice to any further action which may be appropriate under the terms of this decision."

It seems clear that a superior may issue a letter critical of an individual's performance and place a copy of such a letter in the individual's personnel file without initiating disciplinary action where the document deals with a relatively minor shortcoming and urges or directs better performance on the part of the individual in the future.

Another concern involves the concept of double jeopardy. A "counseling memorandum" is placed in an individual's personnel file and later disciplinary charges involving the same event(s) are served upon the individual. Does including the events set out in the counseling memorandum in the charges constitute "double jeopardy?" No, according to the Court of Appeal's ruling in Patterson v Smith, 53 NY2d 98.

In Patterson the court said that including charges concerning performance that were addressed in a counseling memorandum was not double jeopardy. The court's rationale: as a proper counseling memoranda contains a warning and an admonition to comply with the expectations of the employer, it is not a form of punishment in and of itself.

Clearly, case law indicates that giving the employee a counseling memorandum does not bar the employer from later filing disciplinary charges based on the same event and the memorandum may be introduced as evidence in the disciplinary hearing or for the purposes of determining the penalty to be imposed if the individual is found guilty.

Another possible complaint is that the subject of a counseling memorandum that is later included in disciplinary charges constitutes "double jeopardy" in that as the individual is being "punished" for the same offense twice.

This is not the case, as a counseling memorandum containing a warning and an admonition to comply with the policy of a school district is not a form of punishment in and of itself.

Accordingly, issuing such a memorandum does not prevent a school district from later instituting disciplinary action based on the same event. Further, the memorandum itself could be introduced as evidence in the course of the disciplinary proceeding.

As to the use of counseling reports in a disciplinary case, sometimes the issue of compliance with a contract requirement mandating "progressive discipline" is raised.

The introduction of "counseling memoranda" to demonstrate that the employee was advised of his or her violation of rules or misconduct or inappropriate or inadequate performance and instructed as to the corrective action to be taken may prove critical in determining the guilt of the party charged and, if found guilty, the penalty to be imposed.

The same standards apply in off-duty misconduct cases. If an employee is charged with misconduct because of an off-duty incident, in most instances it probably will be necessary to show that the employee had been previously advised of the standards of off-duty conduct expected of employees by the employer.

Typically, the investigation should be conducted and completed before the decision to initiate discipline is made. Discipline action should be taken as a result of the analysis of the findings of the investigator, and not because of any prejudgment or "instinct" concerning the guilt of an individual on the part of the administrator.

It should be remembered that the decision to discipline a staff member involves the exercise of discretion by the appointing authority. Two decisions by the Commissioner of Education, Gaul, Decisions of the Commissioner #14432 and Matter of Middleton, Decisions of the Commissioner #14431, concerned the challenges to the exercise of discretion with respect to filing disciplinary charges against an employee.

In Gaul the issue concerned the board's filing disciplinary charges; in Middleton the issue involved a decision not to file such charges.

Port Jefferson Union Free School District board member Kenneth Gaul, together with "presumably parents of students" in the district challenged the district's decision to file disciplinary charges pursuant to Section 3020-a of the Education Law against a school principal, Dr. Esther Fusco, and her subsequent reassignment pending resolution of the disciplinary action.

The Commissioner decided that Gaul failed to show that the board "engaged in a willful violation or neglect of duty" by its filing disciplinary charges against Fusco.

Dismissing the appeal, the Commissioner pointed out that Section 1709(33) of the Education Law grants a board of education broad authority to manage the educational affairs of the district. "Inherent in this authority" is the power to abolish administrative positions and alter an administrator's assignment.

The Middleton appeal considered the issue of a school board refusing to initiate disciplinary action against a staff member.

Beatrice Hudgins Middleton's son was exonerated of charges that he brought a "Category I weapon" to his first grade class. Middleton then asked the school district to file disciplinary charges against school officials whom she alleged had lied during the investigation of the incident or at the disciplinary hearing that followed.

Commenting that it is the board of education that has authority to take disciplinary action against a school district employee, the Commissioner said "a board of education has broad discretion to determine whether disciplinary action against an employee is warranted."

All that is required is the board have "a reasonable basis" for its determination not to file disciplinary charges against the individual.

Presumably the rationales applied by the Commissioner would be applied by the courts in cases involving filing, or failing to file, Section 75, Section 3020-a or contract disciplinary charges against an employee.

In contrast, under certain circumstances the appointing authority may be held to have a duty to file disciplinary charges. This was the ruling by the court in Montefusco v Nassau County, Supreme Court, Nassau County, June 6, 2000; Justice Phelan.

The Montefusco case, brought by a schoolteacher against whom disciplinary charges had been served and who then sued the district for malicious prosecution, raised this issue.

The Lindenhurst Union Free School District filed Section 3020-a disciplinary charges against one of its teachers, John Montefusco, after it was told that Montefusco "was a voyeur who looked at photographs [of teenage girls] to sexually satisfy himself."

No criminal charges were filed against Montefusco but the New York State Education Department was advised of the situation and provided with a copy of a statement in which the detective claimed Montefusco had told him that "he was a voyeur who looked at photographs to sexually satisfy himself." Eventually this information was transmitted to the superintendent and school board.

Montefusco was charged with (1) conduct unbecoming a teacher based on allegations that he "took photographs of unknowing females for the purpose of using these photos for sexual gratification; and (2) "lying to the Associate Superintendent about taking the photos...." Montefusco was suspended with pay but ultimately the board dismissed the Section 3020-a charges and reinstated him to his position.

Contending that the board's action violated his civil rights [42 USC 1983], Montefusco sued the district and its superintendent in federal court. Federal District Court Justice Joanna Seybert dismissed his federal claims, holding that the actions taken by the district were reasonable. In the words of the court, "[t]he information these defendants had obtained led them to take appropriate and reasonable actions under the circumstances as they knew them to be."

Montefusco, however, had also filed a "state law claim" against the district and the superintendent for malicious prosecution. The county and the detective were also named as defendants in the State action. State Supreme Court Justice Thomas P. Phelan ruled that Mantifusco's "state law claims" against the district and the superintendent were barred by the doctrine of collateral estoppel as the federal court "clearly determined that defendant School District and Superintendent acted properly in preferring charges pursuant to Education Law 3020-a against plaintiff."

Justice Phelan said that he agreed with the district's argument that "presented with information that a school teacher engaged in sexual self-stimulation with the aid of photographs of school-aged children -- whether ultimately true or not -- the defendants would have been remiss in their duties had they taken no action at all."

Was the district required to file disciplinary charges against Montefusco after receiving the report from the Education Department? Not necessarily, as the decision by the Commissioner of Education in the Covino case indicates [Matter of Covino, Decision 11227]. The Covino decision holds that a board is not required to serve disciplinary charges against an individual simply because it is advised of allegations of "wrongdoing" on the part of the employee.

A parent complained that Covino, a teacher-coach, had been involved in the hazing of a student by other students. The parent wanted the school board to dismiss Covino and a bus driver who was alleged to have been present during the incident. The board's response to the parent's complaint was to suspend the teacher from his coaching duties. It did not initiate formal disciplinary action against either the teacher or the driver.

This, however, did not satisfy the parent and he appealed to the Commissioner of Education in an effort to obtain an order requiring the board to initiate disciplinary action seeking removal of the teacher.

Noting that a resident of a school district may file disciplinary charges against a tenured teacher, the Commissioner said that a board of education must have a reasonable basis for its decision whether or not to proceed with the disciplinary action.

The Commissioner decided that board's investigation of the incident, followed by its relieving the teacher of his coaching duties was sufficient under the circumstances. He ruled that the board had a reasonable basis for the action it took and its decision not to pursue further disciplinary action was neither arbitrary nor capricious.

The test set out by the Commissioner in the Covino decision: did the board investigate the allegations and then make a reasonable determination whether or not to take further action?

The employer, once having completed its investigation, essentially has the following options available to it:

1. Decide that filing disciplinary charges or taking other administrative action against the individual is unwarranted;

2. Decide that there is insufficient evidence to justify the filing of disciplinary charges but that some other administrative action, such as "counseling the individual," is appropriate.

3. Decide that filing disciplinary charges against the individual is appropriate under the circumstances.

If the employer determines that it is appropriate to bring disciplinary action against an employee, may it demand that the individual resign or be served with charges? In a word: YES!

In Rychlick v Coughlin, 63 NY2d 643, a case involving a tenured State employee, the Court of Appeals said the employer could threaten the employee with disciplinary action if he or she did not resign. The court pointed out that threatening to do what the appointing authority had a legal right to do -- file disciplinary charges against the individual -- did not constitute coercion so as to make the resignation involuntary.

Sometimes the employer will agree not to reveal the reasons underlying its demanding the employee's resignation to potential employers in the future. The employer's ability to agree that the reasons leading to the demand for the resignation shall remain "confidential" has been tempered, however.

In response to the so-called "silent resignation" in cases involving "child abuse in an educational setting" by a school employee, the New York State Legislature, in enacting Section 1133 of the Education Law, has declared that making an agreement "to maintain confidentiality" in resignation situations where allegations of child abuse have been leveled against an individual is against the public policy of this State.

Section 1133 bars a school administrator or superintendent from agreeing to withhold the fact that an allegation of child abuse in an educational setting was involved in the separation of the employee or volunteer in return for the individual's resignation or agreement to a suspension from his or her position.[31]

7.07 Procedures in filing charges

If disciplinary action is recommended, it is necessary to consider some procedural requirements:

1. Charges and specifications brought against the educator should be set out in detail. If they are not, the employee can, and probably will, demand "particularization of the charges."

---

[31] Section 1133 of the Education Law provides as follows: Unreported resignation against public policy. 1. A school administrator or superintendent shall not make any agreement to withhold from law enforcement authorities, the superintendent or the commissioner, where appropriate, the fact that an allegation of child abuse in an educational setting on the part of any employee or volunteer as required by this article in return for the resignation or voluntary suspension from his or her position of such person, against whom the allegation is made. 2. Each violation of subdivision one of this section shall constitute a class E felony, and shall also be punishable by a civil penalty not to exceed twenty thousand dollars. 3. Any superintendent of schools who reasonably and in good faith reports to law enforcement officials information regarding allegations of child abuse or a resignation as required by this article shall have immunity from any liability, civil or criminal, which might otherwise result by reason of such actions.

2. The matter must be referred to the school board for its consideration and determination of whether there is probable cause to bring a disciplinary action. The board is to vote on each charge and specification presented to it and a record of its vote concerning each allegation is required.

3. Charges may not be filed against an employee more than five days before the next regularly scheduled meeting of the board. The board, however, may give an administrator permission to file charges more than five days before its next meeting.

4. After the school board's vote the employee is to be given a written statement specifying in detail each charge for which the board found probable cause to bring disciplinary action, together with a report of the board's vote on each charge recommended be brought against the individual.

5. Notice to the employee is to be sent by certified or registered mail, return receipt requested, or given to the individual by personal service or delivery. In addition, the Commissioner of Education is to be sent a copy by first class mail.

6. The statement must contain the maximum penalty that will be imposed by the board if the employee does not request a hearing together with the maximum penalty that will be sought by the board if the employee is found guilty of the charge(s) after a hearing.

7. The statement is also required to outline the employee's rights under Section 3020-a. This, presumably, includes the right to be advised of the availability of an alternate disciplinary procedure if one exists. If no alternative disciplinary procedure has been negotiated, the notice must also including the fact that the individual has (1) the right to request a hearing; and (2) the right to choose either a single hearing officer or a three-member panel when the charges allege pedagogical incompetence or there are issues involving pedagogical judgment. [If there are no "pedagogical related" charges involved, a single hearing officer is to conduct the disciplinary action.]

If an alternative disciplinary procedure has been negotiated under the Taylor Law, the procedures contained in the agreement are to be followed. (See Chapter 5.)

7.08 Use of school attorney

It is appropriate to use the school board's attorney to assist in preparing disciplinary charges. A school superintendent specifically raised this issue when he was served with disciplinary charges. He questioned the propriety of a School Board member "preparing the charges with assistance from the Board's attorney."

The Commissioner of Education said that "absent contrary local procedures, there is nothing in law or regulation precluding a member of a board of education access to the board attorney, so long as the board member seeks advice in his or her official capacity as a school board member in connection with official school district business." [Commissioner of Education Decision 13601]

7.09 Verdict shopping

Can an individual to claim a constitutional right to a statutory disciplinary procedure such as that available under Section 3020-a of the Education Law or Section 75 of the Civil Service Law after being found guilty of charges following a contract disciplinary hearing? This was addressed by the Court of Appeals in Antinore v State [40 NY2d 6]. If an individual has elected to proceed with a disciplinary proceeding set out in a collective bargaining agreement, he or she may not later claim the right to relitigate the charges under a statutory due process proceeding.

Significantly, the Court of Appeals said that a union could bargain away the employee's statutory disciplinary rights in favor of an alternative disciplinary procedure if the alternate procedure provided constitutional due process protections equivalent to those available under the statute it replaced.

7.10 The Section 3020-a process

For the purposes of avoiding repetition and speculation concerning disciplinary procedures negotiated under the Taylor Law, the comments and observations that follow will concentrate on the procedural and other mandates set out in Section 3020-a and the Regulations of the Commissioner of Education. Where appropriate, references to Taylor Law agreements and procedures will be made.

The Court of Appeals has ruled that to determine whether charges were properly brought under Section 3020-a, the proper standard is "preponderance of evidence", not the more rigorous standard of substantial evidence. [Martin v Ambach (1986) 67 NY2d 975]. See Chapter 3, Evidence, especially 3.01.

Charges against an employee must be made individually. "Group charges," whereby charges are filed against two or more individuals in the same document, are barred. However, the Commissioner's Regulations will allow "group hearings" to be held in the event all of the accused employees agree to a joint proceeding.

As indicated earlier, charges involving pedagogical incompetence or judgment may be held by either a single hearing officer or a panel, at the election of the accused. Where pedagogical issues are not involved, a single hearing officer is to preside.

Theoretically it is possible to file a set of charges against an individual limited to pedagogical issues and a second set of charges involving non-pedagogical issues. In most instances, however, such charges would be combined and a single proceeding initiated.

Once the charges are filed against the employee, he or she is required to advise the board if he or she wishes to have a hearing. This must be done in writing. The request must be sent to the board's clerk or secretary within 10 days of receipt of the charges. This should be done by certified or registered mail, return receipt requested, or by personnel service as was the case in the serving of the charges. The reason for this is simple. It may be necessary to establish the fact that a procedural element was complied with in a timely fashion. The "return receipt" or an affidavit of service may become critical to establishing that fact.

Where charges include both pedagogical issues and non-pedagogical issues the individual has the right to choose either a single hearing officer or a three-member panel to hear all charges. In such a situation, the employee must affirmatively act to elect to proceed either with a single hearing officer or a three-member panel.

While not mandated, the employee may indicate the name of his or her attorney in this request for a hearing.

7.11 Informing the Commissioner

If the educator elects to have a hearing, the Commissioner of Education must be advised of that fact. The district is to forward the following information to the Commissioner:

1. Notice that the individual has requested a Section 3020-a hearing.

2. An affidavit indicating that the employee has been served with disciplinary charges.

3. A copy of the employee's request for hearing.

4. Information indicating the place [within the district or the county seat of a county] where the "pre-hearing conference" and the disciplinary hearing will be held. [Any cost associated with the holding of a hearing at the specified site is at the district's expense.]

5. The name and address of the attorney, if any, who will represent the board at the hearing.

6. Whether an expedited hearing is sought. (Under an "expedited hearing" procedure, the hearing officer is to issue his or her determination within 10 days of the last day of hearing rather than within 30-days allowed for "regular proceedings.")

7. Information indicating whether the employee is suspended and if suspended, whether the suspension is with or without pay.

8. An estimate of the number of days needed for the hearing.

9. Where a panel is to conduct the hearing, the notice is to include the name of the panel member selected by the board. If no such member is named, the Commissioner will select the district's panel member.

10. If the employee has told the board the name of the attorney who will appear on his or her behalf, the Commissioner is to be given the attorney's name and address.

The employee is to be sent a copy of this notification by certified mail, return receipt requested.

If there is more than one individual against whom charges have been filed, the Commissioner must be sent a separate notice for each individual.

If an employee has waived his or her right to a hearing, or is deemed to have waived his or right to a hearing, the Commissioner is to be immediately notified of that fact.

Upon receipt of the notice, the Commissioner will take the necessary steps to have a hearing officer designated and a pre-hearing conference scheduled.

Once this is accomplished, the hearing officer will contact the district and the individual charged confirming his or her acceptance of a selection to serve as hearing officer and proceed to hold a pre-hearing conference.

Where the employee elects to have the charges considered by a hearing panel, he or she is required to designate the person whom he or she has selected as the panel member and advise the district and the Commissioner of his or her choice. This must be done within five days after he or she received a copy of the district's notification to the Commissioner. If this is not done in a timely manner, the Commissioner will designate the panel member for the employee.

7.12 Hearing panel members

The designation of panel members by the district and the employee should not be viewed as the selection of a partisan representative. Rather they are impartial, quasi-judicial officials.

This point was made in Syquia v Harpursville Central School District, 568 NYS2d 263, an "old law" Section 3020-a case. In Syquia, the court observed that a school board and a teacher have a statutory right to select a panel member to serve on the three-member board.

However, the court rejected the argument advanced by the attorney for the Harpursville School District suggesting that "a Section 3020-a hearing is, and is intended to be, something other than a fully impartial fact finding hearing...."

The court clearly stated that the panel members selected by the Board of Education and by the teacher are not advocates for the party respectively selecting them, with only the chairman of the hearing panel intended to be impartial.

The court said that it was taking its opportunity in this case to dispel any such "misapprehension in educational circles, if such in fact exists." It is likely that the same rationale would be applied to the selection of panel members by employers and employees under the new law.

In contrast to the Syquia decision, in June 1998 the Appellate Division decided in Meehan v Nassau Community College that "a party-designated arbitrator may in fact be 'partial'" and that by itself this is not grounds for vacating an arbitration award.

The case involved Nassau County Community College's attempt to overturn two arbitration awards under Article 75. One member of a three-person arbitration panel selected by the parties had direct personal knowledge of the disputed facts underlying the grievances and that this arbitrator actually testified concerning these facts during the arbitration. The Appellate Division had no problem with a panel member testifying at the hearing, holding that "dual capacity of arbitrator and witness may serve as a basis for vacatur only if his behavior in this regard can be properly characterized as constituting 'corruption, fraud, or misconduct' (CPLR 7511[b][1][i])."

7.13 Pre-hearing conferences

As to the pre-hearing conference, the Commissioner's Regulations provide that the pre-hearing conference is to be private. This means that the press and the public are to be excluded from observing the proceeding.

In contrast, Section 3020-a provides that "Hearings shall be conducted by the hearing officer selected pursuant to paragraph b of this subdivision with full and fair disclosure of the nature of the case and evidence against the employee by the employing board and shall be public or private at the discretion of the employee."

The Commissioner's Regulations provide that unless the employee notifies the hearing officer at least twenty-four hours before the first day of the hearing that he or she demands a public hearing, the hearing shall be private. This provision appears to be inconsistent with present case law as well as placing a burden on the employee that does not appear to be mandated by law.

Some support for the proposition that disciplinary hearings shall be automatically open to the public unless the employee insists that they be closed can be found in Randall v Toll, 74 Misc2d 315.[32] Here the court held that a disciplinary action taken against an employee pursuant to Section 75 of the Civil Service Law could not be closed to the public unless the accused employee agrees or requests that the proceedings be held privately

The Commissioner's regulations appear to take a different direction, providing that Section 3020-a hearings are automatically closed to the public unless the employee makes a timely demand that they be opened to the public and, presumably, the press.

Some other cases that considered the question of whether or not the public may be barred from an administrative proceedings include Johnson Newspaper Corporation v Melino, 547 NYS2d 915; Matter of Capoccia, 59 NY2d 549 and Rome Sentinel Company v City of Rome, 546 NYS2d 304.

7.14 Characteristics of arbitration

Disciplinary action, whether before a Section 3020-a hearing officer or hearing panel is very similar to proceeding with a disciplinary under a Taylor Agreement that provides for arbitration of disciplinary matters. Essentially the operative law is the same, following the precedents of arbitration.

---

[32] The hearing officer acquitted Randall of all of the charges and specifications the appointing authority filed against him.

Accordingly, in this book the convenient terms "arbitration" and "arbitrator" and their derivatives will be used in describing both Section 3020-a hearing officer and hearing panel activities and Taylor Law disciplinary arbitration proceedings.

Under the current law, a Section 3020-a decision is treated as though it were an arbitration award and processed through Article 75 of the Civil Practice Law and Rules [CPLR] rather than as a challenge to an administrative determination under Article 78 of the CPLR. This is identical to appealing or enforcing arbitration awards under most Taylor Law collective bargaining agreements.[33]

Political subdivisions of the state, including a number of school districts, have earlier entered into Taylor Law alternatives to statutory disciplinary procedures despite the lack of any specific statutory authority to do so. As noted earlier, the courts have approved the substitution of negotiated disciplinary procedures for those authorized by statute [See, for example, Barera v Frontier Central School District, 672 NYS2 218 and Apuzzo v Ulster County, 62 NY2 960].

The new Education Law Section 3020-a, for the first time, specifically authorizes employee organizations and school districts and BOCES to enter into such agreements on behalf of school district employees in the unclassified service. There is no specific authority in law for such agreements to be negotiated on behalf of employees in the classified service by political subdivisions of the State, including school districts and BOCES.

Arbitration in the disciplinary context is the referral of the issue of alleged employee wrongdoing to an impartial party -- the arbitrator. The arbitrator is authorized to make findings of fact and determinations of innocence or guilt. If the employee is determined to be guilty of all or some of the charges alleged, the arbitrator is then authorized to set the penalty.

The arbitrator's ruling is final and binding on the parties. As will be seen below, it may be challenged, but the grounds for appeal, which are set by law, are limited.

---

[33] Although most Taylor Law contracts provide for binding arbitration, a few agreements limit the arbitrator's authority to make a final and binding determination. Such agreements are said to provide for advisory arbitration. In view of the small number of agreements providing for advisory arbitration, references to disciplinary arbitration in this handbook will be to binding arbitration procedures.

CHAPTER 8

SUSPENDING EMPLOYEES PENDING A HEARING

Frequently employers wish to suspend an employee upon whom charges have been served until the disciplinary procedure has been completed.

8.01 Suspension without pay – general considerations

The circumstances under which an employee may be suspended pending a disciplinary hearing vary according to whether the disciplinary procedure involved is Section 75, Section 3020-a or a negotiated procedure.

Section 3020-a. Under Section 3020-a, suspension without pay for tenured teachers and administrators is authorized under two specific circumstances: (1) The individual has been convicted of a felony involving illegal drugs, or (2) the individual has been convicted of a felony involving the physical or sexual abuse of a minor or student. (McKinney's Cons. Laws of NY, Book 16, Education Law Sec. 3020-a[2][b]).

Taylor Law agreements. Agreements vary. Unpaid suspensions may be prohibited altogether, or suspensions could be authorized for reasons other than those set out in state law. The contract could permit the employee to elect to be reassigned to a different position in lieu of suspension without pay. And under some contracts the question of the reasonableness of a suspension may be subject to review by the arbitrator.

Some collective bargaining agreements specifically authorize the suspension of an employee without pay pending a determination of the charges. This, in effect, means that the employee may be suspended for a period greater than the one specified by law, such as the 30-day limit of Section 75 of the Civil Service Law. Such a "contractual suspension without pay" was an issue in Board of Education v Nyquist, 48 NY2d 97. In this case, the court said that the Taylor Law agreement permitted the suspension of a teacher without pay "pending an investigation and recommendation by the Superintendent of Schools".

The school board, however, continued the teacher in "suspension without pay status" after it had received the Superintendent's recommendation. About 10 months later the teacher was dismissed by the Section 3020-a disciplinary hearing panel after it found the teacher guilty of disciplinary charges.

The court directed the school district to pay the teacher back salary for the period from the date the Superintendent made his recommendation to the Board until the effective date of the teacher's dismissal. Why? Because, said the Court of Appeals, "there (was) no [statutory or contractual] authorization for the Board's suspending the teacher without pay after the Superintendent completed his investigation and made his report" to the Board.

Had the contract permitted the Board to continue the teacher on a suspension without pay, it appears that such a suspension would have been upheld based on the ruling in the Antinore case (Matter of

Antinore, 40 NY2d 921). The only limitation appears to be that the employer may not use the suspension without pay as a sword by delaying the proceedings.

Likewise, the provisions of a collective bargaining trump Section 75 regarding whether an employee must be restored to the payroll after 30 days. Section 75.3 limits the period of an employee's unpaid suspension pending disciplinary action to 30 days. But if the relevant collective bargaining agreement contains no such limitation, the employee may be suspended without pay for longer than 30 days. [Robinson v NYC Transit Authority, Appellate Division]

Section 75. Section 75 provides that an individual can be suspended without pay for a maximum of 30 days pending a hearing on the charges and the final determination, but only if "charges have been preferred". [Section 75.3] That is, it is not proper to suspend an employee without pay merely in anticipation of filing disciplinary charges. If the disciplinary proceeding or a settlement has not been completed within 30 days of the beginning of the period of suspension without pay, the individual must be restored to the payroll, even the employee is later found guilty. [Maurer v Cappelli (2 Dept. 1973) 42 AD2d 758, 346 NYS 2d 154]

There are other alternatives for removing the employee from the workplace. The employer may suspend the employee with pay or reassign the individual to another position for which he or she is otherwise qualified. Either of these actions will usually withstand judicial scrutiny.

If the employee refuses to accept a reassignment, it may be possible for the employer to stop paying salary. [Alderstein v Board of Education, 96 AD2d 1077].

What if the employee does not perform adequately in the position to which he or she has been reassigned? May the employer summarily remove the employee from the payroll? New York State Supreme Court Justice Oshrin [Suffolk County] ruled that the answer is "no" in a case involving the Patchogue-Medford Union Free School District. [Brady v A Certain Teacher, _ Misc2d _].

Justice Oshrin also said that "the withholding of salary and benefits prior to hearing and determination would be a deprivation of the tenured teacher's constitutionally protected property interest in continued employment and compensation without due process of law." According to the ruling, if a teacher accepts the reassignment and reports for work as required but fails to adequately perform the work, the employer may serve a second set of charges on the individual. The lesson is clear: the employer must always be cognizant of the need for due process.

Suspensions without pay will be discussed more fully below. It is worth noting that in 1997 the U.S. Supreme Court ruled that if a public employer suspends a tenured public employee without notice and a hearing after a felony arrest, this does not constitute a violation of the due process clause of the 14th Amendment. [Gilbert v Homar, U.S. SupCt No. 95-651, June 9, 1997]

The Gilbert case involved a policeman at East Stroudsburg University in Pennsylvania who was suspended without pay immediately after State Police arrested him on felony charges after a drug raid at the home of a family friend. The High Court reasoned: "like an indictment, the imposition of felony charges, 'itself is an objective fact that will in most cases raise serious public concern.'" The fact that an independent third party has determined there is probably cause to believe the employee committed a serious crime "serve(s) to assure that the state employer's decision to suspend the employee is not 'baseless or unwarranted'."

8.02 Suspensions with pay, Sections 72 and 75

Suspending an employee with pay seldom presents a legal problem. Section 75.3 does not prohibit suspending an employee from his or her position with pay for a period longer than 30 days, nor does it mandate reinstatement if charges have not been determined. [Prezio v DeSantis, 38 AD2d 772]

May an employer require the employee who is suspended with pay to "take a vacation" and charge the employee's leave credits? Under Section 75, the employee may not be compelled to charge leave credits such as vacation during a period of paid suspension.

However, in cases involving disability or illnesses in which the employer finds reason to believe the individual poses a threat to others or property, the employee may immediately place employee on involuntary leave and charge the absence to the employee's leave accruals in accordance with Section 72.5 of the NYS Civil Service Law.[34]

8.03 "Emergency" Suspensions

Suppose an employer wishes to bar an employee from a work site. Courts have usually upheld the immediate suspension of the employee without pay if there would be some danger to the individual, the public or the organization. Courts have permitted such suspensions when charges were served shortly thereafter (within 24 hours). Most arbitrators would probably apply a similar standard.

Such "emergency" situations are considered in Section 72.5 of the Civil Service Law, which concerns situations in which employees are unable to perform the duties of their position because of a disability and the appointing authority believes that their continued presence at work constitutes some type of danger.

Rather than expose itself to the risk of having improperly suspended the employee, the appointing authority often directs the employee to "take a leave" and to charge such absence to appropriate leave accruals.

However, even this action may be challenged later by the employee under a contract grievance procedure. It behooves administrators to reserve "suspensions" for those situations in which it is genuinely necessary to protect the agency, its staff or the public.

---

[34] Section 72 is not a "disciplinary" provision. Rather, it addresses the appointing authority's ability to place an individual on leave without pay in situations involving a non-work related illness or disease that renders the individual unable to perform the duties of the position. See also "Emergency Suspensions," below.

8.04 Suspension without pay, generally

As long as the employer adheres to the statutory requirements in suspensions without pay, probably the only limitation is that the employer may not use the suspension without pay as a sword by delaying the proceedings. [Farro v NYC Transit Authority, 121 Misc2d 716]

If the employee is later acquitted, "he shall be restored to his position with full pay for the period of suspension less the amount of any unemployment insurance benefits he may have received during such period." [Section 75.3]

If the employee is found guilty, Section 75 lists among permissible penalties a suspension without pay not to exceed 60 days. If such a penalty is assigned, the pre-hearing suspension may be considered "time served" but there is no requirement for the employer to do so [Section 75.3]. An employee found guilty has no right to salary for the period of pre-hearing suspension [Paris v City of New York, 1947, 189 Misc. 445, 74 NYS2d 584].

As explained earlier, under Taylor Law agreements and Section 3020-a, suspension without pay pending the disciplinary determination longer than 30 days are possible. However, the employer's ability to suspend an employee depends on the terms of a collective bargaining agreement. However the existence of a "contract grievance procedure," alone does not constitute a substitute for Section 75. [Mancuso v Crew, NYS Supreme Court, January 1998]

If an employee is absent without authorization while disciplinary charges are pending, perhaps because he or she has been incarcerated, the employer may dock the employee's pay. Such action does not constitute "an impermissible double penalty" as the withholding of pay for an unexcused absence has not been viewed as a penalty within the meaning of the law. (Matter of East Williston Union Free School District, Comm. of Ed. Decision 11062).

In such cases, the employee may be permitted to use appropriate leave credits or be placed on leave without pay until he or she is able to report for duty.

8.05 Suspension without pay of unlicensed individual

An employee may be subject to suspension without pay, or even removal from his or her position, if the individual becomes unable to lawfully perform the duties of the position because of a lack of, or the loss of, a required license or similar permit.

The courts have upheld the right of the employer to summarily place the individual who has lost the required license or permit on leave without pay without limitation.

In essence, the courts have viewed such an employee as being "unqualified," in contrast to being "incompetent," to perform the duties of the position.

Common examples include the revocation of a driver's permit to operate a motor vehicle on public roads, the loss of a license to practice law and the expiration of a temporary permit to teach.

All that appears to be necessary in such cases is for the appointing authority to make some reasonable inquiry to determine if the employee may lawfully perform the duties of the position.

This can be done by simply asking the employee to produce a valid license or permit. If this cannot be done, the employee may be suspended immediately and without limitation.

The courts have held that where an individual is required to hold a valid license in order to perform the duties of the position and the employee losses the required license or it expires, the individual cannot be allowed to perform the duties of the position. This proposition was explored by the Appellate Division in Martin ex rel Lekkas, 86 AD2d 712.[35]

As to the employee being continued on the payroll if he or she is not licensed, in Cutler v Poughkeepsie City School District, 104 AD2d 988, the Appellate Division said that would be incongruous if "a teacher could be unqualified for the purposes of teaching in the educational area for which he was hired, but qualified for the purposes of drawing his pay while suspended from teaching."

A different approach is to file formal disciplinary charges (e.g., failure to maintain professional license or qualification requirements) in such cases, then impose disciplinary sanctions.

In addition, in some instances a Taylor Law agreement may provide for an alternative procedure regarding suspension of employees without pay during the pendency of a disciplinary action.

8.06 Suspension without pay in the event of postponement of disciplinary proceeding

Under Section 75, courts have approved the placement of an individual on leaves without pay for periods equal in length to any adjournment in the hearing process requested by the employee. See, for example, DeMarco v City of Albany (3 Dept. 1980) 75 AD2d 674, 426 NYS2d 860. Amkraut v Hults, 21 AD2d 260]

For other exceptions due to collective bargaining agreements or other reasons, see Winkler v Kingston Housing Authority, NYS App. Div, April 10, 1997, Langhorne v Jackson, 614 NYS2d 627, and Robinson v New York City Transit Authority (2 Dept, 1996) 226 AD2d 467, 641 NYS2d 55.

The situation is not the same for educators. The Court of Appeals has ruled it is impermissible to suspend a teacher without pay because a disciplinary hearing has been postponed, regardless of who requested the delay. Citing its 1974 decision in Jerry v City School District of Syracuse, 35 NY2d 534, the court said that a school district did not have any authority to suspend a teacher's salary during

---

[35] In Martin ex rel Lekkas the issue focused on the employer requiring Lekkas to have a valid license to practice medicine while serving as an administrator, a position that did not involve Lekkas' practicing medicine. The appointing authority had terminated Lekkas from his position because he did not hold a valid New York State license to practice medicine. Only where the duties of the position require the incumbent to be licensed may the lack of such a license be grounds for termination.

the period of the adjournment granted at his request, reversing lower court rulings to the contrary [Derle v North Bellmore UFSD, 520 NYS2d 592 and 551 NYS2d 49].[36]

8.07 Suspension of a school superintendent

The Pickney decision, Decisions of the Commissioner of Education Number 13601, concerned a school board to suspending its superintendent without pay pending a disciplinary hearing. The Commissioner found that the school board had acted incorrectly.

Dr. Robert D. Pickney, the Westbury Union Free School District's Superintendent of Schools was suspended without pay following the Board of Education's preferring disciplinary charges against him. Pickney appealed his suspension without pay to the Commissioner of Education and, in addition, asked the Commissioner to direct his reinstatement to his position.

Although the contract of employment between the parties set out certain procedures providing for the removal of the Superintendent "for insubordination; incompetency; misconduct; or neglect of duty," it was silent with respect to the suspension of the Superintendent without pay pending a final determination, after notice and hearing, by the Board of Education.

The Commissioner declined to order the district to reinstate Pickney pending its final determination of the charges filed against him because of "the unsatisfactory relationship that currently exists between the parties." He, however, viewed Pickney's suspension without pay during this period to be a separate issue.

Addressing the question of Pickney's suspension without pay, the Commissioner said that "absent a specific provision in contract authorizing suspension without pay," a board of education must not be permitted to withhold its superintendent's salary prior to a hearing and determination of the charges".

The rationale for the Commissioner's ruling was that "to hold otherwise would, in effect, create a mechanism by which a chief administrative officer may be forced to resign based solely on his or her financial situation, prior to the resolution of the charges."

The only exception to this general rule noted by the Commissioner was that a school superintendent's salary could be discontinued where the superintendent caused an unreasonable delay in the resolution of the matter that is directly attributable solely to his or her actions.

Concluding that under the terms of the employment contract the Superintendent could not be suspended without pay until "due process was satisfied," the Commissioner ruled that the Board of Education "acted improperly" when it suspended Pickney without pay.

---

[36] A close reading of Section 3020-a raises the possibility that the employer may have more leeway than the Derle decision indicates. The law does not specifically authorize a school district or BOCES to suspend a tenured employee without pay pending a disciplinary hearing. But it does state, "If the employee is acquitted he shall be restored to his position with full pay for any period of suspension and the charges expunged from his record." (Section 3020-a [4]) Why would the legislature include this language if it did not contemplate the possibility of suspension without pay?

The board was directed to restore Pickney to the payroll, retroactive to the date on which he was removed, and to continue him on the payroll until the completion of a due process hearing and the Board's issuance of its determination.

8.08 Unpaid suspension past 30 days: Conflict with local law

If a local law gives an employer authorization to suspend an employee having rights under Section 75 for more than 30 days, the local law must be viewed as invalid, a state Supreme Court justice has ruled. While municipal governments may collectively bargain themselves out of certain demands of state law, they do not have carte blanche to unilaterally enact a local law or charter provision that is completely at variance with existing state law. The legislature authorized only one way to circumvent Section 75's proscription against unpaid suspensions for more than 30 days, namely "by agreements negotiated between the State and an employee organization." [Meringolo v Jacobson, NYS Supreme Court, July 7, 1997]

8.09 Suspension without pay, medical

If a teacher refuses to report for a medical exam, can the school district remove her from the payroll? Yes, but only until the teacher reports for the exam, according to the Commissioner of Education. [Decisions of the Commissioner of Education 13005]

If a teacher repeatedly fails to appear for a medical examination ordered in accordance with Section 913 of the Education Law, the school district cannot suspend her without pay unless it goes through the due process of a disciplinary proceeding. Without disciplinary charges being filed and due process, the teacher cannot be deemed suspended within the meaning of Section 3020-a but must, instead, be considered an employee on involuntary sick leave pursuant to Section 913. [Decisions of the Commissioner of Education 13005]

8.10 Suspension without pay

A decision in the Small Claims Part of the New York City Civil Court provides a number of insights into disciplinary suspensions without pay. [Sanders v NYC Transit Authority 130 Misc2d 719]

Sanders had been charged with misconduct and suspended without pay. He had the option of proceeding pursuant to Section 75 of the Civil Service Law or invoking the contract disciplinary procedure. As it turned out, he did both.

Initially he filed a contract grievance. At Step 4 he elected to exercise his right to a departmental hearing and appeal as provided by Sections 75 and 76 rather than proceed to disciplinary arbitration.

After being suspended without pay for 56 days, Sanders was restored to the payroll, only to again be suspended without pay when his request for an adjournment of his departmental hearing was granted.

Sanders then sued to recover 26 days of salary, which represented payment for the period during which he was suspended without pay in excess of 30 days through the date of his request for the adjournment.

The Authority objected, claiming that the 30-day limitation on suspensions without pay set by Section 75 had been modified by the collective bargaining agreement and that it was permitted to suspend employees who invoked the contract disciplinary procedure without regard to that limitation.

The court ruled:

1. Even if an employee is found guilty of charges and is terminated, the employee would be entitled to payment for any period of suspension in excess of that permitted by statute or by the collective bargaining agreement.

2. Any postponement of the disciplinary action at the request of the employee, however, which was in excess of the limitation would not be considered in determining the amount of any back salary due the employee.

3. As Sanders was suspended without pay for more than 30 days, he should be paid for the period in excess of 30 days up to the date he requested the adjournment. This amounted to 26 days of back salary.

The judge rejected the Authority's argument that by initially electing the contract disciplinary procedure, the Section 75 limitation with respect to suspension did not apply.

8.11 Effect of criminal actions on suspensions

If criminal charges are involved, a prosecutor may request that no administrative action be taken while criminal charges are pending. Such a request is not sufficient to overcome the mandates of Section 75, including limitations on suspension without pay, the Appellate Division has ruled. [Levine v New York City Transit Authority, 70 AD2d 900]

Consider this scenario: After disciplinary charges are served, the individual is arrested and jailed. The individual's ability to build a defense is compromised. He or she might be unable to attend the scheduled disciplinary hearing. Even if the individual is released on bail, it is likely that prosecutors would pressure the employer not to proceed for fear of compromising the criminal case. Is the employer forced by such circumstances to return the employee to the payroll after 30 days?

The answer is: not necessarily. The employer has the option of withdrawing the charges pending resolution of the criminal case. [This can also save the employer considerable effort in proving its case, because a guilty verdict in a criminal court automatically serves to establish guilt in a disciplinary forum. See "Impact of criminal action on disciplinary action, generally", below, and Chapter 3, Evidence.]

After withdrawing disciplinary charges, the employer can require the employee to use up all his or her vacation, personal leave and other leave (other than sick leave, unless he or she is sick) while he is in jail, then suspend the employee without pay because he is absent without the employer's authorization and has exhausted his available leave credits. See "Suspension without pay for unauthorized absence," above.

8.12 Mitigation of damages

Courts have ruled that there is no duty on the part of the teacher to "mitigate" the salary being paid by a school district during this period and the district may not withhold compensation because the teacher refuses to seek other employment during the period of suspension.

However, if the district provides the teacher with an assignment, including a non-teaching assignment, "which bears a reasonable relationship to the teacher's competence and training and is consistent with the dignity of the profession," and the teacher refuses to accept the assignment, the district may lawfully suspend payment of compensation for any period of such refusal.[37]

8.13 Taxation of a settlement

If a disciplinary action is "settled," is any monetary portion of the settlement subject to federal or State income tax?

According to one court, a monetary award flowing from the settlement of a disciplinary action may constitute "salary or wages" and therefore may be subject to payroll withholdings for Federal and State personal income tax and other payroll deductions. (Fay v Butcher, 547 NYS2d 464).

8.14 Recoupment of cash advances

In Duffy v Poughkeepsie City School District, _ AD2d _, the court was asked to consider a somewhat rare situation: the recapture of alleged overpayments of cash advances made to an employee.

The Appellate Division decided such overpayments could be recouped by reducing the amounts due to him as compensation while he was suspended with pay following the initiation of disciplinary action under [old law] Section 3020-a. The Appellate Division held that there appeared to be no legal impediment to the district applying Section 77-b of the General Municipal Law to recoup unreimbursed expense funds received by Duffy.

---

[37] Before being revised in 1984, Section 75.3 provided that employee acquitted of disciplinary charges be "restored to his position with full pay less the amount of compensation which he may have earned in any other employment" and any unemployment insurance benefits. But in 1984 Section 75.3 was amended by Chapter 710 and no longer authorizes such an adjustment based on compensation received because of "other employment". Section 75.3 now provides that an employee who is acquitted of disciplinary charges is to be reinstated "with full pay ... less the amount of any unemployment insurance benefits he [or she] may have received during such period." So, Section 75.3 mandates would dictate that an acquitted employee be paid his or her full back-salary for the 30 days he was suspended, less any unemployment insurance received.

The Appellate Division rejected Duffy's claim that the district had violated the terms of his contract by withholding his salary. It said that the district had not "suspended" his salary, pointing out that the district had continued Duffy's health insurance contributions without interruption.

8.15 Bad faith

A teacher's suspension without pay pending disciplinary hearing may not be converted to one without pay without a showing of obstructive conduct or bad faith on the part of the teacher. [Janke v Community School Board, 587 NYS2d 733].

The case involved a New York City tenured teacher who was placed on leave with pay pending a hearing on disciplinary charges. Later it was decided that the disciplinary action should be discontinued, but the School Board did not take any action that was officially recorded. It merely voted in executive session.

When the teacher refused to resume work, he was put on "unofficial leave without pay."

The Appellate Division ruled that this was improper because the teacher had been improperly suspended without pay while charges pursuant to Section 3020-a were pending against him.

The Appellate Division, noting that there was nothing in the record indicating that the board had voted to withdraw the disciplinary action or denial of the claimed excused absence, directed the payment of back salary from the date when Janke was taken off the payroll until the date he was found unfit for duty.

8.16 Employment contracts

As a general rule, school officials may not suspend a tenured teacher without pay pending the disposition of disciplinary charges unless such a suspension is specifically provided for under an agreement negotiated pursuant to the Taylor Law or authorized by law.
Does the same general rule apply in cases where the educator's employment is pursuant to a contract for a fixed term?

This aspect of the suspension without pay was considered by the Commissioner of Education when a school board attempted to suspend its superintendent without pay immediately upon its voting to file charges against him [Decisions of the Commissioner of Education, 12873].

The board took this action during the first month of a new four-year employment contract with its superintendent.

The commissioner reviewed the employment contract between the district and the superintendent and said that he found no authority in the agreement for the district to withhold the payment of the superintendent's salary during any period of suspension. He directed that the superintendent be paid pending the resolution of the disciplinary charges during any period of his suspension from duty at the direction of the board.

This ruling suggests that had the contract between the district and the superintendent included a clause that provided for withholding compensation during any period of suspension pending the resolution of disciplinary charges filed by the board, the commissioner would have deemed such a provision sufficient authority to allow the district to direct the suspension of the superintendent without pay.

8.17 Suspension with pay, pending criminal action

Allegations of sexual misconduct involving students by an employee frequently results in summary action by a school district.

The Raphael decision, [Raphael v Lakeland Central School District, _ AD2d_], indicates that placing an individual on leave with pay pending the resolution of such allegations may be an acceptable course of action in such situations.[38]

Raphael, a school bus driver, a position in the classified service, with the Lakeland Central School District, was arrested and charged with sexual abuse based on a complaint by an 11-year-old special education student. Lakeland suspended him with pay. Raphael was subsequently acquitted of the charges.

Raphael then sued Lakeland, contending that the district "knew, or should have known, that [the boy] was a special education student with severe psychological problems and sexual vexations" and that it should have advised him of "prior problems." He also claimed that the district was required to have held a hearing prior to its suspending him for his position.

The Appellate Division upheld a lower court ruling dismissing Raphael's complaint.

The court said that there was no allegation that Lakeland was in any way responsible for the false accusation made against him nor was there any allegation that any law or Taylor Law contract provision required Raphael to be given a hearing before the district suspended him from his job with pay.

If, on the other hand, a tenured employee is suspended from his or her position without pay under such circumstances, due process typically requires that the employee be provided with a disciplinary hearing.

---

[38] Section 3020-2.2(b), which applies to educators, who hold positions in the unclassified service, in pertinent part, provides "... suspension shall be with pay, except the employee may be suspended without pay if the employee has entered a guilty plea to or has been convicted of a felony crime ... involving the physical or sexual abuse of a minor or student." Section 3020-a does not apply to individuals such as Raphael who are employed in the classified service of the employer.

8.18 Reassignment pending discipline

In the Matter of Isidore Adlerstein and In the Matter of Jac Radoff, the state Court of Appeals considered the question of a teacher's refusal to accept a different assignment while suspended with pay following the filing of disciplinary charges pursuant to Section 3020-a [old law].

The "different assignment" involved performing administrative duties during the pendency of the charges. In both cases the teacher's refusal to accept the reassignment was held to constitute insubordination warranting dismissal.

When Alderstein, a tenured art teacher for 20 years, failed to perform assigned administrative duties following the filing of charges he was suspended without pay. Found guilty of 5 of 13 specifications, he was restored to classroom teaching but in a different school.

He refused to accept the new teaching assignment and was continued on suspension without pay.

Radoff was a social studies teacher with some 18 years of service. He, also, was assigned administrative duties during the pendency of disciplinary charges filed against him. When he failed to report as assigned, a second set of disciplinary charges were filed against him.

The common issue before the Court of Appeals in these cases was whether a teacher against whom charges have been filed could be required to perform non-teaching assignments.

The teachers argued that although they must be paid if suspended pending resolution of the disciplinary charges filed against them, they could not be assigned to do other work because such an assignment would (1) be inconsistent with their suspension; (2) such an assignment was penal in nature; and (3) a teacher may not be required to work outside his or her tenure area.

The Court of Appeals rejected all of these arguments and ruled that non-teaching assignments which bear a reasonable relationship to the suspended teacher's competence and training and which is consistent with the dignity of the profession is permissible.
The court also rejected Adlerstein's claim for back salary for the period of his suspension during which he refused to either perform administrative duties or failed to report to another school following the disciplinary action.

Although suspension without pay following the filing of charges was not authorized by either law or a negotiated agreement, in this instance it was permitted because the teacher had refused to perform what the court considered a lawful assignment.

8.19 Suspension without pay failure to report to work

Sometimes the employee upon whom charges have been preferred cannot report to work because of some intervening force such as incarceration following his or her arrest.

In such cases, the employee may be permitted to use appropriate leave credits or be placed on leave without pay until he or she is able to report for duty. Here the employee is unavailable for work through, presumably, no fault of the employer.

Unless released on bail, or the charges are dropped and the employee is able to return to work, he or she may not claim any right to continuation on the payroll unless the appointing authority agrees to permit the individual to charge the absence to appropriate leave accruals.

8.20 Repayment of salary after being continued on the payroll

In Rensselaer County v Hudson Valley Community College Faculty Association, Appellate Division, Third Dept., 6/17/99, the Appellate Division decided an arbitrator had the power to require a faculty member to repay the college for the salary it had paid to him while an appeal of his dismissal was pending arbitration.

The arbitrator had ordered the college to provide salary during this period, but reserved the right to direct that the salary be repaid if she later determined that the dismissal was warranted.

Initially the arbitrator ruled that the college had violated the collective bargaining agreement by failing to keep Neuhaus on the payroll during the pendency of the termination grievance. Accordingly, the college restored Neuhaus to the payroll retroactive to September 1, 1996.

Subsequently the grievance went to arbitration and in August 1997 the arbitrator rendered her award, concluding that Neuhaus was guilty of the charges and that the penalty of termination was appropriate.

The arbitrator then ruled that Neuhaus was not entitled to salary beyond August 21, 1996 and that Neuhaus should reimburse the college for salary paid to him after that date.

The college subsequently asked a State Supreme Court judge to confirm the arbitration award. Ultimately the Appellate Division ruled that the provision in the termination grievance award requiring Neuhaus to repay the salary the college had paid to him since September 1, 1996 "did not contradict" the salary grievance award.

The court concluded that the salary grievance dealt exclusively with the issue of Neuhaus' right to receive his salary pending the resolution of the termination grievance.

The court commented that in the salary grievance the arbitrator had ordered the college "to continue such payments until the matter is resolved by the issuance of an arbitration decision dealing with the merits of the dismissal, which decision shall then be controlling." Accordingly, said the court, there was nothing to bar the arbitrator from directing Neuhaus to repay the salary he had received from the college since September 1, 1996.

However, there may be limitations with respect to the period during which a person against whom disciplinary charges have been filed may be suspended from his or her position without pay. An example of this is the statutory limitation set out in Section 75 of the Civil Service Law. Section 75 allows an individual against whom disciplinary charges have been filed to be suspended without pay for up to 30 days. The employee must be restored to the payroll after 30 days, even if he or she is directed not to report to work while the disciplinary action is pending.

In some cases a contract provision may allow the employer to suspend an individual without pay pending the determination of the disciplinary action. Such a provision is usually subjected to "narrow interpretation" by the courts. An illustration of such a narrow construction is set out in Board of Education v Nyquist (48 NY2 97). In this case the Court of Appeals noted that the Taylor Law agreement negotiated by the parties allowed a teacher to be suspended without pay "pending an investigation and recommendation by the superintendent of schools."

The board filed disciplinary charges against a suspended teacher after it had received the Superintendent's recommendation. The teacher's "suspended without pay" status was continued by the board. Some 10 months later a hearing panel found the teacher guilty of the charges. The penalty imposed: termination.

As a result of the litigation that followed, the district was directed to pay the teacher back salary for the period from the date of the superintendent's recommendation to the board until the effective date of the dismissal. The Court of Appeals reasoned that "there (was) no authorization [in the contract] for the board's suspending the employee without pay after the superintendent completed his investigation and made his report".

Had the contract permitted the board to continue the teacher's suspension without pay pending a final disciplinary decision, it appears likely that such a suspension would have been upheld by the court. The only limitation on the duration of a suspension without pay when authorized by a Taylor Law agreement appears to be that the employer may not use the suspension without pay as a sword by delaying the proceedings.

CHAPTER 9

PENDING CRIMINAL ACTIONS

An individual may be subject to administrative disciplinary action and criminal action based on the same events.

9.01 Simultaneous prosecution

May administrative disciplinary action be prosecuted at the same time that a criminal action based on the same facts and allegations is pending? Yes. See, for example, the decisions of the court in Nosik v Singe, CA2, 94-7678 (unnecessary to delay administrative disciplinary action in a case of a school psychologist accused of defrauding insurance companies) and Matter of the Haverstraw-Stony Point CSD, 24 Ed. Dept. Rep. 466, (no requirement to adjourn a Section 3020-a hearing when parallel criminal proceedings are underway).

9.02 Acquittal of criminal charges does not bar disciplinary action

An acquittal of criminal charges will not bar an employer from taking administrative disciplinary action against the employee based on the same facts and incident. "[T]he dismissal of the criminal charges brought against [an employee], which were predicated upon the same acts which were the subject of the disciplinary proceeding commenced against him, has no bearing upon the determination terminating his employment." [Bermudez v NYC Transit Authority, _ AD2d _]

The reason is that standard of proof applied in a criminal action is higher than in an administrative hearing: proof beyond a reasonable doubt in the former; substantial or, in some instances, a preponderance of the evidence, in the latter. [See Chapter 3]

This point of law seems clear-cut. But an assiduous legal researcher can often find a case that contradicts even well established judicial precedent. Such is the case with the Arbitration of William Lozano, in which a federal mediator found that a disciplinary proceeding was invalid because a criminal proceeding had taken place, and the disciplinary action therefore placed Lozano in "double jeopardy."[39]

William Lozano, a Miami, Florida, police officer, fatally shot a motorcyclist while on duty. He was acquitted of criminal charges of manslaughter. But he was found guilty in a disciplinary hearing of charges based on the same incident, and Lozano was terminated from his position.

Federal arbitrator Roger I. Abrams ruled that Miami's firing of Lozano under the circumstances was improper. Abrams decided that the city's action constituted "double jeopardy" because a jury in a

---

[39] The underlying concept of common law and constitutional prohibitions against double jeopardy is that no individual shall be subjected to trial twice for the same criminal offense, i.e., he or she is not to be placed in jeopardy of being convicted for the same alleged crime twice.

criminal proceeding acquitted Lozano based on the same allegations. Abrams also said that Miami improperly added new administrative charges after Lozano was found not guilty of criminal conduct. The arbitrator also awarded Lozano almost $1 million in back pay and legal expenses.

In the opinion of the authors, at least part of the arbitrator's rationale is flawed. While it is possible that new administrative charges were improperly added, the assertion that the administrative proceeding constituted double jeopardy is a difficult one to accept, given that the standard of proof is different in an administrative hearing and the many New York court rulings holding that such administrative procedures do not constitute double jeopardy.

Extending Arbitrator Abrams' rationale to its logical conclusion, if the criminal prosecution followed the administrative disciplinary action, regardless of its outcome, could not the accused contend he or she was immune from criminal prosecution for the same acts or omissions by claiming the criminal prosecution would constitute double jeopardy?

9.03 Criminal conviction bars administrative acquittal of the same charge

If an individual is convicted of a criminal charge, he or she is automatically guilty of the same charge brought in an administrative proceeding. New York courts have held that a criminal conviction is res judicata [a decided matter] with respect to guilt in any administrative disciplinary action taken against an individual based on the same event or misconduct.

In such cases administrative tribunals do not have the option of determining that the accused individual is "innocent" of the charges. Its only leeway available to the administrative tribunal is in recommending or imposing a penalty.

Criminal guilt necessitates administrative guilt, if facts and charges are identical. Again, the key is to understand that the standard of proof is greater in a criminal proceeding. If one is found guilty beyond a reasonable doubt, it follows that one is also guilty when measured by the less rigorous standard of substantial evidence or even less demanding "preponderance of the evidence" standard.

The Kelly case demonstrates this. Kelly, a school business administrator, was charged with larcenies of school funds and bringing discredit upon the school district. An [old law] Section 3020-a hearing panel found Kelly guilty of the charge of bringing discredit upon the district, but not guilty of the larceny charges. Kelly, however, had been convicted of two counts of grand larceny for theft of school property prior to being charged under Section 3020-a [People v Kelly, 72 AD2d 670].

The court ruled that the fact that the administrator had committed two larcenies of school property was conclusively established under the doctrine of collateral estoppel. The court reversed the finding of not guilty for the panel's reconsideration of the appropriate penalty to be imposed [Kelly v Levin, 440 NYS2d 424]. As the hearing panel's decision was based on a finding of guilt of "bringing discredit" charge only, the matter was remitted for a new penalty to be assigned.

Another aspect of collateral estoppel was considered in the Jaworowski case [Jaworowski v NYC Transit Authority, 2nd Circuit, July 1999]. The ruling sets out the elements considered by courts when determining whether the doctrine applies in a particular situation with respect to whether or not the identical issue was decided in a previous proceeding or whether there was an opportunity for such issues to be considered.

Leonard Jaworowski was terminated from his position with the New York Transit Authority following a disciplinary arbitration. He brought an Article 75 action in State Supreme Court in an effort to have the arbitration award vacated. Unsuccessful in this effort, Jaworowski next filed a lawsuit in federal district court pursuant to 42 USC Section 1983 alleging "various constitutional infirmities in an arbitration proceeding arising out of disciplinary charges brought against him by the Authority."

The Authority claimed Jaworowski's federal action was barred under the doctrine of collateral estoppel because he already had "his day in court" on these issues as a result his bringing an Article 75 action. The district court agreed, ruling that Jaworowski was estopped from suing on these claims because they had been previously litigated in his Article 75 action brought in New York state court. The Circuit Court of Appeals affirmed the lower court's ruling.

The Circuit Court of Appeals said that Jaworowski "mistakenly conflates two different grounds for setting aside an arbitration under New York law." Although one ground for vacating an arbitration decision is to show that the award is "totally irrational," a court applying New York law will also vacate an arbitration if it finds that the arbitration violated due process, citing Beckman v Greentree Securities, Inc., 87 NY2d 566.

The Circuit Court said that the district court correctly dismissed his 42 USC 1983 action because New York State courts do not review constitutional challenges to arbitration decisions more deferentially than do federal courts.

Although might seem desirable for an administrator to voluntarily delay disciplinary action until a criminal proceeding is complete, because criminal conviction automatically triggers disciplinary guilt, in most situations the employer will be required to keep the employee on the payroll, with or without work assigned, until the disciplinary finding is issued. For this reason, employers usually do not wait for a criminal trial to conclude before proceeding with administrative disciplinary process.

9.04 Use of disclosures in criminal trials

If a public employee is ordered to answer questions about his or her official acts under threat of removal if he or she refuses to do so, the responses automatically are cloaked with immunity and cannot be used in a subsequent criminal prosecution.[40]
Neither the compelled statements nor any evidence derived directly or indirectly from them may be used against the employee in a subsequent criminal prosecution, the Court of Appeals ruled in

---

[40] In People v Corrigan, 80 NY2d 326, the court pointed out that under both state and federal law, any statement made under the threat of dismissal is protected by the privilege against self-incrimination and is "automatically immunized from use in criminal proceedings."

Corrigan [People v Corrigan, 80 NY2d 326]. The U.S. Supreme Court held similarly in Lefkowitz v Turley, 414 U.S. 70.

If the employee lies, the immunity dissolves. It is well settled law that one who is granted immunity in return for his testimony receives no license to swear falsely with impunity under the protection of that immunity. [United States v Apfelbaum, 445 U.S. 115]

If an employer informs the employee that none of his or her answers will be used in criminal prosecution, and the employee refuses to answer, the employee can be dismissed without violating the individual's rights under the U.S. Constitution according to the U.S. Supreme Court's ruling in Garner v Broderick, 392 U.S. 273. To trigger this result, however, the questions must specifically, directly and narrowly related to the performance of the employees official duties.

What if a prosecutor attempts makes use of the statements despite the promise of the employer? Persons who feel shielded information is being improperly used by prosecutors may request a Kastigar hearing[41] to determine whether the prosecution made any use of either a compelled, immunized statement or any evidence derived directly or indirectly from such a statement

An employer may require an employee to provide certain kinds of routine information about the conduct of their official duties without violating his or her Constitutional right against self-incrimination, just as it is Constitutional for "hit and run" statutes requiring a driver involved in an accident to stop at the scene and provide a name and address.

For instance written statements in "use of force" by police officers may fall into that category, according to a New York Supreme Court decision involving New York City correction officers.[42]

Each of the five officers filed affidavits asserting that he was ordered by a superior officer, under threat of job forfeiture, to submit a written "Use of Force Report." Each claimed that at the time the report was submitted he believed that neither the statement nor any information or evidence derived therefrom could be used in a subsequent criminal investigation.

Deciding that a "Use of Force Report" clearly relates to the regulation of lawful activity and is not designed to incriminate, the court concluded that the Department's regulation had only an incidental effect in implicating the five officers with respect the alleged "use of force."

9.05 Probationers and criminal charges

"[A]s a general principle, a probationary employee is not entitled to a pre-termination hearing and may be dismissed without any statement of reasons" for the termination, as long as the dismissal is in good faith and not motivated by unlawful considerations such as discrimination, the Appellate Division ruled in Holmes v Sielaff, _ AD2d _.

---

[41] Kastigar v United States, 406 U.S. 441.

[42] Seabrook v Johnson, Supreme Court, May 1997.

Holmes, a probationary correction officer with the New York City Department of Corrections, had a number of criminal charges filed against her. When she was dismissed from her position, she sued. She claimed that her termination was arbitrary, capricious and made in bad faith. N

Notwithstanding the fact that all of the criminal charges filed against her were later dropped, the Appellate Division decided that Holmes had not met her burden of showing that the department had acted in bad faith in firing her.

9.06 Reinstatement after acquittal

A public officer who is convicted of a felony or a crime involving the violation of his or her oath office is automatically removed from his or her office by operation of Section 30.1(e) of the Public Officers Law.

However, Section 30.1(e) also provides that in the event the individual's conviction is reversed or annulled, he or she may seek a hearing before the appointing authority in an effort to be reinstated to his or her former position in the event the conviction was the sole basis for the officer's termination.

9.07 Settlement to avoid prosecution

It is lawful for an employer to seek a voluntary settlement of disciplinary charges with an employee by informing him or her that criminal charges are possible and will be sought if the individual does not agree to a disciplinary settlement. [Howland v Schuyler-Chemung-Tioga BOCES, _AD2d_]. Similarly, it is lawful for the appointing authority to demand the employee resign or face administrative disciplinary action.[43]

9.08 Administrator's immunity

Sometimes an administrator will file civil or criminal charges against an employee that later prove to be unwarranted or are dismissed because of a lack of proof.

The employee may then sue the administrator because of the action he or she took against the worker. However, a public official did not lose his or her qualified immunity from liability for acts performed in the line of duty if those acts are "reasonably based on the language of the statute." [Weg v Macchiarola, et al, 92-7730; 92-7818].

9.09 Collateral estoppel

Sometimes an employee will sue an employer over the same or similar issues that were previously considered in the course of an administrative or some other legal proceeding. Usually the employer will try to have the action dismissed, claiming collateral estoppel, a legal doctrine that holds that a

---

[43] Rychlick v Coughlin, 63 NY2d 643

party may not attempt to relitigate matters previously decided by bringing the complaint to a different tribunal.

The doctrine is applicable in a civil action to prevent the relitigation of matters determined in a prior criminal action, the court said that the doctrine may be applied where:

1. issues determined in the criminal prosecution were the same as those involved in the pending civil action; and

2. the party against whom the doctrine is to be applied had a "full and fair opportunity to litigate those issues in the earlier criminal trial."[44]

9.10 Disclosure of records

Does an individual brought up on disciplinary charges that involve alleged sexual harassment have the right to review the employer's files for exculpatory information? This was one of the issues considered by the Appellate Division in the Connolly case [Connolly v Williams, _ AD2d _].

Connolly, a court officer employed by the Office of Court Administration [OCA], was charged with committing acts of misconduct directed against three female co-workers. One of Connolly's arguments was that he was denied his right to due process because the hearing officer reviewed certain OCA investigatory files in camera (in private) and Connolly could not see these records or respond to them.

The Appellate Division ruled that the hearing officer's in camera review of these files "protected both the integrity of the on-going criminal investigation as well as [Connolly's] need to determine whether the files contained any exculpatory information" concerning the charges filed against him.

In addition, the court noted that "the hearings held in disciplinary proceedings are not governed by the rules obtaining at a criminal trial." Connolly, said the court, did not have an absolute right to the disclosure of the information contained in these files.

---

[44] Duffy v Poughkeepsie CSD, _ Misc 2d _.

CHAPTER 10

PREPARING FOR A HEARING

Unless the employee has waived his or her right to a hearing,[45] it is necessary for both the employer and the employee charged in a disciplinary action to begin to prepare for the hearing as soon as disciplinary charges against an individual have been served.

If the employee has waived his or her right to a hearing and cannot reinstate that right, then the employee in effect has agreed to settle the matter on the basis of the maximum penalty proposed by the employer under Section 75.[46] The same principle would likely apply under discipline procedures negotiated in accordance with the Taylor Law.

10.01 The settlement option

Perhaps the first thing for the employee and the employer to consider is the possibility of "settlement." There is nothing in law or public policy barring the parties from attempting to settle the disciplinary action prior to the hearing date. However, the initiative for such settlement usually comes from the employee charged or his or her representative.

The option to settle does not expire. If the employee has demanded a hearing or grieves the proposed discipline under a collective bargaining agreement, there is always an opportunity to agree to a settlement -- even after an arbitrator has made an award. In the latter case, the option of settlement might be an alternative to an appeal or an action to "confirm the award."

10.02 Selecting a hearing officer

Section 75.2 of the Civil Service Law permits an appointing authority to designate "a deputy or other person ... in writing" to conduct a disciplinary hearing for the purpose of making findings of fact and recommendations concerning the disposition of the charges filed against the employee and the penalty, if any, to be imposed.

The importance of naming a hearing officer in writing is shown in the Appellate Division's January 1998 decision in Perez v NYS Dept. of Labor, 665 NYS2d 714. Citing the Court of Appeals ruling in Wiggins v Board of Education, 60 NY2d 385, the Appellate Division said that because there was no written designation appointing the hearing officer, the appointing authority "lacked jurisdiction" to maintain the initial disciplinary proceeding" against Perez. Accordingly, the Appellate Division

---

[45] In the case of a disciplinary action initiated pursuant to Section 3020-a of the Education Law the reverse is true. The party charged must request that a disciplinary hearing be held within ten days of being served charges.

[46] An educator served with disciplinary charges pursuant to Section 3020-a must be advised of (1) the maximum penalty which will be imposed by the board if the employee does not request a hearing and (2) the penalty that the board will seek if the educator is found guilty of the charges after a hearing.

"voided" the appointing authority's determination finding Perez guilty of the charges and the penalty imposed.

The court ordered the appointing authority to reinstate Perez to his former position with back salary and benefits. The court said that since the initial disciplinary action was nullified because of a procedural error, there was no basis to return the case to the employer for a de novo determination.

Other cases in which the formal designation of the hearing officer constituted a critical element include: Pieczonka v Village of Blasdell, App. Div., Fourth Dept, June 16, 2000 [the hearing officer had not been so designated in writing]; Wiggins v Board of Education, 60 NY2d 385 [in the absence of a written delegation authorizing a deputy or other person to conduct the hearing, the removing board or officer has no jurisdiction to discipline an employee]; and Stein v Rockland Co., App Div, 2nd Dept, No. 97-09903/5, 3/8/99, ["lack of a proper, written designation of the hearing officer" as required by Civil Service Law Section 75(2)].

The employee may challenge designation of a hearing officer if the employee believes that the hearing officer is prejudiced in any way that would affect the fairness of the hearing. However, this is a heavy burden to prove. Merely claiming that the hearing officer would be unfair is not sufficient as the ruling in Hughes v Suffolk County Civil Service Department, 546 NYS2d 335, demonstrates.

The Court of Appeals has said that in order to establish arbitrator or hearing officer had bias as a matter of fact, there must be support in the record supporting the claim or the bias and proof that the outcome of the administrative proceeding flowed from the bias.

To support allegations of bias, courts tend to look for actions by the hearing officer that raise questions about impartiality. In AAID Transmissions, Inc. v Adduci, _ Misc2d _, a state Supreme Court justice found a allegations of bias were unproven but sufficient to vacate a hearing officer's decision because the hearing officer had amended the charges at the request of the employer. The court said the hearing officer had acted both as prosecutor and as judge.

Additional material concerning this subject may be found below in Chapters dealing with "Challenging a Section 75 decision," "Challenging an arbitration decision," and "Biased Hearing Officers."

10.03 Pre-hearing legwork

Although the basic facts underlying the charges presumably were in hand at the time charges were formally filed against the employee, it is still necessary for employers to make certain they have proof to use to sustain the charges. Likewise, employees should not take a passive role in their defense.

To this end both the employer and the employee should determine the witnesses to be used as well as the testimony that they can be expected to give in connection with specific charges and specifications.

Employers should keep in mind that although charges have been filed, there is no reason to stop any investigation or efforts to find additional witnesses or evidence. Likewise, it should also be kept in mind that the employee against whom charges have been filed may, indeed, be innocent and the victim of an effort to conceal the identity of the true wrongdoer. It is as important to make certain that the correct person has been charged as it is to prove the charges.

In addition, both the employer and the employee should review the expected testimony of their respective witnesses and all written records should be checked for inconsistencies. Any inconsistency must be resolved. If nothing else, the existence of an inconsistency demonstrates a possible weakness in the proof to be relied upon at the hearing. At times an attempt to resolve a minor inconsistency in a "story" reveals a larger inconsistency. This is something that is best considered before the hearing, rather than at it.

Common inconsistencies involve dates, times and places. Some can be attributed to misstatements or lapses in memory. Others, unfortunately, result from deliberate fabrications. Whether the fabrication is to make the witness feel more important, to conceal the guilt of the true wrongdoer or is part of a personal "vendetta" is of little importance except as it may serve as the foundation for new charges against the fabricator.

If it is discovered that the only real evidence against the employee charged is based on such fabrications the charges should be withdrawn. Efforts should be made to corroborate evidence, especially testimony evidence.

Another caution: Witnesses who are most definite in their statements during an investigatory interview sometimes become less certain with respect to their recollection when asked to sign a sworn statement as to the truth of the facts in their statement. For this reason, it would be wise for the statements taken in the course of an investigation to be reduced to writing and signed, under oath, by the individual making the statement.

All employer records and other records or physical evidence to be used at the hearing should be obtained, cataloged and numbered for introduction in sequence at the hearing. Likewise, the accused should do the same for records and evidence her or she plans to present in defending himself or herself against the charges. It is desirable to submit only original documents to the hearing officer. However, material introduced will become part of the record and may not be returned to the custodian for some time. For this reason, one may wish not to present original documents during the hearing but provide "certified" or "verified" copies for inclusion of the record. Extra copies should be made because in all probability the opposing side will ask for copies at the time they are introduced as exhibits or placed in evidence.

Time schedules for witnesses must be coordinated with the hearing date by the parties. It could be embarrassing, to say the least, to discover that a key witness left for an extended vacation and is not available on the designated hearing date.

It may be helpful for employers to mentally "try the case" from the accused's perspective. "How would I defend the employee if I had to?" often leads to thoughts which may demonstrate a weakness in the charging party's case or evidence. By the same token, the employee or his representative should be thinking through what might be the strongest arguments that could be used against him or her and try to anticipate the proof or evidence that might be used in an effort to mount an effective defense. No case is ever so "open and shut" as to justify complaisance.

As the charging party is required to bear the burden of proof, it should be prepared to critically evaluate its case. If it is suspect, it might be better to abandon the disciplinary action. A weak case will probably result in a dismissal of the charges. Bringing charges to "make an example" of the employee is rarely rewarding.

10.04 A pre-hearing checklist

The following is a list of some of the items that should be considered in preparing for a disciplinary hearing before an arbitrator. Although framed in terms of an arbitration, the same considerations are relevant with respect to hearings conducted pursuant to a statutory disciplinary action or, indeed, any similar procedure, regardless of the authority underlying the process.

1. Study the original statement of the complaint(s) against the employee (the charges and specifications) and review the history of the discipline grievance at every stage of the process leading to hearing or arbitration.

2. Determine the nature of the proof required to convince the arbitrator or the hearing officer of the correctness of your position. In addition to having the burden of proof, the charging party initially has the burden of persuasion as well.

3. Review the collective bargaining agreement to make certain that all procedural steps, especially those involving timely notice, have been complied with. If there are issues concerning any interpretation of the contract, determine if the disciplinary arbitrator has the authority to make the decision regarding such interpretation. In some contracts the disciplinary arbitrator has been given the power to make such determinations while under other agreements such questions must be resolved under a different process, usually called the "contract grievance" procedure.

4. Assemble all of the necessary evidence (records, documents, etc.) and identify the witnesses to be used and the testimony that each is expected to give. If the other party's witnesses are known, try to anticipate the testimony they will give and attempt to be prepared to rebut it.

5. If a subpoena is required to obtain documents or the presence of a witness, make certain that it has been properly obtained and served.[47]

6. It is not improper to interview your witnesses to determine the nature of their testimony. NO ATTEMPT should be made to "put words into the mouth of a witness." The only advice that should be given to a witness is "answer the question which is asked of you" and "always tell the truth."

---

[47] The State is only required to respond to a judicial subpoena for its records. A subpoena for records and documents is called a subpoena duces tecum, which roughly translated means "produce the papers." An attorney's subpoena ducas ticum will not suffice for this purpose if the State department or agency declines to provide such materials. The Civil Practice Law and Rules, Section 2308 (b), provides that a judicial subpoena is required to obtain "state papers."

7. Make an outline of what you propose to prove to the arbitrator and a checklist of the items or witnesses that you will rely upon to do this. Then make sure that you do not overlook any of these elements at the arbitration. However, you should guard against being so controlled by this outline that you overlook an unexpected opportunity that arises at the hearing or the arbitration that might be helpful.

8. Witnesses may, and probably should be, sequestered [separated] from the hearing room. In one case, the court found that excluding witnesses other than the accused from the hearing until it was their turn to testify was clearly a proper procedure.

9. Discuss the case with persons having an interest, but who may not be directly involved, in the prosecution of the case. Often a different perspective will be helpful in identifying potential trouble with your presentation.

10. Attempt to develop your opponent's case and arguments and prepare the rebuttal you would make if actually faced with those arguments.

11. Don't "over-try" your case. Make each point as simply and quickly as possible and then move on.

12. It is always risky, and sometimes dangerous, to ask a witness a question to which you do not already know the answer. On more than one occasion, the asking of such a question was sufficient to grasp defeat from the jaws of victory.

13. Never conceal essential facts, even if those facts may be helpful to the other party.

14. While procedural correctness is desired, do not confound the arbitrator with "technicalities." Equally undesirable is attempting to impress the arbitrator by an unnecessarily complex argument or analysis of the facts.

15. Always treat everyone with courtesy and respect. Maintaining proper decorum during the procedure is the arbitrator's responsibility but a party's representative has an obligation to assist by avoiding "personal attacks" on an opponent or a witness. Arguments are to be addressed to the arbitrator or the hearing panel, not to your opponent.

16. Once a hearing is closed, the case generally is over. Sometimes "newly discovered evidence" makes it possible to have the hearing reopened. Such requests should be made to the arbitrator. A stipulation by the parties to reopen the proceeding usually will be honored; a unilateral request may not.

17. To eliminate any possible suspicion that one side may have offered arguments or evidence to the arbitrator without the other party having had an opportunity to offer a rebuttal, all contacts between a parties and a Section 75 hearing officer or an arbitrator should be in the presence of all the parties or be in writing with copies sent to the parties. This procedure should be observed at all times and no effort made to contact the arbitrator or a party or a hearing officer in any manner that might raise any suspicion of undue influence. Unauthorized contacts, however innocent, may result in the administrative equivalent of a "mistrial".

18. Both parties should be prepared to proceed even if other parties do not appear at the time and place designated for the hearing. If the accused is not present, a hearing "in absentia" can take place. (See below.) If representatives of the employer fail to appear, this may jeopardize its ability to proceed with disciplinary charges against the employee.

10.05 Hearing in absentia

An individual may be tried in absentia (in their absence).

However, a reasonable effort to notify the employee of the charges and of the date and place of the disciplinary hearing before a hearing in absentia can take place.[48] It is also probably advisable for the employer to document the efforts it undertakes in its efforts to notify the employee in such a situation.

The facts of the DelBello case, DelBello v NYC Transit Authority, 542 NYS2d 271, may be instructive. DelBello, an employee of the New York City Transit Authority had moved. The authority was aware of this fact as its notice was returned to it unopened and marked (by the U. S. Postal Service) "Moved-left no address." Despite the fact that the authority was aware that the address in its records could not notify DelBello of the charges and hearing, it did not undertake any further attempts to inform him of the pending disciplinary action.

The Appellate Division, Second Department, citing Mullane v Central Hanover Bank and Trust Co., 339 US 306, said that "mailing the notice to [DelBello's] last known address was not 'notice reasonably calculated, under all the circumstances, to apprise [him] of the pendency of the [disciplinary proceeding] and afford [him] an opportunity to present [his] objections.'"

The court concluded that the Authority acted in an arbitrary and capricious manner when it treated DelBello's failure to receive the notice of the charges and the hearing as "his problem."

Before proceeding to try an individual in absentia, the employer is required to make a reasonable effort to locate the employee and serve the charges before it may comfortably proceed with its holding a disciplinary hearing in absentia.

10.06 Leave to attend hearing

Employees who are subject to discipline usually must miss work to attend their disciplinary hearing. Should the employer allow the employee to appear with or without pay? Or is the employee required to use his or her leave credits? Taylor Law agreements usually dictate how such time off will be treated.

Witnesses other than the accused typically are allowed to appear with pay and without having to charge the absence to appropriate leave accruals.

---

[48] DelBello v NYC Transit Authority, 542 NYS2d 271, address issues concerning holding disciplinary hearings in absentia.

10.07 Mitigation of damages in cases of acquittal

Courts have ruled that there is no duty on the part of the employee to "mitigate" the back salary to be paid to an employee in the event he or she is acquitted of disciplinary charges. Section 75 limits any adjustments to back salary to amounts paid to the individual as unemployment insurance benefits; if "back salary" is awarded, the amount of the award should not be adjusted for earnings he or she may have received or could have received as a result of other employment while suspended or after termination.[49]

However, courts also have ruled that where the employer attempts to provide the individual with an assignment which bears a reasonable relationship to the employees competence and training during the pendency of disciplinary proceedings and the employee refuses to accept the assignment, the employer may lawfully suspend payment of compensation for any period of such refusal. For example, in Matter of Isidore Adlerstein and Matter of Jac Radoff, the Court of Appeals held that a teacher's refusal to accept a reassignment to administrative duties while disciplinary charges were pending constituted insubordination warranting dismissal.

10.08 Taxation of a settlement

If a disciplinary action is "settled," is any monetary portion of the settlement subject to federal or State income tax?

According to one court, a monetary award flowing from the settlement of a disciplinary action could constitute "salary or wages" and therefore may be subject to payroll withholdings for Federal and State personal income tax and other payroll deductions. [Fay v Butcher, 547 NYS2d 464]. Fay indicates that awards of back salary are subject to withholding of state and federal taxes as well as employee contributions to Social Security, health benefits and retirement benefits.

10.09 Independent review of facts

After a hearing officer or panel submits a report and recommendation, it is responsibility of the appointing authority to conduct an independent review of the facts before rendering its decision.

In Ligreci v Honors, 162 AD2d 1010, the Appellate Division found that the appointing authority erred by making a determination in a disciplinary action before he received the transcript of the hearing.

10.10 Considering material in a post-hearing brief submitted by a party

What is the potential impact of the statements of an attorney contained in his or her brief on a disciplinary determination? This was an issue in Sisco v Board of Trustees, App. Div., Second Dept., November 5, 2001.

---

[49] For additional information concerning calculating back pay awards under Section 75, see Footnote 33 above.

The Board of Trustees of the Village of Havestraw dismissed police officer Keith Sisco after finding him guilty of disciplinary charges alleging misconduct filed against him.

Sisco appealed, contending that he had been denied a fair hearing because the Board incorporated portions of the Police Department's post-hearing brief in writing its determination. In effect, claimed Sisco, the inclusion of such statements indicated that the Board had ceded it decision-making powers to the Department.

The Appellate Division rejected Sisco's arguments, in effect indicating that there was nothing improper in the decision maker referring to, or including, statements set out in a post-hearing brief to support its conclusions.

It should be remembered that the purpose of the brief is communicate the salient facts and arguments in support of the party's case that the party wishes the hearing tribunal to consider in making its determination. Accordingly, it should summarize the facts and the law relied upon by the party. Any arguments or claims made in the brief, or the conclusion the party wishes the tribunal to reach, should be supported by such facts in the record.

10.11 Stay of arbitration

Sometimes the employee will attempt to prevent the disciplinary action from going forward by seeking a court order preventing the holding of a statutory disciplinary action or a stay of arbitration. In Grossman v Rockland County, Appellate Division, the employer asked the Court to stay an arbitration challenging a Section 75 disciplinary hearing determination.

What evidence must be presented in order to obtain a stay of arbitration? The Appellate Division, citing In the Matter of the United Liverpool Faculty Association, 46 NY2d 509, said it is necessary to show that the subject matter of the dispute is not clearly and unequivocally within the class of claims the parties agreed to submit to arbitration.

George Grossman was found guilty of the charges following a disciplinary hearing held pursuant to Section 75 of the Civil Service Law. The penalty imposed was dismissal from the service.

Grossman's collective bargaining representative, the Rockland County Sheriff's Deputies Association [RCSDA], filed a contract grievance on his behalf. The union contended that the admission of certain evidence at the Section 75 disciplinary hearing constituted a breach of terms contained in the collective bargaining agreement concerning "personnel files."

When RCSDA attempted to arbitrate the question, Rockland County obtained a court order staying the arbitration from a New York State Supreme Court justice. The Appellate Division affirmed Justice Stolarik's ruling.

The Appellate Division first said that the collective bargaining agreement generally provided that the contract grievance procedure applied to "any alleged violation of this Agreement." It then noted that certain matters had been specifically excluded from the grievance procedure. The question to be resolved was whether the issue presented for arbitration involved a matter that had been excluded from the grievance procedure. The Court concluded that it had.

The Court found the key to resolving the problem in the collective bargaining agreement itself. The Appellate Division said the contract specifically excluded matters "reviewable under administrative procedures established by law or pursuant to rules having the force and effect of law" from the contract grievance procedure.

The Court ruled that under the facts here, the contract grievance procedure was not available to Grossman.

Grossman's complaint arose in connection with a Section 75 proceeding, and Section 75 determinations are reviewable by the civil service commission [or personnel officer] having jurisdiction, or by the courts pursuant to an Article 78 action, pursuant to Section 76, Civil Service Law.

Any challenge to the admission of evidence in a Section 75 hearing could be considered by either the appropriate civil service commission or personnel officer or by the courts, depending on the appeal procedure selected by Grossman.

CHAPTER 11

APPEALS

Appeals from disciplinary determinations are available regardless of the disciplinary procedure followed. The grounds for appeal vary depending on the controlling statute or contract.

11.01 Who may appeal?

In cases involving arbitration (such as Section 3020-a hearings and arbitrations authorized by Taylor Law agreements) either party may seek to vacate or modify the award pursuant to Section 7511 of the Civil Practice Law and Rules, usually referred to as an Article 75 appeal.

Section 7511 controls with respect to efforts seeking to vacate or modifying an arbitration award resulting from a Taylor Law contract disciplinary procedure held in lieu of Section 75 of the Civil Service Law. An application to vacate or modify such an award may be made by a party within ninety days after its delivery to him.

In contrast, an appeal seeking to vacate or modify an arbitration award issued by an arbitrator or hearing panel pursuant to a Section 3020-a disciplinary proceeding must be filed by the party seeking to vacate or modify the award within ten days of the delivery of the award.[50]

Under Section 75 it is only the employee who has any appeal rights regarding the original administrative decision. This is understandable because the employer -- or, to be more precise, the "appointing authority" -- makes the final administrative determination, and therefore does not need any right to appeal.

However, if the employee chooses to appeal an administrative decision pursuant to Section 76 of the Civil Service Law, the employer gains the right to appeal the decision by the appellate forum, which is either the Civil Service Commission or Personnel Officer having jurisdiction or the court.

11.02 What may appeals concern?

Appeals may concern:

1. The determination that the employee is guilty,

---

[50] Section 3020-a(5) provides as follows: Not later than ten days after receipt of the hearing officer's decision, the employee or the employing board may make an application to the New York state supreme court to vacate or modify the decision of the hearing officer pursuant to section seven thousand five hundred eleven of the civil practice law and rules. The court's review shall be limited to the grounds set forth in such section. The hearing panel's determination shall be deemed to be final for the purpose of such proceeding. In no case shall the filing or the pendency of an appeal delay the implementation of the decision of the hearing officer.

2. The fairness of the penalty, or

3. Both.

11.03 What standards apply in appeals?

Appeals involve the question of whether or not the decision was supported by evidence in the record, not whether the determination was correct. In other words, a court or other body reviewing a disciplinary finding will not substitute its judgment for that of the hearing officer or panel regarding findings of fact, the veracity or credibility of the witnesses and weight to be applied to the evidence presented.

Findings of guilt must be based on substantial evidence. If a finding of guilt were not based on substantial evidence, or in certain proceedings "a preponderance of the evidence," it would be ruled to be "arbitrary and capricious."[51]

Disciplinary findings must be in such a form and sufficient specificity as to permit an intelligent challenge and adequate judicial review. This issue was considered in Bader v Lansingburgh CSD, Appellate Division, 1995.[52]

Penalties in New York State must meet the "Pell Doctrine,"[53] also known as the Pell Standard: any legally permissible penalty is appropriate unless it is "shocking to one's sense of fairness."

11.04 Forums for appeal

An employee may appeal an adverse decision made under Section 75 to either:

1. The appropriate Civil Service Commission or Personnel Officer, (Section 76, Civil Service Law), or

2. The state Supreme Court (Article 78, Civil Practice Law and Rules)

Arbitration decisions are appealed to the state Supreme Court under Article 75, Civil Practice Law and Rules. Under Section 3020-a, as amended in 1994, disciplinary decisions involving educators are arbitrated.

Local laws may also affect the forums available. For instance, Section 120 of the Mount Vernon City Charter provides that the exclusive vehicle for a police officer seeking review of a determination of the Police Commissioner is a direct appeal to the Appellate Division within 30 days following the Commissioner's decision. The Appellate Division confirmed the primacy of the Charter's provisions

---

[51] Cargill v Sobol, 565 NYS2d 902, addresses this point.
[52] Bader was decided the former Section 3020-a.
[53] Pell v Board of Education, 34 NY2d 222.

in a disciplinary cases involving police officer William Podszus, who had been found guilty of charges of "insubordination and malicious gossip" and received a penalty of the forfeiture of 10 days of pay. The Appellate division ruled that Podszus's Article 78 action in State Supreme Court was improper in light of the City Charter's provision.

However, there is a trap for the unwary individual seeking to challenge an administrative decision as Gomez v Safir, App. Div., First Dept., 3/5/00, demonstrates. This case involved a delay in challenging an administrative decision via an Article 78 proceeding while a "contract grievance" testing the decision is pending. The issue:

Does a pending grievance concerning the administrative denial of an employee's request toll the statute of limitations for filing an Article 78 petition challenging the administrative disapproval action?

Gomez's grievance was denied on the grounds that it did not involve a contractual right subject to the grievance process. Gomez then initiated an Article 78 action seeking a court order vacating the administrative decision.

However, by the time the "grievance ruling" was issued more than four months had passed by since the employer had issued the challenged "administrative ruling."

State Supreme Court Judge William McCooe said it was untimely and dismissed Gomez's petition. Why? Because, said the court, the employer's administrative decision" became final and binding" on Gomez when he was told that his administrative appeal had been denied. Accordingly, the four-month statute of limitations for bringing an Article 78 action commenced to run at that time.

The critical element in resolving the timeliness issue: Judge McCooe said that Gomez's attempt to resort to contractual grievance procedures did not toll the four-month limitations period, citing Lubin v Board of Education, 60 NY2d 974.

The lesson here: delays in filing an Article 78 petition because the employee is awaiting the resolution of a grievance or arbitration concerning the same issue are fatal as the Gomez decision demonstrates.

Similarly, in Roper v NYC Department of Citywide Administration, decided April 6, 2000 by the Appellate Division, Third Department, the court sustained the Unemployment Insurance Appeal Board's dismissed Clyde Roper's appeal of the denial of his unemployment insurance claim as untimely. Clyde testified that he received the ALJ's decision "but did not appeal based upon his attorney's advice to wait for a pending arbitration decision."

Here the court sustained the board's conclusion that Clyde failed to comply with the 20-day filing requirement of Section 621(1) of the Labor Law and dismissed his appeal.

11.05 Challenging a Section 75 decision

As stated above, an employee may appeal an adverse decision made under Section 75 to either:

1. The appropriate Civil Service Commission or Personnel Officer, (Section 76, Civil Service Law), or

2. The state Supreme Court (Article 78, Civil Practice Law and Rules)

If satisfaction is not reached in one of those forums, there is the potential for further judicial review. Only under certain conditions will courts assume jurisdiction, however. A court will assume jurisdiction to review a Civil Service Commission's Section 76 determination in cases where an individual claims that his or her constitutional rights have been impaired or when it is alleged that the agency has acted illegally, unconstitutionally, or in excess of its jurisdiction.

What happens in a "mixed case"? Suppose that a Taylor Law agreement that provides that disciplinary action was to be subject to the contract's grievance procedure "and is also subject to the disciplinary procedures set out in the Civil Service Law." This was the question when an employee was disciplined as provided under the contract, she appealed to the courts pursuant to Section 76 of the Civil Service.[54]

Although the employer argued that the "final and binding" language contained in the grievance provision of the agreement constituted a waiver of further judicial review, the court disagreed.

Although a negotiated agreement could modify or provide a substitute for the disciplinary procedure established by a statute, in this case the court viewed the agreement as incorporating by reference the provisions of Sections 75 and 76 of the Civil Service Law.

Accordingly, it concluded, the disciplinary action was to be governed by the grievance procedure as a substitute for Section 75 but that the employee's right to appeal pursuant to Section 76 had neither been waived by the employee nor limited by the contract provision.

In contrast, in Johnson v Triborough Bridge and Tunnel Authority, the Court of Appeals ruled that a civil service commission does not have jurisdiction to consider an appeal when the challenge involves testing the application of the terms of a settlement of a disciplinary action that resulted in a "disciplinary probation period."

Here the Court of Appeals held that Section 76 "solely authorizes the Commission to hear appeals from hearings in connection with disciplinary proceedings under section 75." As there was no such Section 75 discipline proceeding held in Johnson's case, the Commission had no jurisdiction to hear his application to review his discharge as it was not effected pursuant to Section 75.

The Court also commented that Section 76(2) limits the Commission's review to the record and transcript of the disciplinary hearing. As there was no record or transcript in this instance, the Commission had no jurisdiction to determine the matter. Thus, said the court, Johnson "cannot reassert his contentions by appealing to the Commission because its jurisdiction is explicitly limited to appeals of Section 75 determinations.

---

[54] Stoker v Tarentino, 64 NY2d 994.

The Court of Appeals also noted that Johnson "could have brought an Article 78 proceeding at the time of his dismissal ... challenging the TBTA's conclusion that he was a probationary employee".

11.06 Challenging an arbitration award

Attempting to vacate an arbitration award pursuant to Article 75[55] is difficult. The general rule is that an arbitration award will be sustained unless it violates a strong public policy,[56] is totally irrational or if the arbitrator exceeded a specifically enumerated limitation of his or her power.

Specific grounds for vacating or modifying an arbitrator's award are set out in CPLR Section 7511.

One category of persons or organizations that can protest an arbitration award includes any party who either participated in the arbitration or was served with a notice of intention to arbitrate. However, the courts will not vacate an award unless such a party seeking to have the award vacated can show the award was defective for one or more of the following reasons:

1. Corruption, fraud or misconduct in procuring the award

2. Partiality of an arbitrator appointed as a neutral, except where the award was by confession

3. The arbitrator, or agency or person making the award exceeded his or her power or so imperfectly executed it that a final and definite award upon the subject matter submitted was not made

4. The arbitrator failed to follow the procedures set out in Article 75, CPLR unless the party applying to vacate the award continued with the arbitration with notice of the defect and without objection

For instance, an arbitrator's refusal to admit into evidence or consider a superseding agreement between the parties, which was later determined to have been pertinent and material evidence, would justify vacating the award.[57]

In addition, courts have vacated arbitration awards determined to be violative of strong public policy notwithstanding the fact that such a ground is not enumerated in Article 75 of the CPLR.

Another category of persons and organizations that can protest an arbitration award includes those who did not participate in the arbitration and those who were not served with a notice of intention to arbitrate. However, again the grounds for relief are limited. Courts will vacate an arbitration award for a third party only if the court finds that:

---

[55] Article 75, Civil Practice Law and Rules

[56] It is the "public policy" in place at the time the arbitrator makes his or her award, not the public policy in effect at the time the incident that led to the disciplinary action or at the time of the disciplinary arbitration, that controls. [Greenburgh CSD v Greenburgh Teachers Federation, _ NY2d _].

[57] Matter of Intercontinental Packaging Co., 172 AD2d 637.

1. The rights of that party were prejudiced in the procurement of the award

2. A valid agreement to arbitrate was not made; or

3. The agreement to arbitrate had not been complied with; or

4. The arbitrated claim was barred by limitation under subdivision (b) of Section 7502.

Equally difficult is an attempt to modify an arbitration award. Courts are permitted to modify the award only for the following reasons:

1. There was a miscalculation of figures or a mistake in the description of any person, thing or property referred to in the award; or

2. The arbitrators have awarded upon a matter not submitted to them and the award may be corrected without affecting the merits of the decision upon the issues submitted; or

3. The award is imperfect in a matter of form, not affecting the merits of the controversy.

As an illustration of the few limitations on the authority of the arbitrator, in Kimball v Pine Plains CSD, App. Div., Second Department, May 1, 2000, the Appellate Division said that "[a]n arbitration award may not be vacated unless it is irrational, violates a strong public policy, or clearly exceeds a limitation imposed on the arbitrator as set forth in CPLR 7511(b)" or if the arbitrator exceeds his or her authority.

When does the arbitrator exceed his or her authority? When, said the Second Department, the arbitrator gave a "completely irrational construction to the provisions in dispute and, in effect, made a new contract for the parties." In Kimball's case, said the court, the determinations made by the arbitrator were within his power and not irrational. Accordingly, the Appellate Division held Supreme Court properly confirmed that award.

Under certain circumstances the court may order a rehearing and determination of all or any of the issues. This may remanded to the same arbitrator or a new arbitrator may be appointed. The time for such a hearing or award shall be measured from the date of such order or rehearing, whichever is appropriate, or a time may be specified by the court.

An application for a rehearing neither tolls (stops) nor extends the limitations period. Only where there is a mandatory right to a rehearing or when a request for rehearing is granted can the statute of limitations be extended. This is so because there is a new determination rendered, even if it results in an identical decision. The statute of limitations begins to run from the date of the new decision.

11.07 Biased hearing officers

It is axiomatic that an unbiased hearing officer must conduct an administrative hearing. Courts have determined that administrative due process will not allow an administrative decision maker to sit in review upon his own decisions. As an example, after serving as a hearing officer and making his ruling, the hearing officer then sat as one of the panel members of the board that reviewed, and affirmed, the ruling he had made as the hearing officer. When challenged, the determination was annulled by the court and returned to the agency for a determination by "a properly constituted board".[58]

The Court of Appeals said that in order to establish hearing officer bias as a matter of fact, there must be support in the record for the bias and proof that the outcome of the administrative proceeding flowed from the alleged bias[59]

11.08 Deadlines for appeal

Deadlines for appeal vary depending upon the law under which the appeal is filed.

Appeals pursuant to Section 76 must be filed with the administrative body within 20 days after the service of the determination.

Appeals pursuant to Article 78 of the Civil Practice Law and Rules must be filed within four months of the service of the disciplinary determination on the employee. Service must be done either by registered mail or by delivering the determination personally to the employee.

In both cases a record of the date and time of service should be made as well as to whom the determination was delivered. If service was by registered mail the employee is given an additional three days in which to file a timely appeal.

Under Section 3020-a of the Education Law, appeals of arbitration decisions must be filed within 10 days of receipt of the hearing officer's decision. In contrast, challenges seeking to vacate or modify an arbitration award resulting from a Taylor Law contract disciplinary procedure must be filed within 90 days of the delivery of the award to the disappointed party.

11.09 Timely and untimely appeals

When a statute authorizes an individual to file an appeal from an administrative determination by mail, what is the controlling date: the date the appeal was mailed or the date on which the appeal was received by the appellate body? The traditional view was that the notice of appeal is untimely if it physically received by the appellate body after the Statute of Limitations had passed. However, the Appellate Division in August 1997 offered a different view in McLaughlin v Saga Corp, 657 NYS2d 784.

---

[58] Matter of Pattison, 108 AD2d 1103 Another example of the court overturning a disciplinary determination when it is determined that the appointing authority was personally involved in the process is Hicks v Fortier, 117 AD2d 930.

[59] Hughes v Suffolk County Civil Service Department, 546 NYS 2d 335

Consistent with the traditional view, the Appellate Division decided that the critical date is the date on which the appeal is received by the appellate body, here the Workers' Compensation Appeals Board (WCB).

When Saga asked the court for permission to appeal the ruling to the Court of Appeals, the Appellate Division decided to reconsider its May 1997 determination.

It then reversed its May decision, holding that it is the date of mailing, rather than the date or receipt that controls with respect to determining the timeliness of an administrative appeal. The Appellate Division has now decided that if the party is able to submit "proof of mailing within the limitations period," the application is timely.

The case arose under a provision of the Workers' Compensation Law that allowed a party to "serve" its appeal on the WCB by mailing it to the WCB within 30 days. However, the WCB took the position that unless it received the application for review on or before the last day of the 30-day limitations period, it was untimely.

In Saga's case, although the appeal was posted within the 30-day period allowed for filing the application, WCB did not physically receive it until eight days after the statute of limitations had expired.

The rationale underlying the revised ruling is clear. If a person has a statutory right to make a decision, which may be then filed by mail, this period would necessarily be shortened if the appellate body could insist that it physically receive the mailed notice no later than the last day of the period of limitation. In effect the court concluded that the method of service of a notice of appeal, mail or personal delivery, should not determine the time period available to the party to decide whether or not to appeal an administrative ruling.

One may "prove" that he or she made a timely response by presenting evidence such as a certified or registered mail receipt or a signed delivery document from a private carrier such as the United Parcel Service.

11.10 Outcomes of appeals

If it is determined that the record supports the findings, the question of the appropriateness of the penalty imposed will then be examined. The commission, personnel officer or court may determine that there is substantial evidence to support the decision but the penalty imposed is too harsh.

If it is determined that only some of the charges have been supported by substantial evidence, the matter is usually returned to the appointing authority for reconsideration of the penalty to be imposed.

Sometimes a court or other forum of review will return disciplinary actions for a completely new review of the record . This is a called de novo (anew) consideration. De novo hearings are granted because there has been some form of failure to provide due process. Examples include improper or questionable involvement of the appointing officer in some phase of the proceeding [see Sander v Owens, 82 AD2d 968], or failure to issue a ruling that is sufficiently specific to permit an appeal.

11.11 Vacating or modifying penalties: The Pell Standard

Often appeals focus, in whole or in part, on the appropriateness of penalty imposed.

With the exception the penalty of a reprimand, all disciplinary penalties imposed pursuant to Section 75 may be appealed by the employee. Under a special circumstance even the penalty of reprimand may be appealed, i.e., if the penalty imposed is a reprimand and the employee was suspended without pay for up to thirty days prior to the hearing as authorized by Section 75, the employee may appeal the reprimand if the suspension without pay was not rescinded.

Courts typically do not impose a harsher penalty than that determined by the appointing authority. In some cases, however, a harsher penalty is imposed. There are a number of "old Section 3020-a cases in which the Commissioner of Education increased the penalty imposed by a hearing panel on the grounds that the penalty imposed by the hearing panel was too lenient.

However, the authors are aware of Appellate Division ruling, State University of New York v Young, that changed the penalty imposed by an arbitrator from a suspension without pay to dismissal on the basis of "public policy." The Young case involved a health care worker who persisted in using the same syringe to draw blood from multiple critically ill patients despite having been warned of the dangers of that practice.[60]

If the appeal is taken to the commission or personnel officer having jurisdiction, there is a review of the record of the disciplinary proceeding.

The commission or personnel officer may decide the appeal on the basis of the record and any written or oral arguments submitted or it may provide for a hearing at which the employee may be represented by an attorney. Here only an attorney is authorized to represent the employee while either an attorney or a union representative, who may be either an attorney or a layperson, may appear on behalf of the employee at the Section 75 hearing.

Only rarely will courts alter the penalty or remand the case back to the employer for re-determination of a penalty. Courts have a mandate to accord "much deference" to employers' determinations regarding penalties. The ruling in Ahsaf v Nyquist, 37 NY2d 182, illustrates this.

Courts will only act to reject a penalty if it finds that the penalty imposed is "shocking to one's sense of fairness." This standard is known as the Pell standard, after the landmark case Pell v Board of Education, 34 NY2d 222.

---

[60] The arbitrator decided that dismissal was too harsh a penalty in view of Young's eight years of employment without evidence of other violations of professional performance and imposed a penalty of suspension without pay for two months. SUNY Health Science Center won its challenge of the arbitrator's award on the grounds that it violated a strong public policy -- to protect and care for its patients.

Some examples of violations of the Pell Standard:

Dismissing a librarian with 17 years of service for failing to report her intended absence on two occasions. [Rathburn v Onondaga Co. Library, Appellate Division]

Using excessive force against a prisoner while going to the aid of a fellow officer who was struggling with an inmate. [Allman v Koehler, 554 NYS2d 842]

Suspending an employee without pay for 30 days for her first offense, which was "engaging in conduct which may result in a safety hazard." [Smith v Hager, 586 NYS2d 41]

Demoting a corrections corporal found sleeping on duty on two occasions, where a hearing officer found the officer's superior "had condoned such conduct." [Stapleton v La Paglia, Appellate Division]

11.12 Back pay and benefits

If the determination is that the record does not support the findings and the employee is found not guilty, the employee is entitled to any back pay due him as well as pay for any period of suspension without pay during the pendency of the charges. However, the payment of back pay under these circumstances has been held to be limited to those situations where the statute expressly authorizes the payment of back pay in the event the guilty determination is reversed or the process held invalid.

One back pay case, In the Matter of Michael Okebiyi, App. Div., Second Dept., 2001-04889, holds that back pay available to a tenured individual.

Okebiyi was terminated from the position of Director of Operations based allegations of "mismanagement." He sued, claiming he was entitled to back pay in the amount of $301,464.52 based on court orders issued on August 5, 1998, and November 10, 1999.

The court pointed out that only tenured employees of a school district are entitled to back pay during periods of either suspension or improper termination because such employees, by virtue of their tenured status, have a property interest in their salaries, citing Hawley v South Orangetown Cent. School Dist., 67 NY2d 796 among other cases. Okebiyi, in contrast served as an at-will employee without tenure and therefore neither had a property interest in continued employment not a right to recover back pay.

11.13 Statute of limitations

Failure to satisfy a statute of limitations for challenging a dismissal will bar consideration of the merits of an appeal. However the critical element that sometimes must be determined is the date on which the statute of limitations begins to run. The Hoesterey case, Hoesterey v Cathedral City [Calif.], CA9, 9055141, illustrates this.

Hoesterey, a city employee subject to dismissal only for cause, involuntarily resigned from his position due to alleged coercion and intimidation by his superior. The "resignation" took effect two days later, on November 30, 1986.

Exactly one year later he filed a lawsuit, claiming the denial of a pre-termination hearing violated his rights under 42 USC 1983. A critical issue in this case was whether Hoesterey's claim was time-barred. The district court ruled that it was as the statute of limitations began to run "on the date of the notification of the discharge" November 28, 1986 rather that the effective date of the resignation, November 30, 1986.

The Circuit Court disagreed, hold that the running of the statute of limitations is triggered when the employee receives the notice of the termination decision and that the notice indicates that the decision is final and no further administrative action would be taken.

In the absence of written notice, it would be only on the last day of employment that the employee could become aware that the employer's decision was final and that no further action regarding the termination would be initiated. The Circuit Court ruled that the statute of limitations began to run on Hoesterey's last day of employment, November 30, 1986 and thus the suit he filed on November 30, 1987 was timely.

11.14 Back salary

Unless there is a Taylor Law contract clause or statute that operates to automatically provide for the payment of back salary and benefits upon reinstatement following an unlawful termination [see, for example, Section 77, Civil Service Law], an employee who wishes to receive back pay and benefits must make certain the decision contains a "clear and unequivocal mandate" that the employer is to provide back salary and the other relief demanded or he or she may not be able to obtain such redress. Unless the reinstatement order specifically provides for relief such as the payment of back salary, or the granting seniority and benefits, it appears that the courts are not willing to read such an intent in the order settling the matter.[61]

In addition, it would appear prudent for the individual to present evidence of "damages" he or she suffered as a result of the unlawful termination.[62]

---

[61] Bellman v McGuire, _ AD2d _

[62] See Maio v New York City Civil Service Commission, _ AD2d _

CHAPTER 12

NON-DISCIPLINARY TERMINATIONS

The word "termination" is usually associated with dismissal for cause. Unfortunately, this term is also used when discipline is not a factor, causing misunderstanding and misapprehension. If discipline is not the reason for a dismissal, the dismissal is properly referred to as a non-disciplinary termination.

12.01 Termination for disability

Sections 71, 72, and 73 of the Civil Service Law refer to separation or termination in quite a different sense than disciplinary dismissal. These provisions permit a position to be filled while the permanent incumbent is incapacitated while simultaneously vesting significant rights to return to the position in the disabled worker.[63]

These terminations are authorized under specific conditions. However the employee may not be removed from the position until he or she has been absent for one year or longer because of illness or disability.

Section 71 deals exclusively with such separations in connection with occupational injury or disease (Workers' Compensation Leave) while Section 72 relates only to leaves of absence due to physical or mental disability. Section 73 involves terminations following an absence of one year or more not related to Workers' Compensation claims.[64] The Retirement and Social Security Law, among others such as Sections 207-a and 207-c of the General Municipal Law, control those situations in which the appointing authority elects to file a disability retirement application on behalf of an individual.

Removal under any of these provisions is at the discretion of the appointing authority and not automatic.

While Section 72 specifically authorizes the termination of an employee pursuant to Section 73 after one year of continuous absence, no such specific authorization is set out in Section 71. However, in Duncan v NYS Developmental Center (63 NY2d 128), the Court of Appeals specifically considered "termination" under Section 71 and ruled that it was permitted. While an employee may not be discharged for absence resulting from an occupational injury or disease, he or she may be removed from the position and be replaced by another appointee.

---

[63] Another procedure available to an appointing authority that results in a "non-disciplinary termination" is for the appointing authority to file an employer application for accidental disability retirement, line-of-duty disability retirement or ordinary disability retirement on behalf of the individual.

[64] For the purposes of Section 71, an employee may be terminated after being absent on workers' compensation leave of a cumulative period on one year. In contrast, an employee who has be absent on leave pursuant to Section 72 may be terminated pursuant to Section 73 after being absent for a consecutive period of one year on longer.

Thereafter, the terminated worker is to be accorded the benefits provided by Section 71 with respect to reemployment. This is similar to the rights granted employees terminated pursuant to Section 73.

However, there is no statutory right to a hearing prior to such termination [Hurwitz v Perales, _ NY2d _].

The Hurwitz decision concerns the issue of "pre-termination due process" in Civil Service Law Section 73 termination situations. In Prue v Hunt (78 NY2d 364), the Court of Appeals decided that in a Section 73 termination, due process required notice and "some opportunity to respond" before the termination could be implemented. In the Hurwitz case the court considered "the companion question of what process is due at the pre-termination stage." The Appellate Division concluded that Hurwitz had not been provided pre-termination procedures satisfying the requirements of due process during the "pre-termination" phase of her dismissal -- the medical evaluation conducted by the Civil Service Department's Employee Health Services [EHS] to determine her ability to return to work.

Hurwitz had been employed by the State Department of Social Services (DSS) when she developed labrynthitis and went on continuous sick-leave beginning February 11, 1987. In December 1987, she was told that her sick leave would be extended until February 10, 1988 and that if she wished to return to her position she must provide medical documentation of her ability to perform her duties. She was also told that she could be terminated if she was continuously absent for one year. When Hurwitz's personal physician indicated that Hurwitz would be able to return to work by December 1987, DSS required her to report for an EHS medical examination and evaluation.

The EHS physician observed symptoms of labrynthitis and ultimately concluded that Hurwitz would be unable to perform her job duties. Accordingly, the EHS physician did not certify her as fit to return to work. Hurwitz objected to the EHS determination and attempted to appeal the decision.

She was told that there was no appeal process in existence but that DSS would withhold further action pending discussions of the report with EHS. Both DSS and Hurwitz's personal physician discussed the evaluation with the EHS physician and tried to get her to change her opinion regarding Hurwitz's ability to return to work. Despite these discussions, the EHS physician declined to modify her opinion or to reexamine Hurwitz. DSS decided to terminate Hurwitz pursuant to Section 73.

Section 72 provides the appointing authority with the discretion to terminate an individual who has been continuously absent due to illness continuously for one year or longer in accordance with the provisions of Section 73 of the Civil Service Law. Terminating the employee, however, is not mandatory but rather the result of the discretionary action of the appointing officer.

Hurwitz sued, seeking reinstatement and back pay on the grounds that she had been discharged without being accorded her due process rights. When the Appellate Division remanded the matter for "a hearing on her present ability to perform the duties of her position with DSS" (Hurwitz v Perales, 179 AD2d 586) DSS appealed.

Referring to the Prue decision, the court said that here Hurwitz was given adequate opportunity to respond to the claimed basis of her discharge prior to her termination. It found that Hurwitz was notified that she would be terminated upon her continuous absence for one year "by reason of a disability" and that she had the right to submit medical documentation demonstrating her ability to return to work in order to avoid discharge. It was noted that Hurwitz that used opportunity by (1) having her physician report to DSS that she was able to return to work (2) undergoing and independent EHS evaluation and (3) submitted numerous physicians' reports to EHS for consideration.

In addition, the court said that Hurwitz's personal physician was consulted by EHS. Although Hurwitz disagreed with the conclusions reached by EHS, she was given several opportunities to dispute the correctness of the evaluation with EHS, with her supervisor and with the DSS. She was unable to persuade either that the EHS was erroneous. Under these circumstances, the Court of Appeals concluded that Hurwitz was given a sufficient "explanation of the grounds for the discharge and an opportunity to respond prior to [her] discharge."

The court observed that "The fact that petitioner was not informed of DSS's decision regarding a second evaluation does not diminish the adequacy of her opportunity to be heard for due process purposes." It said that although the reexamination may have finally determined the correctness of the medical opinion issued by EHS, the ultimate validity of the evaluation is matter properly addressed in the post termination hearing. Due process does not require that such questions be finally resolved at the pre-termination stage. It reversed the Appellate Division's ruling, upholding Hurwitz's termination pursuant to Section 73.

The employee terminated pursuant to Section 71 or Section 73 has the right to return to work once the disability or illness abates or otherwise permits such return. The employee is required to make an application to the appropriate agency (such as the Employees' Health Service with respect to state employees) within one year following their recovery. If the person is found qualified to resume the duties of the position, he or she must be reinstated to it, if vacant.

Although there is no requirement that the vacancy be filled, if the employee is not restored to the position the agency may have to show that it was not being arbitrary or capricious in refusing to fill the position at the time. If the position has been filled by another permanent appointment, the employee is entitled to an appointment in another suitable position. If no position is available, the employee is placed on a preferred list, and will remain on the preferred list for four years or until appointed, whichever first occurs.

As can be clearly seen, the so-called "terminated" employee enjoys many rights to reemployment not normally available to a person who has been removed for cause.

Further, each of these sections of the Civil Service Law provides for due process by giving the employee appeal rights. In addition, the courts have imposed certain due process rights not specifically set forth in law.

Section 72.1 as originally enacted was held to be constitutionally defective as it did not provide for notice and hearing before the employee was placed on leave for mental disability by the appointing authority. This was cured by the court ordering the appointing authority to follow the several steps listed below in connection with efforts to place the employee on leave pursuant to Section 72:

1. The employee is to be given a written notice of the reasons why the appointing officer believes the individual is not mentally fit to perform the duties of the position before referring the employee for examination by the employer's physician.

2. The employee or his or her representative is to be given a copy of the physician's findings.

3. If the appointing officer decides to place the employee on Section 72 leave without the employee's consent, a written notice of that determination, together with the reasons and facts relied on by the appointing officer must be sent to the employee or his representative.

4. The employee must be notified, in writing, of his right to appeal the appointing officer's determination and the steps to be followed in connection with such appeal. The employee is entitled to an adversarial type hearing if he or she wishes. The hearing is to be conducted by an impartial person such as an independent arbitrator. The employee may be represented by an attorney and may present evidence and witnesses on his or her behalf, as well as cross-examining the agency's witnesses.

5. Upon request, the employee or his representative must be given copies of the employee's medical records and related data before the appeal hearing takes place.

6. Finally, the employee is to be given written notice of the hearing officer's decision, with the reasons and facts relied upon by the hearing officer.

Appeal to the appropriate Civil Service Commission or Personnel Officer as provided by Section 72 is available to the employee. Should an appointing officer believe it necessary, the employee may be placed on leave immediately (see Section 72.5). The standard that probably should be used in such circumstances is the "clear and present danger" to the employee's co-workers, or the agency's clients, or the employee himself, if the employee is permitted to remain at the work site.

However, the procedural steps outlined above must be implemented immediately if the employee is placed on such involuntary leave. If the employee later is able to show that he or she should not have been placed on leave pursuant to Section 72.5, he or she is to be reinstated. Any leave credits used in connection with the absence and any lost wages will be paid to the employee as well.

In each of the situations provided for by these sections, the employee is not really "fired" but has been placed, in effect, on an indefinite leave of absence without pay. The leave ends when the employee returns to work or dies or in the event of recovery, one year after the end of his or her disability.

Under certain circumstances, the employee may no longer be eligible for reinstatement from a preferred list, but may be reinstated with approval of the Civil Service Commission or Personnel Officer having jurisdiction. However, the employee continues to have rights to be restored to the position or a similar position during this leave period. He or she may have other rights as well, such as the right to participate in promotion examinations if otherwise qualified.

The Section 71 and Section 73 types of terminations, therefore, must be considered quite differently from the separation for cause implicit in a disciplinary action.

Due process and Section 73 of the Civil Service Law was considered in Vecchia v Town of North Hempstead, _ AD2d _.

The Vecchia case discusses the question of the need to provide a due process hearing in connection with the termination of an employee pursuant to Section 73 of the Civil Service Law and the standard to be met by the employer at such a hearing.

Vecchia was a Laborer with the Town. In October 1984, he became unable to work and was hospitalized "because of his schizophrenic condition." About a year later Vecchia's treating psychiatrist determined that he could return to work. When Vecchia attempted to do so, the Town told him that he would have to be evaluated by the Town's psychiatrist.

The Town's psychiatrist determined that Vecchia could not return to work for two reasons: his illness and because he was taking medication which could cause drowsiness. In January 1986, the Town wrote Vecchia advising him that he had been terminated because he had been "continuously absent and unable to perform [his] duties as a Laborer II for more than one year by reason of a disability."

Vecchia challenged this action and won a ruling by a federal district court judge to the effect that "due process required the Town to afford [Vecchia] a hearing to determine whether he was capable of performing his duties" during the period from October 8, 1984, when he attempted to return to work and through October 19, 1985, date on which he was examined by the Town's psychiatrist.

In the hearing that followed the Town's psychiatrist testified that he could not state, with a reasonable degree of medical certainty, if Vecchia was capable of performing his duties during this 11-day period. Vecchia's psychiatrist, on the other hand, testified that he had examined Vecchia on October 3, 1985 and again on October 24, 1985 and on both occasions found him capable of returning to work and performing his duties. Vecchia's psychiatrist also said that Vecchia did not show any signs that his medication was causing him drowsiness.

The hearing officer determined that Vecchia was incapable of performing his duties for a one-year period ending October 19, 1985 and concluded that the Town had properly discharged Vecchia pursuant to Section 73. Vecchia again sued, challenging this action.

The Appellate Division said "in order to annul an administrative determination made after a constitutionally required hearing, a court must be satisfied, after reviewing the record as a whole, that the record lacks substantial evidence to support the determination. The court then indicated that "while the quantum of evidence that rises to the level of 'substantial' cannot be precisely defined, the inquiry is whether 'in the end the finding is supported by the kind of evidence on which responsible persons are accustomed to rely in serious affairs.'"

The Appellate Division concluded that applying these principles, "the Town's determination that [Vecchia] was incapable of resuming his duties between October 8, 1985 and October 19, 1985 is not supported by substantial evidence." After noting that the record, as a whole, fails to establish [Vecchia] was incapable of performing his duties for a continuous period of one year or more, the court annulled the Town's action terminating Vecchia and directed that Vecchia be reinstated with back salary and benefits from October 8, 1985, reduced by any unemployment insurance benefits paid to him during this period.

As a matter of law, due process hearing are required in the event an employer decides to place an individual on disability leave pursuant to Section 72 of the Civil Service Law against the wishes of the employee. As the Vecchia decision indicates, such hearings are essential if an employee challenges his or her termination pursuant to Section 73. Presumably actions taken by employers pursuant to Section 71 of the Civil Service Law [leave for disability resulting from a work related injury or disease] with respect to placing an individual on such leave or terminating the employee would have to meet the same standards.

12.02 Section 73 pre-termination due process requirements

Ever expanding due process requirements, courts have ruled that pre-termination hearings are required in Section 73 cases.[65]

Section 73 of the Civil Service Law authorizes the termination and replacement of civil servants when they have been continuously absent from and unable to perform the duties of their position for one year or more by reason of a disability that did not result from an occupational injury or disease.

The significant questions raised in the Prue case is whether or not the Federal due process clause requires a hearing before an employee may be terminated under Section 73.

The Court of Appeals said that "in light of Cleveland Board of Education v Loudermill (470 U.S. 532)," a Section 73 discharge must be preceded by a pre-termination notice and a minimal opportunity to be heard. The ruling indicates that "to the extent that [the court's] holding in Economico v Pelham (50 NY2d 120) permits a Section 73 discharge with only a post-termination hearing, it is superseded by Loudermill."

Prue, a police officer with the Syracuse Police Department, was seriously injured in an accident unrelated to his work on November 15, 1986. This injury allegedly prevented him from performing his duties as a police officer. Having exhausted all his paid vacation, personal and sick leave by October 15, 1987, petitioner requested reinstatement but failed to submit the medical documentation necessary to show that he was able to perform the duties of his position.

On November 13, 1987, Prue again requested reinstatement, this time submitting a letter from his physician stating that he was able to return to a desk job. The decision notes that for some ten years Prue, as President of the PBA, had been given a desk job in the department pursuant to a collective bargaining agreement. However Prue's request for desk duty was refused and he was terminated his employment pursuant to Section 73.

Although Prue was offered a post-termination Economico hearing to be held within five days of his termination, he declined the hearing and commenced this Article 78 proceeding contesting his termination. The Court of Appeals decided that Prue's termination under Section 73 was controlled by the U.S. Supreme Court's ruling in Loudermill. It said that "the potential for an erroneous discharge

---

[65] Prue v Hunt, as Chief of Police of the City of Syracuse, __ NY2d __

or an inappropriate exercise of the discretion conferred under Section 73" justifies the minimal burden placed on department in requiring it provide Prue with some pre-termination opportunity to respond."

Also noted was the court's view that Prue's discharge raised questions regarding his physical condition and whether his ability to perform the desk job he had filled for the preceding ten years constitutes an "ability to perform the duties of his position" within the meaning of Section 73.

In addition, the court said "like the Ohio statute in Loudermill, Section 73 calls for the termination of employees in the discretion of the employer." Consideration of Prue's contentions concerning his ability to perform the desk job he had previously held could have been a significant factor in the initial discretionary decision of whether to order termination under Section 73. However, he was given no opportunity to make these arguments prior to his discharge under the procedure followed by Department.

As to the nature of the hearing to be given an employee in a Section 73 termination situation, the court said that it concluded that due process requires only notice and some opportunity to respond.

The decision indicates that the formality and procedural requisites of a hearing can vary depending on such factors as the importance of the interest involved, the extent to which that interest may be lost, the hardship imposed by the loss and the availability of subsequent proceedings. The court concluded that a pre-termination hearing was justified in Section 73 cases.

12.03 Arbitrating Section 71 and Section 73 terminations

The submission of the question of termination pursuant to either Section 71 or Section 73 to arbitration is available in some instances as is demonstrated by Matter of the Correction Officers Benevolent Association, _ Misc2d _.

The New York City Department of Corrections initiated action to terminate correction officers who had been on sick leave for one year or longer pursuant to Section 71 of the Civil Service Law with respect to individuals injured on the job and pursuant to Section 73 with respect to individuals absent because of an injury or illness that was not job related.

Under Article X, Section 2 of the controlling collective bargaining agreement, correction officers were entitled "to leave with pay for the full period of any incapacity due to illness, injury or mental or physical defect, whether or not service-connected in accordance with existing procedures."

The association grieved and ultimately the issue was submitted to arbitration. As framed by the parties, the issue before the arbitrator was: "Was the implementation of medical removal proceedings pursuant to Sections 71 and 72 [sic] of the New York State Civil Service Law, whether or not resulting in either unpaid leave of absence or termination, violative of Article X Section 2 of the collective bargaining agreement?"[66]

---

[66] Sections 71 and 72 of the Civil Service Law deal with the right to a leave, with or without pay, in cases of job-related injuries [Section 71] and other than job-related injuries [Section 72]; Sections 71 and 73 deal with the termination of such leaves, respectively.

The association argued that under the terms of the agreement, a correction officer was entitled to unlimited sick leave with full pay until he or she recovers or retires and the limitations contained in the civil service law could not be incorporated into the agreement by reference.

The city, in contrast, contended that the agreement did not impair the department's rights to implement the provisions of the civil service law as Article X Section 2's reference to "existing procedures" incorporates into the agreement "such things as the department's rules and regulations, the Civil Service Law Sections 71 and 72 and the city's managerial prerogatives."

The arbitrator found in favor of the department, ruling that:

1. the association did not prove that the department's past practice had been to provide correction officers with unlimited sick pay, without exception or qualification; and

2. Civil Service Law Sections 71 and 72 [sic] are subsumed within the phrase ... "in accordance with existing procedures."

The union brought an Article 75 action[67] seeking an order vacating the arbitrator's award on the ground that the arbitrator had exceed his authority and that the opinion and award of the arbitrator were so imperfectly executed that a final and definitive award upon the subject matter was not made.

The court confirmed the arbitration award. The decision notes that "it is well settled that when an arbitrator has been authorized to resolve disputes regarding the interpretation of the contract ... his determination will only be set aside ... if it is completely irrational ... or where the document expressly limits or is constructed to limit the powers of the arbitrator, hence narrowing the scope of arbitration...."

Also emphasized by the court was the principle that even though an arbitrator has committed an error of law or an error of fact, such a mistake is not grounds for vacating an award. Citing Matter of Sprinzen, 46 NY2d 623, the opinion indicates that "an arbitrator's award will not be vacated for error of law and fact committed by the arbitrator and even where the arbitrator states an intention to apply a law and then misapplies it, the award will not be set aside."

12.04 Other provisions of law

There are other provisions of law dealing with terminations and separation for disability.

Section 571 of the Education Law authorizes an employer to file an application for disability retirement on behalf of a member of the New York Teachers' Retirement System.

Similar provisions exist with respect to members of the New York State Employees' Retirement System such as set forth in Sections 62 and 63 of the Retirement and Social Security Law.

---

[67] Article 75, Civil Practice Law and Rules

Officers and employees of the State University in the "professional service" (essentially the academic and professional administrative staff of the State University) are subject to regulations that permit the State University to submit an application for disability benefits on behalf of an employee it believes is unable to satisfactorily perform the duties of their position because of a disability.

Except with respect to the State University's procedure, the efforts of an employer to have the employee retire (or be retired) for disability may be frustrated by the employee's refusal to cooperate by submitting himself to the medical examination usually required in such cases. In that event, the only recourse is for the employer to order the employee to submit himself for such examination and to discipline him for insubordination if the employee refuses.

The University's "Disability Insurance Program" avoids the problem of the employee refusing to cooperate. A special committee on disability may discontinue the university staff member who refuses to appear for any required medical examination from service upon a finding that the employee is disabled. The committee may use the record available to it in making its determination.

Another procedure available to an appointing authority in situations were the individual is unable to perform his or her duties because of a disability is for the appointing authority to filed an application for disability or superannuation retirement on behalf of the individual.

12.05 Considering disability claims

The following example illustrates a typical type of disability claim situation that might be experienced by a law enforcement agency. Because the benefits and procedures available to law enforcement and firefighting personnel are among the most comprehensive and complex, this "case study" demonstrates the variety of issues that may have to be considered by the appointing authority in cases of employee disability. Similar considerations, albeit possibly not as complex, will have to be addressed by an appointing authority in situations involving employee disability and due process requirements.

Relevant facts:

Police officer Smith injured his knee while on duty. Smith's personal physician and the Police Surgeon conclude that Smith is permanently disabled from performing the essential duties of a police officer. The Police Department filed a Workers' Compensation report; Smith requested GML Section 207-c benefits and Smith is currently being paid full salary. The Department then decides to file an employer application for disability retirement on Smith's behalf.

Analysis:

Workers' compensation benefits: Having been injured on the job, clearly Smith is entitled to a workers' compensation award based on his disability. The nature of the award is determined by the Workers' Compensation Board.

Smith, however, is not eligible for Civil Service Law Section 71 Workers' Compensation Leave." Why not? Because Section 71 provides that an individual suffering from a disability resulting from occupational injury or disease as defined in the Workmen's Compensation Law is entitled to a leave of absence for at least one year, except in cases where the disability permanently incapacitates the individual from performing the duties of his or her position.

Further, Smith is ineligible for Civil Service Law Section 72 leave, Leave for Ordinary Disability. Section 72 leave is available only to an employee unable to perform the duties of his or her position by reason of a disability, other than a disability resulting from occupational injury or disease as defined in the Workers' Compensation Law.

Other statutory considerations:

General Municipal Law Section 207-c[68]

In order to be eligible for Section 207-c benefits, Smith's disability must have resulted from injuries suffered in the performance of special work related to the nature of heightened risks and duties involved in the criminal justice process [Balcerak v. Nassau County, 94 NY2d 253].

The basic issue to determine: Was Smith engaged in the performance of the special work related to the nature of heightened risks and duties involved in the criminal justice process? If the Department determines that Smith does not meet this standard, Smith is not eligible for Section 207-c benefits.

Retirement and Social Security Law

If an individual receiving Section 207-c benefits is determined to be permanently disabled, "the head of the police department" may file an application for accidental disability retirement benefits or line of duty disability retirement on behalf of the individual.

If the individual is not receiving Section 207-c benefits, Section 363(b) [Accidental Disability Retirement] and Section 363-c(c) [Retirement for disability incurred in the performance of duty] respectively provide that the "head of the department" may file an application on behalf of the individual.

The Retirement System determines whether or not the individual is eligible for such retirement benefits.

Salary continuation:

Smith is continuing to receive full salary. If the Department determined that Smith satisfies the Balcerak test, such payments are being made pursuant to Section 207-c.

If, on the other hand, the Department determined that Smith did not satisfy the Balcerak test and thus is not eligible for Section 207-c benefits, his continuation on the payroll is subject to the Department's

---

[68] Section 207-a of the General Municipal Law provides similar benefits to firefighters injured in the performance of official duties.

rules with respect to sick leave and, or, the applicable provisions of a collective bargaining agreement, if any.

12.06 Termination of a probationary employee

The general rule regarding the termination of probationary employees is that a probationer can be discharge for any lawful reason at any time after the completion of the employee's minimum period of probation and before the end of the employee's maximum period of probation.

Unless otherwise provided by a Taylor Law agreement, probationary terminations may be made without "notice and hearing" and without the appointing authority having to give the probationer any reason for the termination other than that the individual has not completed the probationary period satisfactorily. The only judicial limitations place on the appointing authority in such cases is that the termination not be arbitrary or capricious or based on unlawful considerations.

The Scherbyn case,[69] sets out a significant exception to this general rule. Here the court held that where the rules of a civil service commission specifically set out the reasons for which a probationary employee may be dismissed, the appointing authority's broad discretion with respect to terminating the services of probationers is subject to limitation imposed by those standards.

In Scherbyn the Civil Service Rules of Ontario County probationary rules stated that a probationer could be terminated only for "incompetency or misconduct" or if the "performance of the probationer is not satisfactory".

Scherbyn was appointed as a typist with the BOCES. While serving as a probationer in that position, she was granted a leave of absence from the typist position to accept a temporary appointment as a Data Entry Operator [DEO]. This temporary appointment matured into a permanent one, and Scherbyn commenced her probationary period as a DEO. While serving as a probationer in the DEO position, Scherbyn was granted yet another leave allowing her to serve as a provisional Data Control Clerk [DCC]. All of these personnel transactions where approved by the county personnel officer.

BOCES then terminated Scherbyn's provisional DCC appointment and simultaneously reinstated her to and terminated her from the DEO position in which she still a probationary employee. Next BOCES asked that Scherbyn be terminated from the DEO position and reinstated to her original Typist title where, again, she still was a probationary employee.

On the advice of the State Department of Civil Service, the Personnel Officer refused to approve Scherbyn's reinstatement as a Typist, indicating that Scherbyn had "vacated the position of Typist when she accepted a Leave of Absence from her probationary appointment as Data Entry Operator as it is impossible for an employee to encumber two [permanent] positions" at the same time.[70]

---

[69] Scherbyn v Wayne-Finger Lakes BOCES, 77 NY2d 753
[70] This advice appears to reflect a misunderstanding of the "serial" nature of Scherbyn's employment situations and her rights flowing from each change of status. For example, A State employee permanently appointed to a position in the classified service pursuant to Section 64.4 of the Civil Service Law obviously can attain permanent status in that position while retaining permanent status in the position from which he or she was appointed to pursuant to Section 64.4. The

However, the Personnel Officer told BOCES that Scherbyn's reinstatement as a DEO would be approved. Ultimately BOCES decided not to retain Scherbyn's services as a DEO and terminated her.

The Court of Appeals held that the more stringent and unique Ontario County Rules circumscribed the more general rule regarding the discharge of probationers and "limit the discharge of a probationary employee to the specific reasons set forth therein."

As the record indicated that the sole reason given for dismissing Scherbyn was that "she vacated the position of Typist when she accept a Leave of Absence ... because it was impossible for an employee to encumber two positions" the court said that "dismissal for this reason was arbitrary and capricious."

In so ruling, the Court of Appeals specifically noted that there is "no provision in either the Civil Service Law or the Ontario County Civil Service Rules prohibiting simultaneous leaves of absence from two positions."

This suggests that the court did not have any trouble with a public employee holding a permanent appointment in two different positions at the same time. BOCES was ordered to reinstate Scherbyn to the position of Typist and the matter remanded to the trial court for a determination as to the payment of back salary and other benefits.

Typically a tenured employee who is given a leave of absence to accept a provisional appointment or permanent appointment to another position is entitled to a leave of absence for the duration of the provisional appointment or until the individual completes the required probationary period associated with the new permanent appointment. An example of such a Rule is found in 4 NYCRR 4.5(d) of the Rules of the State Civil Service Commission.

This is necessary in order to preserve the individual's right to return to their original position should they so desire or if their provisional appointment ends or in the event that they do not satisfactorily complete their probationary period in the higher title.

Indeed, in the case of a permanent employee being provisionally appointed to a higher grade position without such a leave from the position held on a permanent basis, the employee could not qualify for a "promotion examination" as permanent status in a lower grade position is usually a minimum qualification for eligibility for such an examination and appointment from the resulting eligible list.

According to the Scherbyn rationale, probationary employees are entitled to the same rights as are persons with tenure in such situations. Further, it appears that the fact that a subsequent appointment is made to yet another position does not dissolve the right of the employee to return to or be reinstated in any of the positions in which he or she had been serving as a probationer where he or she has yet to

---

individual is given a leave of absence from his former position. When the both positions are under the jurisdiction of the same appointing authority 4 NYCRR 411(e) provides that the individual shall have a leave of absence "for the duration of such contingent permanent appointment," thereby demonstrating that the employee holds permanent status in two different positions at the same time. If the two positions are under the jurisdiction of two different appointing authorities, the granting of such a leave is at the discretion of the releasing appointing authority.

complete the probationary period associated with the specific appointment or appointments earlier made.

On another point, frequently the rules controlling probationary appointments provide that the services of a probationer serving as a provisional in a higher level position may be considered by the appointing authority with insofar as satisfying the probationary requirements in the lower level position is concerned.

Unsatisfactory service in the higher level position, however, may not be considered insofar as adverse evaluations of the individual's performance in the lower grade position is concerned. Section 4.5(h) of the Rules of the State Civil Service Commission,[71] provides an example of this type of situation.

Section 4.5(h) also provides that if a probationer is temporarily or provisionally appointed to a higher level position and is later reinstated to a lower level position, he or she is to be given "sufficient time to permit him to compete his probationary term."

In addition, the Section 4.5(h) provides that such a probationer is not to be terminated at the end of the probationary term for unsatisfactory service unless "he shall have actually served in the position, in the aggregate, at least a period of eight weeks."

---

[71] 4 NYCRR 4.5(h)

CHAPTER 13

TERMINATIONS WITHOUT A HEARING

Sometimes termination is not contingent on providing the individual with a pre-termination hearing. One situation in which a hearing is not required results from the expiration, loss or revocation of a license or permit required to lawfully perform the duties of the position. In such cases the employee is, or must be, discontinued from service because his or her ability to continue performing the duties of the position is made impossible or would be unlawful.

Positions or occupations that require the possession a valid license or its equivalent include teaching, operating motor vehicle on public highways, practicing law or medicine and serving as a certified public account. In the event the employee no longer possesses the required permit, he or she can neither lawfully perform, nor be permitted to perform, the duties requiring the possession of a valid permit or license.

Accordingly, the employee must be removed from the payroll regardless of the fact that he or she is competent (although not qualified) and may not be guilty of any misconduct. Here competence is not equated to qualification. In such cases it is not necessary to "hold a disciplinary hearing" unless the employer seeks to discipline the worker on independent grounds.

Due process is met if the employer provides the employee with a reasonable opportunity to show that he or she holds the required license or permit.

If the license or permit is not produced, the employee has, in effect, "removed himself" from the payroll. If the individual obtains the required license or permit, he or she would, presumably, be restored or reinstated to the position.

13.01 Necessity of a license

It should be remembered that the duties assigned must genuinely require the possession of a valid license for the appointee to lawfully perform those duties.

For instance, an Assistant Clinical Physician holding a permanent appointment with the Office of Mental Retardation and Developmental Disabilities was terminated from his position without notice or hearing because he did not obtain the required license to practice medicine issued by the Education Department (Education Law Section 8522).[72]

The Appellate Division affirmed a lower court ruling that the termination was unlawful (Matter of Martin as Administrator (Lekkas), 86 AD2d 712).

---

[72] The issue arose after the Education Law was amended to require persons previously appointed as physicians to obtain a license to practice medicine. Lekkas had been appointed to the position Assistant Clinical Physician prior to the amendment but had not obtained a New York State license to practice medicine within the prescribed time period.

While affirming the lawfulness of summarily discharging an employee without notice and hearing if the worker is unable to produce his or her license, the court held that this could be done only if the duties being performed required the possession of the license. According to the record, Lekkas was performing administrative duties rather than "practicing medicine."

The court said that no license was mandated by law to perform administrative duties, notwithstanding Lekkas' title of "Assistant Clinical Physician." Accordingly, his removal was subject to the notice and hearing provisions of the Civil Service Law.

13.02 Removal by operation of law

Public officers may be subject to removal by operation of law.[73] For example, Section 30(1) of Public Officers Law provides that any of the following events will result in the removal of the officer without recourse to a disciplinary hearing: (1) the officer ceases to be an inhabitant of the pertinent geographic area; (2) the officer refuses or neglects to timely file his oath of office; or (3) the officer is convicted of a felony or a crime involving a violation of his oath of office. If such an event occurs, the law declares that the office is vacant.

No hearing is required in such cases notwithstanding the fact that the public officer (e.g., a police officer), is otherwise entitled to due process such as that provided by Section 75 of the Civil Service Law or some other statute or a contract disciplinary procedure. A person "ineligible" to hold the position cannot be continued in it and therefore it is only necessary to make a determination as to the question of his qualification to hold such office.

Suppose a police officer is convicted of a felony. Clearly, the officer can be removed without a hearing. But suppose the conviction is reversed. Does that give the officer the right to be restored to the payroll?

No, the Court of Appeals ruled in Briggins v McGuire, 67 NY2d 965.[74] Once an office becomes vacant by operation of law, curing the defect (for example, the reversal of a conviction of a crime) will not automatically serve to restore the officer so removed from the position. It is the conviction that operates to bar the officer from the position rather than the guilt or proof underlying it.

After the Court of Appeals handed down its ruling in Briggins, Section 30.1(e) of the Public Officers Law was amended to provide for a limited right to a hearing under certain circumstances.[75]

Under the provisions of Section 30.1(e), as amended, if a public officer (other than an elected official) is convicted of a felony or a crime involving a violation of the individual's oath of office wins

---

[73] Although all public officers are public employees, not all public employees are public officers.

[74] The Briggins case involved a New York City police officer convicted of two counts of criminal possession of a forged instrument. Upon conviction he was summarily terminated from his position. Later the Court of Appeals decided that the documents in question (1) were not forged instruments and (2) their possession was not a violation of the Penal Law.

[75] Chapter 454, Laws of 1987, effective July 27, 1987.

reversal of the conviction or the conviction is vacated, he or she may request reinstatement where the conviction was the only basis for the termination.

While the appointing officer is free to grant such reinstatement upon receiving such a request, if reinstatement is denied the individual is entitled to a hearing to determine "whether reinstatement is warranted."

13.03 Disqualification for employment because of a criminal conviction

Sometimes the issue of a criminal conviction and disqualification for public employment is raised. Rodgers v NYC Human Resources Administration, 546 NYS2d 581, is a case that involves the termination of a public employee because he allegedly made false statements on his application for public employment. The decision indicates the potential interrelationship of portions of the Civil Service Law, the Human Rights Law and the Corrections Law.

Rodgers had been appointed as a caseworker in 1985. Two years later he was discharged of the grounds that he did not "admit his conviction record on his employment application." According to the ruling, Rodgers allegedly made a false statement on his application for employment when he stated that his did not have any criminal record. This alleged false statement was claimed to be the "sole basis of [Rodgers'] termination." Rodgers sued, claiming that his termination was arbitrary, and that his discharge was in violation of Section 296 of the Human Rights Law.

Although the statutory authority for the termination is not specified in the decision, it is assumed that Rodgers was disqualified pursuant to Section 50.4 of the Civil Service Law. Section 50.4 permits the State Department of Civil Service or a municipal commission or personnel officer to "investigate the qualifications and background of an eligible after he [or she] has been appointed ... and upon finding facts which if known prior to appointment, would have warranted his [or her] disqualification ... direct that his [or her] employment be terminated." Except in cases of fraud, there is a three-year statute of limitation on disqualifications pursuant to Section 50.4.

Rodgers had been convicted of two misdemeanors. However, he said that he had provided his employer with actual notice of the existence of his history of conviction of these misdemeanors when he submitted a copy of his Certificate of Relief from Civil Disabilities[76] together with "the dispositions of his criminal cases along with his application."

Although the courts of this State have generally upheld the termination of an employee upon a finding that he or she falsified a material fact in his or her application form, here the Appellate Division, Second Department, decided that some fact-finding was required. It remanded the matter to the Supreme Court for a hearing. The opinion indicates that the court believed that Rodgers "should be enabled to continue to be a valuable member of society, rather than be relegated to a life of crime due to this baseless allegation that he was anything less than forthcoming about his past."

The Appellate Division appeared troubled by the summary dismissal of Rodgers' case by the lower court in this instance.

---

[76] Section 702, Correction Law

The opinion includes a number of footnotes, including one indicating that "it is beyond dispute that [the City] had actual notice of the subject convictions and permitted [Rodgers] to retain his position after questioning;" and a second stating that the file of investigator originally involved in the case, whom Rodgers claimed told him that "there would be no further problems with his application" despite the inconsistency regarding his criminal record, "had been misplaced."

Another case in which the individual challenged his disqualification for making misrepresentation on his application for employment form is Martin v Marchiselli, App. Div., 6/17/99

Clearly Section 50.4 of the Civil Service Law authorizes the state department of civil service or the responsible civil service commission to disqualify and terminate an applicant or an employee if he or she has materially misrepresented his or her qualifications on the application form.

The Martin case involved a New York City police officer that was terminated pursuant to Section 50.4 for making a material misrepresentation on his application form.

The New York City Civil Service Commission found New York City police officer Kevin A. Martin unfit for such employment following a post-appointment investigation where "undisputed evidence" showed that Martin had falsified his employment application "to conceal his using a social security number not his own to obtain a second New York State drivers' license after his first license had been revoked."

The Appellate Division ruled that the Commission's action was neither arbitrary nor capricious since "the evidence warranted [Martin's] retroactive disqualification for employment ... on grounds of both fraud and unsatisfactory character."

In the event an appointing authority believes that an appointee should be disqualified for appointment, or having been appointed, removed from the position, it should write the responsible civil service commission of the situation, setting the reasons why the individual should be disqualified and ask that it take appropriate steps to disqualify the individual in accordance with the provisions of Section 50.4 of the Civil Service Law.

13.04 Irrelevance of criminal history

As to the protections contained in the State's Human Rights Law in cases involving an individual's "criminal history," except with respect to applicants for employment as a police officer or peace officer, Section 296.16 of the Executive Law makes it an unlawful discriminatory practice to inquire about an applicant's "criminal history" except with respect to matters then pending or where the individual was convicted.

Additional protections against discrimination based on a criminal conviction are contained in Section 752 of the Corrections Law. Section 752 prohibits "unfair discrimination" against persons previously convicted of one or more criminal offenses. The individual may not be refused employment unless "there is a direct relationship between one or more of the previous criminal offenses and the ...

employment sought; or ... granting employment would involve an unreasonable risk to property or to the safety or welfare of specific individuals or the general public."

Another aspect of this case relates to the issuance of a Certificate of Relief from Civil Disabilities pursuant to Section 702, Correction Law. Rodgers had obtained such a Certificate from a State court judge. The granting of such a Certificate by a court removes any bar to employment automatically imposed by law because of conviction of a crime. One exception, however is that such a Certificate does not excuse the impact of the conviction with respect to such an individual's right to retain or be eligible for holding a public office. This exception with respect to public office may be important in certain employment situations. As indicated earlier, although all public officers are public employees, not all public employees are public officers.

The Board of Parole is also authorized to issue such Certificates.[77]

Other methods available to a person convicted of a crime by which he or she may seek to obtain relief from certain disabilities imposed by law as a result of such conviction is the granting of a Certificate of Good Conduct by the State Board of Parole pursuant to Section 703-a, Correction Law, or the granting of an Executive Pardon by the Governor pursuant to Article 4, Section 4, State Constitution.

In the Rodgers case the Appellate Division said that the action taken against Rodgers by the City "seems contrary to the intent of both the legislature which enacted the statutory relief for the furtherance of public interest [Correction Law Section 702(2)(c)] and the courts which saw fit to grant [Rodgers] a second chance at life."

This suggests that in a Section 50.4 disqualification proceeding the courts expect the State Department of Civil Service and local commissions and personnel officers to give due weight to the fact that an applicant or an employee may offer a Certificate of Relief from Civil Disabilities or a Certificate of Good Conduct or an Executive Pardon in opposing his or her proposed disqualification for certification or employment.

13.05 Removal after convictions

In Graham v Coughlin, 72 NY2d 1014, the Court of Appeals upheld the removal of a State Correction Officer following his conviction of a felony under federal law -- mail fraud. The Appellate Division had ruled that Section 30.1(e) applied in cases of the officer's conviction of a felony under any jurisdiction. Although a majority of the Court of Appeals affirmed the Appellate Division's ruling, some members concurred in the decision because they felt that the offense for which Graham was convicted was a felony under New York State law as well as federal law.

When a New York State Senator, Israel Ruiz, Jr., was convicted of a felony under Federal law, the State Comptroller removed him from the payroll, relying on an Attorney General's opinion concerning Section 30.1.e of the Public Officers Law. Ruiz sued, seeking restoration to the payroll and back salary. He claimed that under the State Constitution only the State Senate could determine

---

[77] Section 703, Correction Law sets out the scope and effect of the issuance of such a Certificate by the Board of Parole.

the status of its members and that Section 30 did not diminish or limit the Senate's authority in this respect.

Judge Conway, Supreme Court, Albany County, rejected the argument. He said that Section 30.1.e provides that a public office becomes vacant upon the incumbent's conviction of a felony or a crime involving a violation of his [or her] oath of office. Citing Toro v Malcolm, 44 NY2d 146, Judge Conway ruled that under the circumstances Ruiz' conviction constituted "an abridgment of the office, automatically terminating its duration." The Judge also observed that Section 30.1(e) does not require that the conviction take place in a State Court nor does it expressly mandate that the crime be classified as a felony under New York's Penal Law.

Accordingly, "the Comptroller did not impermissibly remove [Ruiz] from office; rather, by the time the Comptroller acted (some ten days following the date of the conviction), the Legislature had already deemed [Ruiz'] seat vacant upon his felony conviction."

As earlier indicated, Section 30.1.e of the Public Officers Law provides that a public officer is automatically removed from the position upon his or her conviction of a felony or a crime involving a violation of his or her oath of office. To repeat earlier observations, in such cases there is no need to provide the individual with administrative due process such as might otherwise be the case under Section 75 of the Civil Service Law or a Taylor Law agreement.

In Hays v Ward, 542 NYS2d 949 a Supreme Court justice ruled that this amendment to Section 30.1.e was to apply retroactively. Hays, a New York City police officer, was convicted of a felony and removed from his position. Although the decision indicates that administrative disciplinary action was filed against Hays but is silent as to the disposition of these charges. Presumably the department abandoned prosecuting the disciplinary action as the record reports that "the Police Department never conducted a hearing on these charges. As a result of his conviction of manslaughter, in the second degree, Hays was removed pursuant to Section 30.1(e). This conviction was later reversed.

Hays was again indicted and tried for manslaughter, but was found not criminally responsible by reason of mental disease or defect by the jury. He then asked to be reinstated to his position as a police officer. The Department refused to reinstate him and also refused to provide any hearing concerning the issue. It based its decision not to provide Hays with a Section 30.1.e hearing on the fact that Hay's conviction was reversed on July 13, 1987 and the effective date of the amendment was July 27, 1987.

The court said that Section 30.1.e should be given a liberal construction. Thus "although [Hays'] situation does not technically fall within the wording of the statue, permitting [him] to take advantage of the 1987 amendment which entitles officers to a reinstatement hearing ... it is undisputed that his conviction was reversed before July 27, 1987, he was re-indicted based upon the same occurrence that resulted in the conviction, and subsequently acquitted after the effective date of the statute."

Thus, after the amendment took effect, he was ultimately found not to be criminally responsible for the act that first led to a felony conviction, and the vacation of his office pursuant to Public Officers Law Section 30." Based on this reasoning the court concluded that Hays was entitled to a Section 30 reinstatement hearing.

In the case of an elected officer, the courts have ruled that an elected public officer who is removed from their position pursuant to Section 30.1.e is ineligible for reelection to the unexpired term in the event an election to fill the vacancy is held.[78]

In this case Alamo attempted to have the nominating petition of Israel Ruiz, Jr. for State Senator invalidated. Ruiz had been convicted of a felony and removed from his seat as State Senator. He then filed as a candidate for reelected to the unexpired term of the Senate seat that he had forfeited following his conviction.

The Appellate Division said that this attempt by Ruiz to seek election to the position that he had forfeited because of his own malfeasance would nullify the legislative intent of Section 30.1.e. It held that Section 30.1.e must be read to disqualify any elected official from any entitlement to hold office for the duration of the unexpired term.

Presumably the same rule would apply in cases where a "non-elected" public officer who was appointed for a fixed term and was removed from public office pursuant to Section 30.1.e seeks reappointment to such office for the "unexpired term.

If a "non-elected" public officer was removed from a position pursuant to Section 30.1.e and, in addition was served with disciplinary charges that resulted in his or her removal from their position after being found guilty of one or more of such charges, the reinstatement procedures set out in Section 30.1.e may not always apply.

Only if the criminal conviction was the sole basis for finding the officer guilty in the administrative disciplinary hearing such as was the case in Kelly v Levin, 440 NYS2d 424.

Under such circumstances it appears that if the conviction is later reversed or vacated the Section 30.1.e reinstatement procedures become available to the former officer.

If, however, the individual was removed from his or her public office as a result of being found guilty of disciplinary charges that were filed against the officer and a due process hearing was provided, it seems likely that the review procedures set out in Section 30.1.e are not applicable, regardless of the nature of those charges.

Where a hearing is held in order to make such a determination, the entire employment history of the individual and any other information may be considered in deciding if reinstatement should be granted or denied. In addition, the final judgment of the court that reversed or vacated the conviction is to be included as part of the record.

In the event the appointing authority elects to reinstate the individual, back salary may be awarded as a matter of discretion. If the individual is to be reinstated but his or her former office is no longer available, Section 30.1(e) permits the individual to be appointed to a similar office.

---

[78] Alamo v Strohm, 545 NYS2d 1

13.06 Contract violation

In the Ennis decision, Ennis v Somers CSD, NYS Supreme Ct., Westchester County, one of the issues addressed by Justice Fredman, concerned allegations that the District breached its contract with Ennis.

Ennis, the Somers Central School District's Superintendent, alleged that the district had breached its contract with him when the Board of Education "unilaterally divested [him] of his duties and responsibilities."

According to Ennis, the School Board had adopted a resolution "reallocating the majority of [his] duties as superintendent" on January 6, 1993. He also alleged that on January 11, 1993, four members of the School Board voted to "literally strip me of all my powers as superintendent" and transferred them to the assistant superintendent. These actions by the board, Ennis argued, prevented him from performing the duties of his position as set out in the contract of employment between the parties. The court concurred, holding that "it is hornbook law that where one party to an executory contract prevents the performance of the contract he has committed a breach of the contract." There is an implied condition of every contract that one party will not prevent performance by the other. According to the court, by divesting Ennis of his duties, the board terminated his contract.

13.07 Denial of equal protection?

In a federal district court decision which may have an impact on the provisions of Section 30.1(e) of the Public Officers Law, the New York City Transit Authority's policy of rejecting applicants and terminating employees who have been convicted of a felony has been declared a violation of Equal Protection (Furst v NYC Transit Authority, USDC, EDNY).

Furst, an authority dispatcher, had been suspended following his being charged with a felony. Upon his conviction of the crime, he was terminated in accordance with Transit Authority policy. The district court opinion indicates that although a public employer has broad discretion in setting employment classifications, a policy of prohibiting the employment of felons is simply too broad to "accomplish any legitimate governmental purpose." As a result of this ruling, Furst may seek reinstatement and, presumably, back pay.

13.08 Employees-at-will

Although a relatively rare type of appointment, some public employees are termed "employees-at-will." When one such employee, the Executive Director of the Ilion Housing Authority, was terminated, he challenged his dismissal, claiming that he had been fired in retaliation for exercising his right to free speech. He also claimed that the State "Open Meetings Law" had been violated when the City's Housing Authority voted to dismiss him by secret ballot, thereby voiding his dismissal.

The Court of Appeals upheld the termination.[79] It said that Smithson had failed to show that his employment was terminated for "a constitutionally impermissible reason." It then indicated that the

---

[79] Smithson v Ilion Housing Authority, 72 NY2d 1034

claimed violation of the Open Meetings Law, under the circumstances, did not require the annulment of Smithson's termination.

13.09 Withdrawing resignations

Smith v Kunkel, 152 AD2d 893, considers the issue of an employer's refusal to permit an employee to withdraw a resignation following its delivery to the appropriate appointing authority.

Smith, a permanent state employee with the State Division of Equalization and Assessment, submitted his resignation for "personal reasons." The resignation was dated August 21 and was to take effect the following September 3. On August 29 Smith wrote the Division "seeking to withdraw and rescind" his resignation. Kunkel, the Division's Administrative Officer, noting that the resignation had been "accepted on August 21," refused to approve Smith's request to withdraw his resignation, citing 4 NYCRR 5.3(c) of the Rules for the Classified Service.

All that is required for a resignation to become operative is its delivery to the appointing authority; approval or acceptance of the resignation is not required for the resignation to take effect.[80] At most, all that an appointing authority might do is to "acknowledge the receipt" of the employee's resignation. Further, Section 5.3 of the Rules provides that if an effective date is specified in the resignation it takes effect on that date; if no date is specified it takes effect "upon delivery or filing in the office of the appointing authority."[81]

Under the Rules, however, the appointing authority may disregard the resignation in the event disciplinary charges have been filed, or are about to be filed, against the employee and proceed with the disciplinary action notwithstanding the receipt of the resignation.

Smith sued, claiming that Kunkel's refusal to permit him to withdraw his resignation was arbitrary and capricious. In addition, he contended that 4 NYCRR 5.3(c) was unconstitutional as it deprived him of his public employment without notice and hearing.

Although the action Smith brought was determined to be untimely, the Appellate Division did consider the merits of his Constitutional challenge to the Rule. It held that Smith's argument that the Rule was unconstitutional because it allows the appointing authority to deny the withdrawal of a resignation without providing any due process safe guards was incorrect. It said that the argument overlooked a crucial fact: Smith was not terminated but had voluntarily resigned his position with the division.

The court said that the "voluntariness of [Smith's] resignation is not vitiated [rendered legally ineffective] by the fact that Kunkel rejected his withdrawal request prior to the effective date of his resignation... Having relinquished his position [Smith] did not retain any constitutionally protected property interest in it."

---

[80] Hazelton v Connelly, 25 NYS2d 74

[81] 4 NYCRR 5.3 tracks Public Officers Law Section 31.2 as to the submission of resignations by public officers.

On the issue of resignation, cases involving employee efforts to withdraw a resignation that initially was clearly voluntary are not uncommon.

Many jurisdictions have adopted rules providing that in the event an officer or employee resigns from his or her position, regardless of the underlying reason for such resignation, that individual may not with rescind or withdraw the resignation, unless the appointing authority is willing to allow the resignation to be withdraw or rescinded.

These general propositions, although considered in the Davila case, were not followed because of what the court termed "a bizarre set of circumstances."[82]

According to the decision, Davila, a NYC Housing Authority police officer, was directed to take a random urine drug test." The sample proved "positive" for drugs. About a month later Davila was served with disciplinary charges alleging that (1) he had "possession or use of a controlled substance," which charge was apparently based on the earlier positive drug test; and with respect to an earlier incident that (2) he had filed a false report concerning his loss of "an off-duty firearm."

Davila was advised of his rights with respect to these charges, including his right to a hearing before a hearing officer, his right to representation by counsel or an authorized representative and his right to call witnesses on his behalf.

According to the judge, Davila, "rather than utilizing [the disciplinary] process, submitted his resignation apparently feeling at a loss as to what to do and feeling under emotional stress...." He then retained an attorney who requested a rescheduling of the disciplinary hearing so that [Davila] "would have a chance to vindicate himself." When the request was denied, Davila sued seeking a court order for the limited purpose of his being "reinstated solely for the purpose of appearing at a rescheduled disciplinary hearing" in order to defend himself against the charges.

The decision notes that Davila contended that he was not a drug user but had mistakenly ingested some drugs at his sister-in-law's home instead of aspirin two days before he was required to submit to the random drug test. His sister-in-law admitted she used drugs and attended a methadone clinic. She generally corroborated Davila's explanation for the positive drug test. [Davila also claimed that there was "a ready explanation" for the second charge regarding the submission of a false report.]

The judge, noting that under certain circumstances resignations will be set aside, decided that the events here alleged justified his granting an order "so that Mr. Davila can be reinstated solely for the purpose of providing him with a hearing on the disciplinary charges with all the rights attendant such a hearing."

This was apparently based on the court's view that although Davila did not claim that he resignation was obtained as the result of duress, the agency's refusal to reschedule a disciplinary hearing following his resignation when requested to do so could be construed as being arbitrary and capricious. Also indicated was the court's view that the charges here brought "are unrelated to [Davila's] job" and that Davila's petition "also give rise 'to a disquieting feeling that an injustice may have occurred'".

---

[82] Davila v NYC Housing Authority, _ Misc2d _

However, a number of questions as to the ultimate impact of this order are left unanswered. One such critical question is "What will happen if Davila is acquitted of all of the charges?"

Having been reinstated "solely for the purpose of providing him with a hearing on the disciplinary charges," this court order would not, of itself, appear to serve as authority to rescind the resignation. If so, the acquittal would apparently result in nothing more that Davila's "clearing his name." A name clearing hearing, however, serves only one purpose to clear the accused individual's good name and reputation. It does not result in the individual obtaining any right to reemployment. Presumably this means that having been provided with a hearing and having cleared his name, Davila has obtained all the relief to which the court found he was entitled.

If, on the other hand, there is an implication in this ruling to the effect that the authority is expected to reinstate Davila if he successfully defends himself at the disciplinary hearing, "what is the basis for the corollary implication the revocation of the resignation?"

The resignation presumably is, and continues to be, a lawful one, not having been obtained from Davila as the result of duress by the authority or as the result of other unlawful means, according to the court.

13.10 Name-clearing hearings

The availability of a name clearing hearing was the issue in Iritano v NYC Transit Authority, _ AD2d _,

Iritano, a provisional Principal Administrative Associate III terminated by the Authority, attempted to compel the Authority to reinstate him and to give him a name clearing hearing.

The Appellate Division said that "it is firmly established that provisional employees 'may be [discharged] at any time without charges being preferred, a statement or reasons being given or a hearing being held."

Moreover, "absent a violation of a constitutional or statutory provision, reinstatement is not an available remedy" to a discharged provisional employee even if vindicated at a name clearing hearing.

Although an employee may have been submitted a resignation in error, by mistake, in anger or for any reason or, indeed, no reason at all, this alone does not appear to serve to provide a former officer or employee with any special right to have the resignation rescinded or withdrawn if the employee changes his or her mind. Indeed, such an implication could have some far reaching effect. Consider, for example, the potential impact of such a result on an individual whom the agency, in good faith, appointed as the replacement for its former employee upon receipt of the resignation.

Another means by which an office may be deemed to be vacant is when the officer fails to file a required oath of office in a timely manner. Further, the failure to file a timely oath cannot be cured by subsequently filing the required oath.[83]

---

[83] Opinion of the Attorney General, 86-41, Informal

Sometimes any required hearing becomes "pro forma" in that there will be a predetermined result. As an example, a school business administrator was charged with larcenies of school funds and bringing discredit upon the school district.

The disciplinary panel (Education Law Section 3020-a) found the administrator guilty of the charge of bringing discredit upon the district, but not guilty of the larceny charges. However, the employee had already been convicted of two counts of grand larceny for theft of school property prior to the Section 3020-a hearing.[84]

Accordingly, the guilt of the administrator had been already conclusively established. The court said that under the doctrine of collateral estoppel, (a person cannot argue the same thing twice) the hearing panel could not find the employee not guilty of the larcenies. The judge reversed and returned the case to the panel for reconsideration of the appropriate penalty to be imposed.[85]

In another case involving a crime, the Commissioner of Education, in Decision 10479, held that a school district had to do more than merely present evidence of the conviction of a tenured teacher on a conspiracy charge in connection with discipline for "conduct unbecoming a teacher."

In order to present a prima facie case, the school district would be required to present evidence of the effect of the conviction of the crime upon the teacher's performance or effectiveness as a teacher. The decision indicates that conviction created a rebuttable presumption that the teacher had engaged in conduct unbecoming a teacher but it was still the burden of the employer to demonstrate the relationship of the crime to the employee's performance as a teacher at the hearing.

13.11 Noncompetitive class employees

Sometimes the date of an event or a final disciplinary determination could be a consideration. An example of this is found in Matter of Voorhis, 429 NYS2d 325.

Voorhis, a school bus driver, was dismissed without a hearing following a number of complaints regarding her performance of her duties. As she was a "permanent" noncompetitive class employee, she claimed her dismissal was in violation of her civil service rights as well as her right to due process under the 14th Amendment.

The Appellate Division disagreed noting that the legislature did not (yet) include noncompetitive employees of the political subdivisions of the State among those covered by Section 75 of the Civil Service Law, the court concluded that Voorhis did not establish any liberty or property interest in (continued) employment by the school district. Section 75 has since been amended to provide due process rights to employees serving in noncompetitive class positions in a political subdivision of the State, including school districts.

---

[84] People v Kelly, 72 AD2d 670

[85] Kelly v Levin, 440 NYS2d 424

Although noncompetitive class employees such as Voorhis are protected from discharge in bad faith in contravention of the fundamental purposes of the civil service system (discharge for political patronage purposes, for example) such persons are otherwise "at will" employees. As such, they are subject to dismissal upon the proper exercise of the appointing officer's discretion. In Voorhis' situation, "permanent" indicated only that Voorhis had successfully completed her probationary period.[86]

13.12 Disqualification, Section 50.4 CSL

A hearing is not required when an employee is terminated pursuant to Section 50.4 of the Civil Service Law. This was illustrated when the Wayne County Civil Service commission disqualified an employee and removed him from his position as police officer with the Village of Palmyra without any hearing.

The commission had determined that the police officer had "intentionally made false statements of material facts in his application or (had) attempted to practice (a) deception or fraud in his application. The employee sued, claiming he could not be removed from the position without a hearing.[87]

The Court of Appeals rejected Mingo's argument, stating that Section 50.4 "requires no more than that the person be given a written statement of the reasons therefore and afforded an opportunity to make explanation and to submit facts in opposition to such disqualification." No hearing is required. The reason for the Commission's action: the Commission had determined that Mingo had falsified his application with respect to his experience as a police officer and concealed facts related to his separation from previous employment.

Similarly, the Appellate Division in the case of Stewart v Civil Service Commission, City of New York, 84 AD2d 491, upheld the disqualification of a candidate who failed to include the fact that he had been convicted of a number of crimes in his application form for the position of traffic enforcement agent.

The commission's reason for the disqualification was not the criminal conviction but because Stewart misstated a material fact in his application form.[88] Neither Section 296.15 of the Executive Law (unlawful discrimination because of a criminal conviction) nor Section 752 of the Correction Law (unlawful denial of employment because of prior conviction or lack of "good moral character") was viewed by the court as controlling.

---

[86] Section 63, Civil Service Law

[87] Mingo v Pirnie, 55 NY2d 1019

[88] Civil Service Law Section 50.4(d) deals with disqualification where the applicant has been guilty of a crime; Section 50.4(f) permits disqualification for intentionally making a false statement on the application form.

13.13 Nature of the offense

Section 50.4 of the Civil Service Law permits an applicant or appointee to be disqualified if he or she falsifies any material facts in their application for examination. Is the failure to indicate the conviction of a "violation" in response to the question "Have you ever been convicted of a crime?" a falsification within the meaning of Section 50.4? According to the decision of the Appellate Division in Maymi v Sorrento Cheese Company, failure to indicate the conviction of a violation may not constitute a falsification of the examination application form.

Maymi had filed an application form with Sorrento in which he answered "no" to the question "Have you ever been convicted of a crime?" It was later found that he had been convicted of disorderly conduct and was suspended from his employment. He then filed a complaint with the Division of Human Rights alleging unlawful discrimination because he was rejected for employment because of his criminal record.

The division accepted the employer's explanation that Maymi had been terminated because he gave false information on his application form as to his criminal conviction rather than because he had been convicted of a crime.

It then concluded that there was insufficient evidence to demonstrate that Sorrento had unlawfully discriminated against Maymi because of his criminal record.

The Appellate Division reversed this determination and returned the complaint to the division for further consideration. The court pointed out that it is a violation of the Human Rights Law to discriminate against a person because of an arrest or a conviction of a criminal offense.[89]
The court then concluded that Maymi had not falsified his application form as under Section 10.00(6) of the Penal Law a crime is defined as a "misdemeanor or a felony." Disorderly conduct, Section 240.20(7) of the Penal Law, on the other hand, is an "offense," not a "crime."

For this reason, said the court, Maymi had truthfully answered the question on the application form as to any criminal conviction. It then indicated the Maymi had clearly demonstrated probable cause that the company had unlawfully discriminated against him on account of his conviction of criminal offense.

13.14 Violation of oath of office

Public Officers Law Section 30.1.e provides that a public office becomes vacant when the incumbent is convicted of a felony or "a crime involving a violation of his oath of office". The Court of Appeals has ruled that Section 30.1.e clearly applies in situations involving a felony conviction. In Duffy v Ward, _ NY2d _, the issue concerned whether the statute applies in misdemeanor convictions arising outside the line of duty. In other than felony convictions summary termination is permitted only if the crime if found to constitute a violation of the individual's oath of office. Duffy, a New York City

---

[89] Executive Law Sections 296.15 and 296.16

police officer, was found guilty of the misdemeanor of criminal trespass in the second degree after an off-duty scuffle with another man. Following the conviction, Ward, the police Commissioner, summarily terminated him.

The court said that in such cases the courts should look not to the facts of the particular case but solely to the elements of the crime. Here it found that the elements of criminal trespass in the second degree, Penal Law 140.15, as charged here, couldn't be read to constitute a crime involving a violation of petitioner's oath of office. Accordingly, the court held that he should have been afforded a hearing before termination.

The court noted that summary termination pursuant to Section 30.1(e) is not a punishment for the office-holder's crime, and reversal of the conviction on appeal does not automatically entitle the office-holder to return to the vacated position. The automatic vacation of a public office upon conviction reflects two legislative concerns - (1) governmental work should not go unattended, or a position unfilled, while a convicted office- holder pursues a potentially lengthy appeal and (2) the public has a "right to rest assured that its officers are individuals of moral integrity in whom they may, without second thought, place their confidence and trust."

The court then explained that when an office-holder's termination is premised on a "crime involving a violation of [the] oath of office," two questions are raised. "First, should a court, before sustaining a vacatur, look solely to the elements of the crime as set forth in the Penal Law or may it permissibly review the underlying facts of the particular incident leading to the criminal charge" and "second, what type of misdemeanor comes within the terms of the statute?"

In analyzing this case the court said that "understanding that overall statutory scheme is critical to understanding the purposes of Section 30.1.e. The decision indicates that "in making convictions upon certain crimes grounds for immediate dismissal, the legislature implicitly acknowledged that no factual showing by the office-holder was needed, for under no circumstances could facts unique to the incident mitigate the violation of the public trust confirmed by, and arising from, the criminal conviction. Thus, all felony convictions, whether on duty or off duty, whether crimes of violence or crimes of deception, trigger automatic dismissal." The court said that it follows that the second category of offense in Section 30.1.e. "a crime involving a violation of [the] oath of office," should likewise be interpreted in such a way that no factual inquiry is needed to trigger automatic dismissal."

In this case, however, the court distinguished between the automatic termination resulting from a felony conviction and termination following a misdemeanor convictions for conduct outside the line of duty on the grounds that it constitutes "a crime involving a violation of [the] oath of office" under Section 30.1.e. Such automatic termination will result only if the violation is apparent from the Penal Law's definition of the crime.

Where it is not "apparent" that the crime involved constitutes a violation of the individual's oath of office, misdemeanor convictions arising outside the line of duty, a hearing is required and automatic termination pursuant to Section 30.1.e is not authorized.

Applying this analysis to Duffy's situation, the court concluded that his automatic termination must be vacated. The court said that criminal trespass is not the sort of misdemeanor that can be construed facially as a crime "involving a violation of [the] oath" for purposes of Section 30.1.e and summary dismissal was not warranted. Accordingly, a hearing is required so that the extent and nature of Duffy's misconduct can be resolved before he is disciplined.

13.15 Reversal of felony conviction

A city attorney asked the Attorney General whether its former police chief, who had been convicted of various crimes, including the misdemeanors of obstructing governmental administration and attempted hindering of prosecution and felonies, was barred from being employed as a chief of police or a police officer or from being elected to other public office. The city attorney indicated that the felony convictions had been reversed on appeal.

The attorney general[90] indicated that Section 30.1.e of the Public Officers Law declares that a public office becomes vacant upon the conviction of the incumbent "of a felony, or a crime involving a violation of his oath of office".[91]

Thus, he said, the office of police chief became vacant upon the conviction of its incumbent by operation of law. As to the possible impact of the reversal of the felony convictions, the attorney general said that this did not change the situation and the reversal of such a conviction does not automatically require the reinstatement of the former public officer. Section 30.1(e), however, does set out the procedures to be followed in the event the individual asks to be reinstated to his or her former position. It provides that where the underlying conviction was the sole reason for the individual's termination, a public officer, other than an elected officer, who applies for and is refused reinstatement following the reversal of the conviction is to be given a "reinstatement hearing" to determine whether reinstatement is warranted.

As to the former chief's conviction for "obstructing governmental administration," the attorney general indicted that as such an action would tend to undermine the integrity of government, it constitutes a violation of a public officer's oath of office.

The opinion also notes that case law indicates that were a public officer is removed under color of Section 30.1.e, that individual is disqualified form holding that office for the duration of its unexpired term. Accordingly, such a former officer holder is prohibited from being elected or appointed to the same office for any unexpired term of office remaining following his or her removal.[92]

In response to the possibility of the former chief's reemployment as a police officer, the attorney general indicated that Sections 50 and 58 of the Civil Service Law would control. Section 58 provides that an individual is ineligible for employment as a police officer unless he or she is of "good moral character."

---

[90] Opinions of the Attorney General, Informal Opinion 93-13

[91] For the purposes of Section 30.1.e, a plea of guilty is the equivalent of a conviction.

[92] Alamo v Strohm, 153 AD2d 542

Under Section 50.4, a civil service commission may refuse to examine an applicant for a position "who is found to lack any of the established requirements for admission to the examination or for appointment to the position ... or who has been guilty of a crime." The opinion, however, notes that a civil service commission's determination under Section 50.4 must be reasonable, based on the facts and circumstances relating to the applicant's character and fitness.

CHAPTER 14

REDRESS AND REMEDIES

Section 77 of the Civil Service Law provides that an employee who was wrongfully removed from his or her position and is then reinstated to the position pursuant to a court order is to receive back pay for the period from the date of the wrongful removal to the date of his or her restoration to the payroll, less any unemployment insurance received by the individual. If, however, there was any delay in the disciplinary proceeding caused by the accused employee, the salary otherwise payable for the period of such delay is to be deducted from the amount of back pay to be awarded the employee.

Similarly, where the accused employee has been suspended without pay as authorized by Section 75 of the Civil Service Law, if there is a delay in proceeding with the disciplinary hearing caused by the employee during while suspended without pay, the appointing authority may extend the period of such suspension without pay for an equal period of time.

14.01 Delays in reinstatements

The Boylan case, Boylan v Town of Yorkville, _ AD2d _, involves another aspect of determining the back pay due an employee restored to the position pursuant to a court order: the effect of a delay in actually reinstating the individual to his or her position.

Apparently Boylan was to be reinstated to his former position effective June 1, 1987. However he was not restored to the payroll until June 24, 1989. Noting that "where the 'delay in proceeding is occasioned by the conduct of the accused,' he will be denied the right to recover wages for the period involved," the Appellate Division said that there was nothing in the record indicating that Boylan was responsible for the delay in restoring him to his position during the period June 1, 1987 through June 24, 1989.

Other aspects of the case involved the payment of interest and reductions in the amount of the back pay award for earnings from "outside employment" during this period. The lower court did not award any interest on the award of back pay and, in addition, reduced the amount to be paid Boylan for back salary by the amount of money he had earned in "outside employment" during the period involved.

The Appellate Division said that interest should have been awarded, citing its ruling in Kohler v Board of Education, 142 AD2d 260, and, in addition, held that the amount due Boylan as back salary should not have been reduced by earning from outside employment.

Although back pay awards are to be reduced to reflect any payments for unemployment insurance received by the individual during the period involved, in 1984 subdivision 3 of the Section 75 of the Civil Service Law was amended to eliminate wages from outside employment as a factor in adjusting such back pay awards.[93]

---

[93] Chapter 710, Laws of 1984, effective August 3, 1984

14.02 Back pay

NYC Dept. of Personnel v NYC Civil Service Comm. and White, _ NY2d _, concerns the authority of the NYC Civil Service Commission to award an employee back pay in connection with its directing the employee's reinstatement to his or her former position.

In January 1985 White was appointed to the New York City Housing Authority Police Department, subject to a background check. He was terminated during his probationary period for allegedly failing to provide certain information on his application and because he was believed to be medically disqualified. Presumably the termination was accomplished without recourse to any formal disciplinary hearing or procedure in view of White's probationary status.

White appealed his termination to the NYC Civil Service Commission, which overturned the Authority's decision and restored White to his position. It also awarded him back pay for the period he had not worked for the Authority, less any amounts earned or received as unemployment benefits.

The Authority challenged the award of back pay, contending that the Commission had no power to grant that form of relief in the absence of a statutory or a Taylor Law contract provision authorizing it to do so. The Court of Appeals agreed, indicating that "an administrative agency has only those powers expressly or impliedly given it."

It said that under the Section 812.c of the City Charter the Commission's power is that of "an appeals board: to hear and decide appeals by those aggrieved by an agency's personnel determination and to hear and decide appeals in disciplinary proceedings."

In hearing such appeals the Commission may only "affirm, modify or reverse" petitioner's determination -- the power to award back pay is neither expressly given nor may it necessarily be implied as a part of the Commission's delegated powers.

In view of this, the Court of Appeals ruled that the absence of specific authority in law or contract to do so prohibits the Commission from granting a prevailing employee back pay.

The Court of Appeals rejected White's argument that the authority for the award was set out in Section 77 of the Civil Service Law. The court pointed out that Section 77 concerns compensation of employees reinstated "by order of the Supreme Court" and thus was inapplicable in cases such as this as White was reinstated by the Commission's action and not by a "court order."

Section 77 provides that "any officer or employee ... restored to such position by order of the Supreme Court ... shall receive from the state or such civil division ... salary or compensation he would have been entitled by law to receive but for such unlawful removal ... less the amount of any unemployment insurance benefits...."

However, Section 76.3 of the Civil Service Law authorizes the State Civil Service Commission as well as municipal Civil Service Commissions "to direct the reinstatement" of an employee within the context of a successful disciplinary appeal.

In such cases an employee who is so reinstated is to "receive the salary or compensation he [or she] would have been entitled by law to have received ... for the period of removal ... including any prior period of suspension without pay ... less the amount of any unemployment insurance benefit ... received during such period."

It would appear that who is reinstated pursuant to Section 76.3 is entitled to receive "back salary" by operation of law, pointing out the similarity of the language contained in Section 76.3 and that contained in Section 77 in this regard.

14.03 Reinstatement

A request for reinstatement was a key issue in Pinto v Town of Greenburgh, 567 NYS2d 98

Pinto was found guilty of misconduct after a disciplinary hearing in November, 1986. The penalty imposed was dismissal from his position as a Recreation Supervisor with the Town of Greenburgh.

In December, 1988 Pinto asked the Town to reinstate him to his former position. When his request was denied, Pinto sued the Town. His petition seeking reinstatement was dismissed. The court held that his 1988 request for reinstatement was nothing more than an application for reconsideration of the Town's determination dismissing him from his position.

The Appellate Division affirmed a lower court ruling that Pinto's action was "time-barred," having been brought more than four months after the completion of the disciplinary action in 1986. Further, the general rule is that a request for "reconsideration" of a disciplinary determination does not stop the statute of limitations from running for the purpose of filing a timely appeal.

The Greiner case, Greiner v Greene County Dept. of Fire Prevention and Control, _ AD2d _ #65974, 3rd Dept.; Greiner v Greene County, 177 AD2d 907, is another case involving an individual's applying for reinstatement to his former position following criminal action with some interesting twists.

Greiner, a fire dispatcher and part-time fire investigator and deputy sheriff, was accused of wrongfully retaining a firearm found at the scene of a fire. Found guilty by the disciplinary hearing officer, the appointing authority concurred and adopted the penalty recommended by the hearing officer -- immediate dismissal from service, subject to reinstatement [or placement on a preferred list] should Greiner by acquitted of pending criminal charges involving the same incident.[94]

According to the Appellate Division, reinstatement would be allowed only if Greiner were found "not guilty." Conviction of a reduced charge or the entry of a plea bargain or a decision not to prosecute would not satisfy the "not guilty" requirement.

---

[94] This penalty is similar to the procedure set out in Section 30.1.e of the Public Officers Law in cases involving the removal of a public officer following a conviction of a felony or a crime involving a violation of the officer's oath of office in the event the conviction is later overturned or vacated.

The criminal charges were presented to a grand jury, which return a "no bill" verdict. The department, concluding that the grand jury's finding "no bill" was, in effect, a decision not to prosecute, declined to reinstate Greiner. The Appellate Division agreed with the lower court's ruling that the return of a "no bill" by the grand jury was the equivalent of a "not guilty" verdict.

The court pointed out that to obtain an indictment, the prosecutor merely had to present a prima facie case that a defendant committed the crime charged; proof beyond a reasonable doubt was not required. Where, as here, this lesser standard has not been met, it must be viewed as a lack of enough creditable evidence to warrant a prosecution.

The Appellate Division ruled that Greiner was entitled to back pay from the time the first vacancy became available following the dismissal of the criminal charges against him, October 15, 1990, rather than the date on which he was reinstated pursuant to a court order, November 1, 1991. The Appellate Division held that under the circumstances, the department's failure to reinstate Greiner to the "first available position ... effectively subjected him to an "unlawful removal." Accordingly, he was entitled to back pay from that point in time to the date on which he was actually restored to the payroll.

Another opportunity for seeking reinstatement is to challenge the penalty imposed. In the White case, White v Department of Law, 584 NYS2d 555, the thrust of the appeal was an attempt to vacate an arbitration award that imposed the penalty of dismissal.

White brought an Article 75 [Article 75, Civil Practice Law and Rules] in which he asked the court to vacate the arbitrator's award. The court denied his motion and dismissed the action.

White then appealed, contending that the failure of the department of law to enter the judgment constituted an abandonment of the lower court's order. The Appellate Division disagreed and dismissed the appeal. The decision states that although Section 7510 implies that an application to confirm an arbitration award must be made within one year after the delivery of the award, there was no need to do so in this instance.

The court cited Section 7511(e) of the CPLR as mandating an automatic confirmation of an arbitration award upon the denial of a motion to vacate or modify the award. The failure to enter judgment was viewed by the Appellate Division as "a mere procedural irregularity" that had no effect on the viability of the Supreme Court judge's determination dismissing the action.

CHAPTER 15

DRUGS, DRUG TESTING AND DISCIPLINE

Courts in New York are allowing public employers greater flexibility in mandating employees submit to involuntary testing for drugs, provided the employer provides due process and uses accurate and reliable testing methods.

A growing a body of case law suggests that public safety officers are to be held to a high standard and that dismissal for drug use or refusal to submit to such tests is not likely to be overturned by the courts on the issue of fairness of the penalty.

Routine, random testing of officers for drug use generally has not been viewed by courts as compromising Constitutional rights, especially if the process has been agreed upon through a collective bargaining process.

Although alcoholics and drug abusers can qualify for special treatment and accommodations under state and federal disabilities laws, generally those protections are not applicable to public safety officers.

15.01 Reasonable suspicion

For many years courts looked for a "reasonable suspicion" of drug use to support involuntary testing. See, for instance Shepard v Ward, 547 NYS2d 57 (anonymous tips, along with glassy, bloodshot eyes and history of mood swings constitute reasonable suspicion); and Jackson v Gates, CA9, 90-55728 (being seen with another officer who was involved with drugs is not reasonable suspicion).

More recent decisions suggest that courts do not require that periodic, random testing is permissible and that departments that use such testing protocols need not show a reasonable suspicion existed before an officer was tested. See, for instance, Caruso v Ward, 72 NY2d 432 (random testing of "elite" police officers assigned to an organized crime unit is permissible); Seelig v Koehler, 546 NYS2d 828 and Seelig v Koehler, 146 AD2d 486 (supporting involuntary testing of New York City Correction officers every five to six years); McKenzie v Jackson, 547 NYS2d 120 (involuntary testing of probationary corrections officers was not an unreasonable search and seizure under the Fourth Amendment); Chicago Firefighters Local 2 v Chicago, 4 IER 970 (locker searches do not violate the Fourth Amendment because expectation of privacy was diminished).

Through collective bargaining, unions have the power to give members' legal consent to submit to randomly drug tests [Battaglia v NYC Transit Authority, Appellate Division; Ballentine v Koch, Appellate Division]

A case dealing with teachers shows that a lower standard applies to non-law enforcement personnel. In Patchogue-Medford Congress of Teachers v Patchogue-Medford Union Free School District, 119 AD2d 35, the Court of Appeals held that random searches by public employers without reasonable suspicion of the illegal use of drugs is subject to close scrutiny and are generally permissible only when "the privacy interests implicated are minimal, the government's interest is substantial, and safeguards are provided to insure that the individual's reasonable expectations of privacy is not subjected to unregulated discretion." The Patchogue case arose after the school district imposed passing a test for illegal drugs as a condition for acquiring tenure without any evidence that probationary teachers were using illegal drugs.

Frequency of testing can be an issue. The Appellate Division held that monthly testing of randomly selected members of Nassau Police Department's Narcotics Bureau and other special units was an impermissible intrusion on privacy rights. [Delaraba v Nassau Co. Police Dept., _ AD2d _)

Other cases involving the question of requiring an employee to submit blood and urine samples for the purpose of testing for the use of controlled substances include:

Krolick v Lowery, 32 AD2d 317 (firefighters); Division 241, ALT v Suscy, 429 U.S. 1029 (bus and train operators); City of Palm Bay v Bauman, 475 So.2d 1322 (police and firefighters); Turner v Fraternal Order of Police, 500 AD2d 1005 (police); Council 82 v Carey, 737 F2d 187 (security personnel); Colonnade Catering v United States, 397 U.S. 72 (liquor handlers); Shoemaker v Handel, 608 F. Supp. 1151 (horse racing); and Matter of Martin, 447 AD2d 1290 (casino gambling).

15.02 Pre-employment testing

Federal District Court Judge Michael B. Mukasey, USDC, Southern District of New York, has ruled that the pre-employment medical testing of applicants for public employment for drugs is not a search within the meaning of the Fourth Amendment (Fowler v NY Dept. of Sanitation, 704 F. Supp 1264).

The case involved the Department's requirement that prospective employees submit to a test to determine the presence of drugs in their urine to determine their fitness for employment. This decision runs counter to a number of rulings by federal Circuit Courts holding that any such testing is a "search and seizure" under the Fourth Amendment.

This ruling could affect eligibility for unemployment insurance benefits. The individual would probably be disqualified for benefits if he or she refuses or cannot pass the test for drugs "ineligible for benefits." In such a situation the individual would most likely be deemed to be "unavailable for suitable employment" if such employment is conditioned on passing a test for drugs.

Courts evaluate Fourth Amendment privacy issues in the context of the requirements of the job and the degree to which privacy expectations are reasonable. In Skinner v Railway Labor Executives' Association, 109 S.Ct. 1402, the U.S. Supreme Court ruled that the privacy expectations of railway workers were diminished by the fact that employees were working in an industry that was closely regulated to ensure safety.

California's Supreme Court has ruled that it is permissible for public employers in that state to screen applicants for initial appointments to the public service, but that employers cannot require candidates for promotion to pass a test for illegal drugs.[95]

15.03 Due process guidelines

In the McKenzie case,[96] the Appellate Division indicated the employer met the following five standards in the manner indicated:

1. Notice - the examination announcement gave appropriate notice that probationers could be required to submit to periodic substance abuse testing;

2. Duration - the random testing for drugs was limited to only that period during which the employee was a probationer;

3. Privacy - appointees were aware of the scrutiny to which the employer subjects probationary employees and therefore a probationer's expectation of privacy is correspondingly lower than that of a tenured employee;

4. Employer's interest - the employer involved, a Department of Corrections, has a substantial interest in the security of its facilities and in ensuring that probationary correction officers who abuse drugs to not gain tenure; and

5. Exercise of discretion - the promulgation, announcement and posting of the employer's guidelines concerning the use of illegal drugs, drug testing policies and the impact of a finding that a probationer was using illegal drugs satisfied the requirement the employer not possess "unregulated discretion" in such matters.

The Appellate Division concluded that under the relevant facts of this case, "the specific requirements for finding that the random urinalysis drug-testing program falls within the narrow expectation identified by [Patchogue-Medford Congress of Teachers v Patchogue-Medford Union Free School District, 119 AD2d 35] have been satisfied."

Key factors, which the court described as "peculiar to this case," and which it found sufficient to warrant the substantial intrusion of random testing searches, included the following:

1. The employment is in a unique, high-risk, hazardous setting;

2. The guards have voluntarily agreed to submit to a previously enacted series of urinalyses, both random and suspicion based;

---

[95] Loder v City of Glendale, Calif. Sup. Ct., 1997, citing the U.S. Supreme Court's ruling in Treasury Employees vs. Van Raab, 109 S.Ct. 1384

[96] McKenzie v Jackson, 547 NYS2d 120

3. The guards are already subject to a host of intrusive searches of person and property with no suspicion predicate;

4. The Commissioner has demonstrated drug use in his ranks and an inability to stop it with currently available procedures;

5. A guard's usage increases substantially the inherent dangerousness of illicit drugs, putting at risk the lives of inmates and fellow officers;

6. A drug-compromised guard establishes a two-way security breach -- drugs and weapons are more easily smuggled into jail and prisoners can more easily "elope;"

7. The challenged testing procedures guard the privacy and dignity of the subjects as carefully as possible;

8. The accuracy and integrity of the test results are meticulously circumscribed; and

9. A significant appeals process is granted to those who test positive.

15.04 Guidelines on employee privacy

Law enforcement personnel cannot expect the same level of privacy as other employees. However there must be appropriate and sufficient procedural safeguards with respect to the administration of the drug tests in order to pass judicial scrutiny.

In its decision in King v McMickens, 120 AD2d 351, the Appellate Division listed a number of guidelines dealing with a government employer requiring correction officers, and presumably other law enforcement personnel, to submit to tests for drugs. These include the following:

1. Information obtained from an informant concerning the alleged use of drugs by a correction officer provides a reasonable basis for requiring the employee to provide a urine sample for use in testing for drugs.

2. Probable cause is not required where the purpose is not aimed at the discovery of evidence for use in a criminal trial - reasonable suspicion is sufficient even if the information is later to be used in a disciplinary hearing.

3. Refusal to comply with a lawful order to submit to a test for drugs is insubordination.

4. Hearsay information concerning the use of drugs by a correction officer provided by an informant may be used in a disciplinary hearing.

The court observed that a correction officer occupies a sensitive position and is subject to paramilitary discipline. The critical duties of a law enforcement position cannot be satisfactorily performed if the individual's ability to perform his or her duties is impaired by drugs. In view of this, the court concluded that a correction officer's reasonable expectation of privacy as a private citizen must yield to compelling governmental interests when he or she becomes a law enforcement officer.

King and his brother, both correction officers with the New York City Department of Corrections, were under investigation for drug use based on information alleging that the brothers frequented a known drug trafficking location and were observed using drugs at that location. When they refused to submit samples of their urine for the purpose of testing for illegal drugs, they were served with disciplinary charges pursuant to Section 75 of the Civil Service Law. They were found guilty and dismissed.

They then challenged their dismissals on the grounds that (1) the order to provide a urine sample was unconstitutional; (2) the order was not based on reasonable grounds; and (3) the order had not been issued by the appropriate superior officer. The Appellate Division rejected all three arguments.

15.05 Observer's presence during testing

Firefighters may be required to urinate in the presence of an observer as part of municipal drug testing program, according to a federal court decision involving the City of Wilmington, Del. A female firefighter failed in her effort to have the court order a less intrusive method of collecting urine samples.[97]

15.06 Drug testing and collective bargaining

The Court of Appeals has ruled that "constitutional rights may be waived by voluntary employment agreements"[98] In other words, a union can bargain away individual members' constitutional rights.

Likewise, the Taylor Law conceivably could prevent an employer from establishing an involuntary drug-testing program without agreement from the union. PERB ruled that an order by a school district requiring a member of the negotiating unit, bus driver Theresa Davies, to undergo involuntary urinalysis testing for drugs constituted a unilateral change in the terms and conditions of employment that were subject to mandatory collective negotiations.[99]

It is worth noting, however, that both PERB and the courts may establish different standards for public safety agencies.

Although the U.S. Supreme Court now appears disinclined to distinguish between government workers on the basis of their involvement in public safety when it comes to involuntary testing for drugs, New York courts seem disposed to do so. Based on present New York case law, the rules with

---

[97] Wilcher v City, USDC DC, CIV A-94-137-JJFb2

[98] Antinore v State of New York, 40 NY2d 921

[99] CSEA v Arlington CSD, 25 PERB 3001

respect to the involuntary drug testing of law enforcement personnel and other employees involved with the public safety, would not be viewed as uniformly applicable to government employees in general. It would not be surprising if similar distinctions based on the actual duties of the positions involved would be made regarding the question of the impact of the Taylor Law on an employer's authority to unilaterally establish and implement a drug testing policy as well.

15.07 Penalties

Disciplinary action for illegal drug use may result in a termination. The courts appear to be receptive to such a penalty under certain circumstances. For example, the Appellate Division, Second Department, sustained the termination of a New York City Transit Authority when it was found that his urine tested positive for marijuana.[100]

The Appellate Division rejected McCoy's argument that dismissal was too harsh a penalty, the court said that here termination "was not so disproportionate to the offense as to be shocking to one's sense of fairness," citing Pell v Board of Education, 34 NY2d 222.

15.08 Refusal to participate in a drug treatment program

What may an employer do if an employee fails to cooperate with respect to the employer's drug counseling or drug treatment program? The Hill and Akers cases consider a number of issues that could be involved in such situations.[101]

In the Hill case, the employer terminated one of its workers because of the employee's failure to follow through with an employer-sponsored drug treatment program. Hill had agreed to a number of conditions with respect to his continued employment in a settlement of a disciplinary grievance.

Among the conditions was his participation in a company sponsored [drug] treatment program. Another term of the settlement provided that he would be subject to immediate termination if he tested positive for illegal drugs. Hill failed to participate in the treatment program as required. In addition, when he was subsequently tested for drugs, the test proved positive. He was terminated.

Hill then applied for unemployment insurance benefits. He was disqualified for benefits on the basis that his employment had been terminated for misconduct. The Appellate Division, Third Department, affirmed the disqualification, noting that under the circumstances, that there was substantial evidence that Hill's actions constituted misconduct disqualifying him for unemployment insurance benefits to support the determination of the Unemployment Insurance Board.

---

[100] McCoy v Gunn, 545 NYS2d 583

[101] Hill v Hartnett, 568 NYS2d 234; Akers v New York City Transit Authority, 569 NYS2d 137

The Akers case involved similar facts. Akers was dismissed from his position as a motorman with the New York City Transit Authority after he tested positive for cocaine and failed to attend a drug-counseling program to which he had been assigned.

According to the case record, Akers had been placed on probation earlier because of his "inconsistent record in attending [drug] counseling." He was told, and acknowledged in writing, that he could be dismissed from the counseling program if he continued to miss scheduled meetings.

Akers returned to work. While still on probation he apparently reported for work when he was scheduled for a counseling session. Akers claimed that he had called a drug counselor and informed him that there was a conflict between the scheduled drug counseling session and his duty to report to work at the Authority. Akers was told that the counseling session would not be rescheduled and if he missed the meeting he would be discharged from the program.

Notwithstanding this warning, Akers elected to report for work and did not attend the scheduled counseling session. According to the record, Akers also failed to attend other drug counseling meetings that were scheduled for him. Akers was told that he was not in compliance with the drug counseling program requirement and was dismissed from his job.

When he asked for a review of his dismissal by a contractual "tripartite arbitration board," the arbitration board rejected his appeal, indicating that "although [Akers] had been warned, upon penalty of dismissal, not to miss any more [drug counseling] meetings, he nevertheless failed to appear at the October 15, 1988 meeting and did not attend meetings scheduled subsequent to that meeting."

The Appellate Division declined to modify this determination. It held that "it is well settled that an arbitration award 'may not be vacated unless it is violative of a strong public policy, is totally irrational or clearly exceeds a specifically enumerated limitation on the arbitrator's power.'" It said that the arbitration board was not required to accept Akers' "self-serving" explanations for his failure to attend the October 15 meeting.

The court indicated that it was permissible for the board to reject Akers' claims despite the fact that it was aware of his allegations that he was unfairly subjected to conflicting work and counseling obligations as it was aware of the fact that he had missed other counseling sessions in addition to the one he failed to attend on October 15.

Akers also attempted to process a second arbitration grievance in which he claimed that the board had failed to issue a timely determination regarding his original grievance. The court ruled that the board's apparent failure to adhere to the contractual time limits for issuing an arbitration award did not result in any prejudice to Akers and it declined to overturn the award on those grounds. It also held that he was not entitled to file an additional grievance as to the alleged untimely issuance of the award.

These rulings imply that the courts will not be sympathetic to employees who are dismissed after having been given an opportunity to participate in a drug counseling or rehabilitation program and after having agreed to participate, fail to cooperate by attending program meetings or classes.

15.09 Libel and slander

Drug allegations may result in an employee suing the employer for alleged libel or slander. Harris, a Metro North Railroad employee, made such a claim.[102]

Harris, a crew dispatcher with Metro North, alleged that her supervisor, Paul Hirsh, had falsely accused her of using drugs "with malice and reckless disregard of the truth." She also complained that he made these false statements in the presence of other officials.

A jury agreed and awarded her $500,000 in compensatory damages plus $700,000 in punitive damages. Although it is often said that "truth is a complete defense" in cases such as these, here the jury found that the statements made by Hirsh were, in fact, false.[103]

However, under certain conditions a false statement made by a superior concerning an employee may subject to what is termed a "qualified privilege" or a "qualified immunity" if it was made in the course of a public officer's or employee's performance of official duties. In such cases the employer may defend itself on the basis of "good faith" notwithstanding the fact that the statement is later shown to be false.

Here any claim by Metro North that there was a "qualified privilege" or a "qualified immunity" was not viable in view of the fact that it was decided that the statements were made "with malice and reckless disregard of the truth." Accordingly, any rebuttal to Harris' allegations on the basis of "good faith," thereby triggering the possibility of a defense claiming privilege or immunity, was unavailable to Metro North.

In American Federation of Government Employees v Martin, CA9, 91-15829, a case involving off-duty employee behavior, the U.S. Circuit Court of Appeals for the 9th Circuit held that the testing of government workers for drugs on the basis of a "reasonable suspicion" that the employees tested engaged in off-duty drug use did not violate the constitutional rights of the individuals tested.

The case involved the testing of U.S. Department of Labor employees having responsibilities in safety, health care, motor vehicle operators and individuals working in "security-sensitive" areas. Conceding that such testing could constitute an invasion of privacy, the court indicated that here public safety and national security were more important and thus resulted in a diminished expectation of an employee's personal privacy.

The employer and the union may provide for drug testing in a collective bargaining agreement. Such provisions are becoming common. For example, an agreement between the City of Wilmington Delaware and its police union provides for the mandatory, random testing of police officers for drugs. Police officers testing positive for illegal drugs or who admit that they use illegal drugs will be dismissed under the terms of the agreement.

---

[102] Harris v Metro North Railroad, _ Misc2d _

[103] On July 5, 1995 the Court of Appeals reinstated this award after earlier ruling that federal law controlled [Calendar #287].

15.10 The ADA and human rights laws

When considering problems involving alcoholism or the use of illegal drugs by employees, the employer should ensure that actions do not run afoul of federal or state laws that protect the rights of the disabled, as it is conceivable that drug and alcohol addicts could qualify for protection under these laws. In addition to New York State's Human Rights Law, Section 504 of the Rehabilitation Act of 1973 prohibits public employers receiving federal funds from discriminating against an individual on the basis of the disability and Subtitle A of Title II of ADA, which extends the prohibitions of Section 504 to public Rehabilitation Act of 1973 to all employers of a certain size regardless of their receiving or not receiving federal monies, may for the basis for claims of unlawful discrimination because of the individual's use of drugs or alcohol.

Numerous court decisions suggests that generally employers will not be viewed as violating such laws in cases in which drug or alcohol users are discipline or dismissed, depending upon the circumstances. For example:

An employee who refuses long-term treatment for alcoholism is not protected by the Rehabilitation Act.[104]

In Copeland v Philadelphia Police Department, 840 F2d 1139, the court ruled that the employer did not violate the Rehabilitation Act's "reasonable accommodation" requirements when it did not allow the employee to enter a drug rehabilitation program.

In Heron v McGuire, 803 F2d 67, a police officer dismissed because of his heroin addition was not a "handicapped" person within the meaning of the Rehabilitation Act because his addition resulted in his being unfit to perform the duties of a police officer.

In Little v FBI, 2 AD Cases 1109, a U.S. Circuit Court of Appeals ruled that the termination of an FBI agent because the individual was intoxicated while on duty did not violate the Rehabilitation Act, even though the agent was an alcoholic. The court ruled that the Rehabilitation Act protects workers where adverse action is taken against an individual "solely by reason of his or her handicap." In this instance the court decided that Little's termination was based on his misconduct, not his handicap.

The U.S. Department of Justice/EEOC "ADA Handbook" indicates that ADA does not prohibit an employer from refusing to hire an applicant or firing an employee currently engaged in the use of illegal drugs. As to drug tests, the manual indicates that "a test for illegal drugs is not considered a medical examination" for the purposes of ADA. However, ADA does not encourage, prohibit or authorize drug tests for applicants or employees.

The following summarizes some of the Americans with Disabilities Act of 1990's provisions, regulations and the guidelines concerning the illegal use of drugs.

Section 35.131(a)(2) of the ADA provides that "a public entity shall not discriminate on the basis of illegal use of drugs against an individual who is not engaging in current illegal use of drugs and who --

---

[104] Crewe v US Office of Personnel Management, 834 F2d 140; Gallagher v Catto, 778 FSupp 570

1. Has successfully completed a supervised drug rehabilitation program or has otherwise been rehabilitated successfully; or

2. Is participating in a supervised rehabilitation program; or

3. Is erroneously regarded as engaging in such use.

With respect to health and drug rehabilitation services, Section 35.131(h) provides:

Public employers may not deny health services, or services provided in connection with drug rehabilitation, to an individual on the basis of that individual's current illegal use of drugs, if the individual is otherwise entitled to such services.

A drug rehabilitation or treatment program may deny participation to individuals who engage in illegal use of drugs while they are in the program.

As to drug testing, Section 35.131(c) states that a public employer is not prohibited from adopting or administering reasonable policies or procedures, including but not limited to drug testing, designed to ensure that an individual who formerly engaged in the illegal use of drugs "is not now engaging in current illegal use of drugs."

The regulations, however, specifically state that "Nothing in paragraph Section 35.131(c) of the regulations shall be construed to encourage, prohibit, restrict, or authorize the conduct of testing for the illegal use of drugs."

In addition, to the above-mentioned federal laws, employers must adhere to the Drug-Free Workplace Act of 1988 [42 USC Section 701-707], which requires federal contractors and grant recipients are concerned include establishing a "drug awareness" program; advising employees that drugs are prohibited at the work site; and imposing sanctions on employees convicted of drug violations in the work site.

In addition, public employers may be subject to the provisions of the Nuclear Regulatory Commission [10 CFR 26.1-90] and the Department of Transportation's regulations [49 CFR 40.1-39] dealing with the use of alcohol and illegal drugs by employees.

CHAPTER 16

SOME SPECIAL PROVISIONS OF LAW

While Section 75 and contract disciplinary provisions cover the majority of public employees, disciplinary action to be taken against the incumbents of certain positions is sometimes set by a special statute. In a number of cases more than one statute law may be applicable. For example, a police officer of a town could be disciplined pursuant to Section 75 or pursuant to Section 155 of the Town Law.

Why two provisions providing for discipline? Possibly Section 155 was not repealed when Section 75 was enacted. An argument could be made that where there is a specific provision of law with respect to disciplinary procedures for a particular type or class of public employees, that procedure must be used.

Nevertheless, due process is usually held to have been provided if one of the statutory procedures (or contract procedure available in lieu of the statutory provision) is provided the officer or employee. Among those positions for which special provisions of law are applicable are the following:

APPOINTED OFFICERS (Section 32, POL);
APPOINTED OFFICERS 3rd CLASS CITIES (Section 4, GCL);
ASSESSORS (Section 1522, RPT Law)
COMMISSIONER, OFFICE OF GENERAL SERVICES (Section 21 PBL)
CONFLICT OF INTEREST (Section 810, Gen. Mun. Law)
CORONER (Section 33, Public Officers Law)
COUNTY CLERK (Section 33, Public Officers Law; Article 13, State Constitution.)
COUNTY OFFICERS (various) Section 33, POL)
EMPLOYEES 2nd Class Cities Section 137, 2nd CCL)
GRAND JUROR (by Court Rules)
HEADS OF DEPARTMENTS (Section 33-a, POL);
HOUSING FINANCE AUTHORITY (Section 34, PHL);
JUDGES (various Constitution Art. 22, 23; Other laws i.e: Uniform District Court Act 103(c); NYC Criminal Court Act 22, et cetera.
LABORERS, Salt Springs Authority, Section 33, SSL)
MUNICIPAL OFFICERS, general (Section 36 POL);
POLICE OFFICERS, WESTCHESTER COUNTY, 5711q, UnConL)
POLICE OFFICERS of towns Section 155, Town Law)
PUBLIC AUTHORITY, (Section 2527, PAL);
PUBLIC HOUSING AUTHORITY. (Section 34, PHL);
PUBLIC OFFICERS, in general, (Section 30, POL);
PUBLIC SAFETY COMMISSION (Section 33, POL) and
SOCIAL SERVICE, DEPUTY COMMISSIONER, (Section 34, SSL)
SUPERINTENDENT OF HIGHWAYS (Section 101, Section 160, Highway Law
UNIFIED COURT SYSTEM 25NYCRR32)
VILLAGE POLICE (Section 8-804, Village Law)

WORKERS' COMPENSATION BOARD. Section 149, WC Law)

If the officer or employee is subject to both a "tenure" statute with respect to removal and to a removal "by operation of law" provision, it is generally held that the latter provision controls. The reasoning behind this is that the officer or employee is no longer qualified to hold the position regardless of his guilt or innocence of the charges or even in the absence of charges being brought against the individual.

As an example, if a public officer is charged with misconduct, due process as to guilt may be irrelevant to being continued in office if it is also determined that the officer is not a resident of the jurisdiction when such residence is required by law. The individual, however, may be entitled to a hearing to resolve the residence question if he or she contests the residence determination.

Section 30 of the public officers Law lists a variety of "automatic" disqualifications for holding public office. Notwithstanding any automatic removal provision, most authorities agree that an employee may be subjected to disciplinary action as well.

Another case involving the special status of persons holding public office is Sealy v Joseph, _ Misc2d _.

Sealy, employed as a Public Health Sanitarian by the New York City Department of Health, was served with disciplinary charges pursuant to Section 75 of the Civil Service Law. The Section 75 hearing was adjourned by agreement "until the completion of related criminal charges pending against [him]." Sealy was convicted of the criminal charges in March 1985. In 1986 Sealy was tried "in absentia" and found guilty of certain of the charges filed against him pursuant to Section 75 by a hearing officer. He was notified of this determination and of his dismissal from his position by the appointing authority in January 1987.

When Sealy applied for retirement benefits in December 1988, his application was denied on the grounds that "he was terminated as of January 15, 1987." Sealy then attempted to vacate the decision terminating him and asked to court to reinstate him to his former position with back salary and benefits on the theory that his Section 75 dismissal was in violation of the stipulation of adjournment and in bad faith. Sealy argued that he was entitled to a hearing on the charges.

The court held that the arguments raised by Sealy concerning his right to a Section 75 hearing were moot. Sealy was deemed a "public officer" within the meaning of Section 30 of the public officers Law as he, among other things, was authorized to exercise certain police powers, including authority "to proceed as a police officer in serving summons for Health Code violations. Section 30.1.e provides that a public office shall become vacant as a matter of law upon the conviction of the encumber of "a felony, or a crime involving a violation of his oath of office." Accordingly, his conviction in 1985 resulted in his position becoming vacant" by operation of law."
The decision then notes that Sealy's "forfeiture occurred on the date of his conviction, prior to appeals ...." For the purposes of Section 30, the date of conviction would be the date of final judgment or sentencing date. When the Department held the disciplinary hearing in absentia in December 1986, its actions "were nullities since no hearing was required to vacate the position." However, the court ruled

that Sealy was entitled to collect retroactive pay from January 1985 when, "presumably, he was voluntarily suspended, up to the date of conviction date, less 30 days...."

As to the removal of public officers, the Attorney General has advised a village board of trustees it has the authority to adopt a local law establishing a procedure for the removal of an appointed village officer for cause.[105]

Section 30 of the public officers Law provides that a public office automatically becomes vacant if incumbent (1) is convicted of a felony, or (2) is convicted of a crime involving a violation of the individual's oath of office or (3) fails or neglects to file the required oath of office. Section 36 of that law establishes a procedure for applying for the removal of a public officer by making an application to the Appellate Division. However, there is no specific state law providing for the removal of a village officer for cause.

Under the circumstances, however, the attorney general concluded that there was statutory authority for a village to enact a procedure for removing its officers for cause.

He said that Section 10(1)(ii)(a)(1) of the Municipal Home Rule Law provide the statutory authority for a village to adopt such a procedure. That section allows a local government to adopt and amend local laws with respect to the powers, duties, qualifications, number, method of selection and removal, terms of office, compensation, hours of work and the welfare and safety of the officers and employees of that local government.

While the exercise of such authority must be consistent with the State Constitution and general State laws, the adoption of a procedure for the removal of a village officer for cause falls within the grant of authority set out in Section 10.

In some instances the statute creating an agency, authority, public benefit corporation, special district or related type of a public or quasi-public entity may itself contain "appointment and removal" provisions. As an example, the removal of certain personnel of the Albany Light, Heat and Power Authority is specified by Section 1027 (members of the Authority's Board of Directors), Section 1029 (certain employees of the Authority), Section 1031 (Board Members) and Section 1040 (Trustees of Bondholders) of the Public Authorities Law, respectively.

There are also removal provisions for such persons as fiduciaries (Estates, Powers and Trusts Law) and Guardians appointed under the Mental Hygiene Law, as well as disciplinary procedures concerning medical societies (Not For Profit Corporations Law Section 1406(f), and physician's assistants (Education Law Section 6544).

The State Constitution provides for impeachment of certain elected officials. The Constitution sets out procedures for the removal of certain state and local officers by the governor.
It is sometimes important to determine the appropriate appointing authority in disciplinary situations. In more than one instance a person was "removed" from office by someone other than the appropriate appointing authority. Such a removal, if challenged, is generally ruled a nullity and void as a matter of law.

---

[105] Opinions of the Attorney General, 92 Informal 45

In some cases the incumbent may have forfeited his or her office pursuant to either Section 63-a of the Executive Law or Section 23-a of the Town Law. A person charged with malversion[106] or misconduct may be subject to removal pursuant to Article 13 of the State Constitution. Other provisions enacted cover such areas as:

State officers are authorized to inquire into the official conduct of any subordinate officer or employee and may issue a subpoena for the production of records and to compel the appearance of witnesses.[107] In the same fashion, Section 209 of the County Law authorizes Boards of Supervisors to inquire into the conduct and performance of county officers and employees,

Although many statutes may include a statement to the effect that "officers and employees (of the agency, authority, corporation, organization, district, etc.) serve at the pleasure of the appointing officer," such persons holding a permanent appointment are generally viewed as subject to removal only for cause and in accordance with due process. In the absence of a specific statute, the courts have often viewed provisions of the Federal and State Constitution as mandating administrative due process including notice and hearing. It is also to be expected that the recently announced right to a "name clearing" hearing will be applied to public officers and employees not specifically covered by a "tenure" provision of law.

If the officer or employee is subject to both a "tenure" statute with respect to removal and to a removal "by operation of law" provision, it is generally held that the latter provision controls. The reasoning behind this is that the officer or employee is no longer qualified to hold the position regardless of his guilt or innocence of the charges or even in the absence of charges being brought against the individual.

As an example, if a public officer is charged with misconduct, due process as to guilt may be irrelevant to being continued in office if it is also determined that the officer is not a resident of the jurisdiction when such residence is required by law. Section 30 of the Public Officers Law lists a variety of "automatic" disqualifications for holding public office. Notwithstanding any automatic removal provision, most authorities agree that an employee may be subjected to disciplinary action as well.

It is sometimes important to determine the appropriate appointing authority in disciplinary situations. In more than one instance a person was "removed" from office by someone other than the appropriate appointing authority. Such a removal, if challenged, is generally ruled a nullity and void as a matter of law.

---

[106] Malversion includes grave faults such as corruption in public office or bribery in connection with the performance of a public office.

[107] Section 6l, public officers Law

CHAPTER 17

PROVISIONAL AND PROBATIONARY EMPLOYEES

The due process rights of employees depend upon the status of the employee, as described in detail in Chapter 1. The reader may wish to review that chapter to ensure familiarity with the due process rights flowing from various types of appointments that may be made in the New York State public service such as permanent, term appointment, contingent permanent, provisional, or temporary. Likewise, the reader should be familiar with the importance of the jurisdictional class of an employee's position (competitive, noncompetitive, exempt, labor or unclassified) to which the individual is appointed may have in the context of a disciplinary action.

This chapter will focus on the due process requirements applicable in situations involving disciplinary action involving provisional, temporary and probationary employees.

Temporary and provisional employees

Typically a temporary appointment is made to a position temporarily vacant or to a position that is not expected to be continued for any extended period of time. Section 64 of the Civil Service Law addresses temporary employment in the State and its political subdivisions.

In contrast, a provisional appointment can only be made to a wholly vacant position. Section 65 of the Civil Service Law addresses provisional employment in the State and its political subdivisions.

A long list of decisions support the holding that an individual "temporarily appointed" to a position pursuant to subdivisions 1, 2 and 3 of Section 64 of the Civil Service Law cannot attain permanent status by operation of law. This is true regardless of the duration of the temporary employment, even if the temporary appointment has been made from an appropriate eligible list. In fact, a temporary appointment from the eligible list may lawfully have been made without regard to rank on the eligible list, thus avoiding the provisions of Civil Service Law Section 61, which sets out the so-called "rule of three."

Accordingly, it seems clear that except as provided by Section 64.4, a temporary appointment cannot mature into permanent status.

The general rule is that provisional employees and temporary employees enjoy no tenure rights.[108] As the court held in Matter of Gaiser, 15 AD2d 793, a provisional appointee need not be given any notice and hearing if such an individual is to be terminated or dismissed. Further, a provisional appointment cannot ripen into a permanent one unless the individual is qualified for permanent appointment.[109] The terms and conditions of provisional appointments are set out in Civil Service Law Section 65.4.

---

[108] One type of "temporary appointment" – a contingent permanent appointment pursuant to Section 64.4 of the Civil Service Law can result in the appointee attaining vested tenure rights. A contingent permanent appointee may be removed from his or her position only after notice and hearing except in the event the permanent incumbent of the position is reinstated to the position to which he or she has been appointed on a "contingent permanent" basis.
[109] Russell v Hodges, 470 F2d 212

The only limitation on the appointing authority's discretion in terminating a provisional or a temporary employee is that it may not do so for a constitutionally improper or discriminatory reason or purpose.[110]

Under the state's Civil Service Law, the employer does not even have to give a reason in firing a provisional. However, the appointing authority may be sued by the employee and be required to show it was not arbitrary or capricious in terminating the provisional's employment with the agency. But, as the court said in Matter of Ginnandrea, 68 NY2d 612, "Judicial review of such a termination is limited to an inquiry of whether the termination was made in bad faith and was therefore arbitrary and capricious."

At times former provisional employees have persuaded courts to order "name clearing hearings" for them.

While a provisional employee ordinarily does not have any right to remain in his or her position, it should be remembered that under certain circumstances provisional employees in the competitive class become entitled to the protections of tenure and have due process rights. This occurs when a provisional is retained in the position beyond the required probationary period after becoming eligible for permanent appointment. In such cases, the provisional is deemed to have received a permanent appointment to the position "by operation of law."

In contrast, collective bargaining agreement cannot provide provisional employees tenure as City of Long Beach v Civil Service Employees Association, Inc., Long Beach Unit, 8 N.Y.3d 465 [Judge Kaye and Judge Ciparick dissenting in part], demonstrates.

In March 2004, the New York State Civil Service Commission criticized the City of Long Beach for its poor control over provisional appointments in the classified service. The Commission noted that "a number of competitive class positions had been improperly filled with and retained by provisional employees; at least one for as long as 19 years."

Following this, Long Beach advised a number of employees serving as provisional appointees that it believed that they were serving in a provisional capacity beyond the statutorily prescribed time. Civil Service Law Section 65.2 provides that "No provisional appointment shall continue for a period in excess of nine months."

These employees were provided with an opportunity to meet with Long Beach officials to discuss their employment status prior to the City's taking any final employment action. Ultimately, Long Beach determined that the continued employment of certain provisional employees violated applicable the civil service law and regulations and terminated them.

CSEA filed grievances on behalf of the terminated provisional employees. CSEA alleged that pursuant to the terms of its collective bargaining agreement [CAB] with Long Beach, these provisional employees were "tenured" and thus entitled to be rehired in another position. According to CSEA, the following provisions in the CAB controlled:[2]

---

[110] Miller v Ravitch, 60 NY2d 527

Section 6-1.0 - Definition of Tenure
Employees with one (1) year of service in the annual employment of the City, regardless of classification, will be deemed tenured employees. This period of tenure is to be computed retroactively and only employees enumerated in Section 2-1.0 shall be deemed non-tenured.

Section 6-1.1 - Rights of Tenured Employees
All tenured employees will be protected from separation from employment with the City for any reason other than (a) voluntary withdrawal; (b) dismissal for disciplinary reasons after a hearing pursuant to Section 75 of the Civil Service Law; (c) provisional employees in the competitive class will be protected by tenure with the exception that their employment may be terminated pursuant to Civil Service Law should it be necessary pursuant to Civil Service Law to appoint a qualified candidate from a Civil Service eligible list to their position. In that event, the displaced employee will be transferred by the City to another position in the City for which he/she qualifies, should such a position be open. A position will be deemed open if it was vacated within six (6) months of a tenured provisional employee's displacement by a candidate from an eligible list certified by the Civil Service Commission."

In response to CSEA's demand for arbitration, Long Beach filed a petition in an effort to get a court order staying arbitration.

Supreme Court granted the City's petition, holding that the CAB's provisions providing for grievance and arbitration are not enforceable due to the provisional status of the employees. The Appellate Division agreed, ruling that "[b]ecause the provisions of the parties' collective bargaining agreement upon which [CSEA] relies have the effect of limiting [Long Beaches'] ability to discharge provisional employees, those provisions are against public policy and unenforceable as a matter of law" (see Long Beach v CSEA, 29 AD3d 789 at 790).

The Court of Appeals affirmed the rulings by the two lower courts, noting that "the central issue in this case is whether the subject claims are arbitrable under the terms of a Collective Bargaining Agreement (CBA) between the parties."

The Court of Appeals noted that although the general rule in such cases is that the "public policy in this State favors arbitral resolution of public sector labor disputes", a dispute is not arbitrable when the subject matter of the dispute violates a statute, decisional law or public policy.

Here, said the court, the issue for which arbitration is demanded "is not arbitrable because granting the relief sought on behalf of the provisional employees under the so called 'tenure' provisions of the CBA would violate the Civil Service Law and public policy."

Noting the State Constitution's mandates that civil service appointments and promotions "shall be made according to merit and fitness to be ascertained, as far as practicable, by examination which, as far as practicable, shall be competitive" (NY Constitution, Article V, Section 6), the Court of Appeals said that with respect to provisional appointments: "the Civil Service Law authorizes such appointments only when there is no eligible list available for filling a vacancy in a competitive class, and then only for a maximum period of nine months."

The court also pointed out that Section 65.2 requires that in the event a provisional employee has been in a position for one month, the jurisdiction must hold a civil service examination for permanent appointment to the position.

As to the provisions set out in the CAB, the court said that: "The statutory scheme contained in Section 65 by its very terms prohibits any right of tenure to provisional employees. Properly construed, the Civil Service Law renders the provisions of the CBA upon which CSEA relies meaningless."

The opinion then continues:

"We have long held that appointments made pursuant to Civil Service Law §65 carry no expectation nor right of tenure (see Montero, 68 NY2d 253; Hilsenrad v Miller, 284 NY 445 [1940]; Koso v Green, 260 NY 491 [1932]). Provisional employees "though in a sense holding positions in the competitive class, are, for reasons of necessity, exempt from the civil service requirements for appointment; and similarly, so long as they hold such positions, they are entitled to none of the advantages secured by a period of tenure under the [Civil Service Law]" (Koso, 260 NY at 495). Such appointments "are mere stop-gaps, exceptions of necessity to the general rules with respect to the filling of such positions" and "[w]hile such appointments may on occasion be succeeded by a permanent appointment, this may only be by virtue of examination and eligibility under the civil service laws, and not by reason of any ripening of the temporary or provisional appointment into a permanent appointment" (id. at 496). "

Significantly, the Court of Appeals held that the appointing authority cannot agree to provide superior rights to provisional employees holding positions beyond that statutory time period. Accordingly, said the court, "… the provisions under the CBA are unenforceable as a matter of law …."

The court explained that "The failure to administer timely examinations prevents the identification and hiring of qualified candidates from eligible lists, as required by the Civil Service Law, and misleads provisional appointees into having expectations of continued employment beyond that permitted by law."

As the terms of the CBA that attempted to provide "tenure rights to provisional employees after one year of service" such a provision is contrary to statute and decisional law and thus an arbitrator may not grant any relief pursuant to such a provision.

Judge Kaye, in her dissent, agreed that "an arbitrator may not rely on the portion of the CBA that purports to grant tenure to provisional employees after one year of service (section 6.1-0), or on the section that prohibits termination until and unless the City appoints from an eligible list (section 6-1.1[c]), and a stay should be granted with regard to arbitration of section 6.1-0 and the first part of 6-1.1."

She, however, concluded that "the second component of the bargained-for section 6-1.1 (c) — that a displaced provisional worker will be transferred into an open position for which he or she is qualified — is arbitrable." See, also, County of Chautauqua v. Civil Service Employees Ass'n., 8 N.Y.3d 513

Another case addressing a conflict between a Taylor Law contract provision and the Civil Service Law is City of Plattsburgh v Local 788, 108 AD2 104. As the result of the abolishment of a position, one of the two incumbents in the title, Mousseau, was "demoted" to a lower grade position. His date of permanent appointment was in April, 1979, while a co-worker, Racine, had an earlier date of permanent appointment, in February, 1978.

The collective bargaining agreement provided that in determining seniority in the event of demotions in connection with a layoff the "date hired" was to be used. §80 of the Civil Service Law provides that the date of "permanent appointment" controls.

Under the contract, Mousseau would be the senior employee since he had been hired before Racine while Racine was the more senior worker as defined by §80 because he received his permanent appointment first. The Union sought to arbitrate the alleged contract violation. The City resisted and won an order prohibiting arbitration. The Court ruled that the Civil Service Law "reflects a legislative imperative" that the City was powerless to bargain away. Accordingly, it was required to follow the provisions of §80 of the Civil Service Law notwithstanding any Taylor Agreement provision to the contrary. The Court also noted that the contract specifically stated that the arbitrator did not have the power to rule on the legality or illegality of any provision of the agreement and, therefore, the arbitration was properly prohibited by the lower court. This decision is significant in that it calls attention to the fact that the Courts will not favor a Taylor Law contract provision over a statute when there is any substantial conflict between the two. The Appellate Division's decision in this case also notes that unless there is a clear indication in the agreement that a contract provision is subject to arbitration, Courts will "take (it) for granted" that the public employer did not intend to have a particular matter made subject to the contract's arbitration process (see Matter of Liverpool Central Schools, 42 NY2d 509.)

17.01 Tenure of provisionals by operation of law

In rare instances a provisional employee can acquire tenure and due process rights through the simple passage of time. If the provisional appointee passes the required examination and the eligible list is inadequate to fill all of the available positions or the list is immediately exhausted, and the provisional employee is continued in service beyond the required probationary period, he or she may not be thereafter removed except for cause after notice and hearing. The provisional attains what is called tenure by operation of law.[111]

However, case law in New York State holds that a provisional or temporary appointment cannot mature into a permanent one unless the incumbent satisfies the requirements set out in the Civil Service Law for permanent appointment to the position [Matter of Gaiser, 15 AD2d 793; Russell v Hodges, CA2, 470 F2d 212].

Tenure by operation of law as a result of retaining a provisional for more than nine months after his or her name is certified on the eligible list was considered in the landmark case of Roulett v Hempstead Civil Service Commission, 40 AD2d 611. The Appellate Division ruled in Roulett that if a person on a nonmandatory eligible list is provisionally appointed to a position, or is continued as a provisional

---

[111] Civil Service Law Section 65.4

employee after being certified from a nonmandatory list, he or she will be deemed to have been permanently appointed to the position.

The Roulette decision is consistent with Section 65.4 of the Civil Service Law, which provides that a provisional employee is automatically "afforded permanent appointment" in the position if either:

1. The provisional employee (a) takes and passes an examination for the position and (b) the resulting list is not a "mandatory list" and (c) he or she is continued in the position for a period greater than the required probationary period for the position; or

2. The individual is (a) on a nonmandatory eligible list (i.e. having two or fewer qualified candidates interested in the position) for the position and is (b) provisionally appointed to the position or continued in the position based on an earlier provisional appointment and (c) is continued in the position beyond the maximum probationary period for the position.

The reasoning behind this legislative language was the legislature's intent to avoid the perpetuation of untenured employment when the individual is eligible for permanent appointment but the appointing authority declines to use an eligible list on the grounds that it is not a mandatory list. To avoid the conversion of a provisional appointment into a permanent one by operation of law, the appointing authority must remove the provisional from the position before the eligible list is promulgated and either (a) keep the position vacant or (b) appoint an individual not on the eligible list.

Stated differently:

Where there is a nonmandatory list, a provisional appointee attains tenure if he or she is continued as a provisional when otherwise eligible and reachable for permanent appointment within the meaning of Section 61 of the Civil Service Law (or is reappointed to the position) for a period equal to or greater than the required probationary period after becoming eligible and qualified for appointment to the position on a permanent basis.

A number of cases show how courts have consistent applied these rules to a variety of types of situations. In Lelio v Rutkowski, 127 Misc2d 383, the state Supreme Court found a provisional employee is deemed to have automatically acquired permanent competitive status as of the effective date of the eligible list if:

1. the employee has served as a provisional appointee in excess of nine months; and

2. the employee is in such status when the eligible list is published; and

3. there are only two [or fewer] qualified and interested candidates for the single vacancy to be filled.

The court in Lelio said that the provisional appointee may not be removed from the position unless he or she fails to satisfactorily complete the required probationary period. The court refused to permit the appointing authority to terminate Lelio pursuant to the provisions of Section 65.3 although Section 65.3 allows the appointing authority to terminate a provisional employee within two months following the establishment of an appropriate eligible list. The court ruled that because Lelio had already served as a provisional in the position for a period greater than the probationary period otherwise required and was in the position on the day the eligible list was promulgated, he automatically became a permanent appointee on that day.

What if the list, although mandatory, is inadequate to fill all the vacancies that exist? This was the situation in the LaSota case.[112] In this case it was argued that the eligible list was exhausted because there were more vacancies to be filled than there were names certified on the list. LaSota, a provisional employee, was eligible for appointment from the list. He was retained in the position as a provisional. What was his status?

The court said that if a person has (a) served as a provisional appointee for more than nine months and (b) is in such status when the eligible list is published and (c) there are fewer qualified and interested candidates than there are vacancies to be filled, the provisional employee is deemed to have automatically acquired permanent competitive status as of the effective date of the eligible list. However, the individual must satisfactorily complete any required probationary period.

The LaSota and Lelio decisions suggest that appointing authorities must give careful attention to the quality of service of provisional employees and the wisdom of continuing their employment. If a provisional employee is retained for more than nine months, his or her subsequent eligibility for permanent appointment from a nonmandatory list will eliminate any possibility of choice by the appointing authority with respect to filling the position.

However, if a provisional employee passes an examination for the position and is reachable for appointment from a mandatory list, he or she does not automatically attain permanent status.

There are a number of cases dealing with this issue. One key decision is Becker v Civil Service Commission, 61 NY2d 374. In Becker the Court of Appeals held that Section 65.4 of the Civil Service Law is to be strictly construed and the section applies only where there are two or fewer persons willing to accept the appointment on the eligible list.

Becker, a long-term provisional employee, passed the required examination for permanent appointment and was immediately reachable for appointment. Although continued in the position beyond the two-month period allowed by Section 65.3 following the certification of the list, she was later reinstated to her permanent, lower grade position. Becker sued, contending that she had attained permanent status by operation of law, citing Section 65.4.

The court ruled that provisional employees do not attain permanent status, even if continued in the position for more than the two-month period set by Section 65.3, unless the list is a "nonmandatory list."

Similar complications were considered in Matter of Haynes, 55 N.Y2d 814, a case involving the dismissal of a long-term provisional after the promulgation of the eligible list but before the statutory two-month period expired.

---

[112] LaSota v Green, 53 NY2d 631

In Haynes, the Court of Appeals ruled that where there is a mandatory list, the appointing authority may remove a person even if he or she has (a) served in excess of nine months as a provisional and (b) is serving as a provisional when the eligible list is certified and even if the provisional employee is one of the top three eligibles for the single vacancy to be filled.

Another case in which the status of the appointee was critical was Snyder v Civil Service Commission, 72 NY2d 981.

In the Snyder case the Court of Appeals considered the impact of Section 65.4 on a contingent permanent appointment. The decision illustrates the differences between various types of appointments and the rights, or lack of rights, that result.

Snyder had been "officially" reported as having been "provisionally" appointed to a higher-level title. The permanent incumbent was on leave of absence without pay from the position.[113] About two years later Snyder's "provisional appointment" was rescinded and he was reinstated to his permanent title in a lower grade. The individual on leave from the higher-level position, however, had not returned to the position.

In reality, Snyder held a temporary appointment to the higher-level title while it was encumbered, a point that was to prove critical in the decision by the Court of Appeals.

Claiming that he could not be removed from the higher-level position unless found guilty of misconduct or incompetence, Snyder sued the Department, seeking reinstatement and back salary.

Snyder advanced the theory that he had attained "contingent permanent status" [see the Rules of the State Civil Service Commission, 4 NYCRR 4.11] in the higher level position pursuant to Section 65.4 of the Civil Service Law because (1) he was qualified for the promotion to the title pursuant to Section 52.6 of the Civil Service Law and (2) he had been retained as a provisional in the higher position for more than nine months.

The Department, on the other hand, maintained that an appointment on a contingent permanent basis was discretionary and therefore Snyder could not claim "contingent permanent status" unless he had been actually appointed to the position on that basis by the appointing authority.

The court ruled against Snyder, pointing out that Snyder had been appointed to the higher-level position as a "temporary" employee rather than as a provisional employee. This disposed of the "automatic promotion issue," as, according to the court, Section 65.4 is not relevant in "temporary appointment" situations.

Section 65 provides for "filling a vacancy" in the competitive class when no eligible list is available. Section 64 of the Civil Service Law, in contrast, authorizes a temporary appointment for up to three months without regard to any eligible list, except that "when an employee is on leave of absence a temporary appointment ... may be made (to that position) for a period not exceeding the authorized duration of such leave...."

---

[113] In this situation Snyder's appointment should have been designated as a "temporary appointment" rather than as a "provisional appointment" as the position to which he was appointed "was not wholly vacant."

In Snyder's situation there was no "vacancy" to be filled as the position involved was encumbered due to the leave of the permanent incumbent. Therefore Snyder was a temporary appointee, eligible to serve, at most, for the duration of the permanent incumbent's leave. Further, Section 64 does not provide for the conversion of a "temporary appointment" into a permanent one as could result in a Section 65.4 situation.

Critical to the resolution of the Snyder case was the existence of a vacancy -- a position to which a permanent appointment could be made. Although the term "to fill a vacancy" is sometimes used to describe a situation where an appointment to an encumbered position is made, for the purposes of Section 65 it means a position wholly vacant and for which an examination must be held if an individual is appointed to it.

These cases demonstrate the critical importance that an employee's "status" has in determining his or her rights to due process and a pre-termination hearing if he or she decides to challenge the separation.

17.02 Tenure

The date of permanent appointment is critical in many personnel situations as it determines whether or not the individual has rights to a hearing pursuant to Section 75 of the Civil Service Law or its contract or other statutory equivalents. This is usually referred to as "tenure." Once probation has been completed, an employee having "tenure" rights is entitled to notice and hearing before he or she may be removed from the position.

The tenure issue was the subject of the Court of Appeals in its decision in Montero v Harlem Valley Center, Division for Youth, 68 NY2d 253. The principal question presented involved the date an employee began to serve his probationary period. Was it the date on which the employee started working or was it on the date he was actually appointed as a permanent employee? The latter event controls, according to the Court of Appeals.

Montero had been appointed "temporary" to a noncompetitive class position. A few months later the facility "permanently appointed" Montero to the position.

Under the Rules of the State Civil Service Commission, persons permanently appointed as noncompetitive class employee are required to serve a probationary period. Although Montero had started working at the facility, the required physical examination and agility test for the position was not administered to him immediately upon his "permanent appointment" to the position by the facility.

About two months later Montero took and passed these tests and was certified by the Civil Service Department has having been permanently appointed to the position (Youth Division Aide IV). This appointment was subject to a one-year probationary period. The agency terminated Mongtero for failing to satisfactorily complete this probationary period within one year of the date of his permanent appointment. Montero then sued and convinced the trial court (Supreme Court) judge that his termination was unlawful as he had completed the required probationary service.

On appeal, the Appellate Division decided that Montero could not have attained permanent status in his position prior to the date on which he had passed his qualifying examination (January 13, 1983) and that his previous temporary appointment "could not have ripened into a permanent appointment" until that date. The Appellate Division concluded that the probationary period had not begun until January 13 and therefore his termination on January 12, 1984 was lawful.

The Court of Appeals agreed, noting that probation is triggered by the employee's "original permanent appointment."

The high court indicated that the trial court was probably disturbed by "the possibility of an appointing authority arbitrarily expanding an employee's probationary period by first designating the employee temporary and then postponing the qualifying examination that would lead to 'original permanent appointment'." However, this did not prove critical. The Court of Appeals said that whether (Montero's) initial appointment as a temporary was proper or improper, (he) was not, and could not have been, appointed to a permanent position in the noncompetitive class, since he had not yet taken and passed the examination prescribed for that position at the time of his initial appointment "...we cannot by judicial fiat convert what was necessarily a temporary appointment into a permanent one."

The court then concluded that an unlawfully extended period of temporary service cannot ripen into a permanent appointment "...nor can an appointee's successful completion of the qualifying examination.

17.03 Reviewing probationary employee terminations

The basic policy of the State Civil Service Commission [and that of many municipal commissions and personnel officers] is that it will review appeals filed by probationers who have been terminated only if the appeal contains allegations of procedural defects in a Department's or an Agency's administration of the Commission's probationary rules [see 4 NYCRR 4.5]. Simply stated, the State Civil Service Commission does not review the merits of an appointing authority's decision to terminate a probationer and, therefore, does not accept appeals challenging the accuracy of an employer's evaluation of probationary performance.[114]

17.04 "Permanent probationers"

Probationary employees have certain tenure rights as well. As was indicated earlier, provisions of law such as Section 75 of the Civil Service Law and Section 3020-a of the Education Law apply only to "permanent" employees. Probationary employees, however, hold permanent appointment to their positions.
If this sounds contradictory, one need only consider the date from which "seniority" is determined for the purposes of the law. In a layoff situation, for example, seniority dates from the date of initial appointment. It is not the date on which the employee completed the probationary period successfully.

---

[114] Hawkes v Bennett, 155 AD2d 766

Thus probationers in the classified service, (but not, to date, those in the unclassified service), have been given limited due process rights.

A probationer may be dismissed without notice and hearing only within a certain window of time: after the end of his or her minimum period of probation (usually eight weeks for entry-level positions) and before the end of the maximum period of probation (usually 26 weeks for entry-level positions). In other words, a probationary employee cannot be removed without notice and hearing if he or she has either (a) not yet served the minimum period of probation, or (b) successfully completed their probationary period, or (c) served the maximum period of probation and are still working in the position without being removed by the appointing authority ("tenure by estoppel") [Section 75.1(c)]

This was illustrated in Gray v Bronx Developmental Center, 65 NY2d 904. The court ruled that dismissing a probation worker whose performance is not up to standards is permissible without notice and hearing as long as the decision is made in good faith and the probationer has completed the minimum period of probation but not the maximum period of probation.

In another case involving a probationary termination is Application of Evelyn Chow, decided March 13, 2003. New York City Health Department probationary employee Evelyn Chow sued after she had been terminated for unsatisfactory service during her probationary period. The Appellate Division, First Department, found that there was "ample evidence" in the record to support the Department's determination sufficient to rebut her claim that she had been terminated in bad faith. Here the court noted that there is no question that Chow had been given "considerable advice, much of it in writing, concerning her job requirements and her repeated failure to fulfill them."

17.05 Standard of review

In dealing with the termination of a probationer, a different standard of review is applied. A probationer may be dismissed without a pre-termination hearing and without any statement of reasons "in the absence of any demonstration that the dismissal was for a constitutionally impermissible purpose or in violation of statutory or decisional law." In such cases judicial review is limited to determining whether the dismissal was made in bad faith.

17.06 Bad faith determinations

The burden of showing bad faith existed is on the employee.

In Brown v Condon, 587 NYS2d 648, a probationary police officer allegedly left the scene of an accident and refused to submit to a breathalyzer test when ordered to do so by a superior officer. He claimed that his subsequent dismissal was made in bad faith. The Appellate Division rejected Brown's allegations that the department had acted in bad faith notwithstanding the fact that he was subsequently acquitted of charges of having violated the Vehicle and Traffic Law. The court held that Brown's acquittal of the charges in and of itself did not satisfy Brown's burden of showing that he was terminated in bad faith.

A similar case was Soto v Koehler, _ AD2d_. Soto, a permanent NYC Correction Officer, was alleged to have been involved in an automobile accident when driving while impaired by alcohol. Served with disciplinary charges, he entered in a settlement by agreeing to serve a one-year probationary period.

On the day before the end of this probationary period Soto was terminated without any reason being given. Soto challenging his termination on the ground that the Department acted in bad faith in dismissing him prior to the end of the probationary period. The Appellate Division dismissed his appeal.

17.07 Separation pay for probationary teachers

Section 3019-a of the Education Law provides that probationary teachers are to receive notice of termination at least 30 days prior to the effective date of their termination. What happens if this required notice is not given to a probationer who is to be terminated?

In Tucker v Board of Education, 82 NY2d 274, the Court of Appeals said that the teacher is entitled to one day of pay for each day that the notice was late.

In Delphin v Bronxville UFSD, NYS Supreme Court ruled that a teacher was entitled to extra pay for this reason. On June 5, 1995 the Bronxville School Board voted to terminate Delphin effective June 30, 1995. Delphin was never told of the board's action, however, and apparently was not given any notice of the board's decision prior to the effective date of her termination.

Citing the lack of the notice required by law, Delphin claimed that she was entitled to a full 30 days of [additional] pay. The School Board contended that it only should have to pay her for "four additional days" since it had already paid Delphin for the period June 5 through June 30.

The court ruled that Delphin was entitled to an additional 30 days of pay because the legislature intended "to provide additional protection for probationary employees by giving them a period of thirty days in which to seek other employment before being removed from the payroll...." According to the ruling, "no notice thirty days prior to the effective date of termination is equivalent to notice that is thirty days late."

As to the district's contention that it was entitled to "credit" for salary payments made to Delphin even though it had not provided her with the required pretermination notice, the court said to allow such credit "would create the incongruous result that the Board would be better off providing no notice [rather] than a late notice" in such cases.

In a related issue: when can a probationary teacher challenge a decision to be dismissed? In Perlin v South Orangetown CSD, the Appellate Division ruled in June 1997 the teacher cannot receive a court hearing until a "final determination" has been made subject to review pursuant to Article 78 of the Civil Practice Law and Rules, and that a superintendent's recommendation to dismiss is not a "final determination."

The case facts: the superintendent of the Orangetown Central School District wrote to Joan Perlin, a probationary teacher, advising her that he was going to recommend that the Board of Education discontinue her employment. Perlin sued, seeking a court review of the superintendent's decision recommending her termination.

The Appellate Division dismissed her petition as "premature." The court said the superintendent's action did not constitute a "final determination" subject to review pursuant to Article 78 of the Civil Practice Law and Rules.

In some cases, however, the superintendent's recommendation may be subject to a grievance procedure set out in a Taylor Law agreement. Typically such a grievance will allege that there was some omission in the teacher's "evaluation" or some other procedural defect leading to the recommendation.

17.08 Disciplinary probation

Frequently the settlement of a disciplinary action provides for the employee to serve a disciplinary probationary period. If an employee is to be dismissed for violating the conditions of the disciplinary probation, it behooves the employer to ensure that the actions or inactions involved do indeed violate the specific conditions enumerated in the disciplinary settlement.

In Taylor v Cass, 505 NYS2d 929, a Suffolk County employee won reinstatement with full retroactive salary and contract benefits after he was improperly dismissed while serving a disciplinary probation. The terms of his probation said he could be terminated without any hearing if, in the opinion of his superior, his job performance was "adversely affected" by his "intoxication on the job" during the next six months. He was subsequently terminated without a hearing for "failing to give a fair day's work" and "sleeping during scheduled working hours." The Appellate Division said the dismissal was improper because Taylor was not terminated for the sole reason specified in the earlier settlement: intoxication on the job.

It is important that the employee's acceptance of probation be made openly, knowingly and voluntarily. See Matter of Sepulveda, 507 NYS2d 69.

Another disciplinary probation case is Ramos v Coombs, decided by the NYS Appellate Division on March 6, 1997.

On August 8, 1994, Tina Ramos, a New York State Department of Correctional Service correction officer, was charged with misconduct as the result on an incident that occurred while she was escorting a prison inmate. Informed that the department proposed to dismiss her, the disciplinary action was settled when Ramos agreed to pay a $1,000 fine and serve a 12-month disciplinary evaluation.

Under the terms of the settlement, Ramos agreed that the department could terminate her "if her service was unsatisfactory during the evaluation period."

Ramos was observed carrying her weapon in a hospital examination room in violation of Department rules. In April 1995 she was dismissed. She sued, contending:

1. The decision was made in bad faith; and

2. The decision was in retaliation for her having filed a complaint with the Division of Human Rights.[115]

The Appellate Division sustained a State Supreme Court's dismissal of her petition. The court said that Ramos had the burden of proving that her dismissal was made in bad faith, and this she failed to do.

The record showed that there were signs in the examination area proclaiming no weapons beyond this point and all armed officers wait outside the waiting room. Ramos admitted that she was aware of the signs and was, in fact, "at least briefly" in the restricted area while armed.

The court said that because Ramos was still within the 12-month disciplinary evaluation period, "her failure to comply with proper procedures constituted a violation of the settlement agreement, justifying her termination."

Finding no evidence of either bad faith or pretext in her dismissal, the Appellate Division ruled that "the only conclusion that may be drawn ... is that [Ramos'] performance was, indeed, unsatisfactory and thus her discharge was made in good faith."

Another case involving termination during a disciplinary probation is Fortner v NYC Dept. of Corrections, App. Div., First Dept., February 20, 2001.

Corrections terminated him, contending "he violated the terms of his limited probation as set forth in his negotiated plea agreement." Fortner sued, alleging that he had been terminated in bad faith. The court disagreed, finding that Fortner produced no evidence to support his claim that his dismissal was motivated by bad faith.

Fortner had also asked the court to annul his termination and have the matter remitted to the Department "for reconsideration of the sanction." The Appellate Division decided that under the circumstances such relief was unwarranted as Fortner's termination did not "shock the judicial conscience."

Further, said the court, terminating Fortner for violating the terms of his disciplinary probationary period did not constitute an abuse of discretion on the part of the appointing authority.

The lessons here is that the courts will sustain the termination of an individual serving a disciplinary probation period without a hearing if the employee is discharged for violating or failing to comply with the terms of the disciplinary probation agreed upon.

---

[115] The decision indicates that in January 1995 Ramos filed a complaint with the New York State Division of Human Rights alleging that several incidents of sexual harassment, including one that occurred August 8, 1994 - the date she was originally served with charges.

Sometimes the disciplinary probation established resulting from the settlement of the disciplinary action does not limit the appointing authority's discretion in terminating the employee. The Wright case demonstrates such a situation.

In Wright v City of New York, 596 NYS2d 372, the Appellate Division ruled that an employee who had agreed to a disciplinary probation in settlement of disciplinary charges filed against him that provided that his probation status would be the same as any other probationary employee was not entitled to a pre-termination hearing when he was dismissed because of subsequent incidents.

In other words, under the terms of Wright's disciplinary probation he was treated as a "new employee" and he could be summarily terminated for any lawful reason.

17.09 Light duty and probationary requirements

If a probationary employee is injured on the job and is given a light duty assignment, can the employee achieve tenure by operation of law? If the light duty work performed by the appointee is not appropriate for the purposes of probationary service, a light duty assignment is not sufficient to satisfy probation requirements, according to the holding of the Appellate Division, Second Department in Boyle v Koch, 68 NY2d 601.

The Boyle case considered a situation where two probationary firefighters were injured on the job. They were given extended sick leave and later provided with light duty assignments for more than a year. When they filed for disability retirement, the Commissioner extended their probationary periods. They sued, claiming that they had acquired tenure rights. This was significant consideration as they would received greater (disability) retirement benefits if they retired as "tenured firefighters" than would be paid to them if they retired as "probationary firefighters."

The court ruled that the extension of the probationary period was proper. The employees, not having performed the duties of firefighter for the required period of probation, could not claim tenure rights on the basis of their satisfactory performance of "light duty."

The granting of tenure to any probationer who does not successfully complete a probationary period "frustrates the function of probation." Further, said the court, the employer is entitled to evaluate the worker's fitness for appointment in terms of probationary performance and this, in this case, was not possible "since neither was on the job long enough to demonstrate his or her ability." The court then upheld the Commissioner's decision extending the probationary period.

Typically probationary periods are automatically extended for a term equal in length to the probationer's absence during his or her probationary period. In many jurisdictions the rules allow the appointing authority, at its discretion, to deem part or all of such absence[s] "time served" as a probationer.

One notable exception to this general rule: a probationer who is called to active military duty is deemed to have satisfactorily served in his or her probationary period while on military leave if he or she is honorably released from military service and is subsequently timely reinstated from such leave.

17.10 Drug use and probation

The use of illegal drugs may have an impact in probationary situations. For instance, a state Supreme Court justice upheld the termination of a probationary corrections officer when a sample of his urine tested positive for the presence of cocaine.[116] [Claiming that he had never used cocaine and that the positive test resulted from the use of improper sample collection techniques, the former corrections officer sought reinstatement to his position.

The court decided that there was no substance to the claim that improper sample collection procedures had been followed on the basis of an affidavit submitted by medical personnel describing the sample collection procedure followed.

Holding that an appointing officer has the power to terminate a probationer subject only to the requirement that such termination be made in good faith, the judge ruled that a dismissal as a result of the positive test for illegal drugs was permitted. The employee, said the court, had the burden of showing that his termination was made in bad faith or that it was arbitrary or capricious. The individual's inability to demonstrate that his termination was made in bad faith or that the determination of the appointing officer was arbitrary or capricious mandated that his appeal be dismissed.

17.11 Probation and alcoholism

A related issue involves the alcoholic probationer. A police officer that had been terminated at the end of his probationary period sought reinstatement to his position. He claimed that he had been discharged because he had sought treatment for alcoholism. This, he argued, violated Section 33.01 of the Mental Hygiene Law.

The Court of Appeals affirmed an Appellate Division's ruling that the termination did not violate that provision of the Mental Hygiene Law.[117] The Court of Appeals indicated that Section 33.01 prohibits termination of employment solely because an employee sought and received treatment for alcoholism - it did not prohibit termination if there were other reasons or illnesses requiring treatment.

In this case it was determined that the Commissioner of Police had been advised that the officer's major problem seemed to be his inability to deal with emotionally charged issues. This, in turn, appeared to be due to "his obsessive compulsive nature." Such a diagnosis was held to show that the officer's illness "may affect his ability to properly discharge the duties of a police officer." Therefore, ruled the court, "the termination was not for a constitutionally or statutorily proscribed reason."

---

[116] Roulhac v NYC Department of Corrections, Supreme Court, New York County

[117] Matter of John B., 113 AD2d 225, affirmed 68 NY2d 682

17.12 Probation and stress

Similarly, a probationary officer's termination because of stress problems was upheld by the courts. According to the Appellate Division, Second Department, the legislature did not intend to tie the hands of civil service employers when dealing with a mentally disabled person.[118]

The case arose when the Police Commissioner terminated John B., a probationary police officer, because the Commissioner believed that the officer had a deep-seated emotional problem and an inability to deal with stressful situations. The Commissioner had read a report of the physician who had treated the officer in which this inability to cope with stress was indicated. The statement had been made in connection with the physician's evaluation of the officer after the officer had voluntarily sought assistance in connection with his alcoholism.

While John B. argued that his termination violated the Mental Hygiene Law, which provides that no person shall be deprived of any civil right solely by reason of receiving assistance for a mental disability, the court ruled that this was not the basis for the Commissioner's determination. Rather, said the court, the Commissioner's determination was based on a belief that the John B. could not deal effectively with the stress involved in police work.

The court said it would not substitute its judgment for that of the Commissioner, who is charged with the duty of overseeing law enforcement, where that decision is based on the Commissioner's good faith belief that the officer may not be able to meet the stringent requirements of a police officer.

17.13 Extension of probation: modified duty

If a probationary police officer is placed on modified duty pending an investigation of suspected wrongdoing, is his or her probationary period extended by the length of time he or she is on modified duty?

In Garcia v Bratton, et al., the Appellate Division ruled the answer was yes. This permitted the police department to lawfully dismiss the officer without a hearing.

Garcia, a member of the New York Police Department, was accused of failing to take proper police action at a double homicide in which she apparently knew the perpetrator. When a member of department is place on modified duty in the context of a disciplinary investigation, the officer surrenders his or her firearm, shield and identification card, and the individual is directed to report for work in civilian clothing.

Garcia argued that she had achieved tenure in her position because she was employed beyond the maximum period of probation. But the police department cited New York City Personnel Department

---

[118] John B. v Rockville Centre, 113 AD2d 225

Rule 5.2.8(b), which provided that "the probationary term is extended by the number of days when the probationer does not perform the duties of the position."

The question for the court, then, was whether an officer assigned to "modified duty" pending the completion of the investigation was still performing the duties of his or her position. The Appellate Division ruled 3 to 2 that although an officer on modified duty continues to receive pay and accrue vacation time as a police officer, he or she is "not perform[ing] the duties of the position," namely, "police duties," during that period.

The thrust of dissenting opinion is that the fact that the police department neglect to inform Garcia that her reassignment to modified duty constituted an extension of her probationary period. Justice Murphy concluded that, as matter of due process, the department was required to inform Garcia that her modified assignment status was not to be counted towards the completion of her probationary period because "public employees are entitled to know definitely when their probationary period end."

17.14 Traineeships

A case that distinguished between probation and traineeships is Sergeants v Brooklyn Developmental Center, 56 NY2d 628. When a number of probationary employees were terminated at the end of the probationary period, they sued for reinstatement contending that they had not been provided with the 200 hours of training required by department regulations.

The Court of Appeals ruled that "...the employment of a probationary employee may be terminated at the end of the probationary term without a hearing and without specific reasons being stated."

It rejected the employees' claims, on the grounds that training would not have addressed their particular demonstrations of poor performance. The evidence in the record indicated that the poor performance which was related to fitness for the position rather than something that the training provided for by regulation could remedy.

Among the examples of poor performance cited by the court were sleeping on the job, habitual lateness, unscheduled absence, failure to perform overtime assignments and similar poor work habits. The decision also indicated that the only issue for review was whether the appointing officer acted in good faith in terminating the employee.

Another case addressing the issue of training and performance during probation is Gordon v SUNY at Buffalo, 35 AD2d 868.

17.15 Extensions of the probationary period

If the probationary period is extended, may the employee be terminated at any time after the completion the minimum period of probation prior to the end of the maximum period of the probationary period?

Sometimes the extension of a probationary period is automatic. A state employee was to serve a 52-week probationary period. He was absent 24 days because of an injury he suffered while on the job. He was then advised that his probationary period was extended "24 days." Later he was dismissed for failure to satisfactorily complete the probationary period.

The court rejected the argument that the employee became permanent at the end of 52 weeks, holding that the (state's) Rules for the Classified Service for state employees provided that the "Maximum period of probationary term of any employee shall be extended by the number of work days of his absence which ... are not counted as time served in the probationary term.[119] The rationale of the regulation is to add to the expiration date of the probationary period the same period of time that the employee had missed during his probationary period, so that his performance of duty could be fully observed and evaluated for an entire 52-week period.

Civil Service Rules of the state and many local jurisdictions permit an employer to excuse an employee's absence during a probationary period under certain circumstances. For example, the State Civil Service Commission's rule permits an appointing officer to consider up to 20 days of absence during a probationary period as "time served" as a probationer. This is discretionary on the part of the appointing authority and not mandated by the rule.

As an example, consider the following situation. An employee, Malinoski, was promoted by his agency. He was absent for 39 days during his probationary period. Although there was no question that the absences were proper and approved, the agency decided not to consider any of Malinoski's absence as time served as a probationer. The probationary period was automatically extended by 39 days. When Malinoski was later restored to his lower grade position because it was determined that he did not satisfactorily complete his probationary period, he sued, claiming that the extension was improper as he had completed the probationary period before termination was effected.

The court held that a rule such as Section 4.5(f)[120] required the automatic extension of the probationary period in excess of the maximum "excusable" period in cases where the employee was absent for more than 20 days. While the appointing officer had the authority to deem up to 20 days as time actually served as a probationer it was not required to do so. The Appellate Division then dismissed the appeal, finding that there was no evidence that the refusal to waive all or part of the 20-day discretionary period was made in bad faith.

In a similar type of situation, a police lieutenant was absent for 14 workdays during his probationary period. In accordance with a local Commission's Civil Service Rule, the lieutenant's probationary period was extended for an additional 14 workdays. He was then terminated during the period of the extension for failure to satisfactorily complete the probationary period. Among other things, the officer claimed that he had satisfactorily completed the probationary period prior to the effective date of his termination and therefore could not be removed except after a hearing.

---

[119] Hongisto v Fisher, 75 AD2d 973
[120] 4 NYCRR 4.5(f)

Although the rule also provided that up to 10 days of absence during a probationary period could be excused at the discretion of the appointing authority, the Appellate Division again held that the termination was proper.[121]

According to the decision, the appointing authority is entitled to evaluate an employee for an additional period equal in length to the number of workdays the employee was absent during the probationary term. Although the rule permits the appointing officer to waive absences up to 10 days, such a waiver was not automatic.

17.16 Attaining permanent status

When absence during probationary period is involved, it is not always a simple matter to determine the effect of an absence. The Court of Appeals ruled that a provisional employee who has passed the required examination [which resulted in a mandatory eligible list for his or her position] does not automatically become permanent in the position on the date on which the list is established.[122]

The Court of Appeals reversed the Appellate Division ruling in Reis v NYS Finance Agency, 519 NYS2d 355, and, at the same time, apparently affirms the Appellate Division, Third Department's ruling in a similar case, Van Dyke v NYS Department of Education, 146 AD2d 85. Both cases involved provisional employees permanently appointed from the eligible list and then terminated for failing to satisfactorily complete the required probationary period.

The decision resolves an important question regarding the status of a person who is serving as a provisional employee when a mandatory eligible list is certified and he or she is then appointed permanently to the position. The Reis and Van Dyke cases involved determining the effective date the permanent appointment when these two provisional employees were permanently appointed from the list. This is a critical date as it will determine the beginning of the individual's probationary period.

The Court of Appeals said a provisional employee's probationary period commences on the date on which he or she is appointed as a permanent employee, and not the date he or she passed the qualifying examination. In Reis's situation, the court ruled that he did not become entitled to the protection of Section 75 of the Civil Service Law, or its Taylor Law contract equivalent, until "one year from [the date of his permanent appointment], adjusted for absences, and the agency was entitled to remove him, as it did, without formal charges or hearing."

In deciding the Reis case the Appellate Division, First Department, said it was relying on the Montero decision[123] when it ruled that Reis had become a permanent employee "when the agency [learned] that he had passed the examination" rather than on the date on which his permanent appointment was actually processed by the Agency and directed his reinstatement with back salary. The Court of Appeals ruled that this was not correct and reversed that determination.

---

[121] Matter of Mazur, 98 AD2d 974
[122] Reis v NYS Finance Agency, 74 NY2d 724
[123] Montero v Lum, 68 NY2d 253

The Court of Appeals noted that it had rejected Montero's argument that the one-year period of his probation should be measured from the date of his temporary appointment. The high court said "the one year period [for probationary service] could not commence until the applicant became eligible for permanent appointment, which could only occur after successful completion of the qualifying examination."

It indicated that there might have been some misunderstanding of its ruling in Montero because Montero's date of permanent appointment to a position in the noncompetitive class and the examination date were the same and so it "spoke of the date of examination to distinguish it from the date of the temporary appointment." However, it noted that its "decision in Montero did not change the statutorily fixed rule that the date of permanent appointment controls for the purposes of measuring the probationary period."

As to rights of provisional employees to be continued in the position following the establishment of an eligible list, the courts have ruled that where there is a mandatory eligible list certified for a position, the provisional, regardless of the length of his or her provisional status, has no special right to be continued in the position on a permanent basis even if he or she is one of the top three candidates on the eligible list.[124]

Another special situation exists in connection with military duty. A probationary employee who is ordered to military duty will have his or her military service counted as satisfactory probationary service and, in most cases, will be deemed to have successfully completed the required probationary period if he or she is honorably discharged or released from the military and reinstated to public service within the time period permitted.

17.17 Date of permanent appointment and traineeships

The date of permanent appointment determines when the required probationary period commences. The significance of this is illustrated in Garypie v Incorporated Village of Sag Harbour, 551 NYS2d 570.

Garypie was appointed as a "police officer trainee" on January 6. In the following March he was selected to fill a newly created police officer position. In April he completed the examination for police officer and on June 30, the Village was notified that he had passed.
Sag Harbour permanently appointed Garypie to the position effective July 1. The following February he was terminated without notice and hearing. Arguing that his probationary period began when he was appointed as a police officer trainee, Garypie sued claiming that his termination without notice and hearing was unlawful as he already completed his one-year probationary period prior to his dismissal.

The court rejected the argument, finding that his probationary period commenced when he was permanently appointed to the position in July. Accordingly, Garypie was still a probationer when he was dismissed and because he was serving as a probationer, he was not entitled to notice and a pre-termination hearing. "A temporary employee cannot attain permanent status without first qualifying

---

[124] Matter of Haynes, 55 N.Y2d 814

for the position." In Garypie's case this did not occur until June 30 at the earliest. Accordingly, his termination without notice and hearing was consistent with Civil Service Law.

Such a termination is only subject to judicial inquiry with respect to whether the termination was made in bad faith and was therefore arbitrary and capricious. As Garypie had not alleged that his dismissal was motivated by bad faith, his termination without notice and hearing, and without explanation was upheld.

Another case involving the timeliness of the dismissal of a probationary police officer is DiFiglia v Ward, 551 NYS2d 245. DiFiglia had been appointed on July 15, subject to an 18-month probationary period.

Four days prior to DiFiglia's completion of his probationary period he arrested and charged with assault, reckless endangerment, obstructing governmental administration and resisting arrest. As a result, he was immediately suspended from his position. Twenty-seven days later he was terminated. DiFiglia appealed, claiming that as he had already completed his probationary period, he could only be dismissed after notice and hearing.

The court held that under the Rules of the New York City Personnel Director, DiFiglia's probationary period was automatically extended by virtue of his suspension. Thus, he was still a probationer when he was terminated. The probationary rules of many Civil Service Commissions and Personnel Officers provided that absences during a probationary period automatically extend the term of probation for a period equal length of such absences.

17.18 Non-competitive class employees

A special case exists with respect to noncompetitive class employees in state or local government service. Such employees do not acquire tenure rights insofar as Section 75 of the Civil Service Law is concerned until they have had five years of service.[125]

Accordingly, such employees have the protections of Section 75 during their minimum probationary periods, only to lose it until the completion of their fifth year of State service. In contrast, if a noncompetitive class appointment is made without a minimum period of probation being specified in the appointment letter, the appointee has attained "instant tenure" as the minimum and maximum periods of probation have been merged and the individual is entitled to a pre-termination hearing pursuant to Section 75 if he or she is to be removed for cause during the "minimum" period of his or her probation.

Many disciplinary procedures negotiated pursuant to the Taylor Law have granted due process rights to noncompetitive class employees upon completion of one year of service.

---

[125] Civil Service Law Section 75.1(c)

17.19 Good faith determinations concerning probationary service

Courts have ruled that the final decision with respect to discharging a probationary employee without giving the probationer a hearing or any specific reasons for the discharge is the employer's. The court in Rollick v Ambach pointed out that "this well recognized principle" applies unless a prima facie case of bad faith is presented.[126]

The State University of New York at Stony Brook terminated Rollick, an "excellent" probationer. According to the events described in the decision, his "outstanding" rating was reduced to "excellent" on instructions by the Director of Public Safety. No reasons were given for the termination. Rollick sued the university. The lower court judge, without holding a hearing, ordered Rollick's reinstatement to the position.

When the university appealed, the Appellate Division decided that Rollick had made a sufficient showing to support his claim that his termination was made in bad faith and was therefore arbitrary and capricious. It also held that the lower court should have held a hearing to determine if the discharge was motivated by bad faith or was made on the basis of Rollick's job performance.

The case was then sent back to the lower court to determine if the termination was made in bad faith and lacks a "rational basis." The point here is that while no reason need be given in dismissing a probationer, if the action is challenged, the employer will have to show that there was a rational basis for the action. If not, the court will conclude that the termination was in bad faith, or was arbitrary, both of which constitute improper grounds for termination.

As noted earlier, persons in the unclassified service who are being terminated do not have any statutory right to a hearing during their probationary term of service. Probationary teachers are not entitled to a hearing if they are not to be continued in service or given tenure. In some school districts, however, negotiated agreements include what might be called "due process" procedures that must be followed if a probationer is to be terminated.

17.20 Notice of termination

Any probationary employee who is continued in service beyond the last day of the maximum probationary period and who has not been given timely notice that he has not completed the probationary period satisfactorily or that his probationary period has been extended beyond the maximum period acquires tenure and thereafter may only be removed for cause. If the notice of termination is timely given, the last day of service need not coincide with the last day of the probationary period.

So long as the termination is effective within a reasonable time, such as to coincide with the end of the next payroll period, the courts will not deem the probationer to have obtained permanent status because of the "carryover".[127]

---

[126] Rollick v Ambach, 97 AD2d 637

[127] Mendez v Valenti, 101 AD2d 612

17.21 Second probationary periods

In some cases, an employee may be given an opportunity to serve a second probationary period in lieu of separation at the end of the initial period of probationary service. This second probationary period must be served in a "different" assignment to be valid. Otherwise, the employee may be deemed to have acquired tenure as a result of being continued in service beyond the end of the original period of probation if he or she is continued in the same assignment unless the individual agrees that such continuation shall not result in "tenure by acquisition."[128]

When Martin DeSapio, a New York City probationary Correction Officer, was terminated because it was determined that he had failed to satisfactorily complete his probationary period, he sued, claiming that he had been dismissed without a hearing and without reasons being stated.[129]

The Appellate Division, First Department, upholding the lower court's ruling dismissing his complaint, said that as a probationary employee, DeSapio could be terminated without a hearing and without reasons being stated, provided the termination was made in good faith and not capricious. The decision indicates that DeSapio was terminated because he took advantage of a knee injury to remain on restricted duty an excessively long time, and then improperly sought a full-duty assignment at a location with minimal, if any, inmate contact. This, said the court, did not constitute bad faith or capricious action.

Holding that the record "supports the conclusion that neither disability nor injury was the reason for [DeSapio's] dismissal, but rather his misuse and evasion of the liberal leave and restricted duty policies of the Correction Department, the Appellate Division affirmed the lower court's dismissal of DeSapio's complaint.

17.22 Good faith probationary decisions

A probationary termination will survive judicial scrutiny if it is made in good faith. In York v McGuire, 63 NY2d 760, the Court of Appeals indicated that "it is well settled that a probationary employee may be discharged without a hearing and without a statement of reasons" where the decision is made in good faith and not for a constitutionally impermissible purpose.

In Cortijo v Ward, 551 NYS2d 36, the Appellate Division, First Department considered Cortijo's claims that her probationary termination was made in bad faith.

---

[128] For example, 4 NYCRR 5.5(ii), which applies with respect to the extension of the probationary period of a State employee provides as follows: "If the conduct or performance of a probationer is not satisfactory, his or her employment may be terminated at any time after eight weeks and before completion of the maximum period of service. The appointing officer may, however, in his discretion, offer such probationer an opportunity to serve a second probationary term of not less than 12 nor more than 26 weeks in a different assignment, in which case the appointment may be made permanent at any time after completion of 12 weeks of service, or the employment terminated at any time after the completion of 8 weeks of service and on or before the completion of 26 weeks of service."

[129] DeSapio v Koehler, 551 NYS2d 1

According to the record, Cortijo speculated that she had been terminated either because of "her performance on the shooting range" or for "psychological reasons." The court said that Cortijo had the burden of presenting evidence that her termination was made in bad faith. "A mere belief of bad faith does not satisfy the requirement or warrant a hearing."

As to the causes Cortijo suggested as the underlying basis for her termination, the Appellate Division seemed satisfied with these as reasons, holding that "neither reason would support a finding of bad faith even where the agency is in receipt of conflicting opinions."

17.23 Name-clearing hearings

If facts related to a termination have been publicly disseminated, the employee may be entitled to a name-clearing hearing. This pertains to probationary employees as well as non-probationary employees.

In another probationary termination case, Carlo v City of New York, 549 NYS2d 160, the Appellate Division, Second Department, ruled that a probationary police officer who had been terminated had failed to show that his termination was made in bad faith. As to Carlo's demand for a name clearing hearing concerning his probationary termination, the court said that he did not show that he was entitled to such a hearing.

The court indicated that a name clearing hearing is not required when there is not evidence was disseminated to the public and Carlo did not offer any evidence of such public dissemination. The opinion notes "the mere possibility of dissemination in the future is only speculative and is insufficient to warrant a hearing."

The Appellate Division also rejected Carlo's claim that he was entitled to a hearing in an attempt to persuade the New York City Police Department to reinstate him.

However, it should be noted that such a "reinstatement hearing" is required in the event a public officer is removed from his or her position pursuant to Section 30.1.e of the Public Officers Law upon the officer's conviction of a felony or a crime involving a violation of the officer's oath of office and the conviction is later reversed "where the conviction is the sole basis" for the termination.

17.24 Tenure by operation of law

Permanent status may result because the appointing authority fails or neglects to terminate a probationary employee in timely fashion. Gould v Sewanhaka, _ NY2d _ illustrates such "tenure by estoppel."

The Gould decision considers two basic issues: did a teacher acquire tenure by estoppel as a special education high school teacher and, if so, whether her resignation submitted on the mistaken belief that she had not yet acquired tenure precludes her from regaining her teaching position. The Court of

Appeals said that under the facts of this case, Gould "acquired tenure by estoppel and that her resignation is without legal effect."

Gould was granted tenure in 1965 as a "common branch" elementary school teacher in a New York City District. Her application for employment with Sewanhaka indicated this fact. Sewanhaka appointed her for a three-year probationary term as a Special Education teacher at a high school.

On February 24, 1989, six months before the expiration of her three-year probationary term, Gould was told that the superintendent would recommend that her probationary appointment be terminated as of June 23, 1989. Gould asked for, and received a statement of reasons for the superintendent's decision. She then offered to resign in order to avoid have a "probationary termination" reflected in her file. The superintendent told her that if her resignation was submitted and accepted by the school board in a timely fashion, her personnel record would reflect a "resignation" rather than a "termination."

Was this a voluntary, valid resignation? In this instance the court concluded that when Gould submitted her resignation and when the board accepted it, all of the parties assumed that Gould was resigning as a probationary teacher.

According to the ruling, none of the parties was aware that Gould's New York City tenure had entitled her to a reduction in her probationary term from three to two years by operation of Education Law Section 3012 and that, therefore, she might already possessed tenure by estoppel. By letter dated May 17, 1989 -- after her resignation was accepted, but before its effective date -- Gould notified the board that she believed that had acquired tenure by estoppel and asked it to rescind its acceptance of her resignation. The superintendent and the school board took no action on this request.

The Court of Appeals noted that under Section 3012 (1)(a): "Teachers ... shall be appointed ... for a probationary period of three-years; provided, however, that in the case of a teacher who has been appointed on tenure in another school district within the state, ... and who was not dismissed from such district or board ... the probationary period shall not exceed two years." It said "the language of the section is plain and the meaning unambiguous," concluding that because of Gould's previous tenure in New York City, the required term of her probationary service had been reduced from three-years to two years. Further, the court said that made no difference that her tenured status was in a different tenure area in another School District or that she had left her tenured position more than twenty years before.

According to the ruling, tenure by estoppel "results when a school board fails to take the action required by law to grant or deny tenure and, with full knowledge and consent, permits a teacher to continue to teach beyond the expiration of the probationary term," citing Lindsey v Board of Education of Mt. Morris Central School District, 72 AD2d 185, 186. The court found that although the district had "constructive knowledge of the facts pertaining to [Gould's] 1965 tenure from the information contained in her application, they were presumably not cognizant of the legal implications of continuing to employ petitioner beyond September 1, 1988 when her two years of probation ended." This, however, did not serve to excuse its failure to act prior to the end of Gould's "two year probationary period."

The court rejected the district's contention that Gould's resignation was voluntary and, therefore, could not be withdrawn without its consent. It said that the question was whether a teacher should be held to have voluntarily relinquished rights in a tenured position where the teacher, the superintendent and the board mistakenly believes that the teacher is resigning not from a tenured position but from an unprotected probationary position. It held that under the circumstances in this case, such a resignation is ineffective and may be rescinded.

17.25 Transition from probationer to tenured

As discussed earlier, the keys to attaining tenure in the public service are:

1. Permanent appointment.

2. Successful completion of any probationary period required by law, rule or regulation.

The process evolves as follows:

1. Section 63.1 of the Civil Service Law provides that "every original appointment to a position in the competitive class is subject to a probationary period." The individual's probationary period begins on the effective date of the appointee's permanent appointment. Stated another way, although a probationer, the individual is a permanent employee.

2. The probationary period is usually set in terms of a minimum period and a maximum period of probation.

3. The courts have ruled that a probationer is entitled to a pre-termination hearing before he or she may be removed from the position during the minimum probationary period. In contrast, a probationer may be removed without notice and hearing after completing the minimum period of probation and before completing his or her maximum period of probation. Additionally, under certain circumstances, a probationer may be offered the opportunity to serve a "second probationary period" in lieu of termination.

4. The appointing authority determines if and when the employee has satisfactorily completed his or her probationary period, and, in appropriate situations, whether to offer to extend the individual's probationary period beyond the maximum period.

Here is the critical point. The consequences of inaction could be considerable. Should the appointing authority fail, or neglect, to timely notify a probationer that he or she is to be terminated for failure to satisfactorily complete the probationary period on or before the end of the individual's probationary period, the employee is deemed to have obtained tenure by "operation of law," sometimes referred to as tenure by estoppel or tenure by acquiesce.

As an example: Nicholas Tartaglione sued the Westchester County director of personnel when the director refused to approve Tartaglione's permanent appointment as a police officer with the Village of Briarcliff.[130]

---

[130] Tartaglione v Giambruno (NYS Supreme Court)

Tartaglione's personnel history indicated that he had served as a police officer with a number of jurisdictions. He was initially appointed as a police officer by the City of Mount Vernon in January 1993. This permanent appointment was subject to a probationary period.

In December 1993 the Mount Vernon Civil Service Commission told Tartaglione that he could transfer to the Yonkers Police Department because "he was a permanent employee." He resigned his position in Mount Vernon and joined the Yonkers police force.

Three months later Tartaglione resigned from Yonkers because he did not, or could not, meet its residence requirement.

On September 14, 1994 the Village of Pawling appointed Tartaglione as a police officer. Pawling is located in Dutchess County. In the course of obtaining this appointment, Tartaglione asked for, and received, a letter from the Mount Vernon Civil Service Commission stating he was "a full time permanent police officer during the time he worked for the City of Mount Vernon until he resigned on December 22, 1993 [after] successfully completing [his] probationary period."

On May 20, 1996 Tartaglione resigned his position with Pawling to accept an appointment as a police officer with the Briarcliff Manor police department. Briarcliff Manor is located in Westchester County. Briarcliff, however, did not clear the personnel transaction with Westchester County Personnel Office [Personnel] before Tartaglione resigned from Pawling.

Westchester Personnel refused to approve Briarcliff's "reinstating" Tartaglione, indicating that despite the Mount Vernon Commission's letter to Pawling confirming that Tartaglione had successfully completed his probationary period with that jurisdiction, his "civil service roster card from the City of Mount Vernon indicated that he had not." Briarcliff suspended Tartaglione but elected to hold the position open for him "pending a decision" by Supreme Court.

Did Tartaglione complete his probationary period before leaving Mount Vernon? Both Westchester and Mount Vernon cited regulations providing that a police officer's probationary period can range from 3 months to 18 months.

Both jurisdictions' claims also contended that Tartaglione was supposed to have received a letter indicating he completed his probationary period and the fact that he did not meant that he was still a probationer when he left Mount Vernon.

Tartaglione, on the other hand, argued that Mount Vernon's Civil Service Commission declared him permanent after 12 months, fully within the three to 18 month probationary range set forth in its own rules. Tartaglione also claimed that Westchester had the power, under its own rules, to approve his selection by Briarcliff Manor.[131]

Tartaglione won! The court decided that Westchester's refusal to approve Tartaglione's rehiring "on the basis of Mount Vernon's records or lack thereof" was arbitrary and capricious because:

---

[131] Nothing in the decision indicates what action, if any, Mount Vernon Police Department, the appointing authority, had taken concerning Tartaglione's probationary status.

1. Neither Westchester nor Mount Vernon offered any explanation concerning the basis for either Mount Vernon's oral advisories to Tartaglione or its letter to Pawling other than to claim that it was a "clerical error."

2. Westchester County personnel "never even attempted to determine if any separate certification of permanency [sic] was issued by the appointing authority in Yonkers for the minimum three months status period of petitioner's employment there."

3. Westchester did not consider the impact, if any, of Tartaglione's completion of any "additional probationary period" while serving with Pawling as required by Dutchess County and any relation back of Dutchess' determination with respect to his present status with Briarcliff Manor.

The court ruled that these omissions made the personnel director's "non-discretionary" refusal to approve Tartaglione's reinstatement or transfer "arbitrary and capricious."

The court also said that Westchester was "estopped" from refusing to approve Tartaglione's appointment. Applying the doctrine of estoppel bars an entity from speaking against or ignoring the impact of its own actions.

Although the doctrine of estoppel is not generally available against governmental agencies in connection with their performing their governmental functions, courts will apply it "under unusual circumstances where the facts compel it to prevent manifest unfairness or injustice."

Noting that Tartaglione [and his several employers] relied on the information provided to them by Mount Vernon, the court decided that "for both legal and equitable reasons," the non-discretionary decision by Westchester that Tartaglione was not qualified under County rules for reinstatement or retention as a police officer with permanent status with the Briarcliff Manor Police Department should be "set aside."

Westchester was directed to approve Tartaglione's appointment with Briarcliff Manor, subject to "any probationary period the Village may impose under its own rules, but only if so advised."

17.26 Suspension of a probationer

Another situation, although encountered infrequently, concerns the suspension of a probationary worker during his or her probationary period. In Quinn v Brown, _ AD2d _, the court was asked to determine the rights of such employees in that type of situation.

Quinn, a New York City police officer, challenged the penalty imposed following disciplinary action - suspension without pay for 8 days and "warning probation" for one year. He claimed that the failure of certain individuals to cooperate in the investigation of the charges or to testify at the disciplinary hearing meant that the appointing officer's determination was not supported by substantial evidence. Quinn also claimed that the administrative law judge conducting the hearing should not have credited the testimony of the single witness called by the appointing authority to testify against him.

The Appellate Division rejected Quinn's arguments, noting that "issues of credibility [of witnesses] are for the administrative agency, not the courts, to determine." Finding that the conclusions of the appointing officer were supported by substantial evidence, the court dismissed Quinn's appeal.

17.27 Rights under a Taylor Law agreement

Many negotiated agreements may contain provisions that give probationers and provisional employees special benefits or rights in regard to employment, the relevant agreement provisions must be considered in the event a probationary or provisional employee is to be terminated.

As to interpreting labor contracts in connection with a probationary termination, such an issue was considered in Schenectady County v Lainhart, 576 NYS2d 441.

Lainhart was terminated during his probationary period; reinstated after he protested; and again terminated prior to the expiration of his one year probationary period. The union filed a grievance, claiming Lainhart's discharge violated the Civil Service Law and was in retaliation for his earlier protest. Schenectady objected to arbitration, arguing that neither a probationer nor a terminated worker was an employee within the meaning of the "just cause" termination of the collective bargaining agreement.

The Appellate Division ruled that under the terms of the agreement the parties had agreed that arbitrable grievances included those concerned with "claimed violation, misinterpretation or inequitable application of any existing law, rules, regulations or policies." Accordingly, the court ruled that the underlying question -- were probationers "employees" under the "just cause" article of the agreement? -- was for the arbitrator to determine.

As to the rights of a "terminated employee," the decision cites the Baker case[132] in which the Court of Appeals held that "An employer cannot extinguish an employee's rights under a collective bargaining agreement by simply terminating the employment.

17.28 Distinguishing between temporary and provisional appointment

Typically a temporary appointment is made to a position temporarily vacant or to a position that is not expected to be continued for any extended period of time as generally set out in Section 64 of the Civil Service Law.

A long list of decisions support the holding that an individual "temporarily appointed" to a position pursuant to subdivisions 1, 2 and 3 of Section 64 of the Civil Service Law cannot and does not attain permanent status by operation of law regardless of the duration of such status and regardless of the fact that under certain circumstances the temporary appointment has been made from an appropriate eligible list. Indeed, such an appointment from the eligible list may lawfully have been made without regard to rank on the eligible list, thus avoiding the provisions of Civil Service Law Section 61, which sets out the so-called "rule of three."

---

[132] 70 NY2d 314

Except as provided by Section 64.4, a temporary appointment cannot mature into permanent status.

An appointment pursuant to the exception set out in Civil Service Law Section 64.4 is typically referred to as a "contingent permanent appointment." This may be viewed as a "special form of temporary appointment" -- one that provides many of the benefits incumbent upon permanent appointment to the individual appointed to an encumbered position in the competitive class of the classified service but (1) requires that the appointing authority affirmative act to provide for such a "contingent permanent" appointment and (2) requires that the appointee otherwise satisfies the mandates of Section 61.

As the Court of Appeals indicated in Snyder v Civil Service Commission, 72 NY2d 981, a temporary appointee, even if otherwise eligible for such appointment pursuant to Section 64.4, must be appointed specifically as a contingent permanent employee by the appointing authority, which status is granted solely at the discretion of the appointing authority.

In contrast, a provisional appointment authorized by Civil Service Law Section 65, [a provisional appointment may be made only to a position that is wholly vacant], may, under certain conditions, mature into a permanent appointment by operation of law.

Section 65.4 sets out the terms and conditions pursuant to which a provisional appointment matures into a permanent appointment. The various terms, conditions and circumstances under which such permanent status obtains are explained in such decisions as Matter of Roulette, 40 AD2d 611, Haynes v Chautauqua County, 55 NY2d 814, Becker v New York State Civil Service Commission, 61 NY2d 252 and La Sota v Green, 53 NY2d 491.

CHAPTER 18

CASE SUMMARIES

An effective means of developing an understanding of the analytical process used by the courts in arriving at its rulings in the complex area of employee discipline is to study the explanation of the decision by the court itself. Frequently the decisions will, in addition to setting out the facts and reasons underlying its rationale in making its determination, contrast or distinguish the case it is deciding with other cases or similar situations.

The following are summaries of decisions by the courts and administrative bodies selected to illustrate the reasoning behind the ruling in a variety of disciplinary situations that may confront an employer or an employee organization or an individual involved in a disciplinary action. Each summary sets out the basic facts involved and the determination of the court in resolving the issue presented by the plaintiff, typically the employee or the union.

These decisions have been selected from among the thousands available as, in the opinion of the authors, they illustrate the most common issues that arise in the context of a disciplinary action. The summaries are presented alphabetically as a "quick index" to a topic that may be of interest to the reader.

Quick Topic Index

18.01 Attorney fees awarded to the employee
18.02 Authority of the arbitrator
18.03 Automatic termination
18.04 Bringing discredit on the employer
18.05 Challenging a Section 75 settlement agreement
18.06 Challenging administrative decisions
18.07 Challenging administrative rulings
18.08 Challenging arbitration awards
18.09 Chronic absenteeism alleged to be caused by a disability
18.10 Chronic absenteeism policy violations
18.11 Classified service disciplinary procedures
18.12 Collateral estoppel
18.13 Concealing misconduct
18.14 Conducting a private business
18.15 Confrontations with a superior
18.16 Confidentiality of disciplinary records
18.17 Constructive dismissal
18.18 Constructive dismissal
18.19 Continuation on the payroll
18.20 Contract disciplinary procedures and Section 72
18.21 Court modification of disciplinary penalty
18.22 Credibility of witness
18.23 Criticism of employee performance
18.24 Criticism of employees by a coworker
18.25 Defamation and disciplinary action
18.26 Demotion in grade
18.27 Designating a disciplinary hearing officer

18.28 Determining probation status
18.29 Disciplinary arbitrations
18.30 Disciplinary action and wrongful discharge
18.31 Disciplinary action claimed filed with malice
18.32 Disciplinary appeals must be to the forum having jurisdiction
18.33 Disciplinary dismissal not discrimination
18.34 Disciplinary hearings held in absentia
18.35 Disciplinary probation
18.36 Disciplinary settlement payments
18.37 Discipline for 20-year-old misconduct
18.38 Disciplinary settlements
18.39 Discretion to discipline staff
18.40 Dismissal of a provisional employee
18.41 Dismissing a probationer
18.42 Drafting disciplinary charges
18.43 Due process and administrative hearings
18.44 Due process and negotiated agreements
18.45 Duty to file disciplinary charges
18.46 Electing a disciplinary penalty
18.47 Election of remedies
18.48 Employee personnel files used to set penalty
18.49 Employment agreements
18.50 Evaluating conflicting testimony
18.51 Exhausting administrative remedies
18.52 Failing to appear at the hearing
18.53 Failure to file a timely appeal
18.54 Failure to meet contract deadlines

18.55 False official reports
18.56 Filing a timely Article 78
18.57 Final determination for purposes of making a claim
18.58 Fitness of a witness
18.59 Fraud a valid basis for removal from position
18.60 Free speech by public employees
18.61 Hearsay testimony in disciplinary action
18.62 Impartiality of discipline panel members
18.63 Imposing a harsher disciplinary penalty
18.64 Internal investigation reports
18.65 Involuntary leave under Section 72
18.66 Involuntary resignation
18.67 Judicial review of a disciplinary determination
18.68 Jurisdiction to hear a disciplinary appeal
18.69 Leave approval
18.70 Lie detector tests
18.71 Limit on questioning by hearing officer
18.72 Limiting the selection of arbitrators
18.73 Loss of a driver's license
18.74 Malpractice by union's attorney
18.75 Malpractice in disciplinary actions
18.76 Material misrepresentations
18.77 Misconduct off the job
18.78 Misuse of the employer's records
18.79 Mitigation of damages
18.80 Mitigation of the recommended penalty
18.81 Name-clearing hearings
18.82 Negotiated disciplinary procedures
18.83 Negotiating disciplinary procedures
18.84 Notice of a final administrative determination
18.85 Notice of claim
18.86 Off-duty misconduct
18.88 Patronage dismissals
18.89 Payment for unused leave credits
18.90 Payroll decertification
18.91 Personnel records used in setting penalty
18.92 Placement on involuntary leave
18.93 Policy makers
18.94 Pornography and the Pell Standard
18.95 Positive drug test
18.96 Preparing a defense
18.97 Probation after re-hiring
18.98 Probationary termination
18.99 Processing a disciplinary appeal
18.100 Property interest in public employment
18.101 Protected speech
18.102 Providing a "Bratton hearing"
18.103 Proving disciplinary charges
18.104 Public worker to answer work related inquiry
18.105 Random drug tests
18.106 Random searches at work
18.107 Reappointment to public office
18.108 Reassignment pending discipline
18.109 Recommendation of the hearing officer
18.110 Reinstatement from Section 72 leave
18.111 Rejecting a hearing officer's findings
18.112 Rejecting a disciplinary settlement offer
18.113 Removal from the payroll
18.114 Representation by an attorney
18.115 Request for reconsideration
18.116 Request for union representation
18.117 Requesting a disciplinary hearing
18.118 Rescinding a letter of resignation
18.119 Rescinding a letter of retirement
18.120 Rescinding a resignation
18.121 Rescinding tenure status
18.122 Reviewing disciplinary action
18.123 Right to counsel
18.124 Same offense, different penalties
18.125 Section 3020-a disciplinary appeals
18.126 Section 72 leave
18.127 Selective prosecution
18.128 Settlement agreement
18.129 Settlement agreements and FOIL
18.130 Standing to appeal
18.131 Statute of limitations
18.132 Statute of limitations for disciplinary action
18.133 Stipulating a settlement
18.134 Subpoena Duces Tecum
18.135 Suppressing evidence in a disciplinary action
18.136 Suspension without pay during administrative discipline
18.137 Suspension without pay penalty interrupted
18.138 Tainted testimony
18.139 Tenure by estoppel
18.140 Term Appointments
18.141 Terminating an interim appointee
18.142 Terminating temporary appointees
18.143 Termination by operation of law
18.144 Termination hearing - Section 73
18.145 Termination of a probationer
18.146 Termination of employment
18.147 Termination pursuant to Section 73
18.148 Termination without a hearing
18.149 Testimony by the appointing authority
18.150 Testing for drugs
18.151 Testing for illegal drugs
18.152 Threats by employees
18.153 Timeliness of evidence
18.154 Tolling of the statute of limitations
18.155 Unemployment insurance and Section 75
18.156 Use of a videotape as evidence
18.157 Using personnel records in setting a penalty
18.158 Vacating a disciplinary arbitration
18.159 Vacating arbitration awards on grounds of public policy
18.160 Vacating arbitration awards on grounds of public policy
18.161 Violating department rules
18.162 Violating the use of the Internet policies
18.163 Violating workplace rules
18.164 Violating the terms of a disciplinary probation
18.165 Volunteering to provide due process
18.166 Whistle blowing
18.167 Whistle blowing pre-disclosure notice
18.168 Whistleblower law covers provisional employees
18.169 Who is the employer?
18.170 Withdrawing a resignation
18.171 Witness creditability determinations
18.172 Work related investigations
18.173 Workers' Compensation Leave
18.174 Wrongful termination
18.175 Zero tolerance drug policy

18.01 Attorney fees awarded to the employee

Perez v Department of Labor, 244 AD2d 844

Served with disciplinary charges pursuant to Section 75 of the Civil Service Law, Hilton Perez was found guilty of misconduct and terminated from his position. The Appellate Division, however, annulled the determination as there was no evidence that the hearing officer who presided over his disciplinary hearing had been so designated in writing. The Appellate Division directed that Perez be reinstated to his former position with back salary and benefits

Following this victory, Perez asked the Supreme Court to award him attorney fees and expenses. He argued that as the "prevailing party," he was entitled to such payments under Section 8601 of the Civil Practice Law and Rules.[133]

Supreme Court agreed and awarded Perez $19,907.84, $9275 of which reflected Perez's legal expenses attributable to the Section 75 administrative disciplinary action. The Labor Department appealed.

Rejecting the department's argument that the failure to designate the hearing officer in writing was "a mere technicality" and its actions resulting in Perez's termination were otherwise "substantially justified," the Appellate Division affirmed the lower court's award of attorney fees and expenses.

In addition, the Appellate Division ruled that Perez was entitled to the fees and expenses incurred in connection with the department's appeal to the Appellate Division challenging the Supreme Court's decision. It returned the case to Supreme Court for further action concerning this aspect of the case.[134]

18.02 Authority of the arbitrator

Kimball v Pine Plains CSD, 272 A.D.2d 332

Kimball involves two common proceedings brought pursuant to Article 75 of the Civil Practice Law and Rules [CPLR]: one to confirm an arbitrator's award; the other to vacate the award. State Supreme Court Judge John R. LaCava had confirmed the award.

Affirming Judge LaCava's ruling, the Appellate Division said that "[a]n arbitration award may not be vacated unless it is irrational, violates a strong public policy, or clearly exceeds a limitation imposed on the arbitrator as set forth in CPLR 7511(b)" or if the arbitrator exceeds his or her authority.

---

[133] Section 8601 (a) of the Civil Practice Law and Rules provides, in relevant part, that [A] court shall award to a prevailing party ... fees and other expenses incurred by such party in any civil action brought against the state, unless the court finds that the position of the state was substantially justified or that special circumstances make an award unjust.

[134] Judge Mugglin dissented in part. He said that Section 8601 does not provide for the awarding of fees and expenses incurred by an employee in the administrative disciplinary action that typically precedes a judicial action. While Perez was entitled to his legal expenses for his court action, and the department's appeal, Judge Mugglin said the award should be modified to "exclude that portion of the counsel fees ($9,275) attributable to the administrative hearings."

When does the arbitrator exceed his or her authority? When, said the Second Department, the arbitrator gave a "completely irrational construction to the provisions in dispute and, in effect, made a new contract for the parties." Here, said the court, the determinations made by the arbitrator were within his power and not irrational. Accordingly, the award was properly confirmed by the lower court.

18.03 Automatic termination

Bowman v Kerik, 271 A.D.2d 225

Section 30.1(e) of the Public Officers Law provides that a public office becomes vacant upon the conviction of the incumbent "of a felony, or a crime involving a violation of his oath of office." The significance of this provision is that no "pre-termination hearing" that may otherwise be mandated by law such as Section 75 of the Civil Service Law or a Taylor Law disciplinary grievance procedure is required to effect the termination.

In Bowman, Section 30.1(e) was the basis for the court's sustaining the termination of several New York City correction officers without a hearing. As the Appellate Division noted, Section 30.1(e) is a self-executing statute and no pretermination hearing was required.

Bowman and other correction officers had challenged their dismissal without notice and hearing, claiming that administrative "due process" entitled them to a pre-termination hearing. The corrections officers previously pleaded guilty to an "intent to evade any tax imposed under [an] income or earnings tax statute...."

The Appellate Division found that their "public offices were vacated automatically on conviction" by operation of law because of the misdemeanors to which they had pleaded guilty. The point here is that for the purposes of Section 30(1)(e), a plea of guilty is the equivalent of a conviction. As noted in Kelly v Levin, 440 NYS2d 424, even if these individuals were given a "due process hearing," the only penalty that could be imposed by an appointing authority or hearing officer was dismissal.[135]

18.04 Bringing discredit on the employer

Wilburn v McMahon, 296 AD2d 805

From time to time disciplinary charges alleging misconduct because the employee's actions discredited the employer in the eyes of the public are filed against an employee. The Wilburn case is an example of such a case.

---

[135] Other cases involving automatic termination include: Schirmer v Town of Harrison, USDC, SDNY, February 1999; Foley v Bratton, Court of Appeals, 92 N.Y.2d 781; and Griffin v Bratton, Court of Appeals, 92 N.Y.2d 781

Douglas A. Wilburn, a New York State Trooper, was charged with, among other things, "engaging in conduct that tended to discredit [the] Division of State Police." Other charges alleged that Wilburn had left his assigned post without the approval of his superiors and that he used his position as a member of the Division of State Police to obtained and use information for a personal rather than an official reason.

Wilburn admitted that he had obtained the e-mail addresses of two college students who had asked him for directions. He also admitted that he had sent e-mail to the students using the name "like2tryu2" with a subject heading of "BI MALE HERE."

Wilburn conceded that he had no "law enforcement" reason to obtain the names of the students nor their e-mail addresses and further acknowledged that the students had probably divulged their names to him when he has stopped them while he was on highway patrol only because he was a State Trooper.

The students became upset, angry and alarmed by these messages, especially since "like2tryu2" indicated that he knew the students. When they discovered Wilburn's identity, the students registered complaints with the Division of State Police.

Wilburn's defense: his motivation was altruistic and, at worst, constituted excusable poor judgment. Found guilty of the charges, Wilburn was dismissed from his position. He then initiated an Article 78 action, claiming that (1) there wasn't substantial evidence in the disciplinary record to support a determination of guilt and (2) the penalty imposed -- termination -- was too harsh.

The Appellate Division found that there was substantial evidence in the record to support the Superintendent's determination and, further, under the circumstances termination did not violate the Pell standard[136] in that it was not so disproportionate as to shock one's sense of fairness.

The court said that regardless of the merit of Wilburn's testimony regarding his motivation, which testimony was specifically rejected by the disciplinary hearing panel, "the fact remains that he used his position as a State Trooper to obtain information for personal reasons, i.e., purposes unrelated to his law enforcement duties." Further, one of the students he contacted testified that he "didn't expect that to happen from a State Trooper" and the other "wonder[ed] what kind of people they hire if they're going to do that". Such testimony, said the Appellate Division, supported a finding that Wilburn's conduct tended to discredit the State Police.

As to Wilburn's argument that the penalty imposed, dismissal from the service, was disproportionate to the offenses he had committed, the court noted that the Division "did not rely solely upon the subject charges in determining the penalty." Rather, said the court, the Division "properly considered [Wilburn's] employment record over 10 years which contained approximately 16 founded complaints, including, neglect of duty and incompetence."

The court commented that the Superintendent "properly considered" Wilburn's employment history with the Division in setting the penalty.

---

[136] Pell v Board of Education, 34 NY 2d 222

Sometimes the use of the employee's personnel record by the disciplinary hearing officer or arbitrator to determine the severity of the penalty to be imposed on an employee found guilty of one or more of the charges filed against him or her is challenged by the individual. The general rule applied by the courts when asked to determine if the employee's personnel record was lawfully considered in setting the disciplinary penalty is that the employee's personnel records may be considered in setting a penalty, provided the employee is advised that this will be done and is given an opportunity to comment on the contents of his or her personnel file.

The case usually cited as authority for this proposition is Bigelow v Trustees of the Village of Gouverneur, 63 NY2d 470. Further, the employee's consent is not required in order for the hearing officer or arbitrator to consider the employee's personnel record in determining an appropriate penalty.

In some cases the employee's work history may serve to mitigate the imposition of a harsher penalty than would be appropriate under the circumstances because of the individual's otherwise exemplary performance record. Sometimes the individual may request that his or her entire personnel record be considered in order to mitigate the penalty to be imposed.

In contrast, a history of a series of petty offenses by the individual may have a cumulative impact in the determining the appropriate penalty to be imposed. The courts have sustained the dismissal of an employee for a series of misdeeds that if considered individually would not have been viewed as justifying termination.

18.05 Challenging a Section 75 settlement agreement

Johnson v Triborough Bridge and Tunnel Auth., 97 N.Y.2d 627

Edward P. Johnson, an employee of the Triborough Bridge and Tunnel Authority [TBTA], was involved in an after-hours altercation during which his service revolver discharged. As a result, disciplinary charges were filed against him pursuant to Section 75 of the Civil Service Law.

On April 12, 1989, Johnson and the TBTA settled the disciplinary action and Johnson signed a "Waiver of Section 75 Hearing and Acceptance of Recommended Penalty." The waiver included the following provisions:

1. Johnson agreed to waive his right to a disciplinary hearing pursuant to Civil Service Law Section 75 and his right to file an appeal pursuant to Civil Service Law Section 76;

2. Johnson agreed to serve a probationary period of 12 months "exclud[ing] all time during which he was not on duty;" and,

3. During this disciplinary probationary period, the TBTA, in its sole discretion, could dismiss him for any new violation of its rules or regulations.

Johnson, while serving his disciplinary probationary, was injured while on duty. As a result he was absent from work from August 19, 1989 until October 1996. In June 1997, following allegations that he had abandoned his post without authorization, TBTA dismissed Johnson without a hearing.

Johnson appealed his termination to the New York City Civil Service Commissioner, arguing that he was no longer on probation on the effective date of his dismissal. This, he contended, meant that was entitled to a hearing pursuant to Civil Service Law Section 75 before he could be terminated.

Johnson based his claim on the theory that his probationary period should be calculated in calendar days. TBTA, on the other hand, contended that the calculation should be based his workdays --only on the days Johnson actually worked, in this instance 253 days. Thus, TBTA argued, Johnson was still serving his disciplinary probation when he was dismissed.

As to Johnson's right to appeal to the City's Civil Service Commission, TBTA contended that the Commission lacked jurisdiction to hear the appeal because the settlement agreement specifically provided that Johnson waived his Section 76 rights of appeal.

The Commission agreed, dismissing Johnson's appeal on the ground that it did not have jurisdiction. The Appellate Division, however, sustained a lower court's ruling that "the Commission was bound to construe the 1989 agreement to ascertain whether the waiver therein remained effective at the time of petitioner's termination" [Johnson v TBTA, 278 AD2d 34-35]. The Court of Appeals reversed this holding.

The Court of Appeals held that Section 76 "solely authorizes the Commission to hear appeals from hearings in connection with disciplinary proceedings under section 75." As there was no such proceeding in Johnson's case, the Commission had no jurisdiction to hear his application to review his discharge that was not effected under Section 75.

The Court also commented that Section 76(2) limits the Commission's review to the record and transcript of the disciplinary hearing. As there was no record or transcript in this instance, the Commission had no jurisdiction to determine the matter.

In contrast, the Court of Appeals noted that Johnson "could have brought an Article 78 proceeding at the time of his dismissal in June 1997 challenging the TBTA's conclusion that he was a probationary employee, which he failed to do. Accordingly, the Court held that Johnson "cannot reassert his contentions by appealing to the Commission because its jurisdiction is explicitly limited to appeals of Section 75 determinations.[137]

---

[137] Typically probationary periods are automatically extended for a term equal in length to the probationer's absence during his or her probationary period. In many jurisdictions the rules allow the appointing authority, at its discretion, to deem part or all of such absence[s] "time served" as a probationer. One notable exception: a probationer who is called to active military duty is deemed to have satisfactorily served in his or her probationary period while on military leave if he or she is honorably released from military service and is subsequently timely reinstated from such leave.

18.06 Challenging administrative decisions

Gomez v Safir, App. Div., First Dept., 3/5/00

The Gomez case points out a procedural trap that an individual may encounter in the event he or she delays challenging an administrative decision. The Gomez case involved such a delay in challenging an administrative decision denying a police officer permission to engage in "off-duty employment."[138]

Section 208-d of the General Municipal Law allows police officers to be employed by another employer while off-duty, provided that the "extra work" does not: (1) exceed 20 hours a week; (2) does not interfere with or impair their ability to perform their regular duties; (3) does not affect the officer's ability to be available for emergency duty; and (4) does not constitute a conflict of interest. In addition, "the type of employment" to be performed while off-duty is subject to the prior approval of the department or police commissioner.

In some instances the department's "off-duty work policy" has been incorporated in an agreement negotiated pursuant to the Taylor Law. An employer's restriction on employee's use of their nonworking time is generally a mandatory subject of negotiations and the union's acquiescence to limitations concerning off-duty work does not constitute a waiver of the right to bargain subsequent prohibition.[139]

The denial of his request for administrative approval to engage in off-duty employment was the genesis of the Gomez case. There two basis issues involved in this case:

1. Did a pending grievance concerning the denial of his administrative application for "off-duty employment approval" toll the statute of limitations for filing an Article 78 petition challenging the administrative disapproval action? and

2. Was the determination of the commissioner in denying Gomez's request reasonable?

New York City police officer Felipe Gomez wanted to be a professional boxer. When his administrative request to work off-duty in pursuit of a boxing career was denied, he appealed the administrative determination to the commissioner. He also filed a grievance protesting the denial of his request for permission to engage in "off-duty employment" as a professional boxer.

First the commissioner denied Gomez's administrative appeal concerning permission to participate in boxing while off-duty. Gomez did not immediately challenge the commissioner's administrative decision but decided to wait for commissioner's decision concerning his grievance. The grievance was denied because, said the commissioner, it did not involve a contractual right subject to the grievance process, Gomez then initiated an Article 78 action seeking a court order vacating the commissioner's administrative decision.

---

[138] Many police agencies have adopted a policy setting the nature of off-duty employment that its officers may accept and generally require the officers to obtain prior approval before accepting "off-duty employment."

[139] Sheriff's Association and Ulster Co. Sheriff, 27 PERB 3028

However, by the time the commissioner issued the "grievance ruling" more than four months had passed by since the commissioner had issued his "administrative ruling" on Gomez's administrative appeal. As a result the first issue to be resolved by the court was a procedural one -- was Gomez's Article 78 petition appealing the commissioner's administrative ruling timely; i.e., was it filed within four months of the final administrative determination?

State Supreme Court Judge William McCooe said it was untimely and dismissed Gomez's petition. Why? Because, explained the court, the commissioner's administrative decision" became final and binding" on Gomez when he was told that his administrative appeal had been denied by the commissioner. Accordingly, the four-month statute of limitations for bringing an Article 78 action challenging the Commissioner's decision commenced to run at that time.

The critical element in resolving the timeliness issue: Judge McCooe said that Gomez's attempt to resort to contractual grievance procedures did not toll the four-month limitations period, citing Lubin v Board of Education, 60 NY2d 974.

The lesson here: delays in filing an Article 78 petition because the employee is awaiting the resolution of a grievance or arbitration concerning the same issue could be fatal as the Gomez decision demonstrates.

Similarly, in Roper v NYC Department of Citywide Administration, 271 A.D.2d 737, the court sustained the Unemployment Insurance Appeal Board's dismissed Clyde Roper's appeal of the denial of his unemployment insurance claim as untimely. Clyde testified that he received the ALJ's decision "but did not appeal based upon his attorney's advice to wait for a pending arbitration decision." The court sustained the board's conclusion that Clyde failed to comply with the 20-day filing requirement of Section 621(1) of the Labor Law and dismissed his appeal.

Although the Appellate Division dismissed Gomez's complaint for technical reasons, it also elected to comment on the merits of his claim. The court pointed out that although Section 208-d of the General Municipal Law allows a police officer to accept off-duty employment, such employment must not "affect his physical condition to the extent that it impairs his ability to efficiently perform [his or her regular] duties".

The court's conclusion as to merits of Gomez's appeal: "given this qualification, it cannot be said that the blanket prohibition against professional boxing apparently applied here is so lacking in reason as to be arbitrary."

18.07 Challenging administrative rulings

Malitz v NYC Transit Authority, NYS Supreme Court, Justice Stallman

The Malitz case points out the differences in the standards that are used by the courts when reviewing different types of agency or administrative determinations.

In cases involving challenges to an agency's administrative determination made without having held an administrative hearing, the test applied is whether or not the agency's determination can be supported on any reasonable basis. Stated another way: was the administrative determination arbitrary or capricious?

The arbitrary and capricious standard involves a review of whether a particular administrative action is justified. In effect, the "rationality of the decision" is reviewed under this standard.

In contrast, Justice Michael D. Stallman pointed out that when a court considers a challenge to an administrative determination resulting from a "quasi-judicial proceeding," i.e., an administrative hearing, it applies the "substantial evidence" test. "The substantial evidence standard arises only when there has been a quasi-judicial hearing, and evidence taken pursuant to law," said Justice Stallman, citing Colton v Berman, 21 NY2d 322.

The issue before the court in the Malitz case: which was the appropriate test to be applied in addressing Malitz's Article 78 petition?

The case arose as a result of the New York City Transit Authority [NYCTA] filing disciplinary charges against one of its railroad clerks, Bryan Malitz. NYCTA alleged that Malitz failed to properly relieve another railroad clerk, Holmes.

According to the decision, on August 1, 1997 Holmes had incorrectly tallied fare cards resulting in a $2,100 shortage. Malitz did not detect this error and carried over the same incorrect information during his shift. Malitz's relief, Bayo, repeated Holmes' and Malitz's error. Holmes then relieved Bayo without detecting the error. Finally the $2,100 error was discovered by Malitz when he relieved Holmes for a second time.

The Authority terminated Malitz. The grievance arbitration panel upheld the termination, ruling that Malitz "did not make a 'proper relief' [and] this failure did warrant dismissal since the per se procedural violation went to the heart of a railroad clerk's responsibilities and was a serious failure of duty." Neither Holmes nor Bayo were terminated as a result of the error that Holmes made on August 1.

Malitz then filed a complaint with the New York State Division of Human Rights [NYSDHR] contending that he had been unlawfully terminated from his position due to his "sleep apnea" disability in violation of the New York State Human Rights Law [Section 296, Executive Law]. He also asserted that the charges leading to his dismissal were false. NYSDHR dismissed his discrimination complaint, finding that there was a "lack of probable cause."

NYSDHR decided that Malitz had been terminated because of performance infractions unrelated to his sleep apnea. In reviewing Malitz's complaint, the division "took into consideration" various performance infractions set out in Malitz's personnel record. These other infractions included episodes involving insubordination, arguing with customers, closing his window, refusing to sell tokens, exposing himself while on duty and sleeping on duty."

NYSDHR also held that NYCTA's decision to penalize but not terminate Holmes or Boyd did not support a claim that NYCTA's termination of Malitz constituted unlawful discrimination. NYSDHR noted that Holmes' and Boyd's employment dossiers, unlike Malitz's, did not contain any reports of "procedural violations" prior to the August 1, 1997 incident.

Malitz appealed NYSDHR's determination. His Article 78 petition alleged that NYSDHR's dismissal of his complaint was not supported by substantial evidence. The court rejected this theory, indicating that Malitz's reliance on the "substantial evidence" test in his case was misplaced.

The decision states that NYSDHR has the discretion to (1) determine how an investigation will be conducted and (2) to dismiss a complaint for lack of probable cause without a hearing where appropriate. As there was no hearing held concerning Malitz's complaint, the appropriate test to be applied was whether the division's determination was "rational," not whether it was supported by substantial evidence.

Justice Stallman ruled that the division's action satisfied the "rational" test. He said that the "NYSDHR dismissed petitioner's discrimination claim for lack of probable cause after a thorough investigation and review of all factors, including his sleep apnea diagnosis." Under the circumstances the court concluded this result was reasonable.

Clearly, since Malitz's complaint was dismissed for lack of probable cause and a quasi-judicial hearing was not held by the NYSDHR, the "substantial evidence" test was not applicable. As to his challenge to the administrative dismissal of his complaint, the court said that because he did not present any evidence that NYSDHR's dismissal of his complaint was arbitrary or capricious, his petition had to be dismissed.

18.08 Challenging arbitration awards

Carroll v Perkle, Appellate Division, 3rd Dept. Docket 91115

Judicial review of an arbitration award has been statutorily limited by Article 75 of the Civil Practice Law and Rules [CPLR]. Essentially an arbitration award stands unless the court determines that:

1. there was corruption, fraud or misconduct in procuring an award;

2. the arbitrator was not impartial;

3. the arbitrator exceeded his or her authority;

4. the procedures set out in Article 75 were not followed.

In addition to these statutory reasons for vacating the arbitration award, the courts have declared awards found to violate a strong public policy to be null and void.

The Discipline Book

In Carrol, however, the Appellate Division adopted a different standard of review in considering a dismissed employee's effort to vacate an Education Law Section 3020-a disciplinary arbitration award. Citing Matter of Bernstein [Norwich City School Dist. Bd. Of Education], 282 AD2d 70, the Appellate Division said:

Where, as here, the parties are forced to engage in compulsory arbitration, judicial review under CPLR Article 75 requires that the "award be in accord with due process and supported by adequate evidence in the record".

Accordingly, concluded the Appellate Division, the applicable standard for review of the arbitration award in Carroll's case is whether there was substantial evidence in the record to establish the employee's guilt with respect to the charges levied against him. The court also pointed to CPLR Section 7803 as authority to adopt a "substantial evidence" standard in appeals from a 3020-a determination. In the words of the court:

[W]e must determine "whether there is a rational basis in [the whole record] for the findings of fact supporting the [Hearing Panel's recommendation]," citing 300 Gramatan Ave. Assocs. v State Div. of Human Rights, 45 NY2d 176.[140]

Christopher Carroll was a tenured guidance counselor. He had 19 years of service with the Rondout Valley CSD. As a guidance counselor he was responsible for, among other things, creating individualized academic plans for students, planning students' courses for the upcoming academic year, analyzing student report cards to determine whether students passed, adjusting academic plans if students failed, and performing annual reviews of student records.

After several students failed to graduate in 1998, the Board of Education filed Section 3020-a disciplinary charges against Carroll alleging that he failed to maintain required records, he neglected to provide required remedial assistance for students who failed a Regents Competency Test; he failed to schedule students for required courses; and he falsified a student's record.

The Hearing Panel found Carroll guilty of some, but not all, of the charges. It then determined that under the circumstances, dismissal was the appropriate penalty to be imposed. Carroll was terminated from his position on December 28, 2000.

Carroll filed a motion to vacate the arbitration award pursuant to Article 75. Supreme Court, relying on CPLR 7511, dismissed his petition, finding that disciplinary arbitration panel neither exceeded its power nor executed an imperfect award.

Carroll appealed the Supreme Court's ruling, contending that the Supreme Court applied too strict a standard when it limited its review only to those criteria specifically set out in CPLR 7511. The Third Department agreed, ruling that the appropriate standard of review was whether there was substantial

---

[140] In contrast, the individual may appeal an adverse Civil Service Law 75 disciplinary decision to the court pursuant to Article 78 of the CPLR or the individual may elect to appeal the determination to the responsible civil service commission rather than to the courts. In such cases the court applies the substantial evidence in the record test to determine whether or not to sustain the administrative decision.

evidence to support the panel's determination with respect to those charges for which the panel had found him guilty.

The Appellate Division held that all but one of the Hearing Panel's determinations met the substantial evidence in the record standard.

Carroll raised two additional issues in his appeal. He contended that (1) he was denied administrative due process because the Hearing Panel found him guilty of charges that had not been filed against him; and (2) the Hearing Panel failed to consider the school board's failure to provide "remediation" when it determined the penalty.

According to the Appellate Division, the panel found Carroll guilty of intentionally recording that a student had passed a course although the student had failed the course.

Although Carroll contended that he was never charged with intentionally falsifying records. The charge filed alleged that Carroll was guilty of misconduct when he marked a student's plan card to indicate that the student had passed a course without having taken the course. The Appellate Division ruled that the charge adequately apprised Carroll that the alleged misconduct amounted to his intentionally falsifying the student's record and dismissed this branch of Carroll's appeal.

The court, however, agreed that Carroll had been denied administrative due process because the Hearing Panel failed to consider "mitigating circumstances" in determining the penalty. The Appellate Division said that the Hearing Panel failed to honor Carroll's request that the Board of Education's "lack of effort to correct his behavior," be considered by the panel in determining appropriate penalty to be imposed.

Section 3020-a(4) provides that "At the request of the employee, in determining what, if any, penalty or other action shall be imposed, the hearing officer shall consider the extent to which the employing board made efforts towards correcting the behavior of the employee which resulted in charges being brought under this section through means including, but not limited to, remediation, peer intervention or an employee assistance plan."

The Appellate Division said that there was nothing in the record to indicate that the Hearing Panel considered the Board's efforts, if any, to correct Carroll's unacceptable behavior. The Appellate Division vacated the Hearing Panel's "recommendation" as to the penalty to be imposed and directed that the panel reconsider its recommendation.

Although the Court used the term "recommendation" in reference to the disciplinary panel's decision as to the penalty to be imposed, Section 3020-a provides for the Panel's deciding the appropriate penalty to be imposed rather than its recommending a penalty to be imposed to a school board.

Section 3020-a.4 provides that "[t]he written decision shall include the hearing officer's findings of fact on each charge, his or her conclusions with regard to each charge based on said findings and shall state what penalty or other action, if any, shall be taken by the employing board"[141]

---

[141] In contrast, the individual may appeal an adverse Civil Service Law 75 disciplinary decision to the court pursuant to Article 78 of the CPLR or the individual may elect to appeal the determination to the responsible civil service commission

Although Section 3020-a clearly states that CPLR Article 75 controls with respect to appeals involving 3020-a decisions, in deciding the Carroll appeal the Appellate Division concluded that 3020-a appeals are to be treated as though they were Civil Service Law 75 disciplinary appeals.[142]

If the Appellate Division's rationale is ultimately sustained by the Court of Appeals, courts would be required to make a finding that a 3020-a Hearing Panel's determination was supported by substantial evidence in the record in order to confirm an arbitration award.

Further, if the Appellate Division's view that a 3020-a hearing constitutes compulsory arbitration and thus is subject to the substantial evidence test is correct, its determination raises some additional issues.

Section 3020-a.1 authorizes a school district and an employee organization to negotiate an alternative to the statutory disciplinary procedure set out in 3020-a. These alternative procedures are usually referred to as "contract disciplinary procedures" and typically are processed as "disciplinary grievances." Practically all contract disciplinary procedures mandate, as the final step, binding arbitration.

Does Carroll mean that Article 75 motions to vacate or modify a disciplinary arbitration award resulting from "compulsory" arbitration in a contract disciplinary procedure negotiated pursuant to the Taylor Law is subject to a court's review based on the "substantial evidence" standard rather than limited to the reasons for vacating an award set out in Article 75 notwithstanding the parameters for appeal set out in Section 3020-a.5 of the Education Law?

In any event, it would be good practice for a disciplinary hearing panel, statutory or negotiated, to explicitly set out its findings of fact and the reasons for its imposing a particular penalty based in its finding that the individual was guilty of one or more of the charges filed against him or her.

Except with respect to the most egregious acts of misconduct, the Carroll decision clearly signals the need, and reasons, for the employer to attempt to undertake remedial efforts to correct or improve an educator's unsatisfactory behavior and performance prior to its filing formal disciplinary charges against the individual. This type of action is usually referred to as "progressive discipline," i.e., the individual is to be provided with notice of his or her need to improve performance and offered assistance, and a reasonable opportunity, to attain this goal.

Are progressive discipline efforts such as issuing a "counseling memorandum" disciplinary in nature" and thus mandate that an employer file formal charges as a condition precedent to attempting to correct unacceptable employee behavior or performance by issuing such a memorandum? Not necessarily. The test is whether the employer's effort to correct or improve the employee's performance via its issuing counseling memoranda to an individual involves imposing a penalty.

---

rather than to the courts. In such cases the court applies the substantial evidence in the record test to determine whether or not to sustain the administrative decision.

[142] Section 3020-a.5 provides that "... the employee or the employing board may make an application to the New York state supreme court to vacate or modify the decision of the hearing officer pursuant to section [7511] of the civil practice law and rules. The court's review shall be limited to the grounds set forth in such section."

In a number of instances counseling memoranda have been challenged on the theory that the employer's issuing a counseling memorandum, in and of itself, constitutes disciplinary action. The courts have rejected the notion that such an effort on the part of the employer to correct employee behavior constitutes discipline. In Hoffman v Village of Sidney, 652 NYS2d 346, the Appellate Division ruled that an employee is not entitled to a hearing before a letter critical of his or her performance is placed in his or her personnel file, where no punishment is involved.

Accordingly, as observed earlier, the absence of the imposition of any punishment on the employee is the key. Further, courts typically view term "penalty" to mean one of the statutory penalties authorized by 75 of the Civil Service Law or a similar statute.

May the employer subsequently file disciplinary charges against an individual based on the same actions or omissions that motivated the employer to issue a "counseling memorandum" in the first instance or would the inclusion of such charges constitute the administrative disciplinary action equivalent of "double jeopardy" in a criminal proceeding?

In Holt v Board of Education, 52 NY2d 625, the Court of Appeals ruled that should the employer include allegations based on the employee's conduct that resulted in the issuing of a counseling memorandum in the charges or specifications filed against the individual in a statutory or contractual disciplinary proceeding, the inclusion of allegations in charges and specifications involving such prior conduct does not constitute "double jeopardy."

18.09 Chronic absenteeism alleged to be caused by a disability

Sirota v NYC Bd. of Ed., 283 A.D.2d 369

The Sirota case points out that a serious, chronic health condition may not necessarily constitute a disability within the meaning of the Americans With Disabilities Act and other civil rights enactments.

New York City special education teacher Rochelle M. Sirota suffered from cancer. She sued the NYC Board of Education contending that it had unlawfully discriminated against her because of disability and, in addition, unlawfully retaliated against her following her requests for a "reasonable accommodation" because of her disability.

The Appellate Division dismissed her appeal. The court said that Sirota's "cancer and attendant surgeries do not constitute a disability within the meaning of the relevant discrimination statutes (2 USC 12112; New York's Executive Law Section 292[26]; and the Administrative Code of City of New York, Section 8-107[15]) as they did not substantially limit her in any major life activity." In support of this determination, the court pointed to statements in letters prepared by Sirota's personal physician "affirming her ability to work on a regular, full-time basis."

Further, said the court, assuming Sirota does have a disability, her chronic absenteeism, tardiness and unsatisfactory performance evaluations establish that she was unable to perform the essential functions of her job as a special education teacher and thus was not otherwise qualified for the position as required by the discrimination statutes.

As to Sirota's claims of retaliation, the Appellate Division ruled that the refusal to accommodate her requests for a schedule modification or transfer and her being given negative performance evaluations do not show an adverse employment action as required by the discrimination statutes, but only a permissible refusal to change the terms and conditions of her employment.

Another element involving Sirota's claims of unlawful discrimination was based her theory that the school district's conduct constituted a "continuing violation." In addressing this aspect of her petition, the court noted Sirota claimed that she was the victim of "alleged discriminatory conduct preceding her second, 15-month medical leave of absence." Under the circumstances, said the court, the continuing violations exception that might otherwise be applicable is unavailable to her "since the leave of absence, which was voluntary and therefore cannot be considered an act of discrimination, interrupted the alleged pattern of discrimination."

18.10 Chronic absenteeism policy violations

Seabrook v New York, NYS Sup. Ct., Ia Part 5, Justice Stallman.

In an effort to control what it characterized as chronic absenteeism, the New York City Department of Corrections adopted a "Chronic Absence Policy".[143]
The policy, which applied to any New York City correction officer who was out sick more than 12 days in a 12-month period (excluding absences for certain specified reasons), provided that an individual determined to have a "chronic absenteeism" problem could lose of one or more of the following discretionary benefits and privileges:

1. Assignment to a steady tour;

2. Assignment to a specified post or duties;

3. Access to voluntary overtime;

4. Promotions;

5. Secondary employment;

6. Assignment to preferential/special units or commands; and

7. Transfers.

---

[143] Department of Corrections Directive 22583-A

Norman Seabrook, as president of the New York City Correction Officers' Benevolent Association, sued the City on behalf of all of the City's correction officers. Seabrook contended that the directive violates Sections 75 and 76 of the Civil Service Law [CSL].

Seabrook's theory: The directive imposes disciplinary sanctions without providing the individual with the notice and hearing required by Section 75 as a condition precedent to initiating a disciplinary action.

The City, on the other hand, contended that its directive did not authorize the imposition of any of the penalties set forth in CSL Section 75(3) and thus does not, on its face, violate CSL Section 75. It also argued that its directive did not violate Section 76, which applies only to persons "aggrieved by a penalty or punishment ... imposed pursuant to [CSL Section 75]."

The court agreed with the City's argument and dismissed Seabrook's petition.

The City conceded that its directive was promulgated unilaterally and does not afford certain of the protections that CSL Sections 75 and 76 provide to employees. However, argued the City, Sections 75 and 76 are inapplicable here because the provisions of the Directive do not include any of the sanctions or penalties set out in CSL Section 75(3) with respect to a correction officer deemed to be a "chronic absentee."

Justice Stallman said that CSL Section 75 specifically limits the imposition of disciplinary penalties to those set out in the section. The employer may not impose penalties exceeding those set by statute. As an example of this principle, Justice Stallman cited Cepeda v Koehler, 159 AD2d 290. In Cepeda the court held that a penalty consisting of forfeiture of 15 vacation days plus the payment of $1,500 fine violated the penalty provisions of Section 75, which only sanctions the imposition of a "single penalty" from among those enumerated.

In another multiple penalty case, Matteson v City of Oswego, 588 NYS2d 472, the Appellate Division overturned the penalties imposed by the appointing authority and remanded the matter for the imposition of a new, appropriate penalty.

Oswego had imposed the following penalties on Matteson: (1) suspension without pay for 30 days; and (2) demotion to a lower grade position; and (3) restitution of $3,699.48.

The Appellate Division held that the penalty given was contrary to law in that "the imposition of multiple penalties was improper" under 75.3 of the Civil Service Law.

As to the issue of the directive providing for restitution of the $3699.48, "restitution" is not one of the authorized penalties set out in 75.3. Thus it may be necessary for the employer to attempt to recover this amount through a separate proceeding if the employee does not elect to make such restitution.

In contrast, in cases involving the imposition of a penalty by an arbitrator pursuant to a "contract disciplinary procedure" the courts have held that the only limitations on the penalty to be imposed is the sound judgment of the arbitrator.

However, said Justice Stallman, the "[f]acial validity of the Directive does not leave the Union and its members entirely without recourse." The decision notes that the Union had filed an Improper Practice Petition, administratively challenging DOC's unilateral imposition of the Directive with the New York City Office of Labor Relations.

Further, said the court, "implementation of the Directive in a specific individual case may be challenged as arbitrary and capricious."

The decision also points out that "if transfers pursuant to the Directive constitute demotions within the meaning of CSL Section 75, or if actions pursuant to the Directive otherwise constitute substantive penalties enumerated by CSL Section 75, they may be challenged in specific cases where appropriate.

18.11 Classified service disciplinary procedures

Guadagnino v Lancaster CSD, CEd 14080, 2/18/99

The Lancaster Central School District filed disciplinary charges against Anthony P. Guadagnino pursuant to Section 75 of the Civil Service Law. The charges alleged that Guadagnino, a custodian, made false, baseless and damaging statements concerning alleged inappropriate conduct by a building principal, the president of the school board and others to various district officials and staff members.

Found guilty of all charges, Guadagnino was dismissed from his position. His appeal to the Erie County Civil Service Commission pursuant to Section 76 of the Civil Service Law was denied.

Guadagnino next filed an appeal with the Commissioner of Education pursuant to Section 310 of the Education Law contending that the school district violated federal and state law protecting "whistle blowers" by terminating him in retaliation for his making and pursuing his allegations of "inappropriate conduct."

The Commissioner dismissed the appeal for lack of subject matter jurisdiction. He said that with respect to Guadagnino's claims concerning "whistle blowing" [Civil Service Law Section 75-b], such claims may be asserted as a defense in a Section 75 hearing. However, nothing in the Education Law authorizes an appeal to the Commissioner from disciplinary action taken under Section 75. The Commissioner noted that "it is well established ... that the suspension or termination of classified employees is not an appropriate subject of an appeal brought pursuant to Education Law Section 310."

As to Guadagnino's federal claims, the Commissioner pointed out that the federal law cited, 5 USC 1213, is generally applicable to federal employees and those in federally related employment.

18.12 Collateral estoppel

Jaworowski v NYC Transit Authority, 2nd Circuit, July 1999

The judicial doctrine of collateral estoppel prevents a party from relitigating issues previously considered by one forum in a second forum. The doctrine is based on the concept that a party may not relitigate an issue if the identical issue was necessarily decided in a previous proceeding, provided that the party against whom collateral estoppel is being asserted had a full and fair opportunity to litigate the issue in the prior action.

The Jaworowski case demonstrates the elements considered by courts when determining whether the doctrine applies in a particular situation with respect to whether or not the identical issue was decided in a previous proceeding or whether there was an opportunity for such issues to be considered.

Leonard Jaworowski was terminated from his position with the New York Transit Authority following a disciplinary arbitration. He brought an Article 75 action in State Supreme Court in an effort to have the arbitration award vacated. Unsuccessful in this effort, Jaworowski next filed a lawsuit in federal district court pursuant to 42 USC Section 1983 alleging "various constitutional infirmities in an arbitration proceeding arising out of disciplinary charges brought against him by the Authority."

The Authority claimed Jaworowski's federal action was barred under the doctrine of collateral estoppel because he already had "his day in court" on these issues as a result his bringing an Article 75 action. The district court agreed, ruling that Jaworowski was estopped from suing on these claims because they had been previously litigated in his Article 75 action brought in New York state court. The Circuit Court of Appeals affirmed the lower court's ruling.

Jaworowski's major argument was that the doctrine of collateral estoppel should not bar his federal suit because the claims he was asserting in his Section 1983 complaint were not identical to those he litigated in state court. His contended that the standards of review of arbitrations differ between New York state courts and federal courts and thus he had a viable action in federal court.

According to Jaworowski, to prevail in state court he would have had to prove that the alleged due process violations rendered the arbitration irrational, while in federal court he need only show that the arbitration violated due process.

The Circuit Court of Appeals said that his argument "mistakenly conflates two different grounds for setting aside an arbitration under New York law." Although one ground for vacating an arbitration decision is to show that the award is "totally irrational," a court applying New York law will also vacate an arbitration if it finds that the arbitration violated due process, citing Beckman v Greentree Securities, Inc., 87 NY2d 566.

The Circuit Court said that the district court correctly dismissed his Section 1983 action because New York State courts do not review constitutional challenges to arbitration decisions more deferentially than do federal courts.

18.13 Concealing misconduct

Application of Gonzalez, App. Div., First Dept., June 22, 2000

The lesson in the Gonzalez case is that an employee's efforts to suppress his or her misconduct may result in a harsher penalty than might otherwise be imposed.

The Appellate Division, First Department, sustained the dismissal of New York City police officer Antonio Gonzalez after he was found guilty of charges that he had "wrongfully discharged his firearm, and thereafter lied about and attempted to conceal evidence of his misconduct." Citing Berenhaus v Ward, 70 NY2d 436, the court said that under the circumstances, "[t]he penalty of dismissal does not shock our sense of fairness."

In La Chance v Erickson, 522 US 262, the US Supreme Court said that federal employees being investigated for alleged employment-related misconduct who knowingly give false answers to the investigators may be given stiffer penalties than might otherwise be imposed on them for such misconduct.

The court said that an individual "may decline to answer the question, or answer it honestly, but he [or she] cannot with impunity knowingly and willfully answer with a falsehood."

As to a "Fifth Amendment" defense in such cases, in Brogan v United States, 522 US 398, the Supreme Court upheld the conviction of a former union official who falsely answered a federal investigator's questions. The Court held that the Fifth Amendment privilege against self-incrimination does not bar prosecuting an individual who answers questions falsely in contrast to his or her refusing to answer the same inquiries.

18.14 Conducting a private business

Cook v Von Essen, 283 A.D.2d 214
Sometimes a public employee will operate a private business "on the side." Typically the individual is required to obtain the prior approval of his or her appointing authority in order to conduct such activities. The failure to obtain such approval could have serious consequences, as New York City firefighter Darren Cook learned.

Cook was dismissed from his position after a disciplinary hearing. The Administrative Law Judge [ALJ] found that Cook had concealed his operating an outside pool business from the Department and then, at the disciplinary hearing, continued his attempt at concealment by advancing "the less than creditworthy claim that his pool services were rendered free of charge."

In addition, the ALJ found that had Cook conducted his pool business while on a paid medical leave. In the words of the ALJ, it is a "gross abuse of public trust for uniformed workers to engage in unauthorized employment while on medical leave."

The Appellate Division said that the record demonstrated that Cook "had violated Department rules and regulations by engaging in extra-departmental employment while on medical leave on four separate dates, and that he operated an outside pool maintenance business for three years without seeking the necessary departmental approval."

Notwithstanding his unblemished 13-year record with the Department, the court said that "[t]here is no basis upon which we can interfere with the determination to terminate [his] from his employment with the City.

18.15 Confrontations with a superior

Muniz v Giuliani 282 A.D.2d 246

The Appellate Division, First Department, sustained the penalty of a suspension without pay for twenty days imposed on New York City police officer Clifford Muniz after Muniz was found guilty of continuing to argue with his desk sergeant after the sergeant had instructed him to leave the precinct house following the morning roll call and the assignment of duties. Noting that Muniz's testimony supported a finding of guilty, the court said that the penalty imposed "does not shock our sense of fairness."

18.16 Confidentiality of disciplinary records
Sangirardi v Nassau County, NYS Sup. Ct., Justice Alpert, 7/1/02

In deciding the Sangirardi case, Supreme Court, Nassau County, considered the right of a student complainant to see the "Final Results" of a college disciplinary hearing held following her filing her complaint.

A Nassau County Community College women's basketball team member alleged that she had been sexually assaulted by members of the college's men's basketball team. She asked for audiotapes, videotapes and transcripts of the disciplinary proceeding conducted by the college. The college declined to provide her with these materials, claiming that the federal Family Educational Rights and Privacy Act, 20 USC 1232g, frequently referred to as the Buckley Amendment, although allowing students and parents access to "education records," prohibits their dissemination to the public.

Justice Alpert agreed in part, ruling that the student complainant was entitled to a copy of the "final results" of the disciplinary proceedings. Justice Alpert noted that the Buckley Amendment authorizes the disclosure of disciplinary records to teachers and school officials and of the "final results" of any disciplinary proceeding to an alleged victim.

Suppose a disciplinary action is "settled" and the parties agree to keep the terms of a disciplinary settlement confidential. Is such an agreement a defense to a demand to disclose the terms of the disciplinary settlement?

Reading the Sangirardi decision together with the ruling in LaRocca v Jericho UFSD, 220 AD2d 424, it appears that there is neither a federal nor a state shield to honoring such a confidentiality agreement.

In LaRocca, the School District had filed disciplinary charges against the principal of one of its schools. Subsequently the Jericho School Board authorized its superintendent to negotiate a settlement that would dispose of the matter. A settlement was reached and the Board adopted a motion withdrawing its charges against the principal without prejudice.

Anthony LaRocca, vice-president of the Jericho Teachers Association, asked for a copy of the settlement agreement on behalf of the teachers supervised by the principal. LaRocca's request was denied on the grounds that (a) providing the teachers with a copy "would constitute an unwarranted invasion of personal privacy" and (b) the document relates to "intra-agency or inter-agency materials which the School District is not required to disclose."

LaRocca then sued under the Freedom of Information Law [FOIL] (Article 6, Public Officers Law), contending that all records of a public agency are "presumptively accessible" and the settlement agreement did not fall within any of the recognized exceptions set out in FOIL.

Although a Supreme Court justice dismissed LaRocca's petition [LaRocca v Jericho UFSD, 159 Misc2d 90], the Appellate Division reversed, ruling that the settlement agreement did not constitute an "employment history" as defined by FOIL and therefore is presumptively available for public inspection.

Significantly, the Appellate Division said that "as a matter of public policy, the Board of Education cannot bargain away the public's right to access to public records." The court ruled that the settlement agreement or any part of it providing for confidentiality or purporting to deny the public access to the document "is unenforceable as against the pubic interest."

Moreover, the decision indicates that a public employer may not, by private agreement, limit the public's right to access to records which are otherwise subject to disclosure under FOIL, citing Anonymous v Board of Education of the Mexico Central School District, 62 Misc 2d 300. In the Mexico Central School District case the court said that an agreement to keep secret that to which public has a right of access under FOIL unenforceable as against public policy.

There may be some aspect of a disciplinary settlement confidentiality agreement that is enforceable, however. In LaRocca, the settlement agreement contained references to charges that the principal denied or were not admitted, together with the names of certain teachers. The Appellate Division ruled that disclosure of such parts of the settlement agreement would constitute an unwarranted invasion of privacy within the meaning of FOIL.

The Court said that the settlement agreement must be redacted [censored] to eliminate such references -- i.e., the disputed charges and the names of the teachers -- prior to its release to LaRocca.

However one member of the Appellate Division panel reviewing the appeal rejected the concept of providing for confidentiality in such cases by means of redaction of some of the contents of the records. Judge O'Brien said that in his view, "Although disclosure of the charges might cause some embarrassment, that is an insufficient basis under FOIL to deny disclosure."

Sometimes the employer will agree not to reveal the reasons underlying its demanding the employee's resignation to potential employers in the future. The employer's ability to agree that the reasons leading to the demand for the resignation shall remain "confidential" has been tempered, however.

In response to the so-called "silent resignation" in cases involving "child abuse in an educational setting" by a school employee, the New York State Legislature has declared that making an agreement "to maintain confidentiality" in resignation situations where allegations of child abuse have been leveled against an individual is against the public policy of this State.

Section 1133 bars a school administrator or superintendent from agreeing to withhold the fact that an allegation of child abuse in an educational setting was involved in the separation of the employee or volunteer in return for the individual's resignation or agreement to a suspension from his or her position. A violation of Section 1133 is a Class D felony and, in addition, "shall also be punishable by a civil penalty not to exceed $20,000."

In addition, Subdivision 3 of Section 1133 provides that "[a]ny superintendent of schools who in good faith reports to law enforcement officials information regarding allegations of child abuse or a resignation as required by this article shall have immunity from any liability, civil or criminal, which might otherwise result by reason of such actions."

With respect to the availability of public documents pursuant to FOIL, it is well settled that FOIL imposes a broad duty of disclosure on government agencies as noted by the Court of Appeals in Fink v Lefkowitz, 47 NY2d 567.

The general rule: All agency records are presumptively available for public inspection and copying, unless they fall within 1 of 10 categories of exemptions that, as a matter of the exercise of discretion, permit agencies to withhold certain records.

In other words, the fact that certain records may properly be viewed as falling into an "exemption" category does not require that the custodian bar the disclosure of the material in response to a FOIL inquiry. The statute merely permits the agency to elect to withhold disclosing an "exempt" document or record.

The Court of Appeals has repeatedly stated that FOIL is to be liberally construed and its exemptions narrowly interpreted so that the public is granted maximum access to the records of government.

Expressly exempted from mandatory disclosure are records that "if disclosed would constitute an unwarranted invasion of ... privacy" (Public Officers Law Section 87[2][b]), including but not limited to "disclosure of employment, medical or credit histories or personal references of applicants for employment."

Although it is clear that a record is not considered an "employment history" merely because it records facts concerning employment, the term "employment history" for purposes of FOIL exemptions is not defined in the statute, nor well interpreted by case law.

However, as the court said in Hanig v State of New York Dept. of Motor Vehicles, 168 AD2d 884, aff'd 79 NY2d 106, its companion term "medical history" has been defined as "information that one would reasonably expect to be included as a relevant and material part of a proper medical history."

By this the court presumably meant that term "employment history" means that "information" that one would reasonably expect to be included as a relevant and material part of a proper personnel record system.

18.17 Constructive criticisms or discipline?

Matter of Fusco, Comm. of Ed. Decision 14,396, June 27, 2000
Matter of Irving, Comm. of Ed. Decision 14,373, May 25, 2000

Sometimes it may be difficult to determine the location of that thin line that separates lawful "constructive criticism" of an individual's performance by a supervisor and supervisory actions addressing an individual's performance that are disciplinary in nature.

As the Court of Appeals indicated in Holt v Webutick Central School District, 52 NY2d 625, a "counseling memorandum" that is given to an employee and placed in his or her personnel file constitutes a lawful means of instructing the employee concerning unacceptable performance and the actions that should be taken by the individual to improve his or her work.

In other words, comments critical of employee performance do not, without more, constitute disciplinary action. On the other hand, counseling letters may not be used as a subterfuge for avoiding initiating formal disciplinary action against a tenured individual.

In the opinion of the Commissioner of Education, the employers "crossed the line" in both the Fusco and Irving situations.

The Fusco Case

Two questions were raised by Esther Fusco, a tenured Jefferson Central School District school principal, in her appeal to the Commissioner of Education challenging her the 1998 performance evaluation that was prepared by the school board itself.

1. Is a school board authorized to conduct "performance evaluations" of school district administrators?

2. If a school board may undertake such evaluations, did the board's 1998 performance evaluation of her work constitute disciplinary action?

First Fusco contended that only a school superintendent was authorized to undertake a performance evaluation of school administrators and teachers. Her second complaint: her 1998 was evaluation by the board was unlawful because it constituted disciplinary action within the meaning of Section 3020-a of the Education Law and she was not served with charges or given a hearing.

According to the ruling, Jefferson's superintendent, Dr. Wayne Jones, prior to his leaving the district in October 1997, had evaluated school administrators. Fusco was not evaluated by any of the district's acting superintendents who served following Jones' departure.

On July 29, 1998 the school board gave Fusco a memorandum entitled Board Evaluation of Principal Work Performance in which the board characterized Fusco's performance during both academic 1996-1997 and 1997-1998 as "unsatisfactory." The board's examples of Fusco's unsatisfactory performance set out in the evaluation included allegations that Fusco:

1. Demonstrated "unsuitable judgment;"

2. Exhibited unsuitable behavior;

3. Engaged in insubordinate and disrespectful behavior; and

4. Exhibited poor leadership.

The board placed a copy of its evaluation in Fusco's personnel file and Fusco appealed to the Commissioner. Fusco argued that:

1. Only the superintendent of schools is authorized to evaluate her performance and thus the board's action constituted a violation 8 NYCRR 100.2(o); and

2. Assuming that board could conduct such evaluations, the evaluation, when placed in her personnel file, constituted "an impermissible disciplinary reprimand, issued without complying with the procedural protections of Education Law Section 3020-a."

The board defended its action, contending that (1) it did, in fact, have authority to evaluate Fusco's performance and (2) its action was "constructive criticism" of Fusco's performance permitted by law and thus did not constitute disciplinary action within the meaning of Section 3020-a.

The Commissioner agreed with the board in part. First he pointed out that while 8 NYCRR 100.2(o) requires that the superintendent "develop formal procedures for the review of the performance of all personnel of the district", there is nothing in the regulation that requires the superintendent to conduct the evaluation. Accordingly, the Commissioner ruled that in the absence of a provision that would "prohibit a board of education from doing so," a school board may itself conduct such an evaluation.

What of Fusco's second claim -- that the evaluation constituted unlawful disciplinary action and thus must be removed from her personnel file?

The Commissioner said that while the general rule is that personnel given critical administrative evaluations by a supervisor is not entitled to Section 3020-a protections, a disciplinary reprimand may not be issued without a finding of misconduct pursuant to Section 3020-a.

Did Fusco's evaluation constitute disciplinary action without the benefit of the protections of Section 3020-a? Yes, ruled the Commissioner, it did.

The Commissioner said that "contents of the memorandum" did not fall within the parameters of a "permissible evaluation" and despite the board's representation that it was "intended to encourage positive change" in Fusco's performance, it "contains no constructive criticism or a single suggestion for improvement." Rather, said the Commissioner, the memorandum focused on "castigating [Fusco] for prior alleged misconduct." Instead of "constructive criticism," the Commissioner concluded that the evaluation "chastised [Fusco] for serious misconduct," including "improper release of confidential information, harassment of staff members, damaging district/union relationships...and poor leadership."

The district was directed to remove the evaluation from Fusco's personnel file as it "does not constitute a performance evaluation" but rather "an impermissible reprimand."

Two other procedural points were considered by the Commissioner.

The district had also argued that portions of Fusco's appeal concerned Taylor Law matters and thus the Commissioner should defer to the Public Employment Relations Board. PERB, it contended, had "exclusive jurisdiction" over such issues. The Commissioner decided that his "disposition of the appeal ... is upon grounds unrelated to the Taylor Law" and thus dismissal of Fusco's appeal was not required.[144]

In addition, the district asked the Commissioner for permission to submit two additional documents it claimed addressed "substantive issues" related to Fusco's conduct after it had filed its answer to Fusco's petition:

1. An affidavit by an individual; and

2. "[A]n affirmation" by an attorney.

The Commissioner agreed to accept both documents because "that information was not available to the [district] prior to [the] submission of its answer."

The Irving Case

Troy City School District Superintendent Armand Reo, after discussing letters of complaint received from parents and other concerns with the school board and Elementary School Principal Mozella Irving, gave Irving a "letter of counseling" in which he, among other things, said:
You are hereby counseled that in future dealings with the parents of our students you must avoid a confrontational attitude ... avoid making rude or inappropriate comments to parents and you should generally make every attempt to accommodate reasonable requests [received from] parents.

A copy of this letter was placed in Irving's personnel file.

The next day, October 8, 1999, Reo gave Irving a second letter in which he told her that she was transferred to a different school, where she would serve as assistant principal effective October 14, 1999 and that such action was being taken "in the best interest of the school district."

---

[144] As to Taylor Law considerations, PERB has recognized the difference between criticism of employee performance and disciplinary action. In Port Jefferson Union Free School District v United Aides and Assistants, U-5713, PERB rejected a union's claim that every written criticism of an employee was a "reprimand."

Protesting that her involuntary reassignment and demotion "was disciplinary in nature" and illegally deprived her of her rights to due process as set out in Section 3020-a of the Education Law, Irving appealed Reo's action to the Commissioner of Education.

The Commissioner sustained Irving's appeal, holding that "[t]he record convinces me that disciplinary action was taken and that Irving was deprived of her rights under Education Law Section 3020-a."

Conceding that Sections 1711 and 2508 of the Education Law authorize a superintendent to transfer personnel, the problem here, said the Commissioner, was that Irving's alleged "staff mistreatment" and "parental mistreatment" were the only reasons for reassigning and demoting Irving set out in the record. The Commissioner pointed out that the several meetings between Reo and Irving, and Reo and the board, and the two letters given to Irving by Reo, "are all part of a single process, and it is inescapable that the sole reason for [Irving's] transfer was her alleged misconduct as a principal."

Considering all of these circumstances as a whole, the Commissioner concluded that Irving was entitled to the protections of Section 3020-a, including the right to contest formal charges, "and those rights have been violated here."

Another consideration that the Commissioner found persuasive: all of the materials submitted by the board in responding to Irving's appeal were "directed toward demonstrating misconduct on the part of [Irving]. This, the Commissioner pointed out, was exactly the type of proof that the district would have been expected to introduce in a Section 3020-a disciplinary hearing.

Rejecting the district's argument that Irving's "transfer was for the good of the district" and thus not disciplinary in nature, the Commissioner said this theory "misses the mark." He observed that "one would hope that every school district disciplinary action or proceeding, taken in good faith, is for the good of the district."

The Commissioner annulled Irving's reassignment from her position as principal of School 2 to assistant principal of School 14 "without prejudice to any further action which may be appropriate under the terms of this decision."

The standard used by the Commissioner in formulating his ruling: A superior may issue a letter critical of an individual's performance and place a copy of such a letter in the individual's personnel file without initiating disciplinary action pursuant to Section 3020-a where the document deals with a relatively minor shortcoming and urges or directs better performance on the part of the individual in the future.

Had Reo's letter of October 7, 1999 been the only action taken by the district, said the Commissioner, a plausible argument that Irving had not been subjected to disciplinary action could have been made. However, this letter, coupled with the letter of October 8, 1999 demoting and transferring Irving to another school, together with the discussions of the matter by the board, persuaded the Commissioner that Irving had been disciplined within the meaning of Holt.

Another concern: A "counseling memorandum" is placed in an individual's personnel file and later disciplinary charges involving the same event(s) are served upon the individual. Does including the events set out in the counseling memorandum in the charges constitute "double jeopardy?" No, according to the Court of Appeal's ruling in Patterson v Smith, 53 NY2d 98.

In Patterson the court said that including charges concerning performance that were addressed in a counseling memorandum was not double jeopardy. The court's rationale: as a proper counseling memoranda contains a warning and an admonition to comply with the expectations of the employer, it is not a form of punishment in and of itself.

Clearly, case law indicates that giving the employee a counseling memorandum does not bar the employer from later filing disciplinary charges based on the same event and the memorandum may be introduced as evidence in the disciplinary hearing or for the purposes of determining the penalty to be imposed if the individual is found guilty.

18.18 Constructive dismissal

Graziano v NYS Division of State Police, USDC, SDNY, Justice Connor, received July 14, 2002

One of the elements in the Graziano case was Graziano's representation that although he had resigned from his position, his separation, in fact, constituted a constructive dismissal.

John R. Graziano, a Caucasian male sued the New York Division of State Police [DSP] alleging violations of Title VII. Graziano claimed that he was the victim of unlawful discrimination and harassment because of his gender and that this resulted in his constructive discharge. Graziano's complaint: female co-workers had subjected him to ongoing harassment and discrimination following a sexual harassment complaint that was filed against him but never proceeded to trial.

Finding that "no rational factfinder could determine that [Graziano] suffered adverse treatment on the basis of gender since no nexus could be established that attitudes directed towards plaintiff, accused of sexual harassment, relate to animus directed at gender," Justice Connor dismissed his complaint.

According to the decision, in October 1992, a female co-worker, Patricia Kantha, filed a sexual harassment complaint against Graziano. DSP investigated and ultimately found that Kantha's allegations could not be substantiated and that it would take no further action concerning the matter.[145]

Addressing the issue of constructive dismissal, the court, citing Dean v Westchester County District Attorney's Office, 119 F. Supp. 2d 424, said that: "[a] constructive discharge claim is established by showing the employer deliberately created intolerable working conditions in an effort to force the employee to resign."

In determining whether there has been a constructive discharge, "the trier of fact must be satisfied that the . . . working conditions would have been so difficult or unpleasant that a reasonable person in the

---

[145] Although Kantha pursued her sexual harassment claim with the New York State Division of Human Rights and the Division found "probable cause" that Graziano had committed sexual harassment against Kantha, the matter never proceeded to trial.

employee's shoes would have felt compelled to resign." In contrast, mere dissatisfaction with work assignments, unfair criticism, or working conditions that can be categorized as unpleasant does not constitute a constructive discharge.

According to the court, Graziano's constructive discharge claim fails for the same reasons that his hostile work environment claim failed. Other than alleging that DSP sided with his female co-workers, and failed to adequately address his complaints concerning their harassing conduct, Graziano did not assert any independent basis for imputing gender discrimination against the DSP.

Thus, said the court, because Graziano failed to present evidence to support his claim that his co-workers' conduct was gender-related, any neglect by DSP in remedying the situation is not actionable under Title VII and thus his election to resign could not be deemed a constructive dismissal.

Justice Connor also commented that while Graziano "may (or may not) have been the unfortunate target of a conspiracy of his fellow employees who didn't like him and who tried to and did make his work experience extremely unpleasant ... however malicious and contemptible such conduct might be, if it was not gender-motivated, it would not give rise to an action against their employer under Title VII, without which there is no basis for federal jurisdiction." Accordingly, Justice Connor granted DSP's motion for summary judgment and dismissed Graziano's petition with prejudice.

18.19 Continuation on the payroll may require restitution by the employee

Rensselaer County v Hudson Valley Community College Faculty Association, 262 A.D.2d 843

In the Hudson Valley case, the Appellate Division decided that an arbitrator had the power to require a faculty member to repay the college for the salary it had paid to him while an appeal of his dismissal was pending arbitration.

The arbitrator had ordered the college to provide salary during this period, but apparently reserved the right to direct that the salary be repaid if she later determined that the dismissal was warranted, which she did.

Hudson Valley Community College dismissed a tenured member of its faculty, Thomas P. Neuhaus, and removed him from the payroll effective September 1, 1996.

The college alleged that Neuhaus had violated the collective bargaining agreement between the college and the Hudson Valley Community College Faculty Association when he gave each of the students in his electronics communication course a grade of 100 percent in lieu of an examination that had been scheduled but was not administered. Neuhaus was also charged with "improperly selling electronics equipment to students in exchange for special considerations."

The Faculty Association filed two grievances on Neuhaus' behalf. The first challenged Neuhaus' termination. The second grievance concerned the college's removing Neuhaus from the payroll and failing to continue his benefits while the disciplinary grievance was pending.

As to the salary grievance, the arbitrator ruled that the college had violated the collective bargaining agreement by failing to keep Neuhaus on the payroll during the pendency of the termination grievance. Accordingly, the college restored Neuhaus to the payroll retroactive to September 1, 1996.

The termination grievance then went to arbitration. In August 1997 the arbitrator rendered her award, concluding that:

1. Neuhaus was guilty of Articles VII.A and XI.B.3 of the collective bargaining agreement;

2. The penalty of termination was appropriate;

3. Neuhaus was not entitled to salary beyond August 21, 1996; and

4. Neuhaus should reimburse the college for salary paid to him after that date.

The college asked a State Supreme Court judge to confirm the arbitration award [see Section 7510, Civil Practice Law and Rules]. Neuhaus cross-petitioned the court seeking (1) to vacate the termination award and (2) to confirm the award in the salary grievance.

The Appellate Division rejected Neuhaus' appeal seeking to overturn his termination. The court then said that it was "unpersuaded" that the arbitrator exceeded her authority in ordering Neuhaus to repay salary received for the period following August 21, 1996.

The Appellate Division ruled that the provision in the termination grievance award requiring Neuhaus to repay the salary the college had paid to him since September 1, 1996 "did not contradict" the salary grievance award. The court concluded that the salary grievance dealt exclusively with the issue of Neuhaus' right to receive his salary pending the resolution of the termination grievance.
The court commented that in the salary grievance the arbitrator had ordered the college "to continue such payments until the matter is resolved by the issuance of an arbitration decision dealing with the merits of the dismissal, which decision shall then be controlling". Accordingly, there was nothing to bar the arbitrator from directing Neuhaus to repay the salary he had received from the college since September 1, 1996.

However, there may be limitations with respect to the period during which a person against whom disciplinary charges have been filed may be suspended from his or her position without pay. An example of this is the statutory limitation set out in Section 75 of the Civil Service Law. Section 75 allows an individual against whom disciplinary charges have been filed to be suspended without pay for up to 30 days. The employee must be restored to the payroll after 30 days, even if he or she is directed not to report to work while the disciplinary action is pending.

In some cases a contract provision may allow the employer to suspend an individual without pay pending the determination of the disciplinary action. Such a provision is usually subjected to "narrow interpretation" by the courts. An illustration of such a narrow construction is set out in Board of Education v Nyquist, 48 NY2 97. In this case the Court of Appeals noted that the Taylor Law agreement negotiated by the parties allowed a teacher to be suspended without pay "pending an investigation and recommendation by the superintendent of schools."

The board filed disciplinary charges against a suspended teacher after it had received the Superintendent's recommendation. The teacher's "suspended without pay" status was continued by the board. Some 10 months later a hearing panel found the teacher guilty of the charges. The penalty imposed: termination.

As a result of the litigation that followed, the district was directed to pay the teacher back salary for the period from the date of the superintendent's recommendation to the board until the effective date of the dismissal. The Court of Appeals reasoned that "there (was) no authorization [in the contract] for the board's suspending the employee without pay after the superintendent completed his investigation and made his report".

Had the contract permitted the board to continue the teacher's suspension without pay pending a final disciplinary decision, it appears likely that such a suspension would have been upheld by the court. The only limitation on the duration of a suspension without pay when authorized by a Taylor Law agreement appears to be that the employer may not use the suspension without pay as a sword by delaying the proceedings.

18.20 Contract disciplinary procedures and Section 72

Williams v NYS Executive Department (Division for Youth), __ Misc2 __,

Drug abuse by public employees continues to be an issue of critical concern to public employers as indicated by the Williams decision. The case involved a number of significant issues concerning public personnel administration including:

1. treating employees suspected of alcohol or drug abuse as having a disability within the meaning of Section 72 of the Civil Service Law;

2. requiring employees to submit to involuntary tests for drugs as part of a Section 72 medical examination; and

3. taking disciplinary action against employees who fail to report for a Section 72 medical examination that involves their submitting to urinalysis for illegal substances.

According to the decision, Williams was directed him to report to the New York Civil Service Department's Employee Health Service and to provide a urine sample in order to determine the presence or absence of narcotics or other substances in his urine. Williams was told that this action as being taken pursuant to Section 72 of the Civil Service Law following observations of his behavior at work by the director of the facility.[146] The facility director reported that she observed Williams "with bloodshot eyes, perspiring profusely, anxious, speaking inappropriately loud, inappropriately laughing, swinging his arms in the air and repeatedly shouting 'Let me out, let me out.'"

---

[146] Section 72 provides for the placement of an employee on a leave because of a disability, other than a disability resulting from an occupational injury or disease, in the event it is determined that he or she is unable to satisfactorily perform the duties of the position because of that disability.

After Williams refused to comply with this and a number of similar directives given to him by the facility director, he placed on involuntary leave of absence as authorized by Section 72.5 of the Civil Service Law. A few days later he was served with a Notice of Discipline in accordance with the contract disciplinary procedure set out in the collective bargaining between CSEA and the State.

Williams sued, claiming that he could not be compelled to submit to urinalysis in connection with a Section 72 medical examination. His major arguments: (1) the Division had improperly used Section 72 in order to compel him to submit to a urinalysis; (2) it was not misconduct for him to refuse to submit to a urine test that was illegally requested; and (3) Section 72 was unconstitutional as applied to him.

The Division argued that "possible drug and/or alcohol abuse can be considered a disability [under Section 72] and encompasses one who is unable to function at one's job effectively...." The Division also contended that Section 72 provide it with a legal basis for directing Williams to submit to the urinalysis and that disobeying its order(s) to report to the Employee Health Service constituted misconduct subjecting him to disciplinary action under Article 33 of the Taylor Agreement between the State and CSEA. In addition, the Division claimed that a urinalysis can be included as part of a Section 72 medical examination.

The court decided that "the statute allows the [public employer] to require an employee undergo a medical examination, which medical examination could include a urinalysis, and that a disability which renders an employee unable to perform the duties of his or her position could result from alcohol and/or drug abuse."

The court also said that "clearly, the standard of reasonable suspicion must be met before [the employer] may exercise Civil Service Law Section 72 to compel [an employee] to submit to a medical examination, including a urinalysis," citing Patchogue-Medford Teachers Association v Board of Education, 70 NY2d 57, among other cases, in support of this rule.

The court decided Williams was subject to the disciplinary procedure set out in the Taylor Law agreement between the State and CSEA and dismissed his lawsuit.

18.21 Court modification of disciplinary penalty

MacFarlane v Village of Scotia, 274 A.D.2d 643, appeal dismissed, 95 N.Y.2d 930

May a court modify the disciplinary penalty imposed by an employer after affirming the employer's finding that the employee is guilty of the charges and specifications filed against the individual? Yes, as the MacFarlane decision demonstrates.

Village of Scotia police officer Timothy MacFarlane was found guilty of "the majority of charges" filed against him. This determination was affirmed by the Appellate Division.

However, in the course of considering the matter, the Appellate Division said that it viewed the penalty imposed on MacFarlane -- a 10-day suspension without pay -- "unduly harsh and excessive" and remanded the matter to Scotia "for the purpose of reconsidering the penalty."[147]

Scotia reconsidered it decision as to the punishment to be given MacFarlane and then "reimposed the original penalty." MacFarlane appealed and a State Supreme Court justice vacated the 10-day suspension, directing Scotia to place "a written reprimand," one of the penalties authorized by Section 75 of the Civil Service Law, in MacFarlane's personnel file instead. Both Scotia and MacFarlane appealed the ruling.

MacFarlane argued that "no penalty should be imposed" and that Supreme Court's decision directing the placement of a written reprimand in his file constitutes an abuse of discretion.

Scotia, on the other hand, contended that the Supreme Court's decision should be overturned because the court did not find that the penalty imposed by respondent was "shocking to one's sense of fairness." As an alternative, Scotia claimed that its reimposition of the original 10-day suspension "is not so shocking to one's sense of fairness as to require vacatur."

The Appellate Division affirmed the lower court ruling, indicating that in its earlier determination it "made it abundantly clear" that it determined that the penalty 10-day suspension without pay was disproportionate to MacFarlane's misconduct. The court noted that it made this ruling after "a careful assessment of the offending conduct and its impact on [Scotia's] police force, balanced against [MacFarlane's] unblemished service record." By using the terms "unduly harsh" and "clearly excessive" the court said it conveyed its finding that the penalty imposed was disproportionate to the offense and, thus, shocking to one's sense of fairness. The Appellate Division said that the Supreme Court "appropriately found that reimposition of a 10-day suspension without pay was impermissible."

As to a court's authority to change the disciplinary penalty imposed by the employer, the court said that a Supreme Court justice has the necessary power to determine the penalty to be imposed when the original penalty is found to constitute an abuse of discretion and where the record is sufficient for the reviewing court to assess the permissible punishment, citing Pell v Board of Education, 34 NY2d 222 at 234.

18.22 Credibility of witness

Saunders v City of New York, 273 A.D.2d 103, motion to appeal denied, 95 N.Y.2d 766

New York City police officer Brian Saunders was terminated from his position after being found guilty of having "assaulted and caused physical injuries to two former girlfriends."

Sauders appealed, contending that the Commissioner's determination was not supported by substantial evidence because it was based on hearsay. The Appellate Division disagreed, holding that

---

[147] The court commented that it its view "a reprimand was a sufficient penalty under the circumstances (MacFarlane v Scotia, 241 AD2d 574).

"[t]he hearsay statements of the complainants were sufficiently probative to constitute substantial evidence."

According to the decision "[h]earsay may constitute substantial evidence where, as here, it is sufficiently reliable and probative on the issues to be determined." This, in turn, depends on the credibility of the witnesses. The issue of the credibility of the witnesses at Sauders' departmental disciplinary hearing, said the court, "was a matter to be assessed by the Deputy Commissioner who presided at the trial."

Accordingly, said the court, determinations concerning the credibility of witnesses "is largely beyond our power of review."

18.23 Criticism of employee performance

Brackman v City of New York, Supreme Court, August 15, 2000

If a public employee does not have tenure, he or she may be dismissed at any time, for any reason, or for no reason, provided that the termination does not otherwise constitute an unlawful act on the part of the public employer. At best, such an individual may demand, and receive, a "name clearing hearing" if there has been publication of the alleged disparaging remarks concerning his or her work performance.[148]

The Brackman case involved a novel variation of this type of situation -- the rights of a terminated employee of an "independent contractor" performing work for a public entity.

The contractor, Data Industries, was to perform certain data processing related services for the City of New York. City officials were extremely critical of the work being done under the contract by Brackman, one of Data Industries' employees. City officials complained that Brackman was "(1) "screwing up"; (2) [had] "no idea what he is doing;" and (3) "sold us a bill of goods he couldn't deliver on." This criticism resulted in Brackman's dismissal from the project and from Data Industries.

Brackman sued for damages for the alleged "defamation ... arising in the context of [his] work as a computer consultant for New York City's Department of Employment." The court granted the City motion to dismiss Brackman's petition for two reasons:

1. Brackman had signed a release "in exchange for a sum of money" when he was terminated by Data Industries covering "all actions, causes of action [and] suits [...] by reason of any matter, cause or thing whatsoever" against Data Industries, the City of New York, the Department of Employment and its Management Information System Division; and

2. The "allegedly defamatory remarks are quintessential expressions of opinion which are fully protected by the state and federal constitutions."

---

[148] Being cleared in a "name clearing hearing," however, does not entitle the individual to reinstatement to his or her former position.

Justice Stallman said that all of the statements concerning Brackman's abilities and his performance on the project use loose, figurative language, and none of the statements are objectively capable of being characterized as true or false."

Citing Williams v Varig Brazilian Airlines, 169 AD2d 434, the court said that "[d]isparaging remarks concerning a person's job performance are routinely held to be constitutionally protected opinion."

Dismissing Brackman's petition, Justice Stallman said that as an at-will employee in the private sector there was "no tort liability for wrongful or abusive discharge."

The lesson gleaned from Brackman:

As an "at-will employee" -- the private sector equivalent of a provisional or temporary public employee -- Brackman did not even have a right to a name clearing hearing, much less the right to sue the City or it officials for damages after being fired by the Data Industries.

18.24 Criticism of employees by a coworker

Sheehan v. Anderson, CA3, unpublished

An individual may complain about a co-worker's job performance; a supervisor may place a memorandum criticizing the work of a subordinate in the individual's personnel file. Do these and similar types of criticisms allow the target of the comments to sue if he or she contends that the statements are false? This was the significant issue in the Sheehan case.

In deciding Sheehan's appeal, the U.S. Circuit Court of Appeals, Third Circuit, upheld a lower court's ruling that Pennsylvania law does not permit an employee to sue his or her co-worker for slander simply because the co-worker made remarks to a supervisor that are critical of the employee's job performance.

The court's rationale: criticism of an individual's job performance, standing alone, does not constitute defamation within the meaning of Pennsylvania law. According to the ruling, such statements by co-workers are protected by a "conditional privilege" when made to a supervisor or manager.

John Sheehan, a Federal Reserve Bank employee, sued three of his co-workers for defamation. Sheehan complained that he had been disciplined as a result of his co-workers making false statements about him to a superior. According to Sheehan, the co-workers told the supervisor that he sat around drinking coffee and "talking for more than an hour every morning" and that he was responsible for an "antagonistic" work situation at the facility.

The Bank argued that Sheehan's defamation claim should be summarily dismissed because all of the statements concerned, or were related to, Sheehan's behavior at the work site and only related to his performance on the job.

According to the Third Circuit, the statements about Sheehan's work activities and performance were given to Bank officials and were not disseminated to the public. Accordingly, "while the statements were critical of Sheehan and thus may annoy or embarrass him, they are not sufficient as a matter of law to create an action for defamation."

This decision is consistent with the rule followed by New York State courts in determining if an individual is entitled to a "name-clearing hearing."[149] Typically a name-clearing hearing is available to public workers only if stigmatizing or critical statements affecting individual's good name or reputation has been disseminated to the public by the employer. In contrast, the individual is not entitled to a name clearing hearing if he or she was responsible for the disclosure of the offending statements to the public.

What have the courts considered to be stigmatizing? Courts have ordered "name-clearing hearings" in cases involving dismissals because of alleged mental instability, dishonesty, incompetence, rape and sexual molestation, narcotic addiction, being psychologically unfit, and misconduct involving public funds.

In addition, courts have ruled that a name-clearing hearing is warranted even if the reasons for dismissing the individual have not been publicly disseminated in cases where it finds that a discharge for a stated reason stigmatizes the individual and may adversely affect his or her prospects for future employment.

18.25 Defamation and disciplinary action

Monroe v Schenectady County, 266 A.D.2d 792

Sometimes an employee will contend that information contained in his or her personnel files is derogatory. May the individual sue the agency if the information is made available to other governmental officials? Part of the Monroe case concerned the dissemination of information contained in a personnel file alleged to be derogatory.

David Monroe, a Schenectady County corrections lieutenant, sued the sheriff and the county following his termination from his position of lieutenant. After a Federal court dismissed his complaint alleging a deprivation of due process under the 14th Amendment of the US Constitution, Monroe filed a lawsuit in State court.

According to the decision, Monroe was served with a written notice of discipline on July 15, 1994. He was charged with sexually harassing a Schenectady police officer and endangering "the security of the county jail by playing ping-pong and smoking." The proposed penalty: dismissal.
Monroe, union representatives and department personnel met to discuss settlement of the disciplinary action. The proposed terms of the settlement: Monroe would accept a demotion to correction officer

---

[149] As a general rule, name clearing hearings are available to a public employee who is dismissed from his or her position and who does not have a constitutionally protected property interest in the position entitling him or her to either a pre-termination or a post-termination hearing.

and the department would reinstatement him as a correction officer without retroactive pay or the restoration of any lost benefits. Monroe rejected the offer.

As described by the court, after he rejected the settlement, Monroe was told that if he should press for and win the disciplinary arbitration, charges alleging consorting with a prostitute, having sex with her and his being present when she purchased cocaine would be filed against him and this information would be revealed to the press. At this point Monroe decided to withdraw his disciplinary grievance and accepted the settlement offer, which he signed on January 6, 1995.

One of the issues in this rather complex litigation involved Monroe's "ninth cause of action" which set out allegations of defamation. Monroe contended that the sheriff had defamed him when he stated that he intended "to pursue further disciplinary action against [Monroe] based on [Monroe's] alleged connection with a prostitute" if Monroe refused to the settle the then pending disciplinary action.

According to Monroe, "the defamatory words were published by the sheriff to County officials and disseminated throughout the Sheriff's Department by the placing of a note about the event in [Monroe's] file."

The Appellate Division dismissed this branch of Monroe's action, ruling that "[i]t is obvious that the Sheriff was acting wholly within the scope of his duties (as alleged in [Monroe's] complaint) in publishing the charges in a disciplinary action and thus was protected by an absolute privilege providing him immunity from a suit for defamation. The court cited Mahoney v Temporary Commission of Investigation of New York, 165 AD2d 233, in support of its holding.

18.26 Demotion in grade

Pagano v Port Authority, 270 A.D.2d 206

The Employment Relations Panel of the Port Authority of New York and New Jersey approved the disciplinary penalty imposed on Authority Police Sergeant Frank Pagano: demotion to patrol officer.

Pagano sued, seeking reinstatement to his former position claiming that his agreement to the demotion was coerced. The Appellate Division rejected his petition, holding that "the challenged determination may not be disturbed since substantial evidence supports the Panel's decision that the Port Authority did not unduly influence or coerce petitioner's request for demotion from the rank of sergeant to that of police officer."

Coercion is an issue that sometimes emerges in the course of a "disciplinary settlement." An individual may claim that he or she was threaten with disciplinary action if her or she declined to resign or refused to agree to some personnel change demanded by the appointing authority.

The Court of Appeals addressed this question in Rychlick v Coughlin, 63 NY2d 643.

Rychlick, a state correction officer, was told that unless he immediately submitted his resignation, formal disciplinary charges would be filed against him. He submitted his resignation.

Claiming that he had been "forced" to submit his resignation, a few days later Rychlick tried withdraw it. The department refused to allow him to withdraw the resignation and Rychlick sued on the grounds that it had been obtained under duress and thus was void.[150]

The Court of Appeals, upholding Corrections refusal to allow Rychlick to withdraw the resignation, said that threatening an employee with disciplinary action if he or she did not resign did not constitute duress since the appointing authority had the legal right to file such charges.

The basic principle: threatening to do what one had the legal right to do does not constitute duress.

18.27 Designating a disciplinary hearing officer

Pieczonka v Village of Blasdell, 273 A.D.2d 842

If nothing else, the Pieczonka demonstrates the importance of the parties dotting all of the "i's" and crossing all of the "t's" in processing a disciplinary action brought pursuant to Civil Service Law Section 75.

The Town of Blasdell served Robert Pieczonka with disciplinary charges. It later wrote to him informing him of the date, time and location of the hearing and the name of the hearing officer. The hearing officer found Pieczonka guilty and the Town terminated him.

Pieczonka appealed, contending that his termination was unlawful because:

1. The Village failed to comply with Section 75(2) of the Civil Service Law since it had not designates the hearing officer in writing;

2. The determination made by the hearing officer was not supported by substantial evidence; and

3. The penalty imposed was excessive.

The Appellate Division never got to consider Pieczonka's second and third arguments because it ruled that the disciplinary action taken by the Town had to be annulled because the procedure was defective: the hearing officer had not been so designated in writing. Citing Wiggins v Board of Education, 60 NY2d 385, the court said that "[i]n the absence of a written delegation authorizing a deputy or other person to conduct the hearing, the removing board or officer has no jurisdiction to discipline an employee."[151]

---

[150] The general rule is that a resignation must be in writing and once submitted requires the approval of the appointing authority to be withdrawn.

[151] Section 75(2), in relevant part, provides that the hearing of charges preferred against an employee shall be held by the officer or body having the power to remove the person against whom.

The Appellate Division rejected the Town's contention that its written notice to Pieczonka advising him of the name of the hearing officer and the time and place of the hearing constituted the required written delegation of authority.

A failure to comply with the "written notice" requirements set out in Section 75(2) may have other serious consequences.

In Perez v NYS Dept. of Labor, 244 AD2d 844, the Appellate Division, Third Department, annulled a Section 75 disciplinary determination because there was no evidence that the hearing officer who presided over his disciplinary hearing had been so designated in writing. The court ordered Perez reinstated to his former position with back salary and benefits.

Perez then asked for attorney fees and expenses, contending that as the "prevailing party," he was entitled to such payments under Section 8601 of the Civil Practice Law and Rules. A State Supreme Court justice agree and awarded Perez $19,907.84, $9275 of which was for Perez's legal expenses incurred in the Section 75 administrative disciplinary action. The Labor Department appealed.

The Appellate Division sustained the lower court's ruling. It specifically rejected the department's argument that its failure to designate the hearing officer in writing was "a mere technicality" and its actions that ultimately resulted in Perez's termination were otherwise "substantially justified."

In addition, the Appellate Division ruled that Perez was entitled to the fees and expenses incurred in connection with the department's appeal challenging the Supreme Court's decision.

Another designation of a hearing officer case: Stein v Rockland Co., App Div, 2nd Dept, No. 97-09903/5, 3/8/99. Here the court observed that "in the absence of a written delegation authorizing a deputy or other person to conduct the hearing, the removing board or officer has no jurisdiction to discipline an employee." Again Wiggins v Board of Educ. of City of New York, 60 NY2d 385 was cited as the authority for the court's decision.

18.28 Determining probation status

Johnson v Triborough Bridge and Tunnel Authority, 278 A.D.2d 34, Reversed, 97 N.Y.2d 627

Typically an individual serving a "disciplinary probation" may be terminated from his or her position in accordance with the terms of his or her probationary status.

The lesson of the Johnson case: it is essential to determine if the individual is actually serving as a probationer at the time he or she is dismissed for unsatisfactory service as a probationer -- probationary status should not be assumed.

In 1989 Triborough Bridge and Tunnel Authority [TBTA] police officer Edward P. Johnson settled disciplinary charges filed against him by agreeing to be placed "on probation for a period of one year." A few months later Johnson was injured while on duty and did not return to work until October 1996.

In June 1997, following new allegations of misconduct, TBTA dismissed Johnson from his position without a pre-termination hearing. TBTA's justification for its action: Johnson is not entitled to a pretermination hearing since the one-year probationary period agreed to in 1989 had not yet expired.

According to TBTA, Johnson's period of probation was tolled during his Johnson's extended absence from work. Essentially TBTA argued that as it had not "waived" any portion of Johnson's disciplinary probation, he was required to actually complete one year of such service.[152]

Johnson protested his termination without notice and hearing but the New York City Civil Service Commission dismissed his appeal. The Commission said that it does not have "subject matter jurisdiction to consider the appeal" since Johnson's termination had been pursuant to the 1989 settlement agreement in which he waived the protections of Civil Service Law Section 75 mandating pretermination hearings for tenured employees.

The Appellate Division, First Department, disagreed with the Commission's analysis. It said the Commission apparently "assumed that the waiver contained in the 1989 agreement was still operative" -- it never actually made a finding to that Johnson was still a probationary employee – and remanded the matter.

The Court of Appeals reversed the Appellate Division's determination. It said that "Section 76 of the Civil Service Law solely authorizes the Commission to hear appeals from hearings in connection with disciplinary proceedings under section 75. Here, there was no such proceeding and the Commission therefore had no jurisdiction to hear petitioner's application to review his discharge which was not effected under section 75 (*see, Matter of Montella v Bratton*, 93 NY2d 424, 426). Moreover, section 76 (2) limits the Commission's review to the record and transcript of the disciplinary hearing. Because no record or transcript existed here, the Commission had no power to determine the matter."

18.29 Disciplinary arbitrations

Town of Newburgh v CSEA, 272 A.D.2d 405

Although an arbitrator sustained the Newburgh's dismissal of an employee who was found guilty of testing positive for marijuana, this did not end the matter.
The employee's union, the Civil Service Employee's Association [CSEA], filed a second grievance alleging that the Town had violated the collective bargaining agreement because it had suspended the

---

[152] This view is consistent with the Rules of the New York State Civil Service Commission with respect to absences of employees of the State during a probationary period [4 NYCRR 4.5(g)]. The rules provide that an appointing authority may, in its discretion, consider certain absences "as time served in the probationary term." The rule further provides that "[a]ny such periods of absence not so considered by the appointing authority as time served in the probationary term, and any periods of absence in excess of periods considered by the appointing authority as time served in the probationary term pursuant to this subdivision, shall not be counted as time served in the probationary term." A number of local civil service commissions have adopted a similar rule.

individual for more than 30 days without pay prior to the arbitrator's determination. CSEA demanded that the second grievance be submitted to arbitration.

In effect, CSEA argued that because the final resolution of the charges occurred upon the issuance of the disciplinary arbitration award on December 4, 1999, the employee in question was wrongly suspended without pay for a period of more than 30 days prior to the issuance of the award.

The Town, contending that considering a "second grievance necessarily presents a risk of inconsistent awards," filed a petition pursuant to Article 75 of the Civil Practice Law and Rules seeking an order staying the arbitration. State Supreme Court Peter C. Patsalos to grant the Town's petition to stay the arbitration; the Appellate Division, Second Department, reversed.

The Appellate Division pointed out that the arbitrator in disciplinary action apparently did not directly address the question of whether, pursuant to the parties' collective bargaining agreement, the employee could be suspended without pay for more than 30 days pending disposition of the disciplinary charges against him.

The Appellate Division rejected the Town's argument that "arbitration of the second grievance necessarily presents a risk of inconsistent awards."

Accordingly, the court said that under these circumstances "the correct rule to apply is that which holds that it is for a successive arbitrator to decide any res judicata [an already decided issue] or collateral estoppel effect is to be accorded to a prior arbitration award."

18.30 Disciplinary action and wrongful discharge

Cooks v NYC Transit Auth., 289 A.D.2d 278

Donald Cooks sued the New York City Transit Authority to recover damages, alleging that he was wrongful discharged from his employment because of his race. Supreme Court dismissed Cooks' petition and he appealed. The Appellate Division sustained the Supreme Court's decision.

The Appellate Division noted that a prior disciplinary arbitration award, which was confirmed by the Supreme Court, determined that Cooks was guilty of misconduct justifying his discharge from employment. Thus, said the Appellate Division, in this action Cooks could not relitigate any matter litigated in the course of the prior arbitration proceeding, including whether the misconduct actually occurred.

Once the Authority established that it had valid, nondiscriminatory reasons for discharging Cooks from its employment, the burden shifted to Cooks to raise a triable issue of fact: i.e., whether the stated reasons for his discharge were pretext for racial discrimination. Cooks, said the court, failed to raise such an issue.

Accordingly, it found that the Supreme Court properly granted the Authority's motion for summary judgment dismissing Cooks' cause of action seeking to recover damages for wrongful discharge from employment based upon race.

18.31 Disciplinary action claimed filed with malice

Howard v City of New York, App. Div., 1st Dept., 1069

An agency files disciplinary charges against an employee only to later withdraw the charges. Is the employer guilty of malicious prosecution? As the Howard case demonstrates, it depends on the circumstances.

The New York City Department of Corrections filed disciplinary charges against one of its correction officers, Cheryl Howard. The basis for these disciplinary charges: allegations that Howard had appeared in a pornographic video.

When it was subsequently discovered that Howard had neither appear in, nor was involved with, the pornographic video, the Department rescinded and withdrew the disciplinary charges it had filed against her. Howard, however, sued the Department, charging it with malicious prosecution because, she alleged, the Department had conducted a "deficient investigation into the grounds for initiating the disciplinary proceeding against her."

The Appellate Division sustained the Supreme Court's dismissal of her charge of malicious prosecution because Howard did not allege any "special injury." According to the ruling, Howard did not allege any "concrete harm ... considerably more cumbersome than the physical, psychological or financial demands of defending" the disciplinary proceeding. Further, said the court, Howard did not demonstrate that she had suffered "a highly substantial and identifiable interference with person, property or business."

Another case involving alleged malicious prosecution is Covert v County of Westchester, 608 NYS2d 516. Covert, a Westchester County corrections officer, sued the County for malicious prosecution after he was acquitted of criminal charges of assault base on allegations made by a prisoner that he had been subjected to a beating by Covert and two other correction officers.

The Appellate Division said that in order to recover damages for malicious prosecution, the aggrieved party had to show:

1. Initiation of an action;

2. The action was terminated in favor of the employee;

3. There was no probable cause for bring the action; and

4. The charges were filed with malice.

The court dismissed Covert's complaint, holding that "[i]n this instance there was ample evidence in the record to find, as a matter of law, that there was probable cause to believe that Covert had committed the assault."

Although the Covert case involved a criminal complaint being filed against the employee, presumably the same standard would be applied by courts in cases alleging malicious prosecution in connection with administrative disciplinary actions.

18.32 Disciplinary appeals must be to the forum having jurisdiction

Montella v Bratton, Court of Appeals, 93 N.Y.2d 424

Although Section 75 of the Civil Service Law sets out what is probably the best-known procedure for initiating disciplinary action against employees in the classified service, other statutory procedures are available for this purpose. The Montella decision by the Court of Appeals points out the fact that one must consider the basis for the underlying disciplinary action in order to determine the body having jurisdiction to consider appeals.[153]

Peter Montella, a New York City police officer, was served disciplinary charges pursuant to Section 14-115 of New York City's Administrative Code following his testing positive for drugs. Found guilty, Montella was dismissed from the force.

As a result of litigation challenging the disciplinary action, Montella obtained a second hearing, only to again be found guilty and dismissed. This time, however, Montella filed his appeal with the New York City Civil Service Commission rather than challenge the determination in court by filing an Article 78. The Commission reversed Montella's dismissal and ordered his reinstatement.

Although the department had participated in Montella's appeal before the Commission, it subsequently refused to reinstate Montella and asked the Commission to "withdraw its determination because [the Commission] lacked subject matter jurisdiction to hear appeals from discipline imposed pursuant to the Administrative Code."

The Commission rejected the department's application, taking the position that "the Legislature intended Section 76 to provide alternative appeal routes for disciplined civil service employees, regardless of their position ... [and that] in the absence of explicit language precluding appeal by Police Officers" it had authority to review departmental discipline taken against officers pursuant to Section 14-115 of the City Code.

Montella sued to compel the department to comply with the Commission's directive while the department filed a petition to have the Commission's determination annulled on the ground that the Civil Service Commission lacked subject matter jurisdiction to entertain Montella's appeal.

---

[153] In some instances an alternative to Section 75 disciplinary action has been negotiated in accordance with Section 76 of the Civil Service Law. In such cases the "contract disciplinary procedure" will typically set out the appeal procedure to be followed.

The Discipline Book

Did the Commission have jurisdiction to hear and decide appeals by uniformed police officers disciplined pursuant to section 14-115 of the Administrative Code of the City of New York? The Court of Appeals ruled that because the Civil Service Law explicitly limits the Commission's jurisdiction to appeals from discipline imposed pursuant to Civil Service Law Section 75, and because punishment imposed by the New York City Police Commissioner pursuant to section 14-115 is not the same as disciplinary action pursuant to Section 75, the Commission did not have jurisdiction to hear Montella's appeal.

The decision points out that "the Civil Service Law further evidences the Legislature's intention that New York City police officers be disciplined pursuant to the Administrative Code," rather than pursuant to Section 75 when it amended Section 75 by adding subdivision 3-a which provides that if "such officer is found guilty of the charges, the police commissioner of such department may punish the police officer pursuant to the provisions of sections 14-115 and 14-123 of the administrative code of the city of New York." This, the Court of Appeals concluded, acknowledges that New York City police officers are disciplined pursuant to a statutory scheme separate and distinct from Civil Service Law Section 75.[154]

The court concluded that the Commission was not authorized to hear Montella's appeal and its determination was void.

18.33 Disciplinary dismissal not discrimination

Myrick v NYC Employees' Retirement System, USDC, SDNY, Justice Lynch, received July 11, 2002

According to Albert Myrick, his former employer, the New York City Employees' Retirement System [NYCERS] fired him in retaliation for his charging that his superiors discriminated against him in violation of Title VII. Myrick alleged that the reasons given for terminating him were a "pretext for [the] underlying motivation to terminate [him] for charging supervisors and superiors with discriminatory behavior...."

NYCERS, on the other hand, advanced a significantly different version of the situation. It said that although Myrick claims that he suffered years of harassment, discrimination, and eventually, retaliatory termination for complaining about race discrimination within the agency, Myrick was an incompetent employee whose insubordinate behavior and repeated failures to complete his assigned tasks led to his discharge.

The System pointed to Myrick's "long series of poor performance evaluations and an equally lengthy string of grievance complaints filed during the last ten years of Myrick's employment."

Ultimately NYCERS filed disciplinary charges against Myrick setting out twenty specifications of incompetence or misconduct, including his failure to fulfill the tasks of his job, disrupting "the discipline, efficiency and morale" of the agency, insubordination, and absences without leave.

---

[154] Section 76(4) provides that nothing "contained in Section 75 or 76 "shall be construed to repeal or modify any general, special or local law or charter provision relating to the removal or suspension of officers or employees in the competitive class of the civil service of the state or any civil division."

NYCERS later amended the charges, adding more allegations of a similar nature, resulting in a total of thirty-six specifications of misconduct.

The Section 75 hearing officer found that NYCERS "had carried its burden and demonstrated Myrick's guilt on twenty-nine of the thirty-six specifications of incompetence and insubordination.

Notwithstanding Myrick's long-term service with NYCERS, the hearing officer concluded that, as with other employees "who have demonstrated fundamental incompetence, engaged in repeated insubordination, and shown little inclination to change," termination would be "the only appropriate penalty for respondent." NYCERS adopted the hearing officer's Report and Recommendation in its entirety, and terminated fired Myrick on April 28, 1995.

Justice Lynch observed that although Myrick alleged retaliatory motivation on the part of his supervisors, the decision to fire him was not made by them. Rather, said the court, "[t]he decision [to terminate Myrick] was based on findings of fact made by an administrative law judge [ALJ] following an evidentiary hearing."

The decision notes that guarding against dismissal "on the whim or caprice of [an] employer," allegations of misconduct or incompetence "must not be a `mere subterfuge to get rid of the person,'" quoting from Van Tine v Purdy, 221 NY 396. Here, said the court, Myrick had "received the full benefit of these procedural protections."

Myrick filed a discrimination complaint with the New York State Division of Human Rights [SDHR]. SDHR gave preclusive effect to the determination of the ALJ in the disciplinary proceeding, concluding that "the record is clear that ... NYCERS disciplined, and ultimately terminated, [Myrick] for legitimate, non-discriminatory reasons and not in retaliation for his engaging in any protected activity under the Human Rights Law."

The bottom line, Justice Lynch said that he agreed that NYCERS has presented legitimate reasons for Myrick's termination, and that Myrick has not presented sufficient evidence to permit a reasonable fact-finder to conclude that these reasons were pretextual, granting NYCERS' motion for summary judgment.

18.34 Disciplinary hearings held in absentia

Vazquez v NYC Civil Service Commission, Supreme Court New York County, 2002 N.Y. Slip Op. 50076(U),

In Vazquez, the court to consider a number of issues rarely encountered in processing disciplinary actions pursuant to Section 75 of the Civil Service Law, including the question of the proper forum. Some of the questions addressed are rather rarely encountered, involving the.

Jose Vazquez was employed as a Caretaker "J" by the New York City Housing Authority [NYCHA]. On March 16, 1998 Vazquez was charged with being absence from work without approval since

March 2, 1998, and with subjecting the 12 year-old daughter of a NYCHA resident, Vazquez's former girl friend, to unlawful sexual contact.

A Section 75 hearing "in absentia" was held on April 2, 1998 after Vazquez failed to appear at the appointed time at the place designated for the disciplinary hearing. The Hearing Officer issued a report finding that the charges were proven and recommended that Vazquez be terminated. On May 5, 1998, NYCHA adopted the Hearing Officer's findings and recommendation and dismissed Vazquez.

Vazquez filed an appeal with City's Civil Service Commission seeking to reopen the hearing because "he had not absented himself from the original hearing voluntarily." The Commission granted his request and a "continued hearing" was held in June and July of 1999. On August 20, 1999, the hearing officer issued a report and recommendation to NYCHA, after which it again ordered that Vazquez be terminated from his position.

Vazquez filed a second appeal with the Commission challenging the department's determination. In November 2000, the then four member Commission stated that was split 2-2 and lacking a majority for an affirmative reversal, it was required sustained the Department's determination.

The first issue concerned the question of the timeliness of Vazquez's appeal. The City claimed it was untimely since it was commenced more than four months after the Commission's original determination was issued. Vazquez, however, had received a "corrected copy" of the Commission's determination on November 10, 2000. Four months from that date, March 10, 2001, fell on a Saturday and the first business day thereafter was March 12, 2001, which is the date on which his petition was filed. The court said that the date of the "corrected decision" is the operative one for purposes of determining timeliness because it constituted the final administrative determination. Thus Vazquez's petition was ruled timely.

Another issue: Was Vazquez denied due process because only 4 members of the Commission heard his appeal that resulted in a split decision?

The City contended that the fact that four, rather than five, members of the Commission heard the appeal did not deprive Vazquez of due process.

The court said that Section 41 of the New York General Construction Law addresses the question of the consideration of matters by less than a full board. It provides that "Whenever three or more public officers are given any power or authority, or three or more persons are charged with any public duty to be performed or exercised by them jointly or as a board or similar body, a majority of the whole number of such persons or officers ... shall constitute a quorum and not less than a majority of the whole number may perform and exercise such power, authority or duty."

Although a majority of the "whole number" of the five person City Civil Service Commission heard Vazquez's appeal, the Commission, because it was evenly divided, by its own admission did not reach any determination. Did this have any impact on Vazquez's claim? In the eyes of the court it did. According to the ruling, when there is a vacancy, or an inability of a Commissioner to act, the Commission can easily postpone action on the appeal until the fifth Commissioner is able to take part in the deliberations. The court ruled that "As a matter of fairness, [Vazquez] is entitled to have this matter remanded to the Commission, which now has five Commissioners, to hear and decide the appeal filed on his behalf."

The court pointed to Section 76.3 of the Civil Service Law which, in pertinent part, provides that if an employee elects to appeal to a state or municipal commission, as Vazquez did in this case, the decision of such civil service commission shall be final and conclusive, and not subject to further review in any court.[155]

The court commented that in a footnote in its "decision," the Commission said that because it was split 2 to 2, "the determination [below] must be affirmed." In the view of the court, this meant that the Commission had not made a decision as required by Section 76.3, thus justifying its remanding Vazquez's appeal for consideration by the full panel.

The Mari decision,[156] another disciplinary hearing in absentia case, demonstrates that an individual against whom disciplinary charges have been filed cannot avoid the consequences of disciplinary action being taken against him or her by refusing to appear at the disciplinary hearing. The decision also provides an opportunity to explore a number of factors that should be kept in mind when involved in a disciplinary or other administrative action held "in absentia."

New York City police officer Robert A. Mari was served with disciplinary charges alleging that he (1) engaged in unauthorized off-duty employment; (2) knowingly associated with a person believed to be engaged in, likely to engage in, or to have engaged in criminal activities; (3) intentionally disclosed an informant's identity to a target of police activity; and (4) harassed "a former paramour."

When Mari failed to appear at his disciplinary hearing, he was "tried in absentia" and was found guilty of the several disciplinary charges filed against him. The penalty imposed: termination. Mari appealed, contending that he should be given a "new hearing" because he was not actually present during the disciplinary proceeding.

The Appellate Division, First Department, dismissed Mari's appeal. Conceding that Mari not present at the disciplinary hearing, the court said that "a new hearing is not warranted since [Mari] avoided service of the notice of the revised hearing date, and thereafter intentionally absented himself from the hearing."

The general rule in such situations is that if the employee fails to appear at the disciplinary hearing, the charging party may elect to proceed but must actually hold a "hearing in absentia" and prove its allegations rather then merely impose a penalty on the individual on the theory that the employee's failure to appear at the hearing as scheduled is, in effect, a concession of guilt.

---

[155] As the Court of Appeals held in New York City Department of Environmental Protection v New York City Civil Service Commission, 78 NY2d 318, judicial review of Commission decisions is precluded in all but the "exceedingly limited" circumstance in which the Commission is alleged to have acted "illegally, unconstitutionally, or in excess of its jurisdiction."

[156] Mari v Safir, App. Div., 1st Dept., #285, Feb. 19, 2002

In such case, however, the appointing authority is required to make a reasonable effort to contact the employee before proceeding to hold a disciplinary hearing in absentia. It may be that the employee has a valid excuse for his or her nonappearance such as a family emergency or personal illness that would justify the hearing officer granting an adjournment.

The following are factors that should be kept in mind in connection with holding a disciplinary hearing in absentia:

1. Was the employee properly served with the disciplinary charges and advised of the date, time and place of the hearing?

2. If the individual fails to appear at the hearing as scheduled, a diligent effort must be made to contact the individual to determine if he or she has a reasonable explanation for his or her absence before the hearing officer proceeds with holding the hearing in the absence of the accused employee.

3. A formal hearing must be conducted and the employer is required to introduce evidence proving its charges to the hearing officer.

4. A formal record of the hearing must be made and a transcript provided to the appointing authority and, if requested, to the employee.

5. The employee must be advised of the appointing authority's determination and his or her right of appeal if he or she has been found guilty of one or more of the charges.

It should be remembered that it is not may always be a case of the employee being "tried in absentia" -- sometimes the employer fails to appear at the scheduled hearing. The decision of the Appellate Division, Third Department, in Aures v Buffalo Board of Education, 272 A.D.2d 664, involved just such a situation.

In Aures, the employer, the Buffalo City School District, failed to appear at an unemployment insurance hearing as scheduled. The hearing officer proceeded to hold the hearing "in absentia" and awarded unemployment insurance benefits to Aures. Rejecting Buffalo's appeal challenging the award of benefits, the Appellate Division ruled that the determination was binding on the parties.

In yet another hearing in absentia case, Hall v Environmental Conservation, the Appellate Division held that an arbitrator may proceed with a contract disciplinary arbitration notwithstanding the fact that the employer refused to participate in the proceeding. The court said that the arbitrator's decision was final and binding notwithstanding the fact that the employer did not participate in the proceeding.

In its appeal Environmental Conservation [DEC] claimed that its termination of Hall was not subject to being challenged pursuant to the "contract disciplinary procedure." DEC's argument: the State Department of Civil Service had disqualified Hall for employment. Thus Hall's appointment was void and therefore he could not claim any rights under Section 75 of the Civil Service Law or the collective bargaining agreement.

A Supreme Court judge granted the union's motion to confirm that portion of the award providing for back pay, holding that the disciplinary proceeding was not rendered moot by the Civil Service Department's action but refused to confirm that part of the award that directed DEC reinstate Hall to his former position. The Appellate Division affirmed the lower court's ruling.

In contrast, participating in arbitration when one need not do so may have consequences equally serious to those flowing from the failure to appear and participate in the arbitration proceeding. In Suffolk County v SCCC Faculty Association, the Appellate Division pointed out that if a party participates in arbitration when "it did not have to," it cannot later seek to vacate the arbitration award "because it was not required to submit to the arbitration of the issue."

Considering a related matter, assume that an individual served with disciplinary charges pursuant to Section 75 of the Civil Service does not file an answer to the charges and specifications. May the appointing authority impose the proposed penalty without holding a disciplinary hearing? Probably not.

Although Section 75 requires the appointing officer to allow the accused employee at least eight days to file his or her answer to disciplinary charges in writing, this simply allows, but does not mandate, an employee at least eight days in which to prepare and submit his or her answer to the charges. This suggests that the individual may remain mute -- i.e., decline to file an answer to the charges -- without jeopardizing any of his or her Section 75 rights to administrative due process.

Second, and perhaps critical to due process considerations in connection with taking disciplinary action against a public employee, Section 75 provides that "the burden of proving incompetency or misconduct ... (is) upon the person alleging the same."

In other words, the failure of an employee to file an answer to the disciplinary charges, appear at the disciplinary hearing or his or her even refusing to defend himself or herself against the charges at the hearing does not excuse the employer of its duty to prove the employee's incompetence or misconduct before imposing an appropriate disciplinary sanction.

Turning to the merits of the disciplinary determination in Mari's case, the court said that "that there was substantial evidence ... to support the hearing officer's findings." As to the penalty imposed, the Appellate Division found that it was not so disproportionate to the offenses of which Mari was found guilty "as to shock this Court's sense of fairness," citing Kelly v Safir, 96 NY2d 32.

Mari also alleged that the department acted in "bad faith" when it accelerated the date of his disciplinary hearing. He contended that the hearing date was improperly accelerated and as a result his pension was forfeited since his termination took place before the effective date of his retirement.[157] The Appellate Division dismissed this branch of Mari's appeal. According to the ruling, that Mari "was found guilty of conduct that took place, and the resulting disciplinary charges were filed, long before [he filed his] application for retirement."

---

[157] Section 13-173.1 of the Administrative Code of the City of New York requires an employee to "be in service" on the effective date of his or her retirement or vesting of retirement benefits. If the employee is not "in service" on that date, he or she forfeits his or her retirement benefits.

18.35 Disciplinary probation

Gluck v Suffolk County Community College, Supreme Court, Ia Part 26, received January 4, 2002

Joshua Gluck was terminated from his position of laborer by the Suffolk Community College [SCCC]. He sued, seeking reinstatement with full back pay and benefits.

The court noted that in connection with an unrelated matter, Gluck and SCCC entered into a stipulation in lieu of a disciplinary proceeding that provided as follows:

The employee will receive a (12) twelve-month period of probation beginning upon the full execution of this agreement. During the period of probation the employee shall be subject to random drug and alcohol testing, wherein should the employee test positive on a drug/alcohol test, he shall be immediately terminated without the benefit of a hearing or any other protection afforded under Civil Service law or the Collective Bargaining Agreement.

The settlement agreement also provided that Gluck's probationary period would begin upon his return to work in a full duty capacity. On April 3, 2001, Gluck reported for work and was asked to submit to a drug and alcohol test. According to the ruling, Gluck's urine specimen registered a temperature that was "out of range." He was asked to provide another urine sample for testing.

Gluck was told that his refusal to take the test would be considered an automatic positive test result, which in turn would bring about his immediate suspension without pay. He agreed to provide a second urine specimen. However, he did not allow his supervisor to witness his providing the sample. The second sample was also "out of range" and Gluck left the laboratory.

SCCC argued that Gluck's failure to provide a witness-validated urine sample constituted a failure to cooperate with the sample collection procedure. This, SCCC said, was tantamount to Gluck's refusal to submit to the test and Gluck had been warned that his refusal to submit to the test would be deemed a positive test and would result in his immediate suspension without pay. Ultimately SCCC terminated Gluck.

Gluck sued, contending that he willingly gave both samples and was told by laboratory personnel that he was free to leave. He claimed that he had "no qualms about giving the samples because he had no history of drug use and does not abuse alcohol" and thus SCCC's decision to terminate him was arbitrary and capricious.

The court decided that "the record here, which must include the federal guidelines that apply to drug testing in the workplace," demonstrates that SCCC's decision to terminate Gluck was neither arbitrary nor capricious.

Gluck, said the court, had agreed, as part of the disciplinary settlement stipulation he signed in February, to submit to random drug and alcohol testing. What happened on April 3, under the guidelines utilized by the laboratory facility conducting the test, was tantamount to a refusal to submit to such testing. As Gluck was told what would happen under the circumstances, his conduct violated the terms of the stipulation. The court's conclusion: there was a rational basis for SCCC's terminating Gluck and his petition had to be dismissed.

Fortner v NYC Dept. of Corrections, 280 A.D.2d 381, is another disciplinary case that was "settled" by the employee agreeing to serve a "disciplinary probationary period." The majority of such settlements, as was true in Fortner's case, set out the terms and conditions of the probation and typically provide for the termination of the individual without any further hearing if he or she violates the terms of the settlement.

Steven T. Fortner was serving a disciplinary probation period following the settlement of disciplinary charges that had been filed against him by the New York City Department of Corrections.

The department terminated him, contending that "he violated the terms of his limited probation as set forth in his negotiated plea agreement."

Fortner sued, alleging that he had been terminated in bad faith. The court disagreed, finding that Fortner produced no evidence to support his claim that his dismissal was motivated by bad faith.

Fortner had also asked the court to annul his termination and have the matter remitted to the Department "for reconsideration of the sanction."

The Appellate Division decided that such action was not appropriate under the circumstances since Fortner's termination did not "shock the judicial conscience."

Further, said the court, terminating Fortner for violating the terms of his disciplinary probationary period did not constitute an abuse of discretion on the part of the appointing authority.

The lesson here is that the courts will sustain the termination of an individual serving a disciplinary probation period without a hearing if the employee is discharged for violating or failing to comply with the terms of the disciplinary probation agreed upon.

Suppose the court finds that the employee's termination was inconsistent with the terms and conditions of his or her disciplinary probationary period? As the Taylor decision[158] indicates that in such a situation the individual will be reinstated with back salary.

The Taylor court determined that under the terms of Taylor's disciplinary probation, he could be terminated without any hearing if, in the opinion of his superior, Taylor's job performance was "adversely affected" by his "intoxication on the job."

The court said the appointing authority set out two reasons for its terminating Taylor:

1. Taylor's "failing to give a fair day's work"; and

2. Taylor's "sleeping during scheduled working hours."

Taylor's termination, said the court, was improper because Taylor was not terminated for the sole reason specified in the settlement: intoxication on the job.

---

[158] Taylor v Cass, 505 NYS2d 929

Sometimes the disciplinary probation established resulting from the settlement of the disciplinary action does not limit the appointing authority's discretion in terminating the employee. The Wright case demonstrates such a situation.

In Wright v City of New York, 596 NYS2d 372, the Appellate Division ruled that an employee who had agreed to a disciplinary probation in settlement of disciplinary charges filed against him that provided that his probation status would be the same as any other probationary employee was not entitled to a pre-termination hearing when he was dismissed because of subsequent incidents.

In other words, under the terms of Wright's disciplinary probation he was treated as a "new employee" and he could be summarily terminated for any lawful reason.

Other decisions involving disciplinary probation include Gonzalez v Safir, 270 AD2d 103; Dillon v Safir, 270 AD2d 116; Wilson v Bratton, 266 A.D.2d 140 and Williams v NYSOMH, 259 A.D.2d 623.

18.36 Disciplinary settlement payments are not considered payments of annual salary

Horowitz v NYS Teachers' Retirement System, 293 A.D.2d 861, motion to appeal denied, 98 N.Y.2d 614

The Horowitz case concerns the impact of making a lump-sum payment to an employee as an inducement to his or her submitting a resignation in lieu of being served with disciplinary charges in determining his or her final average salary for retirement purposes.

In July 1988, the Jericho Union Free School District offered Marc W. Horowitz the opportunity to resign from his administrative position in lieu of his being served with disciplinary charges. As part of the settlement negotiations related to Horowitz's separation, Horowitz was to receive a lump-sum payment of $123,789 consistent with a benefit set out in a then expired agreement between the District and the Jericho Administrators Association entitled the "Resignation-Retirement Incentive Benefit Program."

The Teachers' Retirement System [TRS] refused to include the $123,789 lump-sum payment to Horowitz as part of his "final average salary" [FAS] for the purpose of determining his retirement allowance. TRS viewed the payment "as an inducement for [Horowitz's] immediate resignation" rather than "compensation for accumulated sick time" as claimed by Horowitz.

Horowitz sued, seeking a court order directing TRS to include the $123,789 in calculating his FAS. The Appellate Division, Third Department, sustained the Supreme Court dismissal of Horowitz's petition. Citing Section 501.11(a) of the Education Law, the Appellate Division said an individual's FAS is defined as "the average annual compensation earnable as a teacher during any five consecutive years of state service." As noted in Moraghan v New York State Teachers' Retirement System, 237 AD2d 703, the purpose of the statute is to prevent artificial inflation of an individual's final average salary by payments made in anticipation of a member's resignation.

Accordingly, said the court, "a lump-sum payment may be excluded from the calculation of a teacher's five-year final average salary where the circumstances support the conclusion that the payment was made in exchange for resignation rather than in satisfaction of accumulated sick leave", citing Hall v New York State Teachers' Retirement System, 266 AD2d 638, [leave to appeal denied, 94 NY2d 759].

Although Section 5003.2 of the Rules of the Commissioner, [21 NYCRR 5003.2 (b)], provide that "termination pay" is includable computation if it constitutes compensation earned as a teacher," the Appellate Division ruled that 21 NYCRR 5003.2 did not apply in Horowitz's case.[159]

Why not? Because, said the court, the timing of Horowitz's resignation rendered him ineligible for the lump-sum payment provided by the then expired collective bargaining agreement between the District and the Association. This apparently resulted in the District and the Association entering "into a separate agreement designed to facilitate [Horowitz's] resignation."

According to the decision, the so-called "Horowitz Incentive Agreement" provided Horowitz with the same financial benefit that the expired collective bargaining agreement provided to eligible retirees for accumulated sick leave. However, the Horowitz Incentive Agreement described its benefit as "a pay differential equal to one year's salary" rather than the payment of accumulated sick leave credit and Horowitz's resignation was specifically conditioned on the receipt of this payment.

Other distinctive elements noted by the Appellate Division: The Horowitz Incentive Agreement was executed on the same day as the stipulation, provided a benefit for which Horowitz was the only recipient and required Horowitz to act within two business days in order to obtain its benefit.

The Appellate Division ruled that the language and circumstances of the agreements involved here rationally support TRS' findings that the Horowitz Incentive Agreement was tailored to Horowitz's particular situation and was created "solely to induce his resignation." Under these circumstances, said the Appellate Division, Supreme Court did not err in upholding TRS' determination and dismissing Horowitz's petition.

18.37 Discipline for 20-year-old misconduct

DeMichele v Greenburgh CSD #7, 2nd Cir., 2/17/99

Section 3020-a(1) of the New York State Education Law provides that "no charges ... shall be brought more than three years after the occurrence of the alleged incompetency or misconduct, except when the charge is of misconduct constituting a crime when committed.

In the DeMichele case, a teacher in the Greenburgh Central School District #7 was found guilty of having inappropriate sexual contact with female students in incidents occurring more than 20 years

---

[159] The fact that the amount paid to the employee in connection with a disciplinary settlement was not deemed wages for the purposes of calculating the employee's FAS for retirement should not be viewed as suggesting that such a payment is not subject to withholdings for income tax and other purposes.

earlier. The Second Circuit U.S. Court of Appeals sustained the school board's decision to dismiss the teacher, even though the teacher had not been convicted of any "criminal act."

Following the same logic as New York State courts that have addressed similar issues involving statutes of limitation under various disciplinary provisions, the federal court observed that the law does not require the individual to be found guilty of a felony in a criminal court for disciplinary charges to be filed after the three-year statute of limitations has expired.

Rather, the law merely characterizes the nature of the allegation. The law says that if a Section 3020-a hearing officer or disciplinary panel finds an individual guilty of an act that fits the definition of a felony under relevant criminal statutes, then a penalty may be imposed even if the disciplinary charges were brought after the three-year statute of limitations has expired.[160]

The 20-year-old sexual misconduct charges arose after a newspaper reported that Greenburgh #7 teacher Robert DeMichele had been restored to the payroll in 1996 after serving one and one-half year disciplinary suspension. The article noted that the suspension without pay was imposed as a penalty after DeMichele was found guilty of having inappropriate conduct with female students during the 1991-92 and 1992-93 academic years.

After the article appeared, two women contacted district officials and alleged that DeMichele had sexually abused or molested them when they had been students in the district decades earlier -- during the 1972-73 and 1974-75 school years. There was no dispute that the district was unaware of these allegations prior to its receiving the February 1996 reports. On March 11, 1996 the district initiated a second Section 3020-a disciplinary action against DeMichele. The hearing officer found DeMichele guilty of all but one of seven specifications set out in the charges. As a result DeMichele was dismissed. The disciplinary determination was reported to the press.

The hearing officers ruled that (1) each instance of misconduct alleged in the second disciplinary proceeding constituted a crime when committed and (2) Section 3020-a does not require that the misconduct actually be the subject of a criminal prosecution. Rather than appeal the hearing officer's determination, DeMichele sued in federal district court claiming that the second disciplinary action violated his rights under 42 U.S.C. Section 1983. He contended that his rights were violated because:

1. The district forced him to defend charges concerning events that occurred more than 20 years ago, which left him unable to defend himself in violation of his right to due process under the Fourteenth Amendment; and

2. He was deprived of a liberty interest without due process under the Fourteenth Amendment when the district's prosecutor disclosed the results of the hearing to the media.

In an unpublished decision, a federal district court judge granted the district's motion for summary judgment and thus dismissed DeMichele's petition without a hearing on the merits of the complaint. The Circuit Court of Appeals affirmed the lower court's decision.

---

[160] Re Board of Education of City School District of the City of New York, Opinions of the Commissioner of Education No. 11353 [1984]

The Circuit Court said that to show a violation of due process as a result of delay in a hearing, New York State law requires the subject of an administrative disciplinary proceeding demonstrate that delay in initiating proceedings caused "actual prejudice" to his or her ability to defend against the charges. The court suggested that if the school district had known about the 1970s allegations before 1996 but delayed proceeding with discipline, DeMichele might have been able to show that his ability to defend himself had been compromised.

The court also addressed DeMichele's claim that the dissemination to the media of the results of his second disciplinary hearing stigmatized him and wrongfully deprived him of his liberty interest under the Fourteenth Amendment. The court noted that this argument rested on the assumption that the results of the disciplinary proceeding were not a matter of public record, but instead were part of his "employment history" which could not be released under New York's Freedom of Information Law, [Public Officers Law, Article 6, ("FOIL")].

However, the decision noted that New York courts have found that the disposition of misconduct charges does not constitute part of an employee's "employment history" as that phrase is used in FOIL, citing LaRocca v. Board of Educ. of Jericho Union Free School District, 632 N.Y.S.2d 576. The Circuit Court ruled that under the circumstances, the dissemination of the background and result of the first disciplinary hearing to the press did not deprived DeMichele of any liberty interest and dismissed the appeal.

Section 75 of the Civil Service Law, a statutory disciplinary procedure covering employees in the classified service, also provides that there is no statute of limitations with respect to bringing disciplinary action against an individual where the charges of incompetency or misconduct "constitute a crime."

18.38 Disciplinary settlements by subordinate may not bind appointing authority

Alfred v Safir, 283 A.D.2d 280

In the course of settling a disciplinary matter, the employee typically agrees to plea guilty to some or all of the charges in exchange for a negotiated penalty that the employee and the employer's representative agree will be imposed. The hearing officer usually makes this settlement a part of the record and the hearing is then "closed."

The Alfred decision sets out the proposition that in the context of the settlement of a disciplinary action, the penalty to be imposed agreed upon by the employee and employer's representative, and made part of the record by the disciplinary hearing officer, may not be binding on the appointing authority.

According to the decision, New York City Police Commissioner Howard Safir suspended Gary Alfred for 30 days without pay and placed him on disciplinary probation for one year following the settlement of disciplinary charges filed against Alfred.

Alfred objected, contending that he, the department's representative at the disciplinary hearing and the disciplinary hearing officer had all agreed to the imposition of a different disciplinary penalty.

The Appellate Division, First Department, unanimously affirmed Safir's decision, commenting that "[t]he various determinations and penalties agreed to by [Alfred] and [the department's] advocate and/or hearing officer were not binding" on Safir, the appointing authority, citing Silverman v McGuire, 51 NY2d 228.

Further, said the court, there is no basis for Alfred to claim that Safir's rejection of the penalty "agreed upon" in the course of settling the disciplinary action was based on racial and other arbitrary considerations.

As to the penalty ultimately imposed by Safir in the course of the disciplinary action, the court ruled that it was "not so disproportionate to [Alfred's] failure to perform the most basic aspects of his assignment as to shock our sense of fairness."

This ruling suggests that where the appointing authority makes the final determination, it would be prudent for:

1. The employer's representative to insist that any settlement of a disciplinary action include a statement to the effect that the settlement is subject to the approval of the appointing authority; and

2. The employee or the employee's representative to insist on a provision spelling out what is to happen if the appointing officer does not agree to imposed the penalty set out in the settlement proposal.

The Appellate Division's decision in the Lyons case [Lyons v Whitehead, 291 A.D.2d 497] demonstrates the importance of making certain that the terms and conditions of a disciplinary settlement agreement clearly indicate the expectations of the parties.

Carol Lyons, an employee at the Letchworth Developmental Disabilities Service, and James J. Whitehead, the Director of Letchworth, had entered into a disciplinary settlement agreement that provided that Lyons would participate in a treatment program to treat her abuse of prescription drugs. The settlement required Lyons to follow the program's attendance requirement, and to complete the program.

The agreement also provided that Lyons would be placed on "general probation status" for one year, and that her employment could be terminated for a violation of her probation without any further hearing "except for time and attendance infractions".

Lyons failed to attend a scheduled "medication course." Whitehead viewed this as a breach of the Settlement Agreement and terminated Lyons' employment. Acting on behalf of Lyons, the Civil Service Employee's Association, Inc., sued. They asked for a court order reinstating Lyons to her position. CSEA argued that Lyons' failure to attend the medication course was a "time and attendance infraction" and thus she could not be summarily terminated under the terms of the Settlement Agreement.

Although the Supreme Court directed that Lyons be restored to her employment, the Appellate Division reversed and remanded the case to the lower court to determine whether Lyons' failure to attend the "medication course" was a "time and attendance infraction" under the Settlement Agreement.

The Appellate Division ruled that "[b]ecause the Settlement Agreement is a contract between the parties, it must be construed according to ordinary contract law." Accordingly, the court must "determine the intention of the parties as derived from the language employed in the contract", and it "should strive to give a fair and reasonable meaning to the language used," citing Abiele Construction v New York City School Construction Authority, 91 NY2d 1.

It is clear that the appellant could terminate Lyons' employment for a violation of her probation, "except for time and attendance infractions." Was Lyons' absence from the "medication course" a breech of the Settlement Agreement?

Whitehead maintained that attending the medication course "was part of the treatment program" that Lyons agreed to attend as part of the Settlement Agreement. CSEA, on the other hand, argued that it was "a mandatory course for all employees working at [Lyons'] grade and title for recertification to perform the duties of dispensing medication to patients" and thus her absence was a "time and attendance" problem excluded under the Settlement Agreement.

The court decided that the nature of the medication course could not be determined from the record and therefore it could not decide whether or not Lyons' failure to attend it was a "time and attendance infraction" or a breach of the disciplinary settlement agreement.

Thus, said the court, "the matter must be remitted to the Supreme Court, for a hearing on the question of whether the medication course was the same as the treatment program, and if not, whether her absence falls within the category of "time and attendance infractions." The Appellate Division said that the lower court "had to make a new determination" based on its answer to these questions.

18.39 Discretion to discipline staff

Matter of Gaul, Decisions of the Commissioner #14432
Matter of Middleton, Decisions of the Commissioner #14431

The Gaul and Middleton appeals both involve the challenges to the exercise of discretion involving the filing of disciplinary charges against an employee. In Gaul the issue concerned the board's filing disciplinary charges; in Middleton the issue involved a decision not to file such charges.

The Gaul case

Port Jefferson Union Free School District board member Kenneth Gaul, together with "presumably parents of students" in the district challenged the district's decision to file disciplinary charges pursuant to Section 3020-a of the Education Law against a school principal, Dr. Esther Fusco, and her subsequent reassignment pending resolution of the disciplinary action.

Also challenged was the abolishment of the position encumbered by the district's former director of special education, Carole Noren.

The district's superintendent, Dr. Edward J. Reilly, had recommended a reorganization plan that would involve the abolishment of Noren's position but before the board acted Noren was offered, and accepted, a retirement incentive.

Among the issues considered by the Commissioner was the question of Gaul's "standing" to appeal a personnel determination by a school board. The Commissioner observed:

1. An individual may not maintain an appeal pursuant to Section 310 of the Education Law unless he or she "has suffered personal damage or injury to his or her civil, personal or property rights."

2. Status as a resident of a district or as a parent of a student in the district does not operate to "automatically confer ... the capacity to seek review of personnel actions by a board of education."

Ruling that the "unsubstantiated assertion that their children have been negatively impacted by Fusco's removal is insufficient to confer standing" to challenge the board's decision, the Commissioner dismissed this aspect of the appeal.

The Commissioner also ruled that the assertion that expenditures to replace Fusco were "wasteful" in contrast to be "unlawful" did not establish "the direct personal harm" essential to conferring "standing" to appeal.

The Commissioner further found that Gaul failed to show that the board "engaged in a willful violation or neglect of duty" by its filing disciplinary charges against Fusco.

Fusco, the district conceded, had received both the Principal of the Year Award in New York State in 1997 and the National Distinguished Principal Award in 1998. However, it filed "49 specifications ranging from relatively minor offenses ... to the more serious" against her.

This, said the Commissioner indicated that "from the breadth and length of the disciplinary charges, as well as the remoteness of some of the allegations, the [board] pursued Fusco's removal with considerable zeal" but there is insufficient evidence that "any board member willfully violated or neglected a legal duty in approving Fusco's reassignment."

Dismissing the appeal, the Commissioner pointed out that Section 1709(33) of the Education Law grants a board of education broad authority to manage the educational affairs of the district. "Inherent in this authority" is the power to abolish administrative positions and alter an administrator's assignment.

As to Gaul's challenging the "retirement incentive" accepted by Noren, the Commissioner rejected his claim that the incentive was "an unconstitutional gift of public funds."

This argument, said the Commissioner, is without merit, noting that in Antonpoulou v Beame, 32 NY2d 126, the Court of Appeals ruled that providing such a benefit, if statutory or contractual, is lawful. He said the retirement incentive offered Noren was authorized by Chapter 41 of the Laws of 1997.

The Middleton appeal

After Beatrice Hudgins Middleton's son was exonerated of charges that he brought a "Category I weapon" to his first grade class, Middleton asked the school district to file disciplinary charges against school officials whom she alleged had lied during the investigation of the incident or at the disciplinary hearing that followed.

The Commissioner, after dismissing Middleton's appeal for technical reasons, addressed the merits of her complaint -- the failure of the district to initiate the requested disciplinary action against its staff members.

Commenting that it is the board of education that has authority to take disciplinary action against a school district employee, the Commissioner said that "a board of education has broad discretion to determine whether disciplinary action against an employee is warranted."

All that is required is that the board has "a reasonable basis" for its determination not to file disciplinary charges against the individual.

18.40 Dismissal of a provisional employee

Miggins v City of New York, 286 A.D.2d 258

Cheryl Miggins was appointed as a provisional caseworker by the New York City Administration for Children's Services in June 1997. Although her performance evaluation for 1997 was "good," in January 1999, presumably reflecting the quality of her services during 1998, Miggins received a "conditional" performance evaluation. In March 1999 the agency terminated her employment.

Claiming that her dismissal was made in bad faith, Miggins sued. She asked the court to order her reinstatement to her former position with back pay. She claimed that her second, "conditional" evaluation "reflected a personal conflict between [herself] and a friend of her supervisor's" and, therefore, the evaluation "constituted bad faith."

The Appellate Division said that as a provisional employee, Miggins could be discharged at any time, without a hearing, for any or no reason, in the absence of a showing that her dismissal was (1) in bad faith or (2) for a constitutionally impermissible purpose or (3) otherwise in violation of law.

Finding that Miggins alleged only that her termination was made in bad faith, the court dismissed her petition. Why? Because, said the Appellate Division, Miggins failed to meet her burden of presenting competent proof that her dismissal was, indeed, made in bad faith.

18.41 Dismissing a probationer

Weintraub v NYC Board of Education, 298 A.D.2d 595

The Weintraub case succinctly sets out what could be characterized as "black letter law" concerning the dismissal of a probationary employee.

The New York City Board of Education dismissed probationary teacher David H. Weintraub. Weintraub sued, only to have his petition summarily dismissed by a State Supreme Court judge.

The Appellate Division affirmed the lower court's ruling, indicating that: "As a probationary employee, [Weintraub] could be terminated without a hearing provided that the termination was not in bad faith, a consequence of constitutionally impermissible reasons, or prohibited by statute or case law."

The probationary employee bears the burden of establishing such bad faith or unlawful reason for his or her termination. Conclusory allegations of bad faith are insufficient to meet this burden and apparently all that Weintraub presented was what the court characterized as "conclusory allegations of bad faith."

In addition to confirming the lower court's dismissal of Weintraub's petition without a hearing, the Appellate Division commented that "[t]he termination of the petitioner's employment was not in bad faith or illegal."

The court's reference to the bar of termination prohibited by statute or case law includes the prohibition against terminating a probationary employee during his or her minimum period of probation without notice and hearing.

Where a probationary period has been set in terms of a minimum and a maximum period of probation, case law holds that if the appointing authority elected to terminate a provisional employee during his or her minimum period of probation, such an individual is entitled to a notice and hearing in the same manner as a tenured individual.

18.42 Drafting disciplinary charges

Fella v County of Rockland, 297 A.D.2d 813

How important it to properly draft disciplinary charges? According to the Appellate Division, even in situations where discipline may be warranted, the failure to properly word the charges and specifications may be fatal to the employer's attempt to discipline an employee.

Peter Fella, Rockland County's Commissioner of Hospitals, was suspended for 30 days without pay for allegedly violating the County's Equal Employment Opportunity Policy [EEOP].

According to the court's decision, following an investigation, the Rockland County Director of Employee Rights and Equity Compliance [Director] concluded that Fella had created a hostile work environment by promoting a person with whom he was then having a romantic relationship to a vacant assistant director of nursing position.

The Director held that the Commissioner's action violated the County's EEOP based on a finding that some employees said that they felt uncomfortable at work because Fella had this "romantic relationship" with a co-employee. This, according to the Director, created a hostile work environment and, as such, violated the EEOP. The County Executive adopted the Director's findings and suspended Fella for having created a hostile work environment in violation of the EEOP.

In its decision the Appellate Division noted that the County's EEOP defined sexual harassment as "unwelcome sexual advances, requests for sexual favors, sexual demands or conduct of a sexual nature which 'had the purpose or affect [sic] of unreasonably interfering with an [affected] person's work performance or creating an intimidating, hostile or offensive work environment.'" Citing DeCinto v Westchester County Medical Center, 807 F2d 304, the court explained that there is no sexual discrimination or harassment involved "where the conduct complained of by the employee involves an isolated act of preferential treatment of another employee due to a romantic, consensual relationship."

The Supreme Court judge commented that while Fella's decision to promote an individual with whom he was having a romantic relationship may constitute poor judgment, it did not constitute a violation of the County's EEOP - the alleged basis for bring the disciplinary action. As the County failed to establish any violation of its EEOP, the Supreme Court annulled the determination of the Rockland County Executive. The Appellate Division affirmed the ruling.

Of particular interest is the Supreme Court's noting that Fella's actions may have served as a basis for discipline, albeit based on other theories of alleged misconduct. While the Court concluded there was no violation of the EEOP and thus the County could not sustain the charges it filed against Fella, the decision suggests that Fella's behavior might constitute a legitimate basis for subjecting him to disciplinary action based on other specifications.

In other words, it is possible that had the County charged Fella with misconduct based on specifications other than violating the EEOP, the court might have allowed its disciplinary action against Fella to survive.

What might constitute such a charge and specification? Perhaps charging Fella with misconduct based on his alleged selection of a person for appointment to a position in the public service solely because of a personal relationship rather than making the selection on the basis of the Constitution's mandate that selection for appointment to the public service be based on "merit and fitness."

What lesson can be learned from Fella? While the charges and specifications filed against an employee should clearly apprise the individual the alleged "misconduct or incompetence" giving rise to the charge, the specifications should constitute acts or omissions that, if proven to have occurred, would support a finding that the employee was guilty of misconduct or incompetence. In any event, the employer should be certain that it will be able to prove the allegations, whatever they may be, before initiating disciplinary action.

18.43 Due process and administrative hearings

Goohya v Walsh-Tozer, 292 A.D.2d 384, appeal dismissed as untimely, 99 N.Y.2d 551

The Goohya decision sets out a number of pitfalls that an administrative hearing officer must avoid if his or her determination and recommendation is to survive judicial review.

Mary Ann Walsh-Tozer, Rockland County Commissioner of Mental Health, filed disciplinary charges against Indrakumar Goohya. Commissioner Walsh-Tozer subsequently adopted the findings and recommendations of the disciplinary hearing officer and dismissed Goohya from his employment as a psychiatrist with the Rockland County Department of Mental Health. Goohya appealed.

The Appellate Division, Second Department, annulled Walsh-Tozer's determination and returned the matter to the Department "for a new hearing before a different Hearing Officer and thereafter for a new determination" by the Commissioner.

The court said that "[d]ue process considerations mandate that findings of fact be made in a manner wherein the parties are assured that the decision is based on evidence in the record, uninfluenced by extralegal considerations, and that both an intelligent challenge by a party aggrieved by the determination and an adequate judicial review are possible," citing Simpson v Wolansky, 38 NY2d 391.

The problem here, said the court, was that:

1. Under the guise of making findings of fact, the Hearing Officer merely reiterated the parties' testimony and other evidence submitted at the hearing.

2. Other than the Hearing Officer rejecting one or two portions of the testimony of Goohya's expert, there is no indication of the evidence he relied upon in reaching his ultimate conclusions in deciding the matter.

3. After setting forth all of the evidence in the record, the Hearing Officer merely stated, in conclusory fashion, that each charge was supported by substantial evidence.

Acknowledging that "while it is clear that strict rules of evidence are not applicable to administrative hearings," the Appellate Division pointed out that an administrative determination may be annulled "where prejudice so permeates the underlying hearing as to render it unfair."

Here, said the court, the Hearing Officer "committed errors which so prejudiced Goohya that a new hearing is warranted."

Among the faults attributed to the Hearing Officer by the court was the Hearing Officer's rejection of Goohya's request for disclosure of the medical records of the two patients who testified at the hearing, despite the fact that the Department had access to, and used, these same records at the hearing.

According to the decision, the Hearing Officer had determined that the records were confidential. On this issue -- the confidentiality of patient records -- the Appellate Division said that:

The need for maintaining the confidentiality of the patients' records must be balanced against the concern for [Goohya's] rights and any adverse impact on his reputation, livelihood and future employment. Clearly, confidentiality, on these facts, must yield to [Goohya's] right to conduct an effective defense to the disciplinary action ... [t]he confidentiality accorded the hospital records of mental patients by the Mental Hygiene Law is not absolute. In a proper case, it must yield to the needs of justice.

Presumably the Appellate Division would apply the same principle and criteria to other types of "confidential records" in appropriate situations.

The Appellate Division also noted that the Hearing Officer ruled that while Goohya's witness qualified as an expert in psychiatry, "his testimony would be accorded diminished weight and he would not in fact be given expert status because he had never before testified in an administrative proceeding." In the words of the Appellate Division: "this ruling has absolutely no basis in law".

In addition, the court faulted the Hearing Officer because he "failed to indicate in his report what weight, if any, he gave to Goohya's expert's testimony."

The Appellate Division concluded that these errors, together with the failure of the Hearing Officer to make findings of fact, prevented it from properly reviewing the final administrative determination by the Commissioner.

The Appellate Division decided that granting Goohya's appeal and annulling the disciplinary determination was warranted.

18.44 Due process and negotiated agreements

Ciambriello v Nassau County, CA2, 01-7556

The Ciambriello case involves a situation not uncommon in labor relations: a union filing a grievance on behalf certain members in the negotiating unit that adversely affects other members in the same unit. The major disciplinary issue in this case: an employee's right to a pre-termination hearing in situations involving his or her demotion after an arbitrator ruled that the employer selected that individual for promotion in violation of seniority provisions set out in the collective bargaining agreement [CBA].

Nassau County promoted Daniel J. Ciambriello to the non-competitive class position of Plant Maintenance Mechanic II [PMM-II]. Upon learning of Ciambriello's promotion, his collective bargaining representative, CSEA, filed a grievance with the County on behalf of four other employees - Ron Roeill, Eugene Romanger, Anthony Saponaro, and Joseph Scali - claiming that the County had promoted Ciambriello to PMM-II in violation of the seniority provisions set out in the CBA.

Significantly, although the grievance ultimately was submitted to arbitration, Ciambriello did not receive any notice of the grievance filed by CSEA, the arbitration, or any of the intervening steps, and as a result he did not participate in any of the grievance proceedings.

CSEA and Nassau stipulated that the issues to be resolved by the arbitrator were:

 1. Did the County violate the Collective Bargaining Agreement when it promoted Daniel Ciambriello to the position of PMM II? and

 2. If so, what is the appropriate recommended remedy?

The arbitrator issued an advisory award holding that (1) the County had violated the CBA in promoting Ciambriello to PMM-II, (2) Ciambriello's position must be vacated and refilled within sixty days, and (3) the County must consider Roeill, Romanger, Saponaro, and Scali for the PMM-II position.

CSEA filed an Article 75 action to confirm the award. The County defaulted and State Supreme Court confirmed the award.

On March 6, 2000, Ciambriello was told that he was removed from the PMM-II position and would be reassigned to an Equipment Operator I [EO-I] position - the position that he had occupied prior to his promotion - effective March 10, 2000. Roeill was appointed to the PMM-II position.

Ciambriello sued the County and CSEA, contending that his demotion in grade and resulting reduction in salary and benefits deprived him of a property interest without due process of law in violation of the Fourteenth Amendment. Ciambriello also contended that he was the victim of an "unlawful conspiracy" in violation of 42 USC 1983.

A federal district court judge summarily dismissed Ciambriello's petition, ruling that his promotion to PMM-II violated the CBA's seniority provision and thus could not be effected. In the words of the district court: "Because the right sought to be protected here is a right finding no support in the CBA, it is not a right to which [Ciambriello] had a 'legitimate claim of entitlement' and therefore, not a property right upon which a Section 1983 claim can be sustained."

The Circuit Court said that while Nassau and CSEA contend that Ciambriello had no property interest in the PMM-II position because he was promoted in violation of the CBA, this issue could not be resolved at this point. Why not? Because, explained the court, although CSEA and Nassau "may well prove that Ciambriello's promotion violated [the CAB] ... they cannot do so on the current record." Thus the District Court was premature in concluding that the CBA did not support Ciambriello's property interest in the PMM-II position.
Reading the word "discipline" broadly to include any adverse personnel action, not simply dismissal or demotion, the Circuit Court decided that the CAB give Ciambriello "a substantive right not to be

dismissed or demoted (or be subjected to any of the other disciplinary actions identified in [the CBA]) except in the event of incompetence or misconduct." Because, said the court, "the only permissible issues in a disciplinary arbitration are whether incompetence or misconduct existed, it naturally follows that the only permissible grounds for discipline are incompetence and misconduct."

Finding that Ciambriello served in the higher position for well over two years, only to be returned to his original position and salary, the court said that it did not have any trouble concluding that this right was a property right of sufficient importance to Ciambriello to warrant constitutional protection.

In the words of the court, "Ciambriello's expectation of continued employment in the PMM-II position rises to the level of a constitutionally protected property interest." Accordingly, the court ruled that Ciambriello was entitled to a due process hearing under the terms of the CBA before he could be dismissed or demoted from his PMM-II position notwithstanding the arbitration award.

According to the ruling, "the governmental interest in not providing a pre-demotion hearing is particularly minimal in this case because the County actually held a hearing prior to Ciambriello's demotion; it simply failed to invite Ciambriello's participation."

As to CSEA's role in the action, the Circuit Court said that although it has no particular interest in furthering the career of one employee at the expense of another, it undoubtedly has an interest in ensuring that the County complies with the collectively bargained for seniority provision in making promotions. Protecting that interest was only hindered by not including Ciambriello in the contract grievance proceeding.

The balance of these factors tips decidedly in favor of affording Ciambriello a pre-demotion hearing and the court decided that Ciambriello had to have notice of the charges against him and the opportunity to be heard before he could be demoted.

CSEA argued that even if Ciambriello would otherwise have a right to notice and an opportunity to be heard prior to being demoted, he waived that right (or, rather, his union waived it on his behalf). The court rejected CSEA's theory, holding that "[a] public employee's right to a pre-deprivation hearing derives from the Fourteenth Amendment, not from any statute or regulation." citing Cleveland Board of Education v Loudermill, 470 U.S. 532.

Turning to Ciambriello charges of "conspiracy," CSEA argued that as a "labor union" is was not a "state actor" and thus could not be sued for its action under 42 USC 1983. Ciambriello, on the other hand, contended that "CSEA acted under color of state law by conspiring with the County." The court decided that CSEA is not a state actor and Ciambriello did not alleged sufficient facts to support the conclusion that it acted under color of state law.

The bottom line: the Circuit Court affirmed the dismissal of CSEA from the action with respect to Ciambriello's 42 USC 1983 claims but vacate the dismissal of his 42 USC 1983 claims against the Nassau County. The case was remanded to the federal district court for further consideration.

18.45 Duty to file disciplinary charges

Montefusco v Nassau County, Supreme Court, Nassau County, June 6, 2000; Justice Phelan

From time to time the question of whether a public employer acted reasonably when it filed disciplinary charges against an individual is raised in the course of litigation. The Lindenhurst case, brought by a schoolteacher against whom disciplinary charges had been served and who then sued the district for malicious prosecution, raised this issue.

The Lindenhurst Union Free School District filed Section 3020-a disciplinary charges against one of its teachers, John Montefusco, after it was told that Montefusco "was a voyeur who looked at photographs [of teenage girls] to sexually satisfy himself."

A Nassau County police detective had found two envelopes of developed photographs in a parking lot. The pictures were of women, mostly teenagers, clothed or in bathing suits. The detective determined Montefusco, using a fictitious name and address, had brought the film to a processor for developing. Ultimately, the photographs were determined to have been taken from Montefusco's home.

No criminal charges were filed against Montefusco but the New York State Education Department was advised of the situation and provided with a copy of a statement in which the detective claimed Montefusco had told him that "he was a voyeur who looked at photographs to sexually satisfy himself." Eventually this information was transmitted to the superintendent and school board.

Montefusco was charged with (1) conduct unbecoming a teacher based on allegations that he "took photographs of unknowing females for the purpose of using these photos for sexual gratification; and (2) "lying to the Associate Superintendent about taking the photos...." Montefusco was suspended with pay but ultimately the board dismissed the Section 3020-a charges and reinstated him to his position.

Contending that the board's action violated his civil rights [42 USC 1983], Montefusco sued the district and its superintendent in federal court. Federal District Court Justice Joanna Seybert dismissed his federal claims, holding that the actions taken by the district were reasonable. In the words of the court, "[t]he information these defendants had obtained led them to take appropriate and reasonable actions under the circumstances as they knew them to be."

Montefusco, however, had also filed a "state law claim" against the district and the superintendent for malicious prosecution. The county and the detective were also named as defendants in the State action. State Supreme Court Justice Thomas P. Phelan ruled that Mantifusco's "state law claims" against the district and the superintendent were barred by the doctrine of collateral estoppel as the federal court "clearly determined that defendant School District and Superintendent acted properly in preferring charges pursuant to Education Law 3020-a against plaintiff."
Justice Phelan said that he agreed with the district's argument that "presented with information that a school teacher engaged in sexual self-stimulation with the aid of photographs of school-aged children -- whether ultimately true or not -- the defendants would have been remiss in their duties had they taken no action at all."

Was the district required to file disciplinary charges against Montefusco after receiving the report from the Education Department? Not necessarily, as the decision by the Commissioner of Education in the Covino case indicates.[161] The Covino decision holds that a board is not required to serve disciplinary charges against an individual simply because it is advised of allegations of "wrongdoing" on the part of the employee.

A parent complained that Covino, a teacher-coach, had been involved in the hazing of a student by other students. The parent wanted the school board to dismiss Covino and a bus driver who was alleged to have been present during the incident. The board's response to the parent's complaint was to suspend the teacher from his coaching duties. It did not initiate formal disciplinary action against either the teacher or the driver.

This, however, did not satisfy the parent and he appealed to the Commissioner of Education in an effort to obtain an order requiring the board to initiate disciplinary action seeking removal of the teacher.

Noting that a resident of a school district may file disciplinary charges against a tenured teacher, the Commissioner said that a board of education must have a reasonable basis for its decision whether or not to proceed with the disciplinary action.

The Commissioner decided that board's investigation of the incident, followed by its relieving the teacher of his coaching duties was sufficient under the circumstances. He ruled that the board had a reasonable basis for the action it took and its decision not to pursue further disciplinary action was neither arbitrary nor capricious.

The test set out by the Commissioner in the Covino decision: did the board investigate the allegations and then make a reasonable determination whether or not to take further action?

The employer, once having completed its investigation, essentially has the following options available to it:

1. Decide that filing disciplinary charges or taking other administrative action against the individual is unwarranted;

2. Decide that there is insufficient evidence to justify the filing of disciplinary charges but that some other administrative action, such as "counseling the individual," is appropriate.

3. Decide that filing disciplinary charges against the individual is appropriate under the circumstances.

If the employer determines that it is appropriate to bring disciplinary action against an employee, may it demand that the individual resign or be served with charges? In a word: YES!

In Rychlick v Coughlin, 63 NY2d 643, a case involving a tenured State employee, the Court of Appeals said the employer could threaten the employee with disciplinary action if he or she did not resign. The court pointed out that threatening to do what the appointing authority had a legal right to

---

[161] Matter of Covino, Decision 11227

do -- file disciplinary charges against the individual -- did not constitute coercion so as to make the resignation involuntary.

18.46 Electing a disciplinary penalty

Public Employees Federation v NYS Workers' Compensation Board, NYS Supreme Court, December 2000, Judge Mason

This decision by Judge Reynold N. Mason resolves an appeal from a disciplinary arbitration. In addition to explaining substituting negotiated disciplinary procedures for statutory procedures such as those set out in Section 75 of the Civil Service Law, it provided a rather unusual remedy: the employee is given a choice of the disciplinary penalty to be imposed.

While conducting a hearing, a Workers Compensation Board Judge, Herbert L. Levy, told a claimant's attorney to "shut up." An investigation followed and Levy admitted to using this language, explaining that he had been "attempting to say something dramatic to break th[e] emotionalism that [the attorney] was involved in," and to get her, the attorney, to stop talking and "get the hearing back on track." Levy also conceded that his plan was "perhaps ill-conceived."

Disciplinary charges were filed charges against Levy alleging "misconduct and/or incompetence." The Board claimed that he had violated it policy "that Board employees maintain a civil, courteous, respectful and professional attitude and practice" and proposed a penalty of a ten-day suspension from work without pay.

Levy rejected the proposed penalty/settlement and his disciplinary grievance was submitted to arbitration in accordance with the terms of the collective bargaining agreement [CBA].

Arbitrator Max M. Doner found Levy guilty of misconduct and/or incompetence in the performance of his duties as law judge. The penalty imposed: a fine of $2,400.

Levy filed an Article 75 petition seeking to vacate the arbitrator's award on the grounds that the arbitrator had exceeded his powers and thus his determination is "arbitrary, capricious and irrational. Levy also contended that the award violates the strong policy of the State of New York and denies petitioner his Constitutional right to due process of law...."

The Board, on the other hand, filed a motion to confirm the arbitration award.

Levy major arguments: (1) The collective bargaining agreement provides for "compulsory" binding arbitration and accordingly "the award would have to be in accord with due process and supported by adequate evidence in the record in order to be sustained;" and (2) The penalty imposed, a fine of $2,400, violates public policy.

Addressing the collective bargaining agreement, Judge Mason rejected Levy's "compulsory" binding arbitration theory.

Citing Antinore v State of New York, 40 NY2d 6, the court said that "a provision in a public employee's CBA which provides for binding arbitration as the method for disposing of challenges to disciplinary action in lieu of a statutory disciplinary procedure such as Section 75 of the Civil Service Law is deemed to have been consented to by the employee (as such provision was voluntarily agreed to by the employee's representative, the union)...."

Accordingly, Levy's submission to arbitration pursuant to his CBA is deemed to be consented to, not compulsory.

Turning to the public policy issue, Judge Mason also rejected Levy's argument that the arbitrator's imposition of a $2,400 fine is in excess of his authority and is "arbitrary, capricious and irregular" in that it violates the "strong public policy" of New York State because Section 75 provides for a fine of not to exceed $100.

Judge Mason explained that because the CBA's disciplinary grievance procedure replaced Section 75 and provides that the arbitrator is to determine guilt and the appropriate penalty, the arbitrator is neither subject to nor limited by the penalties contained in Section 75.

As to the public policy issue, the court said that a fine to be imposed against a public employee not to exceed $100, does not constitute an expression of "public policy" such that the arbitrator's imposition of a fine greater than $100 is violative of public policy and must be set aside.

According to Judge Mason, the fine of $2,400 imposed by the arbitrator appears to be a reduction from the original penalty imposed -- a 10-day suspension without pay. But, said the court, if Levy disagreed and "would actually prefer to suffer the 10-day suspension rather than pay $2,400," he may elect the suspension since he "should not be worse off for having sought review of the original finding and penalty" by an arbitrator."

Sustaining the determination of guilt, Judge Mason modified the award to allow Levy to elect the penalty he preferred.

Judge Mason applied the following standards in reaching his determination:

1. An arbitrator is free to apply his own sense of law and equity to the facts as he has found them to be in resolving a controversy, including consideration of the employee's personnel file in setting the penalty to be imposed.

2. The court's authority for overturning an arbitration award is limited to those provided under Article 75 of the Civil Practice Law and Rules.

3. Any limitation upon the remedial power of the arbitrator must be clearly contained in the arbitration clause.

4. Although an award that is violative of public policy will not be permitted to stand, courts must be careful not to decide the dispute on the merits under the guise of public policy.

The Discipline Book

18.47 Election of remedies

Matter of Coughlin, Comm. of Education Decision 14,751

When there are two or more procedures available to an individual seeking redress for an alleged wrong, his or her selection of one particular remedy will generally foreclose seeking one of the alternative remedies otherwise available at a later date. The Section 310 appeal filed by Kathleen M. Coughlin with the Commissioner of Education challenging an employment decision made by a school district illustrates, in part, the impact of such an "election of remedies."

The Webster Central School District announced that it was seeking applicants for a new ".5 Teacher on Special Assignment" position. Two applicants applied for the vacancy, Coughlin, who had been employed by Webster for 18 years and Johanna Siebert, a teacher then employed by the Rochester City School District. Siebert was selected for the appointment.

After learning of Siebert's appointment, Coughlin filed a "non-contractual grievance" in accordance with the collective bargaining agreement then in place. This provision in the agreement permits an employee to, among other things, challenge an alleged violation, misinterpretation or inequitable application of rules and policies, or to express dissatisfaction with such an alleged action by the District. This procedure, referred to as the "Fair Treatment Procedure," involves a three-stage process leading to a final decision by the school district.

Webster dismissed her Fair Treatment Procedure [FTP] grievance and Coughlin filed an appeal with the Commissioner of Education.

Coughlin alleged that:

1. While she possessed permanent certification as a school district administrator, Ms. Siebert lacked "appropriate certification" and thus by hiring Siebert the District violated Education Law Sections 3001, 3009(1) and 3010, and Section 80-5.10 of the Commissioner's Regulations; and

2. Because there were certain discrepancies and irregularities in the interview process, Coughlin concluded that "the entire posting and interview process were the only formalities."

Applying the doctrine of election of remedies, the Commissioner dismissed Coughlin's appeal alleging alleged unfairness, bias, or other irregularities in the interviewing/hiring process. Coughlin had conceded that her grievance concerning this element of her appeal had been processed through all stages of the FTP. Accordingly, said the Commissioner, "[i]t is contrary to the orderly administration of justice to have multiple tribunals making determinations concerning the same controversy."[162]

The other branch of Coughlin's appeal involved allegations that Siebert was not qualified for appointment to the position. Coughlin contended that because Siebert only held an "internship certificate" issued pursuant to Section 80-5.9 of the Commissioner's Regulations, rather than a

---

[162] The Commissioner also indicated that "[t]he doctrine of res judicata also compels the dismissal of this portion of the appeal because the grievance process has been finally determined and the collective bargaining agreement cannot confer jurisdiction upon the Commissioner of Education to review that final grievance determination."

permanent administrative certificate issued pursuant to Section 80-2.4, she was an "uncertified teacher" within the meaning of Section 80-5.10(a)(1). The Commissioner said that he disagreed with Coughlin's conclusion. The Commissioner noted that "internship certificates are, and have been for many years, issued by the Office of Teaching Initiatives of the State Education Department, not by institutions of higher learning [and] an internship certificate is recognized by the State Education Department as a valid credential authorizing the holder to act within the area of service for which the certificate is valid."

18.48 Employee personnel files used to set penalty

Pettengill v Sissman, NYS Supreme Court, Justice Vincent J. Reilly, Jr., August 13, 2001

The employer decides to introduce an employee's personnel file in the course of a Civil Service Law Section 75 disciplinary proceeding. May it do so? This was the critical issue in the Pettengill case.

New York State Department of Health Associate Budget Analyst Donald Pettengill was dismissed after being found guilty of eight acts of incompetence and insubordination. Claiming that the Section 75 hearing officer had unlawfully considered materials contained in his personnel file in determining the penalty to be recommended to the appointing authority, Pettengill asked his attorney to appeal.

Pettengill's basis for appeal: the hearing officer considered his prior work history and previous performance evaluations "reciting deficiencies in [his] work similar to those for which the charges were based." This, Pettengill contended, meant that he had been "prosecuted for five years of misconduct" in violation of the time limits for initiating disciplinary action set out in Section 75.

The appeal was not timely filed due to "law office failure" and Pettengill sued his attorney for malpractice. As Sissman conceded that his law office was at fault, Justice Reilly granted "partial summary judgment" to Pettengill.

Justice Reilly then considered Sissman's motion to dismiss Pettengill's complaint. Sissman's theory: even if the appeal were timely filed, Pettengill would have lost the case. Justice Reilly agreed and granted Sissman's motion to dismiss as well. The court observed that:

1. The rules of evidence followed in court proceedings are not controlling in processing an administrative disciplinary action;
2. The determination of guilt must be based on proof of the specific charges filed against the employee pursuant to Section 75;

3. Matters not charged could not be considered at the Section 75 disciplinary hearing; and

4. Past misconduct recorded in the employee's personnel file may be considered in the determining the penalty to be imposed for more recent acts of misconduct charged and proven at the hearing.

According to the ruling, Pettengill had been given "ample notice, time and opportunity ... to challenge the contents of his personnel file." Justice Reilly ruled that the hearing officer did not abuse her discretion when she considered Pettengill's personnel file for the limited purpose of imposing a disciplinary penalty after she found Pettengill guilty of incompetence and insubordination.

Thus, said Justice Reilly, granting Sissman's motion to dismiss the malpractice action filed against him by Pettengill, was appropriate as:

In other words, because the Appellate Division would have sustained the appointing authority's Section 75 decision even if Pettengill's appeal had been timely filed by Sissman, the court concluded that Pettengill could not substantiate the elements of his cause of action for legal malpractice.

Perhaps the leading case concerning the use of an employee's personnel records in disciplinary procedures is Bigelow v Trustees of the Village of Gouverneur, 63 NY2d 470.

In Bigelow the Court of Appeals held that if a civil service employee is found guilty of misconduct, a public employer may consider material included in the employee's personnel files in determining the appropriate sanction. The employee, however, must first be advised of the information in his or her personnel record that the appointing authority will consider in determining the penalty and then must be given an opportunity to submit a written response concerning that information.

18.49 Employment agreements

Dillon, et al, v City of New York, 261 A.D.2d 34

Typically an individual is given a letter of appointment upon initial employment setting out the effective date of appointment and some other points such as title and salary. In some instances the parties may enter into a contract. The employment of a school superintendent by a school district is an example of this. The Dillon case concerns another type agreement that the parties may enter -- one in which the employee agrees to perform service for a specified period of time.

John T. Dillon, Jr. and his co-plaintiffs were appointed as Assistant District Attorneys in Bronx County. Prior to being hired, and as a condition of employment, they each signed a statement acknowledging that: "Assistant District Attorneys are required to abide by a commitment to give four years of initial service to the Office of the District Attorney. Failure to honor that commitment may result in a loss of benefits and an unfavorable termination from the Office."
This four-year commitment was subsequently changed to three years. Dillon, Michael Newman and Eileen Koretz each submitted their resignations before completing their three-year service obligations. These resignations were apparently disregarded by the District Attorney and notations indicating "Terminated - Did Not Fulfill Commitment" were placed in their respective personnel files. In other words, their separation was deemed a termination, not a resignation.

Among the claims made by Dillon and the others in this litigation was that they had been defamed because of the characterization of their respective departures as a termination rather than a resignation. A State Supreme Court justice denied the district attorney's motion for summary judgment.

In considering the district attorney's appeal from this ruling, the Appellate Division, with respect to Dillon's "employment commitment," said: "To allow an employee who contractually commits to work a number of years, which is common in many prosecutors' offices, to "resign" prior to satisfaction of the commitment period, and then threaten to sue for defamation if the employer characterizes the employee's departure as termination, would render meaningless the contractual commitment."

The Appellate Division rejected Dillion's contention that the District Attorney's own, unilateral, reduction of the commitment period from four years to three years, abrogated the contractual commitment. The court said this argument was meritless as the district attorney's action only reduced the extent, and not the obligation, of employees' time commitments.

The court also considered the several other claims made by Dillon and decided that none stated a viable "cause of action." The Appellate Division commented that many of the statements that the plaintiffs argued were defamatory were "true" and that "truth is a complete defense," while other statements, in this day and age, did not constitute derogatory speech. The Appellate Division reversed the lower court.

18.50 Evaluating conflicting testimony

Cass v Commissioner of Labor, 296 A.D.2d 759

It is not uncommon for an administrative body to receive conflicting testimony during a hearing. Such was the situation in the Cass case.

Donald M. Cass applied for and was granted unemployment insurance benefits. While he was collecting unemployment insurance benefits, however, Cass was also serving as a member of the Geneva City Council and received a salary of $208.33 per month. On January 1, 2000, while continuing to receive unemployment insurance benefits, Cass was sworn in as the Mayor of the City of Geneva, a part-time position for which he was paid $625 per month.

The Unemployment Insurance Appeal Board [Board] ruled that Cass was ineligible for benefits because he was not totally unemployed during the time he was receiving unemployment benefits and, in addition, it concluded that he had made willful false statements in order to receive these benefits.

According to the Appellate Division's decision, Cass testified that he had mentioned his status as an elected official when he first applied for benefits and was told, by a clerk at the local unemployment insurance office, not to "worry about it". Thus, he contended, he did not reveal that he had received these payments when he made his weekly certifications for benefits.

In contrast to Cass' testimony, the record before the Board included testimony from the clerk who took Cass' application that if claimant had mentioned his status as an elected official, she would have made a note of it on his application for benefits, and she had not done so.

In addition, the record included testimony from another Labor Department representative indicating that she had spoken to Cass concerning his benefits and had specifically instructed him that he was required to report any activities performed by him as an elected official during the benefit period.

The Appellate Division sustained the Board's determination. It concluded that there was substantial evidence in the record to support the Board's finding that Cass was ineligible for benefits because he was not totally unemployed at the time and its further finding that he willfully made false statements in order to obtain benefits.

In the event there is conflicting testimony presented at the administrative hearing, the administrative body, not the court, must resolve any such conflict. In other words, the hearing officer or the administrative body is responsible for making determinations concerning the credibility of the witnesses.

18.51 Exhausting administrative remedies

Kropp v Village of Freeport, 277 A.D.2d 289

Leonard Kropp sued the Incorporated Village of Freeport in an effort to recover damages for an alleged "breach of contract."

The issue before the Appellate Division: could the failure to comply with a provision set out in a collective bargaining agreement requiring the submission of an employee's complaint to a third party bar initiating litigation concerning the matter?

When State Supreme Court Judge Segal refused to grant the Village's motion for summary judgment, Freeport appealed. Not only did the Appellate Division reverse the lower court's decision, it dismissed the Kropp's complaint in its entirety.

The Appellate Division said the Kropp "failed to exhaust his administrative remedies."

According to the decision, Section 28 of the collective bargaining agreement between Freeport and Kropp's employee organization, Kropp's claims "should have been addressed first at the administrative level." This, said the Appellate Division, required that the matter first be submitted for review by the Nassau County Civil Service Commission.

Because Kropp failed to do so, the Appellate Division dismissed his petition on the grounds that he had failed to exhaust his administrative remedy as provide by the collective bargaining agreement. In other words, Kropp's filed a lawsuit against Freeport for the alleged breach of contract was premature.

Jardim v PERB, 265 A.D.2d 329, is another "exhaustion of administrative remedies" case. The Jardim case demonstrates the importance of exhausting one's administrative remedies before initialing litigation challenging an administrative determination.

A Public Employment Relations Board administrative law judge [ALJ] dismissed improper practices charges filed by Leroy Jardim. Jardim claimed that he had been subjected to disciplinary action as a result of his performing his union duties. In effect, Jardim alleged that he had been disciplined for performing "protected activities" within the meaning of the Taylor Law -- an unfair labor practice. The ALJ decided that the disciplinary action had not been taken against him because of his union activities.

Jardim then filed a petition with a State Supreme Court appealing the ALJ's determination. This proved to be a fatal procedural error. His petition was dismissed because the court determined that Jardim had not exhausted his administrative remedies. It seems that Jardim elected to file a petition appealing the ALJ's decision in State Supreme Court pursuant to Article 78 of the Civil Practice Law and Rules instead of filing his "exceptions" to the ALJ's ruling with PERB.

The Appellate Division, Second Department affirmed the lower court's ruling. The court said that "administrative review" was available to Jardim. Thus the dismissal of his petition by the Supreme Court was appropriate.

The court pointed out that PERB's rules provided for such an administrative review, citing Section 204.10[163] of the rules. Section 204.10(a) permits a party to appeal a determination by an ALJ to the board, provided such an appeal -- referred to as "exceptions" to the ALJ's determination -- is filed within 15 working days after the individual has received the ALJ's decision.

Section 204.10 (b)(4) of the rules requires the party filing exceptions to specifically state them in the appeal. Any basis for an exception to a "ruling, finding, conclusion or recommendation" made by the ALJ "which is not specifically urged is waived".

18.52 Failing to appear at the hearing

Aures v Buffalo Board of Education, 272 A.D.2d 664

The Aures decision demonstrates the problem that could result if a party fails to appear at an administrative hearing as scheduled -- the hearing officer may proceed and hold the hearing "in absentia" and the hearing officer's determination will be binding on the parties.

Although it had not participated in the administrative hearing, the Buffalo Board of Education [Buffalo] attempted to overturn a determination by an Unemployment Insurance Administrative Law Judge [ALJ] holding that Karen M. Aures was eligible for unemployment insurance benefits.

Aures, one of number of temporary teachers employed during academic 1996-1997, had applied for unemployment insurance benefits at the end of the school year. The local office of the Division of Unemployment Insurance found that Aures had "received reasonable assurances of continued

---

[163] 4 NYCRR 204.10

employment" for the next academic year and disapproved her application for benefits. Aures appealed.[164]

An administrative hearing was scheduled but Buffalo failed to appear at the hearing. The Administrative Law Judge [ALJ] elected to proceed to hold the hearing notwithstanding Buffalo's absence. The bottom line: the ALJ overruled the initial determination, holding Aures was eligible to receive benefits.

When Buffalo learned of the decision, it asked the ALJ to reopen the case. The ALJ denied Buffalo's motion and the Unemployment Insurance Appeals Board [Board] affirmed the ALJ's ruling. Buffalo subsequently asked the Board to "reconsider" its decision concerning Buffalo's motion to reopen the matter. The Board agreed to do so, but ultimately decided to adhere to its previous ruling that sustained the ALJ's determination denying Buffalo's request to reopen the hearing. Buffalo appealed.

Why didn't had Buffalo appear at the hearing before the ALJ? According to the court, Buffalo's excuse for its not appearing at the hearing as scheduled: "the unavailability of certain key witnesses."

The Appellate Division was not impressed by this argument. Noting that the "key witnesses" in question were under Buffalo's control, the court said that "[h]aving elected to assign such witnesses to their regular duties rather than directing them to attend the scheduled hearings, [Buffalo] cannot now be heard to complain."

The court affirmed the Board's rejection of Buffalo's motion to reopen the matter, explaining that the decision to grant an application to reopen lies within the discretion of the Board. Unless it can be shown that the administrative tribunal abused its discretion, the tribunal's decision will not be disturbed by the courts. The Appellate Division decided that the record supported a finding that Board had not abused its discretion and dismissed Buffalo's appeal.

18.53 Failure to file a timely appeal

Rodriguez v Yonkers, 279 A.D.2d 632

The facts in the Rodriguez case are simple enough: the City of Yonkers terminated Frank Rodriguez, an environmental maintenance worker, for excessive absences effective March 16, 1999. Later Rodriguez decided to file a petition pursuant to Article 78 of the Civil Practice Law and Rules challenging his termination.

In the words of the court: "the gravamen of the [petitioner's] claim [is] that he was fired by the city without notice of the charges, a hearing, or other due process."

---

[164] The key to a teacher's eligibility for unemployment insurance between school years depends on his or her receiving a "reasonable assurance" of reemployment for the next school year within the meaning of Section 590(10) of the Labor Law.

This, said the court was "the classic formulation of an Article 78 proceeding" -- whether the administrative determination was made in violation of lawful procedure, was affected by error of law or was arbitrary, capricious or an abuse of discretion.

The court never got to consider the merits of Rodriguez's appeal. Why? Because, said the court, Rodriguez filed his Article 78 petition more than four months after he received the final determination dismissing him from his position. The statute of limitations for filing a timely Article 78 petition is four months from the date on which the final determination was served on the individual or his or her representative.

This, said the Appellate Division, meant that any appeal was time-barred and that Rodriguez's petition had to be dismissed. The basic rules concerning effective service of a final determination for the purposes of filing a timely appeal are as follows:

1. If the individual is not represented by an attorney or by a union official, the individual must be served to begin the statute of limitations running.

2. If an employee is represented by an attorney, the administrative body may send a copy of the determination to the employee but it must serve the attorney to begin the running of the statute of limitations.

3. If the employee is represented by a person who is not an attorney, the administrative body may send a copy to the representative but it must serve the employee to start the statute of limitations running.

To illustrate this point, in Weeks v State of New York, 198 AD2d 615, the Appellate Division refused to recognize the date of the delivery of a decision to an employee's union representative as the date from which to measure when the statute of limitations began to run.

The Podszus[165] decision is another example of the difficulties that could arise as a result a failure to a timely appeal – a malpractice action against the attorney.

Mount Vernon police officer William Podszus was found guilty of charges of insubordination and malicious gossip. The penalty imposed: forfeiture and withholding of 10 days' pay.

Podszus' attorney, Sussman, failed to file a direct appeal to the Appellate Division within 30 days of the rendering of the determination, as specified in Mount Vernon City Charter Section 120. Podszus then sued the attorney contending that had Sussman filed a timely appeal he would have prevailed and won the vacatur of the determination and penalty against him.
When the Supreme Court denied Sussman's motion for summary judgment to dismiss the malpractice action, finding an issue of fact existed with regard to whether the Podszus would have prevailed on the appeal, Sussman appealed.

The Appellate Division sustained Sussman's appeal, holding that the lower court should have granted Sussman's motion for summary judgment. Why? Because, the Appellate Division explained, the

---

[165] Podszus v City of Mount Vernon Department of Public Safety, 246 AD2d 548

Hearing Officer's determination was supported by substantial evidence and thus Podszus would not have won his appeal. The court's conclusion: As Podszus would not have prevailed on appeal, Sussman's failure to file a timely appeal did not constitute malpractice.

The court also sustained the penalty imposed as consistent with the Pell Doctrine.[166]

18.54 Failure to meet contract deadlines set for disciplinary arbitration

Covino v Kane, 273 A.D.2d 380

The significant issue raised in the Covino case concerns the impact of the employer's failing to meet a contract-specified deadline in issuing a disciplinary determination.

A member of the Nassau County Police Department, Craig S. Covino, was found guilty of violating seven departmental rules and regulations and a disciplinary penalty was imposed.

Covino objected, complaining that the Police Commissioner, issued his decision "late" in violation of Section 6.3-1 of the collective bargaining agreement between the Police Department and the Covino's union. This failure to make a timely determination as to Covino's guilt and the penalty to be imposed as punishment, Covino argued, required that the disciplinary action be rescinded. Section 6.3-1 of the collective bargaining agreement.[167]

According to the decision, Covino was served with charges and specifications and his disciplinary hearing was concluded in September 1998. The hearing officer's report, dated November 20, 1998, recommended that Covino be found guilty of all of the charges preferred against him. On January 4, 1999 the Commissioner concurred with the findings of the hearing officer as to Covino's being guilty of the charges filed against him and imposed penalties based upon those findings and recommendations.

Should the Commissioner's determination be overturned because he failed to meet the 60-day deadline for issuing a decision as required by the agreement?

No! said the Supreme Court, Nassau County, dismissing Covino's petition. The court ruled that in the absence of "specific language barring further action, an employer's failure to act within the time frame contemplated in a collective bargaining agreement does not preclude further action by the employer". The Appellate Division, Second Department, agreed.

In affirming the lower court's ruling, the Appellate Division pointed out that in interpreting similar contractual provisions, the Second Department has repeatedly held that, in the absence of prejudice, "the failure to timely render a determination pursuant to the terms of the parties' contract does not

---

[166] Pell v Board of Education, 34 NY2d 222

[167] Section 6.3-1 of the collective bargaining agreement provides that a determination as to guilt or innocence and punishment, if any, shall be made within sixty (60) days after the hearing is concluded unless an employee or the [Superior Officers Association] consents to a longer period.

warrant vacatur of the determination," citing Correctional Unit Employees v State of New York Department of Correctional Services, 236 AD2d 546.

The decision by the Appellate Division suggests that the Supreme Court decided, or assumed, that the 60-day period for the Commissioner to issue a timely decision in accordance with relevant contract provision started when the "hearing was concluded" in September 1999. If, on the other hand, the disciplinary hearing is not deemed concluded until the hearing officer issued his or her determination and recommendations, this 60-day period would begin to run not before the date the hearing officer issued his or her report -- November 20, 1998.

Another case involving "contract time limits," City of Newburgh v DeGidio, was decided by the Appellate Division, Second Department [273 A.D.2d 468]. In this Article 75 action to stay arbitration, the Appellate Division to the parties to "proceed to arbitration" to resolve the issue. Reversing the Supreme Court's ruling to the contrary, the Appellate Division, citing County of Rockland v Primiano Construction Co., 51 NY2d 1, held:

Where the collective bargaining agreement does not contain an express provision making compliance with the time limitations set forth in the grievance procedure a condition precedent to binding arbitration, the issues related to compliance with the time limitations set forth in the grievance procedure are matters of procedural arbitrability for the arbitrator to decide.

In other words, the arbitrator is to decided whether if the demand for arbitration was valid under the terms of the agreement.

18.55 False official reports

Sweeney v Safir, 267 A.D.2d 99

New York City police officer Kevin Sweeney lost his job after being found guilty of giving false testimony and falsifying official reports.

Sweeney appealed only to have Appellate Division affirm the findings of the police commissioner as to guilt and the penalty imposed -- dismissal. The commissioner found that Sweeny was guilty of "knowingly" making false statements in police reports and in his testimony before a Grand Jury.

Sweeny had testified that "he was the victim of a gunpoint robbery of his fiancée's car when, in fact, the car was simply stolen from the street when [Sweeney] left it double-parked with the keys in the ignition and the engine running."

Another false statement made in an investigation case is Abbate v Safir, 279 A.D.2d 260. Here the court pointed out that not being truthful in responding to questions posed in the course of an official investigation may result in disciplinary action.

New York City police officer Anthony Abbate was found guilty of charges that he "lied at his official interview" when he denied that he had "uttered profanities to another officer," and, in a separate incident, "was discourteous and disrespectful to another officer in uttering racial epithets in an argument." The penalty imposed: dismissal from the force.

Abbate's appeal from the determination and the penalty imposed was dismissed by the Appellate Division. The court said that there was substantial evidence to support a finding that Abbate was guilty of the charges.

As to Abbate's challenge to his dismissal, the Appellate Division decided that in view of Abbate's "poor disciplinary record" the penalty of dismissal satisfied the Pell standard [Pell v Board of Education, 34 NY2d 222]. In the words of the court, "the penalty does not shock our sense of fairness."

18.56 Filing a timely Article 78

Budihas v Board of Education, 285 A.D.2d 549
Bonilla v Board of Education, 285 A.D.2d 548

When does the four-month Statute of Limitation to file a timely Article 78 petition begin to run? This critical issue involving the State's adjective law is explored in the Budihas and Bonilla cases.

The Budihas Case

On April 8, 1998, Stephen J. Budihas was told that his employment as a probationary principal would be terminated "as of the close of business on May 1, 1998". Ultimately the decision to terminate Budihas was sustained by the Chancellor of the Board of Education of the City of New York on April 8, 1999. On July 30, 1999 Budihas filed a petition pursuant to Article 78 of the Civil Practice Law and Rules seeking to overturn the Chancellor's decision. The Appellate Division, Second Department, affirmed a Supreme Court decision holding that Budihas' petition was untimely.

The court pointed out that "a determination to terminate probationary employment becomes final and binding on the date the termination becomes effective," citing Frasier v Board of Education, 71 NY2d 763. Accordingly, said the court, Budihas' petition, filed on July 30, 1999, is clearly time-barred.

Courts in cases involving employee timeliness claims in civil rights litigation, typically have ruled that the Statute of Limitations commence to run when the decision to terminate an employee is communicated to the individual rather than the effective date of the termination. The leading case addressing this: Delaware State College v Ricks, 449 US 250,

The Bonilla Case

The Bonilla case, however, in addition to the issue of the "timeliness" of an Article 78 challenging an employee's dismissal, concerned the timeliness of an appeal from an administrative decision affirming the unsatisfactory performance evaluation underlying the employee's termination.

On June 26, 1998, New York City teacher Carmelo Bonilla was terminated from his position as a provisional [sic] science teacher. Bonilla had received an unsatisfactory rating of his teaching performance. However, the final decision sustaining Bonilla's unsatisfactory performance rating was not issued by the Chancellor of the Board of Education until March 25, 1999. On July 20, 1999, Bonilla filed an Article 78 petition seeking to have his unsatisfactory rating annulled and an order directing his reinstatement to his former position with back pay and benefits.

The Supreme Court dismissed Bonilla's petition in its entirety as time-barred, ruling the Statute of Limitations began to run on the date Bonilla's employment was terminated in June 1998. The Appellate Division disagreed in part with this ruling, holding that the "Supreme Court erred in dismissing the entire proceeding on the ground that it was barred by the Statute of Limitations."

Clearly, said the court, an Article 78 proceeding against a public body or officer must be commenced within four months after the determination to be reviewed becomes final and binding. Thus that part of Bonilla's Article 78 petition seeking a review of determining to dismiss him effective June 26, 1998, is barred by the four-month Statute of Limitations because this determination became final on the effective date of his discharge.

In contrast, said the court, that part of Bonilla's Article 78 petition challenging the March 25, 1999 determination by the Chancellor, sustaining Bonilla's unsatisfactory rating was not time barred.

Bonilla, explained the Appellate Division, had a right to administrative appeal his unsatisfactory evaluation as well as a hearing to test that determination. The hearing panel's recommendation did not become final until the Chancellor issued a decision acting upon it. Accordingly, the determination that Bonilla's teaching performance was unsatisfactory did not become final and binding until the Chancellor denied his appeal and sustained the rating.

The court annulled Bonilla's unsatisfactory rating "since the [Board of Education conceded] that it was not preceded by an inspection of [Bonilla's] work and a consultation with him by the appropriate official."

Assuming his was a probationary appointment in contrast to holding a provisional appointment, Bonilla's Article 78 attack on the Chancellor's determination could survive and he may ultimately prevail in his quest for reinstatement if he can demonstrate that the performance evaluation underlying his termination was arbitrary or capricious or was otherwise materially defective.

If Bonilla was, in fact, a provisional employee, presumably any further proceeding would be solely in the nature of a "name-clearing" hearing.

18.57 Final determination for purposes of making a claim

Skiptunas v State of New York, 290 A.D.2d 868

The Court of Claims Act allows an individual to sue the State, provided he or she files a timely notice of claim or a notice of intention to file a claim. Such a claim or notice of claim must be filed within 90 days from the accrual date of the claim. In Skiptunas, the Appellate Division found that Charles P. Skiptunas did not file either his claim or his notice of his intention to file a claim within the time limits set out in the Court of Claims Act, which begins to run from date of a final administrative decision.

According to the decision, in October 1994, the Middletown City School District investigated a complaint that a probationary teacher had engaged in an inappropriate personal relationship with a student. After the District determined that there was an improper, nonsexual, relationship, the teacher chose to resign from his position rather than be terminated.

On November 7, 1995, the District's Superintendent, Charles P. Skiptunas, reported this event to the Education Department's professional conduct office. Following an investigation by the Department, a charge was filed against Skiptunas alleging that he failed to promptly report the investigation conducted by the District and the circumstances underlying the teacher's resignation as required by Section 83[168] of the Commissioner's Regulations.

The charge against Skiptunas was released by the Department of Education and reported in several newspapers. On October 22, 1996, a three-member Hearing Panel issued its final determination. It found that the Department did not meet its burden of proof and its allegations did not raise any questions about Skiptunas's moral character. The Panel recommended that the charge be dismissed. The Commissioner of Education adopted the Panel's recommendation.

The Commissioner later issued a memorandum dated December 16, 1996 to all school superintendents reminding them of their duty to file timely 8 NYCRR 83 reports and indicating his concern that the Panel's ruling in Skiptunas' case might "send the wrong message" to them, i.e., that simply removing a problem teacher from a district is sufficient to fulfill all legal obligations.

Skiptunas' attorney objected to the Commissioner's memorandum, contending that it appeared to imply that Skiptunas was guilty of an impropriety and asked the Commissioner issue a specific order terminating the proceeding against Skiptunas. The Commissioner replied that as he accepted the Hearing Panel's findings, there was no need for issuance of a separate order.

Skiptunas sued in Federal court, only to have his lawsuit against the Commissioner and others was dismissed on the ground that the defendants were entitled to a qualified immunity. When the Federal court declined to exercise jurisdiction over Skiptunas' State claims, he filed an action in the Court of Claims seeking damages for alleged malicious prosecution, and intentional and negligent infliction of emotional distress. The Court of Claims dismissed his action as untimely and Skiptunas appealed this ruling to the Appellate Division.

In his appeal Skiptunas conceded that he did not file a formal notice of his intention to file a claim at any point. However, he argued, he "substantially complied" with the notice of claim requirement in his May 27, 1998 letter asking the Commissioner "bring public closure to the charges against him".

---

[168] 8 NYCRR 83

The Appellate Division disagreed with Skiptunas' theory, ruling that his lawsuit principally challenged the commencement and investigation of the charges brought against him in January 1996, all of which culminated in the October 22, 1996 recommendation by the Panel to dismiss all charges.

Thus, said the court, the latest possible date on which Skiptunas' claim could have accrued was December 16, 1996, the date of the Commissioner's memorandum to the superintendents of schools concerning the Panel's decision. Since Skiptunas did not send a letter of complaint until May 1998, the Appellate Division said that Court of Claims correctly found that Skiptunas did not meet the filing and service requirements of the Court of Claims Act.

Gibson v NYCPD, CA2, 11/99, is another case that explores the issue of "final administrative determination."

The statute of limitations for appealing an administrative determination begins to run when the individual is notified of the agency's "final determination." However, the agency may not always note the fact that a "final determination" has been made in the written notice sent to the individual. In Gibson, the US Circuit Court of Appeal, Second Circuit, which includes New York State within its jurisdiction, suggested that it would be well for the decision maker to note that the decision is its "final" one.

Pamela Gibson wanted to become a New York City police officer. She took and passed the written test for the position but she failed the psychological examination. The department's letter said that Gibson had 30 days to file an appeal challenging the decision with the New York City Civil Service Commission.[169]

Gibson initiated her lawsuit in federal district court, but the district court justice granted the department's motion to dismissed her petition as untimely. The court explained that Gibson had filed her Title VII complaint with EEOC more than 300 days after being notified of her disqualification by the department [see 42 USC Section 2000e-5(e)(1)]. The Circuit Court of Appeals sustained the district court's ruling that Gibson's petition was untimely.

The Circuit Court rejected Gibson's contention that "her EEOC complaint was timely because the doctrine of equitable tolling applied to the period during which she sought administrative review." The court pointed out that "equitable relief is extended sparingly," noting that it has been allowed in situations where the claimant has actively pursued judicial remedies but filed a defective

In contrast, said the court, an individual's "failure to act diligently is not a reason to invoke equitable tolling." In other words, if an individual has more than one means of seeking redress, he or she must pursue all of them within the controlling statute of limitations and may not rely on the fact that he or she has appealed to one forum to stop the statute of limitations running in another forum.

---

[169] Gibson first appealed her disqualification to the New York City Civil Service Commission, which affirmed the department's determination. She later filed a complaint alleging sex discrimination with EEOC pursuant to Title VII. EEOC found no violation pleading during the statutory period, or where the complainant has been induced or tricked by [her] adversary's misconduct into allowing the filing deadline to pass."

Gibson also argued that the letter notifying her of her disqualification from being a police officer constitutes conduct that requires the application of equitable tolling because it only advised her that she could appeal the department's decision to the Civil Service Commission. As a result, she contended, she appealed to the Commission instead of exploring her other remedies.

The Circuit Court said that Title VII is clear: "regardless of the state and local remedies available to Gibson, she had to file a complaint with the EEOC within 300 days of the allegedly discriminatory conduct." It decided that the department's letter did not hide this fact from Gibson or mislead her into believing that Title VII's filing provision did not apply.

Although the court said that it was not persuaded that the department's letter to Gibson was a deliberate effort to mislead her sufficient to give rise to equitable tolling, it commented that the letter would have been clearer and therefore fairer had it made plain that the Department's decision constituted a final determination, irrespective of Gibson's right to appeal."

In line with this, the court said that it thought that "the Department would be well advised to consider adding such language to its form letter to avoid confusion." The Circuit Court concluded that Gibson filed an untimely complaint with the EEOC and, accordingly, the district court properly dismissed her petition.

The issue of a "final determination" was considered in Sotolongo v NYC Transit Authority, USDC, SDNY. Here Justice Sprizzo denied the Authority's motion to dismiss Sotolongo's appeal as untimely "because the record before the Court ... did not reveal whether the February 15, 1995, employment action constituted a final determination or was merely a recommendation that required further proceedings to become effective." The Authority contended that Sotolongo's appeal was untimely because his time to file began to run on February 15, 1995, when the Authority suspended him and filed disciplinary charges against him.

18.58 Fitness of a witness

Goodman v Safir, 259 A.D.2d 344

In the Goodman case, the Appellate Division considered the value of testimony provided by "corrupt former employees" called by the employer as witnesses against another employee in a disciplinary action.

New York City police officer Keith Goodman was terminated from his position after being found guilty of participating in unlawful searches in violation of the Fourth Amendment to the U. S. Constitution on a number of occasions. Goodman challenged his dismissal, contending that there was no substantial evidence supporting the Commissioner's action because, Goodman alleged, a number of the witnesses testifying against him were corrupt former police officers.

The Appellate Division dismissed Goodman's appeal, commenting that it found "no reason to disturb [the Commissioner's] credibility findings rejecting [Goodman's] version of the events." The fact that some of the witnesses testifying for the employer were characterized by Goodman as "corrupt former police officers" did not mean that their testimony was not "substantial" insofar as the Appellate Division was concerned.

Finding that the penalty of dismissal did not shock its sense of fairness, the Appellate Division sustained the commissioner's determination and his terminating Goodman from his position.

18.59 Fraud a valid basis for removal from position

Schindlar v Village of Lloyd Harbor, 261 A.D.2d 626

Providing false information in his application for appointment as a police officer resulted in Dennis Schindlar's disqualification and removal from his position with the Village of Lloyd Harbor.

The Suffolk County Department of Civil Service, after holding a hearing, revoked the Schindlar's certification and appointment as a police officer. The department's hearing officer determined that Schindlar had "perpetrated a fraud in claiming residency in the Incorporated Village of Lloyd Harbor."

Schindlar had presented evidence that he resided in Lloyd Harbor, including copies of his driver's license and voter registration cards. There was also testimony by the owner of the property on which he allegedly resided.

The Appellate Division noted that notwithstanding such evidence submitted by Schindlar, the hearing officer "credited the persuasive documentary evidence to the contrary." The court said that it was well established that a reviewing court may not weigh evidence or reject the choice made by the hearing officer, especially where there is conflicting evidence and room for choice exists. Finding that there was substantial evidence in the record to sustain a finding that Schindlar did not in fact reside in Lloyd Harbor during the period in question, the court affirmed Schindlar's disqualification by the department.

Section 50.4(f) of the Civil Service Law provides for the disqualification of individuals "who has intentionally made a false statement of any material fact in his [or her] application." A pre-disqualification hearing may be provided where appropriate, it but is not mandated by Section 50.4.

The key due process element in Section 50.4 provides that "no person shall be disqualified ... unless he [or she] has been given a written statement of the reasons ... and afforded an opportunity to make an explanation and to submit facts in opposition to such disqualification."

18.60 Free speech by public employees

Wasson v Sonoma Co. Jr. Coll., CA9, 2/16/00

A public employee may claim that he or she was disciplined as a result of his or her exercising his or her constitutionally protected right of free speech.

This was Sonoma County Junior College instructor Sylvia J. Wasson's argument following her termination from her position. The reason for her dismissal: the College Board decided that she was the anonymous writer of six defamatory letters and "flyers" that "vilified" the college president, Robert Agrella.[170]

Wasson sued, claiming the college's action violated her First Amendment rights. Wasson, however, had denied writing the five letters and the flyer she claimed was the reason underlying her termination. Her denial proved fatal to her "wrongful termination in retaliation for exercising her right to free speech" argument.

The U.S. Circuit Court of Appeals, Ninth Circuit, said that "a free speech claim depends on speech...." In what may be a variation of "Catch 22," the court said that because Wasson denied writing the letters or otherwise being involved in the affair, she had no basis for claiming her right to free speech had been violated.

In the words of the court, "[w]e conclude that the plaintiff fails to state a First Amendment claim in these circumstances because she cannot show the alleged wrongful conduct was in retaliation for any exercise of her free speech rights."

Wasson also presented an alternative argument: she was defending the First Amendment free speech rights of the actual writer of the offending letters and flyer.

The court dismissed this theory as well. The Circuit Court ruled that Wasson "lacked standing" because she did not show that she had any relationship to, or with, the alleged anonymous writer, the "second prong" of the three prong test set out in Powers v Ohio, 499 US 400.

In order to prevail on the basis of a "defending the free speech of others" argument, the individual must show that he or she (1) actually suffered an "injury in fact," (2) had a "close relation to the third party," and (3) there was "some hindrance to the third party's ability to protect his or her own interests."

Further, the courts typically distinguish between a public employee's exercising his or her right to free speech concerning a matter of public interest in contrast to speech that essentially involves the individual's personal interests. Pickering v Board of Education, 391 US 563, sets out the tests applied by the courts in such cases.

Other free speech chase include Council 82, v State of New York, 255 A.D.2d 54, affirmed, 94 N.Y.2d 321 [State Correction Department rules do not trump a correction officer's First Amendment right to fly a Nazi flag at home] and Sheppard v Beerman, USDC, EDNY, Judge Glasser, received March 17, 2002 – [public employee's right to criticizes his or her superior or supervisor].

---

[170] The board subsequently withdrew the Notice of Decision to Dismiss without prejudice and reinstated Wasson to her instructor position pending appeal. She was still so employed on the date this summary was prepared.

18.61 Hearsay testimony in disciplinary action

Brinson v Safir, 255 A.D.2d 247

James Brinson, a New York City police officer, was dismissed after being found guilty of "knowingly and wrongfully associat[ing] with persons know to be engaged in criminal activity."

The evidence against Brinson consisted of hearsay statements of two informants. The statements of the informants were corroborated by police surveillance. The Appellate Division said that such testimony, together with its corroboration, constituted substantial evidence of the charges filed against Brinson and dismissed his appeal.

Another aspect of the appeal involved Brinson's being required to submit to a drug test. The Appellate Division said that "corroborated information" supplied by informants provided a "reasonable suspicion" to require Brinson to undergo drug testing.

18.62 Impartiality of discipline panel members

Informal Opinions of the Attorney General, 99-21, 7/19/99

The impartiality of a disciplinary tribunal is a critical element in any disciplinary action. Further, even the appearance of any impropriety must be avoided. Would it be appropriate for an individual to serve on a disciplinary panel if there was a possibility that his or her son might be called as a witness in the proceeding?

David A. Menken, the Village Attorney, Village/Town of Mount Kisco, asked the Attorney General for his views with respect to such participation after the chief of police advised the board of trustees that disciplinary charges might be filed against one or more Mount Kisco police officers and the son of a trustee, who was a member of the police force, might be called as a witness.

The Attorney General commenced his analysis by noting that Section 5711-q(1) of the Unconsolidated Laws provides that such disciplinary charges must be heard by "at least a majority" of the Board of Trustees and that "even the appearance of impropriety should be avoided in order to maintain public confidence in government."

The Attorney General concluded that the trustee should recuse herself because "the trustee may not be able to make an impartial judgment solely in the public interest if her son is called as a witness." While state law does not bar members of the same family from serving in the same governmental unit, public officers have a responsibility to exercise their duties "solely in the public interest."

The Attorney General said that the difficulty here was that "there was no objective way to verify" that the trustee was able to weigh the credibility of her son fairly and reached an impartial judgment. Under the circumstances, the Attorney General concluded that "there is at least an appearance of impropriety" and thus the trustee should recuse herself and "should not participate in or be present at the hearing, any deliberations, including deliberations conducted during an executive session of the board of trustees, or the determination of the disciplinary proceeding brought by the Mount Kisco Police Department."

18.63 Imposing a harsher disciplinary penalty

Russo v Wantagh UFSD, 259 A.D.2d 703

Smoky conditions prompted school officials of the Wantagh school district to evacuate students from a school building. Investigation showed the fire began in the custodians' area of the school and was caused by cigarettes igniting waste paper in a plastic trash pail that had not been emptied.

The school board dismissed custodian Clement Russo after he was found guilty of "charges of misconduct and incompetence concerning a smoke condition in the school at which he was employed." Russo appealed.

The Appellate Division sustained the district's determination, finding that it was supported by substantial evidence in the record.

Russo also protested his dismissal on the grounds that the hearing officer had recommended a lesser penalty. The court said that "under the circumstances of this case, the termination of the petitioner's employment was not so disproportionate to the offense as to shock one's sense of fairness," quoting the Pell standard in imposing a penalty [Pell v Bd. of Ed., 34 NY2 222].

18.64 Internal investigation reports

Ramirez v MBSTOA, 258 A.D.2d 326

It is not uncommon for an employer to undertake an "internal investigation" of an incident involving alleged negligence or misconduct on the part of an employee in the performance of his or her duties. For example, an internal affairs unit of a police department may conduct an "internal investigation" following allegations of negligence or misconduct filed against a police officer.

If the internal investigator finds that the employee "was at fault" and states this conclusion in his or her final report, may a plaintiff use this as an "admission" by the employer in a lawsuit for negligence?

Not necessarily. In the case of Carmen L. Ramirez v Manhattan and Bronx Service Transit Operating Authority [MBSTOA], a negligence action, Ramirez wanted to use an internal investigation report prepared by MBSTOA investigators that concluded that the MBSTOA's driver who was involved in a particular accident was "at fault". The Appellate Division upheld a lower court's ruling that Ramirez could not use the investigation report as evidence in the lawsuit that Ramirez brought against MBSTOA for negligence.

The court's rationale: the admission of the report into evidence "would be unfairly prejudicial" to MBSTOA and "misleading to the jury." The trial court had barred Ramirez's introduction of the MBSTOA's initial internal investigatory report because it found that the investigator's determination was based on the Authority's "internal rules and policies" and that those rules and policies "exceeded the applicable common-law negligence standard of care." In other words, MBSTOA demanded a higher standard of performance on the part of its drivers than was required under common law. The Appellate Division concurred with the Supreme Court judge's ruling, observing that the initial report's conclusion that the MBSTOA driver "was at fault" was changed on review to a finding of "questionable".

The lesson here is that if an agency wishes to prevent adverse information contained in an internal investigation report from being used in a trial, it must show that the report was prepared in consideration of a standard of care that is higher than that imposed under common [or case] law.

18.65 Involuntary leave under Section 72

NYC Parks and Recreation v Matthews, OATH, 219/00, 11/22/99

The New York City Department of Parks and Recreation wanted to place Rufus Matthews on leave pursuant to Section 72 of the Civil Service Law. Matthews objected.

The department claimed that Matthews, a park maintenance worker, was medically unfit to perform the duties and responsibilities of his position due to a heart condition.

Matthews, on the other hand, contended that he was fully able to perform the duties of his position notwithstanding his "heart condition."

Pointing out that Section 72 places the "burden of proving mental or physical unfitness" upon the entity alleging it, OATH Administrative Law Judge [ALJ] Rosemarie Maldonado held that Parks and Recreation had failed to prove by a preponderance of the evidence that Matthews was "currently unfit" to competently perform his job duties as a city park maintenance worker.

Maldonado said that Matthews personal physician presented "compelling evidence" that [Matthews'] "cardiac rehabilitation was complete, and that physical exertion did not pose an unreasonable risk to his patient."

In response to the department's concern that Matthews "is endangering himself" by insisting that he be reinstated to full duty, the ALJ said while "commendably humanitarian," the legal issue remains the impact of Matthew's condition on his current ability to work.

Maldonado said that unless there is a clear showing of present impairment, the employer cannot place an individual on Section 72 leave "simply because there is some risk" that Matthews' performance of his work might place him in some physical jeopardy.

According to the decision, where it is apparent at the time of the hearing that the employee's condition is in check, or otherwise under control, OATH has declined to find unfitness merely because of the existence of the future potential for relapse or deterioration.

18.66 Involuntary resignation

Shoaf v Dept. of Agriculture, FedCir, 00-3148, August 7, 2001

In the Shoaf case the U.S. Circuit Court of Appeals, Federal Circuit, set out its guidelines for determining whether a federal employee's resignation or retirement was voluntary or whether it should be deemed to be a "constructive discharge."

William Shoaf, an interdisciplinary team leader responsible for preparing large timber sales in southeast Alaska, retired from his position. Following his retirement he sued, alleging that his retirement constituted a constructive discharge and resulted from retaliatory actions that had been taken against him for making disclosures protected under the Whistleblower Protection Act, 5 USC 2308(b)(8).

Observing that "[e]mployees typically ground involuntary resignation or retirement assertions" on claims that the agency:

1. Imposed, or threatened to take, adverse personnel action against the employee;

2. Misinformed or deceived the employee; and, or

3. Coerced the employee to involuntarily resign or retire by creating working conditions so intolerable for the employee that he or she is driven to resign or retire.

The court decided that "Shoaf's claim falls into the 'coercion' category."

As a general rule, to establish "involuntariness on the basis of coercion" the Federal Circuit requires the individual to prove three elements:

1. The agency effectively imposed the terms resulting in the employee's resignation or retirement;

2. The employee had no realistic alternative but to resign or retire; and

3. The employee's resignation or retirement was the result of improper acts by the agency.

This "three-prong" test must be tailored to fit the circumstances of each case and ultimately depends on the court's finding that "working conditions were made so intolerable by the agency that a reasonable person in the employee's position would have felt compelled to resign."

Another factor, said the court, was that in making its determination, courts must consider the employee's entire work history rather than limit its inquiry to the most recent events that were the proximate cause of the employee's decision to resign or retire. Finding that the administrative judge failed to consider the "totality of the circumstances surrounding Shoaf's resignation," the Circuit Court remanded case to the administrative tribunal for a decision "comporting with the precepts delineated herein."

In contrast, suppose an employee entitled to pretermination "notice and hearing" is told that unless he or she immediately resigns from his or her position, he or she will be served with disciplinary charges. Does such a demand constitute unlawful coercion? This issue was considered by the New York State Court of Appeals in Rychlick v Coughlin, 63 NY2d 643.

Rychlick, a State corrections officer, was told that unless he immediately submitted his resignation, formal disciplinary charges would be filed against him. He submitted his resignation. A few days later he asked to withdraw the resignation on the grounds that it had been "forced" from him. When his request was denied, Rychlick sued, claiming the resignation had been obtained under duress and thus was void.

The Court of Appeals upheld the appointing authority's refusal to allow Rychlick to withdraw his resignation, ruling that threatening to do what one had the legal right to do -- file disciplinary charges against an employee -- does not constitute unlawful duress.

Implicit in the Shoaf decision is that his comments were protected under the federal Whistleblower's Act because they involved matters of public concern.

In Craven v University of Colorado Hospital Authority, CA10, 99-1519, decided August 13, 2001, the court held that a hospital safety employee's public comments concerning the disposal of medical waste that resulted in her termination involved issues that were of a professional rather than a public concern and thus not protected by Colorado's whistleblower statute.

In another "whistleblower" case, Huffman v Office of Personnel Management, CA Federal Circuit, 00-3184, decided August 15, 2001, the court ruled that an employee's complaints to his or her own supervisor about the supervisor's conduct were not protected by the federal Whistleblower Act although complaints to a supervisor about another employee's conduct may be protected speech within the meaning of the statute.

18.67 Judicial review of a disciplinary determination

Danahy v Kerik, App. Div., 298 A.D.2d 278

Assuming a public employer follows proper procedure, what must be shown to sustain the discipline it invoked under Section 75 of the Civil Service Law? Historically the courts have indicated that as long as there is substantial evidence supporting the finding(s) of fact and that the disciplinary penalty imposed did not violate the Pell standard,[171] they will not disturb the decision of the employing body."

---

[171] Under the Pell standard, the Court will not substitute its judgment as to appropriate disciplinary action for that of the employing body unless the discipline is so harsh as to "shock one's sense of fairness.

What happens, however, when there is an issue concerning the credibility of a witness's testimony? In Danahy, the Appellate Division reaffirmed its long-standing position that it will not overrule a hearing officer who decides to credit one witness's testimony over another's. In other words, the trier of the case's decision as to creditability will prevail unless the challenging party can demonstrate that such reliance was manifestly improper, a difficult task at best.

Disciplinary charges alleging misconduct were filed against a New York City police officer, Kevin Danahy. The hearing officer found Danahy guilty of the charges -- he used excessive force in making an arrest -- and recommended that Danahy be suspended for 20 days without pay. The Police Commissioner accepting the hearing officer's findings and recommendation.

Danahy had testified that he didn't strike or otherwise injure the complainant, but rather he and the complainant merely fell to the ground while the complainant was flailing his arms in an attempt to avoid being handcuffed. The hearing officer, however, rejected Danahy's version of the event and found him guilty of the charges.

Danahy commenced an Article 78 proceeding challenging the ruling, contending that (1) the decision wasn't supported by substantial evidence and that (2) the discipline imposed violated the Pell Standard. The Court said that it would not disturb the hearing officer's determination as to the credibility of witnesses and that the 20-day suspension did not violate the Pell Standard.

Typically the courts will consistently defer to a hearing officer with respect to the determinations concerning the credibility of the witness testifying in a Section 75 disciplinary hearing. Essentially, where the court determines that there is substantial evidence to support the hearing officer's findings and establish guilt, the critical question becomes whether or not the penalty imposed reasonable under the circumstances.

Sustaining the disciplinary penalty imposed on Danahy, the Appellate Division held that a suspension for 20 days without pay "did not shock its sense of fairness" and sustained the Commissioner's determination.

18.68 Jurisdiction to hear a disciplinary appeal

Pierino v Brown, 281 A.D.2d 960,

The issue in the Pierino case concerns the proper forum to consider a disciplinary appeal.

John Pierino filed an Article 78 action challenging a disciplinary determination based on a hearing officer's finding that Pierino was guilty of violating Section 35-6 of the Buffalo City Code.

The disciplinary charges filed against Pierino were resolved in accordance with the provisions set out in Article 22 -- the contract disciplinary procedure -- of the relevant collective bargaining agreement. Article 22 required the appointment of a hearing officer, who was to hear the charges and make a determination.

Pierino challenged the disciplinary determination by bring an Article 78 action alleging the decision by the hearing officer was not based on substantial evidence. As is typical in such cases, the State Supreme Court transferred the action to the Appellate Division.

The Appellate Division, however, rejected the transfer of Pierino's Article 78 petition to it for review.

What was the basis for the court's action? The Appellate Division ruled that the issue of "substantial evidence" that formed the basis of Pierino's appeal is raised only if an administrative hearing is "required by law." In the words of the Appellate Division, citing Marin v Bensonsi, 131 AD2 100: "Since the hearing was mandated by the collective bargaining agreement and not by Civil Service Law Section 75, the substantial evidence standard of review does not apply and the arbitrary and capricious standard is appropriate. Consequently, the proceeding was erroneously transferred to this Court."

Presumably Pierino's appeal will now be considered by the Supreme Court. In order for Pierino to prevail he will have to prove that the hearing officer's determination was "arbitrary and capricious."

18.69 Leave approval

Renaud v City of New York, 269 A.D.2d 283

An employee is terminated on the grounds that he or she was absent from her position without approval [AWOL] for three months. The employee's defense: the absence was approved by one of the agency's employee relations specialist and therefore the agency cannot deemed the employee to have been AWOL.

This seems to be an easy issue to decide, except for two factors:

1. The employee relations specialist involved was not authorized to approve the leave in the first instance and;

2. The employee relations specialist "was unaware at the time that [Renaud] had been already referred for discipline because of her AWOL status."

May the employee rely on the "unauthorized approval" of her absence? This was the issue considered by the Appellate Division when Leslie Renaud sued the Administration for Children's Services in an effort to be reinstated to her position with the agency.

The court said that Children's Services' decision to terminate Renaud for a three-month absence without leave that was "in flagrant violation of respondent's time and leave rules" was neither arbitrary nor capricious and sustained Children's Services decision to terminate her.

What about Renaud's claim that her leave had been approved by one of the agency's employment relations specialists? In effect, Renaud contended Children's Services was estopped from considering her absence AWOL since it had been approved by the employee relations specialist.

The Appellate Division quickly disposed of this argument. It said that "estoppel is not available against an administrative agency for the purpose of ratifying administrative error."

Accordingly, Renaud could not rely on the approval of her leave by the employee relations specialist to neutralize the agency's decision to discipline her as the employee relations specialist was not authorized to grant leave approvals on behalf of Children's Services.

18.70 Lie detector tests

Escalante v Rapid Armored Corp., NYS Sup. Ct., 12/99, Justice Weissberg

From time to time a public employee may be asked to submit to a polygraph or lie detector test. The Escalante case sets out some of the elements that are relevant in such examinations under the federal Employee Polygraph Protection Act of 1988, 29 USC 2001, [EPPA].

EPPA makes it unlawful for a private employer to require or request any employee to take or submit to a lie detector test.

There is an exemption to this prohibition, however: an employer engaged in an "ongoing investigation involving economic loss or injury to the employer's business, such as theft" may request an employee to submit to a polygraph test. To take advantage of the exemption the employer must provide the individual with a written statement indicating the basis for having the employee to submit to the lie detector test.

The case arose when a bag containing $45,000 was found to be missing from a Rapid Armored Corporation truck. Rapid asked Escalante to take a lie detector test because it felt that he should "be examined because [Escalante] had direct access to the missing bag."

When Escalante said that he first wished to talk to someone before submitting to the polygraph test, he was terminated. Escalante sued for damages, claiming:

1. His rights under EPPA were violated;

2. Defamation; and

3. Emotional distress.

Rapid counter-sued Escalante for the missing $45,000.

Justice Weissberg decided that Rapid violated the EPPA because the statement it gave Escalante when it asked him to take a lie detector test failed to include a statement adequately describing the basis of its suspicion about him.
To demonstrate a reasonable suspicion Rapid was required to do more than simply repeat the fact that Escalante had access to the stolen property. According to Justice Weissberg, "reasonable suspicion" refers to "an observable, articulable basis in fact" given the totality of the circumstances.

In contrast, said the court, access or opportunity, standing alone, does not constitute a basis for reasonable suspicion.

Holding that Rapid "did not comply with the requirements of 29 USC 2006(d)," it was not exempt from the EPPA prohibition on requesting an employee to submit to a lie detector test and on terminating the employee because of the results of the test or because of the employee's response to the request.

Justice Weissberg dismissed Escalante's defamation action, however, ruling that his complaint did not "set forth ... [Rapid's] actual defamatory words." But, said the court, even if such words or statements had been specified, they fell within Rapid's qualified privilege against a claim of defamation since they were allegedly made only to persons having a common interest in the subject matter.

Justice Weissberg also dismissed Escalante's claim for emotional distress.

18.71 Limit on questioning by hearing officer

Bretton v State of New York, 294 A.D.2d 226

An administrative hearing officer has great latitude in his or her conducting a hearing but there are limits as the Bretton decision demonstrates.

James C. Bretton, a Senior Administrative Law Judge employed by the New York State Labor Department, was suspended for 60 days without pay after being found to have exceeded his authority in conducting a hearing involving a claim for unemployment insurance benefits.

The Department disciplined Bretton after it determined that in the course of conducting the hearing he asked the claimant questions "so unnecessarily detailed and repetitive as to cross the line of appropriate questioning" and thus his actions constituted misconduct.

Bretton contended that his questions to the claimant were for the purpose of probing the credibility of her claim that she had been sexually harassed in her employment and therefore had good cause for leaving it, i.e., she was constructively discharged from her position.

The Department rejected Bretton's explanation, holding that the questions he asked "went far beyond the range of relevancy to [his] fact-finding duties" as an administrative hearing officer.

The Appellate Division, dismissing Bretton's appeal, agreed. The court said that Bretton's duties did not include conducting "a sexual harassment inquiry of the type one would find before EEOC or [the Division of Human Rights]."

18.72 Limiting the selection of arbitrators

Suffolk County PBA v Suffolk County, 273 A.D.2d 222

Suffolk County adopted a resolution[172] barring "arbitrators who have served in labor disputes involving Nassau County within the preceding three years to serve in disputes under collective bargaining agreements voluntarily submitted to arbitration or in binding arbitration."

Suffolk County PBA challenged the resolution, contending that it violated both the terms of a collective bargaining agreement [CBA] between it and the county and the Taylor Law. State Supreme Court Judge Jack J. Cannavo, agreed and ruled that the resolution was invalid.

The county appealed and the Appellate Division overturned the lower court's decision. The court said that the CBA and the Suffolk County Administrative Code, which was "substantially equivalent" to the Taylor Law, both contained binding arbitration provisions permitting Suffolk County to select arbitrators at its own discretion.

Pointing out that the county could exercise its discretion in selecting arbitrators, the Appellate Division declared that the PBA "lacks standing to assert that the resolution is arbitrary or capricious, or that the Suffolk County Legislature did not possess the authority to determine how Suffolk County should select its arbitrators."

The court also commented that in contrast to the PBA's contention, the resolution did not prohibit an arbitrator from making comparisons between Nassau and Suffolk County to determine arbitration issues.

18.73 Loss of a driver's license

Lytle v U.S. Postal Service, 257 A.D.2d 779

One of the conditions of Christopher M. Lytle's employment by the United States Postal Service was that he have a valid driver's license so that he could perform his postal duties.

Lytle was arrested for driving while intoxicated and his license was suspended. As he could not lawfully drive a motor vehicle, he was terminated from his position. Finding that he was "terminated due to misconduct," the Unemployment Insurance Appeals Board denied his application for unemployment insurance benefits.

The Appellate Division sustained the board's ruling, holding that since Lytle "engaged in a voluntary act which violated a reasonable condition of his employment, we decline to disturb the Board's decision that [Lytle's] behavior constituted disqualifying misconduct."

Another loss of a required license or permit is Ramsey v Town of Hempstead, Supreme Court, Justice Peck, Received October 22, 2002.

Ramsey served as a Town of Hempstead Building Maintenance Foreman, a position that requires the incumbent to hold a valid Class 5 driver's license.

---

[172] Resolution 377-1998

Ramsey was arrested and charged with driving while intoxicated [DWI]. This charge, by operation of law, resulted in the revocation of his license to drive a motor vehicle. Hempstead "demoted" Ramsey to the position of "Maintenance Mechanic II, a position that did not require the incumbent to hold a valid drivers license.

About three years later Ramsey "reacquired his license" but Hempstead did not restate him to his former position. Ramsey filed a grievance demanding reinstatement to his former position with back salary. The Grievance Board declined to review his complaint, holding that the proper body to consider the matter was the Civil Service Commission. Instead of appealing to the Commission, Ramsey filed an Article 78 petition seeking a court order compelling his reinstatement with back salary.[173]

Ultimately the court dismissed Ramsey petition. Judge Peck concluded that Hempstead had not imposed any penalty or punishment on Ramsey but, instead, it was his own action that was the cause of his demotion -- his being arrested for felony DWI and his subsequent loss of his license.

Presumably the Class 5 drivers license was essential to performance of the duties of a Building Maintenance Foreman in that the incumbent had to operate a motor vehicle that required the operator hold a valid Class 5 license as part of his or her normal duties. Courts have viewed employees who lack licenses as being "unqualified," in contrast to being "incompetent," to perform the duties of the position.

Common examples include the revocation of a permit to operate a motor vehicle on public roads, as was the situation in Ramsey case, the loss of an attorney's license to practice law and the expiration of a temporary permit to teach.

All that appears to be necessary in such cases is for the appointing authority to make some reasonable inquiry to determine if the employee may lawfully perform the duties of the position prior to his or her being barred from performing the duties of the position. In contrast, if the license is not required in order for the incumbent to lawfully perform the actual duties of the position, possession of such a license is not essential to employment or continuation in the position. Perhaps the leading case demonstrating this point is Matter of Martin ex rel Lekkas, 86 AD2d 712.

In the Lekkas case the court ruled that if the license is not essential to the performance of the duties of the position, the incumbent's failure to posses a valid license is not fatal to his or her continuation in service. Lekkas was a "research physician" but did not hold a valid New York State license to practice medicine. The court said that because Lekkas duties involved performing administrative duties, in contrast to practicing medicine involving patients, possession of a State license to practice medicine was not essential to the performance of his duties.

18.74 Malpractice by union's attorney

Mamorella v Derkasch, 276 A.D.2d 152

---

[173] The issue for the Commission to resolve had Ramsey appealed to it: Did Hempstead lawfully removed Ramsey from the Building Maintenance Foreman position thereby extinguishing his right to reinstatement as a matter of law?

Lucille Mamorella asked the Appellate Division "to reject as against public policy the well-established rule that an attorney who performs services for and on behalf of a union may not be held liable in malpractice to individual union members where the services at issue constitute a part of the collective bargaining process."

The Appellate Division "declined to do so," citing Peterson v Kennedy, 771 F2d 1244, in support of its ruling.

The court said that "sound policy reasons as well as established precedent compel the conclusion that attorneys who perform services for and on behalf of a union may not be held liable in malpractice to individual grievants where the services the attorneys perform constitute a part of the collective bargaining process."

18.75 Malpractice in disciplinary actions

Tinelli v Redl, CA2, 12/20/99

After being found guilty of disciplinary charges, an individual decides to sue his or her attorney, contending that the lawyer's action, or failure to act, in the disciplinary hearing or an appeal constituted malpractice. In the Tinelli case, the U.S. Circuit Court of Appeals, Second Circuit considered such a malpractice claim. The decision sets out a test for determining if is a basis for such an action against the attorney.

Joseph Tinelli was served with disciplinary charges pursuant to Section 75 of the Civil Service Law. He retained an attorney, Frank Redl, to represent him in the matter. Following a two-day hearing, the hearing officer found Tinelli guilty of three charges of "misconduct and incompetence."

The appointing authority adopted the findings of the hearing officer and imposed the recommended penalty: termination.

Tinelli appealed. According to the decision, Redl failed to take any "further action ... after the initial filing of the petition for Tinelli's appeal" in New York State Supreme Court. As a result, six months later Tinelli's "appeal expired."

Tinelli sued Redl, contending that the attorney's (1) failure to perfect the Article 78 appeal and (2) his failure to ask the court for an extension of time to perfect the appeal, constituted malpractice. He also charged that Redl's performance at the administrative disciplinary hearing constituted malpractice.

The U.S. Circuit Court of Appeals decided that whether or not Redl's handling the appeal constituted malpractice depended on whether or not Tinelli's appeal would have been successful. In other words, if Tinelli would not have won the appeal regardless of the action or inaction of his attorney, there was no basis for holding the attorney liable for malpractice.

After reviewing the record, the circuit court said that "Tinelli's appeal would not have succeeded because the hearing officer's findings of misconduct and incompetence were supported by substantial evidence and because there was no abuse of discretion in recommending Tinelli's termination under the circumstances."

The court dismissed Tinelli's claim, holding that his attorney could not be held liable for malpractice because he failed to perfect the appeal since Tinelli would not have been able to overturn either the administrative disciplinary determination or the penalty imposed.

As to Tinelli's claim that "Redl's poor performance at the administrative hearings constituted malpractice," Redl's motion for summary judgment dismissing this allegation was also granted.

18.76 Material misrepresentations

Munich v Dept. of Public Safety, 262 A.D.2d 959

A State Supreme Court judge annulled the Lackawanna Department of Public Safety's dismissal of probationary firefighter Steven J. Munich prior to his completing his probationary period.

The Appellate Division reversed the lower court's ruling, pointing out that "[i]t is axiomatic that a probationary employee may be discharged without a hearing and without a statement of the reasons for doing so provided the dismissal was not for a constitutionally impermissible purpose or in violation of statutory or decisional law."

Here, said the court, Munich's "false representations ... concerning his residence at the time of his employment with the City" provided a sufficient basis for his termination.

18.77 Misconduct off the job

Rivera v Farrell, NYS Supreme Court, Justice Stallman, April 5, 2001

From time to time an employee is served with disciplinary charges alleging that his or her off-duty conduct violated a rule or regulation of the employer. The Rivera case involves such a situation.

Rivera, a New York City Department of Sanitation [DOS] supervisor, was "moonlighting" as an income tax advisor. According to the decision, Rivera "promoted a tax-evasion scheme, informed other DOS workers about how to evade taxes, and filled out their payroll forms so that taxes would not be withheld, in return for a fee."

Served with disciplinary charges, Rivera was terminated after being found guilty of violations of the DOS Code of Conduct by his filing a W-4 tax withholding allowance certificate falsely claiming exemptions to which he was not entitled, falsely claiming "tax-exempt status" and failing to a file a tax return for the tax year 1994.
The decision indicates that Rivera had earlier pled guilty to failing to file a tax return for the tax year 1994, a misdemeanor. DOS alleged that Rivera violated Code of Conduct 3.2, by engaging in conduct

prejudicial to good order and which tends to discredit the City or Department, and Code of Conduct 4.4, filing false records or statements.

Rivera appealed, contending that dismissal "was disproportionate compared to sanctions imposed in similar cases." He claimed that (1) others similarly situated, with worse disciplinary records, received suspensions, not termination and (2) three sanitation workers who failed to pay taxes and filed false W-4 forms received 30-day suspensions.

Judge Stallman, after distinguishing the misdeeds of the other DOS workers cited by Rivera with respect to the disciplinary penalties imposed, upheld Rivera's termination. The court said that Rivera had failed to meet his burden of proving that DOS acted arbitrarily, capriciously or contrary to law. Under the circumstances, said the court, the penalty of termination "does not shock the judicial conscience; it was thus not an abuse of discretion."

As an alternative argument for overturning his termination, Rivera submitted a Certificate of Relief from Civil Disabilities he had obtained pursuant to Section 701 of the Corrections Law. Judge Stallman, after commenting that Rivera failed to demonstrate the relevance of the Certificate insofar as this case was concerned, indicated that even if it were relevant, such a certificate does not exempt a civil servant from administrative discipline.

As to a court's authority to overturn or modify an administrative disciplinary decision or a disciplinary penalty imposed on a worker, the Court of Appeals, in its March 22, 2001 decision in Kelly v Safir, 96 N.Y.2d 32, said that:

1. The courts may not modify such a determination if substantial evidence supports it; and

2. A court must uphold an administrative penalty unless it finds that it is so disproportionate to the offense as to be shocking to one's sense of fairness -- the Pell standard [Pell v Board of Education, 34 NY2d 222].

Kelly was terminated after being found guilty of unauthorized "off-duty employment" and falsifying records.

The Appellate Division ruled that the penalty imposes was "disproportionate" based on the officer's service record, notwithstanding the fact that substantial evidence supported the findings of fact.

18.78 Misuse of the employer's records

McKernan v Safir, 292 A.D.2d 281

New York City police sergeant Craig D. McKernan was served with disciplinary charges including charges alleging that he used the Police Department's computer system to run license plate inquiries for purposes other than Department business and that he did so with knowledge that the person making the inquiries was involved in criminal activities. McKernan admitted that he was guilty of the charges related to the misuse of the Department's computer system. The penalty imposed: dismissal.

Dismissing McKernan's appeal, the Appellate Division commenting that:

Notwithstanding [McKernan's] many prior awards for police work, the penalty of dismissal does not shock our sense of fairness, particularly given that [McKernan] was also found guilty of failing to safeguard his firearm while off duty, and also in view of his prior disciplinary record.

The court, however, remanded the case to the Police Department for a determination as to McKernan's entitlement to back pay in view of the fact that he was place on leave without pay for more than the thirty-day period authorized by Section 75 of the Civil Service Law.

Why was it necessary to remand this "back pay" question? Because, said the court, the Department made "no response" to McKernan's claim that the Supreme Court's determination denies him back pay to which he is entitled under Civil Service Law Section 75[3-a].

Section 75[3-a] provides for the suspension of New York City police officers without pay pending determination of disciplinary charges and the determination of the penalty to be imposed. It provides that "[p]ending the hearing and determination of charges of incompetency or misconduct, a police officer employed by the police department of the City of New York may be suspended without pay for a period not exceeding thirty days. If the officer is found guilty of the charges, the police commissioner may imposed any of the penalties set out in Sections 14-115 and 14-123 of the City's Administrative Code.

This is another demonstration of the fact that unless a collective bargaining agreement provides otherwise, an individual suspended without pay pending the determination of disciplinary charges pursuant to Section 75 of the Civil Service Law must be restored to the payroll after thirty days, regardless of whether or not he or she is permitted to return to work.

Another concern: is an employee against whom charges have been filed entitled to leave with pay in order to participate in a disciplinary hearing? Lita Stein complained to the Commissioner of Education that the Monroe-Woodbury Central School District had unlawfully withheld her salary for a number of days during which she had not performed any teaching duties because she was defending herself in a disciplinary proceeding pursuant to Section 3020-a of the Education Law.

The Commissioner said as Stein's absence was job related, pay for such absence "is open to negotiation" or, in the alternative, may be granted at the discretion of school administrators. The Commissioner, however, pointed out that continuing the accused teacher in paid status during his or her absence from work in connection with the disciplinary hearing was not mandated by Section 3020-a.[174]

In contrast, employer and employee witnesses typically will be excused from their regular work assignments to testify in a disciplinary hearing without loss of pay or charges to their leave accruals.

---

[174] Decisions of the Commissioner of Education 11544

18.79 Mitigation of damages

Rongiger v McCall, USDC, SDNY, August 29, 2000

The Rongiger case discusses a somewhat infrequently encountered aspect in litigation involving alleged violations of an employees civil rights: the duty of a dismissed employee to mitigate damages and the proof an employer must produce to show that the employee failed to mitigate, or attempt to mitigate, his or her damages following the termination.

George P. Rongiger sued State Comptroller H. Carl McCall for damages, claiming that McCall had terminated him in retaliation for his exercising his right to free speech in violation of his civil rights. In this phase of the litigation the major issue concerned the question an individual's duty to mitigate damages.

Rongiger, who had been serving in the Office of the State Deputy Comptroller for the City of New York, a division of the Office of the State Comptroller, alleged that he was terminated after making "politically embarrassing statements in deposition testimony" concerning correspondence between McCall and then-Mayor David Dinkins in connection with New York City's efforts to prevent a downgrading of its bond rating.

Did Rongiger have a duty to "mitigate damages" by seeking substitute employment following his dismissal? In a word, yes! As Federal District Court Justice Sweet noted, citing Dailey v Societe Generale, 108 F3d 451, "... an employee who has been subject to discriminatory discharge is required to mitigate his damages."

In Greenway v Buffalo Hilton Hotel, 143 F3d 47, the Second Circuit said that this duty means that the discharged employee "'must use reasonable diligence in finding other suitable employment,' which need not be comparable to [his] previous positions."

Since the employer charged with discrimination is required to prove any failure on the part of the employee to mitigate damages, McCall retained Dr. Charles L. Sodikoff as an expert on the issue of mitigation and asked him to prepare a report as to his findings.

Sodikoff's report set out his opinion concerning the length of time it should have taken Rongiger to find a comparably paying job or to build a profitable consulting practice, and the reasonableness of Rongiger's job search.

Sodikoff concluded that Rongiger should have obtained comparable work within six to ten months of his termination and that he should have built a consulting practice sufficient to replace his compensation in 1994 within two years of his termination. Rongiger challenged the admission of Sodikoff's report.

After noting that such expert testimony was relevant, Justice Sweet discussed the methods used by Sodikoff in preparing his report and his conclusion. Based on his evaluation of the procedures used by Sodikoff Justice Sweet granted part of Rongiger's motion to exclude expert testimony.

In contrast, there seems to be no duty on the part of individual who has been terminated after being found guilty following disciplinary action taken pursuant to Section 75 of the Civil Service Law to mitigate his or her damages.

Civil Service Law Sections 76 and 77, which, respectively, deal with reinstatement by a Civil Service Commission or a court following a successful appeal of as Section 75 dismissal and the annulment of the termination, provide that an employee who is reinstated is to receive the salary or compensation he or she would have been entitled by law to have received in his or her position for the period of removal including any prior period of suspension without pay, less the amount of any unemployment insurance benefits he may have received during such period.

This suggests that mitigation is not a factor as even if the individual obtains employment after being discharged, any monies earned thereby would not be considered in determining the amount of compensation to be paid as "back salary" upon reinstatement -- only unemployment insurance benefits are to be considered in determining the back salary due upon reinstatement.

Significantly, Sections 76 and 77 of the Civil Service Law originally provided for an adjustment in consideration of earnings received from other sources, thereby implying a duty to "mitigate damages." Chapter 710 of the Law of 1984 deleted the phrase "compensation which he may have earned in any other employment or occupation...." from the law.

18.80 Mitigation of the recommended penalty

Winters v Lakeland CSD, 295 A.D.2d 355, motion to appeal granted, 98 N.Y.2d 614 but no further action reported.

Lakeland Central School District Head Custodian Hugh Winters was found guilty of a number of charges alleging misconduct, incompetence, and insubordination including Winters' "removing and photocopying a document from the school principal's desk, and distributing the document to another employee of the Lakeland Central School District."

Winters appealed, contending that the penalty of dismissal was too harsh. The Appellate Division agreed, ruling that "that, under the particular circumstances of this case, the penalty of termination was so disproportionate to the offense as to be shocking to one's sense of fairness," citing the Pell Doctrine.[175] The court said that neither the hearing officer nor the school district gave "sufficient weight to certain mitigating factors, such as [Winter's] 15-year history of working for the School District without incident."

The Appellate Division returned the matter to the school district for the purpose of its "imposition of a penalty other than termination."

Clearly an employee's personnel history may be considered in determining the disciplinary penalty to be imposed once the employee has been found guilty of one or more charges of misconduct. In Bigelow v Village of Gouverneur, 63 NY2d 470, the Court of Appeals held that an employee's

---

[175] Pell v Board of Education, 34 NY2d 222

personnel records may be considered when the setting a disciplinary penalty, provided the appointing authority has complied with two tests set out by the court.

The two tests set out in Bigelow are as follows:

1. The employee must be advised that his or her personnel record will be considered in setting the penalty to be imposed; and

2. The employee must be given an opportunity to submit a written response to any adverse material contained in the record or offer "mitigating circumstances."

Reading the Bigelow and Winters decisions in concert, it appears that:

1. It is a matter of discretion on the part of the appointing authority whether or not to consider an employee personnel record in setting a disciplinary penalty in cases where the charges for which the employee has been found guilty would not, standing alone, justify imposing the proposed penalty; and

2. The appointing authority should review the individual's personnel record to determine if there are any mitigating factors that should be considered in determining the disciplinary penalty to be imposed, particularly in cases where "employee capital punishment" -- dismissal -- is contemplated.

18.81 Name-clearing hearings

Aquilone v City of New York, 262 A.D.2d 13

A public employee who has been terminated from his or her position may be entitled to a name-clearing hearing if the reasons for his or her separation have been made public by the employer and those reasons tend to "stigmatize" the individual.

The Aquilone case addresses whether a retiree who continues to work as a consultant to the employer is entitled to a name-clearing hearing if his or her behavior prior to retirement is criticized in an investigatory report, putting his or her consulting relationship in jeopardy.

Edward Aquilone, a former Executive Director of Personnel for the New York City Board of Education, won a court order in state Supreme Court directing the school board to hold a name-clearing hearing, only to have the order vacated by the Appellate Division.

Aquilone retired from his position in 1989. Two years later, the Deputy Commissioner of Investigation issued a report that concluded that Aquilone had participated in a cover-up of sexual misconduct involving a fellow employee. The report said that Aquilone appointed friends of the employee to a hearing panel to guarantee a result favorable to the accused and "ensure the proceeding's secrecy". He neglected to give a record of the hearing to the Board's Office of Personnel Security or log the file into that office's computer system.

Noting that Aquilone had already retired, the deputy commissioner's report suggested that suspension or termination of [Aquilone] occasional consulting jobs with the board would constitute "appropriate disciplinary action."

A four-judge panel of the Appellate Division, 1st Department, ruled that because Aquilone had been retired for two years when the stigmatizing allegations were made, and he was not fired, suspended or demoted, he is not entitled to a name-clearing hearing.

The court ruled that a name-clearing hearing was not appropriate because such a hearing "is a remedy for the deprivation of a person's due process right when an employee is terminated along with a contemporaneous public announcement of stigmatizing factors, including illegality, dishonesty, immorality, or a serious denigration of the employee's competence," citing Donato v Plainview-Old Bethpage School District, 96 F3d 623, cert. denied 519 US 1150.

In addition, the Appellate Division commented that defamation standing alone does not constitute a deprivation of a liberty interest protected by the due process clause -- some "stigma plus" must be shown before it rises to the level where the individual's constitutional rights may have been adversely affected.

The court also cited Martz v Inc. Vill. Of Valley Stream, 22 F3d 26, in which the Second Circuit U.S. Court of Appeals said: "in the context of defamation involving a government employee, defamation ... is not a deprivation of a liberty interest unless it occurs in the course of dismissal or refusal to rehire the individual as a government employee or during termination or alteration of some other legal right or status ... the 'plus' is not only significant damage to a person's employment opportunities, but dismissal from a government job or deprivation of some other legal right or status."

In addition, the court pointed out that reports such as that issued by the deputy commissioner are protected by an "absolute privilege," referring to the Court of Appeals' ruling in Ward Telecommunications and Computer Systems Inc. v State of New York, 42 NY2d 289.

In the Ward case, the Court of Appeals -- New York State's highest court -- ruled that "official ordered reports issued on behalf of the State Comptroller by the Division of Audit and Accounts are subject to an absolute privilege in any action for defamation based on the content of such reports."

The rationale for this, said the court, was that the public's interest demands that there be no legal or practical constraint placed on the content of the Comptroller's reports or deterrent to their availability for public scrutiny.

Applying this rationale to Aquilone's situation, the Appellate Division said that "the same rule must apply to the results of an official investigation into cover-up of a sex crime committed by a public employee."

18.82 Negotiated disciplinary procedures

Fortune v Div. of State Police, 293 A.D.2d 154

The issue in the Fortune case: May a collective bargaining disciplinary procedure supersede statutory disciplinary due process requirements such as those set out in Section 75 of the Civil Service Law or Section 3020-a of the Education Law? In a word: yes!

The Appellate Division affirmed the principle that an alternative disciplinary procedure negotiated pursuant to the Taylor Law constitutes collateral estoppel to any claim by an employee that he or she is entitled to any disciplinary due process rights otherwise available to an individual under State law.

Roger A. Fortune was given a letter of censure by the Superintendent of State Police after being found to have discharged his weapon and thus "endangered the public and fellow officers" contrary to State Police procedures.

Fortune sued, contending that the State Police regulations violated Section 75 of the Civil Service Law insofar as they permitted the sanction of censure to be imposed on a Trooper without complying with administrative due process requirements.

The Appellate Division rejected Fortune's argument, noting that "the applicable collective bargaining agreement between the union representing [Fortune] and the State provides that management may 'discipline or discharge members in accordance with the Rules and Regulations of the Division.'"[176]

The decision points out that "Both State and Federal Courts have recognized that constitutional protections afforded public employees, including statutory due process rights, may be waived by unions acting on their behalf through entering into collective bargaining agreements with public employers," citing the landmark decision by the Court of Appeals in Antinore v State of New York, 40 NY2d 921.

As the Police Benevolent Association of the New York State Troopers and the Division of State Police had negotiated an alternate disciplinary procedure in lieu of Section 75, Fortune conceded that he was not entitled to rely on the provisions of Section 75 with respect to any alleged violation of his statutory right to administrative due process.

Here the State Police regulations do not provide for a hearing with respect to issuing a letter of censure by the Superintendent. Accordingly, Fortune did not have any right to a pre-determination hearing under the terms of the collective bargaining agreement in cases where the only penalty imposed was a letter of censure.

In addition, the Appellate Division noted that Supreme Court had dismissed Fortune's petition on the merits, finding that the Superintendent's had a rational basis and his action was neither not arbitrary nor capricious. Further, said the court, Fortune was not denied due process as he was permitted to refute the allegations made against him by submitting response letters to be placed in his file.

---

[176] Executive Law Section 215 [3] provides that the Superintendent may establish rules and regulations for the discipline and control of the State Police and provides that permanent State Police appointees may be removed by Superintendent only after a hearing.

18.83 Negotiating disciplinary procedures

Mt. Vernon v PERB, 289 A.D.2d 674, motion for leave to appeal denied, 97 N.Y.2d 613

In considering the appeal of the City of Mt. Vernon, the Appellate Division ruled that under certain circumstances negotiating a contract disciplinary procedure is not a mandatory subject of collective bargaining under the Taylor Law.

Mt. Vernon had appealed a PERB determination that held that its disciplinary procedures were a mandatory subject of collective bargaining in response to the City's claim that its police officers union had submitted a number of nonmandatory or prohibited subjects of collective bargaining for compulsory interest arbitration, one of which involved disciplinary procedures.

The City's argument: Its 1922 City Charter established disciplinary procedures for its police officers and the continuation of such procedures is protected by Civil Service Law Section 76(4). Accordingly, the City said could not be forced to negotiate its disciplinary procedure on the theory that it was a term or condition of employment.

Supreme Court agreed, determining that PERB's decision was "irrational, unreasonable and legally impermissible" and granted the City's motion.

PERB appealed contending that because Section 76(4) was passed years before the Taylor Law, it "could not reasonably be read to reflect 'any intent on the part of the Legislature to exclude or preclude bargaining as to discipline'".

Section 76(4), in pertinent part, provides as follows: Nothing contained in section seventy-five or seventy-six of this chapter shall be construed to repeal or modify any general, special or local law or charter provision relating to the removal or suspension of officers or employees in the competitive class of the civil service of the state or any civil division. Such sections may be supplemented, modified or replaced by agreements negotiated between the state and an employee organization pursuant to article fourteen of this chapter.

The Appellate Division said that although the Taylor Law requires good faith bargaining concerning all terms and conditions of employment which have been held to be a mandatory subject of collective bargaining, here the police officer discipline procedures contained in the City's Charter enacted in 1922 are specifically protected from repeal or modification by Section 76(4).

Affirming the lower court's ruling, the Appellate Division held that under these circumstances, the disciplinary procedures applicable to Mt. Vernon's police officers are not mandatory subjects of negotiation.

18.84 Notice of a final administrative determination

City of New York v DeCosta, 289 A.D.2d 144, affirmed, 95 N.Y.2d 273

The New York City Board of Collective Bargaining [OCB] issued its "final determination." It later sent a "courtesy copy of the decision to the City's Office of Labor Relations [OLR].

The City attempted to appeal the determination. OCB asked a State Supreme Court justice to dismiss the appeal, contending that its appeal was untimely based on the date it initially delivered its ruling to the City. The City, on the other hand, argued that it had filed a timely appeal based on the date OLR had received its "courtesy copy."

The Appellate Division affirmed a lower court's determination that the City's appeal was, in fact, timely. Why? Because, said the court, OCB had created an ambiguity as to the date on which its determination became final and binding. The court's rationale: if a party creates an ambiguity, the ambiguity should be resolved against the party creating it -- here OCB.

According to the decision, OCB had sent OLR a courtesy copy of the decision after the initial copy of the decision had been delivered to the City in response to OLR's asking it if the initial decision "contained the final version of a dissent submitted by two members of the Board."

Holding that granting OCB's motion to dismiss the City's appeal under the facts in this case would deny the City "its day in court," the Appellate Division affirmed the Supreme Court's ruling that the statutory period for filing the appeal did not begin to run until the second decision had been delivered to OLR.

The general rule in such cases is that the statute of limitations to appeal an administrative determination begins to run when notice of the final administrative action or decision is received by the party or, if the party is represented by an attorney, the party's attorney.[177]

The basic rule:

1. If an employee is represented by an attorney, the administrative body may send a copy of the determination to the employee but it must serve the attorney to begin the running of the statute of limitations.

2. If the employee is represented by a person who is not an attorney, the administrative body may send a copy to the representative but it must serve the employee to start the statute of limitations running.

In contrast, a request for reconsideration does not serve to extend the period during which a party can file a timely appeal challenging the administrative action or decision.

This point is illustrated in the Cardo case.[178] In Cardo one of the issues concerned the question of the timely filing of an appeal. The court said that although Cardo asked his employer to "reconsider" its

---

[177] Delivery of a final administrative decision only to the employee's union does not count with respect to the commencement of the running of the statute of limitations. In Weeks v State of New York, 198 AD2d 615, the court held that the statute of limitations begins to run when the decision is served on the employee, not from the date on which the union received its copy.

administrative decision, such a request "did not extend the period \within which the [Article 78] proceeding must be commenced."

In contrast to the legal effect of an individual merely submitting a "request for reconsideration," suppose the administrative body actually agrees to reconsider the matter and issue a new determination. In such a situation the statute of limitations will begin running from the date of the new "final determination." This is the case even if the new "final determination" confirms the original administrative decision.[179]

In any event, at least one court has ruled that the final administrative action must be reduced to writing in order to start the statute of limitations running.

In McCoy v San Francisco, CA9, 92-16319, a federal circuit court of appeals ruled that a public employee's civil rights suit against his employer accrued when the appointing authority issued a written statement suspending him from work rather than from the date of a hearing held earlier at which time McCoy was orally advised that he was suspended from his position.

In contrast, in another case, Mavica v New York City Transit Authority, 289 A.D.2d 86, the court rejected an argument based on an alleged ambiguity created by a collective bargaining agreement and the employer's regulations.

Here the court rejected John Mavica's claim that a provision in his union's collective bargaining agreement with Transit Authority explicitly implementing a disciplinary grievance arbitration procedure in lieu of any other disciplinary procedure that may have previously applied to an employee covered by this Agreement, including, and not limited to, the procedure specified in Sections 75 and 76 of the Civil Service Law, was rendered ambiguous by other provisions of the same collective bargaining agreement and by the Authority's regulations.

Mavica filed an Article 78 petition seeking to have the Authority's action terminating his employment declared null and void.

Here, said the court, the proper way to challenge the Authority's dismissing Mavica from his position following a disciplinary arbitration upholding the Authority's determination was for Mavica to file a motion to vacate the arbitration award pursuant to Article 75 of the Civil Practice Law and Rules, suggesting that the court did not find any ambiguity created by the terms set out in the collective bargaining agreement or in the Authority's rules.

18.85 Notice of claim

Mennella v Uniondale UFSD, Supreme Court, Oct. 2000

---

[178] Cardo v Sielaff, 588 NYS2d 282

[179] Presumably the court did not view OLR's action as a "request for reconsideration." The court, however, may have considered the contents of the "courtesy copy" sent to OLR in response to its inquiry to be OCB's final determination.

As a general rule, Section 3813 of the Education Law requires that in order to sue a school district the plaintiff must file a timely "notice of claim" if he or she plans or expects to sue the district. Such notices are required in order to sue a school district concerning some types of claims related to or involving personnel decisions.

The Mennella case, for example, concerned the termination of a probationary employee and turned on whether the court should excuse a late filing of such a claim pursuant to Section 3813(2-a) of the Education Law.

In July 1998 Vincenza Mennella accepted the position as Dean of Students at Uniondale High School effective September 1, 1998. Her appointment was subject to a three-year probationary period. On May 4, 1999, the Uniondale School Board voted to terminate her employment.

Mennella appealed her termination to the Commissioner of Education pursuant to Section 310 of the Education Law. On November 4, 1999, the Commissioner dismissed her appeal.[180] He found that Mennella "failed to establish that [the district] had violated any statutory proscriptions and that [Mennella] had not articulated any constitutional violations by same."

Mennella did not appeal the Commissioner's decision. She did, however, file a petition in State supreme court seeking permission to submit a late "Section 3813 Notice of Claim" in an effort to sue the district for alleged "discrimination and fraudulent inducement."

The court rejected her application, commenting: "the ability to extend the time to serve a notice of claim is governed by Education Law Section 3813(2-a). Section 3813(2-a) provides that the application late filing must be made within the time for commencing an action and that the school district, its attorney, insurance carrier or agent have knowledge of the essential facts of the claim."

The reasons for the court's rejection of Mennella's petition:

1. Mennella did not show "a reasonable excuse for failing to serve a timely notice of claim;"

2. The district did not have specific knowledge of the essential facts underlying her "discrimination and fraudulent inducement" claims.

3. Allowing the late notice of claim in order to pursue these complaints would substantially prejudice the district.

It appears that Mennella did not allege "denial of tenure." Her Section 3813 Notice of Claim only set out allegations of discrimination and "fraudulent inducement" with respect to her challenging her termination by the district during her probationary period.

Significantly, the courts have held that claims involving "denial of tenure" constitute an exception to the general rule that unless excused in accordance with the provisions of Section 3813(2-a), the filing of a timely Section 3813 notice is essential to a party's being able to sue a school district.

---

[180] Matter of Mennella, 21 Ed Dept Rep 721

For example, in Sephton v Board of Education of the City of New York, 99 AD2d 509, the Appellate Division ruled that "the 'tenure rights' of teachers are ... considered a matter in the public interest and therefore Section 3813 is not applicable to cases seeking to enforce such rights."

In contrast, in Union Endicott CSD v PERB, the Appellate Division, Third Department decided that the union's failure to file a timely notice of claim with a school district as mandated by Section 3813(1) barred it from prosecuting improper practice charges filed against the district with PERB.

In addition, PERB has dismissed improper practice charges filed by a union on the grounds that it failed to filed a notice of claim with the district as required by 3813(1) of the Education Law in cases such as Watertown Education Association and Watertown City Schools, 28 PERB 3033.

However, not every alleged violation of a provision set out in a Taylor Law agreement is subject to the provisions of Section 3813 and a number of exceptions have been noted by courts.

For example, in CSEA v Lakeland Central School District, the Appellate Division rejected the Lakeland's argument that CSEA's action for damages "for breach of a collective bargaining agreement" should be dismissed because CSEA had not complied with the "notice of claim" requirements set out in Section 3813(1).

The Court decided that the collective bargaining agreement entered into by the parties contained detailed grievance procedures and this constituted a waiver of having to comply compliance with that requirement" by the district.

In contrast, in Arthur Stevens v McGraw Central School District, 261 A.D.2d 698, the Appellate Division, Third Department, ruled that a school district bus driver's failure to comply with Section 3813 was fatal to his challenging his dismissal from his position following a disciplinary hearing pursuant to Section 75 of the Civil Service Law.

Insofar as the mandates of Section 3813 are concerned, in both the Union Endicott and Stevens cases the courts appear to have based its decisions on the fact that the plaintiffs sought to vindicate a "private interest" rather than what the court in Sephton characterized as a "public interest."

The lessons here: lawsuits based on what the courts determine involve efforts to vindicate a "private interest" such as the denial of a benefit resulting from an alleged violation of a provision set out in a Taylor Law agreement or a penalty imposed following a disciplinary action must comply with the procedural requirements set out in Section 3813 unless there is clear evidence that the school district has waived its right to such notice as exemplified by the Lakeland decision.[181]

The court also elected to address the merits of Mennella's complaints, commenting as follows:

1. "Fraudulent inducement:" The court said that Mennella served as an at-will employee and her employment was not guaranteed, despite any oral comments to the contrary. "Simply put, [Mennella]

---

[181] While exceptions to the "notice of claim" requirement exist, it would seem prudent for an aggrieved party to file a timely notice of claim with a school district as set out in Section 3813(1) rather than try to persuade a court that it was not necessary to do so in a particular situation at some later date.

left her tenured position for a better one in Uniondale, knowing full well that she was at risk of termination as a non-tenured employee." Thus, the court concluded, there was "no merit to a claim of fraudulent inducement."

2. Unlawful discrimination: The court said that "[f]or racist comments, slurs, and jokes to constitute a hostile environment, there must be 'more than a few isolated incidents of racial enmity,' meaning that '[i]nstead of sporadic slurs, there must be a steady barrage of opprobrious racial comments,'" According to the court, "Mennella alleged two isolated incidents of remarks, one of which is unclear as to any discriminatory motive." In any event, "a racially neutral explanation for [the district's] acts negates recovery." Thus, the court concluded, Mennella's discrimination complaint "appears to be meritless as well."

18.86 Off-duty misconduct

Mahadio v Kerik, 298 A.D.2d 305

New York City police officer Alexander Mahadio was served with disciplinary charges that alleged that while he was off-duty, he "wrongfully and without just cause displayed his weapon while making a threatening remark to a civilian" ... and that he addressed persons ... in an ethnically offensive manner.

Found guilty, Police Commissioner Bernard B. Kerik imposed the penalty of a forfeiture of 25 vacation days. Mahadio appealed, only to have the Appellate Division unanimously confirmed the Commissioner's determination.

The court said that substantial evidence supported the Commissioner's decision and that there was no basis to disturb his determination concerning the credibility of the witnesses testifying. As to the penalty imposed, the Appellate Division said that the forfeiture of 25 days of leave did not shock its sense of fairness, citing Kelly v Safir, 96 NY2d 32.

Another off-duty misconduct case is Smith v Kerik, 292 A.D.2d 223. Here the issue involved whether an employee's off-duty misconduct could be the basis for disciplinary charges being filed against the employee and if found guilty, support the imposition of the penalty of dismissal? This was the issue raised before the Appellate Division when New York City Police Commissioner Bernard Kerick fired detective Robert Smith after he found Smith was guilty of off-duty misconduct.

Smith was charged with striking an individual with his weapon without justification while he was engaged in unauthorized off-duty employment as a security guard at a nightclub.

The Commissioner also determined that Smith subsequently encouraged fellow detectives to arrest the individual he had struck without informing them of the immanency of Smith's criminal trial in which the individual was to testify against him.

Finding that there was substantial evidence to support the Commissioner's determination, the Appellate Division said that "the penalty of dismissal does not shock our sense of fairness," citing Kelly v Safir, 96 NY2d 32, in support of its ruling.

Losada v Safir, 278 A.D.2d 59, is yet another case in which the court considered disciplinary action flowing for alleged off-duty misconduct.

The Appellate Division sustained the disciplinary termination of New York City police officer Fernando Losada based on a finding that Losada, while off-duty, was in a traffic-related altercation during which he "wrongfully punched and kicked the driver of the other vehicle, causing him physical injury."

Another element: Losada was found guilty of filing a criminal complaint regarding the incident "that falsely portrayed the other driver as the aggressor, which resulted in the other driver being arrested and placed in detention." The court said that the penalty of dismissal does not shock its sense of fairness, particularly given that this was Losada's second adjudication of violent misconduct within 16 months.

18.87 Official misconduct

Mieles v Safir, 272 A.D.2d 199

The Mieles case provides an example of the application of the exception to statute of limitations set out in Section 75.4 of the Civil Service Law. Section 75.4 provides that the relevant statute of limitations for bringing disciplinary action does not apply "where the incompetency or misconduct" alleged would "if proved in a court of appropriate jurisdiction constitute a crime."

Manuel Mieles, a New York City police officer, was dismissed from his position after being found guilty of having "used false pretenses to trick the owner of a broken-down vehicle" into giving him the title to the vehicle. Mieles then moved the vehicle from the street and sold it to a salvage company.

The department charged Mieles with "unauthorized exercise of [his] official functions", in violation of Section 104-01, page 3, paragraph 4 of the Police Department Patrol Guide's prohibition against "conduct prejudicial to good order, efficiency or discipline of the department."

Mieles appealed his termination. One of the grounds he contended supported vacating the disciplinary action was that the charges filed against him were untimely as they were "barred by the 18-month Statute of Limitations in Civil Service Law Section 75(4)." The Appellate Division, First Department dismissed Mieles' appeal.

The court said that "[t]here is no merit to [Mieles'] argument" that the charges filed against him were barred by Section 75.4's 18-month Statute of Limitations. As the court explained, "the misconduct charged also constituted the crime of official misconduct" under Section 195.00[1] of the Penal Law.

Accordingly, Mieles was charged with, and found guilty of, acts of misconduct which were "expressly excluded from the time bar of section 75(4)...."

18.88 Patronage dismissals

Bavaro and Hogan v Pataki, CA2, 96-9181; 97-7159, Nov. 1998

The Bavaro and Hogan v. Pataki case involved attorneys removed from their respective exempt class positions in the New York State Health Department following the election of Governor Pataki in 1994. There was no question that both were terminated because of their political affiliation.

The decision by the Second Circuit U.S. Court of Appeals is important as it sets out the various elements that the Second Circuit [New York] considers when deciding if an individual can claim First Amendment protection if he or she is terminated from the public service because of political affiliation, or the lack of such political affiliation.

Ralph Bavaro and Elizabeth Hogan contended that their respective terminations because of their political affiliation violated their First Amendment rights, which protected them from dismissal based on their political affiliation. The Circuit Court affirmed a district court's ruling that "the incumbents of the positions of Associate and Assistant Counsel are not entitled to First Amendment protection against patronage dismissals."

There are limitations on political tests for continuing in the public service however. In Elrod v Burns, 427 US 347, the U.S. Supreme Court concluded that patronage dismissals may infringe upon government employees' First Amendment rights to political belief and association. However, the High Court also noted that a newly elected administration may expect political loyalty among at least some of its employees "to the end that representative government not be undercut by tactics obstructing the implementation of policies of the new administration, policies presumably sanctioned by the electorate."

Subsequently the High Court reaffirmed that patronage dismissals may contravene the First Amendment in Branti v. Finkel [445 U.S. 507]. That case involved a deputy public defender employed by a political subdivision of New York. The test to be applied: has the appointing authority demonstrated that party affiliation is an appropriate requirement for the effective performance of the public office involved?

In Branti the Supreme Court noted that political affiliation is not always relevant even to the job of a policymaker. As an example, the Branti decision notes that the coach of a state university's football team [typically a position in the unclassified service] formulates policy, "but no one could seriously claim that Republicans make better coaches than Democrats, or vice versa...."

The Second Circuit said that it understood Branti as standing for the proposition that "political affiliation is an appropriate [job] requirement when there is a rational connection between shared ideology and job performance" and thus the courts must look to the "inherent duties of the position" rather than the actual duties performed by the employee in a particular case. Accordingly, it is the official job description that controls, not the nature of the actual assignment or responsibilities of the individual.[182]

In determining whether a "rational connection" exists between political affiliation and performance of the inherent duties of a position, the court said that it considers a number of factors, including the following:

1. Is the position exempt from civil service protection [subject to certain exceptions, i.e., veterans who served in time of war and exempt volunteer firefighters who may be subject to the provisions of Section 75 of the Civil Service Law]?

2. Is some technical competence or expertise required to satisfactorily perform the duties of the position?

3. Does the individual supervise the work of others? and

4. Is the incumbent "empowered to act and speak on behalf of a policymaker, especially an elected official"?

The court found that the positions held by Bavaro and Hogan (1) were in the exempt class; (2) required Bavaro, a supervisor, and Hogan, who was not a supervisor, to have "technical competence and expertise;" and (3) that they were not empowered to speak directly on behalf of an elected official. These findings, however, did not end the court's inquiry.

The Circuit Court then found that Bavaro and Hogan represented the State in the performance of their duties, thereby reflecting the views of policymakers. This, the Circuit Court concluded, meant that Bavaro and Hogan were inherently involved in matters of policy extending "well beyond mere ministerial or technical duties."

The court distinguished the role of Bavaro and Hogan from that of Branti. Branti, a deputy public defender, said the court, represented individuals accused of crimes -- not his employer. Accordingly, in a Branti situation the employee's duty of loyalty is to the individual accused of a crime rather than to his or her employer - the Office of the Public Defender and there is no employer "policy issue" involved.

According to the ruling, Bavaro's and Hogan's "inherent duties" indicated a "rational connection between shared ideology and job performance," so that "political affiliation is an appropriate [job] requirement" of these positions. Such was not the case in Branti, where political affiliation was not deemed a consideration to an individual's continuation in public service although the position satisfied the four threshold elements set out by the Circuit Court.

---

[182] In September 1982 the Health Department justified its seeking jurisdictional re-classification of these titles to exempt status on the grounds that the incumbents "must be able to reflect the views of the Counsel and the [Health] Commissioner in oral appearances . . . and demonstrate the utmost discretion in handling these cases. To insure that the Commissioner's views are appropriately reflected, the Agency needs maximum flexibility in selection, retention and remuneration.

18.89 Payment for unused leave credits

Gratto v Ausable Valley CSD, 271 A.D.2d 175

The Gratto case explores the obligation of the employer to pay an individual for his or her unused vacation credits upon his or her involuntary termination. The general rule set out by the Appellate Division, Third Department in dealing with claims for such payment: use it or lose it!

Ausable Valley CSD Superintendent John Gratto's employment contract with the school district provided that Gratto was to receive 25 paid vacation days a year, subject to a maximum accumulation of 45 days of vacation credit. The contract, however, was silent with respect to making any cash payment for any unused vacation time upon the termination of Gratto's employment.

When Gratto was involuntarily terminated from his position he claimed that he was entitled to payment for his unused vacation credits upon his separation as he had "earned it." The district disagreed and refused to pay him for his unused leave credits.

The absence of a statement providing for the cash liquidation of leave credits proved to be one of a number of critical elements in the Appellate Division's resolution of his appeal from a Supreme Court judge's summarily dismissing his complaint.

The Appellate Division said that "[i]n the absence of a statutory or contractual basis for recovery, a public employee may not recover the monetary value of unused vacation time that has accrued as of the date of termination."

Gratto attempted to avoid this general rule by contending that a public employee who is involuntarily terminated, is "constitutionally entitled to receive the cash value of unused vacation days," citing a Fourth Department decision, Clift v City of Syracuse, 45 AD2d 596 in support of his theory.

In Clift, the Fourth Department said that if the employer "discharges an employee without having either given him the opportunity to use the vacation he has earned, or in the alternative, compensating him with its monetary value, it transgresses the due process requirements of both the New York State and United States Constitutions and it should not be permitted to do so."

The Third Department, however, decided that Clift has never been interpreted as meaning that a public employee who is involuntarily discharged is automatically entitled to a cash payment for his or her unused vacation. Rather, it viewed the holding as applying only where there are circumstances requiring "special considerations."

The "special circumstances" in Clift: the employee contended that he agreed to defer using his vacation credits based on promises made by his superior and was then involuntarily dismissed. Similarly in May v Ballston Spa CSD, 170 AD2 920, the Third Department ruled in favor of the employee upon its finding that the employee "was induced to forego vacation" when his superiors assured him that he would be paid for his unused leave notwithstanding his involuntary separation as a result of a layoff.

The Appellate Division rejected Gratto's claim that his "work responsibilities" prevented him from using all of his leave credits for vacations. What was missing in Gratto's situation? Evidence that a "superior or supervisor induced him to forego any vacation time during that year for any reason or that he refrained from using vacation time the entire year because of noncontractual duties."

The Appellate Division affirmed the lower court's ruling, holding that under the circumstances, Gratto was not entitled to the cash value of his 45 days of unused vacation when he was involuntarily separated.

This is similar to the general rule with respect to State workers subject to the State Civil Service Commission's Attendance Rules for the Classified Service, 4 NYCRR 30.1. Section 30.1 states that an employee who is removed from State service as a result of disciplinary action, or who resigns after charges of incompetency or misconduct have been served, is not entitled to compensation for vacation credits.

What about a "voluntary separation," i.e., the State employee is not involved in a disciplinary action when he or she resigns or retires? Section 30.1 provides that "an appointing authority may require, as a condition for such payment" that it be given at least two weeks notice prior to the last day of work.

18.90 Payroll decertification

North Greenbush v Dir. of Pers.,'l., Supreme Court, 9/9/99

Section 100 of the Civil Service Law requires the responsible civil service commission to periodically certify the payroll of all of the public entities under its jurisdiction.

The responsible commission is required to examine the agency's payroll at least once each year "to determine that all persons employed in such department, agency or authority are employed in accordance with law." Section 101 of the Civil Service Law makes it a misdemeanor to pay an individual whom the responsible commission has refused to certify on the payroll.

On May 24, 1999 Rensselaer County Bureau of Personnel Director Christian K. Mahoney wrote to the Town of North Greenbush setting "52 conditions" that the Town had to meet in order for its payroll to be certified. The Town complied with 45 of these conditions. It, however, challenged Mahoney's determination that seven police officers employed by the Town were not eligible to remain on the payroll.

According to Justice James B. Canfield's decision, "these issues [involving the police officers] have been simmering for years in some cases." He noted that North Greenbush and the affected police officers "merely ignored them" until the May 24, 1999 letter rather than "promptly challenge them administratively."

Essentially, said the court, North Greenbush "failed to demonstrate that it was in compliance [with the Civil Service Law] or that either it or the officers pursued their administrative remedies prior to May 24, 1999."

Ruling that North Greenbush failed to meet it burden of proving that Mahoney's efforts "to enforce the civil service law by refusing to certify the payroll at this time is arbitrary, capricious or illegal," Justice Canfield dismissed its petition.[183]

18.91 Personnel records used in setting penalty

Levy v Workers' Comp. Board, 292 A.D.2d 388, appeal dismissed, 98 N.Y.2d 692

In the course of conducting a hearing, Workers' Compensation Board [WCB] Administrative Law Judge Herbert L. Levy told a claimant's attorney to "shut up."

This resulted in disciplinary charges being filed against Levy alleging "misconduct and/or incompetence." The Board charged Levy with violating the Board's policy "that Board employees maintain a civil, courteous, respectful and professional attitude and practice." The Board offered to settle the disciplinary action if Levy accepted a ten-day suspension from work without pay.

Levy rejected the proposed settlement and his disciplinary grievance was submitted to arbitration in accordance with the terms of a collective bargaining agreement [CBA].

Arbitrator Max M. Doner found Levy guilty of misconduct and/or incompetence in the performance of his duties as law judge. The penalty imposed: a fine of $2,400, which award was confirmed by a State Supreme Court Justice Reynold N. Mason.

The Appellate Division, Second Department, sustained Justice Mason's ruling, commenting that the arbitrator found that Levy's behavior violated the WCB's policy and the Code of Judicial Conduct for Administrative Law Judges and that his award was neither irrational, violative of a strong public policy, nor in excess of his authority as the arbitrator.

The court also said that "[c]onsideration of other instances of misconduct in [Levy's] employment record does not provide grounds for vacatur," ruling that "the arbitrator properly considered [Levy's] entire record of employment in determining a penalty."

In Bigelow v Village of Gouverneur, 63 NY2d 470, the Court of Appeals said that if an employee is found guilty of disciplinary charges, the employee's personnel history could be used to determine the appropriate disciplinary penalty to be imposed if:

1. The individual is advised that his or her personnel records would be considered in setting the penalty to be imposed; and

2. The employee is given an opportunity to submit a written response to any material included in his or her personnel file or be allowed to submit an explanation setting out "mitigating circumstances."

---

[183] Council 82, the collective bargaining representative of the seven officers, was permitted to intervene on their behalf in this action over the county's objection, however. Notwithstanding this, Justice Canfield cautioned the town that it should "prepare contingency plans for alternative law enforcement services in the event that a determination is rendered against one or more of the [Council 82's] seven members."

18.92 Placement on involuntary leave

Fronczak v NYS Dept. of Correctional Services, CA2, February 8, 2001

Section 72 of the Civil Service Law -- leave for ordinary disability -- permits an appointing authority to place on employee on involuntary leave without pay if he or she is found unable to perform the duties of his or her position as a result of an illness or a disability that is not an occupational injury or disease as defined in the Workers' Compensation Law.[184]

The Fronczak case involved the placement of a state worker on an involuntary leave pursuant to Section 72 of the Civil Service Law.

Daniel T. Fronczak sued the New York State Department of Correctional Services [DOCS], claiming that this action violated Americans with Disabilities Act, 42 USC Sections 12112-12117 and subjected him to unlawful retaliatory adverse employment actions in violation of 42 USC 1983.

According to the decision by the U.S. Circuit Court of Appeals, Fronczak was a correctional officer employed by DOCS at its Wyoming facility.

Critical of the facility's handling of hazardous waste materials, he began "exhibiting both bizarre and threatening behavior."

In 1993 DOCS asked Fronczak to undergo a psychiatric examination to determine his ability to perform the duties of his job.

Dr. Jeffrey Bernstein, employed by the New York Department of Civil Service's Employee Health Service, examined Fronczak and determined that Fronczak was "in need of psychiatric care ... was a risk for not being able to manage the inmates, possibly even losing control, further control of his emotions and his temper, and having difficulty working with co-workers ... [t]hat he was unable from a psychiatric perspective to continue his duties as a corrections officer."

Based on this evaluation, in 1993 Fronczak was placed on an involuntary leave of absence. He unsuccessfully appealed the determination to the Civil Service Commission.[185]

---

[184] Section 71 of the Civil Service Law provides for leaves of absences in connection with an "occupational injury or disease" within the meaning of the Workers' Compensation Law.

[184] Section 72.2 provides that an employee placed on leave pursuant to Section 72.1 may, within one year after the date of commencement of such leave of absence, or thereafter at any time until his or her employment status is terminated, make application to the civil service department or municipal commission having jurisdiction over the position from which such employee is on leave, for a medical examination by a medical officer selected for that purpose by such department or commission. which such employee is on leave, for a medical examination by a medical officer selected for that purpose by such department or commission.

In 1996, after a further evaluation, Fronczak was found fit to perform the duties of a corrections officer and, in accordance with DOCS policy, was required to undergo seven weeks of retraining prior to resuming active employment as a corrections officer.

During this training period Fronczak had "an altercation with an instructor" and ultimately "gathered his belongings, and departed" the facility.

Fronczak was sent a letter warning him that as provided under the terms of the collective bargaining agreement then in place, his absence for ten days would be considered "a constructive resignation." When Fronczak failed to return with the ten-day period, DOCS notified him by mail that his absence had been deemed a constructive resignation and that his employment with DOCS was terminated.

After losing his administrative appeals before the State Civil Service Commission and exhausting his federal administrative remedies through the Equal Employment Opportunity Commission (EEOC), Fronczak filed a lawsuit in federal district court.

As set out in the Circuit Court's opinion: "A liberal reading of [Fronczak's] complaint reveals the following alleged causes of action: (1) by placing Fronczak on involuntary leave in 1993 and terminating him in 1996, DOCS retaliated against Fronczak's exercise of his First Amendment rights, in violation of 42 USC Section 1983, for his complaints concerning its waste management; (2) the same 1993 involuntary leave and 1996 termination resulted from discrimination on the basis of a perceived mental disability in violation of the ADA."[186]

A federal magistrate judge dismissed Fronczak's petition on the grounds that he failed to establish a prima facie case that he had been discharged either as the result of discrimination on the basis of a perceived disability or in retaliation for his filing waste management complaints.

Instead, the magistrate concluded, "[t]he undisputed record reflects that ... [Fronczak] was discharged because he failed to show up for work." The Circuit Court sustained the magistrate's determination.

However, the Circuit Court went further. The court said that: "assuming arguendo that Fronczak has presented a prima facie case of discrimination on the basis of a perceived mental disability in 1993, DOCS has come forward with a legitimate nondiscriminatory explanation for placing him on involuntary leave at that time, namely that he was not capable of performing the essential job duties of a corrections officer."

In addition, said the court, Fronczak did not present any evidence indicating that DOCS' proffered explanation was a pretext for discrimination.

The court's conclusion: After considering "all of Fronczak's claims and finding them without merit," the judgment of the district court is affirmed.

---

[186] The US Supreme Court ruled that the states enjoy Eleventh Amendment immunity from lawsuit in federal court alleging violations of the Americans With Disabilities Act [Garrett v. University of Alabama, 193 F.3d 1214, decided February 21, 2001

Another involuntary placement on Section 72 leave case is Petix v NYS Off. of Mental Health, 291 A.D.2d 846.

The Petix decision, a case involving the application of Section 72.5 of the Civil Service Law [CSL], provides an opportunity to explore this and a number of other facets of Section 72, Leave for Ordinary Disability.

CSL Section 72.5 authorizes the immediate placement of an individual on an involuntary leave of absence in the event the appointing authority determines that there is probable cause to believe that the continued presence of the employee on the job represents a potential danger to persons or property or would severely interfere with operations.

Section 72 applies in the event an employee suffers an "ordinary disability," i.e., a disability unrelated to any occupational injury or disease. Civil Service Law Section 71 -- Workers' Compensation Leave -- provides for leaves of absences required as a result of an occupational injury or disease as defined in the Workers' Compensation Law.

An employee placed on a Section 72.5 involuntary leave of absence is entitled to use all accumulated unused sick leave, vacation, overtime and other time allowances standing to his or her credit in order to remain on the payroll.[187]

Gerard Petix, a Senior Physical Therapist employed at the Office of Mental Health's Rochester Psychiatric Center [RPC], was placed on an immediate involuntary leave of absence pursuant to CSL Section 72.5 effective October 13, 1999.

Petix objected to his placement of Section 72.5 leave and asked for, and was provided with, a hearing in accordance with the procedures set out in CSL Section 72.1.

A hearing was conducted on October 13, 1999. RPC adopted the recommendations of the Section 72.1 Hearing Officer and found that Petix was unfit to perform the duties of his position on October 13, 1999. In effect, the hearing officer found that RPC had "probable cause" to place Petix on involuntary leave on that date.

RPC also adopted a hearing officer's findings and recommendation that Petix was physically and mentally able to return to work in late February 2000. Petix was actually allowed to return to work in April 2000. RPC restored all the holiday, vacation, and sick leave credits he used from the date of the February 2000 determination until the date on which he actually was permitted to return to work in April 2000.

Petix also asked RPC to restore the leave credits he used while he was on the involuntary Section 72.5 leave of absence from October 13, 1999 until late February 2000. When his request was denied, he filed a petition pursuant to Article 78 of the Civil Practice Law and Rules seeking a court order compelling RPC to restore those leave credits as well.

---

[187] Section 72 leave is leave without pay. If the employee declines to use his or her accumulated leave credits in order to remain on the payroll, or having elected to remain on the payroll, exhausts his or her accumulated leave credits, he or she is placed in leave without pay status.

Supreme Court dismissed Petix's petition based on its reading of CSL Section 72.5.

Section 72.5, in pertinent part, provides that, if "an employee is finally determined not to be physically or mentally unfit to perform the duties of his or her position, he or she shall be restored to his or her position and shall have any leave credits or salary that he or she may have lost because of such involuntary leave of absence restored to him or her".

The Appellate Division sustained the lower court's ruling. The court rejected Petix's theory that he was entitled to restoration of the sick leave credits that he used during the entire period of the involuntary leave of absence because RPC "finally determined" that he was fit to return to work in late February 2000.

Not so, said the court. The Appellate Division noted that Petix, "was allowed to return to work because of an improvement of his condition [in late February 2000] and not because it was 'finally determined' that he was fit to perform his duties" from October 1999 to late February 2000."

In contrast, had the hearing officer determined that RPC did not have "probable cause" to place Petix on involuntary leave pursuant Section 72.5 in October 1999, Petix would have been entitled to all leave credits he used since October 1999.

The "standard Section 72 procedure" is triggered by the appointing officer's determination that the individual is physically or mentally unable to perform his or duties and should be placed on leave of absence. However, CSL Section 72.1 requires completing a number of procedural steps before the individual may actually be placed on Section 72 leave over his or her objections.

In contrast, Section 72.5 essentially sets out an exception to the "standard procedure" that allows it to be truncated only in the event the appointing authority determines that there is probable cause to believe that the continuation of the individual on the job poses a danger to persons, property or the agency's operation.

The "standard procedure" followed under Section 72 may be summarized as follows:

1. The appointing authority determines than an employee is unable to perform the duties of his or her position by reason of an ordinary disability.

2. The appointing authority requires such employee to undergo a medical examination to be conducted by a medical officer selected by the civil service department or municipal commission having jurisdiction.

3. The appointing authority provides the employee and the civil service department or commission, in writing, the facts that constitute the basis for the judgment that the employee is not fit to perform the duties of his or her position prior to the medical examination.

4. If the medical officer certifies that the employee is not physically or mentally fit to perform the duties of his or her position, the appointing authority notifies the employee of any proposed Section 72 leave and the proposed date on which such leave is to commence.

5. The employee is also advised of his or her right to object to his or her placement on the proposed Section 72 leave of absence and to request a hearing.

6. If the employee requests a hearing, the appointing authority is to give the employee a hearing within 30 days of the receipt of the request. The appointing authority is also required to provide the employee and the employee's personal physician or authorized representative, with copies of all diagnoses, test results, observations and other data supporting the appointing authority's decision.

7. The employee is not to be placed on leave until a final determination is made by the appointing authority after the hearing is held.

As is typical in administrative actions of this type, the appointing authority has the burden of proof and must provide the evidence that the employee is mentally or physically unfit to perform his or her duties.

Following the receipt of the hearing officer's findings and recommendations, the appointing authority may decide to (1) uphold the original proposed notice of leave of absence, (2) withdraw such notice or (3) modify the notice as may be appropriate.

If the final determination is to place the individual on Section 72 leave, the employee is to be advised of his or her right to appeal the determination to the civil service commission having jurisdiction as provided by CSL Section 72.3.

Another section of the Civil Service Law may become relevant in connection with absences pursuant to Section 72; CSL Section 73.

Section 73 provides the appointing officer with the discretion to terminate an employee who has been placed on Section 72 leave once the employee has been continuously absent from and unable to perform the duties of his or her position for one year or more.[188]

An employee terminated from employment pursuant to Section 73 is allowed one year after the termination of his or her disability to apply for reinstatement to his or her former position. This request is to be submitted to the civil service department or municipal commission having jurisdiction over the position he or she last for a medical examination.

If the employee is found physically and mentally fit to perform the duties of his or her former position, he or she is to be reinstated to the position, if it is vacant. If there is no vacancy available, he or she is to be appointed to a vacancy in a similar position or to a vacant position in a lower grade in the same occupational field in his former department or agency.

If there is no suitable position available, the individual's name is place on a preferred list for his former position in his former department or agency for a period of four years. Further, if the individual is reinstated to a position in a grade lower than that of his or her former position, his or her

---

[188] In contrast, an individual who has been placed on Workers' Compensation Leave pursuant to CSL Section 71 may be terminated after being on such leave for a cumulative period of one year at the discretion of the appointing authority.

name is placed on a preferred list for his former position, or any similar position, in his former department or agency.

18.93 Policy makers

Butler v NYS Dept. of Law, CA2,

Who is a policy maker? This was one of the issues before the court when former Assistant Attorney General Barbara B. Butler sued then Attorney General Dennis Vacco, contending that she had been unlawfully fired from her position as a Deputy Bureau Chief. Was Butler was a "policy maker" and thus subject to dismissal for reasons of political patronage? The Court concluded that Butler was a policy maker.

In determining whether an individual is a "policymaker" in accordance with the Elrod [427 US at 367] and Branti [445 US 507] standards, the Second Circuit said it considers whether or not the employee:

(1) is exempt from civil service protection,
(2) has some technical competence or expertise,
(3) controls others,
(4) is authorized to speak in the name of policymakers,
(5) is perceived as a policymaker by the public, (
(6) influences government programs,
(7) has contact with elected officials, and
(8) is responsive to partisan politics and political leaders.

18.94 Pornography and the Pell Standard

Schnaars v Copiague UFSD, NYS Supreme Court, July 1999, Judge Floyd

Is dismissal too severe a penalty for a school employee who uses a school computer to find pornographic web sites? Yes, both a Supreme Court Judge and the Appellate Division ruled in the Schnaars case.

A student at Copiague High School turned on a school computer and was immediately confronted by a pornographic image. Schnaars, Copiague UFSD's head custodian, took responsibility. Schnaars admitted that, with his subordinates, he accessed pornographic web sites during two night shift tours of duty.

The district filed disciplinary charges against him, alleging that he had used the district's computers without authorization and neglected his duty. The hearing officer found Schnaars guilty of the charges and recommended that he be demoted to a lower grade position.

Although the board adopted the hearing officer's findings as to guilt, it rejected the penalty recommended by the hearing officer and voted to terminate Schnaars instead.[189]

Schnaars sued, contending that board's rejection of the hearing officer's recommendation as to the penalty to be imposed was arbitrary, capricious, an abuse of discretion, and disproportionate to the offense for which he was found guilty.

New York State Supreme Court Judge Marquette L. Floyd of Suffolk County said that where the finding of guilt is confirmed and punishment has been imposed, the test is whether such punishment is "so disproportionate to the offense, in the light of all the circumstances, as to be shocking to one's sense of fairness," citing the so-called Pell Standard [Pell v Board of Education, 34 NY2d 222].

Although it is quite rare for the courts to find that a penalty violates the Pell Standard, Judge Floyd decided that dismissing Schnaars was a shockingly disproportionate penalty.

The Appellate Division affirmed the lower court's ruling, commenting that Schnaars' actions did not involve "moral turpitude, gross injury to the agency involved or [gross injury] to the public weal."

Noting that "access to the school's computers can be curtailed through adequate passwords and by 'filtering' software, which may also be complicated by First Amendment issues," the Appellate Division said that although it "does not condone [Schnaars'] individual or supervisory behavior, his termination is so disproportionate to the facts that it may not be permitted to stand."

What are some of the factors that should be considered in settling a disciplinary penalty? The Appellate Division said that where there is no "grave moral turpitude" and no grave injury to the agency or to the public weal," the following should be considered:

1. The length of employment of the employee;

2. The probability that a dismissal may leave the employee without any alternative livelihood;

3. The employee's loss of retirement benefits; and

4. The impact upon his innocent family.

In contrast, the court said that no such consideration of "mitigating circumstances" is required in situations involving such actions as a "deliberate, planned, unmitigated larceny, or bribe taking, or [a] demonstrated lack of qualification for the assigned job."

The decision observed that Schnaars "candidly acknowledged his violation of District policy and sought to correct [the] same by informing his subordinates that 'this has got to stop.'" Another consideration, said the court, was Schnaars "otherwise 13 year unblemished record with the District with many letters of recommendation and accolades that exhibit faithful and loyal service."

---

[189] Both demotion and termination are among the penalties an appointing authority may impose on an employee found guilty of misconduct or incompetence pursuant to Section 75.

What penalty would be appropriate in this case? The court said that the district should reinstate Schnaars to his position as Head Custodian with back salary and then impose "an appropriate penalty" suggesting either "demotion and/or suspension without pay for a reasonable period, said period not to exceed ninety (90) days."

The Appellate Division also said that the district "shall be entitled to a credit of any of [Schnaars'] earned income from the time of his termination to the date of reinstatement."

However, Civil Service Law Section 77 -- compensation of officers and employees reinstated by court order -- currently authorizes such adjustment only for "unemployment insurance benefits." In 1985 Section 77 was amended to eliminate the clause allowing adjustments for "compensation which [the individual] may have earned in any other employment or occupation..." [190]

On another point, the court said that the penalty that could be imposed -- demotion and/or suspension without pay not to exceed ninety days. This suggests that the district could demote Schnaars or it could suspend him without pay or it could impose both penalties. Courts, however, have ruled that only one of the several penalties set out in Section 75 may be imposed on an individual found guilty of Section 75 disciplinary charges -- the imposition of multiple penalties is not authorized. In other words, cumulative penalties are not permitted in such cases.

18.95 Positive drug test

McGovern v Safir, 266 A.D.2d 107

New York City police officer John McGovern appealed his termination from the force after testing positive for marijuana.

McGovern had been selected for a random drug test. He did not dispute the fact that he had tested positive for marijuana but explained that his "ingestion of marijuana was unknowing and involuntary." The deputy police commissioner rejected this excuse as incredible, resulting in McGovern's dismissal.

The Appellate Division said that the positive drug test constitute substantial evidence supporting the determination that McGovern possessed and ingested marijuana. Further, the court said that under the circumstances, "[t]he penalty of dismissal does not shock our sense of fairness."

Other positive test for drugs cases include: Williams v Nicoletti, 295 A.D.2d 353.

18.96 Preparing a defense

Guastafeste v NYC Dept. of Sanitation, 282 A.D.2d 398

---

[190] Chapter 851, Laws of 1985

When an employee is served with disciplinary charges, he or she is entitled to be given information concerning such charges sufficient to permit his or her adequately preparing his or her defense.[191] Further, case law has long held that an employee may not be found guilty of acts of misconduct or incompetence that have not been charged.[192]

The Guastafeste ruling focused on the issue of providing the employee with sufficient information concerning the charges in order for him or her to be able to prepare his or her defense so that it cannot rightfully be claimed that the individual was found guilty acts or omissions that were not charged.

Joseph Guastafeste e, a New York City Department of Sanitation employee, was found guilty of misconduct and suspended him for 30 days without pay following his involvement in an accident while operating a department motor vehicle. Gustafeste appealed, contending that the charges of misconduct filed against him by the department did not specifically charge him with having "caused the accident by negligently losing control of his vehicle." Accordingly, he argued, he had not been given an adequate opportunity to prepare his defense against this allegation.

The Appellate Division decided that it was clear from the specifications set out in the charges filed against him that Guastafeste was being charged with "negligently operating his vehicle." This, said the court, meant that Guastafeste had been given sufficient notice of this charge so as to enable him to adequately prepare his defense.

As to the penalty imposed -- 30 days suspension without pay -- the Appellate Division ruled that "for the misconduct proved against [Guastafeste], some of which involved violations of Department of Sanitation safety rules, [such a penalty] does not shock the judicial conscience and accordingly may not be disturbed."

In contrast, in Smith v Davis, a case involving alleged violations of the Americans With Disabilities Act and other civil rights law violations, decided by the U.S. Circuit Court of Appeals, Third Circuit on May 07, 2001, the court found that the explanation provided by Luzerne County [NJ] for terminating county employee Rodney Smith -- violation of its drug and alcohol policy -- did not tell Smith what he did to bring about his termination in sufficient detail as to justify the district court's summarily dismissing his complaint.
The court said that there "does not seem to be anything in the record specifying precisely what aspect of this policy Smith was found to have violated. While the County's brief contended that Smith was fired for absenteeism, his supervisors' declarations did not mention absenteeism as the basis for his termination.

The court also noted that the County's "drug and alcohol policy contains no provision about absenteeism or sick leave that applies to Smith's termination."

According to the Circuit Court, "[w]hile absenteeism may have been what the [County] had in mind when they terminated him, there is a genuine issue as to whether this reason was legitimate or pretextual, particularly since there is evidence that Smith performed his duties to the apparent

---

[191] Pachucki v Walters, 56 AD2d 677

[192] Shuster v Humphrey, 156 NY 231

satisfaction of his supervisors for over six years and carried a case load substantially higher than his coworkers."

The Circuit Court noted that while Smith may have been fired for some other legitimate reason related to alcohol use, it would be improper to grant the County's motion for summary judgment without specific evidence that Smith was fired for such a reason.

A related point involving summary termination pursuant to a disciplinary grievance settlement is clearly illustrated in ruling by the Appellate Division in Taylor v Cass, 505 NYS2d 929.

Under the terms of the disciplinary settlement Taylor was subject to termination without any hearing if, in the opinion of his superior, his job performance was adversely affected by his consumption of alcohol. Taylor was subsequently terminated from his position for sleeping on the job. The court pointed out that the reason given for summarily terminating Taylor -- sleeping on the job -- was not authorized by the settlement agreement and directed his reinstatement with back pay and benefits.

Sometimes an employee will demand "a bill of particulars" requiring the employer to set out the charges and specifications filed against the individual in greater detail. Although Education Law Section 3020-a 3 c(iii)(C) indicates that an administrator or teacher has the right to demand a "bill of particulars" concerning the charges and specifications filed against him or her, no similar provision is included in Section 75 of the Civil Service Law. In some instances the disciplinary grievance procedure set out in a collective bargaining agreement allows the employee to demand a "bill of particulars."

18.97 Probation after re-hiring

Decisions of the Commissioner of Education 13964

As a result of a "take-back" of programs by component school districts of Rensselaer-Columbia-Greene BOCES, Ellen Chernoff was excessed.

Chernoff subsequently accepted a full-time position with the Wynantskill Central School District in Rensselaer County. Later Chernoff resigned from Wynantskill after she was offered full-time employment by the BOCES, also called Questar III. However, she objected to the statement in her letter of appointment indicating that she would be required to serve a two-year probationary period.

Questar III countered by stating that Chernoff had "freely and knowingly" became a full-time Wynantskill employee and thus extinguished her preferred list rights with it. Commissioner of Education Richard P. Mills agreed and dismissed Chernoff's appeal.

Another issue in the appeal involved a BOCES form in which excessed employees, including Chernoff, stated they had been advised that by taking a job with a component school district of the BOCES, they had forfeited their place on a preferred list to be re-hired by BOCES. The form included a statement of resignation: "I have been advised of my rights under Section 3014-b [of the Education Law] and have accepted a full-time position [with the Wynantskill Central School District] in the

Tenure area of General Special Education. As a result, I hereby resign as an employee of Questar III effective June 30, 1997."

The Commissioner found no significance in Chernoff's execution of this form to the issues under appeal. However, he commented that BOCES lacked authority to require such a document be signed when a teacher is excessed pursuant to Section 3014-b. He recommended that Questar III discontinue the practice.

18.98 Probationary termination

Higgins v La Paglia, 281 A.D.2d 679, appeal dismissed, 96 N.Y.2d 854

The Ulster County Sheriff Michael L. Paglia terminated correction officer Bradley Higgins at the end of his one-year probationary period. Higgins filed a grievance and initiated an Article 78 action seeking to overturn the Sheriff's decision.

In the course of his Article 78 action, Higgins claimed that he held tenure and thus was entitled to "notice and hearing" before he could be terminated. He cited a statement in the Ulster County Employees' Handbook that defined the probationary term as being a minimum of eight weeks and a maximum of 26 weeks.

The court rejected this argument, pointing out that the statement in the handbook contravenes the Ulster County Civil Service Rules and Regulations dealing with probation.

Finding that Higgins was a probationary employee at the time of his termination, the court said that he could be dismissed without a hearing unless he proffered sufficient evidence to create a question of fact as to whether his discharge was unrelated to work performance, motivated by a constitutionally impermissible purpose or made in bad faith.

Another probationary termination case is Negron v Jackson, 273 A.D.2d 241. This appeal was filed after the New York State Department of Motor Vehicles terminated Pedro Negron during his probationary period. Negro objected but his appeal was rejected by the Appellate Division. The court pointed out that "A probationary employee may be terminated without a hearing and without a statement of reasons in the absence of a showing that the termination was for a constitutionally impermissible purpose, made in bad faith, or in violation of statutory or decisional law," citing Iannuzzi v Town of Brookhaven, 258 AD2d 651.

Further, the discharged employee has the burden of demonstrating bad faith by competent evidence, not speculation. This apparently was the defect in Negron's appeal. The court said that his petition failed to allege facts that supported his conclusory claim of discrimination, or to otherwise show bad faith. Ruling that this constituted a fatal defect, the court said that his petition was properly dismissed by the lower court.

18.99 Processing a disciplinary appeal

Greenburgh 11 UFSD v Boyer, CEd 14,325, March 16, 2000

Sometimes one legal action involving a school district will have an impact on another action involving the district. The decision by the Commissioner of Education in Greenburgh v Boyer sets out the responsibilities of the parties in such situations, as well as demonstrating the impact that litigation brought in a different issue in a different forum may have on an administrative proceeding.

The Greenburgh 11 Union Free School District filed Section 3020-a disciplinary charges against Stephen Boyer, a physical education teacher. The district alleged that Boyer was guilty of "incompetence, neglect of duty and conduct unbecoming a teacher" in connection with an incident involving two students involved in a dispute during a swimming class. Boyer, said the district, "acted in an unprofessional manner in attempting to control one of the students."

On August 28, 1995 the Section 3020-a hearing panel unanimously found Boyer not guilty of the charges alleging incompetence and conduct unbecoming a teacher. By a 2 to 1 vote it found him guilty of the third charge: neglect of duty. The penalty imposed: a $10,000 fine.

On September 12, 1995 Greenburgh voted to appeal the panel's action. On October 3, 1995 it filed its appeal with the Commissioner seeking to have the Commissioner (1) find Boyer guilty of all of the charges filed against him and (2) authorize the district to terminate him.

About the same time, however, the district's board was involved in a lawsuit that challenged how its meetings were conducted. In Goetschius v Board of Education, decided July 31, 1996, State Supreme Court Judge Aldo A. Nastasi ruled that all actions taken by the Greenburgh 11 board at its meetings on November 11, 1994 and September 12, 1995 were null and void because of "numerous violations of the Open Meetings Law." Accordingly, the board's September 12 vote to appeal the disciplinary panel's was ruled invalid. Judge Nastasi's ruling was affirmed by the Appellate Division in November 1997.[193]

The board, however, attempted to authorize the appeal by readopting its September resolution at its meeting in December 1996. Its December board meeting was challenged in another Article 78 action, resulting in the court annulling actions taken at that meeting as well.

Apparently neither the district nor Boyer told the Commissioner about these court rulings. It was not until February 2000 that the Commissioner learned that the board's votes to prosecute the Section 3020-a appeal had been annulled. The Commissioner dismissed the appeal, ruling that the annulment of the board's actions taken at its meetings on September 12, 1995 and December 6, 1996 meant that "no properly commenced, timely appeal has been initiated within the time limitation set forth in 8 NYCRR 275.16."

The Commissioner, expressing his deep "distress" with the parties' failure to keep his Office of Counsel apprised of the progress of the litigation, admonished the parties "to be more scrupulous in

---

[193] Goetschius v Board of Education 244 AD2d 552

meeting their responsibility to forward relevant information in a timely fashion in future matters before the Commissioner of Education."

18.100 Property interest in public employment

Rivera v Community School District 9 [NYC], USDC SDNY, Justice Stein, May 10, 2001

Anna Rivera, a probationary teacher employed by New York City's Community School District 9, was terminated for allegedly improperly attempting to raise her pupils' standardized test scores.

According to the decision, in December 1999, the New York City Special Commissioner of Investigation issued a report entitled "Cheating the Children: Educator Misconduct on Standardized Tests." The report alleged that educators in the New York City public school system used a variety of inappropriate means to raise their students' scores on standardized tests. It specifically alleged that Rivera was present while a "cheat sheet" was prepared the day before the citywide reading and math tests were to be given to all third graders in 1995.

Notwithstanding Rivera's denial of cheating, the Report said that "interviews with Rivera's students establish that Rivera did in fact cheat on that test." Ultimately Rivera was dismissed from her position with the district.

Claiming that the district violated her right to due process rights by dismissing her without holding a pre-termination hearing and violated her First Amendment rights by terminating her in retaliation for filing a notice of claim against other employees, Rivera sued.

The court granted the Board of Education's motion to dismiss Rivera's Article 78 complaint but said that she could refile her claim provided she presented sufficient facts to establish a causal connection between her filing a notice of claim and her dismissal from her probationary teaching position.

Justice Stein ruled that:

1. Under New York State law, a probationary employee such as Rivera has no property interest in her job which would entitle her to due process rights; and

2. Although a probationary employee, Rivera does have a liberty interest in clearing her name from the stigma of accusations of dishonesty.
As to providing Rivera with a name-clearing hearing, Justice Stein noted that Rivera was terminated because the superintendent of Community School District Nine concluded that Rivera cheated on standardized tests, pressured other teachers into cheating, and attempted to assault another teacher for refusing to cooperate in the cheating scheme. These allegations were disseminated to the public and repeated in letters to Rivera.

As Rivera denied these charges and because these accusations impugn Rivera's honesty, Justice Stein ruled that she has a liberty interest that is protected by the Due Process Clause. As to a remedy, the court said that Due Process Clause of the Fourteenth Amendment is not violated "so long as the state provides a meaningful postdeprivation remedy."

Was such a "postdeprivation remedy" available to Rivera? Yes, said the court. New York's Article 78 proceeding has been held to provide an adequate postdeprivation remedy.[194]

18.101 Protected speech

McKinley v Kaplan, CA11, 00-11653, August 23, 2001

The general rule is that a public employee cannot be disciplined simply for exercising his or her constitutional right to free speech concerning matters of public interest. Where the employee speaks out on matters of public concern, the government bears the burden of justifying any adverse employment action it might take against the individual.

A public employee's speech concerning a private or personal interest, however, is a different matter. The public employer is not required to justify disciplinary action taken in response to an employee's speech regarding personal matters, such as a change in the employee's duties or work location. Further, in Pickering v Board of Education, 391 US 563, the U.S. Supreme Court held that a public employee's right to freedom of speech is not absolute because "the State has interests as an employer in regulating the speech of its employees that differ significantly from those it possesses in connection with regulation of the speech of the citizenry in general."

The McKinley case raises another element to consider concerning the right of a public employer to regulate the speech of its employee -- the employer's expectations with respect to a policy-maker's speech concerning matters of public interest related to the individual's work.

Margaret McKinley, a volunteer and unpaid member of the Miami-Dade County Film, Print, and Broadcast Advisory Board, was removed from her position because, said the County, she had expressed and supported a position that was "inappropriate and insulting to the community" represented by the sponsor of her appointment as well as being inconsistent with County policy.[195]

According to the decision, the County had adopted a policy "prohibiting contracts between the County and any firms doing business either directly or indirectly with Cuba." After determining that an organization planning an Entertainment Conference "was doing business with Cuba by inviting Cuban artists to perform," the County voted against providing any public monies to support the event.

McKinley disagreed with this decision and made a statement at a public meeting held by the Miami Beach Fashion, Film, Television and Recording Committee to the effect that losing the Conference

---

[194] Article 78, Civil Practice Law and Rules

[195] The pay status of the individual has no bearing with respect to an individual's alleged terminated for an improper or unconstitutional reason. As the court indicated in Hyland v Wonder, 972 F.2d 1129, serving as a volunteer constitutes a government benefit or privilege and that "[r]etaliatory actions with less momentous consequences than [the loss of employment], such as loss of a volunteer position, are equally egregious in the eyes of the Constitution because a person is being punished for engaging in protected speech."

would hurt Miami's entertainment industry and that the County's action improperly reflected only the views of the Cuban-American community. She was quoted in the Miami Herald as follows: "While we respect and appreciate the concerns of Cuban-Americans in the exile community, allowing a few people's political standpoint to dictate the potential economic growth of the area is not for the benefit of the community as a whole."

McKinley sued the County after she was dismissed from her position, contending that the county violated her First and Fourteenth Amendment rights because she was fired as a result of the public statement she made concerning a County policy with which she disagreed.

A federal district court judge dismissed McKinley's complaint, holding that the First Amendment did not provide her with any right to continued government employment. The court's rationale: McKinley's role on the Film Board involved public contact and providing input into County policy decisions and she failed to properly represent the views and policies of the County to the public. The Circuit Court affirmed the ruling, pointing out that the Pickering decision sets out a four prong test for determining if an employee's protected speech rights have been violated by a public employer's action:

1. Did the speech involve a matter of public concern?

2. If so, does the government's interest in promoting the efficiency of the public services it performs through its employees out weight the employee's interest in protected speech?

3. If so, did the employee's speech play a substantial part in the government's decision to discharge the employee? and finally,

4. If the speech was a substantial motivating factor in the employer's decision, has the government shown by a preponderance of the evidence that it would have discharged the employee regardless of the protected conduct?

The parties agreed that the only issue to be addressed in this instance was "the balancing prong of the Pickering test" -- weighing the respective interests of the County and McKinley. According to the court:

1. On McKinley's side of the scale is her interest in voicing her opinion on a controversial county resolution.

2. On the County side is its need to maintain loyalty, discipline, and good working relationships with those employees and board members they appoint and supervise.

The Circuit Court's conclusion: the balance tipped in favor of the County based on the proposition that "governments have a strong interest in staffing their offices with employees that they fully trust, particularly when the employees occupy advisory or policy-making roles." Finding that McKinley was a "policy-maker," based on the fact that her duties required her to serve in an advisory capacity with input on policy issues, the court concluded that this factor "gives the County a greater interest in removing her based on her speech."

The Circuit Court then said that "[p]erhaps more important to our decision than [McKinley's] policy influence or public contact, however, is the fact that [McKinley] served as an appointed representative of the County ... and she failed to support [its] interests." According to the ruling:
"It was not [McKinley's] right to free speech that was affected by the County Commission's decision to remove her. Rather, it was her right to maintain an appointed position ... in light of her choice to publicly dissent from [the County's] clearly stated views and policies."

Whistle blowing involves another element that must be considered when determining if the employer's interest in limiting its employees' speech outweighs an employee's interest in free speech. For example, Section 75-b of the Civil Service Law, provides that a public employer:
"shall not dismiss or take other disciplinary or other adverse personnel action against a public employee regarding the employee's employment because the employee discloses to a governmental body information regarding a violation of law ... which violation creates and presents a substantial and specific danger to the public health or safety...."

The statute also includes a provision, Section 75-b.4, that states that nothing in the Section "shall be deemed to ... prohibit any personnel action which otherwise would have been taken regardless of any disclosure of information."[196]

Sometimes it may be difficult to distinguish the line between "free speech" and "whistle blowing." For example, did the McDonald case [McDonald v City of Freeport [TX], 834 FSupp 921] concern the issue of "free speech," or "whistle blowing" or, perhaps, both.

In McDonald the court considered allegations made by police officers that the City fired one police officer and forced another to retire after they spoke to the media about alleged police misconduct. Some might classify this type of activity "whistle blowing." The federal district court, however, made its ruling based on "free speech" concerns, holding that such action violated the police officers' First Amendment rights.

In this instance, said the court, the employee's interest in revealing such matters of public concern outweighed the police department's interest in maintaining "an efficient police department." According to the decision, only a concern for "national security" or similar situations would serve to limit an employee from revealing improper governmental practices to the public.

18.102 Providing a "Bratton hearing"

Roberson v Ward, 278 A.D.2d 180, Motion to appeal denied, 96 N.Y.2d 717

When must a police officer that has been arrested and convicted be given a disciplinary hearing in contrast to being summarily terminated. As the Roberson decision demonstrates, it depends on the nature of the offense.

---

[196] Additional whistleblower protections are set out in New York State's Labor Law 740.

In Bratton v Foley, 92 NY2d 981, the Court of Appeals held that a police officer may be summarily dismissed if he or she is convicted of a particular crime falling under the "oath of office" category, ... under Public Officers Law Section 30.1(e). In contrast, said the high court, for other convictions -- i.e., those not constituting a violation of the police officer's oath of office, or in cases where Section 30.1(e) is not cited as authority for the termination, "a public hearing is required...." If the police officer is not given such a hearing, he or she may demand one.

The lesson in the Roberson decision is that in such situations the police officer must make a timely demand for the hearing.

In 1989 Cedric T. Roberson, was "automatically terminated" from his position as a New York City police officer after his misdemeanor conviction of menacing in the third degree. Apparently the department relied on an administrative rule as authority for his "automatic termination" rather than Section 30.1(e) of the Public Officers Law.

Some ten years later he asked the court to annul his dismissal, claiming that he was entitled to a "Bratton hearing" before he could be terminated from his position.

In response to Roberson's claim that he was entitled to a pretermination hearing as announced in Bratton, the court said that "the proceeding is barred by laches...."

According to the ruling, "[i]t is no excuse for any subsequent delay in challenging his termination that he believed, as a result of advice from his attorney, who opined that any proceeding he might bring to challenge his termination would be futile unless his menacing conviction was overturned on appeal, which did not occur."

What is a "reasonable delay?" It appears that to be "reasonable," it must be a delay of less than two years. According to the decision, Robinson also attempted to obtain a copy of the "order of termination" pursuant to the Freedom of Information Law subsequent to his termination from the police force. However, said the court, this two-year delay "was also unreasonable."

18.103 Proving disciplinary charges

Ferguson v Traficanti, 295 A.D.2d 786

Desiree Ferguson was found guilty of some of the thirty specifications of misconduct and incompetence filed against her. Specifically, the hearing officer found Ferguson guilty of seventeen of these thirty specifications and recommended that she be dismissed from her position of Senior Office Assistant with the Schenectady City Court.

Among the specifications of misconduct and incompetence filed against her: excessive lateness, failure to properly carry out assigned duties, and actions in contradiction of established court procedure. The hearing officer's findings and recommendations were adopted by the appointing authority and Ferguson was dismissed from her position.

In sustaining the determination, the Appellate Division, Third Department noted that: "Findings of a Hearing Examiner will be confirmed if they are supported by substantial evidence in the record even where conflicting evidence may have supported a different determination."

What constitutes "substantial evidence" is the significant issue in such cases. The decision demonstrates some of the factors that courts weigh in determining whether there is substantial evidence to support the finding of the hearing officer.

The hearing officer found Ferguson guilty of seven of the 12 specifications concerning her alleged failure to perform assigned clerical tasks properly. The court said that "only six of the seven specifications should be confirmed based upon the testimony proffered by petitioner's supervisor."

Why? Because, explained the court, testimony that Ferguson had typed the incorrect labels because the witness "recognized the font from [Ferguson's] typewriter was insufficient since testimony also established that there were several typewriters in that office using that particular font."

As the witness could not testify that she witnessed Ferguson preparing these folders and Ferguson denied that the error was hers, the court said it could not conclude that there was sufficient evidence to support this allegation.

The hearing officer also found Ferguson guilty of six of thirteen specifications alleging that she improperly performing her duties by exceeding her authority or violating court policy. In this instance the court held that the record supported the hearing officer's findings, noting that Ferguson was advised of these problems in her performance in various performance evaluation, together with the need for her to improve in these areas.

With respect to disciplinary specifications focusing on Ferguson's use of the workplace to conduct personal business and engage in lengthy personal telephone calls, the Appellate Division ruled that the testimony of her superiors, confirmed by a co-worker, was sufficient to prove the allegations.

The court also said that it did not find any error in the hearing officer finding Ferguson guilty of 36 of the 48 allegations that she had arrived late for work on specified dates. These allegations, said the court were supported either by Ferguson's time sheets or by testimony from her superior or co-workers.

The court also said that it noted that Ferguson was given numerous oral admonitions and counseling memoranda warning her of further disciplinary action, such did not constitute "punishment" such that the present disciplinary proceeding could be deemed duplicative.

The Appellate Division declined to review the penalty imposed, as the more appropriate course is to remit the matter to the appointing authority for its reconsideration.

18.104 Public worker to answer work related inquiry

Delgado v Kerik, 294 A.D.2d 227

One of the issues in the Delgado case concerned the duty of a public officer or employee to answer questions directly related to the performance of his or her duties in the course of an administrative investigation or official interview.

In deciding this appeal, the Appellate Division, First Department, citing Tanico v McGuire, 80 AD2d 297, said that "[A]s a public employee, [a] police officer is required by virtue of his [or her] office to answer questions narrowly relating to his [or her] duties and to account for his [or her] actions."[197]

New York City Police Officer Wilfredo Delgado was terminated from his position as a New York City police officer after the Commissioner of Police determined that he had associated with persons known to the department to have engaged in criminal activities and provided false and misleading statements during official interviews.

Delgado challenged the Commissioner's action, claiming that he was denied representation during the "official interview" conducted by the Department.

Addressing Delgado's claim that he was denied "meaningful representation" during an official interview, the court noted that Delgado, upon the advice of counsel, refused to provide answers to questions relating to his official duties in the course of his interview. Clearly, said the court, relying of his attorney's advice not to answer the questions asked of him in the course of his "official interview" did not excuse Delgado from his duty to respond.

The Appellate Division dismissed Delgado's appeal, ruling that the Commissioner's determination was supported by substantial evidence. This evidence included transcripts of phone conversations between Delgado and two incarcerated individuals.

Finding that dismissal was "not so disproportionate to the offenses that petitioner was found to have committed as to shock our sense of fairness," the court dismissed Delgado's appeal.

18.105 Random drug tests
Seeley v New York City, 269 A.D.2d 205

Are "uncertified toxicology reports" indicating positive drug test results sufficient to support a decision to terminate an employee? This was the issue presented by Clarice E. Seeley, a New York City police officer, who was terminated after being found guilty of testing positive for cocaine in a random drug test.

Seeley argued that due process required the court to vacate the police commissioner's decision because it was not supported by substantial evidence. Seeley contended that the commissioner based his ruling on unreliable toxicology reports because they were not certified copies.

---

[197] A police officer is a public officer. Although all public officers are public employees, not all public employees are public officers.

The Appellate Division was not impressed by this argument. After commenting that "an administrative tribunal is not strictly bound by the rules of evidence," the court pointed out that "foundation testimony" by the toxicologist who supervised the testing and prepared the final toxicology reports was more than adequate to establish the authenticity and reliability of the copies of the reports entered into evidence.

Also noted was the fact that Seeley's attorney "declined the hearing officer's invitation to examine the original toxicology reports before copies of them were received in evidence." The Appellate Division then sustained Seeley's dismissal, commenting that the penalty "does not shock our sense of fairness under the circumstances."

18.106 Random searches at work

Morris v NY-NJ Port Authority, Supreme Court, New York County, August 18, 2000

Robert Morris and the Port Authority Police Benevolent Association [PBA] sued the Port Authority in an effort to obtain a judicial declaration that random searches of the Port Authority police officers' lockers were (1) unconstitutional and (2) a breach of a "Memorandum of Agreement" [MOA] between the PBA and the Authority.

The lockers in question are owned by the Authority and were being used by Authority police officers. A search on October 13, 1999 found radios belong to the Authority in the lockers of two officers in violation of its directive to pass the radios on to their shift replacements. The officers were disciplined for violating the directive.

The court dismissed the complaint citing the Appellate Division's ruling in Moore v Constantine, 191 AD2d 769. Moore challenged his termination as a result of "the search of his personal locker and the seizure of evidence ... which was admitted in evidence at a disciplinary hearing." The court said that the seizure of evidence from Moore's locker did not violate his rights under the 4th Amendment.

According to the decision, in order to be entitled to assert a violation of the 4th Amendment, the individual must establish that he or she possessed a reasonable expectation of privacy as to the searched premises.

The right to privacy in the workplace asserted Moore's situation, said the court, must bend to the superior governmental-societal interest of efficiency in the State Police. All public employees, especially police officers, have a diminished expectation of privacy in the work place.

As the U.S. Supreme Court said in O'Connor v Ortega, 480 US 709, when a public employer conducts such a search, "the court must balance the invasion of the employees' legitimate expectations of privacy against the government's need for supervision, control, and the efficient operation of the workplace."

The court's conclusion: "In light of the foregoing, the searches in question, whether they were consensual or not, did not violate plaintiffs' constitutional rights, and therefore plaintiffs' claim that they have a likelihood of success on this issue is unpersuasive."

As to the PBA's claim that the Authority violated provisions of the MOA, the court ruled that the question was for the arbitrator to determine, as it appears that this dispute is governed by the collective bargaining agreement.

18.107 Reappointment to public office

Gupta v Town of Brighton, 2nd Cir., No. 98-9043, 6/22/99

Is an individual entitled to be reappointed to public office upon the completion of his or her term? The Gupta decision demonstrates that the individual must be able to prove that he or she had a constitutional right to be continued in the office to prevail.

Brijen K. Gupta, a member of the Board of Trustees of the Brighton Memorial Library, was not reappointed to the board by the Town Council when his term expired. Claiming that he was denied reappointment (a) in retaliation for his public criticism of elected officials engaging in extramarital activities and (b) because of racial animus, Gupta sued the Town of Brighton, its Town Supervisor Sandra Frankel and one of its Council members, Robert Barbato, in federal court.

The Second Circuit U.S. Court of Appeals said that Gupta's "claims are without merit" and sustained a federal district court judge's ruling summarily dismissing Gupta's complaint.

As to Gupta's claim that his due process rights had been violated because he was not reappointed, the Circuit Court pointed out that in order to get the issue before a jury, much less prevail, Gupta had to show that he had the constitutionally required "legitimate claim of entitlement" to reappointment, citing Board of Regents v. Roth, 408 U.S. 564.

The court concluded that because Gupta was unable to demonstrate any entitlement to, or property interest in, the reappointment, the lower court properly dismissed his petition.

The Circuit Court commented that while Gupta alleged improper motive on the part of two of the five board members, "he has made no substantiated allegations that the remaining three board members were so motivated." Accordingly, the court concluded, there is insufficient evidence of either discrimination or retaliation, especially since the vote not to reappoint him as a trustee of the library was unanimous.

18.108 Reassignment pending discipline

Gray v Crew, 293 A.D.2d 357, appeal dismissed, 99 N.Y.2d 531

Prior to the filing of disciplinary charges against Dr. Simpson Gray, the Community Superintendent advised Gray of the charges and "the nature of the complaints against him. The Superintendent also told Dr. Gray that he would be transferred to the "district office" and reassigned to perform administrative duties pending the determination of the charges to be filed against him.

Gray challenged the transfer and reassignment to administrative duties but a State Supreme Court justice rejected his petition to rescind the superintendent's decision. The Appellate Division, First Department, sustained the lower court's dismissal of Gray's petition.

The relevant law in this situation: subdivisions 7(c) and 8 of Section 2590-j of the Education Law. Subdivision 7(c) requires the community superintendent, "in advance of the filing of charges and specification," to inform the teacher or administrator and the community board of "the nature of the complaint." The court said that the community superintendent had complied with this requirement.

The court also noted that Subdivision 8 authorizes the community superintendent to transfer teachers and supervisors within the district without their consent for a number of reasons including "disciplinary action pursuant to subdivision 7...."

The Appellate Division said that "[c]ontrary to [Gray's] claims" there were no procedural violations and the community superintendent "properly exercised" discretionary authority when Gray was transferred to the District Office pending the determination of disciplinary charges then pending against him.

The court also concluded held that Gray's right to due process was not violated "since the discretionary transfer to which [Gray] was subject does not implicate due process concerns."

Gray also argued that the reassignment caused him "irreparable financial or professional harm attributable to the Superintendent's action." The Appellate Division disagreed, pointing out "the transfer did not entail any reduction in [Gray's] pay, and [Gray's] lawsuit provides the basis for recovery of damages, if any.

The Appellate Division dismissed Gray appeal, setting out the following three reasons for its determination:

1. Gray failed to show his probability of success on the merits;

2. Gray failed to prove any danger that he would suffer irreparable injury in the absence of the requested relief; and

3. Gray did not demonstrate that the equities balanced in his favor.

18.109 Recommendation of the hearing officer

Spry v Delaware Co., 277 A.D.2d 779 [see, also, 253 A.D.2d 178 involving the same parties]

Delaware County Countryside Care Center ward clerk Valentina Spry was charged with numerous specifications of incompetence, insubordination, conduct un-becoming an employee, serious misconduct and unauthorized use of facility property pursuant to Section 75 of the Civil Service Law.

The hearing officer found Spry guilty of a great many of the charges and recommended that she be demoted in grade and title. Countryside's administrator adopted the Hearing Officer's findings of guilt but rejected the recommendation as to penalty. The penalty imposed: dismissal.

Spry appealed her termination. She, however, did not challenge the hearing officer's finding her guilty of certain charges. She, instead, complained that the administrator's rejection of the Hearing Officer's recommendation of the penalty to be imposed and his subsequent determination to terminate her employment instead is not supported by substantial evidence in the record.

The Appellate Division rejected Spry's argument. It held that the appointing authority "is free to disregard the recommendation of its Hearing Officer, to make new findings and to impose different discipline" and the penalty imposed will not be set aside unless it is found to be shockingly unfair within the meaning of the Pell doctrine.[198]

As to the appointing authority's making new findings, however, such findings must be based on substantial evidence in the record and the court's will uphold such determinations if there is a rational basis for the decision.

The Shurgin case explores this type of situation.[199]

In Shurgin a Section 3020-a disciplinary panel imposed a reprimand as the disciplinary penalty after the panel found Shurgin, a teacher, guilty of "poor judgment" for showing "pornographic films" to his class. The school district appealed to the Commissioner of Education, who found that a reprimand was disproportionately lenient for this "very serious offense" and directed that Shurgin be terminated instead.

The Court upheld the Commissioner's determination.

18.110 Reinstatement from Section 72 leave

An individual on Section 72 leave may make an application for medical examination to determine if he or she is physically or mentally fit to perform the duties of the position "until his or her employment status is terminated." Such termination must be in accordance with the provisions of Section 73 of the Civil Service Law and is at the discretion of the appointing authority.

---

[198] Pell v Board of Education, 34 NY2d 222

[199] Shurgin v Ambach, 83 AD2d 665, affirmed by the Court of Appeals, 56 NY2d 700

Both Section 71 and 73 provide for the termination of employees after the individual has been absent of such leave for one-year or longer at the discretion of the appointing authority -- termination is not automatic.[200]

Once terminated pursuant to Section 71 or Section 73, the individual may apply to the responsible civil service commission if he or she wishes to be reinstated to his or her former position. A request for reinstatement must be made "within one year after the termination of such disability".

Assuming that the appointing authority declines to reinstate the individual when he or she asks to be reemployed, the individual must submit a formal request for reinstatement to the civil service agency having jurisdiction.

This procedural requirement -- the application must be made to the civil service agency and not the employer -- was the key element considered by the court in Armetta v Town of Bethel, 265 AD2 789.

Daniel P. Armetta, a Town of Bethel highway employee, was seriously injured in a work-related accident. Separated from his position after he had been on Section 71 leave for more than one year, Armetta advised the town that he was able to return to work and asked about the procedure to be followed to resume his employment. Armetta was told to contact Richard Greene, Sullivan County's Director of Personnel, concerning the matter. Claiming he had been wrongfully terminated, instead of contacting Greene, Armetta sued the town seeking to "compel" it to give him a medical examination.

According to the decision, the procedure to be followed in such cases is simple. As Section 71 clearly indicates, the individual is to contact the responsible civil service commission, rather than his or her employer, to schedule the medical examination. Since Armetta had not done yet done this, the court dismissed his petition.

Section 73 sets contains similar language: an employee may, "within one year after the termination of such disability, make application to the civil service department or municipal commission ... for a medical examination." Presumably the courts would apply the Armetta rationale in deciding a Section 73 case.[201]

18.111 Rejecting a hearing officer's findings

Perfetto v Erie Co. Water Auth., 298 A.D.2d 932

It is well settled that an appointing authority may reject a Civil Service Law Section 75 hearing officer's finding of fact and penalty recommendation provided that the appointing authority's

---

[200] In the case of the individual on Section 71 leave, the one-year of absence is based on the employee's "cumulative absence;" in a Section 72 leave situation, the employee must be "continuously absent" for at least on year.

[201] In some jurisdictions the procedures to be following in cases involving the application or administration of Sections 71, 72 and 73 of the Civil Service Law have been incorporated in a collective bargaining agreement negotiated pursuant to the Taylor Law.

determination is supported by substantial evidence in the record and that the penalty imposed does not "shock one's sense of fairness."

The Perfetto case demonstrates how important it is for the appointing authority to specify the reasons for its rejection of all or a portion of the hearing officer's findings and recommendation.

Louis J. Perfetto, an employee of the Erie County Water Authority, was charged with three acts of misconduct, all related to absences from work. The first two charges concerned an absence in November of 2000 and Perfetto's alleged failure to provide proper documentation regarding that absence. Because the parties had entered into this settlement agreement concerning the first two charges in December 2000, the Hearing Officer ruled that this settlement precluded considering these two charges in the then current disciplinary action.

The third charge related to Perfetto's alleged misuse of sick time on March 27, 2001. While Perfetto claimed he was sick on March 27, there was evidence in the record establishing that Perfetto had left his home that morning to have a document notarized. The Hearing Officer concluded that the fact that Perfetto left his home on that date did not, in and of itself, "belie [his] claim that he was sick."

The appointing authority, however, rejected the Hearing Officer's findings of fact and recommendation. Although the appointing authority stated that Perfetto's testimony was "disproved by independent sources" in its decision, it failed to cite anything in the record to support this determination.

Insofar as the first two charges were concerned, the Court agreed with the hearing officer, concluding that any consideration as to those charges by the appointing authority constituted an error of law because of a binding settlement had previously been reached regarding the acts underlying the charges.

As to the third charge, the court concluded that the employer's determination was arbitrary and capricious to the extent that the appointing authority failed to set forth any findings of fact supported by substantial evidence in the record to bolster its conclusion. Perfetto was awarded his job back, along with lost wages and benefits.

Substantial evidence is not a difficult burden to meet. The Appellate Division has defined substantial evidence as enough evidence that a "reasonable mind may accept as adequate to support a conclusion."

This definition of substantial evidence allows for different conclusions based on the same evidence, as long as a reasonable person could arrive at same conclusion that the finder of fact did.

Nevertheless, it is vital that in any final decision, whether it is in agreement with the hearing officer's findings of fact or not, that the appointing authority spell out its reasoning and in the event it rejects any or all of the hearing officer's findings, that specific reasons for the rejection be given and that such reasons be supported by substantial evidence in the record. To do otherwise, as the Perfetto case demonstrates, could be fatal to the appointing authority's determination.

In contrast, the individual's entire personnel record, including past disciplinary actions that "were settled" may be considered by the hearing officer in the context of a disciplinary action for the purpose of setting an appropriate penalty provided the individual is advised that his or her personnel records will be so considered and is given an opportunity to rebut any information in that file.

18.112 Rejecting a disciplinary settlement offer

Tetro v Safir, 267 A.D.2d 39, motion for leave to appeal denied, 95 N.Y.2d 753

It is not uncommon for an employee to offer to, or to agree to, "settle" disciplinary charges that have been filed against him or her. Is the appointing officer bound to accept the "settlement?" Not necessarily, as the Tetro case demonstrates.

In Tetro the Appellate Division affirmed the appointing authority's rejection of the terms of the settlement of a disciplinary action previously agreed to by the employee and impose a harsher penalty -- termination -- upon the individual.

Anthony Tetro, a New York City police officer, was dismissed from his position after he was found guilty of giving "false testimony at the criminal trial of a former police officer."[202]

Tetro had "negotiated a plea agreement" in order to settle the disciplinary charges filed against him but the Commissioner rejected it and decided that the appropriate penalty to impose was dismissal from the department.

The Appellate Division ruled that Tetro's "contract rights were not violated" when the Commissioner declined to accept the settlement agreement and imposed a different penalty. The court cited Silverman v McGuire, 51 NY2d 228, in support of its ruling.

18.113 Removal from the payroll

Kahn v SUNY Health Science Center, 271 A.D.2d 656

The employer tells the employee that he or she is off the payroll. The employee sues, seeking a court order barring this action pending the trial challenging his or her termination on the grounds that he or she would suffer irreparable harm if the injunction was not issued because (1) if he or she were removed from the payroll he or she would have no one to support him or her; (2) he or she he would be unable to live in the New York metropolitan area; and (3) he or she would be unable to prosecute the lawsuit challenging the termination.

---

[202] Tetro testified that his partner discovered a gun in their patrol car while he was removing a prisoner from the vehicle. The evidence showed that Tetro and his partner failed to check underneath the back seat of the patrol car and that the weapon was later found by other police officers.

These were the claims made by Mahmood Khan when the State University of New York Health Science told him it was removing him from his faculty position with the university. Although a State Supreme Court judge issued granted the injunction, the Appellate Division, reversed the lower court and vacated the order.

The standards for granting a preliminary injunction is such situations are clear. The party seeking the order must show that he or she (1) is likely to succeed on the merits; (2) he or she would suffer irreparable injury if the provisional relief is withheld; and (3) "a balancing of the equities weighing in favor of the moving party."

The Appellate Division, assuming that Kahn had indeed "made an adequate showing of merit and that the equities balance in his favor," said that he failed to establish irreparable injury, the third element he was required to demonstrate. According to the court, Khan's contentions were "wholly speculative and conclusory, and, therefore, are insufficient to satisfy the burden of demonstrating irreparable injury."

Kahn also argued that if he were to be out of work for an extended period, he would have to return to Australia and would never be able to obtain United States citizenship. As he had not raised this argument before the Supreme Court, the Appellate Division said he precluded from raising it in the appeal because "absent matters that may be judicially noticed, new facts may not be injected at the appellate level."

18.114 Representation by an attorney

Sam v Metro-North Commuter Railroad, 287 A.D.2d 378

One of the issues in the Sam v Metro-North Commuter Railroad was Sam's contention that he was denied administrative due process because a union representative rather than an attorney served as his representative at a disciplinary hearing.

Carlson Sam, an employee of Metro-North Commuter Railroad (Metro-North), was discharged from his employment for conduct unbecoming a Metro-North employee and failing to comply with a lawful order of a Metro-North police officer. The Special Board of Adjustment, which reviewed the disciplinary administrative tribunal's trial and determination, sustained Sam's being found guilty and the penalty imposed, dismissal.

The decision states that Sam was found guilty of leaving his assigned post and becoming involved in an altercation with a homeless man whom he though had stolen his car radio. The altercation, in which both plaintiff and the homeless man brandished weapons, spilled over into the terminal and into the track area of the station. Sam refused to obey the orders of Metro-North Police present during the incident, and Metro-North police officer Barreto had to physically removed the weapon from Sam's control and wrestle him to the ground. The officer subsequently arrested Sam.

In reaching its decision, the Board noted multiple reasons justifying Sam's termination, including the fact that he left his assigned post, engaged in a violent altercation, refused a police officer's lawful order to lay down his weapon, and engaged in conduct requiring his forcible arrest. As to the penalty of dismissal, the Board found that termination was warranted since Sam, who only had three years of seniority, had already been disciplined several times previously.

Sam then sued Barreto and Metro-North asserting claims of assault, false arrest, false imprisonment, malicious prosecution, defamation, as well a claim that his 42 USC 1983 civil rights were violated.

As to Sam's assertions concerning the lack of counsel, the Appellate Division agreed that he was not represented by an attorney at his administrative trial. However, said the court, "here the absence of counsel is not determinative since [Sam] was represented by a union official whose competence and experience were amply demonstrated by the trial record."

The union representative "thoroughly questioned the various witnesses, raised appropriate objections, and requested a continuance to present additional witnesses, a request that was granted." This, in the view of the court, provided Sam with appropriate representation for the purposes of satisfying administrative due process in a disciplinary setting.[203]

18.115 Request for reconsideration

Raykowski v NYC DOT, 259 A.D.2d 367

Sometimes an individual who has been adversely affected by an administrative decision asks the appointing authority to reconsider its determination. However, as the Raykowski decision indicates, such a request will not excuse the individual's failing to file a timely challenged to the decision itself.

Michael Raykowski was terminated from his position with the City of New York Department of Transportation because he failed to "maintain a city residence." Although he asked for reconsideration of the decision terminating his employment, the Appellate Division said that asking for reconsideration "did not extend the applicable four-month [Statute of] limitations...."

The Appellate Division commented that challenges to administrative decision had to be brought pursuant to Article 78.[204] Such an action must be commenced within four month of the final administrative determination.

Significantly, the decision notes that a "fresh, complete and unlimited examination on the merits" will revive the Article 78 statute of limitation. However the Court ruled that the Department's meeting with Raykowski eight months after his termination did not satisfy this test and therefore his petition had to be dismissed as untimely.

This decision points out the danger of a employer's agreeing to reconsider an earlier final administrative decision. If the court determines that the agency's reconsideration is a fresh, complete

---

[203] Section 75.2 of the Civil Service Law provides that an individual against whom disciplinary charges have been preferred may be represented by an attorney or by a representative of a recognized or certified collective bargaining organization.

[204] Article 78, Civil Practice Law and Rules

and unlimited review of the underlying issue, the Statute of Limitations for the purposes of bringing an Article 78 will commence to run from the date the final determination of the agency's "reconsideration."

18.116 Request for union representation

Local 100, TWU and NYC Transit Authority, 35 PERB 4563

PERB Administrative Law [ALJ] Judge Angela M. Blassman ruled that the New York Transit Authority violated Section 209-a.1(a) and (c) of the Civil Service Law [the Taylor Law] when it rejected an employee's request that a union representative be present when he was asked to prepare a written statement in the presence of Authority supervisors.

Authority supervisors asked Igor Komarnitskiy to submit a written report in response to a complaint that he made a "racial remark" to another Authority employee. Although Komarnitskiy submitted the report, the supervisors were concerned that a union representative "may have improperly influenced" Komarnitskiy and insisted that he complete a second report without the union representative being present.

Noting that "[t]he Board has yet to determine whether a public employer engages in unlawful interference under the [Taylor] Act when it refuses an employee's request for union representation during questioning that an employee reasonably believes might result in discipline," ALJ Blassman said that under the National Labor Relations Act [NLRA] "a private sector employee has a statutory right 'to refuse to submit without union representation to an interview which he reasonably fears may result in his discipline.'" Accordingly, said the ALJ, "[a]ny adverse consequences suffered by an employee due to a refusal to cooperate in an interview without representation constitutes unlawful interference and a violation of Section 8(a)(1) of the NLRA."[205]

Commenting that other administrative law judges have found that the Taylor Law gives public employees a parallel right, "while contrary decisions have been issued by the Director and Assistant Director," ALJ Blassman held that "the reasoning in support of finding a parallel right under [the Taylor Law] is more persuasive."

The ALJ directed that the Authority to:

(1) "cease and desist" from requiring employees to submit to questioning without union representation when an employee has requested such representation and there is a reasonable basis to believe that the questioning might lead to discipline and

(2) to remove the second report completed by Komarnitskiy from his personnel file.

---

[205] Section 209-a.6. of the Taylor Law provides that "In applying this section, fundamental distinctions between private and public employment shall be recognized, and no body of federal or state law applicable wholly or in part to private employment, shall be regarded as binding or controlling precedent.

18.117 Requesting a disciplinary hearing

Gagnon v Wappingers CSD, 268 A.D.2d 472

Section 3020-a.2(c) of the Education Law requires the individual against whom disciplinary charges have been filed to advise the district's clerk or secretary whether or not he or she wishes to provided with a hearing. Such a request must be filed within 10 days of the individual's receiving the statement of the charges. If the individual fails to notify the clerk or secretary that he or she wishes to have a hearing within this ten-day period, and this defect is "unexcused," the individual is deemed to have waived his or her right to a hearing.

This was the situation facing Conrad Gagnon. Gagnon had been served with disciplinary charges pursuant to Section 3020-a of the Education Law. He, however, failed to advise the district's clerk or secretary that he wanted a hearing within the statutory 10-day period allowed for this purpose. The district issued its disciplinary determination without holding a hearing.

Gagnon filed a petition pursuant to Article 78 of the Civil Practice Law and Rules contending that "his failure to make a timely demand for a hearing was excusable" and therefore the district's refusal to accept his untimely request for a Section 3020-a disciplinary hearing was arbitrary and capricious and an abuse of discretion. A Supreme Court judge was not persuaded and dismissed Gagnon's petition.

The Appellate Division affirmed the lower court's ruling, noting that Gagnon "failed to proffer any evidence that he in fact requested permission to file a late demand for a hearing, or to rebut the sworn assertions proffered by the Board that no such request was ever made." In other words, not only did Gagnon concede that he fail to file a timely request for a disciplinary hearing, he was unable to demonstrate that he had made any request for such a hearing whatsoever.

The decision clearly demonstrates the importance of both the employer and the employee, respectively, establishing what some refer to as a "paper trail" demonstrating that all procedural elements in such cases were complied with.

In contrast to Section 3020-a, Section 75 of the Civil Service Law mandates that a hearing to consider disciplinary charges filed against an individual in the classified service be scheduled and held if discipline is to be imposed on an employee subject to its provisions.

The holding of a Section 75 disciplinary hearing is not contingent on the employee's requesting such a proceeding. The appointing authority must hold a Section 75 disciplinary hearing even if the individual does not answer the charges.

Further, case law indicates that the hearing must go forward even if the employee fails to appear at, or participate in, the proceeding if the employer wishes to impose discipline on the individual.

18.118 Rescinding a letter of resignation

Grogan v Holland Patent CSD, 262 A.D.2d 1009, motion for leave to appeal denied, 94 N.Y.2d 756

Once a resignation is delivered to the appointing authority, under Civil Service rules it may not be withdrawn without the consent of the appointing authority. This was the lesson that Holland Patent CSD food service worker Gina Grogan learned when she attempted to rescind her letter of resignation.

Grogan sent a letter to the district stating that she was resigning from her position "effective immediately." After the letter had been forwarded to the district's clerk, Grogan decided to withdraw her resignation. When the school board refused to allow her to do so, she sued.

The key question was whether the letter had been delivered to the "appointing authority" before Grogan sought to rescind it. The appointing authority was the school board, the Appellate Division said. Even though the school board had not met and had no opportunity as a body to consider the resignation, the court held that "[d]elivery of the letter of resignation to the clerk of the board constituted delivery to the Board." Therefore, the resignation could not be withdrawn without the board's consent.

Citing Oneida County's Rules for Classified Civil Service, the Appellate Division sustained a lower court's dismissal of Grogan's petition.

The Appellate Division also referred to the Rules of the State Civil Service Commission, 4 NYCRR 5.3 which, in pertinent part, provide that "every resignation shall be in writing" and "a resignation may not be withdrawn, canceled or amended after it is delivered to the appointing authority without the consent of the appointing authority." The Rules of the State Commission only apply to state employees but many political subdivisions of the state have adopted similar provisions.

The court said that "the record reveals a reasonable basis for the [board's] decision not to consent to [Grogan's] withdrawal of [her] resignation, and there is no indication that the decision was affected by an error of law, was arbitrary and capricious, or that it constituted an abuse of discretion."

It should be noted that "acceptance of the resignation" by the appointing authority, unless specifically provided for by law, is not required for the resignation to take effect. For example, the Rules of the State Commission provide that if no effective date is specified in the resignation it takes effect upon delivery to the appointing authority.

The Grogan case implies that acceptance is not required, as clearly the school board had not acted on the resignation, it had merely been "delivered" to the board.

Although acceptance of a resignation may not be required, an appointing authority may elect to ignore a resignation submitted by an individual against whom disciplinary charges have been, or are about to be, filed and proceed with the disciplinary action.

The Discipline Book

18.119 Rescinding a letter of retirement

Elmira CSD v Newcomb, 266 A.D.2d 622, motion to appeal dismissed, 94 N.Y.2d 899

Among the basic general rules applicable to resignation from public service are the following:

1. An individual may rescind his or her letter resignation prior to its delivery to the appropriate authority.

2. The letter of resignation is effective upon delivery to the appointing authority unless an "approval" or "acceptance" of the resignation is mandated by law or a provision in a collective bargaining agreement.

3. Once delivered, the individual cannot withdraw or rescind his or her resignation without the approval of the appointing authority.

4. An appointing authority may elect to ignore a resignation and proceed with disciplinary action against the individual.

Do the same rules apply in cases involving an individual's submission of a letter indicating his or her intent to retire? In the Newcomb case the Appellate Division considered the effort of an individual to rescind his notice of his intention to retire.

James E. Newcomb, a tenured guidance counselor employed by the Elmira City School District, told the district that he could not return to his position due to "medical problems." He was absent for practically all of the fall 1997 semester.

Eventually Newcomb and the district entered into a "settlement agreement" in lieu of district's pursuing disciplinary action against Newcomb. Under the terms of the settlement Newcomb agreed to submit his "written notice of retirement," to take effect February 1, 1998. The district agreed to keep Newcomb on the payroll from December 11, 1997 until January 31, 1998. Newcomb submitted his "retirement letter" in December 1997. For its part, the district continued Newcomb on the payroll.

However, in January 1998 Newcomb sent the district a second letter rescinding his December 1997 letter of retirement. This second letter was delivered to the district before Board of Education had taken formal action on Newcomb's December retirement letter.

The board voted to disregard Newcomb's attempt to rescind his letter of retirement unless he (1) returned "the previously paid leave funds" and (2) "presented medical documentation certifying his ability to work." Newcomb failed to comply with either of these conditions and ultimately was deemed "retired" and terminated from the payroll.

When Newcomb sued to void the board's action and to reclaim his position, the district countered with a petition asking the court to rule that Newcomb "had no right to unilaterally rescind his retirement letter and that his retirement was effective February 1, 1998." The district argued that it had acted in reliance of the settlement agreed to by the parties in lieu of its bringing disciplinary action against Newcomb, pursuant to which Newcomb agreed to retire, when it continued him on the payroll as agreed and had hired his replacement. The Supreme Court justice denied Newcomb's motion for summary judgment and he appealed.

Newcomb's basic argument: This is a simple rescission before acceptance case, i.e., I rescinded my retirement letter prior to its acceptance by the Board and thus the district had no authority to terminate my employment.

The district position: Newcomb's letter of retirement was not a unilateral act on his part but rather reflected a settlement agreement between the parties and therefore it was not obligated to honor the letter Newcomb submitted in a unilateral effort to rescind his retirement letter.

The Appellate Division commenced its analysis be noting that "authority exists to support the general proposition that a retirement letter may be withdrawn prior to a legally binding acceptance by a board of education," citing a number of court decision and rulings by the Commissioner of Education. This, according to the ruling, means that although submitting a notice of an intention to retire simultaneously implies a "resignation" from one's position, delivery of the "retirement letter" is not the operative factor; the appointing authority must take some action to "finalize it."

The Appellate Division, however, concluded that there were questions of fact that barred the application of this general principle -- a retirement letter must be formally acted upon to be effective -- at this stage of the litigation. Among the issues of fact to be resolved:

1. Was Newcomb's retirement letter, submitted in compliance with a settlement of a disciplinary action, essentially a term or condition of the settlement and thus he could not unilaterally rescind it notwithstanding the fact that the board had not formally acted on his retirement letter? and, if not,

2. Was the absence of a formal acceptance by the Board fatal in view of the fact that it had indicated its acceptance of the settlement by continuing Newcomb on the payroll and recruiting his replacement?

The Appellate Division, ruling that the Supreme Court was correct in denying Newcomb's motion for summary judgment, returned the matter to Supreme Court for its consideration of these issues.

18.120 Rescinding a resignation

Otero v Safir, 258 A.D.2d 297

After being served with disciplinary charges involving allegations that subjected him to criminal charges, New York City police officer Louis Otero submitted his resignation from the force rather than testify at a disciplinary hearing. Later Otero asked a New York State Supreme Court justice to direct the Department to rescind his resignation. When the Supreme Court dismissed his petition, he appealed.

The Appellate Division denied Otero's appeal. It said that Otero's resignation was "strategically motivated and not the result of fraud, overreaching or other misconduct on [Department's] part, was not improperly obtained and, accordingly, may not be judicially countermanded," citing Cacchioli v Hoberman, 31 NY2d 287.

This case illustrates the general principle that an individual's request to withdraw a resignation or to have it rescinded is subject to the discretionary approval of the appointing authority. Generally courts will intervene only in situations where the former employee proves that the resignation was the result of fraud or coercion.[206]

18.121 Rescinding tenure status

Remus v Tonawanda City School Dist., 277 A.D.2d 905, affirmed, 96 N.Y.2d 271
Shaffer v Schenectady City School Dist., , 96 N.Y.2d 271

The Remus and Shaffer decisions by the New York State Court of Appeals set out the court's view with respect to the effective date of a teacher's employment rights flowing from holding a tenured appointment.[207]

The ruling, which concerned the tenure status of individuals employed in unclassified service positions, has significant implications with respect to an appointing authority's ability to rescind a permanent appointment to a position in the classified service prior to its effective date as well.

Both the Remus and Shaffer cases involve essentially the same question: May the appointing authority rescind its earlier action granting a probationary teacher tenure if such action is taken prior to the effective date of the teacher's attaining tenure status?

The Remus Case

On June 4, 1998, in accordance with the recommendation of the superintendent, the Tonawanda school board adopted a resolution appointing probationary teacher Jill Remus "to a tenured position effective September 2, 1998."

A short time later, in response to an inquiry by her school principal, Remus admitted that she had joined students in drinking alcoholic beverages while acting as a chaperone during a school-sponsored student exchange program in Costa Rica notwithstanding the school's "zero tolerance" policy as to the consumption of alcohol at school-sponsored events.

---

[206] Courts will also direct the rescinding of a resignation for certain types of "mistakes." For example, a teacher was told that she was a probationer and would not be recommended for tenure. She submitted her resignation solely to avoid having her personal record indicate that she was terminated for failure to satisfactorily complete her probationary period. It was later determined that the teacher had completed her probationary period and had acquired tenure prior to her submitting the resignation. The Court of Appeals approved the rescinding of the resignation on the theory that the teacher had submitted her resignation under the mistaken belief that she was a probationer. [Gould v Sewanhaka CSD, __ NY2 __].

[207] The Remus case challenged a ruling by the Appellate Division, Fourth Department; the Shaffer decision was made in response to the "certification of the question" by the U.S. Circuit Court of Appeals, Second Circuit [NY].

On August 31, 1998, the School Board adopted a resolution rescinding its resolution giving Remus a "conditional tenure appointment" and terminated her employment as a probationary teacher. This action by the board followed Remus' declining an offer to extend her probationary period for an additional year that was made to her earlier in the day. Remus appealed the Board's action, claiming she had attained tenure and could not be summarily dismissed.

The Shaffer Case

The Schenectady Superintendent of Schools told probationer Sharon Shaffer that because of her excessive absences from work, he would recommend that the Schenectady City School District Board of Education discontinue her employment as of June 30, 1998.

On May 29, 1998, the Superintendent submitted a report to the Board recommending that it approve tenured appointments for the 33 teachers he had listed in the report. Shaffer's name was included on the list, with an effective tenure date of September 1, 1998. On June 2, 1998, the Board adopted a resolution granting all 33 teachers listed tenure. This action by the Board was then distributed to the public.

Informed that "Shaffer's name was included on the tenure recommendation list because of a clerical error," the Superintendent told Shaffer that the Board would rescind its June 2 resolution unless she agreed to resign. Shaffer refused to resign.

A special board meeting was held on June 17, 1998, during which the Board adopted a resolution rescinding its action granting tenure to the 33 teachers for the reason that the prior resolution "contained a clerical error." The Board then adopted a new resolution granting tenure to teachers on a revised list. Shaffer's name was not on this new list. Shaffer appealed, contending that she had attained tenure as a result of the Board's action on June 2, and thus was entitled to the protections of Section 3020-a of the Education Law.

The Court of Appeals said that both cases present a common threshold issue: "Does a Board of Education resolution that grants tenure to a teacher effective on a specified future date pursuant to the provisions of Education Law Section 2509[1], immediately entitle that teacher to the benefits of tenure?" The Court of Appeal's conclusion: "A teacher granted tenure effective on a [specified] future date is not entitled to the benefits of tenure until the effective date specified in the resolution."

The Court explained that the Education Law draws a distinction between probationary teachers and tenured teachers. Probationary teachers can be terminated at any time during the probationary period, for any reason and without a hearing while tenured teachers hold their positions during good behavior and competent service, and are subject to dismissal only after formal disciplinary proceedings.[208]

The basic argument advanced by both Remus and Shaffer is that once they were granted tenure by action of the board pursuant to Section 2509 of the Education Law, their employment could not be terminated except for cause after notice and hearing. In their view, their tenure status accrued upon

---

[208] Typically probationers in the classified service may be summarily dismissed from their position only after completing the minimum period of their probationary period and prior to the end of their probationary period. However, there is no bar to granting a probationary employee tenure status at any time during his or her probationary period.

adoption of the resolution granting them tenure by the board and could not be rescinded by a subsequent resolution adopted by the board.

The Schenectady City School District, and the Appellate Division in deciding the Remus case, took the view that a formal offer and acceptance of tenure was required for tenure to become operative before the expiration of the three-year probationary period and such an offer and acceptance was not present insofar as either Remus or Shaffer was concerned.

The Court of Appeals disagreed with this argument, commenting that the Education Law does not require a formal offer and acceptance of a tenure appointment and, "given the express grant of power to make tenure appointments before the end of the probationary period, no reason exists to inject such a requirement into the statute."

Noting that this specific issue -- rescinding an appointment prior to its effective date -- was not addressed in Weinbrown v Board of Education, 28 NY2d 474, a case cited by both school districts in support of their respective arguments, the Court of Appeals held that "A Board resolution granting a probationary teacher tenure effective on a future date (one set either to coincide with the end of or to occur before the end of that teacher's probationary period) confers tenure upon the teacher only as of that specified future date."

These decisions suggest that any permanent appointment, or contingent permanent appointment, that is subject to a probationary period, or an appointment based on reinstatement from a preferred list, whether in the classified service or the unclassified service, may be rescinded prior to its effective date by the appointing authority, provided such action (1) is not otherwise prohibited by law and (2) would not otherwise constitute unlawful discrimination.

It may be significant that the decision refers to the appointing authority's granting tenure effective on a specified future date insofar as trigging the individual's tenure rights are concerned. If, on the other hand, no "future date" is specified, it could be argued that the individual attains his or her tenure rights immediately upon the act granting such status by the appointing authority.

18.122 Reviewing disciplinary action

Horgan v Safir, 273 A.D.2d 135, motion for leave to appeal denied, 95 N.Y.2d 765

A court's review of an administrative decision following a hearing is significantly more limited when a higher court considers an appeal than when a trial court is reviewing the matter. This limitation proved critical in the Appellate Division, First Department's consideration of the Horgan case.

New York City police officer John Horgan was found guilty of "using discourteous and disrespectful remarks concerning race" following an administrative disciplinary hearing. The penalty imposed: forfeiture of 20 days of vacation. Horgan appealed the Police Commissioner's determination.

The Appellate Division dismissed Horgan's appeal. The court, however, specifically commented that it had to dismiss the appeal despite the fact that if the Commissioner's determination was reviewed "under the standards applicable to a trial court decision," it would have been "disposed to annul it as against the weight of the credible evidence."

The Appellate Division said that courts have very limited review powers over administrative agency determinations. Accordingly, it said that it was "constrained to confirm [the Commissioner's] findings" in the disciplinary hearing, citing Berenhaus v Ward, 70 NY2d 436.

18.123 Right to counsel

Elmore v Plainview-Old Bethpage CSD, 273 A.D.2d 307 [other decisions involving these parties: 296 A.D.2d 704; 299 A.D.2d 545]

The Plainview-Old Bethpage Central School District filed disciplinary charges against one of its teachers, Edwin Elmore, alleging that Elmore had "engaged in inappropriate conduct toward a student." Found guilty following a disciplinary hearing held pursuant to Section 3020-a of the Education Law, the district terminated him.

Elmore appealed, contending that he had been unfairly denied his right to counsel when the Hearing Officer ruled that he could not discuss his testimony with his attorney during any adjournments in his cross-examination by the district's attorney. According to the decision, the five days of Elmore's cross-examination extended over a period of 10 weeks. In other words, the hearing officer barred Elmore from discussing his testimony with his attorney for a ten-week period.

A State Supreme Court judge vacated the determination and the penalty imposed. The Appellate Division sustained the lower court's decision. The Appellate Division pointed out that Section 3020-a(3)(c)(i) provides that a teacher facing disciplinary charges "shall have the right to be represented by counsel" at any hearing held on those charges.

However, because there were no cases "discussing the precise issue herein, namely, to what extent a Hearing Officer may circumscribe a teacher's contact with his attorney between adjourned dates of hearings," cited in the briefs submitted by the parties, the Appellate Division applied the rationale followed in criminal prosecutions involving similar situations -- barring the client from conferring with his or her attorney.

Commenting that "teacher disciplinary proceedings are not criminal actions," the court said it was "mindful that a tenured teacher has a protected property interest in his [or her] position which raises due process considerations when a teacher is faced with termination of his employment," presumably deeming the loss of employment the economic equivalent of incarceration.

As New York courts have disapproved forbidding a defendant from discussing his trial testimony with his attorney for all but brief periods of time, the Appellate Division, citing Goldfinger v Lisker, 68 NY2d 225, decided that such a restriction in an administrative disciplinary proceeding was inappropriate in view of the due process considerations involved when a tenured employee is threatened with termination of his or her employment -- particularly in Elmore-type situation, where the time period involved was 10 weeks. The Appellate Division directed the district to hold a new hearing.

The court's rationale would probably be applied in disciplinary actions taken against an individual pursuant to Section 75 of the Civil Service Law.

18.124 Same offense, different penalties

Wagner v Kerik, 298 A.D.2d 322
Jones v Kerik, 298 A.D.2d 308

Two different employees serving in the same agency are charged and found guilty of the same type of misconduct but the appointing authority imposes different penalties on each. Is this something that the courts will find arbitrary? Apparently not, as the Wagner and Jones decisions demonstrate.

New York City police officer John Wagner was served with disciplinary charges alleging that he used excessive force against an individual. Found guilty, the penalty imposed by Police Commissioner Bernard B. Kerik was suspension from duty for 15 days without pay.

Another New York City police officer, Richard Jones was served with disciplinary charges alleging that he "used excessive force against another person." Found guilty, here the penalty imposed on Jones by Police Commissioner Kerik was the forfeiture of seven vacation days.

The Appellate Division, First Department, affirmed the Commissioner's determination that the individuals were guilty of the charges preferred against them and did not object to the fact that different penalty were, respectively, imposed on each despite the fact that the same underlying offense was involved -- use of excessive force by a police officer.

The appointing authority's electing to impose different penalties for essentially the same type of offense sometimes results in an employee filing a lawsuit objecting to the penalty on the grounds that another employee who committed the same offense received a lighter punishment. Case law suggests that such challenges will receive little sympathy from the courts.

If the court find that the penalty imposed does not offend its sense of "fairness" with respect to nature of the offense, it will typically uphold the penalty notwithstanding the fact that a different penalty was imposed on another individual guilty of the same offense, citing the Pell standard set out in Pell v Board of Education, 34 NY2d 222. In other words the courts do not consider the fact that a different penalty was imposed on another employee charged with the same offense relevant in most instances.

In one case, however, Trotman v Ward, 146 AD2d 236, the Appellate Division was persuaded that a certain penalty was unfair because lesser penalties had been imposed on other employees found guilty of more egregious misconduct.

Other types of "same facts, different results" situations have been considered by the courts. For example, City School District of Tonawanda v Tonawanda Education Association, 63 NY2d 846, involved a situation in which the same facts considered by two different arbitrators but involving two different employees produced different results.

The school district had made layoff decisions that adversely impacted on two employees. Both individuals grieved. The grievances were considered by two different arbitrators.

The first arbitration decision handed down ruled in favor of the employer while in the second case, heard by a different arbitrator and handed down after the first arbitrator had made a ruling, the employee prevailed.

The school district claimed that the first arbitrator's decision should be adopted by the second arbitrator since the same facts were involved and thus the second arbitrator was bound by the first arbitrator's findings.[209]

The Court of Appeals rejected Tonawanda's theory, holding that both arbitration decisions were to stand.

Same offense, different penalties was also an issue in Meagher v Safir, 272 A.D.2d 114, reversed, 95 N.Y.2d 762, wherein the Court of Appeals said: Although Officer Ryan forfeited five vacation days as part of a plea arrangement, Meagher should have anticipated the possibility of a harsher penalty in opting for an administrative trial. "Given that the *quid pro quo* of the bargaining process will almost necessarily involve offers to moderate sentences that ordinarily would be greater ..., it is also to be anticipated that sentences handed out after trial may be more severe than those proposed in connection with a plea" (*People v Pena*, 50 NY2d 400, 412 [citations omitted])."

18.125 Section 3020-a disciplinary appeals

Austin v NYC Board of Education, 280 A.D.2d 365

The Austin decision by the Appellate Division, First Department, sets out the standards followed by the courts in considering appeals from Section 3020-a disciplinary determinations. Typically these standards are considered in connection with motions by the parties to confirm or vacate the hearing officer's decision.

The ruling also addresses an issue that is frequently of concern in such disciplinary proceedings: the acceptance and consideration of hearsay evidence by the hearing officer.

Wallace Austin was served with disciplinary charges pursuant to Section 3020-a of the Education Law. He was found guilty of certain of the charges and specifications.

---

[209] Would Tonawanda have been disposed to argue that the second arbitrator was bound by the first arbitrator's award had it gone the other way? It is prudent to consider the future impact of an instant position under alternate circumstances in such situations.

A State Supreme Court justice overturned the hearing officer's ruling on the basis that it was not supported by substantial evidence in the record. The Appellate Division, however, said that the lower court had applied an incorrect standard in reviewing Austin's petition and vacated the lower court's determination.

According to the Appellate Division's decision, the lower court had applied the standard applicable in reviewing challenges to administrative determinations brought pursuant to Article 78 of the Civil Practice Law and Rules [CPLR].

The Article 78 standard for review: Was the administrative determination supported by substantial evidence in the record?

In contrast, the standard of review of Section 3020-a disciplinary decisions is controlled by CPLR Article 75, not the standards to be met in resolving a challenge brought pursuant to CPLR Article 78.[210]

The Appellate Division pointed out that Section 3020-a(5) specifically requires that a court's review of a Section 3020-a hearing officer's decision in accordance with the standard spelled out in CPLR 7511.

The sole grounds set out in Article 75 for overturning such a determination:

1. Proof of corruption, fraud or misconduct in procuring an award;

2. The partiality of the arbitrator;

3. The arbitrator exceeded his or her authority; or

4. The arbitrator failed to follow the procedures set out in Article 75.

In addition to these statutory standards justifying the vacating of the arbitration award, the courts have declared arbitration awards that violate a strong public policy null and void.

The Appellate Division said that since Austin failed to show any misconduct, bias, excess of power or procedural defects on the part of the hearing officer, [or any violation of a strong public policy] his petition must be dismissed.

In addition, the court observed that the rules governing Section 3020-a disciplinary hearing procedures do not require compliance with technical rules of evidence. Accordingly, a hearing officer may accept and consider hearsay evidence in such an administrative proceeding.

The Appellate Division also commented that "the hearing officer credited the testimony of the Principal and Assistant Principal and found [Austin's] testimony to be inconsistent and incredible."

---

[210] Essentially a CPLR Article 75 proceeding concerns challenges to arbitration awards while an Article 78 proceeding tests whether an administrative determination was arbitrary or capricious.

There are other critical elements to be remembered in connection with appealing a Section 3020-a disciplinary determination.

For example, in addition to the limited grounds for vacating the arbitration award listed in Section 7511, Section 3020-a sets a very short statute of limitations for filing a petition to overturn or modify the award as well as setting other limitations in appealing such decisions.

Section 3020-a.5 provides that:

1. Not later than ten days after receipt of the hearing officer's decision, the employee or the employing board may make an application to the New York state supreme court to vacate or modify the decision of the hearing officer pursuant to CPLR Section 7511.

2. The court's review shall be limited to the grounds set forth in Article 75. Further, the hearing panel's determination shall be deemed to be final for the purpose of such proceeding.

3. In no case shall the filing or the pendency of an appeal delay the implementation of the decision of the hearing officer.

Keeping in mind the 10-day limitation for perfecting an appeal from a Section 3020-a decision, it should be remembered that the basic rules concerning effective service of a final determination for the purposes of filing a timely appeal are as follows:

1. If the individual is not represented by an attorney or by a union official, the individual must be served to begin the statute of limitations running.

2. If an employee is represented by an attorney, the administrative body may send a copy of the determination to the employee but it must serve the attorney to begin the running of the statute of limitations.

3. If the employee is represented by a person who is not an attorney, the administrative body may send a copy to the representative but it must serve the employee to start the statute of limitations running.

18.126 Section 72 leave

Lara v City of New York, USDC, SDNY, July 1999, Judge Cote

It is not unusual for an employee placed on disability leave pursuant to Section 72 of the Civil Service Law to allege that his or her employer's action in placing the individual on such leave constituted unlawful discrimination because of a disability. In the Lara case, national origin discrimination was claimed to have motivated placing the employee on "an involuntary medical leave" that eventually resulted in Lara's being placed on Section 72 leave.

Pablo Lara, who was born in the Dominican Republic, was employed as a Program Officer by the New York City Department for the Aging (DFTA). His duties included monitoring contracts between DFTA and community-based organizations.

The New York Foundation for Senior Citizens wrote a letter complaining that Lara "continuously" compared the Foundation administration to "'militant dictatorships in many African countries.'" Throughout a meeting, it was alleged, Lara's voice was raised and "he seemed agitated." He repeatedly mimicked Foundation staff at the meeting.

The department decided to place Lara on an involuntary medical leave of absence effective March 21, 1997. Lara was also instructed to report to Dr. Azariah Eshkenazi for a psychiatric examination. According to the decision, Dr. Eshkenazi diagnosed Lara as having a "personality disorder, paranoid type" and "generalized anxiety."

Lara was also examined by a psychiatrist of his own choosing, Dr. Pedro Rodriguez. Dr. Rodriguez said he found no evidence of "serious psychiatric conditions, including psychosis and personality disorder that could have prevented [Lara] from doing his work."

Administrative Law Judge [ALJ] Ray Fleischhacker was designated to hold a Section 72 hearing. The ALJ decided to adjourn the hearing so that Lara could be examined by a third psychiatrist, Dr. Myron Gordon. Dr. Gordon diagnosed Lara as having "paranoid personality disorder."

On December 3, 1997, the ALJ issued a "Report and Recommendation" in which he concluded that Lara was "mentally unfit to perform the duties of his position." He recommended that Lara be placed on Section 72 leave.

The Department placed Lara on Section 72 leave effective December 15, 1997. While on such leave Lara was re-evaluated by Dr. Eshkenazi, who determined that "Lara's mental condition had not improved and that Lara remained unfit to return to work." The department terminated Lara's employment effective December 15, 1998. Section 73 of the Civil Service Law authorizes the termination of an individual who has been continuously absent on Section 72 leave for at least one year.

Meanwhile, Lara filed a charge of discrimination with the Equal Employment Opportunity Commission (EEOC) on April 16, 1997, contending that the department's decision to place him on involuntary medical leave constituted national origin discrimination. EEOC issued Lara a "right to sue letter" and Lara initiated litigation in federal district court.

A federal district court judge dismissed Lara's petition, agreeing with the department that Lara had failed to perform his duties satisfactorily and, consequently, he failed to satisfy one of the critical elements required to establish a prima facie case of unlawful discrimination -- the individual's ability to satisfactory perform the duties of the position.

Judge Cote said that the city had submitted "uncontroverted evidence" of Lara's inappropriate behavior at staff meetings and that there was unrebutted evidence that "DFTA contractors complained repeatedly about Lara's unprofessional behavior and requested that Lara be replaced by another program officer." Accordingly, said the court, "Lara fails to raise an issue of fact that he was performing his job satisfactorily and [thus] fails to establish a prima facie case."

The decision also notes an important procedural element. Lara had named the City, Shaffer, and DFTA as defendants. Judge Cote said that "[t]here is no individual liability under Title VII and the Title VII claims against Shaffer must be dismissed." In addition, the court ruled that the Title VII claims against DFTA also had to be dismissed because under Chapter 17, Section 396 of the New York City Charter all actions and proceedings for the recovery of penalties for the violation of any law shall be brought in the name of the City of New York, and not that of any agency, except where otherwise provided by law.

18.127 Selective prosecution

Bey v New York City Civil Service Commission, Supreme Court, received January 6, 2002, by Justice Madden

Pedro Rivera Bey, Oba Hassan Wat Bey, Edward Ebanks, Herbert L. Hinnant, and Michael Nichols [hereinafter collectively referred to as Bey] are former tenured New York City Correction Department officers. The lawsuit involved one issue infrequently encountered: allegations of selective prosecution.

Bay identified himself as "Black and of Moorish national origin," and believing he was exempt from federal and state taxes, filed Federal and New York State tax forms claiming exemptions from income tax withholdings. Some of the Bay correction officers also filed IRS forms for nonresident aliens or filed self-made forms entitled "Certificates of Foreign Status for Moorish Americans."

New York City conducted an investigation to determine which employees were claiming tax-exempt status or were claiming an excessive number of exemptions. About 1,400 City employees were identified, including the Bey correction officers.

In April 1998, the Correction Department served disciplinary charges alleging that the Bey employees had engaged in conduct unbecoming an officer by: 1) knowingly submitting Federal and State tax forms falsely claiming exemption from taxation; 2) submitting false tax information with the intent to defraud the State of New York; and 3) violating their oaths of office by submitting documents disclaiming their United States citizenship.

The City's Office of Administrative Trials and Hearings [OATH] held a joint hearing for 17 Correction Department employees pursuant to Civil Service Law Section 75. OATH found that Bey and his co-plaintiffs were guilty of all charges filed against them except their alleged "disclaiming of their United States citizenship." The Department imposed the penalty recommended by OATH: termination.

In response to an appeal filed by the Bey employees pursuant to Section 76 of the Civil Service Law, the City's Civil Service affirmed the Correction Department's dismissal of Bey correction officers.

Bey's appeal to State Supreme Court set out several claims but only one survived: the claim that "[t]he charges, the hearing procedures and the discharge of the [Bey officers] violated their statutory and constitutional rights." The Supreme Court justice ruled that Bey raised a triable issue when he alleged that employees who were not Moorish-Americans and who engaged in the same or similar misconduct, were permitted to change their W-4s and, further, these employees were not discharged.

Justice Madden ruled that assuming that the allegations in Bey's petition were true, it is sufficient to raise the only issue here subject to judicial review pursuant to Article 78 of the Civil Practice Law and Rules: the constitutional claim of selective prosecution.

In making a claim of selective prosecution, the individual alleges that he or she has been denied his or her constitutional right to equal protection of the laws as guaranteed by the 14th Amendment and the New York State Constitution forbidding a public authority from applying or enforcing an admitted valid law "with an evil eye and an unequal hand, so as practically to make unjust and illegal discriminations between persons in similar circumstances."

According to the decision, both the "unequal hand" and the "evil eye" requirements must be proven: i.e., there must be not only a showing that the law was not applied to others similarly situated but also "that the selective application of the law was deliberately based upon an impermissible standard such as race, religion or some other arbitrary classification."

The court said that Bey's petition alleges that he and his co-correction officers were singled out based upon their race, religion and, or, national origin, because the Correction Department and other City agencies permitted "other employees" who were not "Moorish American" to change their withholding forms, and no disciplinary charges were filed against them and they were not discharged.

As these allegations were found sufficient to state a cause of action for impermissible discriminatory prosecution, the court dismissed all of Bey's allegations except those dealing with the selective prosecution claim and said that a trial was required to resolve this issue.

18.128 Settlement agreement

McLean v Village of Sleepy Hollow, USDC, SDNY, 10/24/01

What can an individual do if the terms of a settlement agreement between the employee and the employer fail to provide the benefit or result expected by the employee? In the absence showing that agreement to the settlement was the result of some fraud on the part of the employer, very little, as the McLean decision by a federal district court judge demonstrates.

Gary McLean was a part-time Buildings Code Enforcement Officer in the Village of Sleepy Hollow. He was also employed full time in another position and in view of this, he was permitted to set his own work schedule. McLean was terminated from his position following the election of a new mayor. He sued in federal district court, contending that he had been fired in retaliation for his vocal support of the previous administration.

The Village and McLean settle the case. McLean was to be reinstated with back pay and his attorneys' fees paid -- all the relief to which he would have been entitled had he won his lawsuit. Settlement documents were signed and the Court "so ordered" the Stipulation and Order of Settlement.

The settlement included the following provision:

"IT IS FURTHER AGREED that the plaintiff will be re-employed by the Village of Sleepy Hollow at the annual salary of $10,000 per annum as a part-time Code Enforcement Officer subject to all terms and conditions of employment attendant to that position."

McLean was told that he could return to work by letter dated June 14, 2000. Prior to this date, however, the Mayor endorsed a recommendation that Building Code Inspectors be required to work between the hours of 9 a.m. and 12 p.m. Mondays through Fridays. As McLean's full time job required that he be at work 7:30 a.m. and 3:30 p.m., he was unable to meet the Village's new work schedule set for his position. The possibility of a new policy changing the work hours of his job was not mentioned to McLean during the settlement negotiations.

Although the Village offered McLean the option of working any three successive hours between 8:30 AM and 4:30 PM on weekdays, this would not solve his problem and he did not return to work as contemplated by the settlement. The Village subsequently filed disciplinary charges against McLean for failure to return to work "as scheduled." The hearing officer ruled that the Village had acted within its authority when it changed McLean's work schedule and recommended that McLean be dismissed from his position because he failed to report for work.

The Village Board adopted the hearing officer's findings and recommendations and terminated McLean. McLean filed an Article 78 in state supreme court challenging the Village's action. He also asked the federal district court to enforce the terms of the settlement order.

McLean's argument: he would never have settled the case if he had known that he would have to give up his full-time job in order to go back to work as a Building Code Examiner. He contended that the use of the phrase "subject to all the terms and conditions of employment attendant to that position" in the Stipulation and Order means that the Village had to reemploy him on the terms that were in effect at the time he agreed to settle the case.

The district court said that although the "situation is extremely unfortunate" and McLean did not get what he thought he was entitled to under the settlement to which he agreed, it agreed with the Village that his motion must be denied.

Although it is clear that the court has subject matter jurisdiction to enforce the settlement, "subject matter jurisdiction was only the first hurdle to adjudication" in this case. The federal judge pointed out that McLean participated in a civil service disciplinary hearing, where he litigated and lost the issue of the Village's right to dismiss him notwithstanding the terms set out in the settlement agreement.

According to the ruling, whether the hearing officer's finding against McLean bars his obtaining a different interpretation of the meaning of the relevant language in the settlement Stipulation in federal court is a complicated question. While any decision by the New York State Supreme Court in the

Article 78 proceeding would be entitled to preclusive effect under the Full Faith & Credit Clause, regardless of whether the Supreme Court ruled on questions of fact or of law, here there is only the administrative determination. Is an administrative hearing officer's unreviewed findings entitled to preclusive effect under the circumstances?

According to the ruling, this depends on whether the challenged elements constitute findings of fact, where preclusive effect is accorded, or findings of law.[211]

The judge said that he did not have to decide if there was any "preclusionary effect" with respect administrative findings of law. Instead the court held that even if McLean could relitigate the meaning of the settlement agreement, he agreed "with the conclusions of the hearing officer."

McLean conceded that the Village had the right to set the terms and conditions of employment, including the work schedule, of its employees.

In the words of the court: "The Village is of course free to waive its rights in this regard, but any such waiver must be apparent from the face of the contract between McLean and Sleepy Hollow. The terms of the Stipulation and Order are artless (at least from McLean's perspective), but the relevant sentence is not ambiguous and cannot be read as a waiver by the Village of its right to alter the terms and conditions of its employees' jobs. The Stipulation does not require the Village to maintain the terms and conditions of McLean's employment as they were at the time the settlement was negotiated. It says only that McLean will be reemployed on the terms and conditions that are 'attendant to his position.' While the words 'from time to time' do not appear after the word "position," they do not have to, because the usual rule is that job terms can be changed. McLean's reading of the Stipulation, not the Village's, is the one that departs from the usual rule; thus McLean's reading cannot be adopted unless it is clearly spelled out in the contract. It is not. End of discussion."

This, said the court, leads to a harsh result. However, the fact that McLean and his counsel assumed that everything would go back to the way it was, -- i.e., "that they subjectively intended the settlement would restore the status quo ante" -- is insufficient to bind the Village when that subjective intention is not clear from the objective manifestation of McLean's intent - the words of the Stipulation and Order.

18.129 Settlement agreements and FOIL

Hansen v Wallkill, 270 A.D.2d 390

Sometimes an individual agrees to terminate his employment or settle a disciplinary action in accordance with agreed upon terms and conditions. Typically, such an agreement contains a "non-disclosure" clause. What happens if the terms of the settlement are made public without the expressed consent of the individual? This was the issue raised in the Hansen case.

---

[211] The preclusionary effect of an administrative determination involving findings of law has not yet been considered by the Second Circuit.

Jon Hansen and the Town of Wallkill entered into a "settlement agreement." When the town supervisor, Howard Mills, revealed the amount of the "severance payment" made to Hansen under the terms of the agreement to the town board, Hansen sued for damages, claiming the disclosure constituted a breach of contract.

Hansen pointed to a clause in the agreement that provided that the terms of the settlement were to remain confidential except "as may be required by law or legal process".

Mills, on the other hand, argued that the board was told the amount of Hansen's severance pay in response to a question during a regular meeting and that his disclosing this information was required under the Freedom of Information Law (FOIL).

The Appellate Division sustained a lower court's ruling dismissing Hansen's complaint. The court said that "[i]t is well settled that FOIL imposes a broad duty of disclosure on government agencies," citing Section 84 of the Public Officers Law. Thus all public records are to be disclosed pursuant to a FOIL demand except:

1. When disclosure is specifically prohibited by law or by a court order; or

2. Where a record falls within an exception that permits the entity, as a matter of discretion, to withhold the information and the entity elects to withhold it.

The disclosure of the amount of the severance payment, said the court, does not fall within any of the FOIL exceptions.[212] Further, while the town supervisor did not seek court authorization for the disclosure, the agreement did not require prior court authorization to do so.

Suppose the information sought under FOIL concerns a "disciplinary settlement." Can a public employer agree to keep the settlement document confidential?

This issue was considered by the Appellate Division in LaRocca v Jericho UFSD, 220 AD2d 424. In LaRocca the court decided that the terms of a disciplinary settlement were subject to disclosure under FOIL.

The court held that a disciplinary settlement agreement did not constitute an "employment history" as defined by FOIL and therefore was presumptively available for public inspection. In addition, the court said that "as a matter of public policy, [a public employer] cannot bargain away the public's right to access to public records."

The Appellate Division decided that the settlement agreement, or any part of it, providing for confidentiality or denying the public access to the document "is unenforceable as against the pubic interest."

---

[212] The courts have ruled that although FOIL provides for certain exceptions, honoring such exceptions is a matter of discretion on the part of the custodian of the records; it may elect to provide the records notwithstanding its authority to decline to provide it pursuant to one of statutory exceptions set out in law.

The settlement agreement, however, contained references to charges that the employee denied or were not admitted, together with the names of other employees. The Appellate Division held that disclosure of those specific portions of the agreement would constitute an unwarranted invasion of privacy within the meaning of FOIL.

It should also be remembered that Section 1133 of the Education Law bars the so-called silent resignation, declaring that public policy prohibits agreements not to reveal certain types of resignations. Under the statute a school administrator or superintendent "shall not make any agreement to withhold from law enforcement authorities, the superintendent or the commissioner, where appropriate, the fact that an allegation of child abuse in an educational setting on the part of any employee or volunteer as required by this article in return for the resignation or voluntary suspension from his or her position of such person, against whom the allegation is made."

18.130 Standing to appeal

Delgado v NYC Board of Education, 272 A.D.2d 207, motion for leave to appeal denied, 95 N.Y.2d 768

The basic issue in the Delgado case concerns the right of an individual to bring a lawsuit involving the same issue[s] considered by an arbitrator in resolving a grievance brought in accordance with procedures negotiated under the Taylor Law.

John Delgado was terminated from his position with the New York City Board of Education Office of School Food and Nutritional Services. His grievance protesting his dismissal was denied by an arbitrator.

In an effort to vacate or modify an arbitration decision rejecting his grievance challenging his termination of his employment Delgado filed a petition pursuant to Article 75 of the Civil Practice Law and Rules seeking to vacate the arbitrator's award.

The Board of Education opposed Delgado's motion. The Appellate Division affirmed a lower court ruling summarily dismissing Delgado's petition. The court's rationale: Delgado "lacks standing to bring the instant petition" since he was represented by the union at the arbitration.

Significantly, the Appellate Division said that although the issue of standing was first raised by the Board of Education in its appeal, it presented a question of law -- did the court have jurisdiction to adjudicate Delgado's petition -- that could not have been avoided had it been raised before the lower court. Accordingly, it was proper to raise, and the court to consider, the question of jurisdiction at the appellate level.

In other words, if Delgado did not have standing to bring the Article 75 action, the courts may not consider his petition in the first instance and that issue -- jurisdiction -- may be raised by a party at any stage of the proceeding.

Clearly, had the union filed an Article 75 petition challenging the arbitrator's determination, it would have found to have "standing."

It is generally held that unless the Taylor Law agreement includes an uncommon provision -- allowing an employee himself or herself to demand arbitration of his or her grievance independent of the union -- the right to demand that a grievance be submitted to arbitration is vested exclusively in the employee organization.

Accordingly, as a general rule, only the union has to right to challenge an adverse determination by the arbitrator by filing an Article 75 petition seeking to vacate or modify the award.

18.131 Statute of limitations

Levine v Board of Education, 272 A.D.2d 328

Sometimes an individual will file a grievance in accordance with the grievance procedure set out in a collective bargaining agreement rather than immediately initiate a lawsuit on the assumption that he or she can file the lawsuit "later."

The Levine case is another example of the difficulties an individual may encounter if he or she does not take the steps necessary to protect his or her right to litigate the issue.

The New York City Board of Education terminated Martin Levine from his position as laboratory specialist. When he later attempted to challenge his dismissal by filing a petition pursuant to Article 78 of the Civil Practice Law and Rules, he found that he was time barred.

Levine's problem: he had filed a contract grievance disputing his termination under the assumption that filing a grievance would stop the running of the Statute of Limitations for the purposes of his filing an Article 78 petition until the conclusion of the grievance procedure and a final determination was issued by the arbitrator.

Levine's assumption proved to be incorrect, as the Appellate Division quickly pointed out.

Affirming the dismissal of his petition by State Supreme Court William J. Garry as untimely, the Appellate Division set out the following factors as basic to individual litigating an issue initially submitted for adjudication under a grievance procedure:

1. An Article 78 must be commenced within four months after the determination to be reviewed becomes final and binding.

2. Where, as in Levin's case, a review of an administrative decision is sought, the determination, for the purposes of bringing a timely Article 78, becomes final and binding on the date that the termination of individual's employment becomes effective.

3. The "invocation of an administrative grievance procedure" in accordance with a Taylor Law agreement does not stop the running of the Statute of Limitations.

Levine could probably have avoided this problem by filing a Article 78 petition within the four month Statute of Limitations period even though a final determination on his grievance had not yet been made.

18.132 Statute of limitations for disciplinary action

El Bey v New York City Dept. of Corrections, 294 A.D.2d 164

In the El Bey case, the exception to the statute of limitations for filing disciplinary action pursuant to Section 75 of the Civil Service Law where the charge would otherwise constitute a crime was applied by the Appellate Division in sustaining disciplinary action taken against Yashua Amen Shekhem El Bey.

El Bey was served with disciplinary charges pursuant to Section 75 of the Civil Service Law alleging, among other misconduct, that he falsely claimed exemption from Federal income taxation. El Bey's defense to this particular charge: it was barred by the 18-month Statute of Limitations in Civil Service Law Section 75(4) as it was filed more than 18 months after the alleged act.

The Appellate Division rejected El Bey's claim that the charge was untimely, ruling that the alleged misconduct constituted a crime under 26 USC 7205 (fraudulent withholding exemption certificate or failure to supply information) and under New York State's Penal Law Section 175.30 (offering a false instrument for filing in the second degree). Accordingly, said the court, the filing of such a charge is expressly excluded from time limitations for filing administrative disciplinary charges set out in Section 75(4) as the allegation "described in the charges would, if proved in a court of appropriate jurisdiction, constitute a crime."

The Appellate Division then sustained El Bey's being found guilty of charges of submitting false information on a Certificate of Exemption and Withholding in Lieu of IRS Form W-4; and violating Department rules concerning excessive absences and by his (1) leaving his residence without authorization while on sick leave; (2) failing to log in and out with the Health Management Division; (3) failing to comply with an instruction to present his firearms to the Health Maintenance Division; and (4) attending an administrative hearing in another matter without authorization while on sick leave.

El Bey also challenged the penalty imposed -- termination -- as a result of his being found guilty of these charges. The court said that it found no basis to disturb the imposition of such a penalty as "[t]he penalty of dismissal does not shock our sense of fairness," citing the Pell Doctrine [Pell v Board of Education, 34 NY2d 222].

18.133 Stipulating a settlement

Marpe v Dometsch, 246 A.D.2d 723, [see also 256 A.D.2d 914, 280 A.D.2d 795]

Sometimes the parties to a grievance or disciplinary proceeding agree to "settle" the matter. The terms of the settlement may be read into the record at an administrative hearing or before an arbitrator or the parties may simply "sign an agreement of settlement." The Marpe case shows that the settlement of a pending lawsuit must follow a more formal procedure.

Terri L. Marpe sued Paul Dometsch and Capital Area Community Health Plan Inc. [CHP], alleging that sexual harassment and negligence arising out of psychiatric treatment provided by her supervisor, Paul Dolmetsch. During a pretrial deposition with her attorney, Marpe and CHP entered into an on-the-record oral stipulation of settlement providing that Marpe would execute a written release and confidentiality agreement in exchange for CHP's agreement to pay her a specified sum of money. CHP forwarded the proposed settlement papers to Marpe but she refused to sign them. When a State Supreme Court justice denied CHP's motion to enforce the stipulation of settlement, it appealed.

The Appellate Division affirmed the lower court's determination, commenting that "a stipulation of settlement is not enforceable unless it is made in open court, reduced to a court order and entered, or contained in a writing subscribed by the parties or their attorneys." Since the stenographic record created at the deposition was made outside the presence of a judge, the Appellate Division ruled that it was insufficient to satisfy the requirements of Section 2104 of the Civil Practice Law and Rules.

18.134 Subpoena Duces Tecum

Bd. of Educ. v Hankins, 294 A.D.2d 360, see also 5 A.D.3d 771

From time to time one reads about a case involving the serving of a subpoena duces tecum. The purpose of a subpoena duces tecum is to compel the production of documents that are relevant and material to facts at issue in a pending judicial or administrative proceeding. The Hankins case involved such an issue.

On occasion a hearing officer may be asked to issue a subpoena duces tecum in the course of a disciplinary action. Sometimes an attorney will attempt to obtain such information by serving an "attorney's subpoena" on the employer.[213]

Alfred Hankins, a New York City schoolteacher, was served with disciplinary charges pursuant to Section 3020-a of the Education Law. In the course of the disciplinary hearing, Hankins served a subpoena duces tecum on the New York City Board of Education requiring it to produce the names and addresses of certain students. The Board asked Supreme Court to quash the subpoena duces tecum served upon it by Hankins, The court granted the motion to quash.

---

[213] To obtain state documents a judicial subpoena duces tecum -- i.e., a subpoena issued by a court having jurisdiction -- is required if the State entity holding the documents sought by the employee declines to provide them when requested to do so.

The Appellate Division affirmed the Supreme Court's decision quashing Hankins' subpoena. The problem here, said the Appellate Division, is that Hankin attempted to use the subpoena duces tecum improperly. Such a subpoena, said the court, "may not be used for purposes of discovery or to ascertain the existence of evidence."

In this instance, said the court, Hankins wanted the subpoena in order "to discover the names, addresses, and telephone numbers of the students in the class on the day or days when his misconduct allegedly occurred." Accordingly, concluded the court, the subpoena was properly quashed by Supreme Court.

18.135 Suppressing evidence in a disciplinary action

Section 75 hearing officer's findings, received May 8, 2002

As announced by the U.S. Supreme Court in cases such as Weeks v United States, 232 US 383 and Mapp v Ohio, 367 US 643, evidence obtained by police officers found to have been the fruit of an unlawful search cannot be used in a criminal proceeding. Does this rule apply in administrative disciplinary actions taken against employees?

This was one of the issues addressed by Civil Service Law Section 75 Hearing Officer Howard A. Rubenstein in the course of his considering disciplinary charges filed against Michael Lennon by the North Rockland Central School District.

The School District charged Lennon with misconduct and incompetence, alleging that on or about February 15, 2002, he possessed cocaine on school grounds.

Lennon, a maintenance mechanic employed by the School District, was stopped by Police Detective Thomas Crowe at the entrance to one of the District's schools. Crowe testified that he asked Lennon if he could search his car and Lennon agreed. Crowe found material that he identified as cocaine and placed Lennon under arrest.

Lennon essentially challenged the admission of Crowe's testimony concerning the cocaine found in his car, presumably on the theory that it was the product of an unlawful search and "any evidence of illegal drugs obtained as a result of the search should not be admitted into the record."

Rubenstein noted that although the issue of whether or not the search of Lennon's car was a constitutionally valid search no doubt may be a significant issue if "raised in Lennon's criminal trial," this issue may not be relevant in a civil administrative proceeding involving an employer taking administrative disciplinary action against an employee.

In the Boyd case,[214] the Court of Appeals considered an appeal by a State Police Officer who was found guilty of disciplinary charges based on the introduction of "improperly obtained evidence of possession of marijuana by local police authorities."

---

[214] Boyd v Constantine, 81 NY2d 189

Significantly, criminal charges against Boyd had been earlier dismissed after a Supreme Court justice ruled that the evidence against him obtained by Buffalo police officers was the result of an unlawful search.

The Court of Appeals said that the "improperly obtained" evidence could be used in the administrative disciplinary action because the local police authorities who committed the improper search were not acting as agents of the Division of the State Police and that the Division of State Police was not seeking to discipline one of its members by relying on the unlawful acts of its own agents.

Rubenstein concluded that the School District did not commit any search, legal or otherwise, nor was Detective Crowe acting as the agent of the District when he searched Lennon's car and found the cocaine.

The hearing officer said that in the Boyd case the Court of Appeals "adopted the principle that improperly obtained evidence may be admissible in administrative proceedings which are not concerned with criminal law or its enforcement."

Based on the record, Rubenstein recommended that Lennon be found guilty of the charge of possessing cocaine on school grounds and that his employment with the School District be terminated.

18.136 Suspension without pay during administrative disciplinary action

Elmore v Mills, 296 A.D.2d 704

Among the several issues considered by the Appellate Division, Third Department in Elmore case was the suspension of a tenured teacher without pay in the course of a disciplinary action.

In June 1997, Plainview-Old Bethpage Central School District filed disciplinary charges against Edwin Elmore pursuant to Section 3020-a of the Education Law.

Section 3020-a.2(b) provides that in the event a teacher is suspended during pendency of the hearing, such suspension shall be with pay unless the teacher pleaded guilty to, or was convicted of, one of several enumerated crimes.

However, in this instance the Taylor Law contract between the district and the teacher union, in pertinent part, provided that:

A teacher who has been suspended from school pursuant to Section 3020-a of the Education Law shall receive his/her regular full pay to which he/she would otherwise be entitled pursuant to Article V of the Collective Bargaining Agreement [CBA] and all fringe benefits for a period of a maximum of fifteen (15) school months (1 1/2 years salary).... Thereafter, any suspension may be without pay.

In December 1998, the District, relying on this provision in the CBA, suspended Elmore without pay, effective January 6, 1999, pending the outcome of the disciplinary hearing.

Elmore, however, had neither pleaded guilty to, nor was convicted of, any of the several crimes enumerated in Section 3020-a. Was Elmore's suspension without pay by the District pursuant to the CBA lawful in view of the provisions of Education Law Section 3020-a.2(b)?

Although the Appellate Division declined to rule on the merits of this question, holding that because a final determination in the disciplinary action had been made and thus the issue was "moot," the court did elect to discussing a number of elements concerning the question of suspension without pay in a Section 3020-a proceeding. It said that:

1. A CBA may allow a school district to suspend its teachers without pay as long as the agreement's terms clearly manifest the parties' intent to do so, citing Board of Education of the City of Rochester v Nyquist, 48 NY2d 97.

2. The CBA relied upon by the District in this case clearly circumscribe a teacher's right to full pay during a protracted suspension.

3. The CBA provides for restoration of wages and benefits for any such period of leave without pay if the teacher ultimately is not terminated from employment but here the penalty imposed on Elmore was termination.

Thus, said the court, if the issue of Elmore's suspension without pay was properly before it, it would find that this provision in the CBA was valid and that under the circumstances the District was authorized to suspend Elmore without pay as provided by the CBA.

In another suspension without pay case, Vargo v Safir, 291 A.D.2d 268, although the Appellate Division did not have any difficulty in affirming New York City Police Commissioner Howard Safir's imposing the penalty of dismissal after finding police officer James Vargo guilty of misconduct, it did find that there was a question as to whether Vargo was entitled to back pay.

The court said that it appeared that Vargo had been suspended without pay for more than 30 days after he was served with disciplinary charges filed against him.

Civil Service Law Section 75.3-a, in pertinent part, provides that a New York City police officer may be suspended without pay for thirty days pending the determination of disciplinary charges. CSL Section 75.3-a further provides that if a New York City police officer is found guilty of the charges, the Commissioner "may punish the police officer pursuant to the provisions of Sections 14-115 and 14-123 of the Administrative Code of the City of New York."

Accordingly, said the court, and the Department agreed, it was necessary to remand the matter to the Department to determine if Vargo was entitled to back salary for any period of suspension without pay in excess of 30 days.

The Appellate Division sustained the Commissioner's determination that Vargo was guilty of being the driver of a motor vehicle involved in "a hit-and-run" while off duty and that he used illegal drugs.

Under the circumstances, said the court, "[t]he penalty of dismissal does not shock our sense of fairness, citing Kelly v Safir, 96 NY2d 32, in support of its ruling.

18.137 Suspension without pay penalty interrupted

Manning v Warsaw CSD, CEd 14071, 1/13/99

The Warsaw Central School District served disciplinary charges against a tenured teacher, William Manning, Jr., related to his alleged operating a motor vehicle under the influence of alcohol.

Following a disciplinary hearing and an appeal, on November 22, 1994 former Commission of Education Sobol issued a decision and imposed a penalty of suspension without pay for two years. The decision was sustained by a State Supreme Court justice [Manning v Sobol, August 7, 1995, not officially reported].

Manning, however, was incarcerated in the Wyoming County jail on July 19, 1994. Because he was "unavailable" to work, the district changed his pay status from suspension with pay pending resolution of the Section 3020-a action to suspension without pay effective July 19, 1994.

Released from prison and claiming that his two-year suspension without pay commenced on November 22, 1994, Manning advised the district that he intended to return to work on November 22, 1996. The District said that the two-year suspension period commenced on March 21, 1995, when he was released from prison and therefore he could not return to work earlier than March 21, 1997. Manning appealed.

Commissioner of Education Richard P. Mills said that the two-year suspension imposed by former Commissioner Sobol commenced when Manning was released from incarceration since allowing the suspension to run concurrently with his incarceration "nullifies a portion of the suspension, since [Manning] could not work during that period in any event."

The Commissioner rejected Manning's claim that he was entitled to back salary from November 22, 1996, holding that to do so would abrogate the degree of discipline deemed appropriate by former Commissioner Sobol.

18.138 Tainted testimony

Buric v Safir, 285 A.D.2d 255, [See, also, 4 A.D.3d 160]

John Buric, a New York City police officer, found guilty of administrative disciplinary charges of assault and lying, was dismissed from his position.

The Appellate Division vacated this determination. Noting that "the threshold required to annul the Commissioner's determination is a very high one," the Court said that the Commissioner's findings in this case clearly demonstrate, on this record, the lack of any rational basis.

According to the decision, "The hearing examiner based her decision on the testimony of Mr. Dunham and the allegedly corroborating testimony of Ms. Fwilo, Mr. Small and Mr. Henson. Mr. Dunham, however, told different stories to different people.... The testimony of the three "corroborating witnesses" was incredible since none of them were present ... at the time this incident was alleged to have occurred."

Astonishingly, said the court, the hearing examiner ignored key details set out in the record in making her determination, instead lauding the credibility of Mr. Dunham, Ms. Fwilo, Mr. Small and Mr. Henson.

Annulling the Commissioner's finding Buric guilty of charges of assault and lying, the Appellate Division addressed another charge, Buric's removal of a prisoner from a cell without permission.

Buric, said the court, admitted he was guilty of removing the prisoner as charged. Accordingly, the court found it was necessary to remand the matter to the Commissioner for the purpose of imposing of an appropriate lesser penalty based on Buric's admission of his guilt to this charge.[215]

18.139 Tenure by estoppel

Wamsley v East Ramapo Central School District, 281 A.D.2d 633

If a school board neglects to take timely action to discontinue the services of a probationary teacher or administrator, the individual will attain what is termed "tenure by estoppel." The Court of Appeals addressed the issue of a individual obtaining "tenure by estoppel" in the Sewanhaka case.[216] However, "tenure by estoppel" is not limited to individuals in the unclassified service such as teachers and school administrators -- employees in the classified service also may attain tenure by estoppel as the Wamsley case demonstrates.

On October 5, 1998, East Ramapo appointed George Wamsley to the position of school bus driver, a classified service position in the noncompetitive class. Wamsley's appointment was subject to his satisfactorily completing a 26-week probationary period.

On August 18, 1999 the school district's personnel officer wrote to Wamsley advising him that he was to be dismissed because his service during his probationary period had been deemed unsatisfactory by his supervisors. Wamsley was terminated from his position effective August 25, 1999.

Wamsley sued, contending that his probationary term[217] had expired before he was discharged and he held a tenured appointment. He also claimed that he was entitled to a "pretermination hearing"

---

[215] The language used by the court in remanding the matter appears to signal its view that dismissing Buric for this offense would not be an appropriate penalty under the circumstances.

[216] Gould v Sewanhaka Central High School District, 81 NY2d 446

[217] Although decision indicates that Wamsley "became permanent" after the expiration of his 26-week probationary term, "probationary employees" in fact hold permanent appointments, and may enjoy limited tenure rights. For example, courts have ruled that probationers are entitled to notice and hearing if the appointing authority decides to dismiss the individual

because he was an "exempt volunteer firefighter" within the meaning of Section 75.1(b) of the Civil Service Law.

The Appellate Division agreed with Wamsley's argument that he was no longer a probationary employee at the time he was discharged. In the words of the court, Wamsley's "probationary term began on October 5, 1998, and ended 26 weeks later ... as permissibly extended by his days of absence." Accordingly, Wamsley's 26-week period, not having otherwise been extended as permitted by the rules of the Rockland Civil Service Commission, "expired long before his employment was terminated."

However, there were other elements to consider concerning Wamsley's claim of a right to a pretermination hearing.

The due process procedures set out in Section 75 of the Civil Service Law are not available to a noncompetitive class employee who has less than five years of continuous service unless the individual is a veteran who served in time of war or is an "exempt volunteer firefighter."

According to the Appellate Division, Wamsley claimed, but never established, that he was entitled to the protections of Section 75 because he was an exempt volunteer firefighter. The Appellate Division concluded that although clearly Wamsley was not a probationer at the time of is dismissal, he raised a triable issue of fact with respect to his claim of Section 75 rights based on his status as an exempt volunteer firefighter. According, a hearing on this aspect of this complaint was required and the matter was returned to State Supreme Court "for resolution of that factual issue."

Two technical elements concerning exempt volunteer firefighter status should be noted:

1. The individual claiming exempt volunteer firefighter status has the burden of demonstrating that he or she enjoys such status,[218] and

2. Notice of the fact that the individual is an exempt volunteer firefighter must be given to the employer prior to the individual's effective date of termination.[219]

Other tenure by estoppel cases include Roese v South Country CSD, 283 A.D.2d 580, and Dembovich v Liberty CSD, 296 A.D.2d 794 [See also 25 A.D.3d 908 concerning a related matter involving the parties.]

---

during his or her minimum period of probation. In contrast, a probationer may be dismissed without notice and hearing after completing his or her minimum period of probation and prior to the expiration of his or her maximum period of probation.

[218] People v Hayes, 135 AD 19

[219] Badman v Falk, 4AD2d 149

18.140 Term Appointments

Wheeler v Washington Co., 259 A.D.2d 902

Term appointments are rare in the classified service.[220] The Wheeler case involves such a type of appointment and considers the rights of an incumbent upon the expiration of his or her term of office. Section 100 of the Highway Law provides that a county Superintendent of Highways is appointed for a four-year term and "may be removed from office for malfeasance or misfeasance before expiration of the term.

Kenneth F. Wheeler was initially appointed to the position of Superintendent of Highways for a four-year term in 1987 and was reappointed to an additional four-year term, beginning on January 1, 1993. In 1991 his job title was changed to Superintendent of Public Works. At the conclusion of his term on December 31, 1996, Wheeler was not reappointed but remained as Superintendent until a successor was appointed by the Board of Supervisors on February 3, 1997.

Claiming that his termination was unlawful, Wheeler sued.

According to the decision, Wheeler's most recent term of office as Superintendent of Public Works commenced on January 1, 1993 and expired on December 31, 1996. The issue, as the Appellate Division saw it, was "whether the rights afforded a permanent, competitive employee under Civil Service Law Section 75 extended to [Wheeler] after the expiration of his term of office.

Wheeler contended that his position was wrongfully reclassified in 1996 from competitive to "unclassified" or noncompetitive status and that his position did not meet the requirements for "unclassified" status. Relying on his alleged permanent, competitive status in the classified service, Wheeler argued that Section 75 barred his termination except for misconduct or incompetence.

The court said that contrary to Wheeler's contention, he was not terminated or removed from office but rather, his four-year term pursuant to Highway Law Section 100 merely expired. Since he was not reappointed and his successor had not yet been chosen, the position became vacant at the expiration of his term on December 31, 1996.

However, until his successor took office in February 1996, Wheeler was a holdover and an at-will employee as provided by Section 5 of the Public Officers Law. Therefore, the court concluded, Section 75 was inapplicable and thus Wheeler was not entitled to a review of the County's decision not to reappoint him after completion of his then current term of office.

As to the question of whether Wheeler's position was wrongfully reclassified from the competitive class to another jurisdictional classification, the Appellate Division said that the change in

---

[220] Perhaps the most notable instance of a "term appointment" under the Civil Service Law is the provision set out in Section 15.6.1(b), which provides that "The term of a personnel officer shall be six years."

jurisdictional classification was irrelevant since Wheeler was not removed from his position prior to the expiration of his term of office.[221]

The decision implies that a person holding a term appointment authorized by law, unless reappointed, is to be deemed terminated upon the expiration of his or her term "by operation of law" notwithstanding the fact that he or she may otherwise be protected against removal except for incompetence or misconduct by the provisions of Section 75 of the Civil Service Law.

18.141 Terminating an interim appointee

Amnawah v NYC Bd. of Education, 266 A.D.2d 455
Soleyn v NYC Bd. of Education, USDC, SDNY, 10/99

The Amnawah and Soleyn decisions indicate that a nontenured employee has the burden of proof when challenging his or her termination from public service.

The Amnawah Case

Linda Amnawah, an interim-acting "Special Education Review Specialist," was terminated from her position by the New York City Board of Education effective January 31, 1998. She sued, seeking reinstatement to her former position. A State Supreme Court justice dismissed her case.

In affirming the lower court's determination the Appellate Division quickly disposed of Amnawah appeal, commenting that since she was a "non-tenured, interim-acting employee," the board of education could terminate her employment without any statement of reasons, provided that the termination was not made in bad faith or for impermissible reasons.

The court said that while Amnawah had the burden of proving that her termination was made in bad faith or was for an impermissible reason she only offered "conclusory, unsupported, and irrelevant arguments" to this end. Thus, said the court, Amnawah failed to sustain her evidentiary burden and dismissed her appeal.

The Soleyn Case

In the Soleyn case, a federal district court dismissed Earl Soleyn petition alleging that his employment was terminated by the Board of Education because he was African American and that the reasons given by the board of education for its action were pretextual.

The court said that "[t]he defining feature of this case is the complete absence of any evidence direct, circumstantial, statistical, or otherwise suggesting that race was a motivating factor behind [the principal's] decision to rate plaintiff unsatisfactory and end his employment.

---

[221] Typically the courts have held that an individual cannot be jurisdictionally reclassified out of his or her position [Meenagh v Dewey, 286 NY 292; Fornara v Schroeder, 261 NY 363].

As was the case in the Amnawah, the court found that Soleyn failed to satisfy his burden of proof. The court characterized his allegations of unlawful discrimination because of his color as "(i) conclusory without any evidentiary support, or (ii) in the form of general allegations about the school which do not apply to [Soleyn's] case, commenting that he "failed to meet even the minimal evidentiary threshold required to defeat [the board's] motion for summary judgment."

18.142 Terminating temporary appointees

Sanni v NYS Office of Mental Health, USDC, EDNY, 2/15/2000

Frequently a public employee will challenge his or her termination from a temporary appointment, claiming that he or she is entitled to a pretermination due process hearing. This was one of the issues considered by Federal District Court Judge Gleeson in the course of his deciding the Sanni case.

Thomas Sanni, then employed in a grade 27 project director position at Kings Park Psychiatric Center was served with disciplinary charges pursuant to Section 75 of the Civil Service Law. Simultaneously, he was restored to his permanent grade 18 position and transferred to Queens Children Psychiatric Center.

Ultimately a hearing officer found Sanni guilty of 11 of the 14 charges filed against him. Among the charges for which Sanni was found guilty were the following:

1. "Improperly participating in and supporting the decision" to employ the minister of [Sanni's] church to exorcise a patient "possessed by spirits;"

2. Transporting a patient in his car when he did not hold a valid driver's license;

3. Claiming overtime for work he did not perform;

4. Having his personal automobile repaired by Kingsboro and billing the facility for personal items he shipped overseas "via international Federal Express;" and

5. Lying under oath in the course of being interviewed concerning the charges.

The department accepted the hearing officer's findings and his recommendation that Sanni be terminated. Sanni sued, contending that the Office of Mental Health's disciplinary action against him (1) violated his civil rights, (2) constituted retaliation for his filing a Title VII complaint against it and (3) it terminated him from the grade 27 position in violation of Section 75.

As to Sanni's due process claims, Judge Gleeson pointed out that a public employee who has a property interest or right in his or her position is entitled to a pretermination hearing before he or she may be removed from the position. "By logical extension," said the court, an employee covered by Section 75 has a property interest in his or her civil service grade" since one of the penalties that may be imposed under Section 75 is demotion in grade and title.

The problem with Sanni's argument, however, was that "temporary employees in New York have no property interest in their jobs." Accordingly, Judge Gleeson, citing the Appellate Division's ruling in Jones v Westchester County, 644 NYS2d 640, granted the State's motion to summarily dismiss this branch of Sanni's complaint.[222]

18.143 Termination by operation of law

Maldarelli v Doherty, NYS Sup. Ct., Ia Part 21, Justice Lippman

In some instances a public officer or employee otherwise entitled to a pretermination hearing before he or she may be dismissed is automatically removed from his or her position by operation of law without being given any "notice and hearing."

For example, Section 30(1)(e) of the Public Officers Law provides that a public officer, such as a police officer, automatically vacates his or her position if he or she is convicted of a felony or a crime involving a violation of the individual's oath of office. Here, however, Justice Lippman held that the New York City Department of Sanitation [DOS] removing Louis Maldarelli from his position by "operation of law" because he had been convicted of a crime without his first being served with Section 75 disciplinary charges and without being given a pretermination hearing was unlawful.

DOS's justification for its action: when Maldarelli entered a plea of guilty to the crime of insurance fraud in the third degree, he forfeited his position as a sanitation worker pursuant to New York City Charter Section 1116(a). Maldarelli had filed a claim for "lost wages" with the American Transit Insurance Company following an accident even though he had received paid sick leave during the time he was out of work as result of his injuries and entered a plea guilty to insurance fraud.

Maldarelli, on the other hand, argued that because he was a tenured employee he could not be removed from his position without first being given a hearing upon stated charges pursuant to Civil Service Law Section 75.

Justice Lippman ruled that DOS could not invoke Section 1116(a) and thus deprive Maldarelli of a Section 75 hearing. Accordingly, the court held that Maldarelli's termination was improper because it violated his right to a hearing under the Civil Service Law.

Addressing DOS's alternate grounds for declaring that Maldarelli's position became automatically vacant upon his being convicted of a felony -- Section 30(1)(e) of the Public Officers Law -- Justice Lippman, citing Tepidino v City of New York, 50 Misc2d 324, said that "It has long been the rule that sanitation workers are not public officers but public employees."

---

[222] Sanni's civil rights and retaliation claims based on his "demotion and transfer" to another department facility survived, however. This suggests that the State may try to have the case dismissed on the grounds that it immune from suit in federal court for alleged violations of Title VII in view of the rulings by the Supreme Court of the United States in Kimel v Board of Regents, and Alden v Maine, cases involving employees suing their state employer in federal court for alleged violations of, respectively, the Age Discrimination in Employment Act and the Fair Labor Standards Act.

As it has often been observed, although all public officers are public employees, not all public employees are public officers.

Where, however, the enabling statute does not itself declare the individual to be a public officer, the courts have viewed a public officer as one "whose position is created, and whose powers and duties are prescribed, by statute and who exercises a high degree of initiative and independent judgment." Justice Lippman said that "clearly" the position of sanitation worker does not fall within that definition.

18.144 Termination hearing - Section 73

Conticello v Westchester County, CA2, 11/24/99

Westchester County corrections officer John A. Conticello was terminated from his position effective July 31, 1997 pursuant to Section 73 of the Civil Service Law. Conticello had been "continuously absent from and unable to perform the duties of his position for one year or more by reason of a disability."[223]

According to the decision, Conticello "was absent from work due to serious psychological problems from 1995 until his employment was terminated in July 1997." On March 31, 1997 Conticello had written the department requesting that he be allowed to "return to full duty," and attaching a note from his psychiatrist. The department told him that "he could not return to work until he underwent a psychological examination by a doctor selected by appellees." Although the department scheduled an appointment for Conticello with its doctor, he refused to appear for the appointment.

Although it had terminated Conticello effective June 4, 1997, on July 1, 1997 the department rescinded the termination for the specific "purpose of providing [Conticello] an opportunity to be heard on the appropriateness of [his] termination." Although instructed to contact Luke J. Smith, a department official, if he wished a hearing, Conticello failed to contact Smith.

Conticello sued, contending that his termination without a hearing violated his Fourteenth Amendment procedural due process rights." The Circuit Court disagreed and affirmed a district court's ruling dismissing his case on the grounds that his there was no merit to his contention that he was entitled to a termination hearing.

The court commented that Conticello was "twice provided ... with notice and an opportunity to be heard regarding the termination of his employment" but that he "chose not to avail himself of either opportunity to be heard."

---

[223] Conticello was apparently on leave pursuant to Section 72 of the Civil Service Law due to a disability or illness that was not work-related. Such an individual may be terminated pursuant to Section 73 if s/he has been continuously absent for one year or longer. In contrast, a person who has been absent on workers' compensation leave pursuant to Section 71 of the Civil Service Law may be terminated from his or her position pursuant to Section 71 if s/he has been absent for a cumulative period of at least one year.

The circuit court quoted with approval the district court's observation that "a plaintiff in a Federal Civil Rights action can't use his own voluntary waiver or his own negligence or his own failure to avail himself of due process which is offered as support for a position that he was denied due process or denied an opportunity to a pre-termination hearing."

Holding that Conticello "was thus accorded all process that was due," the Circuit Court dismissed his appeal.[224]

18.145 Termination of a probationer

Miller v Village of Wappingers Falls, 289 A.D.2d 209

In July 1998, Louis Miller, a registered Republican active in local party matters, was appointed as the zoning administrator of the Village of Wappingers Falls by the then Republican-controlled Village Board. Miller's appointment was apparently subject to his satisfactorily completing a probationary period. In April 1999, presumably while still serving as a probationer, Miller was terminated from his position by the newly elected Democratic administration. Miller sued, contending that he was improperly terminated from his employment because of his membership in the Republican Party.

The Village's motion for summary judgment was rejected by a State Supreme Court justice. In response to the Village's appeal challenging the lower court's denial of its motion, the Appellate Division, citing Negron v Jackson, 273 AD2d 241, said that probationary employee may not be fired for constitutionally impermissible reasons. Here, said the Appellate Division, Miller alleged a "constitutionally impermissible reason" for his termination -- his political affiliation.

The court rejected the Village's argument that because Miller was a probationary employee it had the right to terminate his employment for any reason or for no reason. The Appellate Division said that "given the nature of [Miller's] allegations, it was incumbent upon the [Village] to present admissible evidence in Supreme Court showing that [Miller's] political affiliations did not play a substantial part in the decision to terminate him."

In sustaining the lower court's dismissal of the Village's motion, the Appellate Division also noted that the Village "failed to even address these claims before the Supreme Court." This, said the court, meant that it did not carry its burden of proof and its motion was properly denied.

In its appeal the Village apparently also argued that Miller was "a policy-making employee cloaked with considerable discretion, and thus his political affiliation was a relevant consideration" insofar as his dismissal was concerned. The Appellate Division said it could not consider this argument "as [the Village] improperly seeks to interject new facts and theories for the first time on appeal."

Terminations alleged to be based on political affiliation frequently are stated in terms of a violation of the individual's rights under the federal Constitution. The general rule in such cases is that a public employee may not be removed from his or her public employment solely on the basis of his or her

---

[224] The ruling points out that although Conticello's federal claim was dismissed with prejudice while his state law claims were dismissed without prejudice. This allows him to pursue any available state court remedies

political affiliation unless there is proof that the individual's political affiliation was a critical element to his or her performance of the duties of the position.

Among the significant cases addressing this issue are Elrod v Burnssi, 427 US 347; Branti v Finkel, 445 US 507 and Rutan v Republican Party of Illinois, 497 US 62.

Other termination of a probationer cases include: Johnson v City of New York, 281 A.D.2d 322; Morgan v Kerik, 267 A.D.2d 8; and Mennella v Uniondale UFSD, Comm. Ed. Decision 14245

18.146 Termination of employment
Croman v City University of New York, 277 A.D.2d 185

It is well settled that as a matter of public policy an appointing authority such as a board of education may not surrender its ultimate responsibility for making tenure decisions or restrict its exclusive right to terminate a probationary employee's appointment and thus such the denial of tenure is not subject to grievance arbitration.

The Court of Appeals, by way of illustration, observed that "... a board of education may not surrender its ultimate responsibility for making tenure decisions or restricting its exclusive right to terminate probationary teacher appointments" and thus such the denial of tenure is not subject to grievance arbitration.

In contrast, however, in Cohoes City School District v Cohoes Teachers Association, 40 NY2d 774, the Court of Appeals ruled that contractual provisions between an employee association and an appointing authority may set out procedural safeguards concerning the tenure decision that are subject to grievance arbitration procedures without offending public policy.

In other words, while a board's decision involving the "denial of tenure" is not arbitrable, alleged violations of the procedures to be followed in determining whether to grant or deny tenure are arbitrable.

Does public policy prohibit the arbitration of the disciplinary termination of tenured faculty?

This was the issue raised by Linda H. Young, a tenured faculty member, when she challenged her suspension without pay for six months from her position with the City University of New York by an arbitrator following a disciplinary hearing held in accordance with the provisions of a Taylor Law agreement.

Young's argument: As Section 6212(9) of the Education Law "vests the power to remove tenured faculty solely in [University's] Board of Trustees," public policy is violated by a collective bargaining agreement delegating the authority to discipline to an arbitrator at the employee's option.

The Appellate Division, First Department, disagreed. The court said that "[a]bsent clear language in Education Law Section 6212(9) '[i]t is well settled that a contract provision in a collective bargaining agreement may modify, supplement or replace the more traditional forms of protection afforded public employees ...'", citing Dye v New York City Transit Authority, 88 AD2d 899.

According to the ruling, the collective bargaining agreement allowed Young to either accept the disciplinary penalty recommended by appointing authority's designee or take the matter to arbitration. Young elected arbitration.

The Appellate Division dismissed Young's appeal, commenting that "[p]ublic policy does not nullify the choice she made."

The leading cases on "negotiated disciplinary procedures": Antinore v State of New York, 40 NY2d 6 and Abramovich v Board of Education, 46 NY2d 450.

18.147 Termination pursuant to Section 73

Fallon v Triboro. Bridge & Tunnel Auth., 259 A.D.2d 377

An individual who is terminated pursuant to Section 71 or Section 73 of the Civil Service Law because of his or her absence caused by a disability may sue the employer, claiming the termination was unlawful.[225]

The Triborough Bridge and Tunnel Authority terminated Gregory Fallon pursuant to Section 73 of the Civil Service Law after he had been continuously absent in excess of one year. Fallon sued, claiming various violations of his civil rights under federal and state law. The court found that Fallon had been absent on disability leave for 12 years and had never sought to return to work, with or without accommodation, even after he was denied ordinary disability retirement benefits.

The Authority had told Fallon that it would terminate him if he failed to qualify for ordinary disability retirement. This, said the Appellate Division, constituted "adequate pretermination notice," commenting that "[i]n the context of Section 73 discharges, [due process] amounts to no more than an opportunity for the employee to present opposing views as to whether [he] has been absent for one year or more and whether [he] was able to return to [his] position."

As to any post-termination rights, the Authority "in language tracking the provisions of Civil Service Law Section 73," had written Fallon advising him of his termination and "that he could apply for a medical examination within a year of the termination of his disability, and if found fit, could apply for reinstatement." This, said the court, was sufficient to meet due process requirements.

The Appellate Division also ruled that Fallon failed to make a prima facie case of disability-based discrimination under the Vocational Rehabilitation Act (29 USC Section 794) because the Authority "is not a recipient of federal funds."

---

[225] Section 71 provides for leave in connection with a work-connected injury or disease. Section 73 provides for the termination of an individual who is on leave pursuant to Section 72, which mandates leaves of absence in the event an employee is unable to work because of an injury or disease that did not result from a work-related incident.

Fallon also contended that the Authority had violated the Americans with Disabilities Act. The court determined that his ADA rights had not been violated "since he makes no allegation that he requested an accommodation for his alleged disability and was refused."

In view of this, the court ruled, "there is no ground to conclude that [the Authority] violated the New York State Human Rights Law (Executive Law Section 296), prohibiting disability-based discrimination" and dismissed Fallon's appeal.

18.148 Termination without a hearing

Pirozzi v Safir, 270 A.D.2d 2

New York City police officer John Pirozzi was terminated from his position without a hearing after he was convicted of "a crime committed by petitioner in the line of duty and constituting a violation of his oath of office."

Claiming that he was entitled to due process before he could be removed from his position, Pirozzi sued. The department, citing Section 30(1)(e) of the Public Officers Law argued that Pirozzi was removed by operation of law and thus he was not entitled to a pre-termination hearing.[226]

The Appellate Division agreed and dismissed Pirozzi's petition. The court said that Pirozzi "was properly terminated from the Police Department without a hearing in light of his conviction of aggravated harassment in the second degree." The court cited Duffy v Ward, 81 NY2d 127, as authority for its ruling.[227]

18.149 Testimony by the appointing authority

DiMattina v LaBua, 262 A.D.2d 409

One of the issues considered by the Appellate Division in the DiMattina case appeal concerned the fact that the appointing authority both preferred the charges filed against Thomas J. DiMattina and testified against him at the disciplinary hearing that followed.

DiMattina, a Town of Huntington employee, was dismissed from his position after he was found guilty of having "wrongfully obtained and withheld Town-owned lumber, wrongfully obtained and withheld Town-owned tools and equipment, abused his authority, and improperly influenced subordinate Town employees with respect to political activities."

---

[226] Section 30(1)(e) of the Public Officers Law applies only to individuals who are "public officers." A police officer is a public officer. While every public officer is a public employee, not every public employee is a public officer.

[227] If a public officer is terminated pursuant to Section 30(1)(e) as a result of his or her conviction of a felony or a crime in a violation of his or her oath of office and the conviction is later reversed or vacated, he or she may request reinstatement [to other than an elective office] and if such a request is denied, he or she is entitled to a hearing with respect to that decision if the conviction was the only basis for the termination.

The appointing authority, the director of the Department of General Services, had preferred the charges against DiMattina and testified at the subsequent disciplinary hearing. But the Appellate Division noted that "he properly disqualified himself from reviewing the recommendations of the Hearing Officer and acting on any of the charges."

The determination was made by the Deputy Director, who was authorized to act generally in the Director's absence pursuant to local law and who had been properly designated to render a final determination in DiMattina's case. The court said that "it is well settled that when an officer institutes charges of misconduct and testifies at an ensuing hearing, that officer, in the interest of fairness, must disqualify [himself or] herself from reviewing the Hearing Officer's recommendations and rendering a final determination." This was done in this case.

18.150 Testing for drugs

Roy v City of New York, App. Div., 685 NYS2d 668

How much evidence is sufficient to require an employee to take a drug test? And if the employee refuses to take the drug test, is that grounds for dismissal?

The Appellate Division addressed those questions in the Roy case. The court ruled that an informant's statement to a police officer that she had observed Gary Roy, a New York City police officer, using drugs on numerous occasions constituted substantial evidence and provided the amount of reasonable suspicion required for an order directing a drug test for cause.

The Appellate Division said the informant's story was reasonably detailed. The fact that some of information provided by the informant was self-incriminatory also suggested credibility to the court. The Appellate Division also commented that Roy's termination for refusing to submit to a drug test when ordered to do so, under the circumstances, did not shock its sense of fairness, upholding Roy's termination.

However, there was a "back pay" issue to be resolved. The Appellate Division said that Roy had been suspended without pay for more than 30 days pending resolution of the disciplinary action. The decision notes that Roy was suspended without pay on May 2, 1996 and dismissed, following the hearing and determination of the charge supporting the suspension, on July 26, 1996. As there was no evidence that Roy was responsible for the delay in the determination of the charge beyond the 30 days suspension period permitted by Civil Service Law Sections 75(3), he is entitled to back pay for the period from June 2, 1996 to July 26, 1996, less any earnings he may have received from other sources during that period.

This is somewhat troublesome, however. Sections 75, 76 and 77 of the Civil Service Law originally provided for such an adjustment for earnings received from other sources during a period of suspension without pay in excess of 30 days upon the restoration of the individual to his or her former position. But these three sections were amended in 1984. Chapter 710 of the Law of 1984 deleted the phrase "compensation which he may have earned in any other employment or occupation...." These sections now provide that an employee who is acquitted of disciplinary charges or whose reinstatement is directed by a civil service commission or the court is to be "restored to his position with full pay for the period of the suspension less the amount of any unemployment insurance benefits he may have received during such period."

Similar language is used in Education Law Section 3020-a.4(b) with respect to the payment of back salary upon acquittal.

18.151 Testing for illegal drugs
Mack v The Port Authority of New York and New Jersey, USDC, SDNY, Judge Swan [Received October 10, 2002]

One of the issues considered by Judge Swan in the Mack case was Michael Mack's allegation that he was subjected to disparate treatment in violation of Title VII because he was an African-American. Mack alleged that he was required to submit to an involuntary random test for illegal drugs because of his color. Mack also claimed that after he submitted to a random drug test and tested positive for cocaine, the Authority told him that he would be terminated.

According to the decision, Mack was employed as a truck driver by the Authority and was required to posses a valid commercial driver's license in order to perform the duties of his position. Authority employees such as Mack are required to submit to random drug tests under the federal Omnibus Transportation Testing Act of 1991. On July 6, 1996, Mack was tested for drugs and tested positive for cocaine.

Mack and the Authority settled the matter by entering into an agreement that required Mack to submit to random drug testing for a period of sixty months and to enter a drug rehabilitation program. The agreement also provided that if Mack tested positive again, he would be subject to "administrative action."

When Mack again tested positive for cocaine on November 10, 1997, the Authority told him that his employment would be terminated effective November 17, 1997, because of the positive drug test.

Mack's union negotiated a second "disciplinary waiver agreement" and Mack agreed that he would be subject to random drug testing for sixty months and that he would cooperate with the Port Authority's Office of Medical Services. The agreement also stated that Mack's failure to comply with these obligations could result in his termination and that one positive test result would result in his termination.

On May 6, 1998, Mack was asked to submit a urine sample to the Medical Services nurse. When the sample provided proved "unusable," he was asked to supply a second sample. Mack refused to do so and, as a result of this refusal, he was terminated.

Judge Swan granted the Authority's motion to dismiss the complaint, commenting that Mack failed to allege facts sufficient for the court to find that it was the custom or practice of the Port Authority to treat him or other non-white employees differently from non-black employees when imposing sanctions for failure to pass a urine test for illegal drugs.

According to the ruling, Mack presented only conclusory allegations that "race was the determining factor in [his] termination" and thus failed to establish a prima facie case of "wrongful termination."

18.152 Threats by employees

Aviles v Cornell Forge Co., CA7, February 21, 2001

Violence at the work site is a growing concern to both employers and employees. The Aviles case involves an employer's fear of such violence after it learns that a disgruntled employee has threatened a supervisor and is seen standing outside the building.

The police are called and arrest the employee. The employee then sues the employer for alleged unlawful discrimination based on his national origin and claims that the employer called the police in retaliation for his filing a hostile work environment claim.

These were the essential elements alleged in the Aviles case. Alfredo Aviles contended that he was the victim of unlawful discrimination because "calling the police to report that a disgruntled employee is waiting outside the workplace and may be armed is an adverse action as a matter of law."

The U.S. Circuit Court of Appeals disagreed with Aviles' theory, ruling that a truthful, nondiscriminatory report to the police should not subject an employer to Title VII liability.

According to the decision, such theory is "ill-advised." If, said the court, an employer had to face potential Title VII liability for truthfully reporting to the police that a disgruntled employee had threatened a supervisor and could be armed, it probably would discourage employers from taking the most prudent action to protect themselves and others in the workplace.

In contrast, the court said that a false report to the police could be construed as a retaliatory action meant to dissuade Aviles from pursuing his EEOC charge against the company.

The court affirmed the district court's granting a directed verdict in favor of Cornell Forge.

18.153 Timeliness of evidence

Wojewodzic v O'Neill, 295 A.D.2d 670

Section 75.4 of the Civil Service Law requires that disciplinary action against an individual be initiated within eighteen months of the occurrence of the alleged act or acts of incompetency or misconduct except in cases where the alleged incompetency or misconduct charged would, if proved in a court of appropriate jurisdiction, constitute a crime.[228]

---

[228] Except for acts that would constitute a crime, the statute of limitations for State employees designated managerial or confidential pursuant to the Taylor Law is one year after the occurrence of the alleged act or acts of incompetency or misconduct.

In the Wojewodzic case the Appellate Division considered an interesting aspect of Section 75.4: Does Section 75.4 support or imply imposing a statute of limitations with respect to evidence produced in course of the Section 75 disciplinary hearing?

John J. Wojewodzic was terminated from his position after being found guilty of several charges of misconduct including charges that he:

1. Knowingly made false statements concerning an alleged sexual affair involving two Essex County officials;

2. Deliberately provided false answers during the investigation concerning certain of the charges;

3. Created a hostile work environment while on duty and engaging in violent and disruptive behavior while off duty; and

4. Conducted himself in a manner unbecoming a staff development coordinator by using loud, rude, abusive, racist and sexist language in relation to other employees.

Wojewodzic appealed, contending that "the charges sustained against him should be dismissed because they are based upon evidence outside the Statute of Limitations applicable in Civil Service Law Section 75 proceedings." The Appellate Division said that, as a general rule, disciplinary charges had to be filed within eighteen-months of the alleged wrongdoing.

However, with respect to charges [referred to as Charges 6 and 7,] concerning Wojewodzic's alleged creating a "hostile work environment" and his alleged engaging in "behavior unbecoming a staff development coordinator," the court held that the record indicated that many of the underlying incidents alleged by Essex County in support of these two charges "involved wrongdoing occurring outside the 18-month period."

Essex, on the other hand, contended that the testimony of witnesses concerning these "untimely events" was for the purposed of demonstrating a pattern of behavior and was, therefore, admissible in accordance with the Court of Appeals' ruling in Block v Ambach, 73 NY2d 323.

The Appellate Division decided that while such evidence may be admissible under certain circumstances, it could not allow such untimely proof to stand in this case because "it is unduly prejudicial."

According to the ruling, many untimely incidents were relied on in concluding that Wojewodzic was guilty of the charges filed against him. Conceding that "many of the timely incidents were also referenced," the court said that the problem here was that "there is simply no way of knowing to what extent the remote allegations influenced the determination of guilt herein."

The court decided that it would be appropriate to remit the matter to the county for the purpose of a new hearing as to Charge 6 and the remaining specifications of Charge 7 without consideration of the untimely allegations.

In contrast to the prohibition against using "time-barred incidents" to bolster charges of misconduct or incompetence, the appointing authority may consider "stale or untimely incidents" inappropriate for the purpose of filing disciplinary charges contained in the individual's personnel file in determining a disciplinary penalty.

The reason for this is that the appointing authority's ability to use an individual's personnel record in determining a penalty is not triggered until after the employee is found guilty of one or more charges of incompetency or misconduct of charges that have been timely served and then only after the individual is advised of that fact and given an opportunity to respond.

18.154 Tolling of the statute of limitations

Montella v Safir, 290 A.D.2d 261

New York City Commissioner of Police Howard Safir terminated police officer Peter Montella for misconduct after Montella was found guilty of the charges at a departmental hearing held pursuant to New York City's Administrative Code Section 14-115(a). Montella sued and was successful in having the Commissioner's determination annulled [Montella v Kelly, 202 AD2d 241]. The Appellate Division directed the Commissioner to hold another hearing if he elected to go forward with disciplinary action against Montella.

A second Section 14-115(a) departmental hearing was conducted and again Safir found Montella guilty and again imposed the penalty of termination.

Montella appealed his termination to the New York City Civil Service Commission, which reversed the Commissioner's determination. However the Court of Appeals subsequently ruled that the Civil Service Commission did not have the authority to review Safir's Section 14-115(a) determination. The court ruled that the Commission's reversing Montella's dismissal and ordering his reinstatement was "void."[229]

Again Montella sued, this time seeking to annul the Commissioner's second, March 31, 1995 determination. While the Commissioner contended that Montella's Article 78 was untimely because if was filed more than four months after his determination, Montella argued that it was timely because of the six-month extension provided by CPLR 205(a).

The Appellate Division ruled that Montella's "extension" argument was correctly rejected by the lower court because CPLR 205(a) refers to the terminated prior proceeding as an "action" and "an administrative proceeding is not an action." Further, said the court, Montella's appeal to the Civil Service Commission did not qualify as a predicate for a CPLR 205(a) extension.

Also rejected was Montella's argument that by participating in the proceeding before the Civil Service Commission the Commissioner was estopped from later challenging the Commission's subject matter jurisdiction.

---

[229] Montella v Bratton, 93 NY2d 424

The Appellate Division made two additional observations concerning the procedures to be followed in challenging an administrative determination such as a disciplinary decision:

1. The fact that an individual pursues an unavailable grievance procedure does not toll the Statute of Limitations, citing Majka v Utica City School District, 247 AD2d 845; and

2. In Montella's case, the four-month period for filing a timely article 78 proceeding challenging the March 31, 1995 determination dismissing Montella from his position expired before the Commissioner was required to answer his appeal to the Civil Service Commission.

The Appellate Division unanimously affirmed the lower court's granting the Commissioner's motion to dismiss the petition as barred by the Statute of Limitations, and dismissed Montella's appeal.[230]

18.155 Unemployment insurance and Section 75

Dimps v NYC Human Resources Administration, 274 A.D.2d 625

When the Unemployment Insurance Appeals Board ruled that Shirley Dimps was disqualified for unemployment insurance benefits because she had been terminated for misconduct, Dimps appealed the Board's decision to the Appellate Division.

Dimps had been found guilty of 12 of 20 specifications of misconduct by an administrative law judge [ALJ] following a disciplinary hearing pursuant to Section 75 of the Civil Service Law.

The ALJ recommended that Dimps be dismissed and HRA adopted the hearing officer's findings and recommendation regarding the penalty to be imposed. The New York City Civil Service Commission affirmed HRA's Section 75 determination and the penalty imposed.

Dimps then applied for unemployment insurance benefits, which were denied on the ground that her employment was terminated due to her misconduct. A hearing was scheduled and a Unemployment Insurance ALJ allowed Dimps "to explain nine of the specifications on which she was found guilty."

HRA objected, contending that the doctrine of collateral estoppel should apply to the findings of fact made at the disciplinary hearing with respect to Dimps' appeal of her disqualification for unemployment benefits.

Ultimately the ALJ agreed with HRA's argument and did not consider Dimps' explanation in making his determination. The ALJ ruled that Dimps was ineligible for unemployment insurance benefits because she had been terminated for misconduct.

---

[230] In Johnson v Triborough Bridge & Tunnel Authority, 97 NY2d 627, the Court of Appeals held that Section 76 of the Civil Service Law solely authorizes the [Civil Service] Commission to hear appeals from hearings in connection with disciplinary proceedings under Section 75. Section 14-115(a) did not constitute a Section 75 proceeding. The Commission, therefore, had no jurisdiction to hear an individual's application to review disciplinary action in such cases.

Was the application of the doctrine of collateral estoppel appropriate in Dimps' case before the Unemployment Insurance Appeals Board? The Appellate Division, Third Department, ruled that it was and dismissed Dimps' appeal.

In the words of the Appellate Division: "... inasmuch as claimant was given a full and fair opportunity to litigate the issue of misconduct at the disciplinary hearing, the ALJ at the unemployment insurance hearing properly accorded collateral estoppel effect to the ensuing factual findings."

The court noted that at the disciplinary hearing, Dimps was represented by counsel, testified on her own behalf, cross-examined the employer's witnesses and had the opportunity to present and examine relevant evidence.

As an alternative, Dimps argued that the Unemployment Insurance Board's determination was not supported by substantial evidence. The Appellate Division said that it found "to the contrary" and that there was substantial evidence supporting the Board's determination that Dimps "committed disqualifying misconduct, i.e., she continuously refused to abide by reasonable directives of her supervisor...."

18.156 Use of a videotape as evidence

Paulin v City of New York, 288 A.D.2d 153

One of the elements in the Paulin case was the use of a videotape in a disciplinary hearing. Fred Paulin, a New York City police officer, was charged with misconduct. The Police Commissioner found Paulin guilty of having stolen merchandise from a store and imposed the penalty of dismissal. In dismissing Paulin's appeal, the Appellate Division ruled that the Commissioner's decision was supported by substantial evidence, including a videotape of the incident.

Further, said the court, under the circumstances, imposing the penalty of dismissal "does not shock our sense of fairness."

18.157 Using personnel records in setting a penalty

Massaria v Betschen, 290 A.D.2d 602

In the Massaria case the Appellate Division was asked to determine if was appropriate for the Section 75 hearing officer to consider a disciplinary settlement agreement entered into by an employee and his or her employer to resolve disciplinary charges filed against an employee when determining the penalty to be imposed on the employee after he or she was found guilty of misconduct and incompetence in a second, subsequent, disciplinary action.

New Paltz Superintendent of Schools Frederick Betschen filed Section 75 disciplinary charges Kenneth Massaria alleging that he was guilty of misconduct and incompetence based on Massaria's failing to drop a third grade student off at the proper bus stop on two occasions and an incident, captured on videotape, in which Massaria drove his bus in the middle of the road as he approached waiting students at a bus stop.

The hearing officer found Massaria guilty of all of these charges and recommended that he be dismissed from his employment. The School Board adopted the hearing officer's findings and recommendation and terminated Massaria from his position. Massaria appealed, challenging the Board's action. The Appellate Division dismissed Massaria's appeal, ruling that the testimony and evidence presented at the hearing supplied the substantial evidence required to affirm the school district's action.

One the major issues considered by the court involved the "penalty phase" of the disciplinary hearing. At this point in the proceeding the School District introduced Massaria's prior disciplinary record for the hearing officer's to consider in determining the appropriate penalty to be imposed on Massaria.

This record consisted of a "stipulation of settlement" in lieu of disciplinary charges. In executing this stipulation, Massaria admitted to four acts of misconduct and incompetence involving improperly operating his school bus and "his departing from a mandatory meeting without supervisory permission."

Massaria conceded that the stipulation also provided that it constituted Civil Service Law Section 75 discipline, that it could be used in any future disciplinary proceeding against him, and that if he engaged in similar misconduct in the future, the District would seek to dismiss him from his position.

Addressing the hearing officer's consideration of the stipulation documenting Massaria's prior admission of misconduct and incompetence during the "penalty phase" of the disciplinary action, the Appellate Division said that here the hearing officer's consideration of Massaria's employment record met the test set out in Bigelow v Board of Trustees of the Incorporated Village of Gouverneur, 63 NY2d 470. In particular, the court found that:

1. The hearing officer considered the stipulation only after Massaria was found guilty of the charges of misconduct and incompetence filed against him;

2. Massaria "was given ample notice" that the prior stipulated incidents would be submitted to the hearing officer to consider in determining the penalty to be imposed; and

3. Massaria was given an opportunity to be heard regarding those prior incidents.

Significantly, the Appellate Division said that the "prior infractions need not have been included in the statement of charges."

Ruling that Massaria's employment history, including the settlement agreement flowing from the prior disciplinary action taken against him, "was properly taken into consideration in the determination of an appropriate sanction for the proven present acts of misconduct and incompetence," the Appellate Division dismissed Massaria's appeal.

18.158 Vacating a disciplinary arbitration

Roemer v NYC Bd. of Ed., 268 A.D.2d 479, motion for leave to appeal denied, 94 N.Y.2d 763

The Roemer decision serves as a reminder that the grounds for appealing a Section 3020-a disciplinary determination under the new law are very limited. In order to overturn a Section 3020-a arbitration award, it is necessary to prove that one or more of the statutory reasons set out in Article 75 of the Civil Practice Law and Rules for vacating the award exist.

Under Article 75, [Section 7511.b] an arbitrator's award can be vacated if a court finds that the rights of a party were violated because of corruption, fraud or misconduct in obtaining the award; the arbitrator was not impartial; to one party; the arbitrator exceed his or her powers or so imperfectly exercised them that a final determination was not made or the arbitration procedures were not followed, unless the party objecting to the award continued with the arbitration without objection after becoming aware of the defect.

In addition, courts have vacated arbitration awards found to violate strong public policy.

Here David Roemer, a New York City schoolteacher was terminated after the Section 3020-a arbitrator found him guilty of charges of incompetence and insubordination. He attempted to vacate the award. However, the Appellate Division sustained the Supreme Court's dismissal of Roemer's petition to vacate the award because Roemer "did not demonstrate" any basis for vacating the award under Section 7511.

In addition to the limited grounds for vacating the arbitration award set in Section 7511, Section 3020-a set a very short statute of limitations for filing a petition to overturn or modify the award as well as settling other limitations in such cases. Section 3020-a.5 sets out the following limitations with respect to challenging a Section 3020-a disciplinary determination:

1. Not later than ten days after receipt of the hearing officer's decision, the employee or the employing board may make an application to the New York state supreme court to vacate or modify the decision of the hearing officer pursuant to CPLR Section 7511.

2. The court's review shall be limited to the grounds set forth in Article 75. Further, the hearing panel's determination shall be deemed to be final for the purpose of such proceeding.

3. In no case shall the filing or the pendency of an appeal delay the implementation of the decision of the hearing officer.

Point 3 is particularly significant as it allows the appointing authority to imposed the penalty determined by the arbitrator while the decision is being challenged.

18.159 [See 18.160]

18.160 Vacating arbitration awards on grounds of public policy

Nassau Co. v Sheriff's Officers Association, Supreme Court, Nassau County, Justice Ralph P. Franco, March 13, 2001

This Article 75 action arose as a result of Gemelli, a Nassau County corrections officer, being found guilty of assaulting an inmate under his care by a federal district court jury and the Sheriff terminated Gemelli from his position effective March 1, 1999. Gemelli filed a grievance challenging his dismissal and eventually the matter was submitted to arbitration. However, while the disciplinary arbitration procedure was still pending, Gemelli retired.

Notwithstanding Gemelli's retirement, the arbitration proceeded to its conclusion and the Arbitrator made the following award:
1. The County's discharge of the grievant, Salvatore Gemelli, was not time barred.

2. The County did not have just cause to discharge Gemelli.

3. Gemelli shall, forthwith, be made whole for any wages and benefits lost, less any interim earnings, for the period of March 1, 1999, until Gemelli's retirement, effective May 27, 1999.

Nassau County brought an Article 75 action in an effort to vacate the arbitrator's award. The Sheriff's Officers Association, on the other hand, asked the court to confirm the award.

Justice Franco, after reading the arbitrator's decision and award, pointed out that an arbitration award shall be vacated where it is "violative of strong public policy." In this instance, said the court, the arbitrator's award conflicts with strong public policy.

The court explained that Gemelli, in exercising his responsibilities, was required to protect and care for this mentally retarded inmate under his care at the jail. In contrast to Gemellii's actions in the instance serving as the genesis of the disciplinary action taken against him, Justice Franco said that "[t]he inmate was to be protected by [Gemelii], not assaulted by him as the jury found in the Federal trial."

As to the arbitrator's ruling overturning Gemelli's termination, the court ruled that "[a]s his conduct was clearly a violation of public policy, he was justly discharged and is not entitled to be made whole for wages." Based upon all the facts and circumstances presented to him, Justice Franco vacated the arbitrator's award on the grounds that it constituted a violation of a strong public policy.

Accordingly, Gemelli's separation from the Sheriff's Department may now be recorded as a dismissal as a result of disciplinary action taken against him rather than as a "retirement."

18.161 Violating department rules

Malave v Safir, 270 A.D.2d 72

It is not too often that one encounters a court decision involving an employer filing disciplinary charges against an employee alleging that the employee was guilty of "patronizing a prostitute." However, this is exactly the issue before the Appellate Division in the Malave case.

Reubin Malave, a New York City police officer, was charged with violating Section 104.01 of the department's Patrol Guide. Section 104.01 prohibits New York City police officers from patronizing a prostitute. Found guilty, the penalty imposed on Malave was termination.

In the appeal that followed, the Appellate Division decided that the department's determination that Malave was guilty of the charge was supported by substantial evidence -- "including the testimony of two undercover police officers posing as prostitutes."

Applying the Pell doctrine, Pell v Board of Education, 34 NY2d 222, the Appellate Division said that it did not find the penalty of dismissal so disproportionate to petitioner's offenses as to shock our sense of fairness."

18.162 Violating the use of the Internet policies

Schnaars v Copiague Union Free School District, 275 A.D.2d 462

Public employers are adopting policies dealing with its employees using the agency's computers to access the Internet for personal business and transmitting and receiving personal e-mail. Some employee organizations have included demands to negotiate "computer and e-mail policies" among its collective bargaining proposals.

Recognizing the growing concerns of both the employer and employee organizations in this area, the Schnaars case serves to illustrate the problem and its resolution when one employee was found guilty of violating the employer's "computer policy."

The Copiague Union Free School District distributed a written memorandum advising its custodial staff that using its computers to access inappropriate material on the Internet violated district policy after it learned of the unauthorized use of its equipment by district employees.

The memorandum also cautioned that "employees who violated the policy would be subject to disciplinary proceedings which could result in suspension and/or termination."

About three months after promulgating its policy, the district learned that Robert Schnaars, the head custodian of the night crew at Copiague High School, used the school's computers to view pornographic web sites on the Internet with his subordinates during two night shifts in May 1998.

Schnaars was served with disciplinary charges and ultimately found guilty of using the District's computers to view "inappropriate material." Rejecting the hearing officer's recommended that Schnaars be demoted from his position of head custodian, the district imposed the penalty of dismissal.

Schnaars, however, contested his termination on the grounds that the penalty imposed by the district was "disproportionate to the offense." The Appellate Division agreed and remanded the matter to the district with instructions that it impose a penalty other than dismissal in light of Schnaars' previous "unblemished 13-year record of loyal service to the District with many accolades."

The court said that in its view, "the District did not give sufficient weight to these mitigating factors." But for Schnaars' "unblemished 13-year record" of employment with the district, the court might well have sustained his dismissal for violating the policy.

Clearly the court was neither troubled by the fact that the district had adopted a "computer use policy" nor that it had initiated disciplinary action when it learned that an individual had violated the policy. Its only concern in this case was the nature of the penalty imposed in view of Schnaars employment history with the district.

It appears that the courts will not treat violations of policies addressing the personal use of computers by employees lightly.

18.163 Violating workplace rules

Smith v Commissioner of Labor, 296 A.D.2d 803

Violating the employer's policy or work rules concerning sexual harassment may not only result in the termination of the employee. It may also disqualify the individual for unemployment insurance benefits.

The Appellate Division, Third Department, said that it is clear that an employee who is terminated because he or she "knowing" violated his or her employer's established policy or workplace rules may have been dismissed for "disqualifying misconduct" for the purposes of his or her eligibility for unemployment insurance benefits is concerned. In the Smith case, the Appellate Division, citing the Campbell decision, 271 AD2d 787, demonstrated this principle in a case involving an employee's termination for violating the employer's policy prohibiting sexual harassment.

William F. Smith was fired for violating his employer's policy prohibiting its employees from "sending inappropriate communications by e-mail." When his application for unemployment insurance benefits was rejected by the Unemployment Insurance Appeals Board, Smith sued.

According to the evidence introduced in the course of an unemployment insurance administrative hearing, Smith had sent "questionable e-mail" to his co-employees to notify them of a meeting with the subject line reading "NUDE PICTURES - NUDE PICTURES". Smith's explanation for this: he had used the phrase as a means of gaining the attention of his readers.

About a year later Smith was fired following his sending an e-mail to his co-employees containing a list of "Top Ten" sayings at second jobs. One of the sayings listed by Smith: "Another table dance?"

At the unemployment insurance hearing Smith's supervisor testified that after this episode he told Smith that "that this language violated the employer's policy against sexual harassment and the misuse of electronic communications." The supervisor also testified that he had told Smith that his repeating such inappropriate conduct would be severely sanctioned. Smith testified at the hearing that he had never received any such warning.

The Appellate Division sustained the Unemployment Insurance Appeals Board's decision that Smith had lost his employment under disqualifying circumstances -- i.e., he lost his employment due to his misconduct.

The court said that there was substantial evidence in the record to sustain the Board's determination and any issue concerning the credibility of the testimony of witness was for the Board to resolve.

18.164 Violating the terms of a disciplinary probation

Davis v DMNA, 291 A.D.2d 778

Disciplinary action was initiated against Randall Davis by his employer, the New York State Division of Military Affairs and Naval Affairs [DMNA], based on allegations that he was guilty of violating DMNA's Internet policy by visiting inappropriate websites, including pornographic websites and using a State-owned computer for "personal business."

The disciplinary action was matter was settled and the Division and Davis entered into an agreement dated January 19, 2000.

The relevant part of the settlement agreement placed Davis on disciplinary probation for one year and prohibited him from using State-owned computer equipment for personal reasons, including placing personal information on disks or other storage devices owned by the State. The agreement expressly provided that in the event Davis violated any of its terms, he would be subject to "automatic dismissal".

Davis returned to work and shortly thereafter created a file folder in his computer entitled "Rd" and stored various information, including personal information, in that folder.

According to the decision, Davis created this folder after work hours and placed it in a location on his work computer that was considered to be unusual for this type of file. As a result he was summarily terminated from his position on the grounds that he had violated the terms of his disciplinary probation.

Davis appealed, claiming that his termination was arbitrary and capricious and that the decision to terminate him was made in bad faith. However, noted the Appellate Division, Davis neither contested the fact that he created this file in his state-owned computer nor that he moved nonwork-related website addresses into it.

The Appellate Division observed that Davis "voluntarily entered into the settlement agreement which placed him in the status of a probationary employee subject to automatic termination if he violated any of its provisions."

Citing Swinton v Safir, 93 NY2d 758, the court said it had to apply a "stringent standard of review" in considering termination cases of probationary employees. It said that "a probationary employee has no right to challenge the termination by way of a hearing or otherwise, absent a showing that he was dismissed in bad faith or for an improper or impermissible reason."

Dismissing Davis' appeal, the court made the noted the following:

1. The record demonstrates that Davis violated the terms of the disciplinary settlement agreement, which provides a legally sufficient basis to terminate his employment; and

2. Davis did not meet his burden of establishing that his termination was retaliatory in nature and thus made in bad faith.

18.165 Volunteering to provide due process

Eckstrom v City of Ithaca, NYS Supreme Ct., November 21, 2000

In 1997 the City of Binghamton amended the City Code to require "notice and hearing" and proof of incompetence or misconduct before a city official appointed by the Mayor could be removed from his or her office. Prior to the amendment such officials were "employees-at-will" and not entitled to any form of a pretermination hearing.

In the Eckstrom case State Supreme Court Judge Walter J. Relihan, Jr. concluded that having enacted such a provision, the City was required to substantially comply with the principles followed in prosecuting disciplinary charges filed pursuant to Section 75 of the Civil Service Law.

Six disciplinary charges were filed against Richard L. Eckstrom, the city's Building Commissioner, by the Mayor. One was withdrawn by the Mayor prior to the hearing and three were dismissed by the hearing officer. Eckstrom, however, was found guilty of the two remaining charges based on building code decisions he had made. Accepting the findings and recommendations of the hearing officer, the Mayor dismissed Eckstrom. Eckstrom appealed.

In reviewing the record, Judge Relihan noted that the hearing officer had concluded that as to the first charge Eckstrom's actions were "arguably correct" and that his conduct with respect to the second charge "was neither incorrect nor unreasonable."

How then could the hearing officer have found Eckstrom guilty? In both instances, said Judge Relihan, the hearing officer relied on "an uncharged offense in support of a finding of guilt regarding an offense which does appear in the charges."

In the words of the court: "Obtuse to his own prior findings, the hearing officer concluded that Eckstrom should be fired for incompetence and misconduct ... These jarring inconsistencies and departures from well settled principles compel the conclusion that the 'Final Determination' is arbitrary, capricious, affected by an error of law and constitutes an abuse of discretion."

As the Court of Appeals held in Murray v Murphy, 24 NY2d 150, in order to satisfy due process, a notice of the charges must be given to the employee so that he or she may mount an adequate defense, if one is available.

Further, the disciplinary determination must be based on the charges filed against the employee and "no person may lose substantial rights because of wrongdoing shown by the evidence but not charged."

Observing that the city "disabled" itself from dismissing its high-ranking officials on policy grounds "unless, in addition, misconduct or incompetence could be proven at a hearing," Judge Relihan ruled that Eckstrom was to be reinstated to his former position.

Judge Relihan said that this may "complicate the business of the Building Department and cause discomfort elsewhere in City Hall" but "[p]erhaps, with good will, a rational and practical denouement can...be achieved...[which] of course, rests entirely in the hands of the parties."

The lesson of the Eckstrom case: in the event a public employer unilaterally decides to provide a pretermination disciplinary hearing to individuals not otherwise entitled such administrative due process by law or contract, the procedures normally appropriate to conducting such a disciplinary hearing must be followed.

18.166 Whistle blowing

Dobson v Loos, 277 A.D.2d 1013

In Dobson the significant issue before the Appellate Division, Fourth Department, concerned whether or not certain personnel actions alleged taken against an employee could constitute retaliation for whistle blowing in violation of Civil Service Law Section 75-b and Labor Law Section 740.

Richard Dobson, an Erie County Sheriff's Department Sergeant, complained that the Department had retaliated against him because of his "whistle blowing activities" by taking "active and extraordinary measures to preclude his appointment as Lieutenant during the life of the preferred eligibility list until its expiration by operation of law."

The Appellate Division ruled that such alleged conduct falls within the definition of a "retaliatory personnel action".

The court noted that retaliatory personnel action is defined in the statutes as the "discharge, suspension or demotion of an employee, or other adverse employment action taken against an employee in the terms and conditions of employment."

In addition, the court found that the following departmental actions Dobson alleged were taken against him could constitute unlawful retaliation as well:

1. Creating and filling new positions of senior and supervisory detectives, quasi-lieutenant positions "that rightfully should have been offered to [Dobson] but were not."

2. Assigning Dobson to "virtually nonexistent duties."

18.167 Whistle blowing pre-disclosure notice

Brohman v NY Convention Center Operating Corp., 293 A.D.2d 299

The Brohman case discusses the issue of notice to the employer in cases involving alleged retaliation in violation of the Whistle Blowers Law, Section 75-b of the Civil Service Law.

Sheldon Brohman sued the New York Convention Center Operating Corporation alleging he was wrongful discharge in violation of Section 75-b. The Appellate Division affirmed a Supreme Court justice's granting the Corporation's motion for summary judgment dismissing Brohman's complaint. The ruling points out that Section 75-b(2)(b) requires that the individual, prior to disclosing information to a governmental body, "shall have made a good faith effort to provide the appointing authority or his or her designee the information to be disclosed and shall provide the appointing authority or designee a reasonable time to take appropriate action."

Civil Service Law Section 2.9 defines the term "appointing authority" as the "officer, commission or body having the power of appointment to subordinate positions." In this instance, said the Appellate Division, the appointing authority is the Corporation's Board of Directors and its designee would be its president and chief executive officer at the time of the alleged improper governmental actions.

Brohman conceded that he did not communicate his concerns of alleged wrongdoing by the Corporation's president to either the Board of Directors or its president and chief operating officer. Brohman contended that he had satisfied Section 75-b pre-disclosure notice requirement because he communicated his concerns to one of the Corporation's vice-presidents.

However, said the court, even assuming that the vice-president can be considered the Corporation's designee, Brohman's argument was crippled by his own deposition testimony and affidavit. His statements, according to the Appellate Division, demonstrated that Brohman's communications with the vice-president were not for the purpose of informing Corporation of the alleged improper actions of its president. Rather, said the court, Brohman used the vice-president: "As a 'friend and a soundboard,' went to him for 'advice,' did not ask him to put an end to the alleged improprieties, and had a mutual understanding with him that their conversations would "absolutely" go no further."

Accordingly, Brohman's "pre-disclosure" of his concerns neither satisfied his duty to made a good faith effort to provide his employer with the information he proposed to disclose nor provide his employer with a reasonable time within which it could take appropriate action.

18.168 Whistleblower law covers provisional employees

Sisson v Lech, App. Div., 266 A.D.2d 858

The fact that an individual is a provisional employee does not necessarily mean that the individual cannot challenge his or her dismissal in court. For example, the individual may allege that he or she was discharged for "whistle blowing." In such a case the individual has a statutory right to sue his or her former employer. The Sisson decision illustrates this.

Dismissed from his provisional appointment with the Niagara County Department of Mental Health, Joseph A. Sisson sued alleging that "he was terminated from his public employment in violation of Civil Service Law Section 75-b, commonly referred to as the 'whistleblower's law', and that he was terminated in bad faith." Although a State Supreme Court justice summarily dismissed his petition, the Appellate Division reversed and said that the matter should go to trial.

It is well settled that a provisional employee may be "discharged at will" after completing the minimum period of probation and before the end of his or her maximum period of probation unless there was evidence that his or her termination "was for a constitutionally impermissible purpose or in violation of statutory or decisional law." The Appellate Division concluded that Sisson, although a provisional appointee, was covered by Section 75-b and thus he had a statutory right to challenge his dismissal for any alleged "whistle blowing."

Section 75-b defines the term "public employee" as any person holding a position by appointment or employment in the service of a public employer except judges and members of the legislature. It also provides that where the employee is not entitled to due process pursuant to Section 75 or a similar provision of law, or a disciplinary procedure negotiated pursuant to the Taylor Law, the individual may sue under the same terms and conditions as set out in Article 20-C of the Labor Law. Thus Section 75-b covers all public employees, not just those who are "tenured" employees.

According to the Appellate Division, Sisson presented evidence that his termination was related to the fact that "he reported to the Community Service Board that his superior, Antoinette Lech, acted in an improper manner with respect to him and two other employees" to the lower court. Viewing this evidence in the light most favorable to Sisson, the court concluded that there was a "rational basis whereby [a] jury might find for [Sisson] as against [Lech]" and thus neither she nor the department were entitled to summary judgment.

18.169 Who is the employer?

Beers v Village of Floral Park, 262 A.D.2d 315

Who was the employer who fired part-time library clerk Barbara Beers: the Village of Floral Park or the Floral Park Public Library? Such a simple question is not as easy to answer as one might expect.

Barbara Beers was terminated from her position as a part-time clerk by the Floral Park Public Library. She sued both the village and the library, claiming that she had been unlawfully removed from her position without a hearing.

Actually Beers filed a "hybrid proceeding" consisting of an Article 78 to compel the library to reinstate her to her former position and a complaint contending the library violated 42 USC 1983, a federal civil rights statute, when it deprived her of a property right -- her job -- without a due process hearing. She also named the village as a defendant based on representations by its attorney that she had been an employee of the village.

In response, both the village and the library filed motions seeking to have Beers' petition dismissed. The village said it should be severed from the action on the grounds that notwithstanding the village attorney's statements to Beers, it was not Beers' former employer. The village argued that the library was not an agency or department of the village.

The library contended that Beers' Article 78 action was untimely, having been filed more than four months after she had been terminated. A Supreme Court judge granted both motions and Beers appealed.

The Appellate Division commenced its analysis by noting that a public library is an educational corporation chartered by the New York State Board of Regents with the authority to hire, fire, and pay its employees and that the Education Law provides that a public library is an entity that is "separate and distinct from the municipality that created it." It then noted that the relationship between the municipality and the public library may be varied by contract, either express or implied.

Was there an implied contract? Based on the record of the municipality's behavior, the Appellate Division said that there was a triable issue of fact to be resolved as to which entity was Beers' employer. The court noted that the village had offered Beers a comparable clerk's job and sent her a notice directing her to appear on a date certain for employment. In addition, the court said that the village, in its original answer, admitted "that it employed her". Accordingly, said the court, it was not clear if the village assumed responsibility for the library's employees, and thereby responsibility for her termination.

As to Beers' claims against the library, the Appellate Division said that her Article 78 action was untimely because it was filed more than four months after her termination. It commented that Beers "knew that she worked in the library and that the library functioned separately through a board of trustees."

However, the Appellate Division ruled that Beers' complaint contending that the library had violated her civil rights under 42 USC 1983 because it terminated her without a hearing was timely. The question of who is Beers' employer and whether she was denied her rights to due process will now have to be considered by a state supreme court judge.

18.170 Withdrawing a resignation

Martinez v State Univ. of New York, 294 A.D.2d 650; 13 A.D.3d 749

Probationer Odilon Martinez was advised by his supervisors that he was to be terminated from his position as a Laborer, Grade 6 because his performance during his probationary period had been unsatisfactory.

Martinez was also told that he would be simultaneously reinstated to his former position of Cleaner, Grade 5. Martinez then went to the office of the Director of Human Resources [DHR] and submitted a letter of resignation. The next day the DHR wrote to Martinez indicating that "his resignation had been accepted."[231]

Martinez subsequently wrote to the DHR indicating that he wished to withdraw his resignation. The DHR declined to allow Martinez to withdraw his resignation because it "had already been accepted." Martinez sued, seeking to a court order (1) allowing him to withdraw his resignation, (2) annulling the termination of his probationary promotion, and (3) his reinstatement to the Laborer Grade 6 position subject to new probationary term. Supreme Court granted the University's motion for summary judgment, dismissing Martinez's petition without addressing the merits of his allegations.

The Appellate Division commenced its review of Martinez's appeal by noting that 4 NYCRR 5.3(c) provides that a written resignation submitted an employee of the State "may not be withdrawn, canceled or amended after it is delivered to the appointing authority, without the consent of the appointing authority".

The court, citing Edelman v Axelrod, 111 AD2d 468, said that allowing the individual to withdrawal his or her resignation after it has been delivered to the appointing authority is subject to the exercise of "the sound discretion of the appointing authority."

However, said the court, the exercise of such discretion may not be done in an arbitrary or capricious manner. As the issue of whether the University's action met this standard was not considered by Supreme Court because it granted the University's motion for summary judgment, the Appellate Division remanded the case to the lower court for its consideration of whether or not the University's rejection of Martinez's request to withdraw his resignation was arbitrary or capricious.

On a related issue: May an appointing authority refuse to accept an employee's written resignation?

As noted earlier, an employee's written resignation becomes effective upon delivery; neither the appointing authority's acceptance or rejection is a factor insofar the effectiveness of the resignation is concerned.

---

[231] Courts generally have ruled that to be effective a resignation must be in writing and delivered to the appointing authority, or its designee. All that is required for a written resignation to become operative is its delivery to the appointing authority. The approval or acceptance of the resignation typically is not required for the resignation to take effect (see Hazelton v Connelly, 25 NYS2d 74).

The receipt of an employee's resignation may have an effect on other personnel actions under certain circumstances, however. For example, the employee may submit his or her resignation in the anticipation of disciplinary charges being filed against him or her or while disciplinary charges are pending. Will the employee's resignation prevent the appointing authority from proceeding with the disciplinary action?

Not necessarily. The appointing authority may elect to disregard the employee's resignation for the purposes of proceeding with the disciplinary action. The Rules of the State Civil Service Commission [4 NYCRR 5.3(b)], specifically provide that the appointing authority may elect to disregard the resignation and proceed with the disciplinary action. Many municipalities have adopted a similar rule or regulation.

What is the result if the employer wishes to disregard the resignation and proceed with the disciplinary action. It could have a significant impact on the individual. If, for example, the individual is found guilty of the charges and the penalty imposed is dismissal, the official records will reflect that the separation was a "termination for cause" rather than a resignation from the position. Further, the individual will have to report that fact to potential public employers as most employment applications and examination applications include the question that, in effect, asks: "Have you ever been dismissed for cause or resigned in the face of disciplinary action?"

18.171 Witness creditability determinations

CSEA Local 1000 [Vaziri-Cohen] v Tioga County, 288 A.D.2d 802

In an administrative disciplinary action, the hearing officer's determination is frequently based on his or her evaluation of the credibility of witnesses testifying at the disciplinary hearing. In the Vaziri-Cohen appeal the Appellate Division considered the issue of credibility in determining if substantial evidence supported the disciplinary determination resulting in Vaziri-Cohen's dismissal.

Susan Vaziri-Cohen was terminated after being found guilty of charges that she had falsified agency records, repeatedly failed to follow her superior's instructions and made demeaning remarks to a co-worker about her supervisor.

The Hearing Officer recommended that Vaziri-Cohen be dismissed from service based on a finding that her conduct had "hindered the mission of the agency and hurt its credibility" and that she "remained unwilling to concede that her behavior was unacceptable."

CSEA appealed, contending that the hearing officer's findings were not supported by substantial evidence. The Appellate Division disagreed and dismissed the appeal.

The court pointed out that here the finding of the hearing officer with respect to the first charge -- falsification of official records -- turned on issues of credibility and inferences drawn by the hearing officer from the evidence presented. Deciding that the conclusion drawn by the hearing officer was supported by both direct and circumstantial evidence, the court sustained the hearing officer's finding.

Noting that both Vaziri-Cohen and her supervisor testified during the disciplinary hearing, the court said that "it was within the province of the Hearing Officer to implicitly reject the credibility of [Vaziri-Cohen's] exculpatory explanation."

As to the second charge -- Vaziri-Cohen's alleged failure to follow work orders -- her supervisor testified that despite several successive directives by him concerning the inclusion of certain information in a client's medical record over the course of one week -- Vaziri-Cohen failed to add the information as directed.

Vaziri-Cohen, on the other hand, testified that she had made the changes directed by her supervisor. The court said that this conflict in the testimony given at the disciplinary hearing raised an issue of credibility implicitly resolved by the Hearing Officer's ruling against her.

As to the charge alleging Vaziri-Cohen made disparaging remarks about her superior to a co-worker, the Appellate Division said that substantial evidence supported the hearing officer's conclusion that, under the circumstances, her comments were "irresponsible and denigrating" and obviates any claim that they were made in good faith.

According to the decision, "the unrefuted testimony, including [Vaziri-Cohen's] admission, established that ... [she] made a denigrating and explicit comment to a co-worker about her supervisor...."

As to the penalty imposed, dismissal, the Appellate Division wrote that "in view of the nature of the misconduct and insubordination involved in these charges, we see no basis upon which to disturb the penalty of dismissal, which we do not find was so disproportionate [to the offenses to which she was found guilty] as to be shocking to one's sense of fairness," citing the Pell standard.[232]

Creditability was also an issue in the Pelayo case.[233] Henry Pelayo, a New York City police officer, was dismissed from his position after being found guilty of administrative disciplinary charges alleging that he "knowingly gave false material testimony in felony court proceedings, and that he provided false information concerning the events underlying [those] criminal proceedings in departmental ... forms."

The court said that Pelayo "challenges to the credibility determinations of the Assistant Deputy Commissioner are unavailing since, in an Article 78 proceeding, the reviewing court may not weigh the evidence, choose between conflicting proof, or substitute its assessment of the evidence or witness credibility for that of the administrative fact-finder."

18.172 Work related investigations

Cerrone v Cahill, USDC, NDNY, 1/28/00

---

[232] Pell v Board of Education, 34 NY2d 222

[233] Pelayo v Safir, App. Div., First Dept., November 27, 2001

An investigation is being conducted by the appointing authority concerning alleged misconduct by an employee.

1. Do the same rules that apply when the appointing authority conducts an investigation involving alleged work-related misconduct as control when the appointing authority is investigating alleged off-duty misconduct?

2. Is there any difference between an investigation by an appointing authority for the purpose of filing administrative disciplinary charges against an employee and its investigation directed towards bringing criminal charges against the individual?

As the Cerrone case demonstrates, if the focus of the investigation is criminal rather than administrative, different rules and safeguards control.

State Police Sergeant Thomas Cerrone filed a lawsuit in federal district court contending that his Fourth Amendment rights were violated in the course of his being investigated concerning "some sort of cover-up" related to his role in an investigation of a "hit and run accident" that occurred on April 3, 1993.

According to the decision, Cerrone reviewed and signed an accident report prepared by Trooper Robert Gregory that was alleged to be "facially insufficient" and contained "false information." Sometime later a letter signed by "Ed Scott" stating that "Rory Knapp, the brother of State Trooper Timothy Knapp, left the scene of an accident on April 3, 1993" was received by the Division of State Police. Ed Scott denied writing the letter and the letter writer was never positively identified.

On January 19, 1995 Cerrone was stopped by investigators, placed in an unmarked police car and taken to a hotel for questioning about the hit and run incident.

Cerrone was given a "Miranda" warning and advised that he was the target of a criminal investigation. The investigators did not have a warrant for their action. After being questioned for six hours, Cerrone was permitted to leave when he agreed to take a polygraph test.

One of the recognized exceptions to the prohibition against warrantless searches and seizures is "work-related investigations." Cerrone argued that in this case the investigation was criminal rather than work related and thus he was entitled to the protections of the Fourth Amendment against unreasonable searches and seizures.

Noting that the procedures governing "administrative investigations" set out in the applicable Taylor Law agreement were not implemented in the course of Cerrone's interrogation, Judge Thomas J. McAvoy agreed that the basic purpose of the investigation was criminal rather than administrative in nature.

The court said that "the distinction between searches and seizures for the purpose of criminal prosecution and those undertaken for work related or administrative purposes is critical and many courts upholding a standard lower than probable cause [in work related investigations] have recognized that the lower standard is not appropriate in the criminal arena."

Thus, observed Judge McAvoy, if Cerrone "was seized or arrested without probable cause, his Fourth Amendment rights were violated." The court also noted that the available evidence prior to Cerrone's being questioned "revealed little" linking him, as opposed to other officers, to the alleged cover-up.

The decision sets out the following basic principles to be followed in investigation of employee misconduct:

1. Where a search or seizure is conducted by a government employer to further a criminal investigation, the traditional requirement of probable cause is necessary and the individual is protected by the Fourth Amendment.

2. Government employers cannot avoid the traditional Fourth Amendment safeguards applicable in the context of criminal investigations simply by labeling a criminal search work-related.

Law enforcement agencies may have greater difficulty here than other government employers. Typically a non-law enforcement agency's investigation of alleged misconduct looks towards filing administrative disciplinary charges against an individual. As the court ruled in Biehunik v Felicetta, 441 F2d 228, Fourth Amendment rights do not apply in investigations of work-related misconduct.

In contrast, the very nature of investigations by law enforcement agencies of its personnel often tends to blur the line between "administrative investigation" for the purpose of initiating administrative disciplinary action and an investigation of the same or a related incident for the purpose of bring criminal charges against the individual. Accordingly, the distinctions identified by Judge McAvoy in the Cerrone case should be kept in mind when investigations into alleged employee misconduct are initiated by a law enforcement agency.[234]

18.173 Workers' Compensation Leave

House v NYS Office of Mental Health, 262 A.D.2d 929

Martha I. House, a keyboard specialist at Richard H. Hutchings Psychiatric Center, suffered a work-related injury in December 1991. As a result she was frequently absent from work. The psychiatric center deemed these to be absences workers' compensation leave under Civil Service Law Section 71.

When the number of these absences exceeded the one-year cumulative period allowed for Section 71 leave, House was told that her employment would be terminated in 30 days. She was also told that she could apply for reinstatement if she could demonstrate that she was medically fit.

House submitted a note from her physician stating that she was medically fit. The psychiatric center referred her to a physician employed by the State Employee Health Service for an evaluation. The EHS physician stated that House was "too symptomatic to return to work and perform the full duties

---

[234] In Dombrowski v Safir, decided by the Appellate Division, First Department, February 3, 2000, the court sustained the appointing authority's termination of New York City police officer Kenneth J. Dombrowski following his refusal to answer questions "directly and narrowly relating to his official duties".

of her position." As a result House was terminated. House sued, seeking reinstatement to her job and back pay.

A state Supreme Court decided that the psychiatric center had not given House "proper notice of the procedure for requesting a post-termination hearing, resulting in the denial of her due process right to an administrative appeal." It remitted the matter for an administrative hearing on the issue of Houses's medical condition and her ability to perform her job-related duties at the time of her termination. It declined, however, to order either House's reinstatement or back salary at this point in the process.

Both House and the employer appealed. The Appellate Division ruled although House was entitled to a post-termination hearing, until that administrative remedy has been exhausted, a resolution of her other demands would be premature.

The Appellate Division said that once it has been determined by the appointing authority's physician that an employee is unfit to serve, he or she cannot be restored to employment until there is a finding that the employee is medically fit to perform the duties of the position.

Thus the Supreme Court's judgment remitting the matter for an administrative hearing to develop the record regarding petitioner's medical fitness was appropriate.

18.174 Wrongful termination

Lewis v Cowen, 2nd Cir., No. 97-7895, 1/15/99

J. Blaine Lewis, head of Connecticut's lottery, was fired for refusing to publicly support a change in the lottery. Lewis was an unclassified employee and served at the pleasure of the Executive Director of the Connecticut Division of Special Revenue and the Gaming Policy Board.

Lewis had national prominence in the public gaming community. He served as President of the National Association of State and Provincial Lotteries, an association of public gaming executives in the United States and Canada, and had been featured on the cover of Public Gaming International, a trade magazine.

Problems began in 1988, when the state awarded a contract to install a statewide computer system for the sale of lottery tickets to General Instrument Corporation (GIC). Lewis opposed this move. After GIC's system malfunctioned and created a system-wide breakdown of on-line sales, Lewis criticized GIC to the press. The board ordered him and other unit heads to stop all media contact, but this gag order was eventually lifted.

Another change Lewis opposed was increasing the pool of numbers from which the winning Lotto numbers were picked was from 40 to 44. Lewis believed that revenues would decrease and suspected that GIC had recommended the change merely to cover up problems with on-line ticketing.

His superior, the Executive Director, ordered him to present the change to the Board at a public meeting and to cite "all positives and no negatives." Lewis balked and was fired by the board one day after it unanimously approved the change.

He sued, contending that his termination constituted a violation of his First Amendment rights. He won a substantial jury verdict in U.S. District Court -- $2 million in compensatory damages and punitive damages plus $380,000 in attorney's fees.

On appeal, the Second Circuit U.S. Court of Appeals reversed. While "it is by now well established that public employees do not check all of their First Amendment rights at the door upon accepting public employment," the court said that Lewis' case involves a different issue: may a public employer discipline an employee for refusing to speak?

Connecticut argued that it was entitled to terminate Lewis pursuant to the standard announced in cases such as Connick v. Myers, 461 U.S. 138 (1983), and Pickering v. Board of Education, 391 U.S. 563 (1968), and in the alternative, that its decision to terminate Lewis is shielded by a qualified immunity. The Circuit Court applied the so-called Pickering balancing test typically used in considering free-speech cases involving public employees in resolving the issue.

The Pickering test has two elements. The court must first decide whether the speech addresses a matter of public concern. If so, the court then must balance the interests of the employer in providing "effective and efficient" public services against the employee's First Amendment right to free expression. The court addressed two key questions:

1. Did Lewis's refusal to speak to the Board touch on a matter of public concern? and

2. Did the potential disruptiveness of Lewis's refusal to speak outweigh his First Amendment-based interest in not speaking?

Reviewing the evidence, the circuit panel concluded that as a matter of law Connecticut's interest in the effective and efficient operation of its Lottery Division outweighed Lewis's First Amendment interest in refusing to present the proposed Lotto change before the Board in a positive manner.

State officials testified that Lewis's speech would "potentially interfere" with the Division's operations and that his refusal to promote the proposed change would result in negative publicity and decreased morale, in turn impairing the profitability of the lottery. Concluding that under the circumstances Lewis's termination was justified, the Court ruled that:

1. The lower court should have dismissed the action on the ground of qualified immunity.

2. The state defendants are immune from liability on Lewis's state law wrongful discharge claim.

The decision also considered "the exceptional significance of a government employee's interest in testifying truthfully before a legislative committee," referring to the Piesco case.[235] In Piesco the Second Circuit "refused to force employees like Dr. Piesco to choose between answering questions

---

[235] 933 F.2d at 1157

honestly and risk being fired on one hand, and committing perjury on the other" holding that there was no evidence that Dr. Piesco's testimony interfered with government operations in a manner outweighing Dr. Piesco's strong interest in testifying truthfully.

In contrast, the court said although Lewis had a strong First Amendment interest in testifying truthfully before the Board, it "did not believe that interest to have been implicated here because Lewis was directed to present the Division's views, not his own."

18.175 Zero tolerance drug policy

Dept. of Corrections v Robbins, OATH 2030/99, 11/3/99

Many employers have initiated "zero tolerance" policies requiring the automatic dismissal of individuals found to have violated the policy. These policies address a number of situations that the employer views as disruptive or dangerous, the most common involving the use of drugs by employees, on or off the job.

The New York City Department of Corrections had established a "zero tolerance" drug policy providing for the termination of any employee, uniformed (i.e., correction officers), or civilian, who violated the policy. Its justification: the policy serves important functions by acting as a deterrent against drug traffic in its facilities and ensured that "the security of penal institutions is not breached."

Was dismissal the appropriate penalty in a case involving a civilian employee -- a dietary aide -- found to have smoked one marijuana cigarette, off-duty, almost two years before being charged with violating the policy? The administrative law judge did not believe it was, concluding that there are instances, particularly where a civilian employee is involved, when the "automatic penalty" under the department's zero tolerance drug policy should not be applied.

The employee, Anthony Robbins, admitted he was guilty of the charge of using marijuana while off-duty. Although the department wanted him terminated for violating its "zero tolerance" drug policy, the hearing officer recommended that a lesser penalty be imposed. The mitigating circumstances set out by the hearing officer justifying the deviation from the policy included the following:

1. Since the time of the incident, Robbins had been in counseling, had undergone drug testing, and laboratory reports indicated that he tested negative for drugs.

2. The employee has continued in counseling and still undergoes, as part of counseling, drug screening.

3. The risk of Robbins' being involved in drug smuggling at the facility is so negligible as to be speculative and therefore cannot justify termination.

4. In previous cases involving violations of the "zero tolerance" policy by civilian workers, the individuals were not terminated and lesser penalties were imposed by the department.

5. The department did not subject civilian workers to random drug testing procedures although it required uniformed employees to submit to random drug tests.

6. In one instance the department "converted a penalty of termination into a lengthy suspension with random drug testing against a correction officer found to have tested positive for marijuana."

The hearing officer concluded in these "mitigating circumstances" justified a departure from the "zero tolerance" policy's "automatic termination" provision.

APPENDIX I

STATUTORY AND OTHER AUTHORITY FOR DISCIPLINE

Part 1, Civil Service Law Section 75

Section 75. Removal and other disciplinary action.

Section 75-a. Civil service proceeding; commencement upon alleged violation of certain provisions of the labor law relating to police officers.

Section 75-b. Retaliatory action by public employers.

Section 76. Appeals from determinations in disciplinary proceedings.

Section 77. Compensation of officers and employees reinstated by court order.

Section 75.

Removal and other disciplinary action.

1. Removal and other disciplinary action. A person described in paragraph (a) or paragraph (b), or paragraph (c), or paragraph (d), or paragraph (e) of this subdivision shall not be removed or otherwise subjected to any disciplinary penalty provided in this section except for incompetency or misconduct shown after a hearing upon stated charges pursuant to this section.

(a) A person holding a position by permanent appointment in the competitive class of the classified civil service, or

(b) a person holding a position by permanent appointment or employment in the classified service of the state or in the several cities, counties, towns, or villages thereof, or in any other political or civil division of the state or of a municipality, or in the public school service, or in any public or special district, or in the service of any authority, commission or board, or in any other branch of public service, who was honorably discharged or released under honorable circumstances from the armed forces of the United States having served therein as such member in time of war as defined in section eighty-five of this chapter, or who is an exempt volunteer firefighter as defined in the general municipal law, except when a person described in this paragraph holds the position of private secretary, cashier or deputy of any official or department, or

(c) an employee holding a position in the non-competitive class other than a position designated in the rules of the state or municipal civil service commission as confidential or requiring the performance of functions influencing policy, who since his last entry into service has completed at least five years of continuous service in the non-competitive class in a position or positions not so designated in the rules as confidential or requiring the performance of functions influencing policy, or

(d) an employee in the service of the City of New York holding a position as Homemaker or Home Aide in the non-competitive class, who since his last entry into city service has completed at least three years of continuous service in such position in the non-competitive class, or

(e) an employee in the service of a police department within the state of New York holding the position of detective for a period of three continuous years or more; provided, however, that a hearing shall not be required when reduction in rank from said position is based solely on reasons of the economy, consolidation or abolition of functions, curtailment of activities or otherwise.

2. Procedure. An employee who at the time of questioning appears to be a potential subject of disciplinary action shall have a right to representation by his or her certified or recognized employee organization under article fourteen of this chapter and shall be notified in advance, in writing, of such right. A state employee who is designated managerial or confidential under article fourteen of this chapter, shall, at the time of questioning, where it appears that such employee is a potential subject of disciplinary action, have a right to representation and shall be notified in advance, in writing, of such right. If representation is requested a reasonable period of time shall be afforded to obtain such representation. If the employee is unable to obtain representation within a reasonable period of time the employer has the right to then question the employee. A hearing officer under this section shall have the power to find that a reasonable period of time was or was not afforded. In the event the hearing officer finds that a reasonable period of time was not afforded then any and all statements obtained from said questioning as well as any evidence or information obtained as a result of said questioning shall be excluded, provided, however, that this subdivision shall not modify or replace any written collective agreement between a public employer and employee organization negotiated pursuant to article fourteen of this chapter. A person against whom removal or other disciplinary action is proposed shall have written notice thereof and of the reasons therefore, shall be furnished a copy of the charges preferred against him and shall be allowed at least eight days for answering the same in writing. The hearing upon such charges shall be held by the officer or body having the power to remove the person against whom such charges are preferred, or by a deputy or other person designated by such officer or body in writing for that purpose. In case a deputy or other person is so designated, he shall, for the purpose of such hearing, be vested with all the powers of such officer or body and shall make a record of such hearing which shall, with his recommendations, be referred to such officer or body for review and decision. The person or persons holding such hearing shall, upon the request of the person against whom charges are preferred, permit him to be represented by counsel, or by a representative of a recognized or certified employee organization, and shall allow him to summon witnesses in his behalf. The burden of proving incompetency or misconduct shall be upon the person alleging the same. Compliance with technical rules of evidence shall not be required.

3. Suspension pending determination of charges; penalties. Pending the hearing and determination of charges of incompetency or misconduct, the officer or employee against whom such charges have been preferred may be suspended without pay for a period not exceeding thirty days. If such officer or employee is found guilty of the charges, the penalty or punishment may consist of a reprimand, a fine not to exceed one hundred dollars to be deducted from the salary or wages of such officer or

employee, suspension without pay for a period not exceeding two months, demotion in grade and title, or dismissal from the service; provided, however, that the time during which an officer or employee is suspended without pay may be considered as part of the penalty. If he is acquitted, he shall be restored to his position with full pay for the period of suspension less the amount of any unemployment insurance benefits he may have received during such period. If such officer or employee is found guilty, a copy of the charges, his written answer thereto, a transcript of the hearing, and the determination shall be filed in the office of the department or agency in which he has been employed, and a copy thereof shall be filed with the civil service commission having jurisdiction over such position. A copy of the transcript of the hearing shall, upon request of the officer or employee affected, be furnished to him without charge.

3-a. Suspension pending determination of charges and penalties relating to police officers of the police department of the city of New York. Pending the hearing and determination of charges of incompetency or misconduct, a police officer employed by the police department of the city of New York may be suspended without pay for a period not exceeding thirty days. If such officer is found guilty of the charges, the police commissioner of such department may punish the police officer pursuant to the provisions of sections 14-115 and 14-123 of the administrative code of the city of New York.

4. Notwithstanding any other provision of law, no removal or disciplinary proceeding shall be commenced more than eighteen months after the occurrence of the alleged incompetency or misconduct complained of and described in the charges or, in the case of a state employee who is designated managerial or confidential under article fourteen of this chapter, more than one year after the occurrence of the alleged incompetency or misconduct complained of and described in the charges, provided, however, that such limitations shall not apply where the incompetency or misconduct complained of and described in the charges would, if proved in a court of appropriate jurisdiction, constitute a crime.

Section 75-a. Civil service proceeding; commencement upon alleged violation of certain provisions of the labor law relating to police officers.

1. Any police officer alleging a violation of section two hundred fifteen-a of the labor law may institute a proceeding pursuant to the provisions of his collective bargaining agreement. If no such agreement exists a complaint may be filed by a police officer with the state or a municipal civil service commission alleging a violation of section two hundred fifteen-a of the labor law; as a condition of entertaining such complaint the commission may require a police officer to exhaust all remedies available to such employee pursuant to the provisions of a collective bargaining agreement and the rules and regulations of the employer . Upon the filing of such complaint or upon its own initiative the commission having jurisdiction may investigate and upon finding an improper transfer or other penalty in violation of such section, enforce the provisions of such section. The commission may exercise any powers heretofore granted to it by provision of this chapter or by any other provision of law necessary for the enforcement of the provisions of section two hundred fifteen-a of the labor law.

2. Nothing in this section shall be construed to abrogate, impair, alter, or in any way modify any right of action in law that an employee, alleged to have been penalized, may have.

Section 75-b. Retaliatory action by public employers.

1. For the purposes of this section the term:

(a) "Public employer" or "employer" shall mean (i) the state of New York, (ii) a county, city, town, village or any other political subdivision or civil division of the state, (iii) a school district or any governmental entity operating a public school, college or university, (iv) a public improvement or special district, (v) a public authority, commission or public benefit corporation, or (vi) any other public corporation, agency, instrumentality or unit of government which exercises governmental power under the laws of the state.

(b) "Public employee" or "employee" shall mean any person holding a position by appointment or employment in the service of a public employer except judges or justices of the unified court system and members of the legislature.

(c) "Governmental body" shall mean (i) an officer, employee, agency, department, division, bureau, board, commission, council, authority or other body of a public employer, (ii) employee, committee, member, or commission of the legislative branch of government, (iii) a representative, member or employee of a legislative body of a county, town, village or any other political subdivision or civil division of the state, (iv) a law enforcement agency or any member or employee of a law enforcement agency, or (v) the judiciary or any employee of the judiciary.

(d) "Personnel action" shall mean an action affecting compensation, appointment, promotion, transfer, assignment, reassignment, reinstatement or evaluation of performance.

2. (a) A public employer shall not dismiss or take other disciplinary or other adverse personnel action against a public employee regarding the employee's employment because the employee discloses to a governmental body information: (i) regarding a violation of a law, rule or regulation which violation creates and presents a substantial and specific danger to the public health or safety; or (ii) which the employee reasonably believes to be true and reasonably believes constitutes an improper governmental action. "Improper governmental action" shall mean any action by a public employer or employee, or an agent of such employer or employee, which is undertaken in the performance of such agent's official duties, whether or not such action is within the scope of his employment, and which is in violation of any federal, state or local law, rule or regulation.

(b) Prior to disclosing information pursuant to paragraph (a) of this subdivision, an employee shall have made a good faith effort to provide the appointing authority or his or her designee the information to be disclosed and shall provide the appointing authority or designee a reasonable time to take appropriate action unless there is imminent and serious danger to public health or safety. For the purposes of this subdivision, an employee who acts pursuant to this paragraph shall be deemed to have disclosed information to a governmental body under paragraph (a) of this subdivision.

3. (a) Where an employee is subject to dismissal or other disciplinary action under a final and binding arbitration provision, or other disciplinary procedure contained in a collectively negotiated agreement, or under section seventy-five of this title or any other provision of state or local law and the employee reasonably believes dismissal or other disciplinary action would not have been taken but for the conduct protected under subdivision two of this section, he or she may assert such as a defense before the designated arbitrator or hearing officer. The merits of such defense shall be considered and determined as part of the arbitration award or hearing officer decision of the matter. If there is a finding that the dismissal or other disciplinary action is based solely on a violation by the employer of such subdivision, the arbitrator or hearing officer shall dismiss or recommend dismissal of the disciplinary proceeding, as appropriate, and, if appropriate, reinstate the employee with back pay, and, in the case of an arbitration procedure, may take other appropriate action as is permitted in the collectively negotiated agreement.

(b) Where an employee is subject to a collectively negotiated agreement which contains provisions preventing an employer from taking adverse personnel actions and which contains a final and binding arbitration provision to resolve alleged violations of such provisions of the agreement and the employee reasonably believes that such personnel action would not have been taken but for the conduct protected under subdivision two of this section, he or she may assert such as a claim before the arbitrator. The arbitrator shall consider such claim and determine its merits and shall, if a determination is made that such adverse personnel action is based on a violation by the employer of such subdivision, take such action to remedy the violation as is permitted by the collectively negotiated agreement.

(c) Where an employee is not subject to any of the provisions of paragraph (a) or (b) of this subdivision, the employee may commence an action in a court of competent jurisdiction under the same terms and conditions as set forth in article twenty-C of the labor law.

4. Nothing in this section shall be deemed to diminish or impair the rights of a public employee or employer under any law, rule, regulation or collectively negotiated agreement or to prohibit any personnel action which otherwise would have been taken regardless of any disclosure of information.

Section 76. Appeals from determinations in disciplinary proceedings.

1. Appeals. Any officer or employee believing himself aggrieved by a penalty or punishment of demotion in or dismissal from the service, or suspension without pay, or a fine, or an official reprimand, unaccompanied by a remittance of said officer or employee's prehearing suspension without pay, imposed pursuant to the provisions of section seventy-five of this chapter, may appeal from such determination either by an application to the state or municipal commission having jurisdiction, or by an application to the court in accordance with the provisions of article seventy-eight of the civil practice law and rules. If such person elects to appeal to such civil service commission, he shall file such appeal in writing within twenty days after service of written notice of the determination to be reviewed, such written notice to be delivered personally or by registered mail to the last known address of such person and when notice is given by registered mail, such person shall be allowed an additional three days in which to file such appeal.

2. Procedure on appeal. Where appeal is taken to the state or municipal commission having jurisdiction, such commission shall review the record of the disciplinary proceeding and the transcript of the hearing, and shall determine such appeal on the basis of such record and transcript and such oral or written argument as the commission may deter mine. The commission may direct that such appeal shall be heard by one or more members of the commission or by a person or persons designated by the commission to hear such appeal on its behalf, who shall report thereon with recommendations to the commission. Upon such appeal the commission shall permit the employee to be represented by counsel.

3. Determination on appeal. The determination appealed from may be affirmed, reversed, or modified, and the state or municipal commission having jurisdiction may, in its discretion, direct the reinstatement of the appellant or permit the transfer of such appellant to a vacancy in a similar position in another division or department, or direct that his name be placed upon a preferred list pursuant to section eighty-one of this chapter. In the event that a transfer is not effected, the commission is empowered to direct the reinstatement of such officer or employee. An employee reinstated pursuant to this subdivision shall receive the salary or compensation he would have been entitled by law to have received in his position for the period of removal including any prior period of suspension without pay, less the amount of any unemployment insurance benefits he may have received during such period. The decision of such civil service commission shall be final and conclusive, and not subject to further review in any court.

4. Nothing contained in section seventy-five or seventy-six of this chapter shall be construed to repeal or modify any general, special or local law or charter provision relating to the removal or suspension of officers or employees in the competitive class of the civil service of the state or any civil division. Such sections may be supplemented, modified or replaced by agreements negotiated between the state and an employee organization pursuant to article fourteen of this chapter. Where such sections are so supplemented, modified or replaced, any employee against whom charges have been preferred prior to the effective date of such supplementation, modification or replacement shall continue to be subject to the provisions of such sections as in effect on the date such charges were preferred.

Section 77. Compensation of officers and employees reinstated by court order. Any officer or employee who is removed from a position in the service of the state or of any civil division thereof in violation of the provisions of this chapter, and who thereafter is restored to such position by order of the supreme court, shall be entitled to receive and shall receive from the state or such civil division, as the case may be, the salary or compensation which he would have been entitled by law to have received in such position but for such unlawful removal, from the date of such unlawful removal to the date of such restoration, less the amount of any unemployment insurance benefits he may have received during such period. Such officer or employee shall be entitled to a court order to enforce the payment of such salary or compensation. Such salary or compensation shall be subject to the provisions of sections four hundred seventy-four and four hundred seventy-five of the judiciary law for services rendered, but otherwise shall be paid only directly to such officer or employee or his legal representatives.

Part 2, Education Law Section 3020-a

And

The Commissioner's Regulations Implementing Section 3020-a

Section 3020. Discipline of teachers.

1. No person enjoying the benefits of tenure shall be disciplined or removed during a term of employment except for just cause and in accordance with the procedures specified in section three thousand twenty-a of this article or in accordance with alternate disciplinary procedures contained in a collective bargaining agreement covering his or her terms and conditions of employment that was effective on or before September first, nineteen hundred ninety-four and has been unaltered by renegotiation, or in accordance with alternative disciplinary procedures contained in a collective bargaining agreement covering his or her terms and conditions of employment that becomes effective on or after September first, nineteen hundred ninety-four; provided, however, that any such alternate disciplinary procedures contained in a collective bargaining agreement that becomes effective on or after September first, nineteen hundred ninety-four, must provide for the written election by the employee of either the procedures specified in such section three thousand twenty-a or the alternative disciplinary procedures contained in the collective bargaining agreement and must result in a disposition of the disciplinary charge within the amount of time allowed therefore under such section three thousand twenty-a.

2. No person enjoying the benefits of tenure shall be suspended for a fixed time without pay or dismissed due to a violation of article thirteen-E of the public health law.

Section 3020-a.

Disciplinary procedures and penalties.

1. Filing of charges. All charges against a person enjoying the benefits of tenure as provided in subdivision three of section one thousand one hundred two, and sections two thousand five hundred nine, two thousand five hundred seventy-three, twenty-five hundred ninety-j, three thousand twelve and three thousand fourteen of this chapter shall be in writing and filed with the clerk or secretary of the school district or employing board during the period between the actual opening and closing of the school year for which the employed is normally required to serve. Except as provided in subdivision eight of section two thousand five hundred seventy-three and subdivision seven of section twenty-five hundred ninety-j of this chapter, no charges under this section shall be brought more than three years after the occurrence of the alleged incompetency or misconduct, except when the charge is of misconduct constituting a crime when committed.

2. (a) Disposition of charges. Upon receipt of the charges, the clerk or secretary of the school district or employing board shall immediately notify said board thereof. Within five days after receipt of

charges, the employing board, in executive session, shall determine, by a vote of a majority of all the members of such board, whether probable cause exists to bring a disciplinary proceeding against an employee pursuant to this section. If such determination is affirmative, a written statement specifying the charges in detail, the maximum penalty which will be imposed by the board if the employee does not request a hearing or that will be sought by the board if the employee is found guilty of the charges after a hearing and outlining the employee's rights under this section, shall be immediately forwarded to the accused employee by certified or registered mail, return receipt requested or by personal delivery to the employee.

(b) The employee may be suspended pending a hearing on the charges and the final determination thereof. The suspension shall be with pay, except the employee may be suspended without pay if the employee has entered a guilty plea to or has been convicted of a felony crime concerning the criminal sale or possession of a controlled substance, a precursor of a controlled substance, or drug paraphernalia as defined in article two hundred twenty or two hundred twenty-one of the penal law; or a felony crime involving the physical or sexual abuse of a minor or student.

(c) Within ten days of receipt of the statement of charges, the employee shall notify the clerk or secretary of the employing board in writing whether he or she desires a hearing on the charges and when the charges concern pedagogical incompetence or issues involving pedagogical judgment, his or her choice of either a single hearing officer or a three member panel. A single hearing officer shall hear all other charges.

(d) The unexcused failure of the employee to notify the clerk or secretary of his or her desire for a hearing within ten days of the receipt of charges shall be deemed a waiver of the right to a hearing. Where an employee requests a hearing in the manner provided for by this section, the clerk or secretary of the board shall, within three working days of receipt of the employee's notice or request for a hearing, notify the commissioner of education of the need for a hearing. If the employee waives his or her right to a hearing the employing board shall proceed, within fifteen days, by a vote of a majority of all members of such board, to determine the case and fix the penalty, if any, to be imposed in accordance with subdivision four of this section.

3. Hearings. a. Notice of hearing. Upon receipt of a request for a hearing in accordance with subdivision two of this section, the commissioner of education shall forthwith notify the American Arbitration Association (hereinafter "association") of the need for a hearing and shall request the association to provide to the commissioner forthwith a list of names of persons chosen by the association from the association's panel of labor arbitrators to potentially serve as hearing officers together with relevant biographical information on each arbitrator. Upon receipt of said list and biographical information, the commissioner of education shall forthwith send a copy of both simultaneously to the employing board and the employee.

b. (i) Hearing officers. All hearings pursuant to this section shall be conducted before and by a single hearing officer selected as provided for in this section. A hearing officer shall not be eligible to serve as such if he or she is a resident of the school district, other than the city of New York, under the jurisdiction of the employing board, an employee, agent or representative of the employing board or of any labor organization representing employees of such employing board, has served as such agent or representative within two years of the date of the scheduled hearing, or if he or she is then serving as a mediator or fact finder in the same school district. Notwithstanding any other provision of law, the hearing officer shall be compensated by the department with the customary fee paid for service as an arbitrator under the auspices of the association for each day of actual service plus necessary travel and other reasonable expenses incurred in the performance of his or her duties. All other expenses of the disciplinary proceedings shall be paid in accordance with rules promulgated by the commissioner of education.

(ii) Not later than ten days after the date the commissioner mails to the employing board and the employee the list of potential hearing officers and biographies provided to the commissioner by the association, the employing board and the employee, individually or through their agents or representatives, shall by mutual agreement select a hearing officer from said list to conduct the hearing and shall notify the commissioner of their selection.

(iii) If the employing board and the employee fail to agree on an arbitrator to serve as a hearing officer from said list and so notify the commissioner within ten days after receiving the list from the commissioner, the commissioner shall request the association to appoint a hearing officer from said list.

(iv) In those cases in which the employee elects to have the charges heard by a hearing panel, the hearing panel shall consist of the hearing officer, selected in accordance with this subdivision, and two additional persons, one selected by the employee and one selected by the employing board, from a list maintained for such purpose by the commissioner of education. The list shall be composed of professional personnel with administrative or supervisory responsibility, professional personnel without administrative or supervisory responsibility, chief school administrators, members of employing boards and others selected from lists of nominees submitted to the commissioner by statewide organizations representing teachers, school administrators and supervisors and the employing boards. Hearing panel members other than the hearing officer shall be compensated by the department of education at the rate of one hundred dollars for each day of actual service plus necessary travel and subsistence expenses. The hearing officer shall be compensated as set forth in this subdivision. The hearing officer shall be the chairman of the hearing panel.

c. Hearing procedures.

(i) The commissioner of education shall have the power to establish necessary rules and procedures for the conduct of hearings under this section. Such rules shall not require compliance with technical rules of evidence. Hearings shall be conducted by the hearing officer selected pursuant to paragraph b of this subdivision with full and fair disclosure of the nature of the case and evidence against the employee by the employing board and shall be public or private at the discretion of the employee. The employee shall have a reasonable opportunity to defend himself or herself and an opportunity to testify in his or her own behalf. The employee shall not be required to testify. Each party shall have the right to be represented by counsel, to subpoena witnesses, and to cross-examine witnesses. All testimony taken shall be under oath, which the hearing officer is hereby authorized to administer. A competent stenographer, designated by the commissioner of education and compensated by the state education department, shall keep and transcribe a record of the proceedings at each such hearing. A copy of the transcript of the hearings shall, upon request, be furnished without charge to the employee and the board of education involved.

(ii) The hearing officer selected to conduct a hearing under this section shall, within ten to fifteen days of agreeing to serve as such, hold a pre-hearing conference which shall be held in the school district or county seat of the county, or any county, wherein the employing school board is located. The pre-hearing conference shall be limited in length to one day except that the hearing officer, in his or her discretion, may allow one additional day for good cause shown.

(iii) At the pre-hearing conference the hearing officer shall have the power to:

(A) issue subpoenas;

(B) hear and decide all motions, including but not limited to motions to dismiss the charges;

(C) hear and decide all applications for bills of particular or requests for production of materials or information, including, but not limited to, any witness statement (or statements), investigatory statement (or statements) or note (notes), exculpatory evidence or any other evidence, including district or student records, relevant and material to the employee's defense.

(iv) Any pre-hearing motion or application relative to the sufficiency of the charges, application or amendment thereof, or any preliminary matters shall be made upon written notice to the hearing officer and the adverse party no less than five days prior to the date of the pre-hearing conference. Any pre-hearing motions or applications not made as provided for herein shall be deemed waived except for good cause as determined by the hearing officer.

(v) In the event that at the pre-hearing conference the employing board presents evidence that the professional license of the employee has been revoked and all judicial and administrative remedies have been exhausted or foreclosed, the hearing officer shall schedule the date, time and place for an expedited hearing, which hearing shall commence not more than seven days after the pre-hearing conference and which shall be limited to one day. The expedited hearing shall be held in the local school district or county seat of the county or any county, wherein the said employing board is located. The expedited hearing shall not be postponed except upon the request of a party and then only for good cause as determined by the hearing officer. At such hearing, each party shall have equal time in which to present its case.

(vi) During the pre-hearing conference, the hearing officer shall determine the reasonable amount of time necessary for a final hearing on the charge or charges and shall schedule the location, time(s) and date(s) for the final hearing. The final hearing shall be held in the local school district or county seat of the county, or any county, wherein the said employing school board is located. In the event that the hearing officer determines that the nature of the case requires the final hearing to last more than one day, the days that are scheduled for the final hearing shall be consecutive. The day or days scheduled for the final hearing shall not be postponed except upon the request of a party and then only for good cause shown as determined by the hearing officer. In all cases, the final hearing shall be completed no later than sixty days after the pre-hearing conference unless the hearing officer determines that extraordinary circumstances warrant a limited extension.

4. Post hearing procedures.

(a) The hearing officer shall render a written decision within thirty days of the last day of the final hearing, or in the case of an expedited hearing within ten days of such expedited hearing, and shall forthwith forward a copy thereof to the commissioner of education who shall immediately forward copies of the decision to the employee and to the clerk or secretary of the employing board. The written decision shall include the hearing officer's findings of fact on each charge, his or her conclusions with regard to each charge based on said findings and shall state what penalty or other action, if any, shall be taken by the employing board. At the request of the employee, in determining what, if any, penalty or other action shall be imposed, the hearing officer shall consider the extent to which the employing board made efforts towards correcting the behavior of the employee which resulted in charges being brought under this section through means including but not limited to: remediation, peer intervention or an employee assistance plan. In those cases where a penalty is imposed, such penalty may be a written reprimand, a fine, suspension for a fixed time without pay, or dismissal. In addition to or in lieu of the aforementioned penalties, the hearing officer, where he or she deems appropriate, may impose upon the employee remedial action including but not limited to leaves of absence with or without pay, continuing education and/or study, a requirement that the employee seek counseling or medical treatment or that the employee engage in any other remedial or combination of remedial actions.

(b) Within fifteen days of receipt of the hearing officer's decision the employing board shall implement the decision. If the employee is acquitted he or she shall be restored to his or her position with full pay for any period of suspension without pay and the charges expunged from the employment record. If an employee who was convicted of a felony crime specified in paragraph (b) of subdivision two of this section, has said conviction reversed, the employee, upon application, shall be entitled to have his pay and other emoluments restored, for the period from the date of his suspension to the date of the decision.

(c) The hearing officer shall indicate in the decision whether any of the charges brought by the employing board were frivolous as defined in section eight thousand three hundred three-a of the civil practice law and rules. If the hearing officers finds that all of the charges brought against the employee were frivolous, the hearing officer shall order the employing board to reimburse the state education department the reasonable costs said department incurred as a result of the proceeding and to reimburse the employee the reasonable costs, including but not limited to reasonable attorneys` fees, the employee incurred in defending the charges. If the hearing officer finds that some but not all of the charges brought against the employee were frivolous, the hearing officer shall order the employing board to reimburse the state education department a portion, in the discretion of the hearing officer, of the reasonable costs said department incurred as a result of the proceeding and to reimburse the employee a portion, in the discretion of the hearing officer, of the reasonable costs, including but not limited to reasonable attorneys` fees, the employee incurred in defending the charges.

5. Appeal. Not later than ten days after receipt of the hearing officer's decision, the employee or the employing board may make an application to the New York state supreme court to vacate or modify the decision of the hearing officer pursuant to section seven thousand five hundred eleven of the civil practice law and rules. The court's review shall be limited to the grounds set forth in such section. The

hearing panel's determination shall be deemed to be final for the purpose of such proceeding. In no case shall the filing or the pendency of an appeal delay the implementation of the decision of the hearing officer.

Education Title 8, Volume A

(Current through 01/99)

SUBPART 82-1

PROCEDURES FOR HEARINGS COMMENCED ON OR AFTER AUGUST 25, 1994

Section 82-1.1 Application of Subpart.
Section 82-1.2 Definitions.
Section 82-1.3 Filing of charges.
Section 82-1.4 Request for a hearing.
Section 82-1.5 Notice of need for hearing.
Section 82-1.6 Appointment of hearing officer and notice of prehearing conference.
Section 82-1.7 Panel members.
Section 82-1.8 Selection of panel member by employee.
Section 82-1.9 Demand for public hearing.
Section 82-1.10 Conduct of hearings.
Section 82-1.11 Reimbursable hearing expenses.

Section 82-1.1 Application of Subpart.

This subpart applies to hearings on charges against tenured school employees pursuant to section 3020-a of the Education Law that are commenced by the filing of charges on or after August 25, 1994.

Section 82-1.2 Definitions.

(a) As used in this Subpart:

(1) Employee means any person or persons against whom charges may be filed pursuant to section 3020-a of the Education Law, or, except where the context indicates a contrary intent, the attorney designated to represent such person or persons in a hearing pursuant to this Part.

(2) Chief school administrator means the district superintendent of schools of the board of cooperative educational services employing a person against whom charges are made; or the superintendent of schools, community superintendent, chancellor or the principal of the school district employing a person against whom charges are made.

(3) Board means the employing trustee, board of trustees, board of education, community board or board of cooperative educational services.

(4) Commissioner means Commissioner of Education.

(5) Association means the American Arbitration Association.

(6) Hearing officer means a single hearing officer selected to conduct a hearing pursuant to section 3020-a of the Education Law, or the panel chairperson in the case of a hearing before a three-member hearing panel.

(7) Panel member means a member of a three member-hearing panel, other than a hearing officer, who is selected by either the employee or the board.

Section 82-1.3 Filing of charges.

(a) Charges may not be filed by the chief school administrator or other party authorized to file charges against an employee more than five days before the next regularly scheduled meeting of the board except with the permission of the board.

(b) A copy of a written statement specifying in detail each charge as to which the board finds probable cause exists, and a copy of the vote of the board on each charge, shall be forwarded at once to the employee by certified or registered mail, return receipt requested, or personal delivery and to the commissioner by first class mail. Such statement shall state the maximum penalty which will be imposed by the board if the employee does not request a hearing or that will be sought by the board if the employee is found guilty of the charge after a hearing and shall outline the employee's rights under section 3020-a, including the right to request a hearing and the right to choose either a single hearing officer or a three member panel when the charges involve pedagogical incompetence or issues involving pedagogical judgment.

(c) Charges against an employee must be made separately from charges against any other employee.

(d) Where charges concerning pedagogical incompetence or issues involving pedagogical judgment are filed with other charges, the employee shall have the right to choose either a single hearing officer or a three-member panel to hear all charges.

Section 82-1.4 Request for a hearing.

Where the employee desires a hearing, he or she may file a written request for a hearing with the clerk or secretary of the employing board within ten days of receipt of the charges, and where the charges concern pedagogical incompetence or issues involving pedagogical judgment, the employee shall choose either a single hearing officer or a three member panel. In the request for a hearing, the employee may designate an attorney who will represent the employee at the hearing.

Section 82-1.5 Notice of need for hearing.

(a) The notification to the commissioner of the need for a hearing shall contain the following information:

(1) an affidavit of service of the charges upon the employee;

(2) a copy of the employee's request for hearing;

(3) a place within the district or the county seat of a county in which the board is located which will be made available by the board at school district expense for the holding of the prehearing conference and hearing;

(4) the name and address of the attorney, if any, who will represent the board at the hearing;

(5) whether an expedited hearing is sought, and whether the employee is suspended either with, or without pay;

(6) an estimate of the number of days needed for the hearing;

(7) the name of the panel member selected by the board, if applicable; and

(8) where the board has received written notice that the employee will be represented by an attorney at the hearing, the name and address of such attorney.

(b) If the board shall fail to notify the commissioner of its selection of a panel member and the employee has not waived his or her right to a panel hearing, the commissioner shall select the member of the hearing panel for the board.

(c) At the same time that the notification is sent to the commissioner, the board shall, by certified mail return receipt requested, send to the employee the information provided in paragraphs (a)(3), (4), (5), (6) and (7) of this section.

(d) Separate notification of the need for a hearing shall be given with respect to each employee against whom charges have been filed.

(e) Whenever an employee shall be deemed to have waived his/her right to a hearing, the clerk or secretary of the board shall immediately file notice of such waiver with the commissioner.

Section 82-1.6 Appointment of hearing officer and notice of prehearing conference.

(a) Forthwith after receipt of notification of the need for a hearing, the commissioner shall notify the association, obtain a list of potential hearing officers, together with relevant biographical information, and send a copy thereof to the attorneys representing the employing board and employee, or to the employee if he or she is not so represented. Such list shall consist of individuals selected by the association who are qualified to serve as hearing officers. To be qualified to serve as a hearing officer, an individual shall:

(1) be on the association's panel of labor arbitrators;

(2) be a resident of New York or an adjoining state;

(3) be willing to serve under the conditions imposed by Education Law, section 3020-a and this Subpart; and

(4) not be ineligible to serve in the particular hearing pursuant to Education Law, section 3020-a(3)(i).

(b) Not later than ten days from the mailing of the list, the parties or their agents or representatives shall by agreement select a hearing officer and notify the commissioner thereof.

(c) If the parties fail to notify the commissioner of an agreed upon hearing officer within the time prescribed by subdivision (b) of this section, the commissioner shall request the association to select a hearing officer from said list.

(d) The commissioner shall notify the hearing officer selected pursuant to subdivision (b) or (c) of this section, and confirm his or her acceptance of such selection.

(e) The hearing officer shall contact the parties and, within ten to fifteen days of receipt of notice from the commissioner confirming his or her acceptance of a selection to serve as hearing officer, hold a prehearing conference.

Section 82-1.7 Panel members.

(a) The commissioner shall maintain a list of persons eligible to serve as panel members pursuant to Education Law, section 3020-a (3) (b) (iv), which list shall be updated at least annually.

(b) Copies of such list of panel members appointed by the commissioner shall be filed in the office of the school district clerk or secretary of the board of each district and shall be available for public inspection.

(c) No person may be selected from a list to serve as a panel member when that person is serving as a panel member in connection with charges being heard against another employee, except with the consent of the commissioner.

Section 82-1.8 Selection of panel member by employee.

Where an employee has exercised the option to have the hearing conducted before a hearing panel, within five days after receiving the copy of the notification to the commissioner of the need for a penal hearing, the employee shall, in writing by certified mail, notify the board and the commissioner of the name of his or her selection for the hearing panel. If the employee shall fail to notify the commissioner and the board as required and the employee has not waived his or her right to a hearing, the commissioner shall select the employee panel member for the employee.

Section 82-1.9 Demand for public hearing.

Unless the employee notifies the hearing officer at least twenty-four hours before the first day of the hearing that he or she demands a public hearing, the hearing shall be private. The prehearing conference shall be private.

Section 82-1.10 Conduct of hearings.

(a) Cine photographs, still photographs, videotape recordings and audiotape recordings may not be taken at private hearings, and may be taken at public hearings only when permitted by the hearing officer.

(b) Public hearings shall be open to members of the public and to representatives of the news media, except that the hearing officer may, in his or her discretion, exclude any persons other than parties, witnesses, and their attorneys from all or any portion of the hearing where such exclusion is warranted for the protection of the privacy or reputation of any person under the age of 18 years.

(c) The hearing officer shall have the power to consolidate with the pending charges amended or additional charges against an employee as to which the board has found that probable cause exists no later than five days before the date of the prehearing conference, provided that the employee may file a waiver of the right to a hearing on such amended or additional charges with the hearing officer and provided further that charges involving pedagogical incompetence or issues involving pedagogical judgment may not be consolidated with pending charges unless the employee has previously exercised his or her right to choose between a single hearing officer and hearing panel in the request for a hearing.

(d) If the hearing officer determines that the absence of a hearing panel member is likely to delay unduly the prosecution of the hearing, he or she shall order the replacement of such panel member. If the party who selected such panel member fails to select a replacement within two business days, the commissioner shall select such replacement. If the hearing officer needs to be replaced and if the commissioner determines that the parties cannot agree on a replacement, the commissioner shall request the association to select a replacement from the list of hearing officers. In no event shall a panel hearing proceed except in the presence of two panel members and the hearing officer.

(e) Members of the hearing panel may question witnesses and parties, subject to the right of the hearing officer to disallow such questions if he or she deems them improper. Notwithstanding the foregoing, no questions may be addressed to the employee unless he or she has been sworn as a witness with his or her own consent.

(f) At the conclusion of the testimony, the hearing officer may adjourn the hearing to a specified date after conclusion of the testimony, to permit preparation of the transcript, submission by the parties of memoranda of law, and deliberation; provided that such specified date may not be more than 60 days after the prehearing conference unless the hearing officer determines that extraordinary circumstances warrant a later date. The hearing officer shall arrange for the preparation and delivery of one copy of the transcript of the hearing to each panel member, to the employee and the board.

(g) The hearing officer or hearing panel shall render a written decision within thirty days of the last day of the final hearing, or within ten days of the last day of an expedited hearing and shall forthwith forward a copy to the commissioner who shall send copies to the employee and the clerk or secretary of the employing board. Such written decision shall include the hearing officer's findings of fact on each charge, his or her conclusions with regard to each charge based on such findings and shall state the penalty or other action, if any, which shall be taken by the board, provided that such findings, conclusions and penalty determination shall be based solely upon the record in the proceedings before the hearing officer or panel, and shall set forth the reasons and the factual basis for the determination.

Section 82-1.11 Reimbursable hearing expenses.

(a) The commissioner shall compensate the hearing officer with the customary fee paid for service as an arbitrator for each day of actual service rendered by the hearing officer. For this purpose, a day of actual service shall be five hours. In the event a hearing officer renders more or less than five hours of service on a given calendar day, the per diem fee shall be prorated accordingly. Any late cancellation fee charged by the hearing officer shall be paid by the party or parties responsible for the cancellation.

(b) In addition to the statutory fees payable to the hearing officer and panel members for each day of actual service, the commissioner shall reimburse hearing officers and panel members for their necessary travel and other related reasonable expenses incurred at rates not to exceed the rates applicable to state employees.

(c) The commissioner shall arrange for the preparation of a hearing transcript by a competent stenographer and shall compensate the stenographer for the cost of preparing the transcript and copies thereof for the hearing officer, each panel member, the department, the employee and the board. Upon request of one or more parties, the commissioner may arrange to have a daily copy of the transcript prepared and distributed to each party making such request and to the hearing officer, in addition to the final copies to be provided by the commissioner after conclusion of the hearing. Any incremental cost incurred for preparing a daily copy for a party and the hearing officer that is in addition to the base amount payable by the commissioner for preparation of the final transcript shall be paid by the party requesting daily copy, or shall be shared equally by the parties where both parties request daily copy.

(d) Additional hearing costs, other than facilities costs, incurred to make a reasonable accommodation to an employee or a witness based on such individual's disability, including but not limited to the retention of a qualified interpreter for the deaf or hearing impaired, shall be paid by the commissioner. Except as otherwise provided in this Subpart, any other additional hearing costs shall be paid by the board.

Part 3 – Contract Disciplinary Procedures

The following is a typical contract disciplinary procedure negotiated pursuant to the Taylor Law. Taken from a contract between the State of New York and CSEA for the Administrative Services Collective Bargaining Unit, it is provided for illustrative purposes only.

ARTICLE 33 — Discipline

§33.1 Eligibility

The following disciplinary procedure for incompetency or misconduct shall apply to all employees as provided herein in lieu of the procedure specified in the Civil Service Law Sections 75 and 76. This entire disciplinary procedure shall apply to all persons currently subject to Sections 75 and 76 of the Civil Service Law and, in addition, shall apply to any permanent non-competitive class employees described in Section 75(1)(c) and to permanent labor class employees who, since last entry into State service, have completed at least one year continuous service in the State classified service, except that approved leaves of absence or reinstatement within one year of resignation shall not constitute an interruption of such service. The disciplinary procedure provided herein is not applicable to review the removal of an employee from a probationary appointment.

§33.2 Employee Rights

a. Representation
   1. An employee shall be entitled to representation by CSEA or by private counsel selected at his or her own expense at each step of the disciplinary procedure.
   2. CSEA representation may include both a grievance representative and the CSEA Local President or, where the Local President is absent from work, his or her designee, and a CSEA staff representative; however, the absence of the two additional representatives shall not unreasonably delay an interrogation and/or the request to sign a statement made pursuant to this section.
b. Interrogation
   1. The term "interrogation" shall be defined to mean the questioning of an employee who, at the time of such questioning appears to be a likely or potential target or subject for disciplinary action.
   2. If an employee is improperly subjected to an interrogation in violation of the provisions of this subdivision, an arbitrator appointed pursuant to this Article shall have the authority to exclude information obtained thereby or other evidence derived solely through such interrogation. The State shall have the burden of proof to show that, upon the preponderance of the evidence, such evidence sought to be introduced was not derived solely by reason of such interrogation and was obtained independently from the statements or evidence so provided by the employee.
   3. No employee shall be required to submit to an interrogation by a department or agency (a) if the information sought is for use against such employee in a disciplinary proceeding pursuant to this Article, or (b) after a notice of discipline has been served on such employee, or (c) after the employee's resignation has been requested pursuant to Article 35, unless such employee is notified in advance of the interrogation that he or she has the right to have CSEA representation, as defined in Section 33.2(a)(2) - Representation - or private counsel provided at his or her own expense present or to decline such representation and that, if such representation is requested, a reasonable period of time will be afforded for that purpose. If the employee requests representation and the CSEA or employee fails to provide such representation within a reasonable

time, the interrogation may proceed. An arbitrator under this Article shall have the power to find that a delay in providing such representation may have been unreasonable.

c. Recording Devices/Transcripts

No recording devices or stenographic or other record shall be used during an interrogation unless the employee (1) is advised in advance that a transcript is being made, and (2) is offered the right to have CSEA representation, as defined in Section 33.2(a)(2) - Representation - or private counsel provided at his or her own expense present. Unless the employee declines such representation, he or she will be given a reasonable period of time to obtain representation. If the employee requests representation and the CSEA or employee fails to provide such representation within a reasonable time, the interrogation and taking of a record thereof may proceed. An arbitrator under this Article shall have the power to find that a delay in providing such representation may have been unreasonable. A copy of any stenographic record (verbatim transcript) and/or tape recording made pursuant to this provision shall be supplied to the employee.

d. Signed Statement
   1. No employee shall be requested to sign any statement regarding his or her incompetency or misconduct unless the employee is offered the right to have CSEA representation, as defined in Section 33.2(a)(2) - Representation - or private counsel provided at his or her own expense present.
   2. Unless the employee declines such representation he or she will be given a reasonable period of time to obtain such representation. If the employee requests representation and CSEA or the employee fails to provide such representation within a reasonable time, the employee may be requested to sign such a statement. An arbitrator under this Article shall have the power to find that a delay in providing such representation may have been unreasonable. The statement shall be submitted to the employee within a reasonable time after the interrogation. A copy of the statement shall be supplied to the employee at the time the employee is requested to sign the statement. Prior to signing the statement, the employee may make such modifications or deletions in such statement that the employee deems necessary. Any statements or admissions signed by him or her without having been so supplied to him or her may not subsequently be used in any disciplinary proceeding.
   3.
e. Burden of Proof

In all disciplinary proceedings, the employee shall be presumed innocent until proven guilty and the burden of proof on all matters shall rest upon the employer. Such burden of proof, even in serious matters which might constitute a crime, shall be preponderance of the evidence on the record and shall in no case be proof beyond a reasonable doubt.

f. Coercion/Intimidation

An employee shall not be coerced, intimidated or caused to suffer any reprisals, either directly or indirectly, that may adversely affect his or her hours, wages or working conditions as the result of the exercise of his or her rights under this Article.

§33.3 Disciplinary Procedure

a. Notice of Discipline
   1. Where the appointing authority or the appointing authority's designee seeks the imposition of a written reprimand, suspension without pay, a fine not to exceed two weeks' pay, loss of accrued leave credits, reduction in grade, or dismissal from service,

notice of such discipline shall be made in writing and served upon the employee. Discipline shall be imposed only for incompetency or misconduct. The specific acts for which discipline is being imposed and the penalty proposed shall be specified in the notice. The notice of discipline shall contain a detailed description of the alleged acts and conduct including reference to dates, times and places.

2. An employee shall not be disciplined for acts, except those which would constitute a crime, which occurred more than one (1) year prior to the notice of discipline.
3. In those cases where such acts are alleged to constitute a crime, a notice of discipline must be served no later than the period set forth for the commencement of a criminal proceeding against a public employee in the Criminal Procedure Law of the State of New York.
4. If the arbitrator appointed pursuant to this Article finds, upon motion before the commencement of the arbitration, that the notice does not sufficiently apprise the employee of the acts or conduct for which discipline is being imposed, he or she may require that, where the employer has either refused to provide such specificity where the information sought was available or the charges are so vague and indefinite that the employee cannot reasonably respond, the State provide more specificity within thirty (30) days of the ruling. The arbitrator shall proceed immediately with the arbitration hearing on those charges in the notice of discipline where no specificity is required. If the State does not provide such specificity as required by the arbitrator within thirty (30) days, the arbitrator shall dismiss those non-specific charges only, with prejudice, and resolve the remaining charges, if any, contained in the notice. In order for such a motion to be made at the hearing, the employee or his or her representative must have made a request of the employer before the hearing to provide such specificity of the notice and the employer must have failed to do so.
5. Two copies of the notice shall be served on the employee. Service of the notice of discipline shall be made by personal service, if possible. If service cannot be effectuated by personal service, it shall be made by registered or certified mail, return receipt requested.
6. The Arbitration Administrator of CSEA and the CSEA Local President shall be advised by registered or certified mail, return receipt requested, of the name and work site of an employee against whom a notice of discipline has been served.
7. The notice of discipline served on the employee shall be accompanied by a written statement that:
    - the employee has a right to object by filing a grievance within fourteen (14) days;
    - the grievance procedure provides for a hearing by an independent arbitrator as its final step;
    - he or she is entitled to representation by CSEA or by private counsel selected at his or her own expense at every step of the proceeding;
    - if a grievance is filed, no penalty can be implemented until the matter is settled or the arbitrator renders a determination;
    - a copy of this Article shall be supplied.

In the case of an employee who speaks only Spanish, this written statement shall also be given in a Spanish translation.

8. A notice of discipline shall be served in accordance with this section no later than seven (7) calendar days following any suspension without pay or temporary reassignment.
9. If an employee is not able to personally sign and file a disciplinary grievance, CSEA may, at the employee's request, submit such grievance on the employee's behalf. Provided, however, that within seven (7) days of submission, the employee in question must appear to sign the grievance form or CSEA must produce documentation

supporting any reason as to why the employee could not appear. Should neither of these actions occur, the grievance shall be deemed void after seven (7) days.
b. Penalty
   1. The penalty proposed by the appointing authority or the appointing authority's designee may not be implemented until (a) the employee fails to file a grievance within fourteen (14) calendar days of the service of the notice of discipline, or (b) having filed a grievance, the employee elects not to pursue it, or (c) the penalty is upheld by the disciplinary arbitrator or a different penalty is determined by the arbitrator to be appropriate, or (d) the matter is settled.
   2. At any time during the disciplinary procedure after a timely grievance has been filed, the employee may elect in writing to the appointing authority or his or her designee, the agency or department head or his or her designee, or the Panel Administrator that he or she elects not to pursue the grievance. In such event, the proposed penalty may be implemented.
c. Grievance
   1. If not settled or otherwise resolved, the notice of discipline may be the subject of a grievance before the department or agency head and shall be filed either in person or by certified or registered mail, return receipt requested, by the employee within fourteen (14) calendar days of service of the notice of discipline.
   2. The timely filing of such a grievance shall constitute a demand for arbitration unless the grievance is settled or the employee elects not to pursue it.
   3. The filing of such a grievance shall be complete on (a) the date on which it is filed or, (b) the date of mailing by certified or registered mail, return receipt requested. The date of mailing shall be that date stamped on the official postal receipt provided by the U.S. Post Office for registered or certified mail and not any date stamped on the return receipt. Only if the official receipt for registered or certified mail is produced undated by the U.S. Post Office will the date of postmark on the envelope which contained the grievance be acceptable. No other documentation or evidence of the date of such mailing will be acceptable.
d. Agency Level Meeting
   1. The employee shall be entitled to a meeting at the department or agency level to present his or her position to the department or agency head or his or her designee within fourteen (14) calendar days of the filing of the grievance.
   2. The meeting shall include an informal presentation by the department or agency head or his or her designee and by the employee or his or her representative of relevant information concerning the acts or conduct specified in the notice of discipline, a general review of the evidence and defenses that will be presented if the matter proceeds to arbitration and a discussion of the appropriateness of the proposed penalty. The meeting need not involve the identification or presentation of prospective witnesses, the identification or specific description of documents or other formal disclosure of evidence by either party. The employee shall have the right to remain silent at such meeting, except that CSEA or the employee's private counsel provided at his or her own expense shall present a summary of his or her answer to the allegations contained in the notice of discipline.
   3. The meeting provided for herein may be waived, in writing, on the grievance form, only in accordance with Section 33.3(g)(2) - Suspension Without Pay.
   4. The employee has a right to have a CSEA representative or private counsel provided at his or her own expense present or to decline such representation. If such representation is requested by the employee, he or she will be given a reasonable period of time to obtain a representative. If the employee requests representation and the CSEA or employee fails to provide a representative within a reasonable time, the meeting may proceed. The disciplinary arbitrator appointed pursuant to this Article shall have the power to find that a delay in providing a representative may have been unreasonable.
e. Agency Response

1. A response shall be rendered in writing, if possible, in person, or by certified or registered mail, return receipt requested, no later than four (4) calendar days after such meeting. If possible, the department or agency head should render the written response at the close of such meeting. Such response may include a reduction in the proposed penalty.
2. If the department or agency fails to respond within four (4) calendar days, the grievant has the right to notify the Panel Administrator that the grievance is unresolved and request that an arbitrator be appointed and a hearing scheduled.
3. Unless the grievance is settled or the employee elects not to pursue it, the agency or department representative shall notify the Panel Administrator that the grievance is not resolved and request that an arbitrator be appointed and a hearing scheduled.

f. Withdrawal/Amendment

The agency or department head or his or her designee has full authority, at any time before or after the notice of discipline is served by an appointing authority or his or her designee, to review such notice and the proposed penalty and to take such action as he or she deems appropriate under the circumstances in accordance with this Article including, but not limited to, determining whether a notice should be issued, amendment of the notice no later than the issuance of the agency response, withdrawal of the notice or a reduction in the proposed penalty. Amendment of the notice after the issuance of the agency response, or amendment of the notice where the agency or department level meeting has been waived pursuant to Section 33.3 (g)(2) - Suspension Without Pay - or withdrawal of the notice, are subject to the following:

- the withdrawal or amendment must occur no later than fifteen (15) days prior to the disciplinary arbitration hearing provided for in Section 33.4 - Disciplinary Arbitration - of this Article;
- where amended, the employee is entitled to an adjournment where requested by the employee, or his or her representative;
- in the instance where an employee is suspended without pay or temporarily reassigned pursuant to Section 33.3(g)(1) - Suspension Without Pay - the withdrawal of a notice of discipline shall cause the employee to be retroactively reinstated with back pay, if suspended, or returned to his or her original assignment, if temporarily reassigned, upon such withdrawal. The amendment of the notice of discipline in such instances shall end such suspension or temporary reassignment as of the date of such amendment. However, the disciplinary arbitrator shall determine whether there was a probable cause for suspension in accordance with Section 33.3(g)(1) - Suspension Without Pay - and, where in issue whether the amendment is, in fact, a withdrawal of the initial notice of discipline and entitled to be treated as such pursuant to this section;
- in all instances where an employee is suspended without pay or temporarily reassigned pursuant to Sections 33.3(g) - Suspension Without Pay - and (h) - Temporary Reassignment - and the notice of discipline is amended or withdrawn pursuant to this section, such an employee may not be again suspended or temporarily reassigned solely upon those same facts alleged to constitute incompetency or misconduct in the notice of discipline which has been withdrawn or amended;
- where a notice of discipline is withdrawn pursuant to this section, said notice must be reinstituted pursuant to Section 33.3(a) - Notice of Discipline - no later than thirty (30) days from the time of the withdrawal of the notice of discipline or such withdrawal will be with prejudice to the reinstitution of the notice of discipline;
- in those instances where there is an amendment of the notice of discipline after the issuance of the agency response or a withdrawal of the notice of discipline and an arbitrator has been appointed pursuant to Section 33.4(a)(1) - Disciplinary Arbitrators - any hearing on the amended or reinstituted charges shall be held before the arbitrator initially appointed unless that arbitrator is not available within a reasonable time and the parties jointly agree to the selection of a new arbitrator pursuant to Section 33.4(a)(1) - Disciplinary Arbitrators.

g. Suspension Without Pay
   0. Prior to exhaustion or institution by an employee of the grievance procedure applicable to discipline, an employee may be suspended without pay or temporarily reassigned only if the appointing authority determines that there is probable cause to believe that the employee's continued presence on the job represents a potential danger to persons or property or would severely interfere with operations. Such determination shall be reviewable by the arbitrator in accordance with this section to determine whether the appointing authority had probable cause.
   1. Where the employee has been suspended without pay or temporarily reassigned, he or she may, in writing, waive the agency or department level meeting at the time of filing the grievance on the grievance form. In the event of such waiver, the employee shall file the grievance form within the prescribed time limits for filing a department or agency level grievance directly with the Panel Administrator. The Panel Administrator shall give the case priority in assignment and shall forthwith set the matter down for hearing to be held within thirty (30) days of the filing of the demand for arbitration. The time limits may not be extended. The Arbitration Administrator of CSEA and the CSEA Local President shall be notified in writing by registered or certified mail, return receipt requested, within four (4) calendar days of any such suspension.
   2. In the event of a failure to serve a notice of discipline within the time established in Section 33.3(a)(7) - Notice of Discipline - the employee shall be deemed to have been suspended without pay as of the date of service of the notice of discipline or, in the event of a temporary reassignment, may return to his or her actual assignment until such notice is served. In the event of failure to notify the Arbitration Administrator of CSEA of the suspension within four (4) calendar days, the employee shall be deemed to have been suspended without pay as of the date the notice is sent to the Arbitration Administrator of CSEA.
   3. In the case of any suspension without pay, the employee may be allowed to draw from accrued annual or personal leave credits, holiday leave or compensatory leave which shall be reinstated in the event that, in accordance with this Article, the suspension is deemed improper or the employee is found innocent of all allegations contained in the notice of discipline. The use of such credits shall be at the option of the employee. Such use of leave credits during suspension will not be available if the employee is offered a reassignment and declines.
   4. When an employee is suspended without pay or temporarily reassigned pursuant to Sections 33.3(g) - Suspension Without Pay - and (h) - Temporary Reassignment - the disciplinary arbitrator shall, upon the request of the employee at the close of the State's case, issue an interim decision and award with respect to the issue of whether there was probable cause for the suspension without pay or the temporary reassignment. Should the arbitrator find in the interim decision that probable cause did exist, the arbitrator is not precluded from reconsidering the issue of probable cause after the hearing is closed.
   5. In those cases which involve a suspension without pay pursuant to this section, when the disciplinary arbitrator finds the employee innocent of all allegations contained in the notice of discipline and also finds probable cause for such suspension, he or she shall reinstate the employee with back pay for all of the period of the suspension without pay.
   6. In the event an employee is found innocent of all allegations contained in the notice of discipline as a result of a disciplinary proceeding, he or she must be reinstated to the exact shift, work location and pass days that the employee possessed prior to the institution of the disciplinary charges against said employee and prior to any temporary reassignment imposed pursuant to this Article. In all instances where a disciplinary arbitrator reinstates an employee who is found innocent of all allegations contained in the notice of discipline, and the appointing authority later seeks to change the shift, work location or pass days of said employee, the appointing authority must notify the employee in writing of the reason therefore without prejudice. Such action by the appointing authority shall be grievable under the Article 34 contract grievance

procedure, and all such grievances shall be commenced at Step 3 of said contractual grievance procedure.

7. The appointing authority or his or her designee, at his or her discretion, may suspend without pay or temporarily reassign an employee charged with the commission of a crime. Within thirty (30) calendar days following a suspension under this paragraph, a notice of discipline shall be served on such employee or such employee shall be reinstated with back pay. Where the employee, who is charged with the commission of a crime is temporarily reassigned, the notice of discipline shall be served on such employee within seven (7) days after the disposition of the criminal charges as provided in the Criminal Procedure Law of the State of New York or the employee shall be returned to his or her regular assignment. Nothing in this paragraph shall limit the right of the appointing authority or his or her designee from taking disciplinary action while criminal proceedings are pending. Nothing in this paragraph shall preclude the application of the provisions in Article 33.3(h).

8. During a period of suspension without pay pursuant to the provisions of Article 33.3(g)(1) or 33.3(g)(8), the State shall continue to pay its share of the cost of the employee's health coverage under Article 9 which was in effect on the day prior to the suspension provided that the suspended employee pays his or her share. Also, any employee suspended pursuant to the provisions of Article 33.3(g)(1) or 33.3(g)(8) shall be counted for the purpose of calculating the amount of any periodic deposit to the Employee Benefit Fund.

h. Temporary Reassignment

0. Where the appointing authority informs an employee that he or she is being temporarily reassigned pursuant to this Article, and prior to exhaustion or institution of the disciplinary grievance procedure, the employee shall be notified in writing of the location of such temporary reassignment and that the employee may elect in writing to refuse such temporary reassignment and be suspended without pay. Such election must be made in writing before the commencement of the temporary reassignment. An election by the employee to be placed on a suspension without pay is final and may not thereafter be withdrawn. Once the employee commences the temporary reassignment, no election is permitted.

1. Temporary reassignments under this section shall not involve a change in the employee's rate of pay. The provisions of Article 24, Out-of-Title Work, shall not apply to temporary reassignments under this section.

2. The fact that the State has temporarily reassigned an employee rather than suspending him or her without pay or the election by an employee to be suspended without pay rather than be temporarily reassigned shall not be considered by the disciplinary arbitrator for any purpose.

§33.4 Disciplinary Arbitration

c. Disciplinary Arbitrators

1. The State and CSEA jointly agree to the creation of a permanent panel of arbitrators to serve during the term of this Agreement and to be jointly selected and administered by the State of New York and CSEA by an agreed Panel Administrator. The composition of the panel of arbitrators may be changed by mutual agreement of the State and CSEA. In those cases involving an allegation of patient, client, resident or similar abuse, the Panel Administrator of the panel of disciplinary arbitrators must appoint the disciplinary arbitrator from a select panel of arbitrators jointly agreed to by the State and CSEA. Disciplinary arbitrators on the select panel shall receive special training regarding patient abuse and the disciplinary process. The special training shall be jointly sponsored by the State and CSEA.

2. All fees and expenses of the arbitrator, if any, shall be divided equally between the appointing authority and CSEA or the employee if not represented by CSEA.

Each party shall bear the cost of preparing and presenting its own case. The estimated arbitrator's fees and estimated expenses may be collected in advance of the hearing. Where the arbitrator requires that his or her estimated fees and expenses be collected in advance of the hearing from an employee who elects not to be represented by CSEA, and the employee fails to tender such advance as required, the grievance shall be deemed withdrawn.

d. Hearing
   0. The disciplinary arbitrator shall hold a hearing within twenty-one (21) calendar days after selection. A decision shall be rendered within seven (7) calendar days of the close of the hearing or within seven (7) calendar days after receipt of the transcript, if either party elects a transcript as provided in this Article, or within such other period of time as may have been mutually agreed to by the department or agency and the grievant or his or her representative.
   1. Arbitrations, pursuant to this Article, shall be held at an appropriate location at the employee's facility.
   2. Protection of Patient or Client Witnesses
      i. A patient or client witness will be protected, when giving testimony in a disciplinary arbitration hearing, by shielding the employee from view, in one of the following ways:
         - use of a portable screen or partition consisting of one-way glass; or
         - use of a closed circuit television in a live transmission with the employee in a separate room and the arbitrator, the representatives and the witness(es) in another room; or
         - use of a one-way mirrored room with the employee in a separate room with the ability to view and hear the proceedings.

         A patient or client witness will be shielded in one of the described ways when a certified or licensed professional determines that there is a need for such protection for the patient or client witness. A determination that there is a need for such protection is not subject to review.

      ii. Additionally, where the employee is in a separate room during the arbitration hearing, a method of communication will be provided for the employee to communicate with his or her representative.

e. Recording/Transcript
   0. Unless both parties agree, the proceedings in disciplinary arbitrations should not be tape recorded. The use of transcripts is to be discouraged and the fact that a transcript is made should not extend the date the hearing is closed. The party ordering the transcript shall obtain and pay for an expedited or rush transcript.
   1. Either party wishing a transcript at a disciplinary arbitration hearing may provide for one at its own expense and shall provide a copy to the arbitrator and the other party.

f. Ex Parte Hearing

The arbitrator may hold ex parte hearings in cases where an employee fails to attend the hearing after being served with a notice of discipline pursuant to this Article, and has not notified the arbitrator in advance or produced a satisfactory reason for his or her failure to appear.

g. Settlement
   0. A disciplinary matter may be settled at any time following service of the notice of discipline. The terms of the settlement shall be agreed to in writing. An employee before executing such a settlement shall be notified of his or her right

to have a CSEA representative or private counsel provided at his or her own expense present or to decline such representation and, if such representation is requested, to have a reasonable period of time for that purpose. If the employee requests representation and the CSEA or employee fails to provide a representative within a reasonable time, the settlement may be executed. An arbitrator pursuant to Article 34 shall have the power to find that a delay in providing a representative may have been unreasonable. A settlement entered into by the employee, his or her private counsel or CSEA shall be final and binding on all parties. The Arbitration Administrator of CSEA and the CSEA Local President shall be advised of the settlement in writing by registered or certified mail.

1. Offers of compromise or settlement or discussions related thereto, at the agency level settlement conference, or in any attempt at settlement prior to the arbitration, shall not be introduced at the arbitration hearing or accepted as evidence by the arbitrator.

h. Arbitrator's Authority

0. Disciplinary arbitrators shall render determinations of guilt or innocence and the appropriateness of proposed penalties and shall have the authority to resolve a claimed failure to follow the procedural provisions of this Article including, but not limited to, the timeliness of the filing of the disciplinary grievance, and whether the notice of discipline was properly served in accordance with this Article.
1. Disciplinary arbitrators shall neither add to, subtract from or modify the provisions of this Agreement.
2. The disciplinary arbitrator's decision with respect to guilt or innocence, penalty, probable cause for suspension or temporary reassignment, if any, and a claimed failure to follow the procedural provisions of this Article shall be final and binding upon the parties.
3. The disciplinary arbitrator may approve, disapprove or take any other appropriate action warranted under the circumstances, including, but not limited to, ordering reinstatement and back pay for all or part of any period of suspension without pay. If the arbitrator upon review finds probable cause for suspension without pay, he or she may consider such suspension in determining the penalty to be imposed.
4. The disciplinary arbitrator is not restricted by the contractual limits on penalties which may be proposed by the State. He or she has full authority, if the remedy proposed by the State is found to be inappropriate, to devise an appropriate remedy, but shall not increase the penalty sought by the State except that the arbitrator may direct referral to a rehabilitative program in addition to the penalty.
5. The employee's entire record of employment may be considered with respect to the appropriateness of the penalty to be imposed, if any.
6. This disciplinary procedure is not the proper forum for the review of counseling memoranda or unsatisfactory performance evaluations.

i. Back Pay Award

Where an employee is awarded back pay, the amount to be reimbursed shall not be offset by any wages earned by the employee during the period of his or her suspension. Where an employee is awarded back pay, said award shall be deemed to include retroactive reimbursement of all other benefits, including the accrual of leave credits and holiday leave.

§33.5 Time and Attendance Disciplinary Grievances

j. All notices of discipline based solely on time and attendance, including tardiness, which have not been settled or otherwise resolved, shall be reviewed by a permanent umpire in accordance with the attached schedule except as otherwise provided in paragraph (g) below.
k. The determinations of the permanent umpire shall be confined to the guilt or innocence of the grievant and the appropriateness of the proposed penalty. The employee's entire record of employment may be considered by the permanent umpire with respect to the appropriateness of the penalty to be imposed. The permanent umpire shall have the authority to resolve a claimed failure to follow the procedural provisions of this Article.
l. The decision and award of the permanent umpire, with respect to guilt or innocence and penalty, if any, shall be final and binding on the parties and not subject to appeal to any other forum except that, in the case of a decision and award of the permanent umpire which results in a penalty of dismissal from service, the decision and award may be reviewed in accordance with Article 75 of the CPLR. The permanent umpire shall, upon a finding of guilt, have full authority to uphold the penalty proposed in the notice of discipline or to impose a lesser penalty within the minimum and maximum penalties as contained in the attached schedule and appropriate to that notice of discipline. In appropriate cases and in addition to the penalty imposed, the permanent umpire may direct the grievant to attend counseling sessions or other appropriate programs jointly agreed upon by the State and CSEA.
m. Within one (1) month of the execution of this Agreement, the State and CSEA shall mutually select a panel of two or more permanent umpires who shall serve for the term of this Agreement, and shall be jointly administered by the State and CSEA. All fees and expenses of the permanent umpires shall be divided equally between the State and CSEA.
n. Unless the State and CSEA mutually agree otherwise, the permanent umpires shall be available to hold reviews at least once each month on a regularly scheduled basis. At such times, the permanent umpires shall review and finally determine all time and attendance disciplinary grievances which have been pending no less than ten (10) days prior to the permanent umpire's scheduled appearance, and are unresolved in accordance with paragraph (a) above.
o. An employee is entitled to appear at the review before a permanent umpire and is entitled to have a CSEA representative or an attorney provided at his or her own expense present. Matters scheduled to be heard by the permanent umpire may not be adjourned except at the discretion of the permanent umpire for good cause shown. Any matters which are adjourned shall be rescheduled for the next regularly scheduled appearance of the permanent umpire.
p. Where an employee is to be served a notice of discipline related solely to time and attendance and, within three years of such notice, has been found guilty of or settled (or a combination of both) two prior notices of discipline not solely related to time and attendance, the appointing authority may elect either to pursue such time and attendance notice before the permanent umpire in accordance with the attached Schedule or to service a notice of discipline and proceed before a disciplinary arbitrator. This paragraph shall not apply to notices of discipline based solely on tardiness.

For the purposes of the Time and Attendance Schedule only, "prior record" shall mean any notice of discipline based solely on time and attendance where either guilt was found or a settlement occurred or a combination of both occurred. However, for all notices of discipline based solely upon time and attendance issued on or after July 1, 1992, the "prior record" shall not include any notices of discipline based solely upon time and attendance that are three or more years old if the employee has not been served a notice of discipline based solely upon time and attendance within the three years from the date of the resolution of the last notice of discipline based solely upon time and attendance.

Notices of discipline based solely on tardiness shall proceed on the tardiness schedule only and shall not be considered as a prior record for any other offense.

The penalty level for notices of discipline which contain charges of both tardiness and unauthorized absence shall be the appropriate level within the type of unauthorized absence charge.

TIME AND ATTENDANCE SCHEDULE

Type of Offense	Prior Record	Minimum Penalty	Maximum Penalty
Tardiness	1st, 2nd, or 3rd Notice of Discipline	Written reprimand	$300 fine
	4th or more Notices of Discipline	Penalties contained in Article 33.3(a)(1)	
Unauthorized absence including improper use of sick leave of 3 consecutive workdays or less.	1st & 2nd Notice of Discipline	Written reprimand	$150 fine
	3rd Notice of Discipline	$150 fine	Suspension without pay of 4 weeks or equivalent
	4th Notice of Discipline or more	$250 fine	Dismissal
Unauthorized absence including improper use of sick leave of more than 3 but less than 8 consecutive workdays	1st Notice of Discipline	$200 fine	Suspension without pay of 3 weeks or equivalent
	2nd Notice of Discipline	$250 fine	Suspension without pay of 8 weeks or equivalent
	3rd or more Notice of Discipline	$300 fine	Dismissal
Unauthorized absence including improper use of sick leave of 8 consecutive workdays or more	1st Notice of Discipline	$300 fine	Dismissal
	2nd Notice of Discipline or more	Suspension without pay of 8 weeks or equivalent	Dismissal

q. As used in this Article, "time and attendance disciplinary grievances" shall mean those disciplinary grievances based upon notices of discipline which specify tardiness, or unauthorized absence, including improper use of sick leave, and do not contain any other allegations of misconduct or incompetence.

§33.6 Definitions

r. As used in this Article, "days" shall mean calendar days.
s. "Service" shall be complete upon personal delivery or, if it is made by registered or certified mail, return receipt requested, it shall be complete the date the employee or any other person accepting delivery has signed the return receipt or when the letter is returned to the appointing authority undelivered. In addition, in all instances other than personal service, service shall include a concurrent first class mailing.

§33.7 Administration

The State and CSEA may jointly administer the arbitration procedure and panels for the purpose of this Article. The State shall seek an appropriation in the amount indicated in each year of the Agreement: $250,000 in 1999-2000, $261,386 in 2000-2001, $273,607 in 2001-2002 and $286,302 in 2002-2003, to be used for the self-administration of the panels and procedure, the time and attendance procedure, research for and training of the panels in the area of patient abuse, and publication of arbitration decisions. The unexpended portion of each year's appropriation shall be carried over into the succeeding year and added to the appropriation for the succeeding year.

§33.8 Application

Changes in shift, pass day, job assignment, transfer or reassignment to another institution, station or work location shall not be made for the purpose of imposing discipline.

APPENDIX II

Civil Practice Law and Rules

ARTICLE 75 ARBITRATION

Section 7501. Effect of arbitration agreement.
Section 7502. Applications to the court; venue; statutes of limitation; provisional remedies.
 (a) Applications to the court; venue.
 (b) Limitation of time.
 (c) Provisional remedies.
Section 7503. Application to compel or stay arbitration;
 (a) Application to compel arbitration; stay of action.
 (b) Application to stay arbitration.
 (c) Notice of intention to arbitrate.
Section 7504. Court appointment of arbitrator.
Section 7505. Powers of arbitrator.
Section 7506. Hearing.
 (a) Oath of arbitrator.
 (b) Time and place.
 (c) Evidence.
 (d) Representation by attorney.
 (e) Determination by majority.
 (f) Waiver.
Section 7507. Award; form; time; delivery.
Section 7508. Award by confession.
 (a) When available.
 (b) Time of award.
 (c) Person or agency making award.
Section 7509. Modification of award by arbitrator.
Section 7510. Confirmation of award.
Section 7511. Vacating or modifying award.
 (a) When application made.
 (b) Grounds for vacating.
 (c) Grounds for modifying.
 (d) Rehearing.
 (e) Confirmation.
Section 7512. Death or incompetency of a party.
Section 7513. Fees and expenses.
Section 7514. Judgment on an award.
 (a) Entry.
 (b) Judgment-roll.

Section 7501. Effect of arbitration agreement. A written agreement to submit any controversy thereafter arising or any existing controversy to arbitration is enforceable without regard to the justiciable character of the controversy and confers jurisdiction on the courts of the state to enforce it and to enter judgment on an award. In determining any matter arising under this article, the court shall not consider whether the claim with respect to which arbitration is sought is tenable, or otherwise pass upon the merits of the dispute.

Section 7502. Applications to the court; venue; statutes of limitation; provisional remedies.

(a) Applications to the court; venue. A special proceeding shall be used to bring before a court the first application arising out of an arbitrable controversy which is not made by motion in a pending action. The proceeding shall be brought in the court and county specified in the agreement; or, if none be specified, in a court in the county in which one of the parties resides or is doing business, or, if there is no such county, in a court in any county; or in a court in the county in which the arbitration was held. All subsequent applications shall be made by motion in the pending action or the special proceeding.

(b) Limitation of time. If, at the time that a demand for arbitration was made or a notice of intention to arbitrate was served, the claim sought to be arbitrated would have been barred by limitation of time had it been asserted in a court of the state, a party may assert the limitation as a bar to the arbitration on an application to the court as provided in section 7503 or subdivision (b) of section 7511. The failure to assert such bar by such application shall not preclude its assertion before the arbitrators, who may, in their sole discretion, apply or not apply the bar. Except as provided in subdivision (b) of section 7511, such exercise of discretion by the arbitrators shall not be subject to review by a court on an application to confirm, vacate or modify the award.

(c) Provisional remedies. The supreme court in the county in which an arbitration is pending, or, if not yet commenced, in a county specified in subdivision (a), may entertain an application for an order of attachment or for a preliminary injunction in connection with an arbitrable controversy, but only upon the ground that the award to which the applicant may be entitled may be rendered ineffectual without such provisional relief. The provisions of articles 62 and 63 of this chapter shall apply to the application, including those relating to undertakings and to the time for commencement of an action (arbitration shall be deemed an action for this purpose) if the application is made before commencement, except that the sole ground for the granting of the remedy shall be as stated above. The form of the application shall be as provided in subdivision (a).

Section 7503. Application to compel or stay arbitration; stay of action; notice of intention to arbitrate.

(a) Application to compel arbitration; stay of action. A party aggrieved by the failure of another to arbitrate may apply for an order compelling arbitration. Where there is no substantial question whether a valid agreement was made or complied with, and the claim sought to be arbitrated is not barred by limitation under subdivision (b) of section 7502, the court shall direct the parties to arbitrate. Where any such question is raised, it shall be tried forthwith in said court. If an issue claimed to be arbitrable is involved in an action pending in a court having jurisdiction to hear a motion to compel arbitration, the application shall be made by motion in that action. If the application is granted, the order shall operate to stay a pending or subsequent action, or so much of it as is referable to arbitration.

(b) Application to stay arbitration. Subject to the provisions of subdivision (c), a party who has not participated in the arbitration and who has not made or been served with an application to compel arbitration, may apply to stay arbitration on the ground that a valid agreement was not made or has not been complied with or that the claim sought to be arbitrated is barred by limitation under subdivision (b) of section 7502.

(c) Notice of intention to arbitrate. A party may serve upon another party a demand for arbitration or a notice of intention to arbitrate, specifying the agreement pursuant to which arbitration is sought and the name and address of the party serving the notice, or of an officer or agent thereof if such party is an association or corporation, and stating that unless the party served applies to stay the arbitration within twenty days after such service he shall thereafter be precluded from objecting that a valid agreement was not made or has not been complied with and from asserting in court the bar of a limitation of time. Such notice or demand shall be served in the same manner as a summons or by registered or certified mail, return receipt requested. An application to stay arbitration must be made by the party served within twenty days after service upon him of the notice or demand, or he shall be so precluded. Notice of such application shall be served in the same manner as a summons or by registered or certified mail, return receipt requested. Service of the application may be made upon the adverse party, or upon his attorney if the attorney's name appears on the demand for arbitration or the notice of intention to arbitrate. Service of the application by mail shall be timely if such application is posted within the prescribed period. Any provision in an arbitration agreement or arbitration rules which waives the right to apply for a stay of arbitration is hereby declared null and void.

Section 7504. Court appointment of arbitrator. If the arbitration agreement does not provide for a method of appointment of an arbitrator, or if the agreed method fails or for any reason is not followed, or if an arbitrator fails to act and his successor has not been appointed, the court, on application of a party, shall appoint an arbitrator.

Section 7505. Powers of arbitrator. An arbitrator and any attorney of record in the arbitration proceeding has the power to issue subpoenas. An arbitrator has the power to administer oaths.

Section 7506. Hearing.

(a) Oath of arbitrator. Before hearing any testimony, an arbitrator shall be sworn to hear and decide the controversy faithfully and fairly by an officer authorized to administer an oath.

(b) Time and place. The arbitrator shall appoint a time and place for the hearing and notify the parties in writing personally or by registered or certified mail not less than eight days before the hearing. The arbitrator may adjourn or postpone the hearing. The court, upon application of any party, may direct the arbitrator to proceed promptly with the hearing and determination of the controversy.

(c) Evidence. The parties are entitled to be heard, to present evidence and to cross-examine witnesses. Notwithstanding the failure of a party duly notified to appear, the arbitrator may hear and determine the controversy upon the evidence produced.

(d) Representation by attorney. A party has the right to be represented by an attorney and may claim such right at any time as to any part of the arbitration or hearings which have not taken place. This right may not be waived. If a party is represented by an attorney, papers to be served on the party shall be served upon his attorney.

(e) Determination by majority. The hearing shall be conducted by all the arbitrators, but a majority may determine any question and render an award.

(f) Waiver. Except as provided in subdivision (d), a requirement of this section may be waived by written consent of the parties and it is waived if the parties continue with the arbitration without objection.

Section 7507. Award; form; time; delivery. Except as provided in section 7508, the award shall be in writing, signed and affirmed by the arbitrator making it within the time fixed by the agreement, or, if the time is not fixed, within such time as the court orders. The parties may in writing extend the time either before or after its expiration. A party waives the objection that an award was not made within the time required unless he notifies the arbitrator in writing of his objection prior to the delivery of the award to him. The arbitrator shall deliver a copy of the award to each party in the manner provided in the agreement, or, if no provision is so made, personally or by registered or certified mail, return receipt requested.

Section 7508. Award by confession.

(a) When available. An award by confession may be made for money due or to become due at any time before an award is otherwise made. The award shall be based upon a statement, verified by each party, containing an authorization to make the award, the sum of the award or the method of ascertaining it, and the facts constituting the liability.

(b) Time of award. The award may be made at any time within three months after the statement is verified.

(c) Person or agency making award. The award may be made by an arbitrator or by the agency or person named by the parties to designate the arbitrator.

Section 7509. Modification of award by arbitrator. On written application of a party to the arbitrators within twenty days after delivery of the award to the applicant, the arbitrators may modify the award upon the grounds stated in subdivision (c) of section 7511. Written notice of the application shall be given to other parties to the arbitration. Written objection to modification must be served on the arbitrators and other parties to the arbitration within ten days of receipt of the notice. The arbitrators shall dispose of any application made under this section in writing, signed and acknowledged by them, within thirty days after either written objection to modification has been served on them or the time for serving said objection has expired, whichever is earlier. The parties may in writing extend the time for such disposition either before or after its expiration.

Section 7510. Confirmation of award. The court shall confirm an award upon application of a party made within one year after its delivery to him, unless the award is vacated or modified upon a ground specified in section 7511.

Section 7511. Vacating or modifying award.

(a) When application made. An application to vacate or modify an award may be made by a party within ninety days after its delivery to him.

(b) Grounds for vacating.

1. The award shall be vacated on the application of a party who either participated in the arbitration or was served with a notice of intention to arbitrate if the court finds that the rights of that party were prejudiced by:

(i) corruption, fraud or misconduct in procuring the award; or

(ii) partiality of an arbitrator appointed as a neutral, except where the award was by confession; or

(iii) an arbitrator, or agency or person making the award exceeded his power or so imperfectly executed it that a final and definite award upon the subject matter submitted was not made; or

(iv) failure to follow the procedure of this article, unless the party applying to vacate the award continued with the arbitration with notice of the defect and without objection.

2. The award shall be vacated on the application of a party who neither participated in the arbitration nor was served with a notice of intention to arbitrate if the court finds that:

(i) the rights of that party were prejudiced by one of the grounds specified in paragraph one; or

(ii) a valid agreement to arbitrate was not made; or

(iii) the agreement to arbitrate had not been complied with; or

(iv) the arbitrated claim was barred by limitation under subdivision (b) of section 7502.

(c) Grounds for modifying. The court shall modify the award if:

3. there was a miscalculation of figures or a mistake in the description of any person, thing or property referred to in the award; or

4. the arbitrators have awarded upon a matter not submitted to them and the award may be corrected without affecting the merits of the decision upon the issues submitted; or

5. the award is imperfect in a matter of form, not affecting the merits of the controversy.

(d) Rehearing. Upon vacating an award, the court may order a rehearing and determination of all or any of the issues either before the same arbitrator or before a new arbitrator appointed in accordance with this article. Time in any provision limiting the time for a hearing or award shall be measured from the date of such order or rehearing, whichever is appropriate, or a time may be specified by the court.

(e) Confirmation. Upon the granting of a motion to modify, the court shall confirm the award as modified; upon the denial of a motion to vacate or modify, it shall confirm the award.

Section 7512. Death or incompetency of a party. Where a party dies after making a written agreement to submit a controversy to arbitration, the proceedings may be begun or continued upon the application of, or upon notice to, his executor or administrator or, where it relates to real property, his distributee or devisee who has succeeded to his interest in the real property. Where a committee of the property or of the person of a party to such an agreement is appointed, the proceedings may be continued upon the application of, or notice to, the committee. Upon the death or incompetency of a party, the court may extend the time within which an application to confirm, vacate or modify the award or to stay arbitration must be made. Where a party has died since an award was delivered, the proceedings thereupon are the same as where a party dies after a verdict.

Section 7513. Fees and expenses. Unless otherwise provided in the agreement to arbitrate, the arbitrators` expenses and fees, together with other expenses, not including attorney`s fees, incurred in the conduct of the arbitration, shall be paid as provided in the award. The court, on application, may reduce or disallow any fee or expense it finds excessive or allocate it as justice requires.

Section 7514. Judgment on an award.

(a) Entry. A judgment shall be entered upon the confirmation of an award.

(b) Judgment-roll. The judgment-roll consists of the original or a copy of the agreement and each written extension of time within which to make an award; the statement required by section 7508 where the award was by confession; the award; each paper submitted to the court and each order of the court upon an application under sections 7510 and 7511; and a copy of the judgment.

APPENDIX III

SELECTED STATUTES

Public Officer Law

ARTICLE 3

Creation and Filling of Vacancies

Section 30. Creation of vacancies.
Section 31. Resignations.
Section 32. Removals by senate.
Section 33. Removals by governor.
Section 33-a. Removal of heads of departments.
Section 34. Proceedings for removal by governor.
Section 35. Removals from office.
Section 35-a. Removal for treasonable or seditious acts or utterances.
Section 36. Removal of town, village, improvement district or fire district officer by court.
Section 37. Notice of existence of vacancy.
Section 38. Terms of officers chosen to fill vacancies.

Section 39. Filling vacancies in office of officer appointed by governor and senate.

Section 40. Vacancy occurring in office of legislative appointee, during legislative recess.

Section 41. Vacancies filled by legislature.

Section 42. Filling vacancies in elective offices.

Section 43. Filling other vacancies.

Section 30. Creation of vacancies. 1. Every office shall be vacant upon the happening of one of the following events before the expiration of the term thereof: a. The death of the incumbent; b. His resignation; c. His removal from office; d. His ceasing to be an inhabitant of the state, or if he be a local officer, of the political subdivision, or municipal corporation of which he is required to be a resident when chosen; e. His conviction of a felony, or a crime involving a violation of his oath of office, provided, however, that a non-elected official may apply for reinstatement to the appointing authority upon reversal or the vacating of such conviction where the conviction is the sole basis for the vacancy. After receipt of such application, the appointing authority shall afford such applicant a hearing to determine whether reinstatement is warranted. The record of the hearing shall include the final judgment of the court which reversed or vacated such conviction and may also include the entire employment history of the applicant and any other submissions which may form the basis of the grant or denial of reinstatement notwithstanding the reversal or vacating of such conviction.

Notwithstanding any law to the contrary, after review of such record, the appointing authority may, in its discretion, reappoint such non-elected official to his former office, or a similar office if his former office is no longer available. In the event of such reinstatement, the appointing authority may, in its discretion, award salary or compensation in full or in part for the period from the date such office became vacant to the date of reinstatement or any part thereof; f. The entry of a judgment or order of a court of competent jurisdiction declaring him to be incompetent; g. The judgment of a court, declaring void his election or appointment, or that his office is forfeited or vacant; h. His refusal or neglect to file his official oath or undertaking, if one is required, before or within thirty days after the commencement of the term of office for which he is chosen, if an elective office, or if an appointive office, within thirty days after notice of his appointment, or within thirty days after the commencement of such term; or to file a renewal undertaking within the time required by law, or if no time be so specified, within thirty days after notice to him in pursuance of law, that such renewal undertaking is required. The neglect or failure of any state or local officer to execute and file his oath of office and official undertaking within the time limited therefor by law, shall not create a vacancy in the office if such officer was on active duty in the armed forces of the United States and absent from the county of his residence at the time of his election or appointment, and shall take his oath of office and execute his official undertaking within thirty days after receipt of notice of his election or appointment, and provided such oath of office and official undertaking be filed within ninety days following the date it has been taken and subscribed, any inconsistent provision of law, general, special, or local to the contrary, notwithstanding.

2. When a new or an additional office shall be created, such office shall for the purposes of an appointment or election, be vacant from the date of its creation, until it shall be filled by election or appointment.

3. When any member of a board, commission, committee or authority, holding office by appointment of the governor, fails to attend three consecutive regular meetings of such board, commission, committee or authority, unless such absence is for good cause and is excused by the chairman or other presiding officer thereof, or, in the case of such chairman or other presiding officer, by the governor, the office may be deemed vacant for purposes of the nomination and appointment of a successor.

4. Neither the provisions of this section, nor of any general, special or local law, charter, code, ordinance, resolution, rule or regulation, creating a vacancy in a local office of a political subdivision or municipal corporation if the incumbent thereof ceases to be a resident of such political subdivision or municipal corporation, shall apply in the case of a person who is a member of the police force of any political subdivision or municipal corporation of the state and who while a member of such force resides (a) in the county in which such political subdivision or municipal corporation is located; or (b) in a county within the state contiguous to the county in which such political subdivision or municipal corporation is located; or (c) in a county within the state contiguous to such political subdivision or municipal corporation; or (d) in a county within the state contiguous to a county described in item (c) hereof where the former is less than fifteen miles from such political subdivision or municipal corporation, measured from their respective nearest boundary lines; or (e) in a county within the state contiguous to a county described in item (d) hereof where the former is less than thirty miles from such political subdivision or municipal corporation, measured from their respective nearest boundary lines: (1) If such person was appointed as a member of such police force prior to July first, nineteen hundred sixty-one, shall reside in any such county on such date and shall continue to reside in any

such county after such date, or (2) If the police force of which he is a member consists of two hundred or more full-time members or shall have consisted of two hundred or more full-time members when, as a member of such police force, he shall have resided in such county and shall continue to reside in any such county thereafter, or (3) If the police force of which he is a member consists of less than two hundred full-time members; provided, however, that the local legislative body of such political subdivision or municipal corporation having such police force shall have power to adopt and amend local laws, ordinances or resolutions of general application requiring members of such police force, other than those members covered by paragraph one or paragraph two of this subdivision, to reside in such political subdivision or municipal corporation, or permitting them to reside in specified areas of such counties or within specified distances from the political subdivision or municipal corporation provided such local legislative body shall determine that a policeman may respond therefrom promptly and be available to render active service in such political subdivision or municipal corporation.

4-a. Neither the provisions of this section, nor of any general, special or local law, charter, code, ordinance, resolution, rule or regulation, creating a vacancy in a local office of a political subdivision or municipal corporation if the incumbent thereof ceases to be a resident of such political subdivision or municipal corporation, shall apply in the case of a member of the department of sanitation of any municipality who resides in a county within the state contiguous to such municipality.

4-b. Except as otherwise provided in subdivision five of this section, neither the provisions of this section, nor of any general, special or local law, charter, code, ordinance, resolution, rule or regulation, creating a vacancy in a local office of a political subdivision or municipal corporation of the state if the incumbent thereof ceases to be a resident of such political subdivision or municipal corporation shall apply to the appointment or continuance in office or position of an officer or member of a paid fire department in any political subdivision or municipal corporation of the state, if such person resides in the county, or one of the counties, in which such political subdivision or municipal corporation is located.

5. Neither the provisions of this section, nor of any general, special or local law, charter, code, ordinance, resolution, rule or regulation, creating a vacancy in a local office of a political subdivision or municipal corporation if the incumbent thereof ceases to be a resident of such political subdivision or municipal corporation, shall apply in the case of a paid member of the uniformed force of a paid fire department, or in the case of a person employed in a department of correction in the correction service of the classified civil service, or in the case of officers and inspectors employed in a department of health of a city of over one million population who resides (a) in the county in which said city is located; or (b) in a county within the state contiguous to the county in which said city is located; or (c) in a county within the state contiguous to such city; or (d) in a county within the state which is not more than fifteen miles from said city; or (e) in a county within the state contiguous to a county described in item (d) hereof where the former is less than thirty miles from such political subdivision or municipal corporation, measured from their respective nearest boundary lines. 5-a. Any person who resides in this state and who is currently employed as a member of the police force, a paid member of the uniformed force of a paid fire department, or department of corrections in the correctional service classification of the classified civil service, of a city of over one million population, shall be exempt from the provisions of paragraph (d) of subdivision one and subdivisions four and five of this section upon compliance with the procedure set forth in this subdivision. Any

person seeking to benefit from the exemption created by this subdivision shall notify his respective employer in writing of said intention within thirty days from the effective date of this subdivision and shall specify his then current residence address. The exemption created by this subdivision shall be applicable only to said actual designated residence and not to any residence that any subject currently employed member may thereafter establish; provided, however, that any such currently employed member who resides outside this state shall have one year from the effective date of this subdivision within which to establish residence as required pursuant to paragraph (d) of subdivision one, and subdivisions four and five of this section and comply with the notice requirements of this subdivision. Said residence shall constitute a lawful residence for all purposes notwithstanding any provision to the contrary of any general, special or local law, charter, code, ordinance, resolution, rule or regulation.

6. Neither the provisions of this section, nor of any general, special or local law, charter, code, ordinance, resolution, rule or regulation, creating a vacancy in a local office of a political subdivision or municipal corporation if the incumbent thereof ceases to be a resident of such political subdivision or municipal corporation, shall apply in the case of appointed public officers in the city of Troy, except the city manager of such city, who reside in the county of Rensselaer.

7. Neither the provisions of this section, nor of any general, special or local law, charter, code, ordinance, resolution, rule or regulation, creating a vacancy in a local office of a political subdivision or municipal corporation of the state if the incumbent thereof ceases to be a resident of such political subdivision or municipal corporation, shall apply in the case of the city court judge in the city of Hudson, provided that such person resides in the county in which such city is located.

Section 31. Resignations. 1. Public officers may resign their offices as follows: a. The governor, lieutenant-governor, comptroller and attorney-general, to the legislature; b. All officers appointed by the governor alone, or by him with the consent of the senate, to the governor; c. Senators and members of assembly, to the presiding officers of their respective houses; d. Judges and justices of the unified court system, to the chief administrator of the courts; e. Sheriffs, county clerks, district attorneys and registers of counties, to the governor; f. Every other county officer, to the county clerk; g. Every town officer, to the town clerk; h. The officer of any other municipal corporation, to the clerk of the corporation; i. United States senators, to the secretary of state. j. Representatives in the House of Representatives of the Congress of the United States, to the secretary of state. k. Every other appointive officer, where not otherwise provided by law, to the body, board or officer that appointed him, and every other elective officer, where not otherwise provided by law, to the secretary of state.

2. Every resignation shall be in writing addressed to the officer or body to whom it is made. If no effective date is specified in such resignation, it shall take effect upon delivery to or filing with the proper officer or body. If an effective date is specified in such resignation, it shall take effect upon the date specified, provided however, that in no event shall the effective date of such resignation be more than thirty days subsequent to the date of its delivery or filing; except that the effective date of the resignation of a judge or justice of the unified court system may be up to ninety days subsequent to the date on which such resignation is delivered or filed. If a resignation specifies an effective date that is more than thirty days subsequent to the date of its delivery or filing, or more than ninety days subsequent thereto where such resignation is that of a judge or justice, such resignation shall take

effect upon the expiration of thirty days from the date of its delivery or filing, or upon the expiration of ninety days therefrom, as appropriate.

3. A resignation addressed to an officer shall be delivered to him at his place of business or filed in his office. A resignation addressed to the legislature or to the presiding officer of either house thereof, shall be delivered to and filed with the secretary of state, and he shall forthwith communicate the fact of such resignation to the legislature or to such house, if in session, or if not, at its first meeting thereafter. A resignation addressed to any other body shall be delivered to the presiding officer or clerk of such body, if there be one, and if not, to any member thereof, and shall be filed with the clerk, or if there be no clerk, with the other records of such body. A delivery at the office or place of residence or business of the person to whom any such resignation may be delivered shall be a sufficient delivery thereof.

4. A resignation delivered or filed pursuant to this section, whether effective immediately or at a specified future date, may not be withdrawn, canceled, or amended except by consent of the officer to whom it is delivered or body with which it is filed.

5. If a resignation from an elective office is received pursuant to the provisions of this section, the official who receives such resignation shall immediately notify the state board of elections of the fact of such resignation and the effective date, if any, set forth in such resignation.

Section 32. Removals by senate. The governor before making a recommendation to the senate for the removal of any officer may in his discretion take proofs, for the purpose of determining whether such recommendation shall be made. The comptroller or attorney-general may be removed by the senate, on the recommendation of the governor, for misconduct or malversation in office, if two-thirds of all the members elected to the senate shall concur therein. No such removal shall be made unless the person who is sought to be removed shall have been served with a copy of the charges against him and have an opportunity of being heard. On the question of removal, the yeas and nays shall be entered on the journal. The governor may convene the senate in extra session for the investigation of such charges. The senate shall have power to make such rules as it may see fit for the practice before it. At the time appointed for the investigation, the senate shall proceed to hear and try the charges against such officer, and may take proofs in relation thereto. The governor may appoint any suitable person to conduct the trial of such charges before the senate. An officer appointed by the governor by and with the advice and consent of the senate, except an officer who is or any or either of the officers who are the head of a department, and except as otherwise provided by special provision of law may be removed by the senate upon the recommendation of the governor. If the senate shall reject a recommendation of removal the secretary of the senate shall, by a writing signed by him and by the president of the senate, communicate the fact of such rejection to the governor. If the senate shall concur in such a recommendation the removal shall take effect upon the passage of the resolution of concurrence, and duplicate copies of such resolution, certified by the secretary and president of the senate, shall be executed and delivered by such secretary to the secretary of state.

Section 33. Removals by governor. 1. An officer appointed by the governor for a full term or to fill a vacancy, whose appointment is not required by law to be made by and with the advice and consent of the senate, any county treasurer, any county superintendent of the poor, any register of a county or any coroner, except as otherwise provided by special provisions of law, may be removed by the governor within the term for which such officer shall have been chosen, after giving to such officer a copy of the charges against him and an opportunity to be heard in his defense.

2. The chief executive officer of every city and the chief or commissioner of police, commissioner or director of public safety or other chief executive officer of the police force by whatever title he may be designated, of every city may be removed by the governor after giving to such officer a copy of the charges against him and an opportunity to be heard in his defense. The power of removal provided for in this subdivision shall be deemed to be in addition to the power of removal provided for in any other law. The provisions of this subdivision shall apply notwithstanding any inconsistent provisions of any general, special or local law, ordinance or city charter.

Section 33-a. Removal of heads of departments. Any officer who is, or any or either of the officers who are, the head of a department, if appointed by the governor by and with the advice and consent of the senate, may be removed from office by the governor whenever in his judgment the public interest shall so require. In case of such a removal the governor shall file with the department of state a statement of the cause of such removal and shall report such removal and the cause thereof to the legislature at its next session.

Section 34. Proceedings for removal by governor. 1. In any proceeding for the removal by the governor of a public officer, he may conduct an investigation into the charges, and may take the evidence as to the truth of the charges at a hearing for such purpose, or he may direct that such investigation or hearing, or both, shall be conducted by a justice of the supreme court of the judicial district, or the county judge of the county, in which the officer proceeded against shall reside, or by a commissioner appointed by the governor, by an appointment, in writing, filed in the office of the secretary of state.

2. The governor may direct the attorney-general or the district attorney of the county in which the officer proceeded against resides, to assist the governor, or the person designated by the governor under the first subdivision of this section, in the conduct of the investigation into the charges, and of the hearing into the truth of the charges. If the hearing provided for in this section shall be conducted by a justice, judge or commissioner, it shall be held at such place in the county in which the officer proceeded against shall reside as the justice, judge or commissioner shall appoint, and at least eight days after written notice of the time and place of such hearing shall have been given to the officer proceeded against.

3. The governor may direct the justice, judge or commissioner to report to him the evidence taken at such hearing, or the evidence and the findings of the material facts deemed by such justice, judge or commissioner to be established. Both in the investigation of the charges and at the hearing into the truth of the charges, the governor or the person designated by him under the first subdivision of this section may require witnesses to attend before him, and may also require the production of any books, papers, or other documents, deemed by him to be material, and shall issue subpoenas for such witnesses for appearance at the hearing as may be requested by the officer proceeded against.

4. At the hearing provided for in this section, the officer proceeded against and his counsel shall be permitted to attend, but such officer or his counsel shall have no right to be present at the investigation provided for unless the governor or the person designated by him to conduct such investigation so directs. No evidence taken in such investigation shall form the basis of any report to the governor by the person designated by him under subdivision one of this section, or the basis of any determination by the governor, unless such evidence is presented at the hearing provided for in this section.

5. The person designated under subdivision one of this section, or the governor, where no person is so designated, is authorized to employ counsel in any case where the attorney-general or district attorney has not been directed to assist the governor or his designee, as provided in subdivision two of this section, and to employ such personnel as may be necessary to assist him in the performance of his duties under this section.

6. If the proceeding be for removal of a state officer, the reasonable expenses incurred in the conduct thereof, including the compensation of authorized counsel and of necessary assistants, in the taking and printing of the testimony, shall be paid by the state, on the certificate of the governor, out of moneys appropriated or available therefor.

7. If the proceeding be for the removal of a county or city officer, the reasonable expenses incurred in the conduct thereof shall be a county or city charge, as the case may be. The board of supervisors of the county, or the board of estimate and apportionment or other board or body of the city vested with the power to make appropriations, on the requisition of the governor, from time to time, shall forthwith appropriate such sum as shall be needed to pay such expenses; and after such appropriation shall have been duly made, the fiscal officer of the county or city, as the case may be, shall pay such expenses, upon vouchers approved by the governor, after audit, in the same manner and by the same authority as other county or city charges are audited and paid.

8. A person designated by the governor to conduct an investigation or hearing, or both, under this section, who is not regularly employed by the state or by a county or city, shall be paid a reasonable compensation for his services, to be fixed by the governor, and paid in the same manner as other expenses for the removal of a state officer, or a county or city officer, as the case may be, as provided in this section.

9. All sheriffs, coroners, constables and marshals to whom process shall be directed and delivered under this section shall execute the same without unnecessary delay.

Section 35. Removals from office. Every removal of an officer by one or more state officers, shall be in written duplicate orders, signed by the officer, or by all or a majority of the officers, making the removal, or if made by a body or board of state officers may be evidenced by duplicate certified copies of the resolution or order of removal, signed either by all or by a majority of the officers making the removal, or by the president and clerk of such body or board. Both such duplicate orders or certified copies shall be delivered to the secretary of state, who shall record in his office one of such duplicates, and shall, if the officer removed is a state officer, deliver the other to such officer by messenger, if required by the governor, and otherwise by mail or as the secretary of state shall deem advisable, and shall, if directed by the governor, cause a copy thereof to be published in the state paper. If the officer removed be a local officer, he shall send the other of such duplicates to the county clerk of the county in which the officer removed shall have resided at the time he was chosen to the office, and such clerk shall file the same in his office, and forthwith notify the officer removed of his removal.

Section 35-a. Removal for treasonable or seditious acts or utterances. A person holding any public office shall be removable therefrom, in the manner provided by law, for the utterance of any treasonable or seditious word or words or the doing of any treasonable or seditious act or acts during his term.

Section 36. Removal of town, village, improvement district or fire district officer by court. Any town, village, improvement district or fire district officer, except a justice of the peace, may be removed from office by the supreme court for any misconduct, maladministration, malfeasance or malversation in office. An application for such removal may be made by any citizen resident of such town, village, improvement district or fire district or by the district attorney of the county in which such town, village or district is located, and shall be made to the appellate division of the supreme court held within the judicial department embracing such town, village, improvement district or fire district. Such application shall be made upon notice to such officer of not less than eight days, and a copy of the charges upon which the application will be made must be served with such notice.

Section 37. Notice of existence of vacancy. When a judgment shall be rendered by any court convicting an officer of a felony, or of a crime involving a violation of his oath of office, or declaring the election or appointment of any officer to be void, or that the office of any officer has been forfeited or become vacant, the clerk of such court shall give notice thereof to the governor, stating the cause of such conviction or judgment. Whenever a public officer shall die before the expiration of his term of office, or shall cease to be a resident of the political subdivision of the state or a municipal corporation in which he is required to be a resident as a condition of continuing in the office, the county clerk of the county in which such officer shall have resided immediately prior to such death or removal, shall immediately give notice of such death or removal to the governor. If the governor is not authorized to fill any vacancy of which he shall have notice, he shall forthwith give notice of the existence of such vacancy to the officer or officers, or to the body or board of officers authorized to fill the vacancy, or if such vacancy may be filled by an election, to the officers authorized to give notice of such election.

Section 38. Terms of officers chosen to fill vacancies. If an appointment of a person to fill a vacancy in an appointive office be made by the officer, or by the officers, body or board of officers, authorized to make appointment to the office for the full term, the person so appointed to such vacancy shall hold office for the balance of the unexpired term. The term of office of an officer appointed to fill a vacancy in an elective office, shall be until the commencement of the political year next succeeding the first annual election after the happening of the vacancy, if the office be made elective by the constitution, or at which the vacancy can be filled by election, if the office be otherwise made elective.

Section 39. Filling vacancies in office of officer appointed by governor and senate. A vacancy which shall occur during the session of the senate, in the office of an officer appointed by the governor by and with the advice and consent of the senate, shall be filled in the same manner as an original appointment. Such a vacancy occurring or existing while the senate is not in session, including offices in which officers are holding over pursuant to the provisions of section five of this chapter or any other law, and offices vacant during the session of the senate, shall be filled by the governor for a term which shall expire upon the appointment and qualification of a successor but in any event such term shall expire at the end of twenty days from the commencement of the next meeting of the senate.

Section 40. Vacancy occurring in office of legislative appointee, during legislative recess. When a vacancy shall occur or exist, otherwise than by expiration of term, during the recess of the legislature, in the office of any officer appointed by the legislature, the governor shall appoint a person to fill the vacancy for a term which shall expire at the end of twenty days from the commencement of the next meeting of the legislature.

Section 41. Vacancies filled by legislature. When a vacancy occurs or exists, other than by removal, in the office of comptroller or attorney-general, or a resignation of either such officer to take effect at any future day shall have been made while the legislature is in session, the two houses thereof, by joint ballot, shall appoint a person to fill such actual or prospective vacancy.

Section 42. Filling vacancies in elective offices. 1. A vacancy occurring before September twentieth of any year in any office authorized to be filled at a general election, except in the offices of governor or lieutenant-governor, shall be filled at the general election held next thereafter, unless otherwise provided by the constitution, or unless previously filled at a special election.

2. A vacancy occurring by the expiration of term at the end of an even numbered year in an office which may not under the provisions of the constitution be filled for a full term at the general election held prior to the expiration of such term, shall be filled at said general election for a term ending with the commencement of the political year next succeeding the first general election at which said office can be filled by election for a full term.

3. Upon the failure to elect to any office, except that of governor or lieutenant-governor, at a general or special election, at which such office is authorized to be filled, or upon the death or disqualification of a person elected to office before the commencement of his official term, or upon the occurrence of a vacancy in any elective office which cannot be filled by appointment for a period extending to or beyond the next general election at which a person may be elected thereto, the governor may in his discretion make proclamation of a special election to fill such office, specifying the district or county in which the election is to be held, and the day thereof, which shall be not less than thirty nor more than forty days from the date of the proclamation.

4. A special election shall not be held to fill a vacancy in the office of a representative in congress unless such vacancy occurs on or before the first day of July of the last year of the term of office, or unless it occurs thereafter and a special session of congress is called to meet before the next general election, or be called after September nineteenth of such year; nor to fill a vacancy in the office of

state senator or in the office of member of assembly, unless the vacancy occurs before the first day of April of the last year of the term of office, or unless the vacancy occurs in either such office of senator or member of assembly after such first day of April and a special session of the legislature be called to meet between such first day of April and the next general election or be called after September nineteenth in such year. If a special election to fill an office shall not be held as required by law, the office shall be filled at the next general election. 4-a. If a vacancy occurs in the office of United States senator from this state in any even numbered calendar year on or after the fifty-ninth day prior to the annual primary election, or thereafter during said even numbered year, the governor shall make a temporary appointment to fill such vacancy until the third day of January in the year following the next even numbered calendar year. If such vacancy occurs in any even numbered calendar year on or before the sixtieth day prior to an annual primary election, the governor shall make a temporary appointment to fill such vacancy until the third day of January in the next calendar year. If a vacancy occurs in the office of United States senator from this state in any odd numbered calendar year, the governor shall make a temporary appointment to fill such vacancy until the third day of January in the next odd numbered calendar year. Such an appointment shall be evidenced by a certificate of the governor which shall be filed in the office of the state board of elections. At the time for filing such certificate, the governor shall issue and file in the office of the state board of elections a writ of election directing the election of a United States senator to fill such vacancy for the unexpired term at the general election next preceding the expiration for the term of such appointment.

5. Whenever the authority to fill any vacancy is vested in a board and such board is unable to fill such vacancy in an elective office by reason of a tie vote, or such board neglects to fill such vacancy for any other reason, the governor may, in his discretion, make proclamation of a special election to fill the vacancy.

Section 43. Filling other vacancies. If a vacancy shall occur, otherwise than by expiration of term, with no provision of law for filling the same, if the office be elective, the governor shall appoint a person to execute the duties thereof until the vacancy shall be filled by an election. But if the term of such officer shall expire with the calendar year in which the appointment shall be made, or if the office be appointive, the appointee shall hold for the residue of the term.

General Index

Absence from hearings 1.20
Absence from work during disciplinary activities 5.03
Acquittal of criminal charges does not bar disciplinary action 9.02
Administrator's immunity 9.08
Admission of guilt difficult to retract 6.09
Admissions 3.21
Affect of criminal actions on suspensions 2.13
Ambiguity of language in Taylor Law agreements 1.18
Anonymous allegations 2.03
Arbitrating Section 71 and Section 73 terminations 12.03
Attaining permanent status 17.16
Attorney fees awarded to the employee 18.01
Authority of the arbitrator 18.02
Authority to discipline 1.26
Automatic termination 18.03
Back pay 14.02
Back pay and benefits 11.12
Back salary 11.14
Bad faith 8.15
Bad faith determinations 17.06
Best evidence rule 3.08
Biased hearing officers 11.07
Bill of Rights in contracts 5.02
Bringing discredit on the employer 18.04
Budgetary classification irrelevant to due process rights of employees 1.11
Challenging a Section 75 decision 11.05
Challenging a Section 75 settlement agreement 18.05
Challenging administrative decisions 18.06
Challenging administrative rulings 18.07
Challenging an arbitration award 11.06
Challenging arbitration awards 18.08
Characteristics of arbitration 7.14
Charges must be specific 6.02
Choice of law 6.11
Chronic absenteeism alleged to be caused by a disability 18.09
Chronic absenteeism policy violations 18.10
Civil rights 1.29
Classified service disciplinary procedures 18.11
Collateral estoppel 18.12
Collateral estoppel 9.09
Competent and incompetent witnesses 3.11
Concealing misconduct 18.13
Conducting a private business 18.14
Confessions and coercion 3.10

Confidentiality of disciplinary records 18.16
Conflicting evidence 3.15
Confrontations with a superior 18.15
Considering disability claims 12.05
Considering material in a post-hearing brief submitted by a party 10.10
Constructive dismissal 18.17
Constructive dismissal 18.18
Continuation on the payroll 18.19
Contract disciplinary procedures and Section 72 18.20
Contract violation 13.06
Court modification of disciplinary penalty 18.21
Court review 4.02
Credibility of witness 18.22
Credibility of witnesses 3.14
Criminal conviction bars administrative acquittal of the same charge 9.03
Criticism is not discipline 6.08
Criticism is not discipline 7.06
Criticism of employee performance 18.23
Criticism of employees by a coworker 18.24
Date of permanent appointment and traineeships 17.17
Deadlines for appeal 11.08
Defamation and disciplinary action 18.25
Defamation of employees 2.21
Delays in reinstatements 14.01
Demotion in grade 18.26
Denial of equal protection? 13.07
Designating a disciplinary hearing officer 18.27
Determining probation status 18.28
Determining the penalty to be imposed 4.09
Disciplinary action and wrongful discharge 18.30
Disciplinary action based on pre-employment misconduct 1.33
Disciplinary action claimed filed with malice 18.31
Disciplinary appeals must be to the forum having jurisdiction 18.32
Disciplinary arbitrations 18.29
Disciplinary dismissal not discrimination 18.33
Disciplinary hearings held in absentia 18.34
Disciplinary probation 17.08
Disciplinary probation 18.35
Disciplinary settlement payments 18.36
Disciplinary settlements 18.38
Discipline for 20-year-old misconduct 18.37
Disclosure of personal records 3.18
Disclosure of records 9.10
Discretion to discipline staff 18.39
Dismissal of a provisional employee 18.40
Dismissing a probationer 18.41

Disqualification for employment because of a criminal conviction 13.03
Disqualification, Section 50.4 CSL 13.12
Distinguishing between temporary and provisional appointment 17.28
Double jeopardy 1.28
Drafting disciplinary charges 18.42
Drug testing and collective bargaining 15.06
Drug use and probation 17.10
Due process and administrative hearings 18.43
Due process and negotiated agreements 18.44
Due process and optional hearings 1.23
Due Process and Progressive Discipline 4.10
Due process guidelines 15.03
Due process rights depend on appointment status and jurisdictional classification 1.01
Due process rights under Section 3020-a 1.04
Duty of fair representation 5.04
Duty to file disciplinary charges 18.45
Effect of criminal actions on suspensions 8.11
Effect of criminal conviction or dismissal on discipline 3.06
Electing a disciplinary penalty 18.46
Election of remedies 18.47
Emergency Suspensions 8.03
Employee must receive opportunity to respond 6.03
Employee personnel files used to set penalty 18.48
Employee surveillance 3.16
Employees-at-will 13.08
Employment agreements 18.49
Employment contracts 8.16
Evaluating conflicting testimony 18.50
Evidence 2.18
Examples of penalties imposed 4.21
Exhausting administrative remedies 18.51
Expiration of the penalty 4.07
Extension of probation: modified duty 17.13
Extensions of the probationary period 17.15
Failing to appear at the hearing 18.52
Failure to file a timely appeal 18.53
Failure to meet contract deadlines 18.54
Fairness in investigations 2.04
False official reports 18.55
Filing a timely Article 78 18.56
Final determination for purposes of making a claim 18.57
First Amendment rights 1.30
Fitness of a witness 18.58
Forms of evidence 3.01
Forums for appeal 11.04
Foundation for testimony 3.13

Fraud a valid basis for removal from position 15.59
Free speech 2.07
Free speech by public employees 18.60
Freedom of information 1.31
Good faith determinations concerning probationary service 17.19
Good faith probationary decisions 17.22
Guidelines on employee privacy 15.04
Handling complaints 2.02
Hearing in absentia 10.05
Hearing panel members 7.12
Hearsay evidence 3.02
Hearsay testimony in disciplinary action 18.61
Immunity from discipline 1.16
Impact of criminal action on disciplinary action, generally 2.14
Impartial tribunals 1.14
Impartiality of discipline panel members 18.62
Imposing a harsher disciplinary penalty 18.63
Indemnification 4.06
Independent review of facts 10.09
Informants 2.17
Informing the Commissioner 7.11
Internal investigation reports 18.64
Interviewing employees 2.05
Involuntary leave under Section 72 18.65
Involuntary resignation 18.66
Irrelevance of criminal history 13.04
Issuing subpoenas, recording evidence 2.16
Judicial notice 3.17
Judicial review of a disciplinary determination 18.67
Jurisdiction to hear a disciplinary appeal 18.68
Jurisdictional misclassification 1.10
Key procedural elements 6.01
Lawful penalties 4.03
Leave approval 18.69
Leave to attend hearing 10.06
Legal representation during investigations 2.11
Libel and slander 15.09
Lie detector tests 18.70
Light duty and probationary requirements 17.09
Limit on questioning by hearing officer 18.71
Limiting the selection of arbitrators 18.72
Loss of a driver's license 18.73
Loss of leave credits and other alternative penalties 4.16
Lying by employees 2.09
Malpractice by union's attorney 18.74
Malpractice in disciplinary actions 18.75

Material misrepresentations 18.76
Misconduct off the job 18.77
Misuse of the employer's records 18.78
Mitigation of damages 18.79
Mitigation of damages 8.12
Mitigation of damages in cases of acquittal 10.07
Mitigation of the recommended penalty 18.80
Name-clearing hearings 1.22
Name-clearing hearings 13.10
Name-clearing hearings 17.23
Name-clearing hearings 18.81
Name-clearing hearings 7.04
Nature of the offense 13.13
Necessity of a license 13.01
Need for investigatory report regardless of merit of allegations 7.02
Negotiated disciplinary procedures 18.82
Negotiating disciplinary procedures 18.83
Noncompetitive class employees 13.11
Non-competitive class employees 17.18
Notice of a final administrative determination 18.84
Notice of claim 18.85
Notice of discipline 5.01
Notice of hearings 1.21
Notice of termination 17.20
Observer's presence during testing 15.05
Off-duty misconduct 18.86
Opinion evidence 3.12
Other provisions of law 12.04
Outcomes of appeals 11.10
Overview: Disciplinary investigations 2.01
Patronage dismissals 18.88
Payment for unused leave credits 18.89
Payroll decertification 18.90
Pell standard 4.01
Pell Standard of Fairness 4.12
Penalties 15.07
Penalty: demotion 4.19
Penalty: fine 4.17
Penalty: reprimand 4.15
Penalty: suspension 4.18
Pending criminal charges 6.10
Pending criminal matters 1.27
Permanent appointments, probation and tenure in the competitive class 1.06
Permanent probationers 17.04
Permanent vs. probationer vs. provisional 1.07
Personnel records used in setting penalty 18.91

Pitfalls for that a hearing officer must avoid 2.25
Pitfalls to avoid 6.07
Pitfalls to avoid 7.05
Placement on involuntary leave 18.92
Policy makers 18.93
Pornography and the Pell Standard 18.94
Positive drug test 18.95
Pre-employment testing 15.02
Pre-hearing checklist 10.04
Pre-hearing conferences 7.13
Pre-hearing legwork 10.03
Pre-hearing suspensions 5.08
Preparing a defense 18.96
Privileged communications 3.23
Probation after re-hiring 18.97
Probation and alcoholism 17.11
Probation and stress 17.12
Probationary termination 18.98
Probationers and criminal charges 9.05
Probationers' due process rights 1.08
Procedures in filing charges 7.07
Procedures under contracts 5.05
Processing a disciplinary appeal 18.99
Property interest in public employment 18.100
Protected speech 18.101
Providing a "Bratton hearing" 18.102
Proving disciplinary charges 18.103
Public hearings 1.32
Public worker to answer work related inquiry 18.104
Random drug tests 18.105
Random searches at work 18.106
Reappointment to public office 18.107
Reasonable suspicion 15.01
Reasons Courts Reject Penalties 4.13
Reassignment pending discipline 18.108
Reassignment pending discipline 8.18
Reassignments 5.06
Recommendation of the hearing officer 18.109
Recommending penalties 4.04
Recording investigation findings 2.19
Record-keeping 2.20
Recoupment of cash advances 8.14
Refusal to answer questions 2.06
Refusal to participate in a drug treatment program 15.08
Reinstatement 14.03
Reinstatement after acquittal 9.06

Reinstatement from Section 72 leave 18.110
Rejecting a disciplinary settlement offer 18.112
Rejecting a hearing officer's findings 18.111
Removal after convictions 13.05
Removal by operation of law 1.24
Removal by operation of law 13.02
Removal from the payroll 18.113
Repayment of salary after being continued on the payroll 8.20
Representation by an attorney 18.114
Request for reconsideration 18.115
Request for union representation 18.116
Requesting a disciplinary hearing 18.117
Rescinding a letter of resignation 18.118
Rescinding a letter of retirement 18.119
Rescinding a resignation 18.120
Rescinding tenure status 18.121
Reversal of felony conviction 13.15
Reviewing disciplinary action 18.122
Reviewing probationary employee terminations 17.03
Right of appeal and timeliness 1.19
Right to counsel 18.123
Right to pre-determination hearing 1.17
Right to union representation 6.04
Rights of employees of quasi-government entities 1.12
Rights under a Taylor Law agreement 17.27
Risk of libel or slander as a result of investigatory report 7.03
Same offense, different penalties 18.124
School attorney, use of 7.08
Second probationary periods 17.21
Section 3020-a disciplinary appeals 18.125
Section 3020-a process 7.10
Section 72 leave 18.126
Section 73 pre-termination due process requirements 12.02
Selecting a hearing officer 10.02
Selective prosecution 18.127
Self-incrimination and immunity 2.08
Separation pay for probationary teachers 17.07
Serving charges 6.06
Settlement 5.07
Settlement agreement 18.128
Settlement agreements and FOIL 18.129
Settlement to avoid prosecution 9.07
Simultaneous prosecution 9.01
Source of documentary evidence 3.22
Specificity of charges 1.15
Standard of conduct 3.20

Standard of proof, Section 3020-a 3.05
Standard of proof, Section 75 3.04
Standard of proof: criminal vs. disciplinary hearing 3.03
Standard of review 17.05
Standing to appeal 18.130
Statute of limitations 11.13
Statute of limitations 18.131
Statute of limitations 6.05
Statute of limitations 7.01
Statute of limitations for disciplinary action 18.132
Statute of limitations on discipline 2.10
Stay of arbitration 10.11
Stipulating a settlement 18.133
Subpoena Duces Tecum 18.134
Substantial Evidence 4.11
Suppressing evidence in a disciplinary action 18.135
Suspension of a probationer 17.26
Suspension of a school superintendent 8.07
Suspension with or without pay 2.12
Suspension with pay, pending criminal action 8.17
Suspension without pay – general considerations 8.01
Suspension without pay 1.25
Suspension without pay 8.10
Suspension without pay during administrative discipline 18.136
Suspension without pay failure to report to work 8.19
Suspension without pay in the event of postponement of disciplinary proceeding 8.06
Suspension without pay of unlicensed individual 8.05
Suspension without pay penalty interrupted 18.137
Suspension without pay, generally 8.04
Suspension without pay, medical 8.09
Suspensions with pay, Sections 72 and 75 8.02
Tainted evidence 3.09
Tainted testimony 18.138
Taxation of a settlement 10.08
Taxation of a settlement 8.13
Temporary and provisional appointments 1.09
Tenure 17.02
Tenure by estoppel 18.139
Tenure by operation of law 17.24
Tenure of provisionals by operation of law 17.01
Term Appointments 18.140
Terminating an interim appointee 18.141
Terminating temporary appointees 18.142
Termination by operation of law 18.143
Termination for disability 12.01
Termination hearing - Section 73 18.144

Termination of a probationary employee 12.06
Termination of a probationer 18.145
Termination of employment 18.146
Termination pursuant to Section 73 18.147
Termination without a hearing 18.148
Testimony by the accused 3.07
Testimony by the appointing authority 18.149
Testing for drugs 18.150
Testing for illegal drugs 18.151
The ADA and human rights laws 15.10
The concept of tenure 1.05
The settlement option 10.01
Threats by employees 18.152
Time and attendance issues 4.20
Timeliness of evidence 18.153
Timely and untimely appeals 11.09
Tolling of the statute of limitations 18.154
Traineeships 17.14
Transition from probationer to tenured 17.25
Unemployment insurance and Section 75 18.155
Unpaid suspension past 30 days: Conflict with local law 8.08
Unsealing criminal records 3.19
Use of a videotape as evidence 18.156
Use of disclosures in criminal trials 9.04
Using personnel records in setting a penalty 18.157
Using polygraph tests in disciplinary actions 2.24
Using the individual's employment history in disciplinary action 4.05
Vacating a disciplinary arbitration 18.158
Vacating arbitration awards on grounds of public policy 18.159
Vacating arbitration awards on grounds of public policy 18.160
Vacating or modifying penalties: The Pell Standard 11.11
Verdict shopping 7.09
Veterans' due process rights 1.13
Violating department rules 18.161
Violating the terms of a disciplinary probation 18.164
Violating the use of the Internet policies 18.162
Violating workplace rules 18.163
Violation of oath of office 13.14
Violations of the Pell standard 4.14
Voluntary resignations 2.15
Volunteering to provide due process 18.165
What may appeals concern? 11.02
What standards apply in appeals? 11.03
Whistle blowing 18.166
Whistle blowing pre-disclosure notice 18.167
Whistleblower law covers provisional employees 18.168

Whistleblower protection 4.08
Who has no due process rights? 1.03
Who is entitled to due process? 1.02
Who is the employer? 18.169
Who may appeal? 11.01
Withdrawing a resignation 18.170
Withdrawing resignations 13.09
Witness creditability determinations 18.171
Work related investigations 18.172
Workers' Compensation Leave 18.173
Wrongful termination 18.174
Zero tolerance drug policy 18.175

ABOUT THE AUTHORS

Harvey Randall is former Counsel, New York State Department of Civil Service. He also served as Director of Personnel for the State University system and as Director of Research, Governor's Office of Employee Relations. He has an MPA from the Maxwell School, Syracuse University and a J.D. from Albany Law School.

Eric D. Randall is the Editor in Chief of ONBOARD, the New York State School Board Association's newspaper. Formerly publisher and CEO of NYPER Publications and a reporter for USA Today, he has also written for the Albany Times Union, The Washington Post, The Dallas Morning News and Newsweek. He has a bachelor's degree from Cornell University and an MBA from the University of Virginia's Darden School of Business.